Shortcut	Method
Create shortcut in Taskbar	Drag and drop shortcut from Desktop or Start menu onto Shortcut bar (usually next to Start button).
Delete shortcut from Start and Programs menus	Right-click Shortcut, and select Delete.
Open Display Properties Control Panel	Right-click Desktop, and select Properties.
Enable cascading Start menu	Right-click Taskbar, select Properties, select Advanced tab, and check Expand next to each item.
Enable Start menu Logoff menu item	Right-click Taskbar, select Properties, select Advanced tab, and check Display Logoff.
File search	Right-click My Computer, and select Search.
Keep Web pages offline	Select Start ➤ Favorites, right-click Shortcut, and select Make Available Offline.
Launch Explorer in Start Menu folder of logged-on user	Right-click Start button, and select Explore.
Launch Explorer for general browsing	Right-click My Computer, and select Explore.
Local computer management	Right-click My Computer, and select Manage.
Make Toolpad out of Taskbar toolbar	Drag vertical bar on left side of toolbar off Taskbar and onto Desktop.

Windows 2000 Server

24seven™

Windows® 2000 Server 24seven™

24seven™

Matthew Strebe

San Francisco Paris Düsseldorf Soest London

SYBEX®

Associate Publisher: Dick Staron

Contracts and Licensing Manager: Kristine O'Callaghan

Acquisitions and Developmental Editors: Maureen Adams and Tom Cirtin

Editor: Anamary Ehlen

Production Editor: Liz Burke

Technical Editor: Dan Renaud

Book Designer: Bill Gibson

Graphic Illustrator: Tony Jonick

Electronic Publishing Specialists: Susie Hendrickson and Maureen Forys

Proofreaders: Laurie O'Connell, Nathan Whiteside, Leslie E.H. Light, Yariv Rabinovitch

Indexer: Nancy Guenther

Cover Designer: Ingalls + Associates

Cover Illustrator/Photographer: Hank Osuna

Library of Congress Card Number: 2001087041

ISBN: 0-7821-2669-3

Manufactured in the United States of America

10 9 8 7 6 5 4 3 2 1

To Christy and Nathan

Acknowledgments

Putting one person's name on the cover of a book doesn't even begin to tell the story of its production. So much work goes into projects like this that there ought to be movie credits on the back cover.

I'd like to thank my wife for handling literally everything in our lives so that I can work full time and then write my work experiences down. Without her help, this book would not exist. I'd also like to thank the people I work with at Connetic for stepping in for me while I write when necessary: Zach Little, Yuri Risovanny, Bryon Pinkston, Merrick Lozano, and (especially) Charles Perkins. Any use of "I" in this book is incorrect; "we" is far more accurate.

Finally, I'd like to thank Maureen Adams for making both this book and this series a reality, and Tom Cirtin for assisting her in that regard. Liz Burke produced this book, and Anamary Ehlen made it palatable for human consumption. Dan Renaud's commentary was invaluable in curing me of obsolescence—the condition that occurs when an old hacker doesn't keep up to date on the latest jargon. There are a lot of unsung heroes involved in the production of this book that I'd like to sing about: Susie Hendrickson, Maureen Forys, Nancy Guenther, Leslie E.H. Light, Laurie O'Connell, Yariv Rabinovitz, and Nathan Whiteside.

Contents at at Glance

Contents

Introduction

Windows 2000 is an amazing operating system. It can also be a very frustrating operating system at times. Supporting Windows 2000 can be easy with the right planning, or it can be difficult when you make architectural decisions that cannot be sustained as your network grows. This book will help you make the right decisions about Windows 2000 networks, and it will steer you away from the pitfalls administrators (including myself) often fall into. Windows 2000 is the most advanced, most highly evolved software produced by any company ever; it is the flagship product of the largest software development company in the world. Its complexity is both a blessing and a curse, but with proper management, you can maximize the blessing and minimize the cursing. This book will show you how.

Although it may seem more similar to Windows 98 in its user interface, Windows 2000 is the successor to Windows NT; in fact, it was called Windows NT 5 until midway through its beta release. Although 2000 is based upon Windows NT, it is the most dramatic improvement and upgrade in an operating system I've ever seen—and a complete overhaul of the administration interface. NT 4 differed from NT 3.51 primarily in its desktop user interface; most of the administration tools remained the same—once you got used to the Start menu and the Windows Explorer, there was little administrative difference between the two operating systems. Every administrative tool in Windows 2000 is different. All the administrative tools have been unified by rewriting them as "snap-ins" to a pseudo-hierarchical management tool called the Microsoft Management Console, which provides both a consistent look and feel and a standard configuration namespace to which documentation (and this book) can easily refer. Additionally, numerous new services and features have been added to the operating system, and the networking stack has been overhauled from top to bottom, with a new driver model, improvements to the network layer transports, and security upgrades and improvements to the Windows networking components, and of course the addition of the Active Directory resource location service.

About This Book

This book contains the essence of my six years of experience as a consultant working with all versions of Windows—both my successes and failures. This book is formatted for ease of use and maximum clarity. It is not an encyclopedia of Windows 2000; it is an operator's manual. It is based mostly on those problems that I've seen affect more than one customer. I've avoided fluffing the book up with the minutiae of every discovered bug in Windows 2000. This book does not explain every esoteric Windows 2000 problem; it explains how to avoid them en masse. It does not toe the Microsoft line; it approaches Windows 2000 with the clarity of skepticism. You'll find solutions to large-scale problems (for example, server rollout and network design) as well as small-scale problems (for example, determining which physical adapter is which in a multi-homed server). This book covers problems where Microsoft's documentation either leaves off or is unclear.

Microsoft's TechNet information CD is my constant companion in my consulting practice and was so during the writing of this book, and it should be yours as well. If you don't have a subscription to TechNet, get one. Without authoritative technical information from the manufacturer of the operating system, you'll be poking around in the dark when you try to fix esoteric problems—no matter how long you've worked with Windows 2000. Think of this book as a companion to TechNet rather than a replacement for it.

This book should also be thought of as a supplement to the Microsoft Resource Kits rather than competition to them. There's little reason for me to rehash Microsoft's recommendations when it comes to configuring software—that's why you'll find my recommendations here and only when they differ from Microsoft's. Where are those differences likely to show up? In the administration of both extremely small and extremely large networks, because I find that Microsoft's documentation speaks right at the medium-sized network, while leaving extreme-case users on both ends to try to infer what should be done. I've placed the most emphasis on smaller networks because these users have fewer resources to turn to and less ability to hire experts for help.

Finally, I'm on support.microsoft.com just about every day. You will be too. About 80 percent of the problems I run into are already solved and explained there. The more bizarre the problem seems, the more likely it is that you'll find the answer there.

Who Should Buy This Book?

This book is for active Windows NT or Windows 2000 system administrators or for those who would like to become system administrators. Although it is written for those who already consider themselves to be expert Windows NT or Windows 2000 administrators, you do not need to be an expert to learn from it. However, you should at least be an MCSE or have equivalent understanding of Windows 2000, because I assume you understand the architecture of Windows 2000, network protocols, and networks in general. To benefit from this book, you should also run Windows 2000 in your company. This book is designed to be useful to all users from large enterprises to small businesses.

Assumptions

This book is primarily about Windows 2000 Server. It covers earlier editions of the operating system (Windows NT) only so far as they are the same. It covers other editions of Windows 2000 only inasmuch as they are similar to the services of Windows 2000 Server, except for an occasional note about a feature that is different between versions. For the most part, this is adequate for troubleshooting purposes, because the various editions of Windows 2000 are remarkably similar, varying only in the included services and a few minor Registry settings.

I've also assumed that you are running Windows 2000 on the Intel platform. I do not have access to an Alpha server and have only worked with one once, so I'm not really qualified to write about them. Other platforms are now completely obsolete, so if you haven't migrated from them to Intel, you should consider doing that now. Sadly, there doesn't seem to be room for more than one microprocessor in the world.

Service Pack 1 was released during the production of this book. There's a slight chance that minor changes may not have percolated throughout the text. Check for errata to the book (in book publishing we call service packs *errata*, being a little more willing to admit our mistakes than the folks in software publishing) at www.sybex.com.

How This Book Is Organized

This book is divided into four parts in the order that you will work with Windows 2000 in the field throughout its service life. Part I, "Windows 2000 in Depth," covers the technology of Windows 2000. Part II, "Windows 2000 Network Planning," covers issues you should plan for before you deploy Windows 2000 and those you'll run into when you bring Windows 2000 online. Part III, "Windows 2000 Every Day," discusses long-term maintenance of Windows 2000 and your support organization. Finally, Part IV, "Troubleshooting and Optimization," details procedures you can use to repair Windows 2000.

The sides of this book are tabbed by section to make it easy for you to refer to these parts as a reference.

Part 1—Windows 2000 in Depth

This section discusses the design and use of Windows 2000 in a networked environment. The emphasis is on proper planning and architecture to support the remaining sections of the book.

Chapter 1, "Windows 2000 Core Technologies," discusses the architecture of Windows 2000 in general. Think of it as a feature guide for those who understand operating systems but are not familiar with Windows 2000.

Chapter 2, "Installing Windows 2000 (the Right Way)" discusses how to install or upgrade to Windows 2000 quickly and easily in even the most difficult environments.

Chapter 3, "Storage and Fault Tolerance," discusses how to use mass-storage devices for storage and archiving. The chapter also deals with Windows 2000's built-in fault tolerance mechanisms and discusses which are useful and which are more trouble than they're worth.

Chapter 4, "Network Protocols," discusses network protocols and routing, along with the architectural differences between switched and routed networks.

Chapter 5, "Network Services," covers the services included with Windows 2000 with an emphasis on which services you should use and why.

Chapter 6, "Windows 2000 Security," discusses both the built-in security mechanisms of Windows 2000 and those security measures that should be included but aren't.

Chapter 7, "Routing and Remote Access," covers connecting your network to the outside world.

Part 2—Windows 2000 Network Planning

This section discusses all aspects of network planning and design, from the physical layer up through server applications. The emphasis is on up-front planning to eliminate systemic problems down the road.

Chapter 8, "Network Design," is a soup-to-nuts discussion of network design. Every aspect of network planning and design is discussed, including an empirical method for determining how many servers and collision domains you'll need based on the sorts of uses your network will support, for all available network technologies.

Chapter 9, "Designing Windows 2000 Networks," is a discussion of Active Directory planning and design. Practical design and flexible choices are stressed, including shortcuts to Active Directory implementation and the periodic need for overhaul as new uses appear.

Chapter 10, "Deploying Windows 2000," provides a template for distributing Windows 2000 Professional and Server throughout your network.

Chapter 11, "Upgrading Networks to Windows 2000," provides answers for those of us who are moving from Windows NT or earlier network operating systems to Windows 2000.

Part 3—Windows 2000 Every Day

This section is about the long-term maintenance of both your network and your network support operation.

Chapter 12, "Supporting Clients," discusses how to manage the client computers in your network—no matter how many you have or what sort of clients you use. This chapter covers establishing a four-tiered support structure for rapidly responding to and fixing problems with client computers.

Chapter 13, "Supporting Servers," discusses how to manage multiple servers in your network. Issues like domain management and high availability are covered in depth.

Chapter 14, "Information Technology Management," discusses your IT support organization and how to troubleshoot it to keep your computers running well.

Part 4—Troubleshooting and Optimization

This section shows you the fastest ways to deal with a wide range of problems, covering both the theory and practice of optimization and troubleshooting.

Chapter 15, "Performance Optimization," covers not only performance theory but which optimizations make the most sense.

Chapter 16, "Troubleshooting Theory," covers the basic tenets of troubleshooting that apply to all systems.

Chapter 17, "Practical Troubleshooting," is a troubleshooting guide written specifically for Windows 2000 that will help you narrowly define what's wrong and how to fix it.

Chapter 18, "The Registry," discusses that holy grail of Windows 2000 gurudom: the Registry. This chapter will help you decipher its cryptic contents and make it a tool you use rather than a problem you fear.

Appendix—Useful Registry Keys

This encyclopedic reference to the Windows 2000 Registry contains those keys I find myself modifying frequently. You will find valuable information that will assist you throughout your practice and as a Windows 2000 administrator. Important Registry keys are highlighted for easy reference.

Watch the 24seven Web site, `www.24sevenbook.com`, for updates, tips, and tricks you can use. See you there!

Part 1

Windows 2000 in Depth

Topics Covered:

- Architecture of Windows 2000
- Versions of Windows 2000
- Services of Windows 2000
- Windows 2000 Installation options
- The Windows 2000 Boot Process
- Using the Windows 2000 Repair Process
- Windows 2000 Disk Storage
- Disk Encryption in Windows 2000
- Managing Storage
- Implementing fault tolerance
- Core Windows 2000 Networking Technologies
- Choosing network protocols
- Network Services
- Windows 2000 Security Model
- Group Policies
- Implementing Network Security
- Internet Access
- Virtual Private Networking

1

Windows 2000 Core Technologies

Windows 2000 is an amazing operating system; it is the most sophisticated and useful operating system ever developed. Most amazing is the relative simplicity of Windows 2000's basic architecture. From a few simple design decisions springs an operating system capable of running the most complex software available across a number of processors in a single machine on virtually any processor architecture.

Before we dive into the complexity of Windows 2000, let's take a look at those simple precepts upon which all the complex services of Windows 2000 are based. Once you understand the architecture of Windows 2000, its sometimes inexplicable behavior becomes quite explicable.

Although I wrote this chapter primarily for administrators migrating from other operating systems like UNIX, I explain the inner workings of Windows 2000 in a concise manner that even the most seasoned Windows NT administrator should appreciate. I also set the stage for the rest of the book and explain terms that will be used throughout the book.

This book should be used in conjunction with Microsoft's official Resource Kits for Windows 2000. The Resource Kits contain very precise administrative procedures to cover just about every task you'd need to perform and numerous utilities that belong in the toolbox of every serious administrator. However, they are extremely focused on Microsoft's marketing view of the network world, so they don't provide a well-rounded discussion of management techniques, they don't discuss the problems you'll find with Windows 2000 services, and they don't contain any significant real-world case studies or scenarios outside Microsoft's own walls.

Think of this book as a reality check for the Microsoft Resource Kits.

This book is primarily about the most important package of Windows 2000: Windows 2000 Server. However, nearly all the information in this book applies to all packages of Windows 2000, so throughout this book, the term *Windows 2000* refers to any current version of Windows 2000, including Windows 2000 Professional. I will refer to more specific products, such as Windows 2000 Advanced Server or Windows 2000 Datacenter Server, when a feature is available only in that package.

Windows 2000 Design Goals

Windows 2000 is the latest incarnation of Windows NT, which Microsoft created to compete directly against OS/2, NetWare, and UNIX in the file server and small application server markets. Windows 2000 was called Windows NT 5 while in the beta process, but Microsoft changed the name to Windows 2000 in order to decrease confusion in the minds of consumers when they end the MS-DOS–based Windows 9x development track. (It's interesting to note that Northern Telecom owns the trademark for NT in the networking market, which may have had something to do with the name change as well.)

Since then, microprocessors have become as powerful as traditional mainframe processors, and the minicomputer and mainframe markets have nearly been replaced by the microcomputer platform upon which Windows 2000 runs, so it now competes as an application server as well.

The market for network operating systems has changed completely since the early days of Windows NT; OS/2 has been completely dispatched as a competitor, and Novell NetWare is losing ground so quickly that the company will likely not be profitable this year. But despite NT's amazing success against its commercial competitors, it is losing ground in the Internet services market to a most unusual competitor: Linux and the open source movement. Started as a student project that evolved into a revolution against commercial ownership of software, Linux has very rapidly become a strong competitor to Windows NT in nearly every aspect. Although NT currently supports more native services and is vastly easier to configure and manage, Linux is catching up fast and gaining momentum and wide industrial support. The development of Linux proves that not only can decentralized, unmanaged development work, decentralization may in fact be a better model for mass-market operating systems and applications.

To succeed as a *network operating system* against strong competition, Microsoft designed Windows 2000 to support some important computing technologies. Those core technologies are:

- Multiprocessing
- Multithreading
- Huge applications
- Platform independence
- Pervasive security
- Backward compatibility

Many functions of Windows 2000, such as disk security and network connectivity, are actually the functions of services and drivers that run on top of this basic architecture. I discuss these functions in the later section, "Windows 2000 Architecture."

Multiprocessing

Multiprocessing refers to using more than one microprocessor in a single computer—in other words, all the microprocessors are attached to a single memory bus. This functionality allows multiple microprocessors to work on a single problem without the overhead of network communication. This is useful for tasks limited by processor performance (such as graphical rendering or trajectory calculations) or for providing more processing power for heavily loaded application servers (such as Web or database servers). Windows 2000 implements *symmetrical multiprocessing* (SMP), meaning that all processors are loaded as equally as possible. Later in this chapter, in the "Incarnations of Windows 2000" section, Table 1.1 shows the relationship between Windows 2000 variants and multiprocessor support.

Multithreading

Multithreading allows more than one program to run simultaneously and allows single programs (*processes*) to have more than one simultaneous thread of execution. You'll find a detailed description of multithreading in the "Windows 2000 Architecture" section later in this chapter.

Reality Check: Multithreaded Applications

The Web service of Internet Information Server (IIS) is an excellent example of a multithreaded application. When you start a Web server, code that runs in a single thread listens on TCP port 80 for connection attempts. When a Web browser sends a connection request, that monitor thread immediately spawns a new thread, which runs code that answers the connection. This frees the monitor thread to continue listening for new connections without interruption and provides a dedicated process for every individual Web connection to the server. Multithreading makes it easy to write server applications, and all multiuser services in Windows 2000 work this way.

Large Address Space

Huge applications that efficiently use enormous amounts of memory require a "flat" or linear memory space of 32 bits (or 4GB). However, Windows 2000 uses the high bit to separate kernel mode from user mode, so only 31 bits are actually available for user processes (2GB).

The developers of Windows NT, the product upon which Windows 2000 is based, didn't feel the need to exceed a 32-bit address space for applications. When Windows NT was developed, 2GB hard disks didn't exist, much less dynamic memory modules large enough to provide 4GB to a single machine. However, new software development always seems to use up the resources provided by new hardware development, and Windows 2000 runs best with copious amounts of RAM. Due to these two factors, the Terminal Service functionality of Windows 2000 and some enterprise applications can use more memory space than Windows 2000 can provide, and some large corporate users have begun to complain about Windows 2000's 2GB limitation.

A temporary reprieve for this problem appeared in Windows NT Server 4 Enterprise Edition. A new /3GB switch added to the boot.ini file configures the kernel to use the top 2 bits of memory to split the user space from the system space, with 3/4 going to the user and 1/4 going to the system. This allowed applications to take advantage of 3GB of application space for a small performance penalty. This switch works in Windows 2000 Advanced Server editions as well.

Windows 2000 Advanced Server and Windows 2000 Datacenter Server address this problem (pun intended) by implementing Intel's AWE (Address Windowing Extensions) extended memory management scheme for the x86 processors.

Remember MS-DOS and the 640KB limit? Ever wonder why there was a 640KB limit? The 8086 processor divided RAM into 16 banks of 64KB (1MB total) because the 16-bit processor could only address a 16-bit address space (64KB bytes). Intel added a "page" register of 4 bits (16 unique values) to indicate which bank of 64KB the computer was working on at that moment. A special processor instruction was required to switch banks, and no other processor instructions could address memory outside the current bank. This was a major pain for program developers who had to make sure their code either fit within a single 64KB bank or always correctly handled the bank switching. The first 10 banks of memory were dedicated to user memory (640KB), and the remaining six banks (384KB) were dedicated to BIOS ROM routines and to I/O hardware plugged into the ISA bus. This problem was further compounded by the 80286 architecture, which added another 4 bits of page space to increase the total available memory to 16MB—still segmented into 64KB chunks.

The flat memory architecture of Windows 2000 prevents all of these bizarre problems, but it's limited to just 32 bits of address space (4GB). While that seems like plenty, some applications could make good use of more memory. Windows 2000 Advanced Server and Windows 2000 Datacenter Server use the same bank register scheme to address 8GB and 64GB, respectively, in 4GB blocks. Individual threads are still limited to the 32-bit address space, and special processor instructions are required to switch memory banks. In other words, applications needing more than 4GB of address space have to work around the 4GB limitation the same way MS-DOS programs had to work around the 64KB bank boundaries. It's déjà vu all over again. Later in this chapter, Table 1.1 shows how much memory the various incarnations of Windows 2000 provide.

Windows 2000 is currently being developed for the new Intel Itanium line of processors that use a 64-bit word size. A true 64-bit version of Windows 2000 will allow applications to again treat huge memory as a flat memory space rather than dividing it into 4GB segments. The new Windows API, Win64, will probably replace the segment-switching model quickly for huge applications, guaranteeing that segment-switching will never gain widespread acceptance before it is rendered obsolete. It will be interesting to see if Microsoft releases Win64 for the Alpha (already a 64-bit processor that runs in 32-bit mode for Windows 2000) and for AMD's Sledgehammer processor that adds 64-bit extensions to the standard x86 family.

Platform Independence

Platform independence allows Microsoft to quickly target emerging machines as platforms for Windows 2000 and to keep from being tied to any specific hardware manufacturer (namely Intel). Windows 2000 runs on an abstract virtual machine (the hardware abstraction layer, or HAL) that translates hardware accesses from Windows 2000 to whatever is required by the hardware machine. This feature allows Microsoft to quickly port Windows 2000 to any machine architecture by creating a unique HAL for the new target machine and then recompiling Windows 2000 for the microprocessor used by the machine.

NOTE Windows 2000 actually only supports microprocessors capable of operating in the little-endian byte order mode used by Intel microprocessors. *Endian* refers to the byte order of a stored 32-bit word: storing a word with the most significant byte first is *big endian*; storing a word with the least significant byte first is *little endian*. Most modern processors (except those made by Intel) can switch between big-endian and little-endian modes, but an actual computer may be hardware-limited to one mode or the other. For example, while the PowerPC processor can run in either mode, the processor is likely hardwired in the big-endian mode on the Apple Macintosh, which would make it impossible to port Windows 2000 to that platform.

At one time, Microsoft supported four microprocessor architectures for the Windows NT kernel upon which Windows 2000 is based:

MIPS   NT was originally developed on MIPS computers, but MIPS development has since been abandoned.

Intel 32-bit architecture   This architecture includes the obsolete 386 and 486, Pentium, and Pentium Pro processors, as well as the current Celeron, Pentium II, Pentium III, and Xeon processors from Intel and the AMD 6x86 and Athlon processors.

Digital Alpha   Now that Compaq owns the processor, its future is uncertain. Hitachi, the second source for Alpha processors, has continued its development past the original Digital development track. Microsoft released a beta version of Windows 2000 for the Alpha, but has yet to release a final version, and there are doubts that they ever will.

IBM's PowerPC   PowerPC development has been abandoned because IBM stopped producing PowerPC-based workstations. Currently, only the Apple Power Macintosh workstations use the PowerPC microprocessor.

Microsoft has dropped support for the MIPS and PowerPC processors for Windows 2000 due to lack of demand. The future of the Alpha processor is now uncertain following the acquisition of Digital's semiconductor divisions by Compaq, so Windows 2000 may never support the Alpha processor. The next version of Windows 2000 for the Itanium is in beta testing as this book goes to press, however, proving that Microsoft's commitment to platform independence is fruitful despite the hegemony of Intel processors.

Pervasive Security

Pervasive security provides an environment wherein an application can be certain that its data has not been modified by another application on the same machine. Applications running on the same machine cannot violate the memory space of other applications, which prevents both accidental crashes and malicious theft of data. Despite the steady stream of news about esoteric bugs in Windows 2000's security implementation, the architecture remains secure, and Windows 2000 is no less secure than any other mass-market, high-end operating system. Unfortunately, vendors (including Microsoft) frequently make mistakes in the security implementations of services and applications that run on top of the secure Windows 2000 kernel. This creates back doors that can be used to exploit a machine. These problems are common to all operating systems, however, and Windows 2000's security architecture actually prevents numerous flaws from expressing.

Reality Check: Windows 2000 Security

It's hard to toe the Microsoft line on Windows NT and Windows 2000 security when Microsoft releases security hot fixes for the operating systems at an average rate of about twice per week. Linux fixes come out just as frequently, however, indicating that these operating systems are simply subject to exploits by vastly more hackers and security researchers now that the Internet is ubiquitous.

Backward Compatibility

Windows 2000 supports backward compatibility with existing applications and standards. It also supports a number of application subsystems that provide backward compatibility to various earlier Microsoft and third-party operating systems. Various subsystems provide compatibility with the following:

- DOS (Windows 2000 Virtual DOS Machine, NTVDM)
- 16-bit Windows applications (Windows on Windows, WoW)
- OS/2 1.3 (OS/2 subsystem)
- POSIX (POSIX subsystem)
- OpenGL (OpenGL API)
- Win32

Programs that are written to these specifications and do not try to access hardware directly or require the services of drivers that do should work correctly under Windows 2000. The OS/2 subsystem is obsolete, and the vast majority of users do not use the POSIX subsystem.

Users of Windows 2000 Professional use the MS-DOS and Windows on Windows subsystems frequently. The Win32 subsystem is required for the operation of Windows 2000 and for that reason is sometimes not considered to be a subsystem.

Pervasive Internet Connectivity

Windows 2000 builds on the Internetworking improvements of its predecessor, Windows NT. The first version of Windows NT didn't even include a TCP/IP stack. From these humble beginnings springs Windows 2000, which includes more Internet compatibility features as part of the operating system than any other operating system ever released, including UNIX and Linux. Unlike Windows NT, TCP/IP is a required part of the Windows 2000 operating system and cannot be uninstalled. Internet connectivity features include:

- Highly optimized TCP/IP stack
- Routing support for RIP, OSPF, and other routing protocols
- Stateless packet filtering
- Network address translation (NAT)
- TCP/IP-based load balancing
- TCP/IP-based Quality of Service bandwidth allocation
- IPSec (IP Security)
- Point-to-Point and Layer-2 Tunneling protocols
- HTTP, FTP, NNTP, and SMTP servers
- Secure Socket Layer support
- PPP and Remote Access Server
- State-of-the-art Web browser

These improvements, many of which existed in a less-integrated fashion in Windows NT 4, make Windows 2000 a very serious contender in the Internet server market and enable a seamless connection to the Internet from a Windows 2000 client.

Windows 2000 Architecture

Windows 2000 is a *preemptive multitasking* operating system, which means it can do more than one thing at a time—whether or not the individual processes are written to cooperate with one another.

The scheduling of these various processes is the domain of the kernel, as is the allocation of memory and communication with input/output (I/O) devices. The kernel manages the three basic components of a computer: memory, processor time, and I/O.

The physical (if you can call it that) implementation of Windows 2000 is a series of system files that are loaded during the boot process. For example, basic kernel services are contained in the file `ntoskrnl.exe`, and the hardware abstraction layer for your machine is contained in a file called `hal.dll`. Each specific system service or driver has its own file associated with it. When a service is dependent upon another service, such as the `cdfs.sys` CD file system's dependency upon the `cdrom.sys` device driver, the dependent module will fail to start if the dependent driver isn't already running. Service and driver dependencies are indicated in the Registry keys that control the service.

The kernel and all drivers share a single memory address space; they are protected from other processes but not from each other. This process memory space is called the *kernel mode*. Most of the kernel is nonpageable, which means that it's always available in RAM and is never paged out to disk. Most of the kernel cannot be paged out, because it contains the code that controls paging and the disk drivers. It is also a performance optimization since the kernel is frequently used. Drivers and services in the executive are pageable (unless configured otherwise) because they're used less often and are not critical to the paging function.

> **NOTE**   Since drivers share the same protected space as the kernel, they can crash Windows 2000. Blue-screen crashes are caused by drivers that either are poorly written or are trying to drive malfunctioning hardware.

The kernel is divided into distinct components:

Process Manager   Creates threads and processes upon request. A *process* is simply a unique virtual address space consisting of one or more threads. *Threads* are unique chains of execution within a process that represent the fundamental, scheduled entity in Windows 2000. Threads have their own kernel stack, user stack, and environmental variables. (A *stack* is a scratchpad area available to threads for quick storage and retrieval of data during calculations.)

Interrupt handlers   Act when called upon by hardware events such as page faults or I/O calls. The kernel establishes an interrupt handler for each possible interrupt call. The kernel handles some interrupts itself; drivers running in the kernel space handle others.

Hardware abstraction layer   Makes all computers appear the same to Windows 2000, whether they are based on the industry-standard PC architecture, the Advanced RISC Computing (ARC) platform, or any other machine. The hardware manufacturer provides the HAL for machines other than standard PCs.

TIP   Think of the HAL as a device driver for the computer's motherboard.

Object Manager   Provides a namespace for various components of Windows 2000, such as files, ports, processes, and threads—virtually anything that the system would need to keep track of. Processes can use the services of the Object Manager to refer to other objects in the system.

TIP   Using the Performance Console, you can view many of the objects managed by the Object Manager.

Virtual Memory Manager   Controls the paging of memory to disk. In addition to the typical processing functions, all modern microprocessors include a device called a *Memory Management Unit* (MMU) that is crucial to the architecture of preemptive multitasking operating systems, including Windows 2000. MMUs facilitate three crucial functions:

    Address abstraction   Creates a unique address space for each process. Each process simply sees a contiguous space of free memory starting at address 0 and going for the length of requested memory, no matter where the process is actually stored in RAM. This allows processes to assume they have control of the entire computer's memory space without conflicting with the memory of another process.

    Page protection   Prevents processes from accessing memory that is assigned to another process (which results in the familiar access violation error message). This ensures that one process can't crash other processes on the machine.

    Virtual memory   Allows the operating system to use I/O storage as memory by recording pages of memory on an I/O device (such as a hard disk drive) and recalling them whenever the memory is accessed. This operation is entirely hidden from the process, so the computer appears to have more RAM than it actually has.

TIP   Use the System applet in the Control Panel to specify how you want virtual memory set up on your computer. Click the Advanced tab, click the Performance button, and then click the Change button.

Interprocess Communications Manager   Provides the local procedure call (LPC) facility, which passes messages between processes. Since processes cannot violate the address spaces of other processes, they use the LPC facility to transfer information. The LPC facility acts as the interface between the kernel mode and the user mode. In concert with the remote procedure call service, it provides the abstraction necessary to interface with processes on remote computers over a network.

I/O Manager   Presents a uniform interface to which all drivers can attach. The I/O Manager handles the passing of data and messages between device drivers, similar to the way the LPC mechanism handles interprocess communication. Drivers can depend upon the services of other drivers through layers called *dependencies*. For example, basic drivers that communicate directly to hardware are called device drivers. Higher-level drivers such as the NTFS file system depend on hard disk device drivers to store data. This layering of drivers allows the abstraction of specific purpose for drivers; for example, various storage mediums can use the same file system, and multiple file systems can use the same storage medium.

Windows 2000 in Depth

PART 1

TIP   The Device Manager in the System Control Panel applet allows you to control the functionality of the I/O Manager.

Cache Manager   Optimizes file access by using RAM to store frequently accessed files. The Cache Manager acts much like a driver layered between the file system driver and user-level processes. When a user requests a file that is in the cache, the Cache Manager returns it rather than accessing the slower storage medium. The Cache Manager works closely with the Virtual Memory Manager to use otherwise unused RAM. Whenever the Virtual Memory Manager needs memory, it deallocates cache memory before paging active processes out to disk.

Drivers   Provide the interface to I/O devices through a layered system of dependencies upon more basic drivers. The next section explains drivers in detail.

Security Reference Monitor   Enforces security by limiting which objects can access other objects. When an object makes a request to access another object, the accessing object provides a security identifier that the Security Reference Monitor checks against the access control list of the referenced object. If the object's security identifier is not present in the control list of the referenced object, access is denied. Through this mechanism, user-level security is implemented pervasively throughout Windows 2000. Chapter 6, "Windows 2000 Security," describes this mechanism in detail.

Plug and Play Manager   Controls Plug and Play drivers, sending them the commands to start and stop as necessary to support hot-swappable hardware and device detection and installation.

Power Manager   Acts as a central point of control for power-related events and messages. The Power Manager is responsible for monitoring battery state; starting, stopping, and pausing hardware resources to conserve power; and controlling the hibernation and standby features of the operating system.

Graphical device interface   Provides the interface through which graphics are represented on the screen. This includes the Window Manager component to provide higher-level content-based regions (windows). Prior to Windows NT 4, this component existed outside the kernel. It was incorporated in Windows 2000 to decrease processor overhead and improve graphical performance of the operating system.

Drivers

Drivers are used to control (or drive) I/O devices such as hard disks, serial ports, or video displays. Every piece of hardware that can work with Windows 2000 ships with a piece of software that Windows 2000 uses to control the device. (In addition, Windows 2000 comes with a number of drivers for common devices).

Drivers allow Windows 2000 to control any type of I/O device—not just those devices that existed when Windows 2000 was written. Drivers also provide a convenient abstraction for various low-level services; for example, file system drivers allow a single computer to use more than one data structure for file storage to more closely fit the characteristics of a specific device.

Drivers are all pretty much the same architecturally, but a few important classes of drivers are made distinct by their importance to the operation of Windows 2000:

Device drivers   Control hardware directly. These include hard disk controller drivers, video device drivers, and so forth.

File system drivers   Control the structure of stored data on a storage device and allow chunks of data, called *files*, to be referred to by a given name. File system drivers control the device drivers for storage devices in order to perform this function.

Network drivers   Perform the various functions necessary to transmit data over data links. These layered functions include chopping up data into addressed packets, providing named storage retrieval, and driving network adapters.

During the early development of Windows 2000, Microsoft released the Windows Driver Model (WDM) specification to manufacturers for device drivers that would be supported both by Windows 98 and Windows 2000. Windows 2000 requires WDM drivers to support power management features in order to place the devices in standby or power them off for hot-swap ability. Some device drivers from Windows NT (sound card drivers, for example) are compatible with Windows 2000 when power management is not necessary.

TIP   If you can't find a Windows 2000 driver for an esoteric device (that isn't a network adapter) try using a Windows 98 driver or a Windows NT driver. This usually fails, but when it works, you can continue using a device you would probably otherwise discard.

Services

Services are simply applications that do not have a direct user interface and are automatically started by the operating system. Services run as if they had been logged in with a defined user security context. The configuration of services is usually managed either by a Control Panel applet or by a Microsoft Management Console (MMC) snap-in. Services differ from drivers in that they run outside the kernel and cannot, therefore, directly affect the operation of Windows 2000 (in the theoretical version of Windows 2000 that is bug-free, of course). They can only make calls to the kernel. Many services are started automatically at boot time, with various security permissions as required by their purpose. Other services are started upon demand. You manage services using the Service snap-in built into the Computer Management console.

Services operate within the protected mode security environment of the executive, but they are not part of the kernel proper; the operating system can actually boot and operate without any services running.

Incarnations of Windows 2000

Microsoft currently maintains five versions of Windows 2000, although only four of them are technically products: Windows 2000 Terminal, Windows 2000 Professional, Windows 2000 Server, and Windows 2000 Advanced Server. As of this writing, the fifth product, Windows 2000 Datacenter Server, has not been released.

Table 1.1 compares key features of each package.

Table 1.1   Windows 2000 Product Options

Product	Available Memory	Processors	Clustersupport
Terminal	Shared	Shared	N/A
Professional	4GB	2	N/A
Server	4GB	4	N/A
Advanced Server	8GB	8	2-node
Datacenter Server	64GB	32	4-node

Windows 2000 Terminal

Windows 2000 Terminal is the client environment provided by the Terminal Services of Windows 2000 Server. It provides services similar to Windows 2000 Professional for users of thin clients and the Microsoft Terminal Services client.

Windows 2000 Professional

Windows 2000 Professional is Microsoft's business-class desktop operating system, and it will form the basis of their next generation of home operating systems when they retire the MS-DOS–based Win32 line of operating systems descended from Windows 95. Because Windows 2000 does not perform as well as Windows 95/98/ME in the video game and multimedia markets (due to the heavy overhead of its graphical rendering subsystem), Microsoft has not yet merged the two operating system lines.

Important services of Windows 2000 Professional include:

File and Print Sharing   Fundamental to network operating systems, the File Sharing service enables a server to act as a large shared hard disk, so that many clients have access to a vast amount of shared storage space. Users can share files ubiquitously in an organization and have a platform for basic multiuser applications. Print Sharing service transmits documents from several clients to a server that queues them up and prints them one at a time.

NetMeeting Remote Desktop Sharing   The NetMeeting Remote Desktop Sharing service allows IT administrators and trainers to connect to a Windows 2000 Professional user's desktop and remotely control it to fix problems and explain how to use software. While the machine is being controlled, however, only the controller's input is recognized—not the input of both users, as the free Virtual Network Computing (VNC) tool from AT&T allows. In addition, the service does not allow the user to "send" control of their desktop to the administrator. This makes it difficult for an admin outside of a network-address-translated network to reach a computer inside it. Otherwise, the service is almost exactly like VNC in its performance and characteristics. NetMeeting operates over the H.323 video teleconferencing protocol, which many firewalls are not capable of translating as well. On the plus side, NetMeeting allows for voice-over networking, whiteboard use, and other simultaneous collaboration. With NetMeeting to control desktops remotely and Terminal Services to control servers remotely, Microsoft has finally provided complete remote control service for all their operating systems in the enterprise.

Windows Installer   The Windows Installer provides a standardized format for describing application installations. By standardizing an installation description format (the .msi installation package file), Microsoft has provided a foundation for remote installation and change control. Unfortunately, Office 2000 is currently the only suite of applications that supports the Windows Installer. Unless every application you're going to install uses the .msi installation package file, you'll have to create your own .msi packages or use other methods to perform remote installation. Until the vast majority of application developers support the Windows Installer, it won't be particularly useful as an administrative convenience.

Windows 2000 does come with Veritas (formerly Seagate) Software's WinINSTALL .msi packaging tool. This software works by saving a "before" snapshot of your computer's file system and Registry to compare to an "after" snapshot taken after the application is installed. The program then creates the installation package by copying the files and Registry keys that are different between the two snapshots. Repackaging existing applications isn't particularly convenient, especially if you need to exclude files. You'll have to maintain a clean computer (or virtual machine) that can be used to create snapshots. The packager is also not flexible about installation location and has no facility to enable or disable portions of an application installation. Until apps come as .msi packages, this isn't really a convenience, except in extremely large environments.

Plug and Play   Plug and Play is a set of device drivers that allows the operating system to manage the computer hardware, reconfigure device resource allocation, and manage power. Combined with power-management-aware device drivers, this allows many peripherals to be *hot-swapped* (added and removed from the system without shutting down the computer). In my opinion, this is the primary improvement in Windows 2000 over Windows NT, and it provides a broad set of new administrative possibilities to both clients and servers. Plug and Play allows entire new technologies to be supported, such as USB and Firewire, and tremendously improves support for existing PCMCIA and CardBus devices. In addition, Windows 2000 consumes the lowest amount of standby power of any of Microsoft's operating systems while running on a laptop.

Internet Connection Sharing   Internet Connection Sharing is a simple version of the Network Address Translation (NAT) component of Windows 2000 Server's Routing and Remote Access Service (RRAS). Internet Connection Sharing provides a very simple interface through which nontechnical users can specify which one of two network connections should be "shared." The service then automatically configures NAT, DHCP, and a DNS proxy service on that interface so that computers connected to it can be set to receive a DHCP address and experience seamless connectivity to the Internet using just a single public IP address.

Windows 2000 Server

Windows 2000 Server is Microsoft's main line server operating system for providing file, print, terminal, Web, and application services to networks from the small business to the large enterprise.

Windows 2000 Server is designed to run on commodity server hardware that is not necessarily specialized and which need not be any different than workstation hardware. The broad range of hardware upon which it can run allows the operating system to be scaled from small departmental servers that handle a few connections a day to massive multi-processing Internet servers that handle hundreds of thousands.

Windows 2000 Server is the direct descendant of Windows NT 4 Server, which was Microsoft's most popular server operating system ever. At the release of Windows NT Server 4, Microsoft held about 4 percent of the server market. By the release of Windows 2000 Server, they held about 50 percent and were selling about 80 percent of new installations. Windows NT 4 completely outcompeted Novell NetWare, OS/2 Warp, and most proprietary versions of UNIX. Only Solaris and Linux retain any significant market share against it.

Windows 2000 Server is poised to close the remaining gap. Microsoft took a long hard look at Linux, the operating system they consider to be their primary competition now, and made certain that everything Linux could do, Windows 2000 Server could do better. The list of network services added to Windows 2000 is impressive: LDAP directory support with Active Directory, operating system integrated DNS, Kerberos secure authentication, IPSec (which Linux does not support), network address translation and numerous routing protocols, and multiuser terminal sessions. Windows NT has always been better at managed-user-based security and administrative convenience. For many sites, UNIX will remain only for inexpensive mail services because Microsoft does not provide lightweight POP3 and SMTP mail tools with their operating system.

Active Directory   Active Directory is essentially a hierarchical database that stores information about both the configuration and network resources, such as computers, users, and groups. Microsoft has integrated this rather simple database into most of its services to store necessary information in a centrally managed location along with other related data. It is the service integration of Active Directory, not the database itself, which makes the concept interesting. When Microsoft and third parties create tools that make Active Directory management more intuitive, Windows 2000 Server will be truly hard to compete against.

Intellimirror   Intellimirror is Microsoft's file replication service, dusted off, renamed, and integrated with Active Directory. Intellimirror components are capable of replicating files and Active Directory objects automatically between different computers, which make distribution of information, application, and data files automatic. Some unfortunate restrictions on the service, however, seriously limit its effectiveness for many environments.

Group Policy   Microsoft has extended the Windows NT 4 security policy concept by allowing multiple policies affecting more than just security to affect the same user based on their association with different security groups. This greatly improves an administrator's ability to fine-tune how various users are allowed to use their computers and network services.

Kerberos   Kerberos is an authentication scheme developed originally to shore up the security of UNIX systems, which apply the concepts of encryption to the problem of user authentication. Microsoft's rather naïve NT Challenge and Response authentication scheme—based only on user passwords—was frighteningly easy to compromise, especially when they integrated it with Internet Explorer. Any Web site on the planet could secretly coax your account name and hashed password out of your computer. Kerberos authentication provides short-term "tickets" or authentication keys that prove you are who you say you are, but whose valid life is so short that by the time they're acquired by a hacker, they're already obsolete and worthless. This eliminates the practical possibility of password theft and impersonation.

Public Key Infrastructure   Microsoft's Public Key Infrastructure (PKI) allows system services like the NTFS Encrypting File Service to work with any PKI-compliant encryption algorithm, which in turn can support many different methods of user authentication. This extensible security system allows organizations to choose at a management level what grade of security is appropriate for them, rather than being forced to rely on frequently inferior security that comes built in to operating system services. PKI provides encryption services to IPSec, the Certificate Manager, Secure Socket Layer, the authentication and login services, disk encryption, and every other encryption-related service of the operating system.

File and Print Service for Macintosh clients   File and Print Service for Macintosh clients was an early market opportunity for Windows NT since Apple had never come up with a compelling server operating system (despite many attempts). Microsoft implemented Apple's AppleTalk network protocol and packaged it with a service to provide file and print services to Macintosh clients. Because the service emulates an Apple file share, no software installation is necessary on the Macintosh client. For this reason, Windows 2000 is the preferred network operating system in most Macintosh installations.

Dynamic Host Configuration Protocol (DHCP)   DHCP address assignment is included so TCP/IP clients can dynamically obtain their IP address and other TCP/IP configuration data from a central server. This eliminates a lot of hassle for network administrators and is easy to use.

Routing and Remote Access   Routing TCP/IP and IPX packets allows Windows 2000 servers to act as routers in an internetwork. Although generally less efficient than special purpose routers, the function adds no additional cost and is an effective way to increase overall network throughput when you use it judiciously.

Remote access dial-up networking allows modem users to attach to a Windows 2000 network to access any of its service features or applications. Windows 2000 supports a practically unlimited number of simultaneous dial-in users as well as dial-out connectivity and demand dialing to connect to the Internet or other networks.

NetWare Connectivity and Gateway Services   Client and Gateway Services for NetWare allows Windows 2000 to operate seamlessly with NetWare file servers. Windows 2000 can operate as a client to a NetWare server and can act as a gateway to "reshare" NetWare shares to other Microsoft clients to ease the migration between systems.

Domain Name Service (DNS) and Windows Internet Name Service (WINS)   DNS and WINS both provide resource location through name resolution to clients by returning the IP address of named resources on the Internet or the local network. DNS works with Internet names (`www.microsoft.com`), and WINS works with Windows NetBIOS names (`MYCOMPUTER`).

Remote Installation Service   This service allows computers with PXE network adapters (the type used in diskless workstations) to download their operating system from a central server. Read-only memory located on the network adapter makes a plea for an address assignment and then installs its operating system files automatically. This sort of installation rarely makes much sense unless your workstations all have remote-boot-compatible network adapters.

File Transfer Protocol (FTP)   FTP allows Windows 2000 to act as an FTP server to FTP clients. FTP is a very simple protocol for transferring files; it does not provide the services of a true file-sharing protocol because it doesn't handle file and record locking. It is a very efficient way to distribute software to a number of clients running virtually any operating system. FTP is a service of IIS provided with Windows 2000.

Hypertext Transfer Protocol (HTTP)   HTTP is the protocol of Web service. Windows 2000 makes an excellent Web server and is especially compelling when combined with other BackOffice applications and the dynamic features of Active Server Pages to create e-business solutions. HTTP is a service of IIS provided with Windows 2000.

Network News Transfer Protocol (NNTP)   NNTP provides message-board browsing and posting functions for an intranet. This function is handy for providing technical support or customer service forums on your server, but the NNTP service provided with Windows 2000 is not capable of participating in the Usenet Internet-based NNTP group. NNTP is a service of IIS provided with Windows 2000.

Terminal Services   Windows 2000 Server integrates the services of a package based on Citrix WinFrame to make Windows 2000 Server a truly multiuser operating system. Terminal Services allows diskless Windows terminals to create multiple user sessions on a single server.

A multiuser operating system is an operating system where more than one person can be logged on locally to the same machine. In traditional mainframe or UNIX environments, these "extra" users would be connected via text terminals attached to serial ports on the actual computer. These terminals are "dumb terminals" in that they don't have any processing power, RAM, or disk drives.

Windows 2000 Server Terminal Service supports "smarter" dumb terminals called *thin clients* or NetPCs. These devices usually have microprocessors, but they aren't used to work on your work problems. Thin clients use their processors to transmit keystrokes and mouse-clicks to the terminal server, to connect to the network, and to interpret the windowing commands sent back from the terminal server. The software applications in use are actually run on the terminal server, not the client. So, for example, if 15 users are all running Microsoft Word, 15 copies of Word are running on the terminal server.

Users on a thin client will experience much the same environment as users of a full-function computer, except that their applications will seem to be a little more sluggish than they would on a normal computer under heavy load conditions.

Terminal servers and thin clients are appropriate for situations where only low bandwidth is available, where maintenance costs are extreme, or where actual computers are too expensive. However, powerful Pentium-class computers are usually cheaper than thin clients because of their mass-market appeal and product maturity, so cost alone is rarely a good justification to use terminal servers and thin clients.

Microsoft includes a terminal server client for 32-bit versions of Windows that can make older 486 and Pentium-class computers viable for continued use in a Windows 2000 network. The new Terminal Services Advanced Client (TSAC), an ActiveX implementation of Terminal Services, can be configured to download automatically to any computer running Internet Explorer 4.01 or greater.

Windows 2000 Advanced Server

Windows 2000 Advanced Server is everything that Windows 2000 Server is with just a bit more: twice as many processors and support for more memory, two-node clustering, and IP load balancing. When your problem is so large that Windows 2000 has a hard time handling it, Windows 2000 Advanced Server is the operating system for you.

Cluster Service   Based on the Wolfpack clustering technology that Microsoft licensed from Digital before they were bought by Compaq, the Cluster Service allows two servers to back each other up for applications written to the clustering specification. Client computers connect to the Cluster Service, which runs on one server or the other, and if one server fails, the other server can take over while the server is restored. Clustering works because the two servers trade "state of the service" information over the network so they both have the data they need to take over in the event that the other server fails.

This fail-over mechanism allows for the possibility of "rolling upgrades," where one machine in a cluster is taken offline so its clients fail over to the running machine. The offline machine is then upgraded and brought back online. Next, the second machine is shut down so its clients fail over to the upgraded server, and then it is upgraded. Entire new operating systems can be deployed in this way without a client losing service. Rolling upgrades are the ideal of which IT administrators dream.

Unfortunately, the cluster server only works with applications written to take advantage of the clustering API—essentially, just Microsoft's BackOffice applications. If the service is compelling, third-party application providers will eventually support it as well.

TCP/IP Network Load Balancing   TCP/IP Load Balancing is a form of "stateless" clustering. It splits the client load between servers, but it doesn't provide state sharing, so the servers can't really take over for one another. If a server crashes, its clients have the option of reconnecting to another server, but that's it. While this may seem limited, it's perfect for stateless protocols like HTTP, where no information needs to be retained from one client request to the next. Load balancing lets you deploy numerous servers that all look like one "virtual" server to the clients.

Windows 2000 Datacenter Server

When Windows 2000 Advanced Server can't handle the load, you get Windows 2000 Datacenter Server. With support for four times as many processors, eight times as much RAM, and four-node application failover clustering, Windows 2000 Datacenter Server will run on hardware as powerful as any mainframe computer. Datacenter Server is designed to provide public services such as Web and streaming multimedia and massive applications such as public databases.

Registry Optimizations

In addition to the services and tools listed in the previous section, the following differences are affected by various changes to default Registry settings between the Professional and Server versions of Windows 2000. Unless otherwise noted, "Server" applies to Advanced Server and Datacenter Server as well.

- All versions of Windows 2000 contain Registry keys that identify the platform license. It is possible to (illegally) patch this Registry value to make one product appear to be the other.

- More of the server service in Windows 2000 (srv.sys) is kept in RAM, thus increasing server performance on a heavily loaded RAM-limited machine. Professional optimizes to keep more RAM available and therefore is less suited to file service.

- Write throttling—the timing values used to determine when write-back disk caches are actually written to disk—is different. The default values for Windows 2000 Server are optimized to reduce disk head movement in an extremely busy environment. Professional writes back data more immediately and is optimized for fewer open files.

- Windows 2000 Professional loads the NTVDM virtual DOS machine at boot time for improved application launch time. Windows 2000 Server only loads the NTVDM when necessary. Your software will be more stable if you load the NTVDM individually for each 16-bit application, as described below.

TIP   Have a separate virtual machine for each running 16-bit application by setting the DefaultSeparateVDM value in HKEY_LOCAL_MACHINE\SYSTEM\ CurrentControlSet\Control\WOW to Yes. This improves application stability and shuts down the NTVDM when no 16-bit applications are running.

- The number and priority of system and blocking threads differ. Windows 2000 Server is optimized for fast response, and Professional is optimized for maximum processor and memory resources.

- Windows 2000 Server is optimized for file service by default. Windows 2000 Professional is optimized for application service by default.

- Windows 2000 Professional will accept only 10 client connections to its server service, thus limiting its usefulness as a server.

- Windows 2000 Server supports up to four microprocessors simultaneously as packaged. Professional supports two. Both can be updated using special hardware abstraction layers provided by the various multiprocessor motherboard manufacturers.

Internet Information Server (IIS) will only accept 10 simultaneous inbound connections when running on Windows 2000 Professional, but this limitation is implemented in IIS rather than in Windows 2000.

Licensing Windows 2000

Licensing Windows 2000 is easier than it seems, especially if you follow some simple rules. Here's how it works:

Every server running Windows 2000 requires a Windows 2000 software license. These licenses cost about $700 retail. In addition to that cost, you'll need Client Access Licenses for the number of users you want to support. Every server running Windows 2000 Advanced Server requires a license that costs about $2,400 retail.

Every computer or simultaneous user that connects to a Windows 2000 Server requires a Client Access License. These licenses cost about $40 retail. Clients also require their own operating system license, so if you were connecting a Windows 2000 Professional client, your total cost per client would be $320 + $40 = $360.

Every thin client or computer running Terminal Services requires a Terminal Server License. These licenses cost about $80 retail. If the computer has an operating system, you'll need a license for that, but chances are you'll be using an obsolete operating system such as Windows 3.11 or Windows 95/98 to host terminal services that you already own. If you intend to use new computers to run Terminal Services, check out www.citrix.com for terminal client software that runs on MS-DOS.

If you want the box, CD-ROM, and packaging, you'll have to purchase the minimum bundle, which is one Windows 2000 Server license bundled with five user licenses at a minimum, with an actual retail price of $900.

Finally, if you will be using Windows 2000 to provide services on the Internet, you'll need a Windows 2000 Unlimited Internet Access License, which costs $1,800. Windows NT did not have a license of this type; you could provide Internet services without an additional license. You can also provide unlimited Terminal Service over the Internet with the Unlimited Terminal Services License, which costs $10,000. In order for this to make sense, however, you'd have to have hardware capable of allowing more than 120 users. This number stretches the limit of what a current server could handle, which is probably exactly why the license fee costs this sum. In a year or two, hardware may be available that can make this license a good deal.

Client Access Licenses can be applied in one of two ways:

Per Server You may apply the licenses to a specific server to limit the number of simultaneous users that the specific server allows.

Per Seat You may apply the license to a specific client computer, allowing that client to access any number of Windows 2000 servers.

You should always use Per Seat licensing to simplify your costs and make your network more flexible. Using this method, you simply purchase a Windows 2000 Server software license for each server in your business and a Client Access License for each client. Compliance is easy, and you don't have to worry about who needs access to which server. Table 1.2 shows license costs when this book was written.

Table 1.2   Windows 2000 Licensing Costs

Product	License Cost
Windows 2000 Professional	$320
Upgrade from Win9x	$220
Upgrade from NT	$150
Server 2000	$700
Server 2000 Upgrade	$400
Windows 2000 Advanced Server	$2,400
Windows 2000 Server Unlimited Internet CAL	$1,800
Windows 2000 Terminal Services Unlimited Internet CAL	$10,000
Server 2000 Upgrade CAL	$20
Windows 2000 CAL	$40
Terminal Service CAL	$80
Terminal Service Upgrade CAL	$40

Summary

Windows 2000 is an amazing operating system. It provides more operating system services than any operating system ever, all utilizing a coherent management interface. Services such as disk and network link encryption, world-class Web services, unmatched security, and broad platform compatibility make Windows 2000 very difficult to compete with.

Derived from Windows NT, Windows 2000 is a kernel-based operating system with pervasive security that provides a multiprocessor, multithreaded platform upon which numerous services can run without any danger of their behaving badly and crashing the machine. While the operating system isn't perfect, it can only be crashed by the kernel and calls made to device drivers, which cohabitate in the executive. Because separate services and user-mode processes run in their own secure process space, Windows 2000 is more stable than most network operating systems.

Windows 2000 comes in five primary variations:

Windows 2000 Terminal   The multiuser mode of Windows 2000 Server that is seen on NetPC thin clients, PocketPC palm computers, and computers running the Terminal client for Windows 2000. This environment simulates a Windows 2000 Professional client.

Windows 2000 Professional   Aimed at business desktop and laptop uses, it provides all the convenience features of Windows 98 with the stability of Windows NT. New support for Plug and Play devices makes it possible to completely eliminate earlier operating systems in the enterprise.

Windows 2000 Server   Provides world-class application services for both private networks and the public Internet. Every service provided by any other network operating system (with the possible exception of e-mail) is provided natively by Windows 2000 Server. By standardizing the encryption services of the operating system, Microsoft has substantially improved the security posture of the operating system over that of Windows NT.

Windows 2000 Advanced Server   Adds clustering and load balancing to the feature set of Windows 2000, providing improved fault tolerance and the ability to handle more clients with a single application. Windows load balancing allows many servers to act as one for stateless protocol services.

Windows 2000 Datacenter Server   Extends the reach of Windows 2000 to the most powerful computers available. With support for 32 processors, 64GB of RAM, and 4-node clustering, even the most massive applications can run on the Windows 2000 platform.

You can check out Microsoft's official specifications for the various versions of Windows 2000 at www.microsoft.com/windows2000/guide/.

Case Study: Choosing a Platform

One of my clients is a "dot-com" — a company that provides their primary product over the Internet. As such, their choice of Internet platform is crucial because their entire business runs over it.

They first deployed their Web services in 1997. At that time, they asked me to recommend an operating system for their production Web servers. These servers needed to be

- Inexpensive to deploy and maintain
- Capable of serving up to one million site visits per month per machine
- Capable of supporting a database

We narrowed our choices to three candidates:

1. Windows NT running IIS 4 and SQL Server 5 on a Dell PowerEdge server
2. Solaris running Apache and Oracle 7 on a Sun Ultra
3. Linux running Apache and PostgreSQL on a custom-built server

After calculating the initial costs and total cost of ownership, we found that options 1 and 2 had high initial costs of ownership while options 2 and 3 had high (roughly equal) maintenance costs. This put option 2 out of the running immediately, and the choice simply became "pay now or pay later."

The company took the "pay later" option and deployed their Web site on Linux running Apache and PostgreSQL. They developed their application in the Perl programming language, and it ran very well.

Fast-forward three years (during which they migrated their existing system to MySQL): Due to burgeoning use of their Web site, their Web servers were bursting at the seams. Because MySQL is not an industrial-strength SQL server, they had to write extra code in Perl to simulate views and transactions, and those hacks still didn't work perfectly. They also reached the performance limits of MySQL, and because it can't be clustered or configured to replicate, their site could no longer grow.

In addition, only two system administrators really understood the system. As the company grew, they became heavily dependent upon those two people. New administrators experienced a very serious learning curve trying to figure out what was going on.

So we decided to reengineer the Web site to use more robust industrial solutions. The options in this round were the same as options 1and2 and before: Solaris and Oracle or Windows 2000 and SQL Server 7.

The assumptions this time were somewhat different: The company now had plenty of capital, so initial costs were not an issue. And for the two original administrators, the learning curve would be about the same either way.

But new administrators could come up to speed far faster on the Windows platform than on the Oracle platform, and SQL Server 7 database administrators have become easier to find than Oracle database administrators because the database software is so much easier to use.

When correctly tuned, the Solaris/Oracle solution could serve two to four times as many users, but the machines upon which they run are also four times as expensive, so the users per dollar rate would be essentially the same.

The company decided to go with Windows 2000 and SQL Server 7 because they could change directions and deploy solutions faster on Windows than they could in Solaris. By using Perl ASAPI modules for IIS 5, they were able to leverage their existing code base and programming talent on the new platform. Windows 2000's multiprocessing, multitasking, performance monitoring, and system administration features made the choice simple.

2

Installing Windows 2000 (the Right Way)

If you're using hardware on the Windows 2000 Hardware Compatibility List, installing Windows 2000 is completely seamless and nearly automatic. Microsoft has made numerous improvements to the installation and boot process that resolve a number of Windows NT's long-standing installation problems.

Unlike Windows NT, Windows 2000 has no problem creating, formatting, and installing to large partitions on IDE disks. Unlike Windows NT, you can boot the Windows 2000 CD-ROM to a running command prompt that can be used to fix file system problems, to disable malfunctioning drivers, and to extract data from a non-booting NTFS system. This simple improvement shaves hours off server downtime and troubleshooting. Finally, Windows 2000 supports safe-mode booting, which loads the operating system with a minimal set of drivers and without starting third-party applications that might cause boot problems. Solving these problems in Windows NT often meant installing another copy of Windows NT into the same partition so you could boot to it to correct the problem in the malfunctioning installation.

The difference between an easy and a difficult installation is standard hardware—especially the hard disk controller. Any regular ATAPI/IDE-compatible hard disk will install easily, as will any typical supported SCSI adapter—but Windows 2000 only supports a few UDMA-66 controllers out of the box and does not support UDMA-100 controllers. Any SCSI controller supported by drivers already on the Windows 2000 installation CD-ROM will install smoothly, but SCSI controllers that are not supported on the CD-ROM present special problems, and many RAID devices are either obnoxiously difficult or impossible to get working correctly using Windows 2000's installation software.

What makes some controllers so problematic? They are cousins of adapters included on the Windows 2000 CD-ROM and for that reason are misidentified in the controller detection phase. That misidentification causes the wrong drivers to be installed, and the computer fails with an inaccessible boot device stop message when the setup program starts the kernel. You can't get around this problem by attempting to provide the correct drivers during setup, because the drivers from the CD-ROM are loaded before any drivers provided by the user. Later in this chapter, I'll present a workaround to this problem, but the best solution is simply to use an adapter that is on the Hardware Compatibility List (HCL), which is provided on the Windows 2000 CD-ROM.

The Installation Process

This section describes a standard installation on generic hardware to provide a foundation for the rest of the chapter. I'm not going to describe the installation process in excruciating detail—on standard hardware it's a fairly straightforward process. Feel free to grab a computer and follow along—preferably a computer you don't need for anything else.

A generic computer for the purposes of this discussion is any platform with a hard disk driver and Ethernet adapter supported by drivers that come on the Windows 2000 CD-ROM. Generally this means an Intel-based PC with an IDE hard disk, but many common SCSI controllers and a few other base platforms also fit the definition.

Installation Source Options

You can choose to begin a normal installation from one of the following sources:

- Boot floppy disks
- A boot CD-ROM
- A running installation of MS-DOS
- A running installation of Windows 95, 98, NT, or 2000

These four methods are broken down into two types: booting the installation program or running the WINNT or WINNT32 setup program. Other source options, such as installing from the hard disk drive or from over a network, are just special cases of the last two options.

When you run the WINNT32 program from within Windows 95, 98, NT, or 2000, you have the option of installing a fresh copy of Windows 2000 or upgrading the running operating system. Performing an upgrade installs Windows 2000 but migrates application and some operating system settings from the Registry of the previous operating system.

> **NOTE**   With Windows 2000, installation from any Win32 (including Windows 95 and 98) operating system is started using the WINNT32 program. This is different than Windows NT, where only installations from Windows NT were started using WINNT32.

When you run the WINNT or WINNT32 programs to install Windows 2000, the WINNT program simply installs the Windows 2000 boot loader and the setup program, copies the Windows 2000 source files on your hard disk, and then reboots. When your computer reboots, it's running the setup program as if it had booted the CD-ROM. So in fact all standard installations of Windows 2000 run through the same setup process no matter what the source media is.

Sage Advice: Easy Standard Installs

Here's an easy way to perform nearly any standard installation if you can't boot the CD-ROM for some reason:

1. Partition and format your disk using an MS-DOS boot floppy. Use a Windows 98 boot floppy to partition the disk with large partition support and format it using FAT32. This will allow you to create installation partitions up to 138GB in size.

2. Copy the contents of the \i386 directory onto the local hard disk.

3. Use the following command to install Windows 2000: `C:\i386\winnt /b`.

This method will allow you to remove drivers from the default installation set if they interfere with your hardware.

Beginning the Installation

By setting the computer's BIOS to boot from the CD-ROM, you can simply insert the 2000 CD-ROM and go. No boot from floppy is required, and Windows 2000 doesn't ship with boot floppies. If you need to make them, you can use the boot floppy creation program located on the Windows 2000 CD-ROM.

Windows 2000's initial setup load phase is a 16-bit process that was created just to support loading 2000. During this phase, drivers for generic devices and hard disk controllers are loaded. This phase is necessary for its compatibility—Windows 2000 cannot start until the appropriate hardware abstraction layer (HAL) and disk drivers are loaded, which must of course be specified somehow. The setup program also is capable of probing hardware resources to determine what hardware is installed.

Press F2 during the initial setup load to specify a different HAL for your computer if a special one is required before Windows 2000 switches to 32-bit mode. Your hardware vendor will have supplied a floppy containing these files if they are necessary. Press F6 if the setup program indicates you need to load a hard disk controller driver that isn't included on the Windows 2000 CD-ROM.

Once the screen switches to the Windows 2000 banner, the kernel has been started and the setup program is ready to begin (see Figure 2.1). If the computer presents a STOP message at this point, it's because the drivers on the Windows 2000 CD-ROM don't support your hard disk controller correctly. You may need to use one of the alternative installation techniques presented later in this chapter if this happens.

Figure 2.1   The Windows 2000 banner indicates that the kernel has started.

Hard Disk Drivers

If you have a SCSI, RAID, or an unusual IDE hard disk controller, you're in for a somewhat more harrowing installation experience. The device driver for your hard disk controller must already be in memory when the Windows 2000 installation program starts for the Windows setup program to install to it. Although you can specify additional hard disk controllers during the normal installation process, you cannot install to a drive managed by any loader that isn't loaded prior to starting the Windows 2000 kernel.

Windows 2000 will give you the opportunity to provide a hard disk controller early in the startup process. Press F6 when indicated by the setup program to specify an alternate hard disk driver for the installation. This method is an imperative for many RAID hard disk controllers. If you get an error stating that Windows 2000 cannot find any drives to install to, you need to use this method to load the disk driver. The disk containing these drivers should have been provided with the hard disk controller.

Some hard disk controllers can appear to be different controllers to Windows 2000 when it loads during the setup program, because they return the same signature codes when Windows 2000 probes the device using a driver included on the Windows 2000 CD-ROM or boot floppies. This means that Windows 2000 will load the wrong device driver and subsequently will not be able to access the controller or any drives attached to it. Specifying the driver as mentioned will not solve this problem because Windows 2000 doesn't look for specified drivers until it has already tried the built-in drivers. You'll have to partition and format the disk from another operating system (DOS or Windows):

1. Copy the \i386 directory to that partition.
2. Remove the offending driver and replace it with the correct driver.
3. Start the installation using the winnt.exe program.

You can usually find out which drivers are causing the problem from the Web site of the hard disk controller manufacturer.

> **NOTE**   The term *built-in driver* simply refers to a driver that ships on the Windows 2000 Installation CD-ROM and is available when the setup program probes for hardware. There is no other technical difference between a driver that comes with Windows 2000 and one provided on a floppy disk or CD-ROM.

Windows 2000's setup program is only capable of loading device drivers from the primary floppy drive. This means that if you use a device other than a floppy as your A: drive (for example, an ATAPI removable media drive such as an LS-120 SuperDisk), your BIOS must be capable of handling it as a floppy disk drive or you won't be able to load drivers during the setup phase. The only workaround to this problem, if your BIOS cannot emulate a floppy with the device, is to install an actual floppy drive.

Sage Advice: Installing to Any Hard Disk

If after attempting to use the F6 method to introduce a device driver to the setup program, you still cannot successfully use your disk controller under Windows 2000, use the following method to install Windows 2000:

1. Install a standard IDE hard disk drive on the motherboard controller (or SCSI controller if your motherboard only has a built-in SCSI controller), and install Windows 2000 to that controller.

2. Once Windows 2000 is up and running, install the disk controller driver for your special hardware using the Hardware Wizard and reboot.

3. Edit the boot.ini file to add entries that will allow you to boot from the other partition.

4. Copy the hard disk driver for your hard disk controller to the system partition on the IDE disk and rename it ntbootdd.sys.

5. Format a floppy from within Windows 2000.

6. Copy the following files from the root directory of the system partition to the formatted floppy disk: ntldr, ntdetect.com, boot.ini, and ntbootdd.sys.

7. Use the Disk Administrator to mirror the system partition that is located on the IDE disk onto the disks attached to the special controller. You will have to upgrade each disk to the dynamic partition scheme in order to activate mirroring.

8. Once the mirror partition has completed, shut the computer down and remove the original IDE (or SCSI) disk.

9. Reboot and select the boot.ini option that will load Windows 2000 from the special hardware.

10. If the computer cannot find the operating system when you attempt to reboot, insert the floppy you created and boot from that. When Windows 2000 is up and running, use Disk Administrator to mark the system partition as active. Correct the boot.ini file to load only the correct operating system.

Partition Decisions

Unlike Windows NT, Windows 2000 can partition and format IDE disks up to 138GB during the setup process. (I'm trusting documentation here—I don't actually have this much space as a single volume to attempt to format, so the number may be higher. I've formatted 104GB as a single partition.) This eliminates one of the most annoying problems with Windows NT's boot loader and makes partition decisions more esoteric.

Unless you have a good reason to do otherwise, partition your entire disk as a single partition and install the operating system there. You'll have fewer problems down the road, and you'll avoid the problem of running out of space on your system partition. Many applications, especially server applications, require installation to the system partition or will copy numerous files to the system partition even if the application is installed elsewhere.

> **NOTE** In Microsoft's early MCSE exams, the technical writers confused the terms *system* and *boot* partitions. Rather than correcting the mistake, Microsoft compounded it by trying to promulgate the use of the term *boot partition* to mean the partition containing the system files, and *system partition* to indicate the partition that was marked active and therefore booted. That meaning applies only to the MCSE exams. In the real world (and in this book), the *boot partition* is the partition that the computer boots. The *system partition* is the partition that contains the operating system.

What good reasons are there to do otherwise? There are a few:

- *You want to separate user data from the system and from applications to prevent users from filling up the system partition and crashing the computer.* In my opinion, you're better off using Windows 2000's Quota Manager to solve this problem, but keeping user data on a separate partition is easier to implement and simpler to manage.

- *You want a separate partition for temp files because you don't want the NTFS directory space to be expanded.* In the event that a very large number of small files are stored on an NTFS partition, Windows 2000 will increase the percentage of the disk used to store directory information. This allocation never decreases even if you delete those files. For this reason, some administrators prefer to create a separate partition for temp files and format it using either the FAT or FAT32 file systems, which don't have this problem.

- *You want to separate shares from the system and application partitions for security reasons.* Some services, like the World Wide Web or FTP service, have had in the past and may still contain undiscovered security flaws that could allow access outside their shared folders. By putting these shares in their own partition, you can attempt to minimize the potential damage caused by a security flaw when it is discovered.

Beyond these reasons, you should think hard about why you're partitioning and make sure that your reasons aren't just old habits from bygone operating systems.

In a well-built server, you install the system and applications to its own mirror set. Mirroring allows you to lose either system disk and still boot the operating system, and it's the only software fault tolerance supported for the system or boot partitions. Shared user data would then be stored on a RAID-5 group of however many remaining disks you need to support your data. In this arrangement, operating system disk access and page swapping happens on a different physical set of disks than user data access, which can improve file, Internet, and application server efficiency by 50 percent. This arrangement automatically provides for separation of system and user data. Figure 2.2 shows the disk configuration described above.

Figure 2.2   A well-designed server disk subsystem

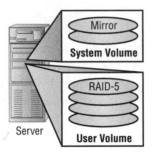

The remainder of the boot process is almost completely automatic. You'll be prompted for some configuration information, like the CD key and the computer's name and network options, but beyond that, the process simply runs by itself. Upon completion, the installer will reboot the computer to a fresh running Windows 2000 installation.

Installation Alternatives

You have to use the Microsoft installation method to install Windows 2000 for the first time, but you don't have to use that method for your remaining installations. Other options for installing Windows 2000 include:

- Upgrading to Windows 2000
- Disk-to-disk sector copying
- Unattended installations

Upgrading

The most important new feature of Windows 2000 for support technicians is its phenomenal support for upgrading. While Windows NT could upgrade earlier versions of Windows NT relatively seamlessly, Windows 2000 Professional is capable of upgrading from Windows 95 or 98 completely automatically—a feature sorely lacking in Windows NT.

> **TIP**   If you already own Windows 95, 98, or NT Workstation, save money by purchasing the Windows 2000 Professional Upgrade edition. There is an upgrade edition of Windows 2000 Server for users of Windows NT Server, as well as upgrade Client Access Licenses. Upgrade editions cost half as much as full editions, but you will have to provide an original CD of your earlier operating system if you perform a fresh install and the setup program can't find an existing copy of the upgradable operating system.

Not only does Windows 2000 support upgrading, it's so completely seamless and automatic that it will truly astonish jaded computer technicians. Windows 2000 will upgrade literally every user setting in the operating system, all the installed applications (with the exception of a few that are known to cause problems under Windows 2000), and all device drivers for equipment supported by Windows 2000. (See the following sidebar, "Sage Advice: Avoiding Upgrade Downfalls," for information about problem applications.)

To upgrade any 32-bit version of Windows to Windows 2000, simply insert the Windows 2000 Professional CD-ROM. If you have CD-ROM autostart enabled, winnt32.exe will launch automatically. Otherwise, you can start it manually by running setup from the root directory on the CD-ROM. Select the upgrade option, enter the CD-ROM key, and just leave the machine to run for about an hour. After rebooting once or twice, Windows 2000 will be installed.

Rebooting is required because the first phase of the installation runs in the original operating system, which copies the Windows 2000 operating system files to the disk. The final act of the first-stage installation is to install the Windows 2000 boot loader in place of the original operating system's boot loader. Upon reboot, the Windows 2000 kernel can load and run, allowing the completion of the installation. Another reboot will be required if you are converting the file system to NTFS, and another if the setup program detects corruption problems with your file system.

Devices for which Windows 2000 could not install a driver will show up with yellow question mark icons in the Device Manager. You can use the update driver function of the Device Manager to install drivers for these devices at your convenience.

TIP   For faster upgrades, copy the \i386 directory from the Windows 2000 CD-ROM to a network share and launch the upgrade from there. With this method, you can go from machine to machine with about five minutes of setup time each to get an upgrade rollout really moving. Schedule this sort of rollout to take place overnight, since the heavy disk load on your servers will lengthen the process for each machine.

Windows 2000 Server will upgrade Windows NT Server as well, but it will not upgrade Windows 9*x*.

Sage Advice: Avoiding Upgrade Downfalls

There is one class of software that the Windows 2000 upgrade process cannot handle well: applications that have software device drivers associated with them. A software device driver is a piece of software that installs as a driver but does not control hardware. These device drivers are usually installed to act as a "wedge" between the application and the operating system in order to perform some function that the operating system would not normally allow the application to perform or to change the functionality of the operating system.

Examples of applications that include software drivers and therefore cause problems during upgrades include:

- Virus-checking software

- Automated "Zip Magic" file compression software

- CD-burning software such as Adaptec EZ CD Creator (Adaptec's ASPI driver for Windows 98 is used by almost all CD-burning software irrespective of its manufacturer, and this software causes problems during the upgrade process.)

- Virtual Private Network clients

- Drivers for laptop convenience features such as power management or BIOS control from within Windows 98

The safest way to handle these sorts of programs during an upgrade is to remove them before the upgrade and then reinstall the latest Windows 2000 compatible version from the manufacturer after the upgrade.

How can you identify this type of software? Using the Windows 95/98 Device Manager, set the option to show hidden devices and then look for software drivers that don't control a physical device. If you can determine what application these drivers are associated with, you can remove the application. Another pretty safe bet is tray icons—although there's no direct correlation, many of these types of programs install tray icons, so by uninstalling the programs that install tray icons, you stand a pretty good chance of removing problematic applications.

You can find some problems in advance by running the upgrade installer from the command prompt using the following syntax:

```
D:\i386\winnt32 /checkupgradeonly
```

The /checkupgradeonly switch indicates that no changes should be made to the computer, so the installation runs and reports upgrade problems but does not attempt to install the operating system. In my experience, this finds most of the problems you'll have, but I've seen a couple of instances where minor problems still slip through.

Disk-to-Disk Sector Copying

For years computer geeks have been using a method called *disk-to-disk sector copying* (also known as *disk cloning*) to copy the contents of a hard disk from one computer to another when they had to install a number of systems. When you buy a new computer from Dell or Compaq, the software that comes on the computer's hard disk was put there using this method. Disk-to-disk copying is handy for migrating from a smaller to a larger disk as well.

This method is amazingly handy for installing Windows 2000. Using the CD-ROM boot installation method on a fast computer, you might install Windows 2000 in 30 minutes. After getting all your drivers loaded, service packs applied, and applications installed, you'll be another two hours down the road if everything goes well. With direct disk-to-disk copying, all these functions can be performed in 10 minutes for your second machine and those that follow.

But there's a small problem: when you copy an installation of Windows 2000 from one disk to another, you get an exact clone of the first installation. Windows 2000 relies upon the installation process to create a unique security identifier (SID) for each computer. Since you've copied the Windows 2000 installation from another installation, the computer's SID is not unique. If left uncorrected, this can cause strange security problems in a networked environment. For example, the local administrator on one machine would have the same SID as the local administrator on another and would therefore be able to access resources inappropriately. Microsoft provides a solution to this problem with the Microsoft System Preparation Tool, which applies unique SIDs and other information to cloned systems. The System Preparation Tool is described in the next section.

After using the System Preparation Tool, you should image the disk to your installation source media or the other hard disks you will be installing it on.

When the cloned computers are booted for the first time, the Setup Wizard will run, asking the user for the machine-specific information. After the user enters this information, the Setup Wizard will apply a new unique SID and reboot the computer, thus completing the system setup and eliminating all of the problems associated with machine cloning.

Sage Advice: The Easiest Way to Install Windows 2000

The most flexible way I've found to do quick and easy Windows 2000 installs is to create a generic Windows 2000 image file using the System Preparation Tool. Copy this image along with your favorite disk-to-disk copying utility to a CD-ROM, and set the burn options to create the CD-ROM as a bootable CD-ROM using floppy drive emulation. Provide the Windows 98 Emergency Disk, which includes a set of generic CD-ROM drivers as well as formatting and partitioning utilities, as the boot image. Then you can simply boot the CD-ROM in a brand new computer and copy the image file from the CD-ROM to the hard disk. It's fast, flexible, and doesn't require swapping hard disks or a network connection.

You needn't install every operating system component prior to creating your source image—in fact, you're better off installing as few specific drivers as you can get away with because this makes your source image applicable to many different hardware configurations. You can always install specific drivers after an image has been copied to your computer.

Windows 2000 Plug and Play will automatically attempt to load all the drivers for your computer upon the first boot after the image is installed. If all your hardware is supported by the Windows 2000 setup disk, you'll just have to wait a few minutes and perhaps reboot once or twice to finish the installation. Otherwise, you'll need to provide drivers for the hardware that Windows 2000 finds. Make sure end-users are prepared to locate drivers if you'll be leaving the final installation to them.

Tools for Disk-to-Disk Copying

So how do you perform a disk-to-disk copy? With third-party sector copying software or by purchasing your machines with your image preinstalled by the manufacturer. It is theoretically possible to use Windows 2000 Server's disk mirroring, but that method is fraught with peril now that the partitioning scheme has changed. As of this writing, third-party software cannot (yet) correctly image a dynamically partitioned disk.

Third-party utilities are fast and flexible. They allow you to connect to an image server, a machine that stores files containing complete hard disk images, and download and install over the network. This method is easy and fast because you don't have to open up machines and swap hard disks around—just boot an MS-DOS floppy with network support and download the image file from an image server. The third-party utilities cost between $30 and $50 for individual use, increasing to about $250 for network-enterprise use.

Some computer manufacturers (such as Dell) now support image provisioning, whereby you can provide a disk image to the manufacturer (on a hard disk or CD-ROM) that they will automatically install on all the computers you purchase from them. The advantage to you is that you can basically drop-ship completely prepared computers to end-users at any facility in the world without ever seeing the machine—you're multiplying your effort for free. The advantage to the manufacturer is that you're now strongly motivated to purchase only from them. The completeness of the service and your ability to specify multiple image classes varies from manufacturer to manufacturer—contact your vendor for specific details on their program.

The System Preparation Tool   With Windows NT, Microsoft originally didn't support the use of disk-to-disk copying, going so far as to say that it simply wouldn't work because of the SID issue. This, of course, deterred no one, and eventually Microsoft got on the bandwagon and even released their own disk-to-disk copying utility and SID management software.

This tool takes a completed Windows 2000 installation, including applications if you install them, and removes the machine-specific information like the SID, the CD-ROM key, the computer name, and the domain. It then modifies the system start-up to run a configuration Wizard that is similar to the original setup program in appearance but which asks only for the hardware key and the computer's name and domain association.

The Microsoft System Preparation Tool is free and is included in the \support\deploy directory of the Windows 2000 Professional CD-ROM in the deploy.cab cabinet file. The utility does not work with the Windows 2000 Server domain controller—the only way to automate Windows 2000 domain controller installations is to image the server and sysprep it before promoting it to domain controller or to use a third-party SID modification tool written for Windows 2000 (none exist at the time of this writing) or an Answer file (see the next section). The utility does not actually perform the image copy, so I recommend going with DriveImage or Ghost for these sorts of rollouts.

DriveImage DriveImage is my personal favorite. It costs about $30 per machine and does everything it's supposed to do without much hassle. It's from PowerQuest and should be available at your local software store. It's an indispensable part of any Windows 2000 administrator's toolbox, in my humble opinion. It supports disk-to-disk copying and disk-to-file creation, so that images can be stored on other local disks or the network. DriveImage also supports creating and resizing NTFS partitions during the copy process so you can use the entire disk rather than be limited to a partition of the same size as the source. Check out DriveImage at `www.powerquest.com`.

Ghost Ghost is the classic disk-copying software—the company pretty much invented the industry. The original version of Ghost was and is available for download from the Internet for free—although it's a bit outdated these days. Ghost was purchased by Symantec, so the name has changed to Norton Ghost. Symantec has updated the software substantially and provides technical support. A demonstration version can be downloaded from the Symantec Web site at `www.symantec.com`.

Ghost makes the mistake of checking for file system errors and then failing if it finds them. This means that every time Microsoft updates its file system (which happens about once every three service packs in my experience with Windows NT), Ghost will fail with an error rather than perform the image, and the problem can only be fixed by upgrading to the latest version of Ghost whenever it becomes available. For this reason, I prefer DriveImage, which reports the error but copies the image anyway.

Sage Advice: Create a Generic Source

Disk-to-disk copying is sometimes maligned because some people believe the destination machine and the source machine must have a somewhat similar hardware configuration to run Windows 2000. In fact, that's not the case at all.

- The HAL must be the same. This is not generally a problem because 99 percent of all Windows 2000 machines use the uniprocessor HAL for standard PCs. In the worst case, a dual processor machine can run with the uniprocessor HAL and then be upgraded by replacing the HAL file manually or with the `uptomp.exe` Resource Kit utility.

- The video display driver must be the same. This is not a problem because all Windows 2000 machines can run with the default VGA driver and will default to this if they can't load the video driver specified. Windows 2000 will also use Plug and Play to detect your video driver, so this isn't usually a problem.

- The hard disk driver must be supported by the installation. This is easy: simply make a different generic installation for each type of disk controller in your organization. ATAPI computers have one generic installation, Adaptec 2940 SCSI controllers another, Promise FastTrak UDMA66 RAID controllers a third. You can determine the specific disk controller by watching the screen during the HDD BIOS boot, so this is never that hard to determine.

No other peripherals are problematic because they can all be Plug and Play–detected by Windows 2000 on the first boot. Peripherals present in the original source machine that aren't present on the imaged machine are automatically disabled by the operating system and don't represent a problem.

Installing Applications

The second major advantage to using disk-to-disk copying, aside from installation speed, is the fact that you can copy entire installations, including installed applications, policy settings, configuration information, and anything else you want. Basically, the copy proceeds from the point you decide you're finished customizing the source computer. And none of this extra information takes much longer to copy.

You can also remove the excess baggage (such as the Channel bar of Internet Explorer or those start-up tip dialog boxes) installed by applications, so your users don't have to do it themselves. Make desktop settings and configure the user policy for your network before creating your source image, too.

Answer Files

Answer files provide installation automation, but they aren't nearly as quick or useful as disk-to-disk sector copying. Unfortunately, Microsoft has limited the System Preparation Tool to work only with servers that are not domain controllers, so if you need to automate the installation of servers, answer files are your best bet.

Answer files work very simply: a normal Windows 2000 installation occurs, but rather than requiring a human to answer the questions raised by dialogs, the answers can be written into a script called an answer file. The answer file simply contains, as the name suggests, answers to the questions the Wizards would normally ask.

Answer files can be written by hand, but rather than learning yet another script format, you're better off using the `setupmgr` program provided on the Windows 2000 CD-ROM in the support folder (`C:\support\`). The `setupmgr` program allows you to create new answer files by answering the setup dialogs manually, by mimicking the configuration of the computer you're running the program on, or by modifying an existing answer file.

Mimicking the configuration of an existing computer is very easy assuming you've already installed a prototypical computer, which is probably the most common usage. Figure 2.3 shows the Setup Manager in action.

Figure 2.3   The Setup Manager allows you to create answer files for unattended installation.

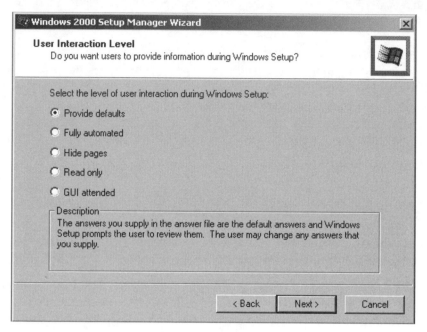

You can select a few different modes of operation for answer files:

Provide Defaults   You supply default answers that the installer can review and change during the installation. This method is appropriate for installations where users have a high degree of sophistication and would be using the answer file as a convenience.

Fully Automated   You supply all of the answers in the answer file, and the installation proceeds without asking the user any questions.

Hide Pages   This mode hides pages you've already answered and presents pages for questions the user must answer. Use this mode when you want to force certain options but must allow the installer to provide some options during setup.

Read Only   For pages that are not hidden, the user may not change answers you've supplied but may provide answers you have not answered.

GUI Attended   Only the initial text mode portion of the setup is automated. The installer must provide answers for the entire GUI portion.

Fully Automated Mode

Since the Fully Automated mode is by far the most useful mode in my opinion, that's the one I'm going to talk about. This is probably the most commonly used mode, since any minor changes can be made after the computer is installed.

Although each computer does need to have (at the very least) a unique name, the answer file can be configured to automatically receive the computer name from the batch file it creates to start the installation process. For example, the user can type:

```
C:\>unattend myserver01
```

Keep in mind that you will be providing such frequently changed variables as the computer name and the user's name. The fully automatic mode of the Setup Manager can be set up to provide unique answers for each computer using a uniqueness database file (with a .udf extension). Creating this file is also automated by the Setup Manager.

To use the answer file for an installation, you simply attach to an installation source on the network or on removable media such as the CD-R that you created with the Setup Manager that contains the answer file, and you launch the setup program using the unattend.bat file that the Setup Manager also created and placed in the installation source directory. You can choose to use a Windows 2000 original CD-ROM as the installation source as well, but there's little reason to do that and you lose some scriptable options relating to Internet Explorer automated installation.

Finally, the Setup Manager allows you to specify the name of an executable program you want to run when the first user logs on to the computer for the first time. This program should be used either to complete the installation of user applications or perhaps to direct new users to support options. Unlike the System Preparation Tool, answer files cannot be used to support the preinstallation of any application. Microsoft applications and those subscribing to the new Microsoft Software Installer (MSI) paradigm can be scripted using their own utilities, but other programs cannot be used. For this reason, answer files should only be used when the more compatible and general purpose System Preparation Tool cannot be used, as with the installation of a domain controller.

Listing 2.1 is a complete unattend.txt file generated for a test server installation. As you can see, the script is fairly easy to understand (it's also completely explained in the unattend.doc file contained in the support directory with the setupmgr.exe program).

unattend.txt

```
;SetupMgrTag
[Data]
    AutoPartition=1
    MsDosInitiated="0"
```

```
    UnattendedInstall="Yes"
[Unattended]
    UnattendMode=FullUnattended
    OemSkipEula=Yes
    OemPreinstall=No
    TargetPath=\WINNT
[GuiUnattended]
    AdminPassword=password
    OEMSkipRegional=1
    TimeZone=4
    OemSkipWelcome=1
[UserData]
    FullName="Matthew Strebe"
    OrgName=Connetic
    ComputerName=*
[Display]
    BitsPerPel=16
    Xresolution=800
    YResolution=600
    Vrefresh=72
[LicenseFilePrintData]
    AutoMode=PerSeat
[TapiLocation]
    CountryCode=1
    Dialing=Tone
    AreaCode=619
[RegionalSettings]
    LanguageGroup=1
[SetupMgr]
    ComputerName0=test1
    ComputerName1=test2
```

```
    ComputerName2=test3
[Identification]
    JoinWorkgroup=WORKGROUP
[Networking]
    InstallDefaultComponents=Yes
```

The unattend.udf file created by the Setup Manager defines those differences between individual computers that you described when you created the answer file. Information common to every computer that will be installed with the answer file is contained in the unattended.txt file; information unique to each computer is described in a separate section for each computer in the unattend.udf file. Listing 2.2 shows the contents of a complete unattend.udf file that describes only name changes for three different computers.

unattend.udf

```
;SetupMgrTag
[UniqueIds]
    test1=UserData
    test2=UserData
    test3=UserData
 [test1:UserData]
    ComputerName=test1
 [test2:UserData]
    ComputerName=test2
 [test3:UserData]
    ComputerName=test3
```

Service Packs—Good and Bad

Service packs are a necessary evil: they fix often-serious problems, but they can also cause serious problems. The record with Windows NT was pretty poor—all of the even-numbered service packs caused fairly serious problems; all the odd-numbered ones were stable.

For example, Service Pack 4 caused some pretty serious disk corruption issues because Microsoft updated the NTFS file system driver that attempted (and occasionally failed) to update core file system structures such as the master file table. This service pack also made it impossible to use the original NT source CD-ROM to recover the system, since once the service pack updated the file system, the NT boot CD-ROM could no longer understand the new format. This left administrators high and dry in the event of a server crash; because the file system format had changed, you couldn't even install a new version of the operating system on the disk.

So why did Microsoft update the NTFS format? Because they were working on the beta version of Windows 2000, and they wanted to make sure that Windows NT could read files written by Windows 2000 so that administrators could load the Windows 2000 beta to evaluate the software. The version of NTFS updated by Service Pack 4 is compatible with the version of NTFS used in Windows 2000. They failed to foresee the troubleshooting problems this could cause, and the serious corruption problems that could occur if the service pack installation was not completed properly.

Once you install a service pack, you can't go back except by using the service pack uninstaller. Many of the original source files are not compatible with later versions from the service pack. With Windows NT, whenever you changed certain components (especially network components), Windows NT requested your original start-up disk and copied the old, original files, replacing newer service pack files. This caused very serious problems in Windows NT, sometimes preventing the computer from rebooting.

With Windows 2000, this problem has been alleviated through the slipstream option, which is also called the integrated installation mode. By running the service pack installer (`update.exe`) and specifying `-s` at the command prompt, the service pack installer will update a copy of the Windows 2000 installation files on the hard disk with the new service pack files. This way, when files from the installation source on the hard drive are updated, files from the latest service pack are copied in, thus eliminating the mixed service pack problem that Windows NT suffered from. If you slipstream your service packs, you won't have to worry about reapplying them after you install software.

The Boot Process

Windows 2000's first-stage boot loader is always contained in the boot sector of the primary partition on the first hard drive on your computer (no matter where Windows 2000 is located, which is a silly flaw, because you may have another operating system on your first drive that you don't want modified, or you may want to boot a hard disk with Windows 2000 on it on another computer for troubleshooting purposes). When you boot your computer, the master boot record loads the Windows 2000 boot loader into memory. The Windows 2000 boot loader reads the contents of the `boot.ini` file (which must be located in the root directory of the first hard disk) and displays a menu of boot options based on its contents. By default, that file contains a reference to the standard Windows 2000 installation and a reference that enables some debugging options.

The Windows 2000 boot loader is capable of loading three operating systems: Windows 2000, Windows NT, and everything else. I'm actually not kidding—it knows how to load Windows 2000 and NT, but for all other operating systems it relies on a special file called `bootsect.dos` that must contain a valid image of a boot sector for the operating system. When you install Windows 2000 on a machine that already has an operating system, the installation program automatically creates that image before it replaces the boot sector. If you select the original operating system in the boot menu, the boot loader chains to that file and expects it to handle loading the foreign operating system.

That covers operating systems installed before Windows 2000, but how about operating systems installed after Windows 2000? Microsoft apparently decided not to support loading other operating systems after Windows 2000, so you are left with some choices, none of which are particularly easy. You can hope the next operating system's boot loader supports chaining to Windows 2000, use whatever native fdisk utility is available to switch the active partition every time you want to change operating systems, hack Windows 2000's boot loader, or install a third-party, multiboot utility such as System Commander.

If you enjoy hacking, you can use sector-editing tools to "lift" the boot sector for foreign operating systems and create `bootsect.dos` files so you can select operating systems installed after Windows 2000. I've done it to support dual booting a Linux system that was installed after Windows 2000.

> **WARNING** For systems you'll be professionally supporting, don't install multiple operating systems on the same computer. This functionality should be reserved for serious computer geeks who understand the implications of multiple booting.

Operating System Installation Order

The order in which you install operating systems is extremely important if you want them all to coexist peacefully with their multitude of boot loaders. Since I can't go through every operating system on the planet, I'll just stick to those systems people actually use (and OS/2, since I have a copy).

First, you can't install MS-DOS or Windows on top of Windows 2000 and still boot Windows 2000. You can't install Windows 2000 to work with an existing Linux installation unless you know how to write your own Linux boot loader. Finally, OS/2 can't be loaded by any other boot loader that I know of. Given these constraints, I've determined that the following installation order actually works:

1. MS-DOS/Windows 95/98
2. Windows 2000/NT

3. Linux (using the master boot record method)

4. OS/2

Of course, when you're done, you get this really strange "chain-o-boot-loaders" effect where the OS/2 boot loader lets you select OS/2 or Linux, the Linux boot loader then lets you select Linux or Windows 2000, and finally the Windows 2000 boot loader lets you select Windows 2000 or MS-DOS/Windows.

NOTE   One easy way around the operating system installation order, if you have to have more than one operating system, is to buy a copy of System Commander by PowerQuest, the authors of much useful software. Recent versions of System Commander have become bloated with features though, so you'll need a FAT partition—annoying if you didn't plan on having one. And I've had it chew up an NTFS partition or two for some reason during installation. Make sure you put System Commander on first and let it detect operating systems as you install them.

The SCSI/MULTI Problem

The last problem with Windows 2000's boot loader is the stupid SCSI/MULTI ARC path syntax in the boot.ini file. ARC (Advanced RISC Computing) paths are supposed to be a universal standard for locating hardware on all computers. The problem is that they are neither universal nor standard. The idea was cooked up in the early '90s as a way to have the new RISC computers boot any operating system. (Remember when RISC was going to save the world from Intel? Those were the good old days.)

Microsoft supported the idea so that the RISC computers Windows 2000 ran on could locate their boot hardware using a standard method. (This was in the days when Windows 2000 ran on a variety of RISC computers.) Because Intel BIOSes didn't support ARC paths, Microsoft wrote the Intel boot loader to support them instead. With the ARC path, the Windows 2000 kernel would know where to find the rest of the operating system once it started. The boot loader just uses the BIOS to find the files. Why the kernel can't do the same is beyond me.

But Microsoft added a feature. Unlike the RISC machines, which always needed a specific device driver to speak to the hard disk, most Intel machines can use the BIOS embedded in the hard disk controller to talk to the machine in a generic fashion, thus obviating the need for a specific hard disk controller driver in the initial load. To indicate that the BIOS should be used, rather than a specific driver, Microsoft invented the MULTI device, which is like the standard SCSI device except that it doesn't require a specific hard disk driver.

This is all fine and good except for one thing—if you install from an ATAPI CD-ROM onto a hard disk that is attached to a SCSI, RAID, or nonstandard IDE controller, the setup program will write the boot.ini file for a MULTI device, because that's what it detects you booted (the CD-ROM). When you try to reboot for the first time, your actual hard disk controller (which requires the SCSI syntax and a hard disk driver) won't be found, and the computer will display a "Stop: Operating System Not Found" error message.

This problem stopped Windows NT cold; Windows 2000 seems to be able to recover from it after a stop in some cases, but not all. The only way to prevent the problem from happening is to install from floppy disks. If it has already happened and you want to salvage the installation, you can install the hard disk in another Windows 2000 machine, fire it up, and correct the ARC paths. You may also need to copy the disk controller's device driver from C:\winnt\system32\devices to the root partition and rename it ntbootdd.sys.

There's another problem with the ARC naming convention. ARC conventions prevent you from booting to removable media. If you sector-copy a working Windows NT installation to an LS-120 floppy and change the ARC paths to boot the A: drive, the boot loader will actually bring the entire Windows NT kernel into memory. But when the kernel starts, it will fail because without a valid ARC path, it can't find the rest of the operating system. And since there's no ARC method to refer to the LS-120 drive, you can't fix the problem using an ARC path name. ARC paths also will fail if you change the drive hardware ID of the disk with Windows 2000 on it.

TIP Format a floppy disk and copy the ntldr, ntdetect.com, boot.ini, and ntbootdd.sys files from the root directory of the boot partition to the floppy. You can use this floppy to boot Windows 2000 if something happens to your master boot record or the boot files of your Windows 2000 machine.

Summary

Installing Windows 2000 is considerably easier than installing any of its predecessors. The typical installation process is very smooth, and with Windows 2000's support for Plug and Play, you don't need to know about every device in your system and its resources in order to get everything functioning correctly.

Besides the typical installation, Windows 2000 supports some very convenient installation options:

- Upgrading
- Disk-to-disk imaging
- Unattended installation using installation scripts

These options provide network administrators with numerous ways to handle even very large scale Windows 2000 deployments with relative ease.

Upgrading from previous versions of Windows is completely automatic—Windows 2000 will import all user settings that can be applied to the new operating system as well as settings for installed applications. Some applications, especially those that rely on drivers, may not survive the upgrade process intact or could cause problems in the new Windows 2000 environment. These applications should be removed prior to the upgrade.

The System Preparation Tool that ships with Windows 2000 makes disk imaging, a popular method of performing mass installations, painless and hassle free. The System Preparation Tool allows you to create an "image master" that can be copied to each computer in the rollout, which is subsequently customized by the end-user or a desktop support technician upon its first boot.

Finally, Windows 2000 supports numerous installation scripting options that let administrators perform controlled normal installations in situations where disk imaging is not appropriate. The installation automation options range from simply providing default values that the user can override to a completely automated and unattended installation.

Case Study: The Invisible Rollout

A medium-sized client of mine was planning a migration to Windows 2000 Professional throughout their organization to replace their current crop of Windows 98 machines. They were not planning to deploy Windows 2000 Server or Active Directory, however, because they ran Linux on their servers.

We had originally decided to perform a full-fledged rollout using the methods documented in this chapter: We would create a generic installation source including applications divided into classes based on the applications that the various types of users required, along mostly departmental lines. We would then move all user data up to the servers on each machine, boot an installation CD-R, and overwrite their current installation with a completely new one. We began planning for training sessions, downtime during the rollout, and the inevitable increase in support calls after the rollout.

In the weeks prior to the upgrade, during our IT evaluation phase, some users began to experience serious problems with their Windows 98 installations. Rather than waste time debugging an operating system we would be moving away from anyway, we ran "temporary" upgrades to Windows 2000 Professional using its upgrade option. We simply inserted the installation source CD-ROM, ran the setup program, selected Upgrade, entered the CD-ROM key, and let the upgrade process run.

Much to our surprise, the upgrade not only ran without a hitch, it properly imported all the user's network settings and solved the problems they'd been having with Windows 98. Support calls from the users we'd upgraded virtually stopped—and they had previously been the largest users of desktop support time.

After a week went by without a single support incident from the upgraded users, we began to question the wisdom of a "true" rollout—it would be cumbersome for the users, since their machines would be completely reconfigured. Although there was the minor possibility that we could wind up moving some problematic applications along with the upgrade, we decided simply to upgrade all the users rather than perform a fresh rollout.

The upgrade process took a bit longer for the IT staff than a rollout would have (about two person-weeks total for 120 machines, including the time spent to solve minor troubles such as unsupported scanners, virus-scanning software, CD-burning software, and the like), but it completely eliminated the rollout burden for the users. For them, the only burden was the hour of lost work time while the installation actually ran.

Since the upgrade, support calls have dropped by at least 50 percent, and we've been able to permanently move a desktop support technician up to back-end operations.

3

Storage and Fault Tolerance

There now exists an array of storage options that tout faster or more secure ways to store your data than the traditional single hard disk method, which has been used since the dawn of computing. Some of these options are effective, while others add more complexity than value and wind up causing more problems than they solve.

This chapter will help you filter the wheat from the chaff in today's rather confusing storage market. Choosing the correct storage devices and fault tolerance methods will make your server rock solid, while choosing incorrectly can make your server a maintenance nightmare.

I'll review disk storage technology, basic concepts, and features built into Windows 2000 before opining on methodologies and explaining the more esoteric fault tolerance options that you'll find in the market. The first quarter of this book may seem a little simplistic for those of you with a hardware background. Persevere—the chapter picks up quite a bit once we've got everyone up to speed.

Sage Advice: Fault Tolerance Axioms

Implementing fault tolerance in your network can either be a breeze or a nightmare. Here are some tips to make it work:

- Keep it simple. Complexity is the enemy of fault tolerance.

- Avoid single points of failure through redundancy.

- Plan for the worst case.

- An ounce of mirrored disks is worth a pound of backup tape.

- Humans are unreliable. Automate everything.

Storage Basics

Many different media are used to store data, but they all fall into just three categories of technology:

Magnetic   Hard disk drives, floppy disk drives, removable cartridge drives of various sizes, including Zip, Jaz, LS-120, SyJet, and SparQ.

Optical   Compact disc read-only memory (CD-ROM), CD-recordable (CD-R), CD-rewriteable (CD-RW), and digital video disc (DVD) and its variants DVD-RAM and DVD-R. DVD is the "second generation CD-ROM" with features such as optical double density and dual-sided disks and readers, which increase capacity from the 650MB of CD-ROM to as much as 17GB for DVD and 5GB for DVD-RAM/DVD-R.

Semiconductor   Random access memory (RAM), read-only memory (ROM), erasable programmable ROM (EPROM), and Flash-EEPROM, which is now available on PCMCIA cards to simulate small, removable cartridge disks.

Some esoteric removable cartridge media devices use both optical and magnetic technologies at the same time, but these devices provide no serious advantage, so they have never made much impact in the market.

Disks

Hard disk drives are the workhorses of data storage. A *hard disk drive* (also called a *fixed disk drive*, a *hard drive*, or simply a *disk*) consists of one or more spinning nonferrous metal (usually aluminum) discs coated with a ferric metal oxide. The coating can be magnetically aligned in minute areas to either the north or south magnetic polarity to indicate a 1 or 0 value for a bit of data storage. Data is read or written to this coating as the disc passes beneath the head (a magnetic coil transducer) located at the end of a swing-arm that can span the radius of the disc. Modern hard disks have heads on both sides of the disc and usually contain multiple discs. If you've never seen the insides of a hard disk, find an old, low-capacity model that you no longer use and take it apart.

Terminology

Disc   Anything round and flat.

Disk   A disc with a magnetic coating that stores data. Hence, CD-ROMs are called *discs* because they are not magnetic (and because they emerged from the audio market), while hard disk drives, floppy disk drives, and even magneto-optical drives are called *disks*. It's okay to be confused about this.

Low-Level Format

Low-level formatting is the process of applying data to a new, empty hard disk to provide points of reference for the retrieval of information, to "zero-out" any random data existing on the disk, and to test each individual bit of storage so that any anomalous areas on the disk that fail to store data correctly can be marked out of use. All modern hard disk drives are already low-level formatted from the factory, so you shouldn't need to worry about this process. However, some controller manufacturers (like Adaptec) don't always conform to industrial standards for low-level formatting, so they may recommend low-level formatting the disk with their controller. You may also need to perform this function with RAID controllers or other esoteric devices.

Drives tend to accumulate errors as they age (these accumulated errors are called *grown defects*), so a low-level format might sometimes be required to get an older drive working correctly.

Low-level formatting utilities are not provided with any operating system because they're usually specific to a certain controller. The low-level formatting utility should be embedded in the BIOS of the controller or provided on a set of utility floppies with the controller. IDE hard disks should never need to be low-level formatted throughout their useful life.

TIP Disks are cheap. Rather than low-level reformatting an old disk, consider replacing it. Chances are the disk is relatively small compared to contemporary drives by the time it begins to fail enough to require a low-level format.

Partitions

Partitioning is the process of apportioning a hard disk for use by multiple operating systems. When hard disks first appeared, there was no way to use more than one operating system on them because the operating system installed first would apply its boot sector, tables, and indexes (a *high-level format*) in the same place all the other operating systems would need to install their own. So you had to have a different hard disk for each operating system that you wanted to install.

Microsoft and IBM developed a standard method for partitioning the hard disk drives of IBM PC-compatible hard disks into partitions that could each hold a different high-level format. A new *master boot record* was devised to store a small table of partitions that allowed four entries and contained a small boot loader that determined which partition was marked active for booting and then chained to that partition's boot sector. This way, you could store multiple operating systems on a hard disk and determine which one you wanted to boot by marking that partition active.

Partitioning also became handy when hard disks became larger than certain operating systems could address. MS-DOS could originally handle only 12 bits of sector address information, which meant that only 32MB of hard disk space could be used for a FAT partition. Disks larger than 32MB had to be partitioned and formatted separately to access their full size. Microsoft then created a 16-bit version of the FAT file system that could access up to 2GB of disk space and recently created a new 32-bit version of the FAT file system that can access up to 138GB of disk space.

Unlike Windows NT, the Windows 2000 setup program is not limited to a 4GB partitioning barrier. This solves a long-standing problem with Windows NT that forced most installations to use separate system and data partitions, even for installations where that scheme provides no advantage.

Microsoft now refers to the classic method of partitioning as "basic" partitioning. Windows 2000 supports the new "dynamic" partitioning, which is incompatible with the classic Microsoft/IBM partitions used by every other major operating system that runs on

Intel-processor-based PCs. Dynamic partitioning makes Windows 2000 fault-tolerant partitions easier for the operating system to manage and supports features like mount points. Dynamic partitions are managed by a different logical disk manager and can be dynamically resized and repaired without rebooting the computer. The dynamic resizing feature cannot be used on partitions that have been upgraded from basic partitions; it only works on partitions originally created as dynamic. This is one reason why resizing does not work on the system partition, which is created by the setup program as a basic partition.

> **NOTE** Microsoft's documentation claims that portable computers do not support dynamic partitions and that the dynamic partitioning option will not be available on them. This claim had no effect on my laptop (a Sony VIAO Z505HS), which allowed me to upgrade its partition to dynamic without complaint. There's no advantage to dynamic partitions on a laptop, however.

While disks with basic partitions are still supported, you cannot create fault-tolerant volumes on them in Windows 2000—you must upgrade hard disks with basic partitioning to the new dynamic partitioning scheme.

> **NOTE** If you upgrade a Windows NT server that had mirror sets or stripe sets, Windows 2000 will continue to support them with basic partitioning. You cannot create new fault-tolerant volume sets under Windows 2000 on basic disks, however.

Volumes

Volumes are the directory and index structures applied to one or more partitions during the process of high-level formatting, which allows files to be stored on the disk and referenced by name. Volumes can only be read by or written to the specific file system to which they are formatted. Windows 2000 supports NTFS volumes, FAT volumes, and FAT32 volumes.

Mirrored Volumes

Mirrors are exact copies of the data in another partition, generally on another disk. Disk mirroring is considered a fault-tolerant strategy, because in the event a single disk fails, the data can be read and written to the still-working mirror partition. Mirroring also can be used to double the read speed of a partition, since data can be read from both disks at the same time. RAID Level 1 describes mirroring. Windows 2000 Server supports RAID-1 mirroring in dynamic partitions.

> ***TIP*** Because the Windows 2000 system and boot partitions can be mirrored, you should use this form of fault tolerance to protect your Windows 2000 system files.

Striped Volumes

Striped volumes (called *stripe sets* in Windows NT 4, and equivalent to RAID-0) are volumes that span across multiple disks and are read and written to simultaneously. This can make disk accesses considerably faster if the disk traffic is handled correctly and if all the disks are synchronized correctly (meaning they are all exactly the same size and make).

RAID Level 0 is striping without parity and is supported in software by all versions of Windows 2000. RAID-0 reduces fault tolerance, because the loss of any one disk causes the failure of the volume.

RAID-5 Volumes

RAID-5 volumes (called *stripe sets with parity* in NT 4) can be used as a form of fault tolerance. The parity information, which is equal to the size of one member of the set, is spread across all disks and contains the mathematical sum of information contained in the other disks. The loss of any disk can be tolerated because its information can be re-created from the information stored on the other disks and in the parity stripe.

RAID Level 5 is striping with parity and is supported in software by Windows 2000 Server. RAID-5 increases fault tolerance over a single disk solution because the failure of any single disk can be tolerated. Mirroring (RAID-1) can be considered a form of striping with parity across only two disks in that the effect is the same, although mirroring is implemented differently. Since the mathematical parity information required to reconstruct a single drive is actually the data itself, the driver can simply copy the data rather than calculate parity.

Windows 2000 cannot boot or load the operating system from a striped or RAID-5 volume because the operating system files would be scattered across numerous disks without any way for the boot loader to find them. This occurs because the files required to recognize the RAID set are not available until the operating system is loaded. Mirroring the system volume is supported because the entire set of operating system files is available on both disks in a mirror. The operating system can load normally and then "switch on" mirroring support once the ftdisk driver is loaded.

Spanned Volumes

Spanned volumes (called *volume sets* in Windows NT 4) are volume structures that are conjoined across two or more partitions, which usually means across two or more disks.

Spanned volume sets make it easy to "add space" to a full volume, which is especially handy on Windows 2000 servers when they run out of space. Unfortunately, the system partition cannot be spanned.

Because spanned volumes often involve more than one disk, they make your volume less fault tolerant; the failure of any one disk in the set will cause the entire volume to be inaccessible. Frequent backup can help insure that you won't lose data in this event. Figure 3.1 shows the various types of volumes available in Windows 2000.

Figure 3.1   Windows 2000 supports mirror volumes, striped volumes, and spanned volumes.

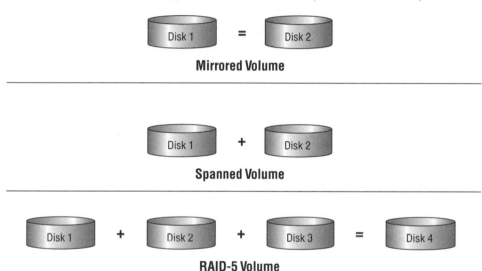

Removable Media

Removable media is an entire category of storage that can be removed while the computer is operating. This is its most important characteristic. The operating system cannot rely on the presence of data stored on removable media, which cannot be write-cached and cannot store active system files.

Magnetic tape   Used since the beginning of time to store computer data. Modern versions are simply smaller, faster, and denser applications of the same old technology.

Floppy disks   Revolving tapes that use the same magnetic powder-coated mylar, but the media revolves around a central axis, so rewinding is never necessary. Data from any portion of the surface of the disk is available every time the disk makes a single revolution. Because floppies added the element of quick access to any portion of the stored data, they quickly became very popular in the workstation market.

CD-ROM   Born of audio compact disc technology and adapted to store any type of digital information instead of just digital audio.

Removable cartridge hard disks   Developed during the mid-eighties, removable cartridge hard disks applied high-capacity hard disk platter technology to the removable market. They operate much like floppy disk drives, but with much greater capacity.

Solid-state memory   Solid-state memory is a relatively old idea, but early forms of it were so expensive that they never really left the lab. Then in the early 1990s, low-power *Electrically Erasable Programmable Read-Only Memory (EEPROM)*— known commercially as *flash memory*—was developed. This technology can permanently store memory in the semiconductor and erase it on a block-by-block basis. This functionality, and its reasonable cost, can be treated much like hard disk drives that have no moving parts. Flash memory has enabled a whole slew of data-related mobile applications such as digital photography and will become increasingly important in traditional computing applications as cost continues to decline.

Modern variations of removable media are based on these five basic technologies.

Tape

The original form of removable media was mylar *tape*, similar to audio tape. (Earlier technologies, such as paper punch cards, were used to load data into memory, not as online storage.) These tapes were booted and used to store the data for mainframe systems.

Tape suffered from the problem of sequential linear access—the tape had to be forwarded and rewound to find specific data. To make data easier to find, timing marks (called a *format*) were applied to the tape at specific intervals, which the read head could find while spooling the tape at high speed. The advantage to tape is that length is not important, so more storage can be had by using longer tapes.

Tape was difficult to handle because it frequently looped off the reels that held it, and it had to be threaded through the tape-reading machines every time it was mounted on the tape reader. To solve these problems, tape cartridges were created that were roughly similar to audiocassettes. Each cartridge contained two reels and a specific length of tape and could be easily mounted and removed from the tape reader. The most popular form of early tape cartridges was the *quarter-inch cartridge (QIC)*, the direct predecessor of the modern mini-QIC and *Travan* backup tapes. QIC and Travan tapes are (currently) capable of handling up to 10MB of data with compression, enough for small servers or workstations.

Digital Audiotape (DAT) is a high-capacity format for digital audio that was adapted for computer use. The significant increase in capacity afforded by the more modern DAT helical recording method made it a natural fit for data archiving and backup.

Finally, *Digital Linear Tape (DLT)* was developed by Digital as a high-capacity medium for backing up their VAX minicomputer. DLT is similar to DAT but uses a thicker tape for higher capacity. DLT also comes in longer lengths than can be stored in a small DAT cartridge, so it is suitable for even the largest of servers. Quantum now owns the DLT specification, and they are currently releasing SuperDLT that has uncompressed capacities up to 500GB per cartridge. With compression, that's about 1TB—plenty for any server.

Tape auto-changers are devices that use some mechanical method to change tapes among a library of installed cartridges. When one tape is filled to capacity, the next tape in the changer is installed, and the archive operation proceeds. With auto-changers, literally any amount of data can be archived. The archive operation can be slow because only one tape is written at a time, and the mechanical devices used to change tapes are (as are all devices with moving parts) subject to failure.

Redundant Arrays of Independent Tapes (RAIT) is the latest development in archiving technology. This technology, also called *TapeRAID*, is a fairly simple adaptation of disk RAID technology. RAIT uses as many tape devices in parallel as your backup requires. RAIT is usually cheaper and always faster than tape auto-changers, which are expensive, low-volume devices. Individual tape units are relatively inexpensive, and the backup is faster because the archival operation is parallel. It takes only the time that a single tape archive takes, no matter how many devices are involved.

Various drivers are used to read or write from tape depending upon the device involved. Microsoft does not provide a file system driver, so you can't access individual files on a tape without using a backup program. You use the Hardware Wizard to install tape devices, and Microsoft provides ntbackup.exe, a tape backup program, for simple archiving to tape or any removable media.

Sage Advice: Tape Technology

DAT is the most convenient and reliable form of tape storage that I've found. The cassettes are more protected than QIC/Travan cassettes, and they are considerably more available than DLT—they can often be found on the shelf at larger computer stores. DAT devices cost more than Travan devices, but the media is cheaper per megabyte.

Select RAIT (or multiple tape devices) over auto-changers whenever possible. Tape auto-changers cost far more than they are worth, depreciate rapidly, and tend to break more often.

Floppy Drives

Mylar tape provided the technology to make mylar discs—floppy disks. *Floppy disks* were a superior format for online storage because data can be accessed quickly at any point on the medium. They became the preferred form of storage in early computers and provided the original medium for software distribution before the CD-ROM. As such, every computer built contains a floppy disk drive (with the notable recent exception of the iMac—the harbinger of a trend, I think).

Three sizes of floppy disk exist: the completely obsolete 8-inch size used in older mainframes and workstations, the all-but-completely-obsolete 5.25-inch format used in the original PC, and the staring-obsolescence-in-the-face 3.5-inch format that debuted on the Macintosh and then became the standard for PCs. These media ranged in capacity from 360K to 1.44MB (a 2.88MB standard exists, but nobody uses it) and are useful for moving files from computer to computer. All computers are still capable of booting from floppy disk, and for many PCs, they are the only removable media that can be booted.

Two new types of floppy disks exist called LS-120 (120MB, Imation) and SuperFloppy (200MB, Sony), which use laser servos (the LS in LS-120) to precisely align a standard magnetic read head. Although these devices can read and write normal floppy disks, they interface through the hard disk bus like a removable media cartridge technology.

Sage Advice: Don't Rely on Floppy Disks

Floppy disks are the least reliable storage medium. Their reliable life is only about two years, and because they usually move from place to place in shirt pockets through various electromagnetic fields, the data on them tends toward a random state. Don't rely on floppy disks to store any important data.

If you have data you must get off a floppy that your disk drive can't read, try reading it in an LS-120 drive. LS-120 drives are more sensitive than regular floppy drives and can read data from a disk long after the magnetic image is too faint for a standard drive to read.

Floppy disks cannot be formatted with the NTFS file system without installing third-party software. Microsoft decided that it would not support the NTFS file system on floppies because NTFS has a relatively high overhead. But with compression, an NTFS-formatted floppy can actually store more than a FAT-formatted floppy and also allow the encryption of documents—which is especially useful on media that can be lost or stolen.

CD-ROM

CD-ROM is currently the most important form of removable media. Nearly all software is distributed on CD-ROM, and the entire software industry is based on it as a distribution medium. DVD will be the successor to CD-ROM and will shortly begin replacing it as the distribution medium of choice. DVD-ROM drives are nearly as inexpensive as CD-ROM drives, and by 2002 DVD-ROM drives may have completely replaced CD-ROM drives in new computers. By 2005, most software will be distributed on DVD.

A single CD-ROM holds 650MB of data in the ISO 9660 industry-standard CD-ROM format. The CDFS (CD-ROM File System, also known as ISO 9660) or UDF (Universal Disk Format, also known as ISO 13346) device driver is responsible for reading data from CD-ROMs. UDF, the successor to ISO 9660, is intended for use across a wide range of removable media optical devices such as DVD, WORM (Write Once, Read Many), and CD-R.

Recordable and rewritable CD-ROM, as well as DVD-RAM and the forthcoming DVD-R, are recent and very interesting developments in removable media. These devices and media allow you to master your own CD-ROMs or DVDs to distribute software. The low cost of the media (about $1 per CD-R disc in bulk) makes it practical to use the medium for permanent archiving. Rewritable (DVD-RAM) devices and media can be erased and reused, but the media is considerably more expensive ($30 per plate) and cannot be read in normal CD or DVD readers, so its primary use is as a periodic backup.

> **NOTE**   DVD-RAM cartridge technology is currently available. True DVD-R is not available, and may never be if movie and music production companies get their way, because they don't want people to be able to copy DVD movies. These groups killed the application of digital tape to audio music in order to prevent music piracy.

Hard Disk Cartridges

Hard disk cartridges are fixed disk drives with removable platters. Because the platter cannot be as precisely aligned in a removable cartridge as a fixed hard disk, the data tracks must be wider and, therefore, less capacious than a fixed disk.

No clear standard has emerged in hard disk cartridges, and many proprietary formats have arisen. Various sizes, even from the same manufacturer, are usually not interchangeable. Currently available popular technologies include:

Zip   100MB per cartridge; recently a 250MB version was released. Zip disks are actually a mylar film floppy disk that uses a laser servo to precisely align the read/write head. Zip drives are, by far, the most popular form of removable cartridge disk.

LS-120   120MB per cartridge. These devices can read and write standard floppy disks. Like Zip disks, LS-120 disks are a mylar film floppy disk that uses a laser servo for head alignment. Contrary to popular opinion, they are not magneto-optical or related to the now obsolete 20MB floptical technology. LS-120 drives can be used instead of floppy drives and are supported by the sfloppy driver in Windows 2000. Sony has an incompatible 200MB version called the SuperFloppy.

Jaz   Originally a 1GB format, a 2GB version now exists. Jaz is made by Iomega, the manufacturer of the Zip drive and the sole major survivor of the volatile removable media market.

SyJet   A 1.5GB format that is both smaller and quieter than Jaz.

SparQ   A 1GB format related to (but incompatible with) SyJet drives. The manufacturer (SyQuest) has recently gone bankrupt, so this medium will probably disappear.

Orb   A 2GB format by Castlewood that is new to the market. Orb disks use a proprietary magneto-resistive technology to achieve high data density and reliability at a lower cost per cartridge than Jaz.

Solid-State Memory

Solid-state memory, now dominated by Flash EEPROM technology, allows you to store data permanently in a semiconductor chip. Although flash memory is very expensive (it costs about twice as much as RAM for the same capacity), it has reliability characteristics that far exceed the capabilities of other types of removable media. These chips can withstand extremes of temperature, humidity, vibration, shock, and magnetism that would render all the previously listed removable media worthless.

Because of their exceptionally small form factor (typical devices are the size of a credit card, and devices the size of a thumbnail are available now at retail outlets) and very low power draw, they're ideal for certain applications where the integrity of data is crucial: storing encryption keys, storing working sets of files, and operating in mobile environments. I recommend flash memory—either PCMCIA, CardFlash, or the new USB Thumbdrive form factor—for anyone who uses a laptop, because these devices will withstand being dropped.

Popular forms of semiconductor memory include:

PCMCIA and CardFlash   These flash devices fully implement the ATAPI specification for removable devices, so they can act just like hard disk drives. In fact, with a passive adapter, you can connect them to the IDE bus of a desktop computer and boot from them. They are ideal for mobile users who need to protect their data from the rigors of mobility or for the storage of crypto certificates for mobile drives. These devices range in capacity from 8MB to 1200MB at the moment and cost about $3 per megabyte.

IDE drives   Built to directly simulate nonremovable hard disks, and with capacities large enough to boot Windows 2000, these drives are used in environmental extremes that would destroy a normal drive or when disk failure cannot be tolerated. These devices are expensive, however; a drive large enough to boot Windows 2000 Server costs about $3,000.

Pure flash devices   Pure flash devices include those form factors that do not simulate a hard disk drive, such as Sony's Memory Stick, Trek's amazingly useful USB product called Thumbdrive, SmartMedia, and SmartCards. These devices simply interface the flash chips directly to a proprietary reader built into the device, and they all require a memory technology driver to operate with Windows 2000.

TIP   Check out www.sandisk.com for information on most forms of semiconductor memory.

Effective Storage Management

Now that we've exhaustively covered the existing market of technology and devices, let's talk about what works and what doesn't in storage management.

The primary rule of storage management is to stay in the mass market—don't get esoteric. Unusual solutions are harder to maintain, are more likely to have buggy drivers, and are usually more complex than they are worth.

Every hard disk will eventually fail. This bears repeating: every hard disk will eventually fail. They run constantly in servers at high speed, and they generate the very heat that destroys their spindle lubricant. These two conditions combine to ensure that hard disks wear out through normal use within about 10 years. Early in the computer industry, the *mean time before failure (MTBF)* of a hard disk drive was an important selling point.

The real problem with disk failure is that hard disks are the only component in a computer that can't be swapped out because they are individually customized with your data. To tolerate the failure of your data, you must have a copy of it elsewhere. That elsewhere can be another hard disk in the same computer or in another computer, tape, or removable media.

Some options don't work well—any medium that's smaller than the source medium will require more effort than it's worth. Usually this means you must either use another hard disk of equivalent or greater size or tape, which can be quite capacious.

NTFS Storage Management Features

Windows 2000 includes an updated NTFS file system with several new features, including disk quotas, mount points, and encryption. Unfortunately, this upgrade makes NTFS incompatible with Windows NT version 4 prior to Service Pack 4. NT 4 Service Pack 4 and later can read and write Windows 2000 NTFS volumes but will ignore the improved features.

WARNING   Because of the significant changes to the NTFS on-disk structure, you should not dual-boot production machines between Windows 2000 and Windows NT 4. If you need to dual-boot workstations, use FAT16 formatted volumes, which are completely compatible with both operating systems.

Compression

NTFS supports file-by-file *compression*, which is controlled via the compression file attribute. To compress or decompress a file, check or clear the compression attribute in the file's Properties window or use the compact.exe command line tool. Files inherit the compression attribute of the folder in which they are stored, which in turn inherits its compression attribute from the volume. Moving a file within the same volume does not change its compression status. Copying or moving it between volumes causes the file system to read and decompress the file and then write it to the new location with compression dependent upon the status of the containing folder's compression attribute.

Compressed files typically take up on average 50 percent of their uncompressed space if they're user-created documents, 75 percent if they're executable files, and 100 percent (uncompressable) if they're stored in an already highly compressed format such as JPEG or ZIP. Actual compression ratios vary widely depending upon the nature of the stored file. NTFS will not compress files that cannot benefit from compression, although it will leave the compression flag set.

Compression in Windows 2000 takes processing power, so it's not recommended for busy file servers or terminal servers because it can create an unnecessary bottleneck. Compression is most appropriate for use on single-user workstations for that reason.

Encryption

NTFS supports file-by-file *encryption* based on the encrypting file system attribute. This attribute is inherited in exactly the same way as the compression attribute; the same rules apply for moving and copying files as well. Files cannot be both compressed and encrypted. Only the user who encrypted the file and the recovery agent for the file can read it; other users will receive an Access Denied error message.

The first time a user attempts to encrypt a file, the certificate service automatically generates an encryption key. A second file recovery key is created for the local administrator (stand-alone machines and workstations) or the domain administrator (domains) in case the user loses the original key. Use the Security Policy Manager to export the recovery key to some type of removable media that you keep in a safe. If all the encryption keys for a file are lost (for example, due to an operating system reinstallation), then the file cannot be recovered.

When an encrypted file is copied or moved to a different volume, its encryption state depends on the inheritable encryption property of the destination volume. Keep this in mind when you copy encrypted files. You don't want to accidentally obviate your security policy by copying encrypted files into an unencrypted volume. Files copied to FAT volumes, including floppies, cannot be encrypted.

There is a special case where encrypted files can be copied to FAT volumes: by using a Windows 2000–compatible backup program (such as the backup program that comes with Windows). When you back up files using a Windows 2000 backup utility, the encrypted contents are written to the tape in encrypted form. That encrypted form can be restored to a FAT volume in encrypted form, but it cannot be decrypted. In order to decrypt the file, it must be restored to an NTFS volume using the same process. While this isn't particularly useful, it works, and it can be used for such purposes as e-mailing a file with the encryption intact. Normally when you e-mail an encrypted file, the file is decrypted before being sent. Of course, the receiver must have an encryption certificate that can decrypt the file as well.

Many applications, including Microsoft office applications, create a copy of a file that is being edited, apply the edits to the copy, and then rename the copy at the end of the editing session. This causes the entire set of attributes, including the encryption attribute, to default to the inherited state of the containing folder. If the file is encrypted on disk, the copy will only be encrypted if the containing folder has its encryption attribute set for the new file to inherit. For this reason, it's important to keep encrypted files in a folder that is marked for encryption. Also be aware that many applications create temporary files in the temp directory, so you should consider encrypting the temp directory as well. To be completely secure, make sure you know how the applications you use behave with respect to temporary files.

WARNING Encrypting a file doesn't protect it from being deleted. Use NTFS permissions for that.

Encryption takes considerable processing power, so you should only encrypt user-created documents that need to be protected from unauthorized disclosure. Create a folder (I call mine crypt) for storing encrypted files and share it. Inside that share you can create whatever directory structure you want.

NOTE The keys used to encrypt disks are located in the Registry, where serious hackers and the government could find them and use them to decrypt your encrypted files. If you want to keep your data safe from security professionals, move your crypto certificates to removable media that you keep on your person, or use a smart card. An easier trick than moving crypto keys is simply to keep your encrypted files on an NTFS-formatted CardFlash or PCMCIA flash memory card. The files will only decrypt on the computer containing the keys in the Registry. Both are secure when separated. Unfortunately, all of the newer flash technology drivers for media, such as Memory Stick and Thumbdrives, only support the FAT file system. More information on security is contained in Chapter 6.

Quotas

Administrators use *quotas* to limit users to a specified amount of storage on shared systems. This prevents users from filling up server disks or using more than their fair share. Quotas are common to most network operating systems, so it's interesting that it took so long for Microsoft to implement them.

In Windows 2000, you can set quotas as either "soft," which informs an administrator when a user has exceeded their limit, or "hard," which actually returns a "disk full" error message when a user attempts to exceed their quota of disk space.

A user's quota is calculated based on the uncompressed size of their stored files, so even though their files may take less space because they're compressed, that additional space is not subtracted from the user's quota amount.

Enabling quotas is easy: simply right-click the NTFS volume on which you want to enable quotas, select the Quota tab, and check Enable Quotas. To create hard quotas, enable the Deny Disk Space to Users Exceeding Their Quota option. You'll need to enter a quota limit for new users of the volume as well.

For quota reporting and to change quota levels for individual users, click the Quota Entries button in the Quota Configuration panel. This will bring up the Quota Entries Manager, which both reports disk usage per user and allows you to customize user quota levels.

Reparse Points

Reparse points are empty folders that act as placeholders for the root of a foreign *installable file system (IFS)*. Reparse points allow third parties to create hierarchical structures that will appear in the file system directory and act as part of the file system without actually being an NTFS file system *per se*.

Reparse points work by directing the NTFS file system to call an installable file system at that "point" in the directory hierarchy. What you see "inside" the reparse point is entirely up to the installed file system.

Mount Points

Mount points are reparse points that specify another volume to be grafted onto the current directory at the folder that represents the mount point. UNIX users will recognize this functionality immediately. Mount points must be created on a Windows 2000 NTFS partition, but the mounted volume may be of any type, including CD-ROM or even removable media. Mount points are indicated with a volume icon in the Explorer, rather than a folder icon. You create mount points by using the Disk Management snap-in to assign the volume to a reparse point (also known as an *empty folder* on an NTFS volume) rather than a drive letter.

Mount points are very useful for extending the size of an existing volume and for managing directory size without using quotas. For example, you can create your temp directory as a moderately sized partition that is then mounted in your normal system volume. This way, you ensure that the space taken by temporary files can only grow to a specific size irrespective of the user who created them. Quotas work only on a per-user basis.

You can also use mount points to add partitions to an existing partition on the same disk (Windows 2000 spanned volumes only support adding whole new disks). Mount points are more fault-tolerant because the failure of a mounted volume does not cause the failure of the host volume, as is the case with spanned volumes. In addition, a manageable set of data is lost in a failure situation because folders separate data thematically in a mounted volume. Mounted volumes can already be formatted and contain data, as well, which cannot happen with spanned volumes. Mount points are the only way to expand the amount of space available to a system partition.

A volume may be mounted in numerous places in a directory structure. For example, you can mount the same partition as `c:\temp`, `c:\tmp`, or `c:\Program files\tempfiles` and also assign a drive letter. This allows you to strictly control the way badly designed programs handle files when the program doesn't allow you to specify or change its default behavior.

Archiving and Backup

Archiving and backup are not the same thing. *Archiving* refers to the permanent storage of information for future reference, whereas *backup* refers to the storage of information for the sole purpose of restoration in the event of a failure. The effective differences are that you can reuse backup tapes but not archive tapes and that you refer to archive tapes to restore deleted files and backup tapes to restore crashed systems.

Backup and archiving are most effectively approached separately—solutions that do both will do neither well. For example, image backup software is vastly better for backups and restoration in an emergency than file-based backup software, which is better for archiving permanently on cheap tape or CD-R media. There is no reason to choose one or the other when you can have both.

The types of failures that cause data loss fall into four categories:

Disk failure   Happens when a single drive fails in a computer. Mirroring and parity striping effectively handle this problem.

Machine failure   Happens when all the storage on a single machine fails for an environmental reason. Tape backup with rotation or server replication effectively handles this problem.

Site failure   Happens when a meteorite the size of a Volkswagen slams into your headquarters at night and destroys all the data at a single site. Fire, flooding, and theft can cause this sort of problem as well. Offsite media storage or network-based remote backup effectively handles this problem.

User failure   Happens when your CEO tells you he deleted a file four months ago—and that he needs it back. Only archiving with tape or CD-R is inexpensive enough to effectively handle this problem. Because of the depth of difference between this failure mode and the others, I recommend handling archiving as a separate process from backup.

It's technically possible for multiple sites to fail simultaneously, but in this event, you'd be hard pressed to find anyone left who cared about your backup problem, so there's no need to worry about it.

The Trouble with Tape

The problem with using tape for archiving and backup is that it is not reliable—in fact, it's highly unreliable. You may find this shocking, but fully 67 percent of attempts to completely restore a system from tape fail. That's two-thirds—an awfully high number, especially for how many people rely upon tape as their sole medium of backup.

Tape software really sucks. From disk-based "catalogs" that can grow so large they fill the very volume they're supposed to back up, to arcane interfaces that are supposed to manage "media sets" of tape and refuse to function if you insert the wrong tape, enterprise-based backup software all seems to have been written by people who hate network administrators and want to kick them when they're down. Of course, I'm exaggerating a tad, but anyone who has worked with Arcserve or BackupExec knows what I'm talking about. These programs are the opposite of intuitive. In my opinion, everyone should be able to figure out how to do an emergency restoration from scribbles jotted on a Post-it note, and that's just not possible with traditional tape backup software.

Traditional Backup   Traditional backup works like this: Every night, you insert a fresh tape into your server. The next morning when you arrive at work, you remove the tape, mark the date, and store it in your tape vault. At larger companies, you'll never use that tape again—it's a permanent record of your network on that date. In smaller companies, that's the same tape you use every Wednesday, and you only keep tapes made over the weekend or perhaps once a month.

Here's a nifty feature of most tape backup software: they won't back up open files. Think about this for a moment: If a file is open, that means it's being used, which means it's an important file, which means it should be backed up. In fact, your busiest, most important documents get skipped the most because they are open quite frequently or because they've been left open overnight by users who forgot to log out.

Traditional backup is okay, except that it has a major failure component: humans. Humans have to change that tape every day. This means that in any organization that doesn't have a dedicated tape operator, the overburdened IT team is bound to forget. And if you've tried to train a non-IT employee to change the tape, you probably feel lucky if it happens at all.

One of two things will occur when the backup software detects that the tape has not been changed. Poorly designed or configured software will refuse to run the backup in a misguided attempt to protect the data already on the tape. Better-configured software will simply overwrite the tape, assuming that a more recent backup is better than no backup at all. So in many cases, the same tape may sit in a server (wearing out) for days or weeks on end while business goes by, and everyone forgets about the backup software.

It is a combination of tape wear, truculent backup software, and this human failure component that contribute to the high failure rate of tape restorations.

Nearly all operating systems, including all Microsoft operating systems, support a backup methodology called *archive marking*, which is implemented through a single bit flag attached to every file as an attribute on the computer. The archive bit is set every time a file is written to and is only cleared by archive software. This allows the system to retain a memory of which files have changed since the last backup.

Most backup software offers a variety of backup options:

Full backup   Archives every file on the computer and clears all the archive bits so that all future writes will be marked for archiving.

Copy backup   Archives every file on the computer without modifying the archive bits. Copy operations proceed faster and can archive open files since the file does not have to be opened for write operations to reset the bit.

Incremental backup   Archives every file that has its archive bit set, meaning it has changed since the last full system backup and resets the bit so that the next incremental backup will not rearchive the file.

Differential backup   Archives every file that has its archive bit set, but it does not reset the bit; therefore, every differential backup tape includes the complete set of files since the last system backup.

Periodic backup   Archives all files that have been written to since a certain date.

A typical restore operation is even more Byzantine. Assuming the worst—you lost your storage system completely—here's what you have to look forward to: After installing new hard disks, you must reinstall Windows 2000 from scratch. Then you must reinstall your tape backup software. Once you've finished these tasks (after a frantic search for the BackupExec installation code that is required to reinstall BackupExec and a panicked call to their tech support to beg forgiveness, mercy, and a new code number), you're ready to completely overwrite all that installation effort with a full restoration from tape. You now get to sit in front of your server providing all the base system tapes, then the Monday incremental tape, the Tuesday incremental tape, and so forth until you hit the current day of the week—the whole time cursing your decision to use daily incremental backups. Once you're completely finished, and assuming that all six tapes involved worked flawlessly, you're ready to reboot your server—an entire workday after you began the restore operation.

Image Backup   Because software vendors have begun to realize how badly tape sucks, a new type of tape backup called *image backup* has become available. In an image backup, a complete sector copy of the disk is written to tape, including all the information necessary to reconstruct partitions. Because the backup occurs below the file level, image archives are capable of archiving open files.

Restoration is where image backup shines. The image backup software will create a set of boot floppies for emergency restoration. By inserting the emergency restore boot floppy and an image tape, the computer will boot a proprietary restore program that simply copies the image on the tape back to disk. One reboot later and you're looking at your old familiar computer.

Image backup is not for archiving—file access is not as good as traditional backup software. But as I mentioned, you're better off using different software for archiving and backup.

Sage Advice: Best Practices for Tape Backup

Don't let some policy document written in the early seventies bind your hands when it comes to backup and archiving. If you are the person who will lose their job when a restoration fails, you should mandate the backup policy that works for you. For tape backups, here are the best practices to work with:

- Backup is a critical security component of any network. Allocate a large enough budget to do it correctly.

- Use tape devices and media large enough to perform an entire backup on a single tape. If this is too expensive, use RAIT software to allow the simultaneous, unattended backup of the entire system.

- Always set your tape backup software to overwrite, without asking, media that may have been left in the machine. Failing to perform a backup is far worse than accidentally overwriting an earlier backup.

- Choose image backup software rather than file-based backup software. Restorations are far easier and faster with this software.

- Turn off storage-based catalogs. They take up far more space than they're worth, and they're never available when the computer has crashed. Use media-based catalogs that are stored on tape. They take longer during individual file recovery operations, but those are (or should be) very rare. It's not worth taking 20 percent of your volume space to store information about backup media sets on disk, especially since these catalogs will be lost in a recovery operation anyway.

- Perform a full-system backup every day. Differential, incremental, and daily backups that don't create a complete image cause headaches and complications during a restoration operation and increase the likelihood of failure by adding more components to the process. If your backup system is too slow to back up your entire data set in the allotted time, get a new one that is capable of handling your data.

- Use the Copy feature to back up opened files or force them closed if you perform your backup at night. Use Windows 2000's force system logoff user policy to shut down user connections at night and force files closed.

- If you reuse tapes, mark them each time they've been written to. Discard tapes after their tenth backup. Saving a few dollars on media isn't worth the potential for loss.

- Pull out a full-system backup once a week or once a month at the longest and store it permanently. You never know when a deleted file will be needed again.

- Instead of buying massive centralized backup software that goes out and backs up every server and workstation in your enterprise directly to tape, either use Intelli mirror to automatically synchronize desktop files or create automated backup scripts that copy changed user files up to servers early in the evening. Later, have every server copy its changed files (including the backed-up workstation directories) to an archive server. Then back up the archive server alone. That machine should contain an archive of every user-created file in your enterprise, from which you can magically undelete files without ever looking at a tape. The servers themselves should have mirrored disks to tolerate disk failure and weekly backups to a simple image file over the network.

Enterprise Backup

Enterprise backup is the problem of backing up all the servers and workstations in a company with some centrally managed resource. As complex as enterprise backup can be, there are some easy ways to make it simple.

Don't bother backing up workstations. Rather, get users comfortable with the idea that no files stored locally on their computers will be backed up—if it's important, put it on a network file server. This reduces the complexity of your backup problem considerably. Workstations should contain operating system and application files only, all of which can be restored from the original software CD-ROMs.

Use enterprise-based backup software that is capable of transmitting backup data over the network to a central backup server. Watch for network capacity, though, because that much data can often overwhelm a network. Schedule each server's transmission so they don't conflict when running over the same shared media. You should put your archive server on your backbone or at the central point of your network.

You don't have to spend a lot of money on esoteric archive servers, even for large environments. When you consider that a good 20GB DAT drive is going to cost $2,000, adding another $1,000 for a motherboard, hard disk, RAM, network adapter, and a copy of Windows 2000 Professional isn't all that big of a deal. The software you have to install is likely to cost more than all the hardware combined anyway. So feel free to have six or eight computers dedicated to large backup problems. They can all run simultaneously to back up different portions of your network without investing in expensive RAIT software or auto-loading tape devices. You'll save money and have a more standard solution that you can fix.

Alternatives to Tape

The alternatives to backing up with tape fall into two major categories: backing up to another disk on the same machine or backing up to another computer over a network. These options are detailed below.

Hard Disks, Removable Media, and Other Computers   Simply storing another copy of your data is an effective form of backup and archive. That other location could be another hard disk in the same machine, a removable cartridge hard disk, or another computer.

Storing to another hard disk (via mirroring) is an excellent primary method for backup and fault tolerance, but it suffers from the problem that any environmental cause for the failure of the first disk will affect the second disk, too. Fire, flood, theft, or a disgruntled employee will kill both drives, leaving you with no recourse if it's your only method of data protection.

Removable cartridge hard disks suffer from always being smaller than the source you're backing up, and so they require human intervention or the selection of a smaller set of backup data. This method of backup is most appropriate for workstations.

Another computer is a really good idea. So good, in fact, that we'll deal with it later on under the "Fault Tolerance" section.

Internet Archiving   An interesting new backup medium has recently emerged: the Internet. A few companies have begun offering remote archiving and backup via the Internet so that your data is stored (presumably safely) off-site. By downloading their backup client and customizing a backup plan to suit your needs, your computer will archive automatically over a constant Internet connection to the disk and tape farms of the backup provider.

They promise encryption, protection, and security—but, of course, they won't be held liable in the event that you actually do lose data. Interesting indeed. This field is so new that it cannot be wholeheartedly recommended by anyone as the sole means of protection for a network—but it is an interesting alternative worth serious consideration and possible implementation as a secondary form of data protection.

Can they promise security? The site I visited touts their use of DES—the government's preferred form of encryption. It has been long suspected (though never proven, and apparently unlikely) that a back door exists to DES and that the National Security Agency knows how to exploit it. It's also been shown to be vulnerable to a key-space decryption in short order. There's no doubt that if the government wanted to see your data and knew that an online archive company had a copy of it, they could get it, and they could decrypt it. Other than that, you're probably pretty safe.

WARNING   Keep in mind that although your data may be encrypted during transit, it may not be encrypted during storage. If the government subpoenas your data, they will get it. If it's important, they can crack it. If this bothers you, don't use outsourced backup.

Finally, if you think a tape restore is slow, sit behind one proceeding at 28.8Kbps over a modem. Unless you have a high-speed Internet connection available, Internet backup is not for you. You'll also have to deal with archiving only user information. In the event of a restore, the operating system and all applications will have to be restored from original media, because Internet archive services charge per megabyte stored, and you'll want to minimize that cost as much as possible.

Disks Are Cheap

Until computers became a household item, hard disks were expensive. The idea of buying extra hard disks just to back up data didn't make sense, and tape was the only cost-effective solution. Because the market for computers (and therefore hard disks) has recently expanded by an order of magnitude or two, hard disks have become cheap. They are now cheaper than tape devices and their media, and they are cheap enough to use for archiving. Hard disks are highly reliable until they fail, and for that reason, they make good archival media.

Use Mirroring

Mirroring is the easiest way to protect your computer from hard disk loss. With two disks, you are protected from normal disk failure, because only one disk is likely to fail at one time, unless the reason it fails is environmental or, though unlikely, one failure causes the next device to fail.

When you use mirroring, put the second drive on a different bus. This will prevent an electrical failure on one disk from affecting the other, because they won't be on the same cable.

You may decide to use a different controller altogether so you can tolerate the failure of a controller, but disk controller failure is extraordinarily rare.

A side benefit of mirroring is that it doubles allowable read speed. It's also the only fault tolerance method available for use on the boot partition where Windows 2000 files are stored, and it is the only way to increase the boot speed of a Windows 2000 server without using hardware RAID controllers.

Avoid Stripe Sets

Stripe sets are a good idea—too bad they don't work that well. Striping to increase performance only manages to double read and write performance at four disks—you can achieve the same performance increase with mirroring—but without worrying about the decrease in fault tolerance that striping causes. Stripe sets with more disks are faster, but if you're going to spend that much money on your disk subsystem, you should get a RAID controller to go with it.

Stripe sets with parity have even more overhead—write operations are considerably slower than mirrored disks. It takes fewer users to burden servers that rely on stripe sets with parity than servers that rely upon mirroring. Beyond the overhead, stripe sets across disks that aren't exactly the same suffer from severe timing problems.

Finally, Windows 2000 does not support booting from a stripe set, so your system files (about 50 percent of normal disk access) won't see any read improvement. Also, Windows 2000 allows you to create stripe sets on partitions that contain other volumes—but accessing those other volumes causes your stripe-set access to fall out of sync and take even more time.

Disk Controllers

Disk controllers are problematic because of the way Windows 2000 supports (or doesn't support) them. If a manufacturer has provided Microsoft with a driver for their controller to include with the distribution of Windows 2000, you'll have no problems. Most likely, Windows 2000's setup program will automatically detect the controller and will have loaded the driver early enough to support installing Windows 2000 on a disk controlled by the controller.

If their disk driver doesn't ship with Windows 2000, you'll have to go through the rigmarole of providing a driver floppy. And if you intend to install Windows 2000 through that controller, you'll need to provide the floppy through a secret method described in Chapter 2, "Installing Windows 2000 (the Right Way)." Unfortunately, some disk controllers don't even work using this method, and you'll have to disk-copy the partition from a more supported controller to them if you ever want to boot Windows 2000 on them.

Sage Advice: Selecting Disk Controllers

Use standard disk controllers, such as UltraDMA IDE controllers or common SCSI adapters like those from Adaptec. Consider checking the Windows 2000 setup disk for supported controllers to provide a pick list from which to shop if you want to use something more esoteric (like a RAID controller). This is important, because when your server crashes in four years, you'll find the floppy with the driver you need to reinstall has also gone bad.

Hardware RAID: Use Caution

Hardware RAID is both the fastest and most fail-safe method of storing data when downtime cannot be tolerated. Hardware RAID is expensive, can be hard to configure correctly, and can easily cause data corruption when failures occur.

Considering these contradictions, you should approach RAID with caution. It's fantastic and a real ally when configured and used correctly, but it's easy to use incorrectly. There are quite a few companies touting RAID solutions that are incomplete at best.

When speaking of RAID in general, most people are actually talking about RAID-5, the most commonly implemented form of RAID that provides both a speed improvement and a measure of fault tolerance. You can assume that whenever someone doesn't specify a RAID level, they're talking about RAID Level 5, and that assumption holds true with this book.

Here's a list of things that I've seen go wrong with RAID:

- The RAID adapter can lose its RAID configuration and suddenly "forget" the configuration of the RAID pack. Many adapters don't include forensic utilities to remedy this problem, and it's most likely to happen after a power-related shutdown.
- A hard disk can have timings that are slightly out of sync with the rest of the pack, causing serious slowdowns of the entire array.
- Hard drive cables can be of lower tolerance than the data bus requires, causing drives to be incorrectly marked bad and forcing the RAID pack to go into fault-tolerance mode.
- Common RAID operations, such as rebuilding a healthy pack, require rebooting to a BIOS-level program or the running of a special utility that requires the server be taken offline for hours.
- Solutions touted as hot-swappable cause the server to crash because the server vendor used the wrong type of bus termination or the adapter is actually more sensitive to termination impedance than it should be to actually tolerate disk insertion.
- The heat from many disks operating in close proximity actually causes the very failures that RAID is supposed to remedy, thus requiring frequent drive replacement.

The real problem with RAID is its snake-oil appeal—once it's installed, everyone seems to think they're protected against all loss, and they don't need other backup measures besides the occasional archive tape. This false sense of security is pernicious in the industry—RAID should be considered nothing more than a high-availability, fault-tolerance measure—it is certainly not a replacement for backup or archiving.

The first thing you should do when you install a server with RAID is simulate failure by (at least) removing the power plug from one of the hard disks in the pack while the computer is running. You won't damage any hardware doing this. If everything doesn't keep humming along smoothly, you don't really have a RAID system. RAID systems simply can't be trusted to operate properly unless they can pass this test.

You should also make certain that every disk is installed in an individually removable carriage. Taking down a server to replace a failed drive causes the downtime you paid so much to avoid. Pay a little extra to do it right.

Be certain the RAID adapters you use are capable of tolerating failure, hot-swapping disks, and rebuilding the failed drive—all without rebooting the computer. Rebuilding a large RAID disk can take hours, so you'll want to make sure you are online while it happens. Many RAID systems recommend using an extra "hot spare" disk that can be spun up and rebuilt whenever any disk fails. This is an excellent idea because the rebuilding begins as soon as the failure is detected and the failed disk is marked out. When you replace the new empty drive, it becomes the hot spare.

Finally, make sure your adapter or software has some method of making you quite certain which drive has failed. (Usually this works by flashing the drive's built-in LED or an LED in the removable carriage.) Nothing will make you feel stupider than pulling one of the good remaining drives out of your RAID pack by accident and watching your server drop like a rock.

Serving CD-ROMs

You will often find a need to serve catalogs of rather static information at your site, and CD-ROM jukeboxes usually seem like a good way to do that. They work well, but they're usually an unnecessary expense. Two other, less expensive methods exist, and one of those methods is technically superior.

When you need to serve a number of CD-ROMs, you have three options:

- Use a CD-ROM jukebox to serve them.
- Use virtual CD-ROM emulation software.
- Use the vast number of CD-ROMs that came with all the PCs at your site.

The first option entails using a server specially configured with a number of CD-ROM drives, usually between 7 and 16, and leaving the CD-ROM media in the CD-ROM drives. This suffers from a few problems:

- Multiple users accessing the same CD-ROM at the same time makes it terribly slow because CD-ROM readers can't seek very quickly.
- CD-ROM jukeboxes are always expensive and usually two or three generations behind in speed. I recently saw 4x CD-ROM jukeboxes being sold in the same catalog that sold 40x CD-ROM readers.
- Your original source discs are in use—not stored for safekeeping.

Virtual CD-ROM emulation software solves all of these problems by installing a special driver that can make CD-ROM image files look like CD-ROM devices to the operating system. By recording the contents of a CD into these compressed CD-ROM image files, the computer acts as if that CD is permanently mounted in its own drive—the virtual CD-ROM reader even gets its own drive letter. You can generally serve as many CDs as you need to from a single machine with the right software. Multiple users accessing the same CD-ROM image file are no more of a problem than any other multiuser function. And because only a few users generally access CDs at once, you can usually get away with using a copy of Windows NT Workstation to serve the files if you're on a budget.

Unfortunately, my favorite virtual CD-ROM software (CD Copy, from IMSI) does not yet support Windows 2000. Considering that IMSI is really just a software packager and not a software developer, it's uncertain when and if they will release a Windows 2000 version. In the meantime, base your CD-ROM jukebox servers on Windows NT 4.

Finally, the absolute simplest method to serve a large number of CD-ROMs in an enterprise is to serve them from the workstations that already have CD-ROM drives. Of course, this method suffers from many of the problems that jukeboxes suffer from, but at least it's free.

If you use any 32-bit version of Windows or UNIX on your workstations, you should be able to serve the CD-ROMs from the workstations that have CD-ROM drives without much hassle. It does mean you have to trust your users not to mess with things, but I've found a hack to get around that problem: mount the CD-ROM farther back in the case and put a blank faceplate in front of it. Then you simply have to trust users not to initiate an eject or shut their computers off.

Fault Tolerance

Now that we've discussed ways to keep a server up, we'll move out a level to the server's purpose: the application. It doesn't matter much that a server runs if the application it serves has crashed. Conversely, it doesn't matter much that a server has crashed if the application it serves still runs. We'll look at solutions that cover both of those eventualities in this section.

Service Monitors

Windows 2000 now includes built-in service monitoring that can alert you to problems with server services and even stop and start the services automatically if they crash. I'm just guessing, but I think Microsoft did this to keep their Exchange servers running without human intervention.

Service monitors are small software applications that run on servers and continuously monitor the state of a software application, such as Exchange or SQL Server. The service monitors simply check to see if the service is responsive to service queries on a periodic basis. Windows 2000's built-in Service Monitor can determine the state of the service using built-in operating system calls, so it's more efficient and safer than third-party service monitors.

In the event that the service fails to respond to a service query within a given time frame, the service monitor will stop the service and start it again (in exactly the same manner as allowed by the Service Control Panel). This is basically equivalent to shutting down and restarting a crashed word processor.

This method of fault tolerance, of course, assumes that whatever caused the service to crash isn't going to happen again and that the service can actually be stopped and restarted (a number of application errors will prevent that).

Sage Advice: Service Monitors

Rather than using Windows 2000's Service Monitor to stop and start Exchange all the time (the service this functionality was really designed for), toss it and look for a better mail server for Windows 2000. POP and SMTP mail services aren't difficult, even when you've got hundreds of thousands of users to support. Don't throw good money after bad to try to prop up bloated and buggy side applications for servers. A frequent problem with monitoring applications is that services which queue batches of information— such as printed documents, e-mail, or faxes—are susceptible to repeating failures because the same malformed document that caused the crash in the first place is stuck in the queue. when the service is restarted, it begins processing the queue again and crashes each time it hits the malformed message. This architectural problem with queued applications explains why Microsoft has always had crashing problems with its print spooler and with Exchange. The solution to these prblems is to clear the queue manually prior to restarting the service.

Server Replication

One step above mirroring and stripe sets is *server replication*—keeping an entire redundant server. This provides complete fault tolerance, since you're protected from any disaster up to and including the complete destruction of a single server.

Intellimirror

Microsoft's Intellimirror technology provides automated file-based replication between Windows 2000 machines, which essentially means that up-to-date versions of files can be automatically copied between machines without user intervention. This provides the ability to make desktop environments consistent for users no matter where they log in, provides offline file synchronization, which is useful for backing up workstation data, and provides the ability to deploy software automatically.

Intellimirror is not capable of automatically synchronizing files that are in use by more than one person, so you'll notice that nearly all of its touted capabilities target either IT administrative deployments or single-user configurations.

Third-Party Standby Servers

Legato (`www.legato.com`) makes StandbyServer for Windows 2000. This server replication system uses a dedicated network link between two servers to handle the mirroring traffic. It installs as a device driver, so from Windows 2000's point of view, you're simply creating a mirror set—one of the partitions just happens to be in another machine.

Since it uses (and requires) its own network link, this product doesn't increase network traffic. StandbyServer can also automatically switch the backup machine into place when the main server goes down.

Legato has also purchased its competitor in third-party fault tolerance for Windows 2000; Octopus allows you to create file-by-file copies of Windows 2000 volumes, or selected files, on one or several servers across the network. Octopus also enables a backup server to automatically take over when the original server goes down.

StandbyServer replicates servers on a sector-by-sector basis, whereas Octopus replicates on a file-by-file basis. File-by-file replication provides better flexibility while sector-by-sector replication is more reliable.

Clusters

True *clustering* is the running of a single application on multiple machines at one time. This allows you to apply the resources of many machines to one problem, and when properly implemented, it is an excellent way to handle large problems such as enterprise databases, commercial Web sites, and serious scientific applications.

Too bad Windows 2000's clustering isn't true clustering. Windows 2000 clustering is really only for failover; only one machine actually processes the application at any given time. Windows 2000 clustering cannot be used to increase the number of machines an application can run on simultaneously. In Windows 2000 clustering, the service fails over to a cluster member when the active application crashes on the primary server. Clients are connected to the cluster rather than to a specific machine, so they see no change when the failover occurs. Windows 2000 Advanced Server supports two-node clustering (an online server and a backup) where as Windows 2000 Datacenter Server supports four-node clustering (an online server and three backups).

Windows 2000's clustering also requires applications that are written for it; only the latest versions of Microsoft's BackOffice applications support it. Considering that the market for clustered applications is small, no applications will be written to support it until it can show some advantage.

Windows 2000's clustering (known as Wolfpack during its development, and based on DEC's original NT clustering solution) is not as good as the high-availability solutions presented in the previous section. Although those solutions also have problems with switching applications, they can be used with many common applications, such as e-mail, as long as a client connection can be interrupted without causing data corruption.

Windows 2000's clustering in its current incarnation is tremendously complicated and without serious merit. Use solutions that work, like StandbyServer from Legato, before considering Microsoft's solution.

Windows Load-Balancing Service

Another type of clustering works quite well for certain problems: load balancing. *Load balancing* is quite simple; it allows multiple machines to respond to the same IP address and balances the client load among that group. For problems such as Web service, this makes all the servers appear to be one server that can handle a massive number of simultaneous connections. Microsoft recently purchased a company that made a load-balancing service for Windows 2000 and has announced that they will roll this product into Windows 2000 Advanced Server to shore up their use of the word *clustering*.

Load balancing is also called *stateless clustering*. Stateless clustering doesn't work for problems such as file service, database, or e-mail, because there's no standard way to replicate data stored on one server to all the rest of the servers. For example, if on your first session you stored a file to the cluster (meaning one of the machines in the cluster) and then connected to the cluster at a later date, there's only a small chance that you would connect again to the machine that had your file. Stateless clustering works only with applications that don't maintain any data transmitted by the client—you can think of them as "output only" applications. Examples of this sort of application are Web and FTP services.

There is a solution to even that problem, though—all the clustered machines can transmit their stored data to a single back-end storage or database server. This puts all the information in one place, where any user can find it, no matter which clustered server they're attached to. Unfortunately, it also means that the cluster is no faster than the single machine used to store everything.

Stateless clustering works well in the one environment it was designed for: Web service for large commercial sites. The amount of user information to store for a Web site is usually miniscule compared to the massive amount of data transmitted to each user. Because some Web sites need to handle millions of simultaneous sessions, this method lets designers put the client-handling load on frontline Web servers and maintain the database load on back-end database servers.

Building Fault Tolerance from Scratch

High availability and clustering solutions are all expensive—the software to implement them is likely to cost as much as the server you put it on. There are easy ways to implement fault tolerance, but they change depending on what you're doing and exactly what level of fault tolerance you need. I'll present a few ideas here to get you thinking about your fault-tolerance problems.

The first question to ask about fault tolerance is whether you need it. Calculations of the cost of downtime are usually based on the assumption that employees in your organization become worthless the moment their computers go down. Sometimes that's the case, but often it's not. I'm not advocating downtime, I'm merely saying that the assumptions used to cost downtime are often flawed, and that short periods of downtime aren't nearly as expensive as data loss or the opportunity cost of lost business if your business relies on computers to transact.

If you can tolerate 15 minutes of downtime, a whole array of less expensive options emerges. For example, manually swapping an entire server doesn't take long, especially if the hard disks are on removable cartridges. For an event that might occur once a year, this really isn't all that bad.

The following inexpensive methods can achieve different measures of fault tolerance for specific applications:

DNS service   The DNS service can assign more than one IP address to a single domain name. If there's no response from the first address, the client can check, in order, each of the next addresses until it gets a response. This means that for Web service, you can simply put up an array of Web servers, each with their own IP address, and trust that users will be able to get through to one of them. This provides fault tolerance because it rarely matters which Web server clients attach to as long as they're all serving the same data.

Firewalls   Another way to solve the load-balancing problem is with firewalls. Many firewalls can be configured to load-balance a single IP address across a group of identical machines, so you can have three Web servers that all respond to a single address behind one of these firewalls.

File service   Fault tolerance for standard file service can be achieved by simply cross-copying files among two or more servers. By doubling the amount of disk space in each server, you can maintain a complete copy of all the data on another machine. The best way to handle this in Windows 2000 is to configure the Distributed File Service to handle it for you. By creating a domain DFS root and using it to create DFS shares in your enterprise, you can choose to physically locate the shares on any servers in your environment. You can also configure DFS to automatically replicate (closed) files between servers that serve the same DFS share.

Fault tolerance doesn't mean you have to spend a boatload of money on expensive hardware and esoteric software. It means that you must think about the problem and come up with the simplest workable solution. Sometimes that means expensive hardware and esoteric software, but not always.

Summary

Windows 2000 Server supports numerous disk storage options to fit just about any storage need in a server. You can use fault-tolerance features, such as mirroring and RAID-5, to ensure that a server will remain online even if a hard disk fails. You can use striped and spanned volumes to increase disk performance or to extend an existing disk volume across additional physical hard disks.

Windows 2000 also supports the standard complement of removable media, such as floppy drives, CD-ROM and DVD-ROM, removable cartridge hard disks, solid-state memory devices, and magnetic tape.

Traditional backup and archiving is performed using magnetic tape due to its extremely low cost per megabyte. Tape has numerous problems, however, chief among them being sequential access, which makes tape operations laboriously slow. As the cost of hard disks drops and their capacity increases, an entire hard disk drive will soon cost less than an equal size tape. At that point, backup and archive operations will probably change dramatically.

On NTFS-formatted drives, Windows 2000 supports compression to reduce the size of files, encryption to obscure the contents of files, and quotas to control disk space usage on a per-user basis. Windows 2000 also supports mount points to allow partitions to be added to existing directory structures and reparse points to allow directories to be constructed from more than one type of file system.

Windows 2000 also supports two types of clustering. Failover application clustering allows applications to run on one machine. If the primary machine in the cluster fails, operations are automatically moved to another machine in the cluster. Load balancing is used to spread connections to a service across a pool of independent machines. Each machine must be serving exactly the same data for this to work, so it's only effective for stateless connections such as Web services.

Case Study: Amok Tolerance

This case study presents an actual incident where a number of in-place fault-tolerance methods failed. The point of this is not to decry the various methods; rather, it is to say that organization and planning are far better fault-tolerance tools than esoteric hardware and expensive software. In this specific case, the operating system was NetWare rather than Windows 2000, but the effect would have been the same with Windows 2000.

A client of mine used two identically configured servers set up to mirror one another through a common high-availability system. In the event that the primary machine failed, the secondary machine would immediately step in and take up the load without dropping client connections or losing data.

These servers stored information automatically generated by scientific recording equipment. Each day's results depended upon the results from the previous day as the study progressed through time.

Each server contained six hard disks configured in a RAID pack. Five volumes participated in a RAID-5 volume and a sixth disk stood by waiting to be made part of the pack in the event that another disk failed.

Tape backups were performed rigorously and without fail, with a full system backup made once per week on three tapes (the tape system was smaller than the RAID pack) and a daily incremental backup performed each night.

A UPS system the size of a walk-in freezer provided smooth uninterruptible power for the system and, in the event of power loss, could power both servers for days.

The system performed flawlessly and ran for years without serious incident until one night when a new employee decided to clean up some space on the servers (which were dangerously full)—a fault none of the in-place fault-tolerance methods could handle. He wrote a batch file to delete files in a temporary directory and ran the batch file.

Unfortunately, he mistakenly included a switch to traverse subdirectories, so the delete operation proceeded to remove study data after it erased the files in the temporary directory. The employee didn't realize he had erased study data, and the operations continued for two more days until the error was discovered. By then, the deleted files had been over-written by new data. Not even NetWare's highly forgiving delete methodology could bring it back.

Of course, the RAID pack and high-availability solutions worked perfectly—they efficiently deleted the data on both machines as requested by the user.

When the error was discovered, we pulled up NetWare's undelete tool and determined that the files were, in fact, gone. So we decided to pull the primary machine out of operation and let the secondary server take over. We would restore the primary machine from tape and then figure out how to merge the data from that day's run, which would be stored on the secondary server.

Being a Thursday, seven tapes composed the complete restore set. We reinstalled the weekly backup and the Monday tapes without incident, but ran into errors with the Tuesday tape. It seems this client had been writing to the same set of weekly tapes for two years. At that point, we realized there was no way to restore the lost data, and since the study was sequential, it would have to be rolled back three days to proceed from the prior Monday.

Three failures contributed to this event:

- The servers were allowed to become full, as no systematic method of detecting or correcting this specific fault existed.

- A human error caused the actual event (but really only highlighted the impending failure due to the full servers).

- A backup system failed due to systematic improper use.

As you can see, not even the most sophisticated fault-tolerance equipment will replace proper design, vigilance, and training.

4

Network Protocols

Network protocols define the way data is transported between computers in a networked environment. Network protocols completely hide their functionality from higher-level services and protocols, which can simply provide the assigned identifier (such as a name or numeric address) of another computer to transmit a message or open a continuous communication stream without dealing with the intricacies of data transport. This is analogous to mailing a letter or calling by telephone—you don't care or even need to know the technical minutiae of how the message is sent or the call is connected. Protocols handle these functions in a network.

Understanding network protocols is necessary to quickly isolate problems in a network. In this chapter, I explain network theory and then describe the major network protocols of Windows 2000. After that, I discuss the best ways to set up networking in your environment.

Network Theory

Early computer communications were fairly simple: Two computers attached to both ends of a digital transport (such as RS-232 serial) communicated by writing data to the serial port. The serial port automatically transmitted the data to the receiving computer, which read the same data in its serial port. Because only two computers participated, there was no real need to address each other—identity was implied by the connection. This simple but effective method of networking remains useful today—it is how dial-up modems work.

But connecting a number of independent computers together presents a serious problem. A direct circuit must exist to talk to a computer. The circuit between the computers is dedicated just to their conversation—no other computers can participate on that channel, and the medium cannot be shared, just like a phone line. Any computer that needs to talk to more than one device requires significantly more communications resources.

The number of circuits required to connect computers together increases exponentially as the number of participating computers increases. Imagine needing a separate phone to talk to each of your co-workers. This exponential increase in circuits requires some method to pass messages among computers in a large-scale network. But a simple data link between computers is not sufficient to implement a message-passing system because a computer cannot simply address another computer to which it is not directly attached, even if a connected path of computers exists. Some sort of unique identifier for each computer must exist to transmit a message to its ultimate recipient.

Network protocols solve these problems. They provide a mechanism whereby multiple computers can both transmit data using shared media and uniquely address one another given any connected path of intermediate computers.

Modern network protocols provide three fundamental networking functions:

Packetizing   Packages data in small independent messages, which alleviates the problem of dedicating a circuit for the duration of a data exchange. More than one computer can participate on the same transport medium because the link is only dedicated during the time that a tiny packet is actually transmitted. TCP/IP was originally developed as a government-funded experiment in packet-based networking—its phenomenal success is proof of the concept.

Addressing   Addresses packets to computers using an addressing scheme that uniquely identifies each computer in the network. Without a unique address, there is no way to ascertain which of the many computers attached to a shared medium should receive a packet.

Error detection   Determines when a packet has become corrupted and discards it.

The simplest protocols, like NetBEUI, stop at this point. More useful protocols, like IP and IPX, add the following feature:

Routability   Identifies both a destination network and client to which a packet should be transmitted. By adding a network number in addition to a client number, gateway computers can keep tables of the networks to which they are connected and share this information among other close routers to determine the most efficient route to transmit a packet along.

More advanced protocols—like TCP, UDP, and IPX—provide the following enhancement:

Multiplexing   Uniquely identifies more than one connection into the same computer to allow for multiple, simultaneous services on the same machine.

TCP (which uses IP as its transport) and SPX (which uses IPX as its transport) provide the following additional features that allow transport protocols to simulate constantly connected circuits:

Guaranteed delivery   Determines when data has been lost in transit and negotiates for its retransmission.

Sockets   Maintain bidirectional streams of traffic seamlessly so the entire network infrastructure is abstracted away from the application. In this way, network transmissions can be handled much like opened files.

Bandwidth throttling   Senses the rate at which data is being transmitted most effectively and tunes the transmission times to maximize the effective use of network resources.

WINS, NetBIOS, and DNS provide the following enhancement:

Name resolution   Automatically accesses an index of names to address so networked resources can be identified easily. In some protocols, this table is built dynamically through a name broadcast mechanism (browsing); in others (DNS), it is maintained statically; and in hybrid systems (WINS and Dynamic DNS), a persistent table is automatically updated by mechanisms such as browsing or DHCP. More recent systems rely less upon automation than static assignment (LDAP, X.500, NDS, and Active Directory) because automated systems do not scale well in large organizations.

Finally, session layer interprocess communications, such as SMB and FTP, support even more complex application support mechanisms, such as the following:

Sessions   Automatically provide security and accounting context for a related series of datagrams between two communicating systems. Sessions provide a method for authenticating a sequence of communications in the beginning and presuming from that point on that those valid credentials are enforced until the session is terminated.

File I/O services   Include opening, closing, and seeking a specific point in a remote file; reading or writing blocks of data; and locking blocks of data so that data integrity can be maintained when multiple users are accessing the same file.

File management   Includes renaming, directory-listing, and deleting files or performing other file directory tasks. By creating semaphores for common functions of file system management, these operations can be performed efficiently over a network. CIFS (Common Internet File System, formerly known as Server Message Blocks or SMB) performs this function in Windows-based networks.

Windows 2000
in Depth

PART 1

NOTE   Windows 2000 now supports CIFS over TCP/IP directly. The NetBIOS session layer is no longer necessary except to communicate with earlier Windows operating systems.

Streaming Transmission   Enables copy operations or other bulk-data communication.

Authentication   Transmits credentials that verify the identity of a network participant. Nearly all session layer or higher protocols include some form of authentication, even when anonymous access is allowed. Authentication may be cryptographically secure, as with the MD5 and SHA authentication protocols, semi-secure, as with LAN Manager authentication, or completely nonsecure, as with Telnet, POP3, and many other application layer protocols. If the security of authentication is deemed necessary, lower-layer security protocols like IPSec or SSL can be implemented to secure the transmission of otherwise nonsecure authentication credentials.

Encryption   Obscures the content of messages in transit so that the intended recipient is the only partly capable of understanding them. Encryption can be handled at the network layer (as with IPSec and other tunneling protocols), transport layer (as with SSL), presentation layer, or application layer (as with PGP).

All of these functions are explained in the following sections except encryption, which is explained in Chapter 6.

Anatomy of a Data Exchange

Data exchanges between computers take place using a number of different protocols, each protocol having a specific purpose in the exchange. Higher-level protocols with more specific purposes, such as name resolution, are contained within lower-level protocols that provide more generic services, such as network delivery and addressing.

The following series of figures elucidates this fundamental concept of encapsulation. This example shows a frame capture of a DNS name request. The lowest-level protocol involved in this exchange is the data-link protocol, Ethernet. I chose to display a DNS name request because the exchange is simple and embodied in a single packet. More complex exchanges, such as reading a file, require far more packets because of the complicated nature of the task. While more complicated, encapsulation is fundamentally the same as the process described here.

Figure 4.1 shows an Ethernet frame containing a payload. The Ethernet frame contains the information necessary to transmit the packet from one participant on the Ethernet collision domain to another. Bridges or switches handle the task of moving frames between collision domains by maintaining tables of all of the Ethernet MAC addresses they've seen. Bridges and switches can also share their address tables, but since forwarding a packet requires that every bridge or switch knows the final location of the packet, these tables grow exponentially, making Ethernet unwieldy and impossible to scale to more than about 10,000 hosts.

Figure 4.1   Network monitor capture of an Ethernet frame

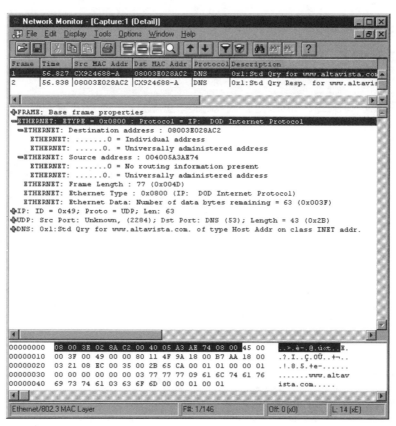

The frame capture displayed in Figure 4.2 shows the IP datagram contained within the Ethernet frame. The IP packet provides only the addressing between computers and other delivery-based information, most of which is actually unused in modern systems. In IP, hosts are identified by both a network number and a client number—typically only the network number is stored in routers, so many hosts can be referred to by a relatively small number of known routes. This provides many orders of magnitude improvement in the maximum size of a network alone. The concept of the default gateway, a route that packets destined for unknown networks take, and increasingly specific network numbering, where large-scale networks are inherently identified inside the network numbers of smaller-scale networks, complete the ideal of an infinitely scalable networking schema.

Figure 4.2   An IP datagram contained in an Ethernet frame

The UDP packet contained within the IP packet is shown in Figure 4.3. The UDP protocol adds port information to provide *multiplexing*, which is additional information needed to route the packet to a specific service on the receiving computer and to retain information about the requesting application on the source machine. In this case, the port information specifies that this packet will be handed to the DNS service.

Figure 4.3   A UDP packet contained within an IP datagram

Finally, the most specific protocol contained within this entire message is the DNS request, shown in Figure 4.4. In this exchange, DNS uses UDP to specify the service port to connect to. UDP uses IP to add addressing information. IP uses Ethernet to be transported to the next router in the path to the destination address.

Figure 4.4   A DNS request contained within a UDP packet

The Transport Protocols

The higher-level services of Windows 2000 are not affected by the particular protocol you choose to use in your network. As long as the transport protocol exposes the Windows 2000 Transport Driver Interface (TDI), which is a superset of the NetBIOS Frames Protocol used in LANs since IBM's introduction of NetBIOS in 1983, you can use it to carry Windows 2000 session information between clients and servers. Most protocols provided with Windows 2000 support TDI.

NOTE The AppleTalk protocol provided with Windows 2000 is now TDI-compliant, so there's no need for a separate file-sharing mechanism as there was in Windows NT.

At the lower end, a transport driver must support the Network Driver Interface Specification (NDIS) in order to connect to a transport driver. All network adapters that support Windows 2000 do this, so it isn't much of a real-world issue.

Four transport protocols are popular enough to warrant default support by Windows 2000:

- TCP/IP
- IPX
- NetBEUI
- AppleTalk

I compare these protocols below and then discuss them in detail in the following sections.

TCP/IP Transmission Control Protocol/Internet Protocol (TCP/IP) is the protocol of the Internet. TCP/IP is required in computers that communicate directly with the Internet and is recommended by Microsoft for use in all networks. NetBIOS over TCP/IP (NBT) is the NetBIOS compatibility layer for TCP/IP. TCP/IP is the slowest of the protocols supported by Windows 2000.

Hosts in TCP/IP are uniquely numbered in their network; networks are uniquely numbered within an internetwork and globally unique within the Internet. The host and network address are combined into a single 32-bit number with the division between host and network defined by a 32-bit subnet mask.

The largest chunk of this chapter is dedicated to TCP/IP, because it is both the most popular and the most complex of network protocols.

IPX/SPX Internetwork Packet eXchange/Sequential Packet eXchange (IPX/SPX) is the protocol of Novell Networks and is implemented by the NWLink TDI driver in Windows 2000. NetBIOS compatibility is provided by the NWBLink compatibility layer. IPX is useful in its own right as a simple, fast, and fairly secure routable protocol and when connectivity with Novell servers is required. IPX is the fastest routable protocol supported by Windows 2000.

Hosts in IPX are numbered by their unique media access control identifier (Ethernet MAC address), which is globally unique and built into the network adapter's firmware. For this reason, host numbers are not assigned in software as they are in TCP/IP. Servers and routers must be additionally programmed with network identifiers, known as *network numbers,* which are attached to packets routed between hosts until they reach their ultimate network.

NetBEUI   Network Basic Input/Output System Extended User Interface (NetBEUI) was designed by Microsoft and IBM for small networks. NetBEUI cannot be routed, but multihomed Windows 2000 servers can "gate" NetBEUI requests between networks much the way an Ethernet bridge can forward requests for remote hosts on to different networks. This function, however, is considerably slower than using a natively routed protocol like TCP/IP or IPX. Since NetBEUI implements NetBIOS natively, no compatibility layer is required. NetBEUI is the fastest network protocol for use with Windows 2000 and is appropriate in workgroup environments consisting of a few machines, a single Ethernet subnet, and no Internet access.

Hosts in a NetBEUI network are identified only by their data-link layer MAC address. There is no network number, so the protocol is not routable.

AppleTalk   AppleTalk is the protocol built into Macintosh computers for file and print sharing. AppleTalk is necessary to support Macintosh clients under Windows 2000 but is not useful for supporting PC clients.

Unlike Windows NT, Windows 2000 implements AppleTalk as a TDI-compliant network protocol—so technically, you could use AppleTalk alone as a network protocol. This might be appropriate in an environment where all the host computers are Apple Macintoshes, and for some reason TCP/IP is undesirable.

NetBEUI

NetBEUI is small and fast. Those are its only benefits. Since it cannot be routed, it's useless except in networks that consist of a single Ethernet network or where a single multihomed server connects all domains. The NBF TDI compliant–protocol driver implements NetBEUI in Windows 2000.

Since NetBEUI is nonroutable, it's virtually free from security problems. If you're not already on the network, you can't gain access to it.

Practical NetBEUI Networking

NetBEUI's only practical uses are derived from its small size and simplicity. Although it is technically the fastest networking protocol included with Windows 2000, it is not fast enough to warrant its use on that merit alone.

Contemporary hardware is capacious enough that small size is rarely useful, but there is an important case when small size is important—booting MS-DOS from a floppy.

The routable protocols are comparatively large, but NetBEUI provides enough remaining MS-DOS memory to perform useful work. By supporting it on your Windows 2000 server, you can use MS-DOS boot floppies to connect to a drive share on your network from PCs that do not yet have operating systems. You can then run disk-imaging software, download a stored installation image file, and easily perform network-based operating system installs. Other network protocols take up so much conventional DOS memory that there's little room left to run an application.

Simplicity is also a benefit. You may run into situations where, for whatever reason, you can't get one of the more complex protocols to work correctly—for example, when setting up a PPTP tunnel over RAS. NetBEUI's simplicity provides a protocol that will nearly always function given the existence of a connected data link. This can make NetBEUI an important troubleshooting tool.

IPX/SPX

IPX, the protocol developed by Novell for use in NetWare, was originally implemented in Windows NT to support connectivity with NetWare networks. It became the recommended protocol for use with Windows NT until Microsoft perfected their implementation of TCP/IP. The NWLink transport driver interface protocol driver implements IPX in Windows 2000.

IPX   Performs the functions of addressing and includes the data elements necessary for routing, as well as packet reordering. In this respect, it is equivalent to IP except that it adds port information, providing the same functionality as UDP/IP.

SPX   Performs flow control functions to ensure that packets arrive to a specific destination in order and do not need to be reordered for purposes such as network printing. *SPX* is equivalent to TCP but is used less often because IPX is complex enough to use for many services.

IPX is nearly configuration-free because it uses the media access control unique identifier as the host number, so clients do not need to have a unique address assigned. In the case of Ethernet, this identifier is globally unique and programmed into the adapter at the factory. For other data-link technologies, the address may be factory-assigned or assigned during installation, but it must always be unique or the data link will not function. Network numbers are assigned to each shared media network, but this information is programmed only into routers and servers. Because IPX is not globally connected, you can use whatever network numbers you deem appropriate.

NOTE   Novell has a globally unique network number registry intended to allow NetWare extranets to interoperate seamlessly. It was never really adopted, however, so it is not important.

IPX has no name-resolution facilities; instead it relies upon higher-level services like NetBIOS or the NetWare Core Protocol (implemented by the NetWare File and Print Services add-on package for Windows 2000) for name resolution.

Practical IPX Networking

IPX is a fairly fast, fairly small, routable protocol that was originally included in Windows NT to support migrating from NetWare. In the early days of Windows NT 3.5, IPX was popular because Microsoft's TCP/IP implementation was buggy and incomplete and because the Internet wasn't a huge deal yet.

Since that time, TCP/IP has surpassed IPX as the protocol of choice for Windows 2000 servers. This is somewhat shortsighted on Microsoft's part. TCP/IP is larger, slower, more difficult to configure, and far more vulnerable to security problems than IPX. The only two benefits of TCP/IP are its massive scalability (IPX begins to bog down in networks larger than 2,000 clients because routed broadcasts take up a considerable amount of network bandwidth) and its seamless Internet connectivity.

Active Directory makes TCP/IP a necessity on servers that participate in a domain, so you can't really choose not to use it. However, you can still mix IPX and TCP/IP in your environment and use IPX on your clients to provide faster connections and easier client administration. Even HTTP Internet access is possible for these clients by using Microsoft Proxy Server. Because IPX is substantially easier to administer than TCP/IP, you should strongly consider using it as your client-to-server networking protocol if specific TPC/IP services are not required.

IPX has some substantial benefits you should consider closely when choosing a primary network protocol:

- It's fast—about 20 percent faster than TCP/IP over the same connections. It has lower overhead and fewer software translation layers to go through. Because it's not subject to Internet attacks, its code contains far fewer time-consuming consistency checks than the code to support TCP/IP.
- It routes broadcasts, which means that all named resources on your network appear correctly and automatically without the necessity for name services like WINS or DNS.
- It uses MAC layer (usually Ethernet) addresses as network layer addresses, so you don't have to assign a unique client number to each machine, and routing pretty much takes care of itself.
- It does not require much specific configuration on either clients or servers, so proper connectivity is nearly guaranteed.
- It can't be routed over the Internet, so machines running only IPX are (almost) completely immune to attack from the Internet.

IPX does have three problems:

- It can't be routed over the Internet, so Internet servers and clients that will access the Internet without a proxy also need TCP/IP.

- It routes broadcasts, so networks larger than 2,000 clients begin to bog down due to excessive broadcast traffic. This problem is somewhat intractable—IPX becomes useless in large networks for this reason.

- Network numbers are not hierarchical as they are in TCP/IP, so routers must have a complete table of network routes in order to route packets. This makes IPX unsuitable for extremely large networks like the Internet.

Since you'll often use TCP/IP to supplement these shortcomings with IPX, most network administrators feel that installing only TCP/IP is easier. Using IPX as the primary protocol will result in faster inside network connections. Establishing TCP/IP connections may take slightly longer, but if you only use TCP/IP for Internet connections, you won't notice the difference.

> **NOTE**   TCP/IP cannot be uninstalled on Windows 2000 servers, but the binding can be disabled on individual network interfaces if you want to prevent TCP/IP connections on that network interface. Since Active Directory requires TCP/IP, however, this isn't an option for many servers.

TCP/IP

The Transmission Control Protocol (TCP) and the *Internet Protocol (IP)* are two distinct protocols that form the basis of nearly all Internet communications. The only exceptions are support protocols like ARP and ICMP that operate at or below the level of IP to create information required for IP to function. Recently they have come to form the basis of most local area network communications. The two protocols are so tightly bound together in their function and purpose that they are often referred to singularly as TCP/IP; however, they can, and often do, function independently of one another.

In common usage, the entire suite of Internet protocols is referred to as the TCP/IP protocol suite. Those protocols include low-level protocols, such as IP, ICMP, ARP, UDP, and TCP, as well as higher-level protocols, such as HTTP and FTP, which rely upon the services of the lower-level Internet protocols. In this chapter, I discuss only the low-level protocols.

Windows 2000 also provides support for encrypted networking with IPSec and SSL (Secure Socket Layer). I discuss these protocols in detail in Chapter 6.

The Internet Protocol

IP is the foundation upon which all other high-level Internet protocols operate. IP provides the basic mechanism for the forwarding of data between two computers on separate networks. IP can fragment packets if they are too large for some older networks to forward, but this feature is largely obsolete because all routers built during the past decade are able to pass large IP packets.

IP packets are simply handed from computer to computer until they reach their destination. The computer sending the packet and the computer receiving the packet are called *end-systems* because they are at the ends of the communication session. The computers between the end-systems are called *intermediate systems*. Intermediate system is a generic term for computers more commonly called routers, gateways, or multi-homed hosts.

IP provides the functions of addressing, fragmentation, and header error checking only to support packet forwarding—no other functionality is presumed or implemented. Therefore:

- IP cannot guarantee that a packet will reach its destination.
- IP has no ability to perform flow control.
- IP performs no error correction.
- IP performs no error detection for the data payload.
- IP does not guarantee that packets will arrive in order and does not order them sequentially.

IP relies on the data link (such as Ethernet or Frame Relay) to transmit data in an error-free condition and does not attempt to provide any guarantees of service. Other protocols, which are transported within IP packets, add information such as packet serial numbers and error-correction codes. The destination system can check to see if all the packets have arrived, arrange them in the correct order, and request that any missing packets be sent again based on this additional information. (TCP performs all these functions, as explained in the next section.)

IP treats each packet as if it existed alone, unrelated to any other packet being transmitted. For this reason, IP packets are often referred to as *datagrams*, which, like a telegram, implies a short but complete transmitted message. IP does not have logical or virtual connections, circuits, sockets, or any other mechanism to provide associations between packets. These functions are all provided by higher-level protocols, such as TCP, or occasionally by lower-level protocols, such as ATM.

IP does not perform error correction. IP does, however, implement limited error checking to verify that the header information is correct. Damaged header information could result in the packet being forwarded to the wrong address. If a router on the path between the sending computer and the receiving computer detects at any time that an IP packet's address header has become damaged (by comparing the header with the header's checksum), the router will simply discard the packet without notification of any kind. Again, higher-level protocols will determine what data is missing and generate a request for retransmission. This header checksum does not detect errors that may have crept into the data portion of the packet. That function is also left up to higher-level protocols. Note that while almost all data-link layer protocols implement error checking to determine whether their frames have become corrupted, IP packets can be corrupted during the routing process before the data-link layer gets the packet. This means that error checking can only be performed reliably by the end-systems in a communication.

IP does include information about how many times and for how long a packet should continue to be forwarded in a routed system. Every IP packet contains a *time-to-live indicator* that is decremented each time a router forwards the packet. (Technically, routers are also supposed to decrement TTL whenever one second of real time elapses, but most do not.) The time-to-live indicator usually starts at around 64, with a maximum possible value of 255. When a packet's time-to-live indicator reaches zero, the packet is discarded. This event can occur in three (rare) cases:

- When the network is too busy to forward packets in a timely manner
- When a circular route exists and packets are just being passed around it
- When the route between two computers is too long to be useful

In all three cases, the route is not useful, so communications should not continue.

Internet Addresses   All computers attached to an IP network (such as the Internet) are uniquely identified by a 32-bit number, usually expressed in dotted decimal notation, with each byte separated by a period. Because each portion of the address specifies eight bits, the decimal range is between 0 and 255 for each of the four bytes. For example:

    10.191.31.10

NOTE   You'll often see bytes referred to as *octets* in other network documents. In this book, a byte is always eight bits long, and an octet is eight singing barbers.

This address must be unique to the specific computer to which it is assigned—no other computer can have this address if it is attached to the same network (usually the Internet). If two computers ever do have the same address, unpredictable routing errors will result. IP addresses are analogous to house addresses in that no two are ever the same and each element (in the case of house addresses, elements would be states, cities, streets, and numbers) is increasingly specific—they become more specific as you read to the right.

IP addresses contain two elements of data: the network number and the host number. The network number is the unique code assigned to your network. This number functions much the way a ZIP or postal code functions for routing mail; it gets the packet to the general area—the network. The host (or station) number determines the specific host on that network to which the packet is addressed. This is similar to your street address.

Internet addresses were originally segmented on byte boundaries. Large networks on which the first byte specifies the network number and the last three bytes specify the host number are called *Class A domains*. Medium-size networks on which the first two bytes specify the network number and the last two bytes that specify the host number are called *Class B domains*. Smaller networks on which the first three bytes specify the network number and the last byte specifies the host number are called *Class C domains*.

Before the advent of *classless interdomain routing (CIDR),* specific address ranges were implied by the network class. The network number and host number were separated based on the address range rather than the network mask. As the Internet grew, this system became rapidly obsolete and was replaced by CIDR. Classes, as applied to Internet networks, now only specify the network size if it happens to be evenly divisible on byte boundaries.

Class-based subnetting is fairly simple. It is also possible to subnet at any point within the 32 bits of the IP address, not just on byte boundaries. This method of dividing network numbers from local addresses is known as *classless addressing*.

Originally, most Internet addresses were segmented on byte boundaries simply because it was easy, but as IP addresses became scarce, CIDR, the more conservative practice of segmenting based on the actual estimated size of a network, became common.

Eight bits can provide 256 addresses (because 2 to the 8th power is 256), but in this case two addresses in every subnet are reserved. The "all zeros" address is used to specify the entire subnet. The "all ones" (binary 11111111 = 255) address is used to specify an IP broadcast, so sending an IP packet to 10.191.61.255 means that all computers in the subnet should receive it. Therefore, to calculate the number of available addresses in a subnet, you raise 2 to the number of bits in the subnet portion of the address and then subtract 2.

Each additional bit of address space doubles the number of hosts allowed on a network but divides the number of possible networks in half. So by adding one bit to an eight-bit subnet, we can address 510 computers ($2^9 = 512 - 2 = 510$). Adding another bit doubles that to 1,022 ($2^{10} = 1,024 - 2 = 1,022$).

TIP When you determine how large an address space should be, add an extra bit to allow for future growth.

Every IP address has two portions:

- The network number
- The local host number

Because both numbers are contained in the same 32 bits and because the size of the network varies greatly from organization to organization, some method is required to determine which part of the IP address is the network number and which is the host's unique identifier. The subnet mask determines which portion of the IP address is the network number and which portion is the local host address. The subnet mask is a 32-bit number—consisting of all ones to the left and all zeros to the right—that specifies how large the network number is. The switch between ones and zeros occurs at the bit size of the network. The following subnet shows an example of a subnet mask for a network with 11 bits of address space:

```
11111111.11111111.11111000.00000000 = 255.255.248.0
```

The ones mean that the network number is 21 bits long, and the zeros mean that an 11-bit range is available for host addresses. You will sometimes see a slash and a number following an IP address, as in 192.168.0.1/24. This is convenience notation that indicates how many bits of the IP address constitute the network number, so /21 is equal to the network mask shown above.

The subnet mask determines whether the destination computer and the source computer reside on the same local network or whether the transmission will require routing. When a computer creates an IP packet, it masks off the host address of the destination computer, leaving only the network number. It compares this network number to its own network number, and if the two are equal, the computer transmits the packet directly to the destination computer because the two computers are on the same local data link. If the two numbers are not equal, the client transmits the packet to its default gateway (or in very rare cases, to another router defined in the host's routing table). The default gateway performs a similar comparison. This process continues until the packet eventually reaches the data link to which it is local and is finally received by the destination computer.

A fundamental (and often overlooked) aspect of classless addressing is the hierarchical nature of network addresses. Network numbers are hierarchical in the sense that to a high-level backbone router, only a few bits of the IP address are interpreted as the network number, whereas at the local level, most of the bits of an IP address may be interpreted as the network number. Consider the following example: A computer with the IP address 10.233.56.74 would be difficult to find from a router with the address 10.1.1.1 without network hierarchy. The router would have to have a specific route to the 10.233.56.0 network in its routing table along with literally millions of other routes. But because classless routing is hierarchical, the router 10.1.1.1 need only know that the network 10.233.0.0 is reachable by forwarding to router 10.233.0.1. That router knows how to reach more specific interior networks through routers that it knows about. This means that 10.1.1.1 need only know 255 routes to interior networks. This concept of network number hierarchy enables the scalability required to operate massive networks like the Internet without requiring every router on the network to maintain a table of every possible route on the Internet.

Routing

Routers, gateways, and multihomed servers perform the routing function. *Routing* is the process of forwarding packets among intermediate systems between two end-systems. Routers forward datagrams received on one network to another network that is closer to the destination. This process repeats until the datagram reaches its destination. Consequently, routers must be attached to both networks and have an Internet address that is local to each network. (Obviously, the devices need more than one IP address.)

IP addresses are assigned to each network interface, not to each computer. If a server has two network interfaces, each attached to a different network, then it is a *multihomed server*. Since most clients have only one network interface, clients have only one IP address and can be referred to by that IP address. Multihomed servers, routers, and gateways all require more than one address; they are generally referred to by the IP address of the adapter through which the default gateway for that multihomed host is reached.

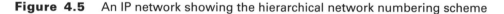

NOTE   You may see the term *host* used to describe either a server or a client. Host means any computer attached to the Internet—either client or server.

Figure 4.5 shows a small portion of a very large Internet. Each interrupted ellipse represents a network. The network number portion of that network is shown in boldface, and the host number portion is shown next to each host. The complete IP address for a host is formed by appending the host number to network number—for example, host number 1.3 on network number 10.191 has an IP address of 10.191.1.3.

Figure 4.5   An IP network showing the hierarchical network numbering scheme

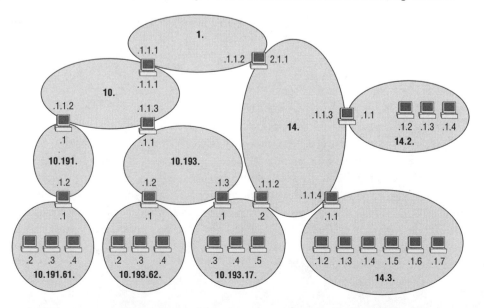

The computers that sit between two networks are multihomed hosts acting as routers—they have more than one IP address. Notice the following about the figure:

- Multihomed computers have an IP address for each network to which they are attached.
- Multihomed hosts connect the networks by forwarding data between them.
- Bottom-tier networks have larger network numbers, usually three bytes long. Host identifiers on these networks are only one byte long.
- Medium-tier networks have two-byte network numbers and two-byte host identifiers.
- Top-tier networks have one-byte network numbers and three-byte host identifiers.
- Multihomed hosts are usually attached to networks with somewhat similar network numbers, but this is not a requirement.
- More than one path can exist between any two end-systems.

A trace route using the `tracert.exe` utility from host 10.191.61.4 to host 14.3.1.7 could produce the following IP address list:

1. 10.191.1.2
2. 10.1.1.2
3. 1.1.1.1
4. 14.2.1.1
5. 14.3.1.1
6. 14.3.1.7

This trace shows that five routers are involved between the two end-systems—an average size for any typical Internet connection. Routers are shown by the network port that the packet travels out of, not by the port that the packet travels into.

The Default Route   In the absence of more specific routing information, the default route specifies which router to send packets to. A router may have any number of network interfaces. For each interface, the router will maintain lists of routes, called *routing tables*, about the network that interface is attached to and the networks that are reachable from that network. The router will forward a packet to the network port (and, therefore, to the network) that is closest to that packet's destination.

If there is no information in a router's routing tables that tells it where a packet should specifically go, the router sends the packet to a default gateway. This route is called the *default route*, because data with no better addressing information is forwarded there. The default route can be followed until the packet reaches a high-level router that has no default route, because it is at the top of the routing hierarchy. The final router either knows where to route the packet, or the packet is dropped and the route is unreachable.

Routing Update Protocols *Routing update protocols* are used to exchange information among routers (also known as *Internet gateways*) about routes, their availability, and their relative congestion. This information provides each router with enough information about its own network environment to make routing decisions for packets. For example, a router may determine that a certain link is not functioning correctly and send packet traffic to another router attached to a working link. The various routing protocols have evolved through time into two basic groups:

Interior gateway protocols   Good at managing small- to medium-scale networks:

- Routing Information Protocol (RIP)
- Open Shortest Path First (OSPF)

Exterior gateway protocols   Used on the Internet backbone for sophisticated traffic management:

- Border Gateway Protocol (BGP)
- Exterior Gateway Protocol (EGP)

Windows 2000 supports RIP and OSPF. These protocols allow Windows 2000 Routing and Remote Access Service to interoperate with other RIP or OSPF routers to maintain a dynamically updated routing table. OSPF is far better at providing fault-tolerant routing than RIP and supports such functionality as automatically routing around failed links or routers. OSPF also checks for the authenticity of routing updates and is much harder to "spoof" than RIP for that reason.

NOTE   Networks large enough to require serious routing protocols like OSPF should probably be using dedicated routers rather than Windows 2000 servers to implement routed connections. While there is nothing inherently wrong with using servers as routers, it reduces the reliability of your network to that of the servers within it. Using dedicated routers is faster, more fault tolerant, and easier to administer.

Transmission Control Protocol

TCP provides a reliable connection using an unreliable transport mechanism by supplying the services that IP is missing. Those services are:

Reliable delivery   TCP will request lost packets until the transmission is complete or will return a valid and useful error message. TCP guarantees that as long as a data path exists between two end-systems, a reliable stream of data can be transmitted.

Sequencing   TCP will put out-of-order packets back in order so a sequential stream of data is maintained.

Constant connection   TCP makes data streams act somewhat like files that can be opened, read, and closed. It abstracts the packet-based protocol away from the user's application.

Error detection and correction   TCP adds a checksum to the data payload. If the checksum shows that a packet is damaged, the packet is discarded and retransmitted automatically.

Flow control and handshaking   TCP implements mechanisms to adapt to the reliability of lower-level systems and improve throughput based on current data-link conditions.

Multiplexing   TCP uses the concept of sockets and ports to create many simultaneous streams of data between the end-systems.

TCP does not need any guarantees of service from lower-level protocols. It can use any packet-switched or connection-oriented network protocol as long as two-way communication actually exists between the two end-systems. The ability to provide a reliable stream of communication between two systems from an unreliable packet-based transport makes TCP the perfect foundation for higher-level services that require error-free communications.

The TCP specification also provides a modicum of security, but those security mechanisms are obsolete (because they don't really work), so they are not discussed here. Encryption services that work above the TCP layer provide true security by reimplementing the socket services with encryption. These services are collectively referred to as *tunnels*, and at the TCP layer they make up the *Secure Socket Layer (SSL)*.

Ports and Sockets   As mentioned earlier, TCP provides a multiplexing mechanism to allow multiple data streams to be transmitted between end-systems. This multiplexing feature is implemented through ports, sockets, and connections. The ability of a computer to provide different services, such as Telnet, FTP, Web, and NetBIOS services, is dependent upon this multiplexing ability. Without multiplexing, a server could not tell the difference between different higher-level protocols connecting from the same client computer.

A *port* is a TCP connection number. TCP has 16 bits for port numbers, so two end-systems may establish up to 65,535 simultaneous, separate communications streams. A *socket* is a port and the IP (or other protocol) address of the end-system that is necessary to form a complete path to data; it is usually specified in the form 10.191.61.2:80, where the first four bytes are the IP address and the number after the colon (:) is the port. A matched pair of sockets between two hosts forms a connection.

NOTE The transmission and reception ports are not the same in a connection. For example, when a connection to port 80 on a server is established, the client may inform the server to respond to port 15543 on the client. This allows the same client to connect to the same service on the same server multiple times.

Once a connection is established, data can be transmitted between systems bidirectionally until the connection is closed. TCP connections are full-duplex, or bidirectional. When you attach your Web browser to an Internet host, the Web browser knows which port to use because the developers of the HTTP service agreed to use the same port number for HTTP servers. This is known as the convention of *well-known ports*.

The well-known port convention specifies that Internet servers of a certain type should "listen" on a certain TCP port for connection requests from client software. The various server software components (such as the Internet Information Server component services) simply open up their ports and wait for connection attempts from remote clients. Table 4.1 lists some common (and some silly) services and the well-known port that each service uses.

Table 4.1 Some Well-Known Ports

Port	Service	Function
17	Quote	Quote of the Day
21	FTP	File Transfer Protocol
23	Telnet	Telnet
25	SMTP	Mail Transfer
37	Time	Time
53	DNS	Domain Name Server
67	BOOTP	BOOTP Server
70	Gopher	Gopher
80	HTTP	World Wide Web
110	POP3	Post Office Protocol 3
135	RPC	Remote Procedure Call
139	NBSession	NetBIOS Session

Many well-known ports are in use, but the majority of them are of little consequence except in special systems. Those listed in Table 4.1 are general in nature and used by many Internet hosting systems. A complete list of well-known ports is contained in the Internet Assigned Numbers document defined in RFC 1700.

The Internet Assigned Numbers Authority of the Internet Engineering Task Force assigns all well-known port numbers below 1024. Port numbers above 1024 are available for public use in any manner. Users of some nonofficial protocols, such as Internet Relay Chat (IRC), have simply chosen their own port numbers (in this case, 8000). By convention, everyone knows to use port 8000 for IRC, so it has become a de facto standard. After all, this type of usage is how the well-known port numbering system came to be.

Dynamic Host Configuration Protocol

The *Dynamic Host Configuration Protocol (DHCP)* makes implementing a TCP/IP network considerably easier than it used to be. DHCP allows computers to request an IP address from an address server, along with other network protocol configuration information such as the subnet mask, default gateway, and IP addresses of important resources (such as name servers).

NOTE   The default gateway is also called the *default route.*

Dynamic allocation makes it easy to reconfigure network addresses across an entire network by simply changing the addresses served by DHCP servers. DHCP also allows you to reuse IP addresses for pools of computers that are only occasionally attached, such as for dial-up users.

DHCP is an outgrowth of the early BOOTP protocol, which was somewhat limited in that it provided only an IP address, subnet mask, and default gateway. More complex networks require additional information, such as the address of a WINS server, or additional gateways. DHCP evolved from BOOTP to provide these (and any other) automatic configuration protocol addresses. DHCP can be forwarded by routers that forward BOOTP requests, thus removing the requirement that a DHCP server exist on each local network. Windows 2000 DHCP can also provide IP addresses and boot file information to BOOTP clients. Although mostly obsolete, this function is still useful for print servers and other network peripherals based on older UNIX operating systems.

DHCP is a client/server protocol in that the booting client requests network information and a server provides that information. The DHCP server is responsible for allocating IP addresses so that no two clients get the same IP address. If you have multiple DHCP servers, you must configure them so that no two servers can provide the same address to different clients.

DCHP supports three models of IP allocation:

Automatic allocation   Assigns a permanent IP address to a host. Whenever a client boots, it will get the same automatically generated but permanently assigned IP address. The DHCP server identifies the client by its MAC address (usually an Ethernet address).

Dynamic allocation   Assigns IP addresses for a limited period of time (lease duration) or until the client relinquishes the address. This model does not guarantee that the same address will be provided to that client in the future.

Manual allocation   Assigns a specific IP address to a specific host permanently. This model assigns IP addresses for resources whose IP addresses must be known because they provide some service to the network, such as a file or name server.

The three allocation methods can be used on the same network, as needs dictate. Dynamic allocation is often the most useful because IP addresses can be conserved. With dynamic allocation, IP address assignment is based on the number of clients actually attached, rather than on the number of clients that exist. In other words, dynamic allocation can reserve IP addresses for those clients that are actually using the network at any one time without reserving them for clients that are not in use.

DHCP will automatically avoid manually assigned addresses already in use on the network. For example, if you have a router with an assigned IP address, DHCP will not assign that IP address. Note that this only applies to manually assigned IP addresses, not to other static blocks that might be assigned by RAS or by another DHCP server. If you have another service that assigns IP addresses dynamically on your network, you need to set up exclusion ranges on your DHCP server to ensure that the same address cannot be dynamically assigned to different devices.

IP addresses are assigned in ranges called scopes. A *scope* is simply a range of IP addresses that the DHCP server is allowed to assign along with the DHCP options that go along with that range. DHCP options are IP parameters (such as the default gateway, WINS server, and DNS server) that would normally be assigned manually. These parameters can also be set as global DHCP options if the same parameters apply to each of your DHCP scopes. That way, you only have to set up the parameter information one time.

You can also specifically exclude IP addresses or ranges when you set up a DHCP scope. Exclusion prevents DHCP from assigning IP addresses in the excluded range. This is useful for situations when more than one DHCP server may assign the IP address, when you want to reserve a range for future expansion, or when you have clients that cannot support DHCP (such as older print servers or obsolete computers).

Internet Control Message Protocol   The *Internet Control Message Protocol (ICMP)* is an integral part of all TCP/IP implementations. As the name implies, it is used specifically to send messages (about the routing of datagrams) between Internet hosts. Essentially, ICMP is the error messenger of the Internet protocols.

ICMP communications are transmitted between gateways (routers or intermediate systems) and hosts (end-systems) under the following circumstances:

- When a gateway cannot reach a destination because a route path does not exist or because the time-to-live indicator of a packet has expired en route.

- When a packet has been discarded because its header information is erroneous.

- When a gateway can't buffer as much information as the host is sending. This controls the rate at which a host transmits TCP/IP information.

- When a shorter route exists.

- When an echo reply has been requested, as in a ping request.

It's important to note that ICMP messages are only transmitted regarding fragment zero of a fragmented IP packet. Hackers can prevent ICMP error messages from being sent about bad packets by creating fragmented packets that have no zero fragment. Windows 2000 checks for and blocks these packets, but many older network devices such as routers and firewalls may not.

Since ICMP has no authentication capability, hackers are able to exploit it for a number of denial-of-service attacks. ICMP redirection messages can be hacked to hijack an existing TCP/IP connection, but this is difficult to accomplish seamlessly, and the data must be sent along generally the same route. Inordinately large ICMP ping packets (about 64K) will crash some older TCP/IP implementations (such as Windows NT prior to Service Pack 3) by overrunning buffers, especially on Intel-based computers.

Sage Advice: Read the RFCs

The Internet Requests for Comment are the source documents developed by and for the loosely organized Internet community. They describe the specific details of every Internet-related protocol. They are unevenly edited and speak to various levels of reader sophistication, but they are required reading if you ever truly intend to understand TCP/IP. Read at least the following RFCs:

- RFC 791 describes the Internet Protocol.

- RFC 792 describes ICMP.

- RFC 793 describes TCP.

- RFC 768 describes UDP.

A reliable source for RFCs in HTML format can be found at http://www.cis
.ohio-state.edu/htbin/rfc/INDEX.rfc.html.

WARNING ICMP attacks are difficult to prevent because many ICMP messages
are crucial to the proper operation of TCP/IP. However, you should set up your firewall to block any access to machines not specifically involved with the external Internet, and make certain you are running the latest version of the TCP/IP software on all
your equipment.

Practical TCP/IP Networking

The benefits of TCP/IP are obvious—it provides the ability to connect massive networks
together, and you can't participate on the Internet without it. Less obvious are the dangers of
TCP/IP—it is very easily hacked because there's no guarantee of authenticity or even data
integrity. Add to that the fact that the evil agents of destruction are attached to the Internet
with you, and you have a full-fledged security problem. The Internet is public. Most networks
are not.

The largest aspect of practical networking with TCP/IP is security—allowing the users
you want to have access while denying access to those you don't. Implementing TCP/IP
security is most easily and rigorously accomplished with a sophisticated firewall and a
strong firewall policy.

But there are a number of practical security measures you can implement in addition to
strong firewalling to further shore up security in your environment, as detailed in the
following sections.

Stay Up-to-Date   Keep current on the latest service packs and hot-fixes for computers
exposed directly to the Internet. Microsoft releases bug fixes and security improvements routinely in service packs. The latest service pack can be downloaded at www.microsoft.com/
windows2000.

WARNING   Microsoft has, on occasion, released service packs that cause more problems than they solve. Case in point: Windows NT 4 Service Packs 2 and 4, both of which caused serious disk corruption problems. You should generally stay about two months behind the release of a service pack for servers so you can hear about any problems a release may cause.

Because services packs update system files, they can cause bizarre problems when the versions of system files don't match. This condition can be caused by reinstalling original system files (especially network drivers and services) from the CD-ROM after a service pack has been installed. Some problems you might encounter include a failure to boot normally or the failure of certain services. To prevent mismatched system files, always reapply service packs before you reboot a computer after software installations.

Windows 2000 provides the ability to "slipstream" services packs by updating a Windows 2000 file set. This prevents the problem of system updates introducing earlier system components that subsequently require a reapplication of the service pack. To use slipstreaming, copy the \i386 directory from your installation CD-ROM to your hard disk drive. Then launch the service pack installer with a -s option. This will allow you to apply the service pack changes to the installation file set on your hard drive, so that further updates that point to that file set will automatically contain the latest service pack updates.

TIP   Perform new installations from slipstreamed file sets to avoid having to apply service packs to brand-new machines.

Use Windows 2000's Internal TCP/IP Security   Windows 2000's internal TCP/IP security can be used to disallow all services except those the server is specifically configured to serve. You can configure the Windows 2000 TCP/IP stack to ignore datagrams from specific host addresses and to refuse connections from specific TCP ports. For servers open to a firewall, you should generally disallow all TCP ports except those you explicitly intend to serve.

You can configure TCP/IP to block addresses using the following tactics:

- Unbind TCP/IP from higher-level services, such as Server and Workstation. This will prevent unauthorized users from attaching to the server as a normal logged-on client and will reduce the number of attack vectors down to TCP/IP services, such as FTP and HTTP, which are harder to exploit and easier to secure.

- Install TCP/IP only on Internet hosts that must participate on the Internet—Web servers and clients. Use IPX on internal servers. This option requires that you base your network on IPX rather than TCP/IP and configure IPX as the first bound protocol, as explained in the earlier section "IPX/SPX." You then install TCP/IP on clients and on Internet servers. Because internal servers do not have a TCP/IP stack installed, any attack on them from the Internet must be vectored through a client having both TCP/IP and IPX, which is very difficult to do and can easily be secured against. To make server connections fast from clients, unbind TCP/IP from the Client for Microsoft networks on client computers. This will cause IPX to be used automatically for connections to servers, and TCP/IP to be used automatically for Winsock connections.

- Use a separate network that is not directly attached to your internal network for Internet connectivity. This is both the most easily implemented and most secure form of TCP/IP security, but it's not that convenient. Users must travel to an Internet-connected client rather than use their desktop PC. However, this can have the effect of reducing casual browsing.

The Interprocess Communications Protocols

Interprocess Communications (IPC) protocols are used to perform higher-level functions such as opening files, connecting to servers to see what services are available, and resolving names to addresses in the network. Windows 2000 supports a number of protocols to perform these services:

- NetBIOS
- Windows Sockets
- SMB/CIFS
- Named Pipes
- Mailslots
- Remote Procedure Call

I discuss each of these protocols in the following sections. You'll notice that I don't cover these protocols as much as others, because there's no configuration information for an administrator to tune, which means they are transparent to the operation of your computer.

NetBIOS

NetBIOS is the basic set of network APIs that perform client-to-server connectivity in a Microsoft network. NetBIOS is a primitive interface that provides the following functionality:

- Name management (add group, check for used, respond used, and report conflict)
- Messaging (datagram and broadcast)

- Session management (locate named resource; establish, transmit, terminate, and flow control)

The data communications facility of NetBIOS is not suitable for many modern applications, but Windows 2000 still uses the name management services of NetBIOS to find networked resources on the network. This is why the unique name of a computer is often referred to as its NetBIOS name.

NOTE   Because the term NetBIOS originally referred to both a network transport and a session protocol, some confusion exists about its correct use. In Windows 2000 parlance, the transport protocol is NetBEUI, and NetBIOS alone refers only to the session-layer protocol.

Sage Advice: NetBIOS Names

Avoid using common real words (like the name of your company) as NetBIOS names for computers, workgroups, or domains. Users who set up their own computers might unwittingly name their computer the same as a domain or workgroup. This can result in strange errors, such as users of a particular network segment being denied access to a domain. Use prefixes or suffixes to keep names unique, such as "OUACCOUNTING" and "CUSERNAME."

Windows Sockets

Windows Sockets (WinSock) enables client/server applications to communicate over a network using an interface compatible with the TPC/IP Berkeley Sockets interface. However, WinSock does not require the use of TCP/IP; WinSock applications can operate over any TDI-compliant transport protocol. For example, Microsoft Proxy Server uses WinSock to proxy information from IPX interior clients to TCP/IP exterior hosts. WinSock was originally created to facilitate the porting of UNIX-based client/server applications to Windows 2000 but remains important for Internet applications such as Web browsers and servers.

Server Message Blocks (SMB)

SMB, alias *Common Internet File System (CIFS)*, is a more complex messaging service that implements client/server communications in a Microsoft/IBM network.

Windows 2000 uses SMB as its core file and print protocol. Microsoft renamed SMB to CIFS when it submitted the protocol to the IETF as a draft RFC. CIFS actually performs remarkably well as an Internet file system, especially considering its small, local area network origins.

SMB provides interfaces for the following functions:

- Connections (start, end)
- Directory management (create, delete, rename)
- File management (create, delete, rename, get/set attributes, search)
- File access (open, close, commit caches, read, write, seek)
- Record locking (lock block, unlock block)
- Printer control (create job, write job, close job, get queue data)
- Messaging (send, broadcast)
- Name service (get machine name)

You can play around with the SMB functions directly using various methods in Windows 2000. When you type the following at the prompt:

```
net send administrator "Hello World!"
```

an SMB message sends the data across the network.

Named Pipes

Named Pipes is a connection-oriented interprocess communication interface designed for more complex, multiuser functions (such as GroupWare and database connectivity) than SMB will support. For example, MS-SQL server uses Named Pipes to transmit data between clients and servers.

Named Pipes provides a functionality similar to the sockets functionality of TCP/IP. But rather than relying upon well-known ports for services, each service is addressed directly by a known service name. This somewhat mimics the functionality of a traditional disk-oriented file system—so much so that Named Pipes is actually implemented as a file system in Windows 2000.

Mailslots

Mailslots is a message-oriented (rather than connection-oriented) interprocess communication protocol. It is used for services that do not require maintaining state (remembering the previously sent data) with a connected computer. For example, Windows 2000's browsing mechanism is implemented using the Mailslots interface. Mailslots is somewhat

Windows 2000
in Depth

PART 1

similar to Named Pipes in that it provides a socket mechanism addressed by name and is implemented as a file system.

Remote Procedure Call

Remote Procedure Call (RPC) was originally developed by Sun as an early attempt at parallel processing to allow certain procedures in a program to spin off to other machines. RPC was designed to be nearly transparent to the programmer. By compiling an application using a library of "stub" procedures that mimic the interface of standard I/O libraries, client/server functionality can easily be added to any application. The stub procedures take care of identifying resources, connecting sessions, issuing parameters, and collecting results. All this activity is completely transparent to the original application.

RPC is unique among interprocess communications mechanisms supported by Windows 2000 because it relies upon other IPC mechanisms (either Named Pipes, NetBIOS, or WinSock) as its transport. It assumes a fully functional guaranteed transport below it, rather than implementing one.

A Local Procedure Call exists to allow functions to operate transparently on the same machine even if they're written to the RPC interface. The network logon mechanism in Windows 2000 is handled using Remote Procedure Call (or the Local Procedure Call facility if you are logging on locally).

Summary

Network protocols provide a common language that allows computers to communicate over data-link circuits. Modern network protocols implement two fundamental methods:

- Packetizing allows many simultaneous communications to occur over the same network link.
- Addressing allows computers to specify different recipients in a connected network and provides the foundation for routing, which makes vast networks possible.

Sophisticated protocols like TCP/IP also provide guaranteed delivery with automatic retry, bandwidth throttling and flow control, and multiplexing, which allows network streams to be assigned to different processes on the same machine.

Network protocols use a hierarchical, layered paradigm in which simpler protocols transport increasingly complex protocols. This allows higher-level protocols to solve specific targeted problems such as encryption or file service, while leaving simpler problems such as routing and addressing to lower-level protocols. This paradigm also makes generic higher-level services apparent only to the end-systems in a communication; intermediate systems need only understand the lower-level transport protocol without interpreting the embedded higher-level protocols, thus allowing new protocols to operate over existing network infrastructures like the Internet.

Windows 2000 supports four true networking protocols:

- TCP/IP is the most complex, least secure, and slowest of the supported network protocols. TCP/IP is required for Active Directory services and Internet access and is installed and enabled by default in all variants of Windows 2000. Microsoft recommends TCP/IP for all networking purposes.

- IPX is required for legacy Novell NetWare access and is a very useful protocol in its own right for small- to medium-sized networks.

- NetBEUI is a small, fast, nonroutable protocol useful in very small networks, for very simple client operating systems such as MS-DOS, and for troubleshooting purposes.

- AppleTalk is required for Macintosh support.

In addition to the networking protocols, Windows 2000 supports various interprocess communications protocols such as Mailslots, Named Pipes, and Remote Procedure Call. These protocols are automatically installed, configuration-free, and called only by the applications that use them. No administration is involved with the operation of these protocols.

Case Study: Know Your Protocols

It amazes me how many organizations call me in to fix network problems that are ultimately caused by very minor TCP/IP configuration problems. Why do these configuration problems occur? Because the IT staffers who set up the network either don't understand how TCP/IP works, or they can't configure IP settings properly on their specific networking devices. This unfortunate dynamic often occurs when outside consultants install the original network configuration. When conditions in the company change, the IT staff lacks the knowledge to properly reconfigure the network.

One of my customers implemented a proxy server for HTTP access to the Internet because they couldn't figure out why their clients couldn't route to the Internet when they had no problem reaching all the internal servers. The problem was that the clients did not have a default gateway configured. The clients had installed DHCP in its default mode without adding the gateway option.

Another client had persistent routing problems because they had left the suggested network mask in place: 255.0.0.0. This made connecting to public Web sites with the same first octet impossible.

Another problem occurred when a client tried to remove an obsolete Token Ring node from one of their sites: when they unplugged either the Token Ring MAU or the last device on the ring, routing to their entire site went down. We discovered that the IP address configured in the routing tables at the other sites was the IP address of the Token Ring interface. The router routed packets according to its internal routing tables, so the fact that they were routed to the IP address of the Token Ring interface was of no consequence. However, when the Token Ring was shut down, the interface changed state to disabled and stopped responding to that IP address. By reconfiguring the routing tables in routers around the network, we were able to remove the obsolete Token Ring equipment.

Not all problems are easy to figure out: One client had recurring name resolution problems, especially when visiting public Web sites. They used a firewall to perform DHCP assignments. The firewall had input boxes for three DNS servers, each of which defaulted to 0.0.0.0. The client configured the first DNS servers with their primary and secondary DNS servers and left the third setting in its default state. The DHCP server served all three DNS server settings— despite the fact that one of them was 0.0.0.0. In turn, Windows 2000 frequently tried to resolve names against 0.0.0.0, causing slow or failed name resolution. The solution was to put valid DNS servers in each input box by repeating the primary DNS server in the third input box.

All of these relatively simple problems were caused because the people responsible for maintaining the network never bothered to learn the intricacies of TCP/IP. A complete understanding of TCP/IP and its major support protocols—such as DHCP and DNS—is crucial to networking now that TCP/IP is everywhere.

24seven **CASE STUDY**

5

Network Services

Services are programs designed to provide specific support to other applications on the computer; *network services* provide support to applications running on any computer in the network. Every useful function of a Windows 2000 computer that can be accessed over the network is implemented by a service. For example, Windows 2000's File and Print Services provide the interface for sharing files and printers on a network. The Workstation service enables a Windows 2000 machine to remotely retrieve shared files from another machine.

Drivers support access to hardware or the implementation of general-purpose protocols for the operating system on the local computer. Services are unlike drivers in that they neither control hardware nor are necessary for the local operation of the computer—a Windows 2000 machine can function perfectly well without any services running.

Before we talk about specific services, let's discuss services in general. I'm not going to provide a lot of lines and boxes covering Windows 2000's services architecture, because (despite the lines and boxes you may have seen in Microsoft documentation) there really isn't much of an architecture to talk about.

Services in Windows 2000 are implemented as executable files (`*.exe`) that run in the executive—that mysterious area that shows up between the kernel and user space in Microsoft's diagrams of the Windows 2000 architecture. The system automatically loads these services during the services load phase of the boot process. The services use specially designated security identifiers rather than the security identifier of the system or the logged-on user. Any executable can be run as a service as long as it does not require a graphical or user interface.

You can identify portions of the operating system that run in kernel mode because they usually have a .sys extension for the files, except in the case of the kernel itself (ntoskrnl.exe) and the hardware abstraction layer (hal.dll).

The only thing that separates services from normal user mode applications is the fact that they're started automatically by Windows 2000 at boot time.

Since they run outside the kernel, they require a security identifier to run. The identifier is provided by assigning a user account to the service when the service is installed.

There are three main differences between running inside the kernel and running outside the kernel:

- Technical programming differences (for example, it's easier to allocate memory in a service, and you cannot call a service from a driver).
- The entire kernel mode executes as a single multithreaded process, which means that any driver can crash the kernel and cause a "blue screen of death."
- Security contexts are not enforced inside the kernel—essentially, once a call makes it into the kernel, security is no longer checked for performance reasons.

Some services are actually implemented as kernel mode drivers that are always running but which have a controller service that executes outside the kernel to control access to the service. These "stub services," such as CSRSS (which controls access to the win32.sys Windows 32 subsystem) and services.exe (which controls access to numerous drivers like rdr.sys and srv.sys), receive the operating system calls from user mode programs outside the executive, perform security checks on the call, and then pass the authorized calls through to the kernel mode driver that actually implements the functionality of the service. Microsoft uses this "half driver/ half service" methodology to improve performance by eliminating the excessive security checking and context switching that would occur if the processes ran outside kernel mode.

Sage Advice: Service Accounts

Create a separate user account for each service (or group of highly related services) you install so that you can fine-tune the permission and rights for that service rather than simply provide wide access to your machine. Most BackOffice programs do this for you—don't override their settings. Using the local administrative account is not wise, because it has no authority outside the local domain, and most services in larger organizations will need to connect to relate services in other domains. Using other user accounts may provide more rights than the service account needs, creating a security problem, or they may provide less rights than the service needs, causing the service to fail in strange ways and creating a problem that is unusual and difficult to troubleshoot.

Don't use the "local system" security context for network services. That security account is not a domain account and has no rights on other machines, so when a client attempts to work with the service, they'll get an "access denied" error because the service's security identifier is an unknown user on their machine. Use domain accounts specifically created to provide a security context for the network service.

The Service Control Manager

Services are started by the Service Control Manager (`services.exe`), which actually also controls a few basic services of Windows 2000, including Alerter, Messenger, Event Log, Scheduler, and the SMB file server service. Some of these services are actually implemented by kernel mode drivers and merely controlled by the Service Control Manager—for example, `srv.sys` for the Server service and `rdr.sys` for the Workstation service.

The Service Control Manager snap-in (Services) allows you to start, pause, and stop a service; to define the how each service will start (automatic, manual, or disabled); and to designate how to handle the service if it hangs (take no action, restart, run as a file outside the executive, or reboot the computer). You can also specify which user account should be used to provide a security context for that service.

You stop or pause a service for different reasons. Stopping a service unloads it from memory and frees up the memory space dedicated to it. Stopping is useful when you no longer need that service or when you need to restart it (stop it and restart it) to eliminate corrupt data that causes it to hang in its allocated memory. Pausing a service merely freezes it to prevent connections to it while maintaining its state and memory allocations. Pausing is useful when you need to prevent clients of a service from using it momentarily or for services that you want available but not running because they may cause a security problem, such as Terminal Services. Pausing a service causes it to become unavailable; the effects of the service being unavailable depends upon the function the service provides.

Services frequently depend upon the functions provided by other services. These dependencies are maintained in the Registry because they affect the order in which services are started by the operating system. Obviously, you can't start a service until the services it depends upon are started, so Windows 2000 uses the Registry to sort them. Dependencies also explain why a problem with one service might affect other services, and why certain services can cause widespread and nonobvious problems. When you stop a service upon which other services depend, the Service Control Manager will tell you that it needs to stop the dependant services. Likewise, when you start a service that depends on other services that aren't running, the Service Control Manager will start those services first.

Sage Advice: Services Best Practices

When a service seems to be unavailable over the network, but the server is operating correctly, try stopping the service and then restarting it. Either the problem will go away, or you'll get a dialog box or Event Log message explaining that the service could not be started, which indicates that something is seriously wrong. Although every third-party service could fail for many different reasons, the default services of Windows 2000 usually fail for one of five simple reasons:

- A driver or another service that the service depends on has not started (due to a hardware malfunction or misconfiguration). This can happen "out of the blue" if a Plug and Play reconfiguration has put two devices on the same IRQ, if termination of a SCSI bus makes devices fail to appear, or if the assignment of high memory has caused a device to fail to allocate enough memory to operate. Or, of course, drivers can fail because some hardware has actually malfunctioned.

- The computer is out of memory or disk space. Make sure the page file is operating correctly and that you have enough memory to support the services you are running on the machine.

- The password for the user account assigned to the service has changed. If this happens, the next time the computer is booted, the service will hang. To prevent this problem, always check the Password Never Expires option and the User Cannot Change Password option for the service user account in the Local Users and Groups snap-in.

- Operating system files are mismatched due to inconsistent application of a service pack. This is especially likely to show up as failures of the Server service or the Remote Access Service. Reapply the most recent service pack to solve this problem.

- A security problem prevents the service's user account from accessing necessary files. Never assign a user account to a service that is actually used by a real user, because the security permissions and passwords for that account could change during the normal operation of the server, which will cause bizarre problems for that service.

Services of Windows 2000

The following services are installed by default in Windows 2000 Server:

Alerter Generates administrative messages about the local computer, which are transmitted via the messenger service. Alerter is provided by the `services.exe` general service manager and depends upon the Workstation service to function. There is no obvious way to configure the Alerter service in Windows 2000, since it's pretty much a vestigial service left over from Windows NT. In Windows 2000 Server, you can run the `srvmgr.exe` program from the Run menu to create alerts. In Windows 2000 Professional, you have to manually edit the Registry as follows:

1. Open the following key using REGEDT32: `HKEY_LOCAL_`
   `MACHINE\System\CurrentControlSet\Services\Alerter\Parameters`.

2. In the dialog box that appears, add the computers or users you want to receive administrative alerts. Put each recipient on a separate line in the Data text box.

Figure 5.1 shows the Registry editor's Multi-String Editor dialog box with name entries.

Figure 5.1   Entering administrative alert receivers for Windows 2000 Professional

Application Management Provides software installation services used by the Windows Installer as controlled by Group Policy. Application Management is provided by the `services.exe` general service and has no dependencies.

ClipBook Transmits the contents of the cut-and-paste clipboard over the network to be viewed by remote clipboard viewers. ClipBook Server is provided by the `clipsrv.exe` general service and depends upon Network DDE (Dynamic Data Exchange).

COM+ Event System Sends COM+ events to subscribed COM+ components. COM is a distributed component object management system that allows applications to distribute information among themselves locally or over a network and is the successor to OLE (object linking and embedding) and DDE. COM+ Event System is provided by `netsvcs` running within the `svchost.exe` service hosting shell and depends upon Remote Procedure Call.

Computer Browser   Maintains a list of the NetBIOS names of machines the computer is aware of and provides that list to services that request it. The Computers Near Me function of My Network Places displays the known list of computers maintained by the computer browser service. Computer browser is provided by the `services.exe` general service manager and depends upon the server and workstation services.

DHCP Client   Requests a plea for an IP address to a DHCP server. The DHCP Client service is also responsible for registering assigned DNS names with dynamic DNS servers. DHCP Client is built into the `services.exe` general service manager and has no dependencies.

Distributed File System (DFS)   Allows the computer to include shared directories on other computers as mount points within the computer's directory structure. DFS shares are managed by the Active Directory in Windows 2000. DFS is implemented by `dfssvc.exe` and depends upon the server and workstation services.

Distributed Link Tracking (DLT) Client   Notifies (and receives notification from) DLT servers when a file stored on an NTFS volume is moved so that links to the file can be updated with the new location. The service runs within the `services.exe` general service manager and depends upon Remote Procedure Call.

Distributed Link Tracking Server   Maintains the link-tracking information so DLT clients can notify and receive notification of linked file changes. The service runs within the `services.exe` general service manager and depends upon Remote Procedure Call.

Distributed Transaction Coordinator   Coordinates transactions involving this computer and others. Transactions are multiple elements of an activity that must be handled as a single unit—in other words, either all the elements must be successfully stored or none must be stored in order for the data store to maintain integrity. The service is implemented by `msdtc.exe` and depends upon Remote Procedure Call and the Security Accounts Manager.

DNS Client   Requests IP addresses for DNS names from a DNS server and caches the result for subsequent reuse. DNS client runs within the `services.exe` general service manager and has no dependencies.

Event Log   Records events posted by other services and applications in the Event Log. Event Log runs within the `services.exe` general service manager and has no dependencies.

Fax Service   Transmits and receives faxes. Fax Service is implemented by
`faxsvc.exe` and depends upon the Plug and Play, Print Spooler, Remote Procedure
Call, and Telephony services.

File Replication   Replicates a specified directory to another computer automatically
and receives replication requests from other computers. File Replication is implemented
by `ntfrs.exe` and depends upon the Event Log and Remote Procedure Call services.

IIS Admin Server   Provides an interface for controlling Internet services (FTP, Web,
SMTP, NNTP). The service is implemented by `inetinfo.exe` and depends upon
Protected Storage and Remote Procedure Call.

Indexing Service   Indexes the document text of HTML and other registered file types
and provides a search interface to receive and respond to content search queries.
Indexing Service is provided by `cisvc.exe` and depends upon Remote Procedure Call.

Internet Connection Sharing   Performs the dial-up network address translation
(NAT) function along with DNS proxy and other related protocol proxy functions
to enable connection sharing. The service is provided by `netsvcs` running within the
`svchost.exe` shell and depends upon the Remote Access Connection Manager.

Intersite Messaging   Automatically sends messages between Active Directory sites
when direct communication links are not available. The service is implemented by
`ismserv.exe` and depends upon the Security Accounts Manager.

IPSec Policy Agent   Starts the IP security driver and the Internet Key Exchange
driver when secure traffic is transmitted. The service is implemented by `lsass.exe`
and depends upon Remote Procedure Call.

Kerberos Key Distribution Center   Distributes Kerberos session authentication
tickets and keys for client/server authentication in Windows 2000 networks. The
service is implemented by `lsass.exe` and depends upon Remote Procedure Call.

License Logging Service   Records the number of simultaneous user sessions for
licensed software on the machine and generates Event Log messages when
installed license numbers are exceeded. The service is implemented by
`llssrv.exe` and has no dependencies.

Logical Disk Manager   Locks disks while they're being managed to prevent
changes to them. When disks can't be locked, LDM queues changes and performs
them at the next shutdown/startup sequence after higher-level services have been
shut down. The service runs within the `services.exe` general services manager and
has no dependencies.

Logical Disk Manager Administrative Service   Provides the interface between the
Disk Management snap-in and the Logical Disk Manager. The service is implemented
by `dmaadmin.exe` and has no dependencies.

Messenger   Transports messages sent by the Alerter service or the `net send` command. The service runs within `services.exe` and depends upon Remote Procedure Call and Workstation.

Net Logon   Performs or passes through logon authentication (and synchronizes the Security Accounts Manager among Windows NT 4 domain participants). The service is implemented by `lsass.exe` and depends upon Workstation.

NetMeeting Remote Desktop Sharing   Provides the ability to allow NetMeeting users to remotely control the local computer for administrative purposes. The service is implemented by `mnmsrvc.exe` and has no dependencies.

Network Connections   Manages the connective state of various network and dial-up interfaces. The service is implemented by `netsvcs` running within the `svchost.exe` shell and depends upon Remote Procedure Call.

Network DDE   Transports Network Dynamic Data Exchange (DDE) requests. The service is implemented by `netdde.exe` and depends upon the Network DDE DSDM.

Network DDE DSDM (DDE Service Data Manager)   Manages multiple NetDDE streams. The service is provided by `netdde.exe` and has no dependencies.

NT LM Security Support Provider   Allows LanManager clients such as Windows for Workgroups computers to log on over the network. The service is implemented by `lsass.exe` and has no dependencies.

Performance Logs and Alerts   Provides an interface between the Performance snap-in and the operating system for the configuration of performance logs and alerts. The service is implemented by `smlogsvc.exe` and has no dependencies.

Plug and Play   Enables activating, changing, and removing Plug and Play devices in Windows 2000. The service runs within the `services.exe` general service manager and has no dependencies.

Print Spooler   Receives print jobs from the local computer and computers attached to shared printers and queues them for printing on the local print device. The service is implemented by `spoolsv.exe` and depends upon Remote Procedure Call.

Protected Storage   Provides an interface for storing passwords and cryptographic keys securely in the Registry. The Registry areas used by Protected Storage are locked down and unavailable to other processes as long as the protected storage service is running. The service is implemented by `services.exe` and depends upon Remote Procedure Call.

Quality-of-Service (QoS) RSVP   Responds to QoS management requests from QoS-aware applications to manage the allocation of bandwidth in network connections. The service is implemented by `rsvp.exe` and has no dependencies.

Remote Access Auto Connection Manager   Automatically dials RAS connections when traffic meeting filter requirements is transmitted or forwarded by the computer. The service is implemented by `netsvcs` running within the `svchost.exe` shell and depends upon the Remote Access Connection Manager and Telephony.

Remote Access Connection Manager   Creates remote access connections as necessary to support dial-up networking. The service is implemented by `netsvcs` running within the `svchost.exe` shell and depends upon Telephony.

Remote Procedure Call (RPC)   Provides the Remote Procedure Call interprocess communications service. RPC allows applications running on one machine to make low-level procedure calls on another machine as if they existed on the same machine, and it is the basic IPC mechanism upon which many services depend. RPC cannot be stopped or started because the operation of the operating system depends upon it. The service is implemented by `netsvcs` running within the `svchost.exe` shell and has no dependencies.

Remote Procedure Call Locator   Provides a service to check for the existence of named RPC procedures on the local machine over the network. The service is provided by `locator.exe` and depends upon Workstation.

Remote Registry Service   Provides a network interface to allow administrators to remotely modify the local computer's Registry. The service is provided by `regsvc.exe` and has no dependencies.

Removable Storage   Manages the allocation of removable media and associated drives and libraries. The service is implemented by `netsvcs` running within the `svchost.exe` shell and depends upon Remote Procedure Call.

Routing and Remote Access   Performs the network layer routing function and listens for dial-up connections from remote access users. The service is implemented by `netsvcs` running within the `svchost.exe` shell and depends upon the entire group of NetBIOS services and Remote Procedure Call.

RunAs Service   Allows users to start processes using other security accounts. RunAs is implemented by the `services.exe` general service manager and has no dependencies.

Security Accounts Manager   Provides account information for the computer's local (non–Active Directory) user accounts. The service is implemented by `lsass.exe` and has no dependencies.

Server   Shares files, printers, and IPC mechanisms such as Named Pipes and Mailslots. The service is implemented by `services.exe` and has no dependencies.

Simple Mail Transport Protocol (SMTP)   Provides SMTP mail send, receive, and relay functions. Note that SMTP does not include the POP3 service required to differentiate users of the mail service and separate inbound mail into various e-mail boxes. The service is implemented by `inetinfo.exe` and depends upon the IIS Admin Service.

Smart Card   Manages Smart Card logon credentials for computers equipped with Smart Card readers. The service is provided by `scardsvr.exe` and depends upon Plug and Play.

Smart Card Helper   Provides additional services for older Smart Card readers. The service is provided by `scardsvr.exe` and has no dependencies.

System Event Notification   Notifies COM+ subscribers of system-level events on the local computer. The service is implemented by `netsvcs` running within the `svchost.exe` shell and depends upon the COM+ Event System.

Task Scheduler   Maintains and executes a list of time-triggered events such as a nightly tape backup. The service is provided by `mstask.exe` and depends upon Remote Procedure Call.

TCP/IP NetBIOS Helper Service   Passes NetBIOS information between NetBIOS and the Sockets interface for certain TCP/IP services. The service is provided by `services.exe` and has no dependencies.

Telephony   Provides an interface to the TAPI telephony programming interface for applications that work with telephones or call centers. The service is implemented by `netsvcs` running within the `svchost.exe` shell and depends upon Plug and Play and Remote Procedure Call.

Telnet   Listens for connection attempts from Telnet clients and provides a command-line interface for remote administration. The service is provided by `tlntsvr.exe` and depends upon Remote Procedure Call.

Terminal Services   Creates user sessions and provides a remote Windows 2000 interface for Terminal Services clients connecting to the local machine. The service is provided by `termsrv.exe` and has no dependencies.

Uninterruptible Power Supply   Listens to a locally connected uninterruptible power supply on a serial port for power events and instigates appropriate emergency actions as necessary. The service is provided by `ups.exe` and has no dependencies.

Utility Manager   Provides configuration for accessibility features of the operating system. The service is provided by `utilman.exe` and has no dependencies.

Windows Installer   Processes MSI files to install, remove, and configure applications. The service is provided by `msiexec.exe` and has no dependencies.

Windows Management Instrumentation   Provides an interface between the operating system and various MMC management snap-ins to report information about the computer's configuration. The service is provided by `winmgmt.exe` and depends upon Remote Procedure Call.

Windows Management Instrumentation Driver Extensions   Provides an interface between the operating system and various MMC management snap-ins to report information about drivers. The service is provided by `services.exe` and has no dependencies.

Windows Time   Sets the computer's clock. The service is provided by `services.exe` and has no dependencies.

Workstation   Redirects network requests to the appropriate server in a network. Workstation provides the client side of a file, print, or IPC communication. The service is provided by `services.exe` and has no dependencies.

World Wide Web Publishing Service   Serves the HTTP protocol to support Web browsers. The service is provided by `inetinfo.exe` and depends upon the IIS Admin Service.

Important Services

The services detailed in the next sections have two things in common: they're important enough that you should know about them, and they're not covered anywhere else in this book. Any service you don't see below is either the subject of another chapter or of little importance to most administrators. If you need to know something about the lesser services, search `support.Microsoft.com`. If you don't find information there, you're not likely to find it anywhere.

Legacy Name Services

Name services resolve network addresses given the network name of a resource such as a computer or a printer. For example, to access `www.altavista.com` or a computer called NTDOM01, a client must have a network address to connect to. Name service providers provide the addresses of named resources that are known to them.

Windows 2000 supports numerous name resolution methods:

- NetBIOS name cache (formed by browsing)
- Windows Internet Name Service (WINS)
- Local data-link broadcast query
- LMHOSTS file entry
- HOSTS file entry
- Domain Name Service (DNS)

DNS is covered in Chapter 4. LMHOSTS and HOSTS are simply text files containing names-to-numbers addresses that are usually found in c:\winnt\system32\drivers\etc\ and are pretty much self-explanatory.

When you request a named resource on your network, the redirector must resolve the name into a network address for the resource. Since the early days of NetBIOS, the process of resolving names has evolved into a somewhat complicated procedure, consisting of internal cache checks, server lookups, broadcast queries, and host file lookups.

A Windows 2000 network uses two types of names:

- A NetBIOS or Windows Networking Name, which consists of up to 15 uppercase letters or numbers only
- A host name, which is up to 255 characters long and consists of a host name and up to 63 hierarchical domain names separated by a period

The complete name resolution process is shown in the following list. Note that the process stops as soon as the name can be resolved, so a step will only be reached if all previous attempts have met with resolution failure.

> **NOTE**   Windows Networking Name and NetBIOS Name are synonymous.

This is the Windows Networking Name lookup procedure:

1. If the name is longer than 15 characters or contains a period, go to step 6.
2. Check the internal NetBIOS name cache.
3. Check a WINS server.
4. Perform a local data-link broadcast query.
5. If the Enable LMHOSTS option is selected, perform a lookup in the LMHOSTS file.
6. If the Enable DNS for Windows Name Resolution option is not selected or if the transport is not TCP/IP, send an error message that the name could not be found on the network.
7. Perform a lookup in the HOSTS file.
8. Query a DNS server.

You can control somewhat how name resolution will occur for various clients by changing the NetBIOS node type, which is assigned either in the Registry or by DHCP. The previous list is the standard name lookup procedure for an H-Node NetBIOS client. A P-Node omits step 4. An M-Node swaps steps 3 and 4. A B-Node omits step 3. Some early NetBIOS clients, such as MS-DOS and earlier versions of Windows and OS/2, may be hard-coded as B-Nodes.

NOTE DNS only works on a TCP/IP network. If you exclusively use IPX or NetBEUI as your network transport, you cannot use DNS for name resolution.

Browsing

NetBIOS browsing is built into all NetBIOS-based operating environments, including MS-DOS, all versions of Windows, and OS/2. Browsing facilitates the automatic discovery of named resources by using the broadcast mechanism of the data-link layer. Computers announce their name and address when they are booted and periodically thereafter. Network clients listen for these names and maintain a list of heard computers in a locally maintained name cache.

Browsing has two problems: it relies upon a broadcast mechanism, which does not usually pass through routed connections, and it relies upon broadcasting from every client, which can consume inordinate amounts of network time in large networks. This makes browsing unsuitable for networks of more than about 200 computers.

WINS

The Windows Internet Name Service (WINS) is Microsoft's attempt at fixing the problems that the name resolution broadcasts create. The WINS service maintains a database of found names permanently, and can be configured to replicate with other WINS servers on the network. Clients are configured to receive their name lists from a WINS server rather than relying upon the traditional broadcast mechanism. WINS is largely self-configuring and is not supposed to require maintenance once it is established.

However, WINS has its own problems. WINS implements NetBIOS names, which are single names that cannot be repeated anywhere in the enterprise. This puts a practical limit on the number of computers that can be deployed before duplication of names becomes a problem. The WINS database can easily become corrupted and require manual intervention. WINS servers must either be physically attached to each segment of a LAN, or clients must have the address of the WINS server specified in their TCP/IP configuration, hard-coded in their LMHOSTS file, or received through their DHCP address assignment.

File and Print Services

File and print services are the foundation upon which networks are built, and the most important services most servers will provide. Because of their importance, they're highly integrated with Windows 2000's user interface and are managed through familiar tools like the Windows Explorer and the Printers Control Panel program. They are robustly stable and not likely to fail, even under a heavy load. For this reason, there's not much to talk about in this section other than to explain their purpose.

Server

The Server service implements the SMB file-sharing protocol (now called CIFS, Common Internet File System) for Windows 2000. This service allows clients (such as the Workstation service), called *redirectors*, to attach to the server and make file requests. The Server service supports the full functionality of a local file system (it is implemented as a file system), so users connecting over the network should notice little difference between a local hard disk and a network share.

The Server service is additionally controlled by the Services Console, which shows file and IPC resources in use, logged-on users, and other interesting information. The Control Panel allows you to close files and disconnect users, as well as transmit messages to users on the network.

If you do not use your Windows 2000 Server as a file or print server (for example, if it's a Web server or a firewall), you should disable the Server service to increase security and free up memory on the machine.

Workstation

The Workstation service is a file system redirector for SMB. Redirectors intercept requests going to the local storage subsystem (hard disk) and transfer them over the network if they actually refer to a network share rather than a local disk. Workstation thus operates as the client to the Server service.

Spooler

The spooler receives print jobs from local and network print clients, spools them to disk, and transmits them to the local print devices attached to the computer. Note that local print devices include network TCP/IP printers and printers attached directly to the LPT or COM ports on the computer.

The purpose of the spooler is to allow a single printer to be shared in a group by receiving multiple simultaneous print jobs from users and transmitting them serially to the printer. The print spooler is also capable of reordering print jobs based on priority settings.

Microsoft can't seem to figure out why the print spooler frequently hangs on print jobs. Rather than spending money improving the print spooler, their solution is to teach administrators to stop and start the spooler service whenever it seems that a print job is stuck in the print manager on the server. This seems to work most of the time, so I'll pass along the tip.

Sage Advice: Avoid Fancy Print Drivers

It seems like every printer sold these days comes with some fancy print driver that has to be installed by a custom installer program, as if you really want some pseudo–back-lit–LCD window popping up in front of your working document just to tell you that you are printing.

Deep in the undocumented folders of the CD-ROMs that come with these printers, you'll usually find a standard Windows 2000 driver that you install using the Add Printers Control Panel. Manufacturers include the standard driver to appease those of us who don't need dancing clowns to announce every page we print. These no-nonsense printer drivers work correctly with the spooler, don't eat up gobs of CPU time or RAM, and work just as well or better on servers than the fancy driver included for desktop users.

If you can't find a standard printer driver on your CD-ROM, you'll find that most laser printers are actually compatible with some common model of HP printer, such as an HP LaserJet 4. You can usually use the printer driver for an HP printer to drive your laser printer. Some printers must have the fancy drivers to perform maintenance (such as changing toner or ink cartridges), so you may have to install both types and only use the silly driver to change ink cartridges.

Internet Services

Internet services vary widely in their purpose and functionality. The two most popular Internet services, FTP and HTTP, are discussed here. Although these services can be stopped and started via the Service Control Manager, they have their own Internet Service Manager snap-in for the Microsoft Management Console. This Service Manager allows you to set all sorts of configuration information for the services to provide a truly useful and secure service environment. In addition to the MMC snap-in, HTML-based administration Web sites are available for performing remote administration, which attach to the IIS Admin Service.

FTP

FTP is the File Transport Protocol for legacy file transfers on the Internet or among UNIX PCs. FTP is somewhat similar to the Server service, except that it does not provide a rich enough API to allow for multiuser write access to a single file. Also, there are no redirectors (like the Workstation service) to provide seamless access to an FTP server (access to FTP is via a user-mode client application), although there's no technical reason why one couldn't be implemented. For these reasons, FTP is used exclusively for bulk file transfers.

World Wide Web (HTTP) Service

HTTP is similar to FTP in that it implements simple read/write data transfers of files over the network. The HTTP service provides a context (called a MIME type) to the receiving client to inform the client what type of data is contained in the file transfer and, therefore, how that data should be presented to the user. HTTP clients, called Web browsers, interpret the transmitted files according to the MIME type to present HTML, pictures, or any other data type for which a registered browser plug-in is available.

Summary

Services provide nearly all the useful functionality of a Windows 2000 server. These services are executable programs that are automatically started by the operating system according to instructions stored in the Registry. You can access services through the Service Control Manager snap-in.

Most services are actually bundled with other services inside executables that provide whole groups of service functionality, such as `services.exe`, `svchost.exe`, `lsass.exe`, and `inetinfo.exe`. These "super services" allow for faster execution and communication among their child services. A problem with one service in these programs, however, can affect other services because they are not protected from each other.

Windows 2000 Server includes a dizzying array of services by default and an equal number of separately installable services. Some services depend upon the functionality of other services, so they cannot be started until the services upon which they depend are running. Likewise, when you need to stop a service, you must stop all the services that depend upon it first.

Windows 2000 gets its personality and a large part of its phenomenal range of functionality from the large number of services that are installed by default or which ship with it. In addition, all properly written back-end software, such as SQL Server, function as services under Windows 2000. A firm understanding of how and why they work the way they do is crucial to administering a Windows 2000–based network.

Case Study: A Lesson in Service Account Security

A client of mine ran into a serious problem when they decided to start managing administrative passwords correctly. Previously, they simply had all administrators use the same administrative account with a fixed password. This policy is rife with problems: the administrative password can't easily be changed unless everyone is told in advance, auditing cannot effectively track the use of administrative privilege, separate user profiles can't be used, and so on. The policy had been implemented when my client switched to Windows NT from another network operating system before anyone was really familiar with the operating system, and the practice had carried over to their Windows 2000 upgrade.

When a new CIO joined the company, he mandated the proper use of user accounts. Every administrator would have their own administrative account, and he alone would have the password to the domain administrator account. Once each administrator had a specific administrative account that was a member of the appropriate administrative groups, he changed the password for the administrator account.

Over the course of the next few days, strange problems cropped up all over the network. Backups failed, various computers wouldn't allow network access to certain services, and all manner of bizarre problems occurred. When I was called in, I was initially very confused about the wide array of sudden problems, until I rooted out the source of the problem: the administrative password change.

To solve the problem, I had the CIO change the password back to its original value. We then rebooted all the servers to get them back online. Then we sat down and identified all the services that should have been set to log in to the local system by installing a new fresh installation on a different server. We also used that installation to determine which services needed user accounts with access permissions across the domain and set them to use accounts we'd created.

By the time we'd finished, all the services were changed to use credentials other than the administrator, and we were able to change the password without affecting anything.

6

Windows 2000 Security

When Windows NT was first introduced in 1993, security meant keeping authorized users from seeing sensitive information stored on a server, and perhaps using callback security for remote access users so that you could control who was able to dial in to your systems from outside your site. Windows NT was considered secure because it used one-way password hashes for user authentication and inherited security tokens for inter-process security.

The Internet changed all of that. Windows NT 4 was released in 1996 with a new and immature TCP/IP stack, just as the Internet was gaining momentum, and the operating system was unprepared for the Internet-based hacking onslaught that ensued for the four years of its release life. Microsoft created hot-fix after hot-fix and service pack after service pack, trying to shore up new breaches discovered in Windows NT's services, protocols, and drivers.

Many of the breaches were caused by new optional components in Windows NT 4, such as Internet Information Server and FrontPage Server Extensions. A big part of the problem was providing Internet service itself: How does a system discriminate between legitimate Web users and a hacker probing the back doors for unauthorized entrance? What is the right balance of useful service and security? How can you be certain of someone's identity when they're connecting from the Internet?

Security in the Internet era means actively blocking sessions from unknown computers, authenticating users based on public key encryption certificates, auditing the use of files and directories, encrypting communications, and preventing legitimate users from unintentionally activating viruses and Trojan horses.

Having learned the lessons of the ill-prepared Windows NT 4, Windows 2000 provides a complex suite of tools to authenticate users, encrypt data, secure connections, block unauthorized access, and manage security holistically. Windows 2000 can be made more secure with its default set of services than any other mass-market operating system—including any version of UNIX or Linux—and it's far easier to manage and use in its secure state.

Windows 2000 can't fix everything, however, because Microsoft and third-party software vendors still put ease of use ahead of security in consumer products such as Internet Explorer, Outlook, and Office. All of these programs have serious security flaws because of their built-in scripting engines that require network administrators to remain vigilant. Windows 2000 can help in fixing these problems as well, but until Microsoft places more focus on security in its end-user products, the only way to prevent these programs from causing security problems on your network is to not use them.

In this chapter, I provide you with all the information you need to understand Windows 2000 security mechanisms, along with some management advice and practical walkthroughs. But no single chapter, and perhaps not even a single book, can cover the wide array of Windows 2000 security mechanisms in complete detail.

Once you've read this chapter and used the information to design a security architecture for your network, consult the Internet RFCs upon which most of these standards are based for technical details of their operation. You'll find an excellent searchable source for Internet RFCs at www.rfc.net. Microsoft's Resource Kit is the authoritative source for the Microsoft implementation of these mechanisms and should be consulted for configuration-specific information.

Security Theory

Security is the sum of all measures taken to prevent loss of any kind. A fundamentally secure system is one in which no user has access to anything. Unfortunately, totally secure systems are useless, so it is necessary to accept a certain amount of security risk in order to provide usability. The goal of security management is to minimize the risk involved in providing the necessary level of system usability.

All modern computer security is based upon the fundamental concept of user identity. To gain access to the system, people identify themselves in a manner that the system trusts. This process is called *logging on*. Once the user has logged on to the system, their access to data and programs can be positively controlled based on their identity.

Of course, to keep this system trustworthy, access to the system must never be allowed without logging on. Even in systems that are open to the anonymous public, an account must be used to control what anonymous users have access to. If access cannot be denied to illegitimate users, security cannot be controlled.

In many cases, users must be allowed to operate on sensitive data that they could potentially destroy, either willfully or by accident. Because usability is the opposite of security, access restrictions must be eased for a system to be functional. In these cases, security is replaced by *accountability*. In pure accountability-based systems, users are given free reign with the knowledge that everything they do is being recorded. This ensures that users will not knowingly cause damage to the system unless they're willing to face the consequences. Because anonymous users cannot be held accountable for their actions, accountability systems cannot function without the ability to correlate a specific person to a user account. In accountability-based systems, every user must have a unique account and no user account can ever be used by more than one person.

Windows 2000 uses a number of mechanisms to secure the local computer against malicious programs, to identify users, and to secure network communications. The major Windows 2000 security mechanisms are listed below:

Control access absolutely   By preventing untrusted computers from connecting to the secure system using packet filtering and network address translation; by ensuring that allowed user sessions cannot be forged, hijacked, or spoofed using Kerberos and IPSec; and by preventing programs from violating the address space of another program using memory protection.

Determine the identity of the user   By using authentication methods such as Kerberos, Message Digest Authentication, smart cards, RADIUS authentication, or third-party authentication protocols such as those that implement biometric methods.

Restrict or permit access based on user identity   With access control lists for security-managed objects such as printers, services, and NTFS stored files and directories; by encrypting files using the Encrypting File System; by restricting access to operating system features that could be abused using Group Policy; and by authorizing remote users from the Internet or dial-up connections using RRAS policy.

Record user activity   With audit logs of especially sensitive information and connection logs for public services such as Web and FTP.

Communicate privately between computers   By using IPSec, PPTP, or L2TP to encrypt the communication stream between computers. PPTP and L2TP are used to enable users to initiate secure communication streams, while IPSec is used to enable two computers to communicate securely over a public medium irrespective of user identity.

Minimize the risk of misconfiguration   By grouping similar security mechanisms into policies and then applying those policies to groups of similar users or computers. Windows 2000's Group Policy, RRAS policy, and IPSec policy management tools allow administrators to make sweeping changes to large portions of a secure system without worrying about individual mistakes.

Security must be managed with the entire network system in mind. Enabling individual security features doesn't provide complete security because there are invariably ways to get around individuated security features.

Windows 2000 in its default state is configured to be useful, not secure. Hard disks are created by default to give full control to everyone, no group policies are in place by default, and most intercomputer communications are not secured. No files are encrypted by default, and no packet filters are enabled by default.

To create a secure system, you must enable all important security features and then ease up on security features to provide access to valid users and to improve performance. Coming from an unsecured posture and attempting to enable individual security features will undoubtedly leave numerous security holes.

There is no "Enable all security features" button in Windows 2000. Despite great strides in holistic management, Windows 2000 still has quite a ways to go, in my opinion, to secure the default configuration. But the tools are easy to find and they do work well together to provide a manageable security interface.

A Cryptographic Primer

Cryptography is the study of codes and ciphers. Windows 2000 uses pervasive cryptography to secure everything from stored files to communications streams to user passwords to domain authentication. Because cryptography and encryption are so important to Windows 2000 security, you need to understand the basic mechanisms of cryptography in order to understand Windows 2000 security. This section is an introduction to cryptography and the cryptographic mechanisms discussed later in this chapter and book.

NOTE   Bruce Schneier's book *Applied Cryptography* (2nd Ed.) is the best mass-market book on cryptography. Consult it for more in-depth information on cryptography.

All of the new security features of Windows 2000 are based on cryptography. In contrast, the first release of Windows NT used cryptography only for password hashing. Over the release life of Windows NT 4, various different cryptographic elements were added to the operating system, but they were not handled in a coherent and secure fashion—they were simply piled on. Windows 2000 changes that by using the Active Directory as the container for nearly all security-related configuration and policy application.

Like any other group of specialists, cryptographers have a language of their own to describe what they do. You don't have to be a theoretical mathematician to evaluate and use cryptography in your network, but it helps to have a general understanding when you are evaluating cryptography options for your network. The following sidebar defines the terms you should be familiar with.

Terminology: Cryptography and Encryption

You should know the precise meanings of these cryptographic terms as they are used in this book:

Algorithm Detailed steps for performing a function.

   Restricted algorithm An algorithm that is kept secret to make it more difficult to break.

   Symmetric algorithm An algorithm in which the same key is used for encryption and decryption. Secret key algorithms are symmetric.

   Asymmetric algorithm An algorithm in which different keys are used for encryption and decryption. Public key algorithms are asymmetric.

Block cipher A cipher designed to operate on fixed-size blocks of data. Block ciphers are used for bulk encryption.

Breakable A cipher that, given a reasonable amount of time and resources, can be compromised by a competent cryptanalyst.

Computationally secure A cipher that, given all the computational power that will be available to the most powerful governments for the forseeable future, is unlikely to be compromised.

Keyspace The range of all possible keys for a cipher. A cipher with a large keyspace is harder to crack than one with a smaller keyspace because there are more keys (numbers or combinations of letters) to try.

Secure A cipher that, even given a reasonable amount of time and resources, most likely cannot be compromised by a competent cryptanalyst.

Stream cipher A cipher designed to operate on a continuous stream of data.

Strong A cipher that, given the computational power that may reasonably be brought to bear on it any time in the near future, is unlikely to be compromised.

Unconditionally secure A cipher that, given an unlimited amount of time and an infinitely powerful processor, cannot be compromised.

Windows 2000 uses encryption for three vitally important purposes:

- To prove the identity of a security principal
- To validate the contents of a message or file
- To hide the contents of a data store or stream

A *cipher* is an encryption algorithm; it protects a message by rearranging it or performing modifications to the encoding, rather than the meaning, of the message. A *code* is an agreed-upon way of keeping a secret between two or more individuals. A *key* is a bit of information that is required to decrypt a message, usually in the form of a value that is used with a cipher to encrypt a message. The key must be kept secret in order for the message to remain private.

Encryption Algorithms

One algorithm that was developed in secret but then released for use by the public as well as the government (but only for "Unclassified but Sensitive" information) is the *Data Encryption Standard*, or *DES*. It is a symmetric algorithm, which means the same key is used for encryption and decryption, and it was designed to use a 56-bit key, although until recently the U.S. government limited export versions of DES to 40 bits. DES is widely used in commercial software and in communication devices that support encryption. There is lingering suspicion, however, that a possible weakness in the DES algorithm could allow the National Security Agency (NSA), which has a vested interest in maintaining its ability to decrypt communications and which cooperated in the development of DES, to more easily break messages encrypted with DES.

RSA (named after its inventors Rivest, Shamir, and Adleman) is an algorithm that was not developed by a government agency. Its creators exploited the computationally difficult problem of factoring prime numbers to develop an *asymmetric*, or *public key*, algorithm, which can be used for both encryption and digital signatures. RSA has since become a very popular alternative to DES. RSA is used by a number of software companies whose products must negotiate secure connections over the insecure Internet (such as Web browsers), including Microsoft, Digital, Sun, Netscape, and IBM. The patent on RSA recently expired, and its owners have placed it in the public domain.

The ciphers described here are not the only ones available for use in computers and networks today. Other governments (such as the former USSR) were just as active as the United States in developing codes and ciphers, and many private individuals (especially in the last decade) have made contributions to the field of cryptography. GOST was developed in the former USSR, FEAL was developed by NTT Japan, LOKI was developed in Australia, and IDEA was developed in Europe. Most of these ciphers use patented algorithms that must be licensed for commercial use, but some (such as Blowfish) do not. Each cipher has strengths and weaknesses.

NOTE   All of the ciphers described in this section have the same weakness: if you know the cipher being used to encode a message but not the key, you can use a number of attacks to attempt to decode the message, including the "brute force" method of trying all of the possible keys.

The purpose of ciphers, after all, is to hide information. Hiding information would not be a useful activity (especially for wartime governments that have other pressing areas to spend time and money on) if no one were interested in the information being hidden. The converse of hiding information is attempting to discover what is hidden, and advances in *breaking* codes (or deciphering codes without the key) have progressed hand-in-hand with developments in creating codes. The practice of attempting to break codes is called *cryptanalysis*, and the people who break codes are called *cryptanalysts*. A number of different types of cryptanalytical attacks can be used against secure systems:

Keyspace attack   This is the hard way to crack an encrypted message. A *keyspace search* involves checking every possible key that might have been used to encrypt the message. This is like trying every possible combination on a bank vault in order to open it. A keyspace search is only feasible when there are not very many possible keys. A cryptanalyst might use this technique if the key length is 40 or 56 bits, and perhaps if it were 128 bits and the message were really worth the millions of dollars of hardware that would be required. Keyspace searches of larger keyspaces are impractical at the present level of computing technology.

Known plain text   A cryptanalyst can reduce the number of possible keys to be searched for many ciphers if the plain text of the encrypted message is already known. (Why would the cryptanalyst want the key if the message is already out? Perhaps there is another message encrypted with the same key.) If even a portion of the message is always the same, especially at the beginning of the message (for example, the headers in an e-mail message are always the same), your cipher text may be vulnerable.

WARNING   In an encrypted file system, if a standard system file is encrypted using the same key as secret documents, it is trivial (for a cryptanalyst) to derive the decryption key using the standard system file. For this reason, you should never encrypt files that were not created by your organization.

Linear and differential cryptanalysis   A cryptanalyst may also look for mathematical patterns in collections of cipher texts that have all been encrypted with the same key. Some ciphers (not all) are vulnerable to either or both of these kinds of analysis, and a cryptanalyst may then have a much smaller range of keys to search.

The Almost Perfect Cipher

There is one encryption cipher—the *one-time pad*—that cannot be compromised if you do not have the key, even with all the time left in the universe and all the compute power that is theoretically possible. It is not simply improbable that the key would be discovered or the message retrieved by using brute force; it is impossible. Unfortunately, the requirements of the cipher make it impractical for use in anything but certain kinds of low-bandwidth communications.

A one-time pad uses a key exactly as long as the message being encoded. The key must be completely random (anything less than random leaves your message open to certain kinds of cryptographic analysis), and no portion of it can be reused without compromising the security of your message. Each letter (or byte) of your message is combined mathematically with an equal-sized portion of the key (often by the XOR mathematical function or the addition with modulus mathematical function) that results in the cipher text and uses up the key.

The one-time pad is so secure because the cipher text being decoded can result in any plain text (of the same length) and associated key. For example, *henryjtillman* encoded with the one-time pad key *lfwpxzgwpoieq* results in the cipher text *tkkhsjafbavfe*. While the cipher text decoded with the correct key produces the original message, the cipher text can also be decoded using the possible key *swgpnmquypciq*, resulting in the message *andrewjackson*, or using the key *gbywrvwcmlkwz*, resulting in the message *milkandcookie*. The attacker has no way of knowing which key and resulting plain text is correct.

The problem with the one-time pad is that it requires a key as big as the message being sent, and both the sender and the receiver must have the same key. If you must encrypt a 10Mbps Ethernet link, you could use up a CD-ROM's worth of key data in just 10 minutes!

NOTE   Clearly, the one-time pad is best used when communication is infrequent or uses very little bandwidth, such as e-mail messages that must have the most secure encryption possible.

Symmetric Functions

If the same key can be used to encrypt or decrypt the message, then the cipher uses a *symmetric function*. Both the sender and receiver must have that same key. Good symmetric ciphers are fast, secure, and easy to implement using modern microprocessors.

Some ciphers are more secure than others. The XOR cipher, for example, is not very secure. A competent cryptanalyst can decode an XOR-encoded message in short order. Two general features of a symmetric algorithm make it secure:

- The algorithm produces cipher text that is difficult to analyze.
- The algorithm has a sufficiently large keyspace.

Cryptanalysts test cipher text for correspondences in the text, an uneven distribution of instances of numbers, and essentially anything that differentiates the cipher text from a series of truly random numbers. A good algorithm will produce a cipher text that is as random-seeming as possible. This is where the XOR cipher fails miserably—an XOR-ed message has a lot in common with a regular ASCII text message. Cryptographers will exploit these commonalities to recover the key and decode the whole message.

A cryptanalyst who cannot exploit nonrandomness in the cipher text has little choice but to simply try all the possible key combinations to decode the message. This is a lot like the hacker trying to guess the password to your system; if they don't know that the password is a birthday or the name of your dog, then they must try all the possible passwords.

NOTE Just as a longer password is safer than a shorter one, a longer key is more secure than a shorter key.

A number of symmetric ciphers are used in both software and hardware. You can get a feel for what is available by comparing the following three ciphers:

DES   IBM and the U.S. National Security Agency cooperated to develop this cipher. It is resistant to differential cryptanalysis but susceptible to linear cryptanalysis. Its key length is only 56 bits, which makes it increasingly easy to perform a brute-force examination of all of the possible keys for an encrypted cipher text. DES is in common use in encryption hardware and software. It is an ANSI standard. Windows 2000 implements both 40-bit DES and 168-bit 3DES (*triple-DES*—DES with three contiguous keys).

IDEA   This cipher has a key length of 128 bits—considerably more than DES uses. While a sufficiently motivated and financed organization or a large cabal of hackers can break a DES-encoded message, the large keyspace makes a brute-force attack on IDEA impractical. IDEA was designed to be immune to linear and differential cryptanalysis, and you can reasonably be assured that not even the NSA can decode an IDEA-encrypted message without the key. IDEA is patented in Europe and the United States.

Blowfish   This cipher can use a key from 32 to 448 bits long, allowing you to select how secure you want to make your message. It was designed to be immune to linear and differential cryptanalysis. Its developer, Bruce Schneier, has not sought a patent on the algorithm so that a good, freely implementable algorithm would be available to both private individuals and public sector.

One-Way Functions

When you type your password to log on to Windows 2000, it is encrypted and compared against the stored encrypted value of your password (see "Windows 2000 Local Security" later in this chapter). The password is stored using a *one-way function* (also called a *hash*, *trap-door*, *digest*, or *fingerprint*) so that it will be difficult to determine your password even if the hacker has gained access to the operating system's stored settings.

Hash functions can also be used for other purposes. For example, you can use a hash to "fingerprint" files (create a digital fingerprint, or hash, that is unique to that file). A hash function can produce a result that is much smaller than the input text; a hash of a multi-megabyte word-processor document, for example, may result in a 128-bit number. A hash is also unique to the file that produced it; it is practically impossible to create another file that will produce the same hash value. You might use this kind of hash to make sure that your Internet-distributed software product is delivered free of viruses and other malicious modifications. You can allow your customers to download the software, and then tell them what the hash value for the software files is. Only your unmodified software files will hash to the same value.

NOTE   One feature of a hash function (especially one that produces short hashes) is that any hash value is equally likely. Therefore it is practically impossible to create another file that will hash to the same value.

Some hash functions require a key; others do not. Anyone can calculate a hash that does not use a key; this kind of hash is good for distributing software or making sure that files have not been changed without you noticing. A hash function with a key can only be calculated by someone (or something) who has the key.

Public Key Encryption

While symmetric ciphers use the same key to encrypt and decrypt messages (that's why they're called symmetric), *public key encryption* (or a *public key cipher*) uses a different key to decrypt than was used to encrypt. This is a relatively new development in cryptography, and it solves many longstanding problems with cryptographic systems, such as how to exchange those secret keys in the first place.

The problem with symmetric ciphers is this: both the sender and the recipient must have the same key in order to exchange encrypted messages over an insecure medium. If two parties decide to exchange private messages, or if two computers' network devices or programs must establish a secure channel, the two parties must decide on a common key. Either party may simply decide on a key, but that party will have no way to send it to the other without the risk of it being intercepted on its way. It's a chicken-and-egg problem: without a secure channel, there is no way to establish a secure channel.

In 1976, Witfield Diffie and Martin Hellman discovered a way out of the secure channel dilemma. They found that by using a different key, certain one-way functions could be undone. Their solution (called *public key cryptography*) takes advantage of a characteristic of prime and almost prime numbers—specifically, how hard it is to find the two factors of a large number that has only two factors, both of which are prime. Since Diffie and Hellman developed their system, some other public key ciphers have been introduced. For example, the difficulty of determining quadratic residues (a subtle mathematical construct that few people other than mathematicians and cryptologists really understand) has been exploited to make a public key cipher.

With a public key cipher, one key (the public key) is used to encrypt a message, while the other one (the private key) is the only key that can decrypt the message. This means that you can tell anyone your public key—even complete strangers and NSA agents. Whoever has your key can encrypt a message that only you can decrypt. Even the NSA agent who has your public key cannot decrypt the message.

One problem that plagues secure public key ciphers is that they are slow—much slower than symmetric ciphers. You can expect a good public key cipher to take 1,000 times as long to encrypt the same amount of data as a good symmetric cipher. This can be quite a drag on your computer's performance if you have a lot of data to transmit or receive.

Although it is much slower than symmetric systems, the public key/private key system neatly solves the problem that bedevils symmetric cryptosystems. When two people (or devices) need to establish a secure channel for communication, one of them can just pick a secret key and then encrypt that secret key using the other's public key. The encrypted key is then sent to the other party, and even if the key is intercepted, only the other party can decrypt the secret key, using the private key. Communication may then continue between the two parties using a symmetric cipher and that secret key. A system that uses both symmetric and public key encryption is called a *hybrid cryptosystem*.

Generating Keys

Most cryptographic systems manage the selection of keys and the negotiation of protocols for you. Systems that do this must be able to select keys that are not easily guessed, because one way to attack a cryptographic system is to predict the keys that might be used in the system. These keys are selected by generating random numbers.

It is difficult for a computer to generate good random numbers. Computers, by their very nature, are extremely predictable, and hundreds of thousands of engineers have labored (collectively) millions of years to make them more so. If you run a computer program twice and give it the same input the second time as you did the first, you will get the same output the second time as you did the first. Since the whole point of a truly random number is not to be able to guess the output based on the input, computers (unassisted) make lousy dice-throwers.

NOTE An example of the randomness problem existed in early versions of Netscape Navigator. In order to generate a random number for the Secure Socket Layer, Netscape used the system time, which provides a 12-bit number, to generate a 40-bit crypto key. Because there was only 12 bits' worth of unique keys in that 40-bit space, hackers were able to crack and exploit secure sessions in a matter of minutes. A 12-bit key is so short that it's worthless for security. It's about as secure as a two-character password.

The best that computers can do by themselves are *pseudorandom numbers*, which are numbers created by a deterministic means (that is, given identical starting conditions, identical numbers will be produced). Good pseudorandom numbers have a long periodicity (it's unlikely that the same number will be generated repeatedly from different seeds) and satisfy the other conditions of random numbers, such as incompressibility (there is no redundant or repeated information in the number) and having an even distribution (generated numbers are equally likely across the possible range of numbers, rather than being clumped together). *Random numbers*, on the other hand, are unpredictable (an identical series of random numbers cannot be reproduced, even from identical starting conditions). Truly random numbers also satisfy other criteria, such as incompressibility and having an even distribution.

In order to get a good random number (to use as a seed value, for example), the computer must look outside itself because computers are inherently deterministic. Many sources of randomness exist in the real (noncomputer) world—the weather, ocean waves, lava-lamp wax gyrations, the times between one keystroke and the next—and a computer can measure these events and use them to generate random numbers. Keystroke timing is commonly used to generate secret keys. Another way is to ask the user to type in a paragraph or two of text. There are no published algorithms that will predict arbitrary user input (yet).

If a random number is going to be used as a seed for pseudorandom numbers, it should have enough bits to make it difficult to guess. For example, you don't want to protect a 128-bit cryptosystem that uses IDEA with a password of eight characters or less for a seed—this is effectively only about 48 bits of security if you just use common printable ASCII characters in the password (the characters used in passwords provide about six bits' worth of uniqueness each).

Uses of Encryption

You can use encryption to protect the following types of network data:

- Private communications
- Secure file storage
- User or computer authentication
- Secure password exchange

You should encrypt any communications containing sensitive or proprietary information that go over an insecure medium such as radio, a telephone network, or the Internet. Use file system encryption to protect sensitive data when operating system features are not effective (when the hard drive has been removed or the operating system has been replaced).

The most common use for encryption with computers is to protect communications between computer users and between communications devices. This use of encryption is an extension of the role codes and ciphers have played throughout history. The only difference is that instead of a human being laboriously converting messages to and from an encoded form, the computer does all the hard work.

Secure File Storage

Encryption can be used to protect data in storage, such as data on a hard drive. All UNIX implementations and Windows NT have many sophisticated security features. You may configure your operating system to allow only authorized users to access files while the operating system is running, but when you turn your computer off, all those security features go away and your data is left defenseless. An intruder could load another operating system on the computer or even remove the hard drive and place it in another computer that does not respect the security settings of the original computer.

You can use encryption software to encrypt specific files that you want to protect and then decrypt them when you need to access them. The encryption and decryption process can be cumbersome, however, and you may end up having to remember a lot of encryption keys. Using encryption in this manner can also leave behind temporary files or files that are erased but still present on the hard drive containing sensitive information. This is obviously not what you want.

A better approach to security is to have the operating system encrypt and decrypt the files for you. Windows 2000 comes with an Encrypting File System (EFS) that will encrypt all the files on your hard drive, even temporary ones created by the applications you use.

To use EFS securely, you must supply the cryptographic key when you start your computer, or use it with a smart card, but otherwise you can treat the files on your hard drive as regular, unencrypted files. This doesn't protect your files from being accessed while the operating system is running—that is what the operating system security features are for—but it does keep the data safe, even if someone steals the hard drive.

User or Computer Authentication

In addition to keeping secrets (either stored or transmitted), encryption can be used for almost the opposite purpose—to verify identities. Encryption can authenticate users logging on to computers, ensure that software you download from the Internet comes from a reputable source, and ensure that the person who sends a message is really who they say they are.

When you log on to a Microsoft operating system such as Windows 95, Windows NT, or Windows 2000, the operating system does not compare your password to a stored password. Instead, it encrypts your password using a one-way cryptographic function and then compares the result to a stored result. Other operating systems such as UNIX and OS/2 work the same way.

This seems a roundabout way of verifying your identity when you log on, but there is a very good reason for the operating system to do it this way. By only storing the cryptographic hash of your password, the operating system makes it more difficult for a hacker to get all of the passwords in your system when they gain access to the system. One of the first things a hacker goes for in a compromised system (that is, one where the hacker has gotten at least one password) is that computer's password list, so that the hacker can get account names and passwords that may be valid on other computers in your network.

With a one-way cryptographic function, it's easy to generate a hashed value from the password, but it's difficult or impossible to generate the password from the hashed value. Since only the hashed values are stored, even a hacker who has complete access to the computer can't just read out the passwords. The best the hacker can do is to supply passwords one by one and see if they match any of the hashes in the password list. The hacker can run a program to do this instead of typing them all in by hand, but it can take a while if the users of the computer have chosen good passwords.

NOTE   Hackers have combined forces to "precompute" password hashes for all possible LAN Manager passwords. A precomputed hash uses the normal hashing function and records the password and its hash in a database. By dividing the keyspace hashing task among thousands of home computers and running as a background application, hackers have created a complete database of passwords to hashes. Hackers can now simply take the hash value (which Internet Explorer will give to any Web site that asks) and look it up in this directory to see which password matches that hash. This is why LAN Manager passwords are not secure.

Digital Signatures

Usually, public key encryption is used to transmit secrets encrypted with the public key and decrypted with the private key. You can also do it the other way: encrypt with the private key and decrypt with the public key.

Why would you want to encrypt a message that anyone can decrypt? That seems a bit silly, but there is a good reason to do so: only the holder of the private key can encrypt a message that can be decrypted with the public key. It is, in effect, a *digital signature*, proving that the holder of the private key produced the message.

Since the purpose of a digital signature is not to conceal information but rather to certify it, the private key is often used to encrypt a hash of the original document, and the encrypted hash is appended to the document or sent along with it. This process takes much less processing time to generate or verify than does encrypting the entire document, and it still guarantees that the holder of the private key signed the document.

Internet e-mail was not designed with security in mind. Messages are not protected from snooping by intermediate Internet hosts, and you have no guarantee that a message actually came from the person identified in the e-mail's From field. Internet newsgroup messages have the same problem: you cannot really tell from whom the message actually came. You can encrypt the body of the message to take care of the first problem, and digital signatures take care of the second.

Digital signatures are useful because while anyone can check the signature, only the individual with the private key can create the signature. The difference between a digital signature and a certificate is that you can check the authenticity of a certificate with a certificate authority.

Secure Password Exchange

When you log on to your network file server, or when you connect to your Internet service provider, you supply a username and password. These two pieces of information control your access to the network and represent your identity on the network. They must be protected from eavesdropping.

Most network operating systems (Windows 2000 and all modern versions of UNIX included) protect your username and password when you log on by encrypting the username and password before sending them over the network to be authenticated. The file server (or ISP host) checks the encrypted username and password against the list of legitimate users and passwords. The host can check the password either by decrypting it and checking the database of passwords stored in the clear, or it can encrypt the stored password and check the result against what has been sent from the client over the network.

To keep the same encrypted data from being sent every time, the client can also include some additional information, such as the time the logon request was sent. This way your network credentials are never sent unprotected over your local LAN or over the telephone system. Windows 2000 does accept unencrypted passwords from older LAN Manager network clients, however, so you should be careful about allowing older clients on your network.

NOTE   Not every authentication protocol encrypts the username and password. SLIP, for example, does not. Telnet and FTP do not, although the Windows 2000 Telnet service can be configured to work only with Windows NT hashes rather than plain-text passwords. PPP may, if both the dial-up client and server are configured that way. Windows NT by default requires encrypted authentication. Windows 2000 uses secure secret-key-based Kerberos for authentication.

Steganography

Cryptography can be very effective at keeping a secret. With a sufficiently powerful cipher and a sufficiently long key, even major world governments cannot read your diary. What if you don't want people to know that you're keeping secrets, though? After all, an encrypted file or an encrypted hard drive is pretty strong evidence that you're hiding something. *Steganography* is the process of hiding those encrypted files where it is unlikely that anyone will find them.

Encrypted files look like random numbers, so anything that also looks like random numbers can hide an encrypted message. For example, in graphic images that use many colors, the low-order bit for each pixel in the image doesn't make much difference to the quality of the image. You can hide an encrypted message in the graphics file by replacing the low-order bits with the bits from your message. The low-order bits of high-fidelity sound files are another good place for encrypted data. You can even exchange encrypted messages with someone surreptitiously by sending graphics and sound files with those messages hidden in them.

A Word about Passwords

Passwords are secret keys. They can be used to authenticate users, encrypt data, and secure communication streams. Kerberos uses passwords as the secret key to prove client credentials to a Kerberos Key Distribution Center.

Having stressed the necessity for randomness in secret keys, it follows that passwords, being secret keys, must also be secure. Of course, telling people your password compromises it, but you can unintentionally compromise your password in a number of other ways.

The most common way is to choose an easily guessable password, such as an empty password, the word *password* itself, slang words or the names of deity, or the names of children or pets. You may think that if a hacker doesn't know you, they won't know the names of your children. Think again. There are only 7,000 baby names at babynames.com. By creating a word list from that site, I was able to crack a Web server over the Internet in just 45 minutes—and that's because I'd gotten all the way to *R*. Last names aren't much more secure; lists of registered voters or phone books can provide a complete set. At just one guess per second (the rate at which commonly available NetBIOS-based crack tools operate over the Internet), it would take less than 12 hours to go through the complete list of 40,000 unique last names in the San Diego telephone book—and automated crack tools can run far faster than one attempt per second by opening multiple simultaneous connections. Using words in the English language is even worse. Shakespeare is estimated to have had a vocabulary of 25,000 words. Mine is only about 15,000. Using any word I know as a password yields a crack time of about two hours from over the Internet.

Using truly random passwords yields much better results. Just a 14-character random password using the standard ASCII keyboard set yields 20 million quintillion (10^{21}) passwords. At once per second, the universe would be cold and dark (or would have collapsed, depending upon which theory is correct) before a hacker got into your network. So the concept of passwords is not fundamentally flawed, but most people choose seriously flawed passwords.

Even if you choose strong passwords, you have probably compromised them many times over. Ever signed up for a service or bought anything off the Web? Sure you have. Ever entered a password to create a new account? Probably. Was it the same password you use everywhere? Probably. How many Web sites have your password now? Lots.

I use four levels of passwords:

Low-quality public password   Usually an English word, I use this password for public services that I don't care about but which require a password anyway, such as my subscription to news Web sites. This password is so unimportant to me that I'll print it here: *Action!*, which is the first compiled programming language I learned.

Medium-quality public password   A short but completely random password, I use this on sites where my money could be spent or actual services could be stolen, such as my online credit card billing site, my favorite e-commerce vendors, and so on. Why just a medium-quality password? Because although it's a hassle, my credit card company is liable for the fraudulent use of my card, not me. I also use this password for nonadministrative access to private networks. This password is seven characters long, yielding about 40 bits of uniqueness.

High-quality password   I use this password for private networks where I'm the administrator and where serious harm could be done to a customer if this password leaked out. I never tell this password to anyone, and I never, ever create accounts on public systems with it. I do use this password at multiple customer sites. This password is 12 characters long, yielding about 70 bits of uniqueness.

Extremely high-quality password   I use this password to encrypt files and store secrets on my personal computers that would seriously disrupt my life if they leaked out. This password never leaves my own systems and has never been written down or spoken aloud. This password is 14 characters long, yielding about 84 bits of uniqueness.

I don't change my passwords frequently, because frankly, it's really hard to remember good random passwords, and if you change truly random passwords, you'll never remember old ones if you have to go back to a system you haven't been to in a while. Although changing passwords often is good in theory, forcing users to use heavy password rotation guarantees that you'll have extremely weak passwords on your network. In my opinion, a good, highly random password should only be changed if you've leaked it by accident.

Windows 2000 Local Security

Windows 2000 security is based on user authentication. Before you can use a Windows 2000 computer, you must supply a username and a password. The logon prompt (provided by the WinLogon process) identifies you to the computer, which then provides access to resources you are allowed to use and denies access to things you aren't.

Windows 2000 also provides group accounts. When a user account is a member of a group account, the permissions that apply to the group account also apply to the user account.

NOTE Even when a group of people does the same job, each user should have an individual account so that when one user violates security, you can track the violation back to a specific user rather than to a group of people who use the same account.

User and group accounts are only valid for the Windows 2000 computer on which they are created. These accounts are local to the computer. The only exceptions to this rule are computers that are members of a domain and therefore trust the user accounts created in the Active Directory on a domain controller. Domain security is discussed in the later section, "Kerberos Authentication and Domain Security."

Each Windows 2000 computer has its own list of local user and group accounts. When the WinLogon process (which logs you on and sets up your computing environment) needs to refer to the security database, it communicates with the Security Accounts Manager (SAM), which is the Windows 2000 operating system component that controls local account information. If the information is stored locally on the Windows 2000 computer, the SAM will refer to the database (stored in the Registry) and return the information to the WinLogon process. If the information is not stored locally (for example, it pertains to a domain account), the Security Accounts Manager will query the domain controller and return the validated logon information (the *security identifier*) to the WinLogon process.

Irrespective of the source of authentication, access is allowed only to the local computer by the computer's Local Security Authority (LSA). When you access other computers on the network, the local computer's LSA establishes your credentials automatically with the LSA on the foreign computer, effecting a logon for each computer you contact. To gain access to a foreign computer, that computer must trust the credentials provided by your computer.

Security Identifiers

Security principals such as users and computers are represented as *security identifiers (SIDs)*. The SID uniquely identifies the security principal to all the computers in the domain. When you create an account using the Local Users and Groups snap-in, a new SID is always created, even if you use the same account name and password as a deleted account. The SID will remain with the account for as long as the account exists. You may change any other aspect of the account, including the username and password, but you cannot change the SID under normal circumstances—if you did, you would create a new account.

Group accounts also have a SID, which is a unique identifier that is created when the group is created. The same rules that apply to account SIDs also apply to group SIDs.

The WinLogon process (part of the Local Security Authority process) checks your username and password (or smart card, if so configured) to determine if you should be allowed to access the computer. If the domain supplied in the logon box is the name of the local computer, the LSA checks the account against the local SAM stored in the Registry. Otherwise, the LSA contacts a domain controller and uses Kerberos (Windows 2000) or NTLM (all other versions of Windows, including Windows 2000 in Mixed Mode) authentication to authenticate the user, depending upon the client operating system.

If the account name is valid and the password is correct, the WinLogon process will create an Access Token for you. The *Access Token* is composed of the user account SID, the

SIDs of the groups the account belongs to, and a Locally Unique Identifier (LUID), which indicates user rights and a specific logon session.

NOTE An Access Token is created each time you log on to Windows 2000. This is why you must log off and then log back on again after making changes to your user account—you need a new Access Token that will reflect the changes you have made.

Special SIDs exist. The *System SID* is reserved for system services; Access Tokens that contain the System SID can bypass all account-based security restrictions. This SID gives system services permission to do things that a regular user account (even the Administrator account) cannot do. The Windows 2000 kernel, not the WinLogon process, starts operating system services, and these services receive the System SID from the kernel when they are started.

Resource Access

Threads (individual chains of execution in a process) must provide an Access Token at each attempt to access a resource. Threads receive their Access Tokens from their parent process when they are created. A user application, for example, usually receives its Access Token from Windows Explorer. Windows Explorer receives its Access Token from the WinLogon process. The WinLogon process is started from a user-generated interrupt (the Ctrl+Alt+Del keyboard interrupt) and is especially able to create new Access Tokens by querying either the local Security Accounts Manager or the Directory Services Agent (DSA) on an Active Directory domain controller.

Through this method, every thread that is started after a user has logged on will have the Access Token that represents the user. Because user mode threads must always provide that token to access resources, there is no way to circumvent Windows 2000 resource security under normal circumstances.

Sage Advice: Mandatory Logons

The foundation of Windows 2000 security is the *mandatory logon*. Unlike in some networking systems, a user cannot do anything in Windows 2000 without providing a user account name and password. Although you can choose to automatically log on with credentials provided from the Registry, a user account logon still occurs.

Although it's not the friendliest of keystrokes, there's a very good reason Windows 2000 requires the Ctrl+Alt+Del keystroke to log on, and it's one of the reasons Windows 2000 is considered secure. Because the computer handles the Ctrl+Alt+Del keystroke as a hardware interrupt, there's literally no way a clever programmer can make the keystroke do something else without rewriting the operating system.

Without this feature, a hacker would be able to write a program that displayed a fake logon screen and collect passwords from unsuspecting users. However, because the fake screen couldn't include the Ctrl+Alt+Del keystroke, users familiar with Windows 2000 would not be fooled.

Because the Access Token is passed to a new thread upon creation, there is no further need to access the SAM database locally or the Active Directory on a domain controller for authentication once a user has logged on.

Inheriting Access Tokens

When you log on to a Windows 2000 server over the network, the Access Token generated by the WinLogon or Kerberos process on the server is not sent back to your client computer. Instead, the Access Token is inherited by a session of the Server service on the Windows 2000 server, which maintains a connection to your client computer and performs the actions on the server (opening files, writing data, printing documents, and so on) for the client computer. Since the Access Token never leaves the Windows 2000 server, there is no chance it will be intercepted on your LAN, and a malicious program on an insecure operating system such as Windows 95 cannot modify it.

Windows 2000 goes through the following steps when a user logs on locally:

1. The user presses Ctrl+Alt+Del, which causes a hardware interrupt that activates the WinLogon process.

2. The WinLogon process presents the user with the account name and password logon prompt.

3. The WinLogon process sends the account name and encrypted password to the Local Security Authority. If the user account is local to that Windows 2000 computer, the LSA queries the Security Accounts Manager of the local Windows 2000 computer; otherwise, the LSA queries a domain controller for the domain in which the computer is a member.

4. If the user has presented a valid username and password, the LSA creates an Access Token containing the user account SID and the group SIDs for the groups of which that user is a member. The Access Token also gets an LUID, which will be described later in this chapter in the "Rights versus Permissions" section. The Access Token is then passed back to the WinLogon process.

5. The WinLogon process passes the Access Token to the Win32 subsystem along with a request to create a logon process for the user.

6. The logon process establishes the user environment, including starting Windows Explorer and displaying the backdrop and Desktop icons.

Objects and Permissions

Windows 2000 maintains security for various types of objects, including (but not limited to) directories, files, printers, processes, and network shares. Each object exposes services that the object allows to be performed upon it, for example: open, close, read, write, delete, start, stop, print, and so on.

The security information for an object is contained in the object's *security descriptor*. The security descriptor has four parts: owner, group, Discretionary Access Control List (DACL), and System Access Control List (SACL). Windows 2000 uses these parts of the security descriptor for the following purposes:

Owner   This part contains the SID of the user account that has ownership of the object. The object's owner may always change the settings in the DACL (the permissions) of the object.

Group   This part is used by the POSIX subsystem of Windows 2000. Files and directories in UNIX operating systems can belong to a group as well as to an individual user account. This part contains the SID of the group of this object for the purposes of POSIX compatibility, as well as to identify the primary group for user accounts.

Discretionary Access Control List   The DACL contains a list of user accounts and group accounts that have permission to access the object's services. The DACL has as many access control entries as there are user or group accounts that have specifically given access to the object.

System Access Control List   The SACL also contains access control entries (ACEs), but these ACEs are used for auditing rather than for permitting or denying access to the object's services. The SACL has as many ACEs as there are user or group accounts that are specifically being audited.

Each access control entry in the DACL and SACL consists of a security identifier followed by an access mask. The *access mask* in the DACL identifies those services of the object that the SID has permission to access. A special type of ACE, called a *deny ACE*, indicates that all access to the object will be denied to the account identified by the SID. A deny ACE overrides all other ACEs. Windows 2000 implements the No Access permission using the deny ACE.

Access is allowed if an Access Token contains any SID that matches a permission in the DACL. For example, if an individual account is allowed read access, and the user account is a member of a group account that is allowed write access, then the Access Token for that logged-on user will contain both SIDs, and the DACL will allow read and write access to the object. Deny ACEs still override any accumulation of permission.

The access control entries in the SACL are formed the same way as the ACEs in the DACL (they are composed of a SID and an access mask), but the access mask, in this case, identifies those services of the object for which the account will be audited.

Not every object has a DACL or a SACL. The FAT file system, for example, does not record security information, so file and directory objects stored on a FAT volume lack DACLs and SACLs. When a DACL is missing, any user account may access any of the object's services. This is not the same as when an object has an empty DACL. In that case, no account may access the object. When there is no SACL for an object, that object may not be audited.

The Security Reference Monitor

Processes do not directly access objects such as files, directories, or printers. The Windows 2000 operating system (specifically, the Win32 portion of it) accesses the objects on behalf of your processes. The primary reason for this is to make programs simpler. The program doesn't have to know how to directly manipulate every kind of object; it simply asks the operating system to do it. Another important benefit, especially from the security point of view, is that since the operating system is performing the operations for the process, the operating system can enforce object security.

When a process asks the Win32 subsystem to perform an operation on an object (such as reading a file), the Win32 subsystem checks with the Security Reference Monitor to make sure the process has permission to perform the operation on the object. The Security Reference Monitor compares the Access Token of the process with the DACL of the object by checking each SID in the Access Token against the SIDs in the DACL. If there is an ACE with a matching SID that contains an access mask that allows the operation and there is no ACE with a matching SID containing a deny mask to the object for the operation, then the Security Reference Monitor allows the Win32 subsystem to perform the operation.

The Security Reference Monitor also checks to see if the object access is audited and should be reported in the Windows 2000 Security Event Log. It checks for auditing the same way it checks for permissions—by comparing each SID in the Access Token with each access control entry's SID. If it finds a match, it checks to see if the operation (or service) being performed is one of those services indicated in the access mask. If it is, and the result of the security check against the SACL matches the kind of auditing being performed (the access failed and failure is being audited, or the access succeeded and the success is being audited, or both), then the audit event is written to the Event Log.

Rights versus Permissions

Some activities do not apply to any specific object but instead apply to a group of objects or to the operating system as a whole. Shutting down the operating system, for example, affects every object in the system. The user must have *user rights* to perform such operations.

Earlier in this chapter, I mentioned that the Local Security Authority includes a Locally Unique Identifier when it creates an Access Token. The LUID describes which of the user rights that particular user account has. The Local Security Authority creates the LUID from security information in the Security Accounts Manager database (local computer account) or the Active Directory (domain account). The LUID is a combination of the rights of that specific user account and the rights of all the groups of which that account is a member.

Rights take precedence over *permissions*. That's why the Administrator account can take ownership of a file whose owner has removed all access permissions; the Administrator has the Take Ownership of Files or Other Objects right. The Windows 2000 operating system checks the user rights first, and then (if there is no user right specifically allowing the operation) the operating system checks the ACEs stored in the DACL against the SIDs in the Access Token.

User accounts have the right to read or write to an object the user account owns even in the case of a deny ACE permission. A user account may also change the permissions to an object owned by that user account.

NTFS File System Permissions

The NTFS file system is the bastion of Windows 2000 security. Being the platform upon which a secure Windows 2000 computer runs, NTFS is the gatekeeper of persistent security.

The LSA makes sure that running programs cannot violate each other's memory space and that all calls into the kernel are properly authorized. But what keeps a program from replacing the files the make up the LSA with an equivalent service that doesn't work? The answer to that question is NTFS, and that example highlights why a secure file system is mandatory for a secure operating system. Without the ability to trust the file system that stores system files, you can't trust the system that executes from those files.

Consider the case of virus strike on a Windows 95 machine. The user executes a program containing a virus. The virus identifies which program started the current program and infects it, thus propagating itself back one level. The next time that program starts, the virus does the same thing, as well as infect every program spawned from that program. Within a few cycles, the virus has propagated back to the core operating system, thereby infecting every file run from it.

In Windows 2000, the user runs a program containing a virus. That program tries to rewrite `explorer.exe` with the virus header, but it is blocked by NTFS file system security because the user doesn't have write permission to `explorer.exe`. Thanks to NTFS, this type of virus is stopped cold by Windows 2000. Granted, some viruses are content to hang out in user mode (such as Word macro viruses and Outlook worms), but those viruses still can't infect the operating system itself—unless the virus was launched by a user account with administrative access to the machine, which is why you should never run nonoperating system software from an administrative account.

TIP   Instead of logging on as administrator, use the Run As feature of Windows 2000 to launch administrative tasks. To easily set this up in the `Adminsitrative Tools` folder, simply right-click the icon in the Start menu, select Properties, and check Run As Different User. Then you can log on using a normal user account and provide your administrative credentials only when performing an administrative task.

NTFS works by comparing a user's Access Token to the ACL associated with each requested file before allowing access to the file. This simple mechanism keeps unauthorized users from modifying the operating system or anything else they're not given specific access to.

Unfortunately, the default state of Windows 2000 is to provide full control to the "everyone" group at the root of all drives, so that all permissions inherited by files created therein are accessible by everyone. To receive any real benefit from NTFS file system security for applications and user-stored files, you must remove the permission granting full control to everyone and replace it with appropriate security for each folder in your computer.

Managing NTFS File System Permissions

Managing NTFS file system permissions in Windows 2000 is simple, and it works like permissions settings did in earlier versions of Windows NT.

To change security permissions on a file or folder, browse to the file or folder object using the Windows Explorer, right-click the file or folder, select the Security tab, select the appropriate group or user account, and make the appropriate settings in the Access Control Entry list.

Inheritance is handled differently in Windows 2000 than it was in Windows NT. In Windows NT, inherited permissions were simply the same as the parent objects and could be immediately modified. In Windows 2000, if the object is inheriting permissions from a containing folder object, you'll have to uncheck the Allow Inheritable Permissions checkbox to create a copy of the inherited permissions and then modify the existing permissions. You can create new ACE entries without overriding the inheritance setting.

Encrypting File System

The Encrypting File System is a file system driver that provides the ability to encrypt and decrypt files on the fly. The service is very simple to use: Users check the encrypted attribute on a file or directory. The EFS service generates an encryption certificate in the background and uses it to encrypt the affected files. When those files are requested from the NTFS file system driver, the EFS service automatically decrypts the file for delivery.

File encryption sounds like a really cool feature, but the current implementation in Windows 2000 is so flawed that EFS is mostly worthless, except perhaps on laptops.

The biggest problem with EFS is that it only works for individual users, making it useful only on client computers. Encryption certificates for files are created based on a user identity, so encrypted files can only be used by the account that created them. Encryption certificates cannot be assigned to group objects, so encryption can't protect general files stored on a server. This architecture would require the exchange of private keys over the network, so an encrypted channel would have to be established to exchange keys.

EFS will not allow encrypted files to be shared because it decrypts them before it delivers them. This too is shortsighted. If encryption certificates were held by a group, the encrypted file could be delivered over the network to the client in its encrypted state, and the client computer could use its participation in the group having the decryption certificate to decrypt the file. Kerberos could create session keys to encrypt the certificates to keep them secure while they're transported to members of the group. File-sharing could be secure enough to use over the Internet without a private tunnel.

Furthermore, loss of the encryption certificate— the Achilles' heel of encryption—would not be such a big deal. As long as any member of the group having the certificate still existed, that user would still have a copy of the certificate to decrypt the files. In its current incarnation, EFS always makes a key for the recovery agent (the local administrator by default) whether or not the user wants the recovery agent to be able to decrypt the file.

Alas, EFS (like file replication) is another example of a service that would have been really cool if Microsoft had done it right. As it is, they did just enough to say they had file system encryption.

Aside from the fact that it only works for individuals, there are a number of other problems with EFS:

- Encryption certificates are stored by default in the Registry of the local machine, where they can be recovered and used to decrypt the files on the machine. For EFS to function correctly as a secure encryption service, certificates must be moved from the local machine to a physically secure certificate server or exported to removable media that isn't left with the machine. Since the vast majority of users don't know or do this, the file system should be more accurately called the Obfuscating File Service.

- The only way to secure local EFS certificates is to use smart card authentication or to use SysKey (select Start ➢ Run ➢ SysKey) to move the System Key (a hash used to encrypt the local SAM accounts database that contains the EFS decryption certificate) to a floppy or use it as a password at boot time—and that password or floppy must be available to everyone who needs to boot the computer.

- Drag-and-drop Copy operations into an encrypted folder will not automatically encrypt the file because move operations do not change the attributes of a file. Cut and Paste operations do, because you're effectively deleting the old file and creating a new one. This is a major problem with the Explorer interface because most people don't know any better and move files using drag and drop, believing their files are secure when in fact they're stored as plain-text files.

- Encrypted files will be decrypted if they are moved to non-NTFS volumes, which do not support encryption. Be certain you know what file system type you're copying encrypted files to. In my opinion, EFS should copy the file in its encrypted state to the non-NTFS store, where it would be useless until it was moved back to an NTFS store. No crypto service should ever automatically decrypt anything without the consent of the user.

- Encrypted files cannot be shared by being located in a shared folder. This restriction is designed to keep them encrypted; shared files are sent as plain text over the wire, so anyone with a network sniffer could decrypt them. A more robust encrypting file system would simply transmit the encrypted file over the wire and trust that the receiver had the appropriate certificate to decrypt it.

- Many programs (most Microsoft Office programs) create temporary files either in the local directory or in a temp directory when a file is being edited. Encryption for temp files follows the normal rule: If the file is created in a folder that has the encryption flag set, the temp file will be encrypted. Otherwise, it will not be encrypted and will foil your encryption security. To solve this problem, simply set the encryption flag on the temp directory to ensure that all temporary files are encrypted. You also need to know exactly where temp files are being created—just because the temp directory exists doesn't mean that every program uses it. Many third-party applications create their own temp directories.

- Printing is another vector for accidental decryption: When you print a document that is encrypted, the file is decrypted by the source application and sent via plain text to the print spooler. If the spooler is configured to spool documents (as most are), then the printed data is written to a file that could be undeleted to recover your encrypted data. To avoid this, you must either configure printing to avoid spooling documents throughout your network or set the encryption flag on the folder that the spooler uses to create spooled documents.

TIP   EFS requires a data recovery agents policy, so you can disable EFS throughout a domain by creating a group policy object for the domain that specifies an empty policy for encrypted data recovery agents. The policy must exist and it must be empty, because a no policy setting will allow the local workstation's policy to override the domain policy.

I don't recommend using EFS except on single-user computers that can't otherwise be physically secured. Its ease of use is a security blanket rather than real security. There are so many holes in EFS and so many accidental decryption vectors that it would be hard for a security expert to remember them all, much less a typical user. EFS is valuable for high-theft computers such as laptops that are configured to encrypt the print spool directory, temp folders, and the My Documents directory. For everyone else, it's worse than nothing because it makes you feel secure when you probably aren't.

Windows 2000 Network Security

Windows 2000 network security is based on a few principal services:

- Active Directory
- Group Policy
- Kerberos

- Share Security
- IPSec

Each of these services works together to form a coherent whole: IPSec is defined by group policies that are stored in the Active Directory and can be configured to use Kerberos for automatic private key exchange. Share Security is based on user identity as proven by Kerberos based on password hashes stored in the Active Directory. Managing security policy through the Active Directory allows administrators to create policies that can be automatically applied throughout the organization.

Active Directory

Active Directory is not a security service, but nearly all the security mechanisms built into Windows 2000 rely upon Active Directory as a storage mechanism for security information like the domain hierarchy, trust relationships, crypto keys, certificates, policies, and security principal accounts.

Because nearly all of Windows 2000's security mechanisms are integrated with Active Directory, you'll use it to manage and apply security. Most of the subjects covered in the following sections could be considered components of Active Directory because they're so tightly integrated with it.

Although Active Directory is not a security service, it can be secured: Active Directory containers and objects have ACLs just like NTFS files do. In Active Directory, permissions can be applied in much the same way as they can in NTFS.

Unlike NTFS file system permissions, you can set permissions for the fields inside specific objects so that different users or security groups are responsible for portions of an object's data. For example, while you wouldn't give a user the ability to change anything about their own user account, you can allow them to update their contact information. This is possible using Active Directory permissions.

Kerberos Authentication and Domain Security

Kerberos authentication was developed by the Massachusetts Institute of Technology (MIT) to provide an intercomputer trust system capable of verifying the identity of security principals (such as a user or a computer) over an open, unsecured network. Kerberos does not rely on authentication by the computers involved or the privacy of the network communications. For this reason, Kerberos is ideal for authentication over the Internet and on large networks.

Kerberos operates as a trusted third-party authentication service by using shared secret keys. Essentially, a computer implicitly trusts the Kerberos Key Distribution Center

(KDC) because they both know the same secret, which has been placed there as part of a trusted administrative process. In Windows 2000, the shared secret is generated when the computer joins the domain. Because both parties to a Kerberos session trust the KDC, they trust each other. In practice, this trust is implemented as a secure exchange of encryption keys that prove the identities of the parties involved to one another.

Kerberos authentication works like this:

1. A client requests a valid set of credentials for a given server from the KDC by sending a plain-text request containing the client's name (identifier).

2. The KDC looks up the secret keys of both the client and the server in its database (the Active Directory) and creates a *ticket* containing a random session key, the current time on the KDC, an expiration time determined by policy, and optionally any other information stored in the database. In the case of Windows 2000, SIDs are contained in the ticket.

3. The ticket is encrypted using the client's secret key.

4. A second ticket called the *session ticket* is created, which contains the session key and optional authentication data that is encrypted using the server's secret key.

5. The combined tickets are transmitted back to the client. Note that the authenticating server does not need to authenticate the client explicitly because only a valid client can decrypt the ticket.

6. Once the client is in possession of a valid ticket and session key for a server, it initiates communications directly with the server. To do so, the client constructs an *authenticator* consisting of the current time, the client's name, an application-specific checksum if desired, and a randomly generated initial sequence number and/or a session subkey used to retrieve a unique session identifier specific to the service in question. Authenticators are only valid for a single attempt and cannot be reused or exploited through a replay attack because they are dependent upon the current time. The authenticator is encrypted using the session key and transmitted along with the session ticket to the server from which service is requested.

7. When the server receives the ticket from the client, it decrypts the session ticket using the server's shared secret (which secret, if more than one exist, is indicated in the plain-text portion of the ticket).

8. The server then retrieves the session key from the ticket and uses it to decrypt the authenticator. The server's ability to decrypt the ticket proves that it was encrypted using the server's secret key known only to the KDC and the server itself, so the client's identity is trusted. The authenticator is used to ensure that the communication is recent and is not a replay attack.

Figure 6.1 shows the entire Kerberos authentication process.

Figure 6.1   Kerberos authentication uses a mutually trusted third party to communicate trust between two security principals.

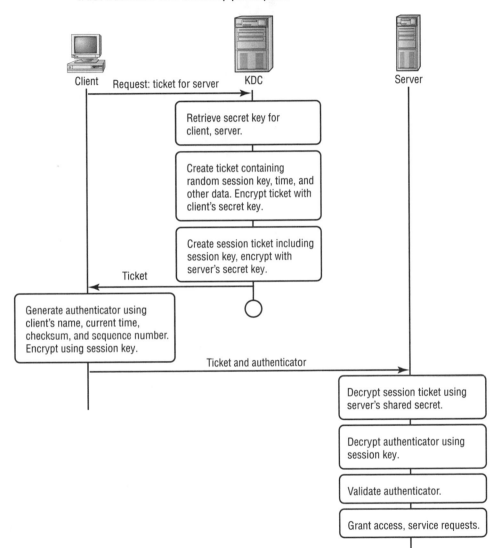

Tickets can be reused for a duration specified by domain security policy, not to exceed eight hours. This reduces the burden on the KDC by requiring ticket requests as infrequently as once per workday. Clients cache their session tickets in a secure store located in RAM and destroy them when they expire.

Kerberos shortcuts the granting of tickets by granting a session ticket for itself as well as the requested target server the first time a client makes contact. The KDC responds to this initial request first with a session ticket for further ticket requests, called a *Ticket-Granting Ticket (TGT),* and then with a session ticket for the requested server. The TGT obviates further Active Directory lookups of the client by pre-authenticating subsequent ticket requests in exactly the same manner that Kerberos authenticates all other requests. Like any session ticket, the TGT is valid until it expires, which depends upon domain security policy.

Kerberos is technically divided into two services: the TGT service (the only service that actually authenticates against the Active Directory) and the Ticket-Granting service, which issues session tickets when presented with a valid TGT.

Trust Relationships between Domains

Kerberos works across domain boundaries (domains are called *realms* in Kerberos terminology; the terms are equivalent).

The name of the domain that a security principal belongs to is part of the security principal's name (for example, `titanium.sandiego.connetic.net`). Membership in the same Active Directory tree automatically creates interdomain keys for Kerberos between a parent domain and its child domains.

The exchange of interdomain keys registers the domain controllers of one domain as security principals in the trusted domain. This simple concept makes it possible for any security principal in the domain to get a session ticket on the foreign KDC.

What actually happens is a bit more complex:

1. When a security principal in one domain wants to access a security principal in an adjacent domain (one domain is the parent; one is the child), it sends a session ticket request to its local KDC.

2. The KDC determines that the target is not in the local domain and replies to the client with a *referral ticket*, which is a session ticket encrypted using the interdomain key.

3. The client uses the referral ticket to request a session ticket directly from the foreign KDC.

4. The foreign KDC decrypts the referral ticket because it has the interdomain key, which proves that the trusted domain controller trusts the client (or it would not have granted the referral key).

5. The foreign KDC grants a session ticket valid for the foreign target server.

The process simply reiterates for domains that are farther away. To access a security principal in a domain that is two hops away in the Active Directory domain hierarchy, the client requests a session ticket for the target server against its KDC, which responds with a referral ticket to the next domain away. The client then requests the session ticket using the referral ticket just granted. That server will simply reply with a referral ticket valid on the next server in line. This process continues until the local domain for the target security principal is reached. At that point, a session key (technically, a TGT and a session key) is granted to the requesting client, which can then authenticate against the target security principal directly. Figure 6.2 shows the Kerberos exchange involved in a complex domain trust transit.

The Ticket-Granting Ticket authentication service is especially important in interdomain ticket requests. After a computer has walked down the referral path once, it receives a TGT from the final KDC in the foreign domain. This ensures that subsequent requests in that domain (which are highly likely) won't require the referral walk again. The TGT can simply be used against the foreign KDC to request whatever session tickets are necessary in the foreign domain.

The final important concept in Kerberos authentication is that of delegation of authentication. Essentially, *delegation of authentication* is a mechanism whereby a security principal allows another security principal with which it has established a session to request authentication on its behalf from a third security principal. This mechanism is important in multitier applications, such as a database-driven Web site. Using delegation of authentication, the Web browser client can authenticate with the Web server and then provide the Web server with a special TGT that it can use to request session tickets on its behalf. The Web server can then use the forwarded credentials of the Web client to authenticate with the database server. This allows the database server to use appropriate security for the actual Web client, rather than use the Web server's credentials, which would have completely different access than the actual client.

Group Policies

Group Policy is Windows 2000's primary mechanism for controlling the configuration of client workstations for security as well as administration. *Policies* in general are simply a set of changes to the default settings of a computer. Policies are usually organized so that individual policies contain changes that implement a specific goal—for example, disabling or enabling file system encryption or controlling which programs a user is allowed to run.

Figure 6.2   The Kerberos-based transitive trust mechanism is simple in Kerberos terms.

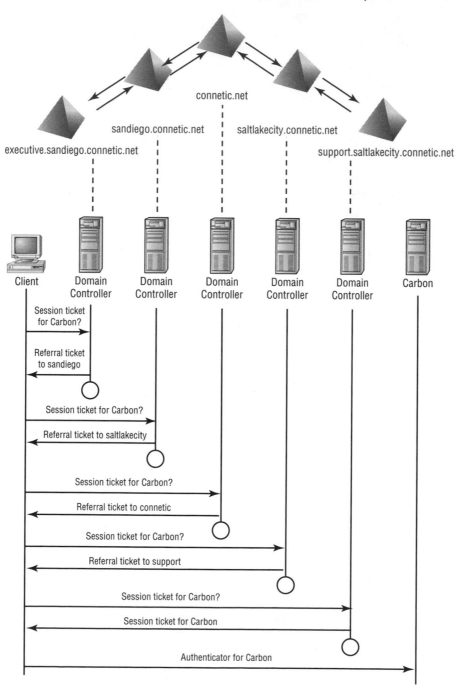

Group policies are applied to members of an Active Directory container (such as a domain or Organizational Unit). Security groups can be used to filter group policies, but policies cannot be applied to security groups. Windows 2000's Group Policy is not strictly a security mechanism—its primary purpose is change and configuration management—but it allows administrators to create more secure systems by limiting the users' range of actions.

Group policies can be used to control the following for *computer policies*:

- Registry settings related to security configuration and control
- Software installation
- Startup/shutdown and logon/logoff scripts
- Services startup
- Registry permissions
- NTFS permissions
- Public key policies
- IPSec policies
- System, network, and Windows components settings

Group policies can be used to control the following for *user policies*:

- Software installation
- Internet Explorer settings
- Logon/logoff scripts
- Security settings
- Remote Installation Service
- Folder redirection
- Windows components
- Start menu, Taskbar, Desktop, and Control Panel settings
- Network settings
- System settings

Mechanics of Group Policy

Group Policy Objects are essentially custom Registry files (and supporting files such as .msi packages and scripts) defined by policy settings that are downloaded and applied to domain member client computers when the computer is booted (computer configuration) and when a user logs in (user configuration). Group Policy Objects and any supporting files required for a group policy are stored on domain controllers in the SysVol share. Multiple group policies can be applied to the same computer, each policy overwriting the previous policy's settings in a "last application wins" scenario—unless a specific policy is configured not to be overwritten.

Each Group Policy Object has two parts: computer configuration and user configuration. You can configure both user and computer settings in a single Group Policy Object, and you can disable the computer or user portion of a Group Policy Object in the policy's Properties window. I recommend splitting all policies to apply either to users or computers, because the policies are downloaded at different times and because the configuration requirements for the two types of security principals are highly likely to diverge over time, requiring the application of different policy anyway.

Computer policies are applied at system initialization before a user logs in (and during periodic refreshes). Computer policies control the operating system, applications (including Windows Explorer), and startup and shutdown scripts. Think of computer policies as applying to the HKEY_Local_Machine portion of the Registry. Computer policies usually take precedence over user policies in the event of a conflict. Use computer policies whenever a configuration is required that does not depend on who logs in to the computer. You can apply company-wide policy easily to computer policies.

User policies are applied after a user logs in but before they're able to work on the computer, as well as during the periodic refresh cycle. User policies control operating system behavior, Desktop settings, application settings, folder redirection, and user logon/logoff scripts. Think of user policies as applying to the HKEY_Current_User portion of the Registry. Use user policies whenever a configuration is specific to a user or group of users, even if those users always use the same computers. By applying security-related settings to users rather than to computers, you can ensure that those settings travel with the user in the event that they use someone else's computer—and that those policies don't apply to administrative or support personnel who may need to log on to the computer (of course, security group membership could be used to filter settings for support personnel as well.)

Group policies are called group policies because they're applied to groups of users; specifically, membership in Active Directory containers like domains or Organizationl Units. Group policies are also hierarchical in nature: many policies can be applied to a single computer or user, and they are applied in hierarchical order. Furthermore, later policies can override the settings of earlier policies. This means that individual elements of policy can be refined from the broad policies applied to large groups such as domains to narrowly focused policies applied to smaller groups such as Organizational Units.

Group polices are configured at the following levels in the following order:

Local machine   Group policy is applied first so that it can be overridden by domain policy. Every computer has one local group policy that it is subject to. Beyond the local group policy, group policies are downloaded from the Active Directory depending upon the user and computer's location in the Active Directory.

Site   Group policies are unique in that they are managed from the Active Directory Sites and Services snap-in. Site policies apply to sites, so they should be used for issues relating to the physical location of users and computers rather than for domain security participation. Since physical location issues are rare, you won't use site policy very often. If your organization has only one site, which policies apply to the site may not be obvious, but you should still apply policies by location if the policy truly relates to location because your organization may some day have multiple physical sites.

Domain   Group policies apply to all users and computers in the domain, and this should be the primary place where you implement global policies in your organization. For example, if your company has a security policy document that requires specific configuration of logon passwords for all users, apply that policy to the domain.

Organizational Unit (OU)   Group policies apply to their member users and computers. Group policies are applied from top to bottom (parent, then child) in the OU hierarchy.

Security group   These work differently than the actual domain containers. Rather than having group policies that can be applied to a security group, group policies that are applied to the user are filtered (allowed or disallowed) by a user's association with security groups. For example, you cannot apply a specific group policy to members of a Sales security group, but you can apply the policy to the Sales and Marketing Organizational Unit and then set security group filters so that the policy would only apply to members of the Sales group. A more coherent (and more easily documented) method, however, would be to create subordinate Organizational Units within the Sales and Marketing Organizational Unit. You should use security group filtering when policies should be applied based on some criterion other than a user's position within the company, such as temporary members of "new employees"—a security status that will quickly change. Only use security group filtering when creating a new OU doesn't make sense.

You cannot link a group policy to generic folders or containers other than those listed above. If you need to create a container for Group Policy, use an Organizational Unit.

Group policies are either all or nothing in their application; you cannot specify that only part of a policy be applied. If you need to implement variations on a policy theme for different users, simply create one policy for each variation and apply the variants to the appropriate Active Directory container or filter by security group.

A single group policy can be applied to more than one container in the Active Directory because group policies are not stored in the Active Directory at the location where you apply them. Only a link to the Group Policy Object is stored; the objects themselves are actually stored in the replicated SysVol share of the domain controllers in the domain.

Creating Effective Group Policy

Group policies give administrators a tremendous amount of flexibility in the application of configuration information on a client computer. This flexibility makes it easy to create group policies that will be difficult to manage in the future because they were applied at the wrong level in the Active Directory domain hierarchy, or were made local when they should have been nonlocal, or were applied too broadly.

Rather than sitting down in front of the Group Policy Manager and clicking away to create policies that seem like a good idea, use requirements planning techniques to create effective policies. To create your requirements, write down the goals you want to achieve. For example:

- Only administrative users should be able to install software. (Applies to the domain, filtered by the Administrator security group.)

- New users should not be able to access the Internet. (Applies to the domain, filtered by the New Users security group.)

- Members of the Sales department should only be able to run the Sales Tracking application. (Applies to the Sales Organizational Unit or domain.)

- Everything transmitted by members of the San Diego Finance group to the UK domain should be encrypted. (Applies to site policy, filtered by Finance group. Why site policy? Because it's geographic in nature; this wouldn't apply to Finance members working in other locations.)

- No desktop users except administrators and people who work in Research and Development should have access to removable media drives. (Applies to the domain, overridden in the R&D Organizational Unit by another policy, and filtered by the Administrators security group.)

- People should change their password at least once per month. (Applies to the domain.)

Notice how these requirements make both the purpose and scope of an individual policy easy to determine? Each of these bulleted items should constitute a group policy, and their applicability should be obvious from the statement.

To whom does this policy apply?   If the answer is "Everyone" or "Anyone who uses this computer," then your configuration should probably be implemented as a computer policy. If the answer is anything else, then it's a user policy.

Is this policy specific to certain locations?   If so, it's a site policy—not a domain policy—even if the two happen to be coincidental. Don't get into the habit of using domain policy for everything, because when your company grows, you'll find yourself deleting links and moving policies around quite a bit.

Is this policy unique to one computer?   Sometimes elements of Group Policy are unique to a single computer—for example, to a computer that operates on the Internet as a public server, or the endpoint to an encrypted tunnel. Also, you may need to use a local policy to control the configuration of laptop computers that aren't always connected to the network. In these cases, local group policy makes sense. It's extremely rare for a local policy to make sense for constantly connected client computers, however, and it's exceptionally rare for user policy to be correctly applied to a local computer in a domain environment. Consider the reasons why you would use a local policy carefully and be sure that the policy wouldn't be more effectively managed as a nonlocal group policy.

Is this policy specific to a group of users?   If so, ask yourself if that group represents an Organizational Unit. If they do, create the Organizational Unit and then apply the security policy to it rather than using a security group to filter the policy. This will allow for easier management of future policies that would apply to the same group and is more easily managed and documented. If the group doesn't represent an Organizational Unit (for example, New Users), then use security groups to filter the application of Group Policy.

Is this configuration one policy, or is it multiple policies?   Policies are all or nothing in their application, so you should get in the habit of making many small policies that are created for specific purposes, rather than creating sweeping policies for people or computers. For example, rather than creating a policy for Sales, create policies that affect certain configurations (such as "Lotus Notes User Application Policy") and apply those many specific configurations to groups. This makes it far more likely that the work you've done to create a policy can be applied to various users and allows you to see at a glance what the effects of policy are applied to various containers in the Active Directory.

Once you've answered these questions, it should be pretty obvious which container in the Active Directory should be linked to each group policy.

There is a downside to using many small, purpose-specific policies: it takes more time at boot time and logon to apply multiple policies. You can optimize the process by combining requirements that are always applied the same way into a single policy. For example, numerous requirements apply to everyone, so it's perfectly fine to combine those into a single policy. I don't recommend optimizing beyond combining policies that apply to the same Active Directory container and security groups, however, because you'll wind up creating confusion as to which combined policies apply to which situations.

Managing Group Policy

Domain group policy is managed through the Active Directory Sites and Services snap-in (for site group policy) or the Active Directory Users and Computers snap-in (for all other nonlocal group policy).

To manage group policy, open the Active Directory Users and Computers snap-in (or the Sites and Services snap-in if you want to apply a policy to a site), right-click the container to which you want to apply the policy (domain or Organizational Unit), and select Properties. Then select the Group Policy tab. Figure 6.3 shows the Group Policy page for the domain controller's OU.

Figure 6.3   Manage the order and application of group policies using the Properties window of the Active Directory container.

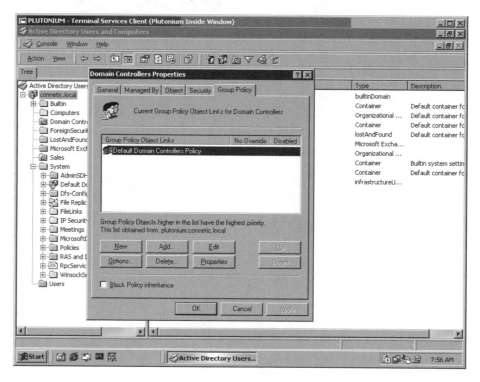

From this page, you can create new Group Policy Objects, add a link to an existing object, edit and delete objects, change the application order, and change the override polices of objects. Creating a new group policy is easy—just click the New button and select the point in the Active Directory where you want the policy to be applied. Once you've created and named the policy, click Edit to modify it.

To change which security groups a policy is applied to (to use security group filtering), right-click the group policy you want to filter, select Properties, and then select the Security tab. You'll see an "Apply Group Policy" Access Control Entry in the ACE list. Simply select the group you want to filter on, select the Apply Group Policy ACE, and check Allow or Deny as appropriate to create the filter.

Editing policies is simple. Simply click the Edit button to open the Group Policy Editor (shown in Figure 6.4) and expand the hierarchy tree to expose the element of policy you want to change. Select the element in the list view you want to change, and double-click it.

Figure 6.4   The Group Policy Editor provides a convenient interface for defining Group Policy Objects.

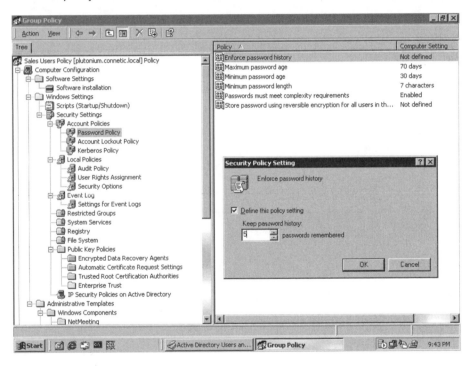

Every policy element must be defined in order to be included the in Group Policy Object. Check Define This Policy Setting to enable the input field for the setting. The input field will vary by setting to allow the correct type of data to be entered.

The same policy can be applied to multiple Active Directory containers, although it is not necessary to explicitly apply a policy to the children of a container to which the policy is already applied because the policy will already have been applied to the security principal.

To apply an existing policy to a security container, right-click the container in the Active Directory Users and Computers snap-in, and select Properties. Select the Group Policy tab, click Add, select the appropriate tab to display the group policy, select the group policy, and click OK to confirm.

Share Security

Shares are directories or volumes on a workstation or server that can be accessed by other computers in the network. Shares can be publicly available, or their access can be controlled with permissions. Shares use *share-level security*, which controls permissions for shared directories but not for anything specific within the directory. File-level security is superior to share-level security but can only be used on NTFS volumes.

Although you can set up a reasonably secure small network with shares, share security techniques don't really scale well for larger networks and environments where security is required. A new share must be created whenever security requirements change, and multiple shares with different security levels can be applied to the same directories.

Using and Securing Shares

The main reason to set up a network is to share files. Any directory on any workstation or server in the network can be set up as a shared directory. Although shares don't have the same level of security as NTFS directories on a dedicated server, Windows 2000 does provide a simple set of security features for shared directories.

NOTE   Although it's often associated with the workgroup model, you can also share files from workstations within a domain. In order to do this, the Server service must be running.

Creating a Share   You can create a share with any volume or any directory within a volume. You can create shares in either NTFS or FAT partitions, although shares in NTFS partitions can be made more secure. To create a share, right-click a drive or directory in an Explorer window and select the Sharing option. The Sharing Properties dialog box is displayed.

From this dialog box you can specify these options:

Not Shared/Shared As   Specify whether the volume or directory should be shared.

Share Name   Choose a name for the share. This name will appear as a directory name when users view a directory listing for the server. If the share will be accessed by users running Windows 3.*x*, or if your users use DOS applications, be sure to use a DOS-compatible name for the share.

Comment   Enter a description of the share's purpose or other information. (This is optional.) The contents of this field are displayed in the Explorer window to the right of the share name in Details view.

User Limit   If Maximum Allowed is selected, the number of users accessing the share is limited only by the Windows 2000 license. If a number is specified, only that many concurrent users can access the share.

Permissions   Clicking this button displays a dialog box that allows you to change permissions for the share, as described later in this chapter in "Share Permissions."

Caching   Click this button to configure caching options for this share. Offline caching allows users to store the file locally on their hard disk so it's available if they're not online or if the server is unavailable.

When a directory or drive is shared, it is listed in the Explorer with a special icon that shows a hand underneath the drive or folder icon.

Accessing Shares   Although a server might have several shares configured—some entire volumes, some directories several levels deep—they all appear to users as a single listing under the server's name. Users can navigate to the server name using the My Network Places icon, and then open it to display a list of shares. Unfortunately, share names are not shown automatically in the Active Directory when you double-click a computer; they must be manually added in the Active Directory hierarchy.

As an example, suppose you created several shares, including VOL_F for an entire NTFS volume, and IE4 for the `\Program Files\Plus!\Microsoft Internet` directory. A user who navigated to the server through Network Neighborhood would see a flat list of shares.

To make access to shares more convenient for users in the workgroup, you can create Desktop shortcuts to particular directories. You can also map a drive letter on the workstation to the share. This method has the benefit of fooling not only users into thinking it's a local drive, but also DOS and older Windows applications that otherwise might not support network access. To map a drive to a share, right-click the My Network Places icon, and then select Map Network Drive. Mapping drives is not normally necessary to access files from Windows Explorer or from Win32 applications.

To use this dialog box, choose a local drive letter, and then choose a server name and path to map the drive to. The window at the bottom of the dialog box displays a list of servers and shares. Select the Reconnect at Logon option to have the drive mapped each time the user logs on.

As an administrator, you have another option for displaying a list of shares on a server. The Computer Management snap-in's Shared Folders extension allows you to list shares on the local machine, add or remove shares, and monitor users who are currently accessing shares. The tool is available in the `Administrative Tools` folder and works just like every other MMC snap-in.

Default Shares   When you look at the Shared Folder Manager, you'll notice several shares with names ending in a dollar sign: C$, ADMIN$, and so forth. These are *administrative shares*—shares automatically configured by Windows 2000 and accessible only to administrators and the operating system itself. These shares are used for remote administration and communication between systems.

Each drive is automatically given an administrative share, with the share name being the drive letter followed by a dollar sign. The ADMIN$ share is connected to the \WINNT directory on each server. There is also an IPC$ share, used for interprocess communication between Windows 2000 servers, and a PRINT$ share, which shares printer information between servers. Domain controllers have a SYSVOL$ share used to distribute group policies, scripts, and installation packages.

As you've probably noticed, these shares don't appear in the browse lists that you can view from the Explorer. The only way to list them is with the Computer Management snap-in, which was described in the previous section.

> **TIP**   You can create your own "administrative" shares. Any share name ending with a dollar sign ($) will be hidden from browse lists. Users (administrators or not) can access the share if they know its exact name.

Administrative shares present a potential security risk. A hacker who has gained access to the Administrator account on a single workstation in the workgroup can access the system drives of other workstations, effectively allowing administrator-level access to the entire workgroup.

You can improve security by disabling the automatic administrative shares created for the roots of hard disk drives (C$, D$, and so on). You can remove the shares from each drive's Properties window, or use the Shared Folder extension's Stop Sharing option. It's best to disable all of these, and then add a share for any specific drives or directories that need to be available across the network. Don't disable the other administrative shares or you will have problems with your machines.

Share versus File Security   Share-level security is similar to file system security, but not nearly as sophisticated (or as secure) because share access control entries can be applied only to the share as a whole. Security cannot be customized within a share.

There is one significant advantage of share-level security: it works with any shared directory, whether it's on an NTFS or FAT volume. Share-level security is the only way to secure FAT directories. However, the share permissions you set only affect remote users. Users logged on to the machine locally can access anything on a FAT volume, shared or not. Share-level security also does not apply to users logged on locally or to Terminal Services clients.

Share Permissions   To set permissions for a share, click the Permissions button from the Sharing Properties dialog box. By default, the Everyone built-in group is given Full Control access to the share—in other words, share security is not implemented by default. The first thing you should do to secure a share is remove Everyone from the list. You can then add any number of users or groups and give them specific permissions. The following are the permissions available for shares, and each can be allowed or denied:

Read   Allows users to list contents of the directory, open and read files, and execute programs.

Change   Allows all Read permissions. In addition, users can create, delete, and modify files.

Full Control   Allows all Read and Change permissions. In addition, users can change permissions and change file ownerships.

Network Layer Encryption

Virtual private networks are a cost-effective way to extend your LAN over the Internet to remote networks and remote client computers. VPNs use the Internet to route LAN traffic from one private network to another by encapsulating the LAN traffic in IP packets. The encrypted packets are unreadable by intermediary Internet computers and can contain any kind of LAN communications, including file and print access, LAN e-mail, Remote Procedure Calls, and client/server database access.

Virtual private networks between LANs can be established using server computers, firewalls, or routers. Client access to the VPNs can be made using VPN software on the client computers, or by dialing in to ISPs that support the VPN protocol. Using this second method, however, makes the ISP a partner in your network security in the same way that relying on an ISP for your firewall does.

Pure VPN systems do not provide adequate network protection. You also need a firewall and other Internet security services to keep your network safe. PPTP in particular has security problems, and you should take steps to correct them in your own network.

Using the Internet to link LANs and give remote computers LAN access causes security, performance, reliability, and management problems. Your LAN is a protected environment that only members of your organization are allowed to use. The LAN clients and servers should be protected from the Internet by a network-address-translating firewall and/or proxy servers so that (ideally) network intruders can't even identify their existence, much less target them for individual attack. In order to make it more difficult for hackers to capture private company information, most firewalls are configured not to pass typical LAN service protocols such as SMB, NetBIOS, the NetWare Core Protocol, or NFS.

SMB works particularly well in the clear over the Internet. Given a high-speed link, you can simply use file sharing without firewalls over the Internet, or you could configure your firewall to pass SMB and Kerberos or NetBIOS traffic and allow your employees to have remote access to file and print services. This would allow hackers to attempt to access your data simply by providing a valid account name and password or by attacking the protocol to exploit a bug that would allow access.

Exposing your LAN's file-sharing traffic in this manner effectively makes the whole Internet your LAN. It is virtual, but not private. Not only can your sales force print to your engineering department's printers or log on to your accounting department's file server, anyone on the Internet can print to the printer or log on to the file server. An intruder would have to guess a password, of course, but hackers have a lot of experience in guessing passwords. Automated password-guessing tools can crack most user account passwords in less than a day over the Internet.

WARNING   You should never leave SMB open to the Internet. Use firewalls to restrict the SMB ports on your corporate network and disable the file and print-sharing service on computers directly connected to the Internet.

VPN Technologies

Virtual private networks solve the problem of direct Internet access to servers through a combination of the following fundamental security components:

- IP encapsulation
- Cryptographic authentication
- Data payload encryption

All three components must exist in a true VPN. Although cryptographic authentication and data payload encryption may seem like the same thing at first, they are actually entirely different functions and may exist independently of each other. For example, the Secure Socket Layer performs data payload encryption without cryptographic authentication of the remote user, and Kerberos performs cryptographic authentication without performing data payload encryption.

IP Encapsulation   You need to protect the data traffic that travels between your LANs over the Internet. Ideally, the computers in each LAN should be unaware that there is anything special about communicating with the computers in the other LANs. Computers outside your virtual network should not be able to snoop on the traffic exchanged between the LANs or be able to insert their own data into the communications stream. Essentially, what you need is a private and protected tunnel through the public Internet.

An IP packet can contain any kind of information: program files, spreadsheet data, audio streams, or even other IP packets. When an IP packet contains another IP packet, it is called *IP encapsulation*, *IP on IP*, or *IP/IP*. You can encapsulate one IP packet in another in several ways; Microsoft does it in two different but related ways as specified in the Point-to-Point Tunneling Protocol (PPTP) and the Layer 2 Tunneling Protocol (L2TP). Microsoft also supports IPSec, which does not necessarily use encapsulation.

Why encapsulate IP within IP? Because it makes it possible to refer to a host within another network when a routed connection may not exist. IP encapsulation can make it appear to network computers that two distant networks are actually adjacent, separated from each other by a single router, when in fact they are separated by many Internet routers and gateways that may not even use the same address space because both internal networks are using address translation.

The tunnel endpoint, be it a router, VPN appliance, or a server running a tunneling protocol, will remove the internal packet, decrypt it, and then apply its routing rules to send the embedded packet on its way in the internal network.

As an example, consider two IP networks linked by a router. Both are Class C–sized IP subnets—one with the network address of 10.1.1.0/24 and the other with the network address of 10.1.2.0/24. In this example, the fourth number in each network is reserved for the station address and can be from 1 to 254. The router must have a network interface adapter on each network so that it can move IP traffic between the two LANs. The .1 and .127 station addresses are typical addresses reserved for routers and gateways, so in this network, the router has one adapter with the IP address of 10.1.1.1 and another with the IP address of 10.1.2.1. All of the computers in both networks have a net mask of 255.255.255.0.

When a computer in the 10.1.1.0 network (for example, 10.1.1.23) needs to send an IP packet to a computer in the 10.1.2.0 network (such as 10.1.2.99), the communication proceeds as follows:

1. The originating computer first notices that the network portion of the destination address (10.1.2.99) does not match its own network address.

2. Instead of attempting to send the packet directly to the destination, the originating computer sends the packet to the default gateway address for its subnet (10.1.1.1).

3. The router at that address reads the packet.

4. The router determines that the packet should be placed on the 10.1.2.0 network.

5. The router sends the packet from its adapter (10.1.2.1) to the destination address (10.1.2.99) on that network.

6. The destination computer reads the packet.

In comparison with the preceding example, consider two IP networks linked by RRAS servers using PPTP. One LAN has the network address 10.1.1.0, and the other has the network address 10.1.2.0. In this example, the RRAS servers on each network provide the network connection to the Internet. One RRAS server has a LAN IP address of 10.1.1.1 and an Internet address of 250.121.13.12 assigned by the ISP it is connected to, while the other has a LAN IP address of 10.1.2.1 and an Internet address of 110.121.112.34 assigned by its ISP.

Communication in the PPTP-connected LANs starts and ends the same way it does in router-connected LANs. The IP packets have further to go, though, so more work is done in the middle. Compare the following example to the previous one:

1. The originating computer (10.1.1.23) first notices that the destination address (10.1.2.99) is not in the same network as itself.

2. Instead of attempting to send the packet directly to the destination, the originating computer sends the packet to the default gateway address for its subnet (10.1.1.1).

3. The RRAS server on the 10.1.1.0 network reads the packet.

4. The RRAS server on the 10.1.1.0 network determines that the packet should be placed on the 10.1.2.0 network subnet, for which it has a PPTP connection established over the Internet.

5. The RRAS server encrypts the packet and encapsulates it in another IP packet.

6. The router sends the encapsulated packet from its network interface connected to the Internet (250.121.13.12) to the Internet address (110.121.112.34) of the RRAS server of the 10.1.2.0 network.

7. The RRAS server of the 10.1.2.0 network reads the encapsulated and encrypted packet from its Internet interface.

8. The RRAS server of the 10.1.2.0 network unpackages and decrypts the IP packet, verifying that it is a valid packet that has not been tampered with and that it comes from a trusted source (another RRAS server).

9. The RRAS server of the 10.1.2.0 network sends the packet from its adapter (10.1.2.1) to the destination address (10.1.2.99) on that network subnet.

10. The destination computer reads the packet.

Note that from the point of view of the two network client computers, it doesn't matter how the packet got from one IP subnet to the other. As far as the network client computers are concerned, a router is the same thing as two RRAS servers and a PPTP connection.

Cryptographic Authentication   *Cryptographic authentication* is used to securely validate the identity of the remote user so the system can determine what level of security is appropriate for that user. VPNs use cryptographic authentication to determine whether or not the user can participate in the encrypted tunnel and may also use the authentication to exchange the secret or public key used for payload encryption.

Many different forms of cryptographic authentication exist, in two general categories:

Secret key encryption   Also called *shared secret* or *symmetric encryption*, relies upon a secret value known to both parties. Simply knowing the value proves to the provider that the requester is to be trusted. Challenge and response can be used to make sure that only hashes of the secret, not the secret itself, are transmitted on the network, and one-time-password variations can be used to ensure that the secret changes each time it's used.

Public key encryption   Relies on the exchange of *unidirectional keys*—keys that can only be used to encrypt data. This means that the decryption key is held on the receiver and never transmitted over a public network, which makes the encrypted data secure during transmission because it can't be decrypted. Tunnel end-systems may exchange pairs of public keys to form a bidirectional channel, or the public key receiver may encrypt a shared secret key and transmit it to the public key transmitter to use for future communications (because secret key encryption is faster than public key encryption).

If a hacker intercepted the public or encrypting key, they could only encrypt data and transmit it to the receiver; they could not decrypt the contents of data they intercept.

Data Payload Encryption   *Data payload encryption* is used to obfuscate the contents of the encapsulated data. By encrypting the encapsulated IP packets, both the data and the internal nature of the private networks is kept secret. Data payload encryption can be accomplished using any one of a number of secure cryptographic methods, which differ based on your VPN solution.

IPSec

IPSec is the IETF standards suite for secure IP communications that relies on encryption to ensure the authenticity and privacy of IP communications. IPSec provides mechanisms that can accomplish the following:

- Authenticate individual IP packets and guarantee that they are unmodified
- Encrypt the payload of individual IP packets between two end-systems

- Encapsulate a TCP or UDP socket between two end-systems (hosts) inside an encrypted IP link (tunnel) established between intermediate systems (routers) to provide virtual private networking

IPSec performs these three functions using two independent mechanisms: *Authentication Headers (AH)* to provide authenticity and *Encapsulating Security Payload (ESP)* to encrypt the data portion of an IP Packet. These two mechanisms may be used together or independently.

The Authentication Headers mechanism works by computing a checksum of all the TCP/IP header information and encrypting the checksum with the secret key of the receiver. The receiver then decrypts the checksum using its secret key and then checks the header against the decrypted checksum. If the computed checksum is different than the header checksum, then either the decryption failed because the key was wrong or the header was modified in transit. In either case, the packet is dropped.

NOTE Because NAT changes header information, IPSec Authentication Headers cannot pass through a network address translator. ESP can still be used to encrypt the payload, but support for ESP without AH varies among implementations of IPSec. Unfortunately, Windows 2000 only supports tunnel mode between gateways with fixed IP addresses and uses transport mode for L2TP connections, so they cannot be network address translated.

With Encapsulating Security Payload, the transmitter encrypts the payload of an IP packet using the public key of the receiver. The receiver then decrypts the payload upon receipt and acts accordingly.

IPSec can operate in one of two modes: *transport mode*, which works exactly like regular IP except that the headers are authenticated (AH) and the contents are encrypted (ESP), or *tunnel mode*, where complete IP packets are encapsulated inside AH or ESP packets to provide a secure tunnel. Transport mode is used for providing secure or authenticated communication over public IP ranges between any Internet-connected hosts for any purpose, while tunnel mode is used to create secure links between routers or other network endpoints for the purpose of linking two private networks.

Microsoft recommends IPSec for use in gateway-to-gateway communications and does not consider IPSec suitable for client-to-gateway communications because the protocol itself does not include user authentication.

TIP Download step-by-step instructions for implementing a client-to-gateway VPN using Windows 2000 IPSec from Microsoft at this URL: www.microsoft.com/TechNet/win2000/win2ksrv/technote/ispstep.asp

The root of the problem is that client and machine authentication are handled separately; use of the correct machine gains access to the network, and then a separate authentication protocol gains access to private network resources. A hacker could exploit the window between machine authentication and user authentication to run probes against the network without logging in or to run automated password attacks against the network.

Consider the following example: A legitimate network user uses an IPSec-configured laptop to gain access to the local network and then simply logs in to the domain over the connection. While traveling, the laptop is stolen at the airport and winds up in the hands of an opportunistic hacker. The hacker uses commonly available password-patching tools to gain local access to the laptop and discovers that it is automatically connecting to a remote network via IPSec. This provides the hacker remote access to the private network, so he uses network-scanning tools to "sniff out" the structure of the network. He then finds a client computer and runs a network-based password-guessing program over the course of a few days to guess the password of the user who lost the laptop.

When user authentication is combined with machine authentication at the security gateway, this attack is not possible because access to the private network is not granted unless both the machine and the user are authenticated.

The bias against IPSec as a client-to-gateway technology is somewhat esoteric, because it can encapsulate secure authentication methods like Kerberos to provide user authentication. When an IPSec tunnel is established between a client system and an IPSec gateway, and then a secure authentication protocol like Kerberos is used for secure authentication of the user at the client station, security remains intact. While a gap between machine authentication and user authentication exists that could technically be exploited, this level of security is sufficient for most business purposes. I've used IPSec for client-to-gateway authentication since shortly after its availability in this mode, and I've found it to be both more reliable and more secure than PPTP.

Microsoft recommends using L2TP/IPSec for client-to-gateway authentication.

Tunnel Mode   In a normal routed connection, a host transmits an IP packet to its default gateway, which forwards the packet until it reaches the default gateway of the receiver, which then transmits it to the end host. All computers in the connection must be in the same public address space.

In IP over IP, or IP/IP, the default gateway (or another router down the line) receives the packet and notices that its route for that packet specifies an IP/IP tunnel, so it establishes a TCP/IP connection to the remote gateway. Using that connection, the gateway transmits all of the originating host's IP traffic inside that connection rather than forwarding it.

IP/IP is useful for virtual networking, so that private IP addresses (in the 192.168.0.0 range, for example) can be passed over the public Internet.

IPSec implements both IP/IP and IPSec/IP. IP/IP provides a nonencrypted virtual tunnel between two end-systems (which can use AH to guarantee authenticity), and IPSec/IP uses ESP to encrypt the payload of the carrier IP, thus encrypting the entire encapsulated IP packet.

Internet Key Exchange   IPSec uses public key cryptography to encrypt data between end-systems. In order to establish an IPSec connection to a receiving host, the transmitting host must know that host's public key. Technically, the transmitter could simply ask the host for a public key, but that doesn't provide authentication—any host could ask for the key and get it. This is how SSL works; the identity of the machine is not important, and SSL relies upon some other protocol to authenticate the user once the tunnel is established. That's fine for public Web sites, but IPSec was designed from the outset to perform host authentication through knowledge of appropriate keys.

NOTE   IPSec is defined by RFCs 2401 through 2409, along with numerous other RFCs that describe supporting protocols.

IPSec uses the concept of *Security Associations (SA)* to create named combinations of keys and policy use to protect information for a specific function. The policy may indicate a specific user, host IP address, or network address to be authenticated or to specify the route for information to take.

In early IPSec systems, public keys for each SA were manually installed via file transfer or by actually typing them in. For each SA, each machine's public key had to be installed on the reciprocal machine. As the number of SAs a host required increased, the burden of manually keying machines became seriously problematic; because of this, IPSec was used primarily only for point-to-point systems.

Internet Key Exchange (IKE) obviates the necessity to manually key systems. IKE uses secret key security to validate their authority to create an IPSec connection and to securely exchange public keys. IKE is also capable of negotiating a compatible set of encryption protocols with the foreign host, so that administrators don't have to know exactly which encryption protocols are supported on the opposite host. Once the public keys are exchanged and the encryption protocols are negotiated, an SA is automatically created on both hosts, and normal IPSec communications can be established. With IKE, each computer that needs to communicate via IPSec needs only to be keyed with a single secret key. That key can be used to create an IPSec connection to any other IPSec host that has the same secret key.

> ***TIP*** In Windows 2000, you can configure IPSec policies to use Kerberos to auto-matically exchange secret keys for IKE. This eliminates the need for manual key-ing and allows for completely automatic secure encryption between members of the same Active Directory in Windows 2000 networks.

The IKE initiator begins an IKE request by sending a plain-text connection request to the remote host. The remote host generates a random number, keeps a copy, and sends a copy back to the initiator. The initiator encrypts its secret key using the random number and sends it to the remote host. The remote host decrypts the secret key using its kept random number and compares the private key to its secret key (or list of keys, called a *keyring*). If the secret key does not match, the remote host will drop the connection. If it does match, the remote host will encrypt its public key using the secret key and transmit it back to the initiator. The initiator then uses the public key to establish an IPSec session with the remote host. Figure 6.5 illustrates this process.

Figure 6.5   Internet Key Exchange uses private key security to simplify IPSec keying.

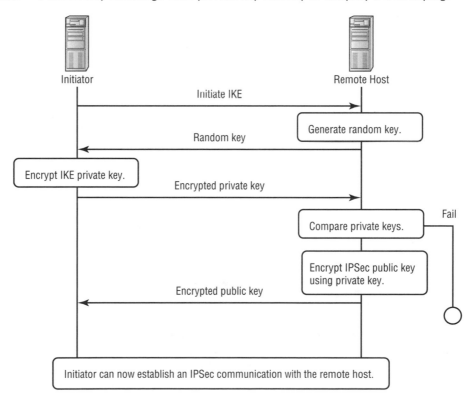

Like nearly everything in Windows 2000, IPSec configurations are managed by creating a policy. For IPSec, you create a different policy for each receiving computer that has unique IPSec requirements. Destination networks, computers, and tunnel endpoints are specified by IP address. For each IPSec policy, you can define the exact encryption protocols used by the policy and the keying method used for IKE.

In Windows 2000, you manage IPSec through the Security Manager snap-in, which is embedded in the Active Directory Users and Computers snap-in (see Figure 6.6).

TIP Use the ipsecmon utility to monitor IPSec traffic to and from your server. From the Start menu, select Run and type **ipsecmon** to start this utility.

Figure 6.6 Manage IPSec policy using the Security Manager.

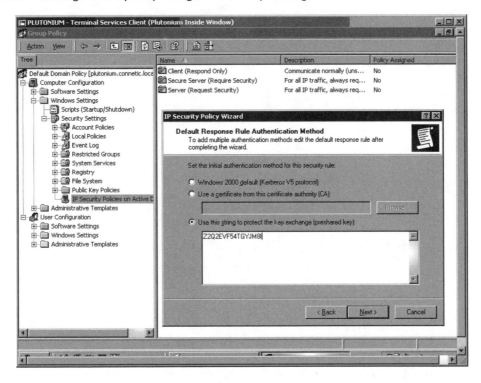

Problems with Windows 2000's IPSec Implementation Microsoft's implementation of IPSec is incomplete because IPSec standards are still emerging. The practical implication of this is that Windows 2000's implementation of IPSec is not compatible with the implementations of most firewall vendors by default. In every case I've tested, I can't configure

IPSec in Windows 2000 to connect to an IPSec-compatible firewall without installing some sort of IPSec client software.

Although Windows 2000 IPSec supports tunnel mode, it disables that support when a dynamic IP address is detected, thus forcing users to use L2TP for remote access to corporate VPNs. If you want to connect a Windows 2000 computer to a third-party firewall IPSec implementation that does not support L2P2, the computer must have a fixed IP address.

Windows 2000 in Depth

PART 1

TIP   Microsoft Knowledge Base article Q252735 describes the mechanism for establishing an IPSec tunnel-mode connection between gateways. Knowledge Base article Q259335 describes basic L2TP/IPSec troubleshooting tactics and has links to numerous other IPSec-related articles.

Windows 2000 automatically disables IPSec communications when transmitting data to Windows 9*x* or NT computers—even when an administrator may think there's an IPSec communication in place and that the communication is secure. It would be far more secure to disallow communication unless an express policy allowing the unencrypted communication was in place. Security features should never be automatically, invisibly disabled by the operating system.

L2TP

The Layer 2 Tunneling Protocol is an extension to the Point-to-Point Protocol (PPP) that allows the separation of the data-link endpoint and the network access point. In traditional PPP, a user (typically a dial-up user) establishes a PPP connection with a remote access server. That server answers the data-link layer connection (modem call) and also serves as a network access point by removing the data encapsulated in the PPP message and forwarding it on the destination network. The encapsulated data might be an Apple-Talk frame, IP packet, IPX packet, NetBIOS packet, or any other network layer packet.

NOTE   In this section, I use the generic term *remote access server* to refer to any L2TP-compatible remote access server, which could be a UNIX computer, a Windows 2000 computer, or a dedicated remote access appliance. In Windows 2000, this service is called RRAS.

L2TP separates the call-answering from the network access routing. With L2TP, a caller can call a modem bank (or DSL Access Module, or whatever), and that equipment can simply encapsulate the received L2TP packets into Frame Relay, ATM, or TCP/IP packets for further transport to a remote access server. Upon reaching the remote access server, the LT2P packets are unwrapped and their payload is forwarded onto the local network.

L2TP is designed to allow for less-expensive ISP equipment by separating the remote access server functions into a hardware function (physically receiving the connection) and a software function (gating the encapsulated PPP data) that can be performed on separate machines. This has a number of important benefits:

- Users can dial a local modem bank that will forward L2TP to a distant remote access server, thus avoiding long distance charges for direct-dial remote access.

- L2TP payloads can be encrypted using IPSec to provide secure authenticated remote access.

- Multilink L2TP sessions can be physically answered by different receivers and correctly bonded on a single remote access server. With current PPP multilinks, all the channels must be connected to the same remote access server.

L2TP can use IPSec to encrypt PPP frames, thus providing what amounts to a secure PPP session for remote users. L2TP was specifically designed to provide remote user authentication and connection to remote networks. Because L2TP is an extension of PPP, any network layer protocol (such as IPX, NetBEUI, or AppleTalk) can be embedded inside L2TP. In contrast, PPTP and IPSec are both specific to IP networks and do not function with other protocols. The use of PPP also provides support for all of the standard user authentication protocols, including CHAP, MS-CHAP, and EAP.

L2TP uses UDP rather than TCP/IP as its data transport because the embedded PPP protocol can provide the necessary guarantee of reliability for the stream. L2TP operates over UDP port 1701.

Microsoft considers L2TP to be the ideal user authentication mechanism for completing the strong security requirements of remote access users. Because L2TP provides secure user authentication and then uses IPSec to provide machine authentication, it allows remote users to connect without the authentication gap that would occur if user authentication is separated from secure tunnel establishment.

PPTP

PPTP was Microsoft's first attempt at secure remote access for network users. Essentially, PPTP creates an encrypted PPP session between TCP/IP hosts. Unlike L2TP, PPTP operates only over TCP/IP; L2TP can operate over any packet transport, including Frame Relay and ATM. PPTP does not use IPSec to encrypt packets; rather, it uses a hash of the user's Windows 2000 password to create a private key between the client and the remote server that (in the 128-bit encrypted version) is salted with a random number to increase the encryption strength.

L2TP is the successor to PPTP—it is more generalized in that it works over any packet transport, and its encryption strength is far stronger thanks to IPSec encryption. PPTP should be used for legacy compatibility, but new installations should favor L2TP for secure remote access.

Summary

Security is the effort taken to prevent the loss or disclosure of information in a network. Because you can't absolutely eliminate the possibility of loss in useful systems, a certain amount of risk is necessary, and your system's security is fundamentally based on providing access only to trusted security principals (users or computers).

To control security, any system must

- Control access
- Identify users
- Restrict or permit access
- Record user activity
- Communicate privately between systems
- Minimize the risk of misconfiguration

Encryption, the process of obfuscating a message using a mathematical algorithm (cipher) and a secret value (key) known only to the legitimate participants, is the foundation of all modern computer security. Encryption can be used to prove the identity of a user or computer, to validate data, or to hide the contents of a data store or communication stream.

Windows 2000 security is based on user authentication. By logging in to Windows 2000, users prove their identity in order to gain access to files, programs, and shared data on servers. Windows 2000 uses a pervasive security model that attaches the user's identity to every action they perform on the computer, rather than providing wide access to the computer once a successful logon has occurred.

For an operating system to be trusted, it must be able to ensure that it has not become compromised and that information can be kept secure from users. Windows 2000 uses NTFS file system permissions to control access to files, including the files Windows 2000 boots from. Permission can be granted to users and to groups of users for each file system function. Files can also be encrypted on disk to ensure that they cannot be accessed, even when the computer is not running.

Windows 2000 network security is managed using the Active Directory as a repository for Kerberos password hashes, Group Policy, and IPSec policy. Active Directory defines the relationship among security principals as well.

Windows 2000 uses Kerberos to validate user identity over the network. Kerberos is a trusted third-party security system. Because both endpoints in a communication trust and are trusted by the Kerberos server, they trust one another. Kerberos servers can trust other Kerberos servers, so transitive trust relationships can be created allowing endpoints from widely separated networks to establish authenticated communication sessions. Kerberos is integrated with Active Directory (all domain controllers are Kerberos Key Distribution Centers), and participation in the same domain tree automatically creates transitive two-way trust relationships.

Group policies are used to define the security requirements and configuration of computers and user accounts in the domain, site, or Organizational Unit. You can use group policies to control nearly every element of user and computer security. You manage group policies through the Active Directory Users and Computers snap-in or through the Active Directory Sites and Services snap-in.

IPSec is the Internet standard for proving the authenticity of IP packets and for encrypting the data payload of IP packets. IPSec works with many different security algorithms and can operate in the normal transport mode or tunnel mode to simulate a private circuit over a public network like the Internet.

Case Study: Windows 2000 VPNs

A client of mine needed secure remote access to their Windows 2000 network for users working in the field with Windows 2000 laptops. Their network was secured by a Sonicwall firewall, which included strong support for IPSec VPN. However, the client software for this device costs about $100 per user. Because my client had a number of users, we decided to try implementing a VPN solution that wouldn't require additional licensing.

As I studied the Microsoft implementation details, I became increasingly discouraged about the project. The major problem was that the client used network address translation inside their network to provide a large enough IP space for all their computers. This usage is very common; every one of my clients uses NAT.

Unfortunately, Windows 2000's implementation of L2TP/IPSec is not compatible with NAT because NAT can't open IPSec-encrypted TCP headers to rewrite address information.

So I decided to look at ESP tunnel-mode pure IPSec connections from the clients that could be connected to the firewall. I then ran into the problem that Windows 2000 only allows tunnel-mode IPSec communications between computers with fixed IP addresses, and the remote clients all had DHCP-assigned addresses from their various ISPs.

We were not willing to expose their server to the Internet by placing it in front of the network-address-translating firewall. After all, it contained all their data, and it was why we needed a firewall in the first place. It looked like we would have to use the firewall's IPSec client software for Windows 2000 due to these mutual incompatibilities.

Then I remembered that the firewall supported a DMZ: a separately firewalled network with a public IP address range that filtered packets but did not translate them. So I configured the DMZ to block all external traffic except IP protocols 50 (ESP) and 51 (AH) and opened UDP port 500 (ISAKMP) to allow L2TP/IPSec traffic through the DMZ. I then put a test Windows 2000 server in the DMZ and configured it to allow L2TP connections.

This worked. Clients from the field were able to establish L2TP connections to the test server. I then tested clients from inside the network to determine if they were able to reach the test server for normal client LAN file access. They were, but connections were slower than they had been because all the internal network traffic flowed through the NAT firewall. The connection speed would be a real problem for actual network access, so moving the actual server into the DMZ was not an acceptable solution.

I then created a static mapping between the server's interior address and an address that the test machine inside the DMZ could reach. This allowed the test machine to connect to the server inside the firewall.

At this point, we had an architecture that allowed external clients to connect securely to a gateway machine in the DMZ, which could then route to the server inside the network. It seemed to me to be a good solution, because it kept connections encrypted until they were inside the building but did not put any burden on interior users.

My client thought differently, however. The cost of installing an additional permanent server (and Windows 2000 Server license)

to solve the problem (the test server belonged to me) was considerably more than the cost of the firewall's IPSec client. They decided to go with the firewall's IPSec client, which connected clients directly to the firewall and allowed them unlimited access to the interior network.

7

Routing and Remote Access

Windows 2000 includes the Routing and Remote Access Service (RRAS), which performs many diverse functions:

- Participates as routers in TCP/IP and IPX networks (routing)
- Provides for the sharing of a single IP address amongst a workgroup (network address translation or NAT, also called Connection Sharing)
- Answers inbound dial-up networking connections from modems, ISDN adapters, and X.25 or Frame Relay
- Functions as an encrypted tunnel end-point (Virtual Private Networking, or VPN)
- Automatically initiates dial-up connections to connect to the Internet or private networks as necessary (dial on demand, also called demand dialing)

For Microsoft, it made good sense to bundle these functions into a single service (with a few ancillary services) to optimize speed. If you think about it, beyond the modem control function, all of these services involve the manipulation of network packets. It wouldn't make sense to roll all this functionality into a network protocol because RRAS can handle multiple packet types (TCP/IP and IPX).

My recommendations in this chapter, however, may seem somewhat deprecating of RRAS. In most cases, it's not good networking practice to use the functions of RRAS on a general-purpose server. Here's why:

- Dedicated routers are best for performing the routing function, if for no other reason than that they rarely crash, so portions of your network don't disappear when servers go down. Routers are far faster, don't suffer from accidental reconfiguration, and are usually obsolete before they fail for the first time. Windows 2000 is still quite a ways from that level of reliability.

- The function of answering inbound dial-up networking calls is usually best handled by a dial-up ISP. They provide a national presence that eliminates phone toll charges, they already have the expensive hardware, and they're capable of answering at 56Kbps, whereas the best you'll do with a modem is 33.6Kbps. Your modem may be able to connect to an ISP at 56Kbps, but it cannot answer a connection from another modem at speeds higher than 33.6Kbps. The V.90 specification requires a pure digital circuit connection on the answering end to achieve speeds above 33.6Kbps. Simply put, analog lines on both ends of the connection introduce too much noise for 56Kbps connections.

- Remote tunneling is best performed by dedicated firewalls. Microsoft's PPTP protocol "leaks" a lot of information in unencrypted headers, it's subject to seemingly random failure, and it's comparatively slow. Dedicated firewalls are fast, built-to-purpose, and have recently become very inexpensive—VPN firewalls can now be had for less than $1,000. The Windows 2000 Server software will cost you that much.

- Network address translation is best handled by dedicated firewalls or simple "NAT routers" that don't pretend to be firewalls. They are faster and more secure, and they correctly manage the difficult protocols such as H.323, FTP, and other multimedia protocols.

In single-server small networks, RRAS can provide great functionality as a collateral duty on a production server—except for the security danger of connecting production servers directly to the Internet or allowing dial-in without going through a firewall. If you can tolerate the risk, then by all means use RRAS, but if your security posture is in the normal-to-strict range, don't even consider installing RRAS on a multipurpose server.

In essence, RRAS is an awesome service, but low-cost dedicated devices or common services can provide all of its functions more reliably and with a lower cost of ownership. This makes RRAS functionally obsolete, except in somewhat rare circumstances such as the case study presented at the end of this chapter. So with that somewhat windy caveat, here's all the stuff about RRAS that you probably won't need to know.

Configuring RRAS

You can configure RRAS most easily with the RRAS Configuration Wizard, available from the Action menu of the RRAS MMC snap-in. You'll encounter the Configuration Wizard when you first run the RRAS snap-in in Windows 2000 Server. Windows 2000 Professional does not have an RRAS snap-in; its limited RRAS functionality is controlled through the Network Interface Control Panel.

As Figure 7.1 shows, The RRAS Configuration Wizard has five options.

Figure 7.1   The RRAS Configuration Wizard has five primary options.

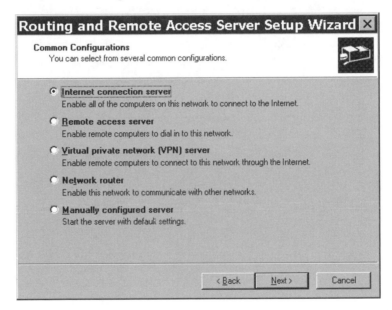

Internet Connection Server   Configures your server to provide transparent network address translation to downstream clients.

Remote Access Server   Configures your server to provide dial-in remote access capability to remote dial-up networking (DUN) users. It also configures your server for five PPTP and five L2TP encrypted tunnel end-points. You aren't limited to 256 ports with RRAS like you were in Windows NT, so add ports to your heart's content.

Virtual Private Networking (VPN) Server   Configures the RRAS server to handle 128 PPTP and 128 L2TP encrypted tunnel end-points. It also configures the DHCP Relay to provide additional client information (such as domain name) to VPN clients, configures the IGMP proxy, and sets up filters on the Internet connection to accept only PPTP and L2TP connections.

Network Router   Configures your server to route TCP/IP and IPX packets. You must manually configure routing protocols such as RIP, NAT, and OSPF after the Wizard has completed.

Manually Configured Server   Allows you to configure any mix of the above options. This option is basically a combination of the network router and remote access settings.

Each of these options is fairly obvious if you understand the underlying technology, and the Windows 2000 online help can guide you through the configuration process.

Configuring RRAS in Windows 2000 Professional

According to Microsoft, RRAS doesn't come with Windows 2000 Professional. According to my Services Control Panel, it does. But the RRAS service in Windows 2000 Professional is limited to providing three inbound remote access connections and to providing the connection-sharing (NAT) and demand-dialing functions.

Accepting in-bound modem connections   To create a network connection that can accept inbound connection attempts, use the Create New Connection Wizard in the Network Connections Control Panel. In the first dialog box, select the Accept Incoming Connections option and then complete the Wizard as you would for any other DUN connection. Inbound connections are assigned addresses in the 169.254.0.0 range.

Sharing network connections   To enable the automatic NAT feature of Windows 2000 Professional called Connection Sharing, right-click the networking connection you wish to share in the Network Connections Control Panel (this works with any type of network connection, not just dial-up connections), and select Properties. Select the Sharing tab, and check the Enable Connection Sharing for This Connection option. You can also enable demand dialing by checking the On-Demand Dialing option, and you can set up protocol filters by clicking the Advanced button and selecting the Services tab.

Establishing demand dialing   You can specify that a DUN connection should be connected automatically by checking the Connect Automatically setting in the dial-up networking Properties window. This provides a similar demand dialing functionality to that of Windows 2000 when you use Connection Sharing.

RRAS Protocols

The RRAS service actually implements a dizzying array of standard TCP/IP protocols. Since these protocols are part of RRAS, you can't individually install or remove them, but you can determine whether or not they function with your RRAS configuration. RRAS directly implements the following routing protocols:

- RRIP
- OSPF
- NAT

RIP and OPSF are discussed in detail in Chapter 4. Network address translation is discussed in the next section.

> **NOTE**   As of Windows 2000 Service Pack 0, the H.323 (NetMeeting and others) protocol NAT editor only allows a single client in the translated range to flow through the NAT. Microsoft has committed to fixing this problem in a future service pack.

RRAS implements the following security-related protocols:

- PPTP
- L2TP
- Extensible Authentication Protocol

These protocols are detailed in Chapter 6.

Network Address Translation

Network address translation (NAT) converts private IP addresses in your private network to globally unique, public IP addresses for use on the Internet. Although NAT was originally implemented as a hack to create more IP addresses for private networks, it has a serendipitous security aspect that is just as important: internal host hiding.

Network address translation effectively hides all TCP/IP-level information about your internal hosts from hackers on the Internet. NAT makes all your traffic appear to come from a single IP address and allows use of any IP address range you want on your internal network, even if those addresses are already in use elsewhere on the Internet. This means you don't have to register a large block from InterNIC or reassign network numbers from those you simply plugged in before you connected your network to the Internet.

NAT hides internal IP addresses by converting all internal host addresses to the address of the RRAS server as packets are routed through it. The RRAS server then retransmits the data payload of the internal host from its own address, using a translation table to keep track of which ports on the exterior interface map to which ports on the interior interface. When an exterior host sends data back to the RRAS server on the interior host's port, the RRAS server performs the reverse translation. If no entry exists in the translation table for the port addressed or if the IP address of the source is different from the address the RRAS server expects to see, then the packet is dropped. To the Internet, all the traffic on your network appears to be coming from one extremely busy computer.

NOTE RFC 1631 describes network address translation.

NAT is actually a fundamental proxy: a single host makes requests on behalf of all internal hosts, thus hiding their identity from the public network.

RRAS is implemented in two ways in Windows 2000: as a routing protocol that you can configure in the Routing and Remote Access Console (NAT is actually the easiest routing protocol to configure, since it requires virtually no configuration) and as Internet Connection Sharing, which can be configured on any network interface through the Network and Dial-Up Connections Control Panel.

RRAS Support Protocols

RRAS implements a few protocols natively that aren't related to networking or security. These protocols are:

DNS Proxy Forwards DNS requests from DUN clients through the RRAS service to a DNS server. The DNS Proxy service can interfere with normal DNS service, so you'll want to disable it if you're also running DNS service on your RRAS server.

DHCP Proxy Allows RRAS routing servers to forward DHCP requests and responses across the networks they connect. The DHCP Proxy service includes its own address in the relayed DHCP request along with clients so that the DHCP server will know which scope to use for the client's IP address assignment.

IGMP (Internet Group Multicast Protocol) Proxy Allows a single host to "broadcast" IP packets to multiple hosts defined by an IP address. Hosts can join and leave the multicast group at will. IGMP operates much like UDP in that hosts are not guaranteed to receive all data packets, and the packets are not guaranteed to arrive in order. IGMP is most suited to data types that can withstand loss, such as streaming audio or video. The IGMP Proxy service allows Windows 2000 RRAS servers to forward IGMP packets from the Internet to their interior networks.

Bandwidth Allocation Protocol (BAP) This is an extension to the multilink capabilities built into Windows NT Server 4. BAP allows a multilink RRAS server to add and remove channels from an existing link to facilitate additional demand or to reduce line charges. BAP only functions correctly between machines that support it, so it's currently exclusive to connections between Windows 2000 machines.

Remote Access

RRAS can solve three problems in private networks:

- Connecting the network to the Internet
- Connecting remote dial-up users to the network
- Connecting remote Internet users to the network

Of these three problems, connecting to the Internet is better done with direct routing. Connecting remote dial-up users is usually done better by ISPs because you don't have to pay toll charges, you don't have to buy remote access equipment, and you don't have to make any special provisions for dial-up users in your security planning—they connect the same way any other user from the Internet would connect: through an encrypted tunnel. And connecting remote Internet users, while very effective, is often more easily and securely managed using tunneling software for your firewall.

The best RRAS practice is not to use it. I make this recommendation after having set up and supported numerous RRAS networks for clients. RRAS accounts for fully 50 percent of the administrative burden in smaller networks, and it allows for a number of different security attacks against your network. RRAS is a complex administrative hassle, and its functionality for private networks is increasingly obsolete in the face of ubiquitous Internet access. The Internet is the only remote access technology you need. With encryption, its security can be better than that of direct-dial or frame-routed point-to-point options.

Using RRAS with PPTP to establish encrypted tunnels over the Internet is still an excellent idea, but it is easy to do incorrectly. It also exposes a network secured only by a password to attack from the Internet. However, in combination with a strong firewall policy, you can limit the range of hosts from which you will accept PPTP connections. Consider using an encryption key-based secure tunneling solution provided with your firewall rather than RRAS and PPTP to support remote connections.

Connecting to the Internet with RRAS

The remote access functionality of RRAS allows you to connect point-to-point dial-up networking devices such as serial links, X.25 or Frame Relay connections, analog modems, and point-to-point tunnels to your Windows 2000 computer. A dial-up networking device is any device capable of establishing a real or virtual communication circuit on demand. This is inherently different than permanent circuits established over unchanging fixed circuits or network links because the software must be able to handle both the establishment of the connection and the possibility that it may suddenly disappear. Analog modems, ISDN, and X.25 devices all establish circuits on demand. Frame Relay uses permanently established virtual circuits to create a constantly connected path, but since it's often done using X.25 links, it's frequently handled as a remote access device.

RRAS integrates with networking software by acting as a virtual network adapter for the connection—it provides an NDIS-compliant wrapper for point-to-point network devices that lack drivers, such as a direct serial link or a modem. RRAS also adds a layer of security and management for these connections to allow you to control how these connections are used. Finally, RRAS handles the connection and disconnection inherent in demand-dialed devices such as modems, X.25, and ISDN.

Connecting to the Internet with a dial-up connection, such as ISDN or a modem, requires using the temporary connectivity features of RRAS in either a permanently connected manner or with automatic session establishment (demand dialing) whenever connectivity is required.

Demand Dialing

Demand dialing automatically connects to the remote network whenever data is requested from the local computer or from any computers that are sharing the dial-up connection. Demand dialing is simple: whenever data needs to flow through the port, the auto-connection manager service dials the dial-up networking connection to provide the link.

In order to eliminate frequent dialing for "chatty" network protocols, spurious broadcasts, or protocol requests that simply aren't that important, RRAS implements demand-dialing filters, which are set up to "ignore" protocols such as name request broadcasts, ARP requests, ICMP echo requests, and so forth. Essentially, the filters wait until they receive a request on "user-initiated protocols" such as HTTP, SMTP, POP3, and FTP. These protocols all indicate that the user has made a specific request, rather than that the system is simply performing some background work. Demand-dialing filters eliminate the unnecessary and seemingly random dialing that plagued the first version of the Remote Access Service for Windows NT 4.

Problems with RRAS Connections to the Net

Temporary Internet connections suffer from a number of problems that make them less than optimal for attaching an entire network. These problems are:

- Low speed
- Single IP address
- Dynamic IP address assignment
- Temporary connections

All RRAS devices are fairly low speed. ISDN tops the pack at 128Kbps, which, although fast enough for a single computer, is far too slow to share among three or more simultaneous users. Higher-speed devices are all permanently connected to the Internet.

Most ISPs provide only a single dynamic IP address for dial-up accounts, so you can only use a dial-up account to connect a single computer to the Internet. However, you can use a firewall to perform network address translation or a proxy to "reshare" protocols of this single server. Windows 2000 supports NAT natively through the NAT routing protocol in Windows 2000 Server and through the Internet Connection Sharing functionality of Windows 2000 Professional.

Most ISPs also provide a different IP address for dial-up accounts each time you connect to the Internet, which means that even private services like PPTP can't be shared easily over the Internet, because clients won't know which IP address to attach to.

Since a demand-dialed account is not constantly connected to the Internet, you cannot use it to provide services such as HTTP or FTP; nor is it appropriate for SMTP, which assumes that mail servers are always available for e-mail delivery. Demand dialing is appropriate only for sharing Web connections in very small networks that will rely upon the ISP to handle Web or mail service.

Routing to the Internet

Routing to the Internet is, by far, the most common and efficient method to connect business networks. Routing to the Internet is generally installed and set up by your ISP. You usually don't need to do anything but attach your network to the Ethernet port on your ISP's Internet router located at your site.

The data-link technology used to connect to your ISP should be invisible to you, but the following technologies are commonly used for this purpose:

X.25/DS0/Frame Relay   Appropriate for slower connection speeds (56Kbps) in areas where more advanced technologies are not available. Modems now approach the speed of Frame Relay connections and usually cost less, so consider using two bonded modem (or multilink) connections instead of 56K Frame Relay.

Integrated Services Digital Network (ISDN)   Appropriate for slower connection speeds (128Kbps) in areas where ISDN is cheap and more advanced technologies are not available. ISDN is a dial-up connectivity technology that is not especially well-suited for permanent connections, but it is often used where low-cost Digital Subscriber Line (DSL) service is not yet available.

T1/DS1/Frame Relay   Appropriate for medium speed (1.5Mbps) connectivity, this is the most common method used to connect businesses to the Internet. T1 connectivity is available everywhere, but special circuit lines and equipment make T1 fairly high in cost.

T3/DS3   Appropriate for high-speed networks (45Mbps) of very large companies, universities, and ISPs.

Digital Subscriber Line (DSL)   Appropriate for medium- to high-speed access (144Kbps to 6Mbps), depending upon loop length and other local factors. DSL is the lowest-cost medium-speed transport.

Broadband cable modem   Smaller businesses located near residential areas may be able to take advantage of the broadband Internet services of the local cable TV provider. Typically, the business-grade services offered by cable TV providers are shared among fewer users so that each has a higher overall bandwidth. If it's available, broadband cable modem is likely to be the least expensive option.

Satellite   Satellite Internet access is a newer option provided primarily by the DirectPC service of Hughes Electronics. DirectPC is related to DSS Satellite television, using the same network of satellites to provide the service. With DirectPC, downloads occur over the satellite link, and uploads occur over a normal modem-based phone line. Obviously, the modem is not capable of providing any high-capacity services, but it is sufficient for uploading e-mail and sending out Web requests. The download service is available in 400Kbps and 2400Kbps, which is enough for any small business with light upload traffic. Satellite service can be provided anywhere in the continental United States, so it's especially compelling for rural areas where other high-speed options are not available.

Alternative access   Includes (currently) rare options such as local proprietary high-speed optical fiber providers over transports such as FDDI (Fiber Distributed Data Interface), ATM (asynchronous transfer mode), and SONET (Synchronous Optical Network). These options vary too widely in their availability, speed, and cost to make general statements about, but they are generally priced to compete against higher-speed telephony options such as T1 and T3.

In any case, a dedicated device will usually route your connection to Ethernet or Fast Ethernet for final connectivity to your network. Otherwise, you'll have to install a proprietary and rare network adapter in your server to connect directly to the ISP's network, which should be avoided.

WARNING   Rare devices suffer from poor driver support, problems with operating system upgrades, and migration problems when new technology emerges. Stay with common mass-market equipment as much as possible.

Firewalls and Remote Access

Whether your network is connected directly to the Internet or through RRAS, you should use a firewall to manage Internet access and to keep the hacking millions at bay. Modern firewalls also support interoperation with encrypted tunnel software. In this case, the encrypted tunnel client software is installed on remote clients, and the firewall serves as the tunnel end-point in the network. This makes remote networking simple and easy (assuming the firewall software is easy to use) and fairly secure (depending on the specific package used). You should consider using the IPSec-based remote tunneling software built into your firewall rather than the PPTP or L2TP protocols of Windows 2000.

Remote Client Access with RRAS

The primary purpose of remote access is to allow remote DUN clients to connect to a Windows 2000 network. This was very important when Remote Access Service was first released, because the Internet was not common or universally available. Now that it is, the importance of RRAS is greatly diminished.

Many network administrators are reluctant to use Internet tunneling because they assume that dial-up networking is more secure than encrypted tunnels over the Internet. This is not the case. With a proper firewall policy, Internet-based remote access can be just as secure as dial-up remote access, which itself introduces a vector of attack into your network. As recently as 1997, dial-up networking still accounted for more than half of all network attacks.

RRAS with X.25, ISDN, or Frame Relay

Don't use RRAS to manage X.25, ISDN, or Frame Relay connections. These connectivity options are very rare, which means there's not a lot of troubleshooting support out there, and even the technicians trained to set them up have problems getting them working.

Instead use dedicated routers designed to connect Ethernet to X.25, ISDN, or Frame Relay networks. By using a router to connect to these data links, the connection is constantly maintained, and you have just another Ethernet segment to attach to your server. You can eliminate the RRAS service entirely in this case. The dedicated hardware to support these functions is fairly inexpensive—between $500 and $5,000, depending upon the data-link technology in use. You'll save far more than that by eliminating the hassle and downtime that you'll inevitably have if you manage these more esoteric connections with RRAS.

Better yet, don't use X.25, ISDN, or Frame Relay at all except to connect directly to your higher-level ISP—and in that case, let your ISP manage the connectivity equipment and connection. These days, DSL is a better choice than any of the three previously mentioned options. It's faster, increasingly available, and costs less.

RRAS with Modems

Whether you should use RRAS with regular modems depends on your requirements. If you are an Internet service provider, consider using RRAS with modems. If you aren't, avoid RRAS with modems.

Why? Again, RRAS is a difficult administrative problem. Even correctly operating RRAS installations are subject to frequent failure. More importantly, you can use the Internet to solve the problem more easily and with less equipment.

Supporting even a few RRAS connections on the RRAS server requires considerable equipment: a modem to match each dial-in modem, a serial port for each modem, and some method to connect the serial ports to the server (either additional serial port internal hardware cards, terminal servers, or Ethernet tunnels). This equipment costs an average of $200 per port.

Using the Internet and a good firewall or the IPSec features of Windows 2000, you can eliminate all of that hardware and use your existing routed connection to the Internet as an endpoint for all RRAS communications. Remote users with modems simply need to dial in to an ISP (at $20 per month) for connectivity on their end. This solution costs the same no matter what distance exists between the remote user and the server—no long distance or local toll charges will apply.

The only case where this method doesn't make sense is when you have a small number of users (less than five) who will dial in from within the telephone toll-free area around the server. Because your users are too close to incur any toll charges, the monthly ISP access charge may be excessive. This use is actually fairly rare.

RRAS for Virtual Private Networking

RRAS is most appropriate for use with PPTP or L2TP. Even though PPTP adds a layer of complexity to RRAS, it eliminates one of the most common causes of failure: special connectivity hardware such as modems, X.25 PADs, and ISDN routers. RRAS with PPTP is a software-only solution to remote connectivity.

Because RRAS with PPTP operates over your existing Internet connection, it requires no additional hardware to implement, which provides considerable cost savings. Although you must pay monthly for ISP connections for remote users, the cost is small and it provides other useful benefits, such as Web and e-mail access. Most remote users will already have these connections anyway.

Using PPTP with RRAS rather than answering dial-up connections directly allows you to automatically support all types of client connectivity. For example, if you have one remote user with a modem and another remote user using ISDN, you'd need both types of equipment on your RRAS server to support both customers. By using the Internet and PPTP, you push equipment support problems to the ISP, which simplifies your network. PPTP also future-proofs your network, because any new method of connecting to the Internet is automatically supported for connecting to your network without any additional equipment. For example, you'll be able to support Cellular Digital Packet Data (CDPD) connections from newer wireless ISP cards for roaming users.

Troubleshooting Dial-Up

Because dial-up networking is so complex, I decided to put its troubleshooting section in this chapter instead of in the more general troubleshooting chapter. RRAS is easy to install but can be very difficult to get working correctly.

Troubleshoot dial-up problems from the bottom up, tackling simpler problems, such as connectivity, before more complex problems, such as protocol establishment. Use this same procedure whenever you have a problem with RRAS, because higher-level problems can be caused by a number of different lower-level failures.

Separate the dial-up networking client and RRAS server and determine which machine is actually having the problem. This is generally pretty easy—if only one remote client can't connect, it's a client problem. If no clients can connect, it's a server problem. If some clients can connect but others can't, find out what's different between the clients and troubleshoot that difference on the server.

To ensure a working dial-up connection, verify the following:

1. The computer can communicate with the modem.
2. The modem can communicate with other modems.
3. RRAS can communicate correctly with the modem.
4. RRAS can communicate with DUN on a remote computer.
5. PPTP or L2TP can establish a session with PPTP or L2TP on a remote computer.
6. The transport protocols are communicating correctly.
7. Dial-in permissions are set correctly.
8. User account information is correct.
9. User permissions are set correctly.
10. Network browsing and DNS are operating correctly.
11. Network routing is operating correctly.

These elements of RRAS troubleshooting are detailed in the following sections.

Can the Computer Communicate with the Modem?

Although this seems rather basic, the inability of the computer to communicate with the modem is frequently the source of remote access problems—especially for a server that has worked with remote access before a hardware upgrade.

Check computer-to-modem connectivity by verifying that the serial port works correctly using the following method:

1. Stop the RRAS service and any other service that might lock down the serial port (such as fax services).

2. Open the Device Manager, select the modem in question, and select Properties.

3. Select the Diagnostics tab, and click the Query Modem button. If the modem fails to respond, one of the following problems has occurred:

   - The modem is not attached to the serial port.
   - The modem is malfunctioning.
   - The port is misconfigured or malfunctioning.

Assuming you're addressing the right serial port and don't have a cable problem, the most likely problem is that the serial port IRQ and port don't match the hardware settings in the BIOS for the port. Try deleting the ports in the Device Manager and then restarting the computer. Upon reboot, enter the BIOS and ensure that the port is enabled and set to the correct IRQ and port. Make sure no other peripherals are set to use the same IRQ. Sound cards and network adapters are frequently assigned to the same IRQs as serial ports. You may need to set your BIOS to reassign Plug and Play IRQ levels by moving a PCI adapter from one slot to another.

When the computer boots to Windows 2000, check to make sure that the port appears and that its IRQ and port settings are correct. Try using the port again.

Can the Modem Communicate with Other Modems?

Once you've ensured that you can communicate with the modem, use HyperTerminal to ensure that you can establish communications with another modem. Use the ATDT 555-1212 command (replacing the phone number with the phone number of a modem known to you) to establish a connection. If the connection goes all the way through, the modem will report the connection speed, thus verifying that the modem is working correctly. You can hang up at this point, because the modem's ability to connect has been verified.

Is the RRAS Service Configured Correctly?

RRAS must be configured to dial out on the machine establishing the connection and must be configured for dial-in on the machine accepting the connection. If you use dial-back security, both machines must be configured correctly to support it.

Check the network settings for each computer and make sure that the computers are both properly set to support dial-in and dial-out sessions.

Each RRAS dial-out port requires a separate memory pool, so you may find yourself running out of memory if you have too many RRAS ports configured to dial out. Since there's usually no reason to have more than one dial-out RRAS connection from a server, set all of your RRAS ports to dial in except one. Dial-in RRAS ports share a common memory pool.

Can RRAS Communicate with RRAS on a Remote Computer?

Establishing a remote access connection with a remote RRAS computer is the next step. If you get an error message stating that a common protocol could not be established or that the user account or password was incorrect, then you've proven that RRAS is communicating correctly between computers.

If you intend to support non-Microsoft PPP clients (such as Macintoshes or UNIX computers), be sure to allow any authentication including clear-text. Third-party clients will not work with Windows 2000 Challenge/Response Authentication.

If you get to this point but still get error messages stating that a connection could not be established, test the connection using the same model modem on both ends. In rare cases, modems by different manufacturers will not communicate correctly or at the highest possible speed.

Are the Transport Protocols Communicating Correctly?

If you get an error message stating that no common protocol could be negotiated or that the protocol you want to use could not be negotiated, make sure the remote client and RRAS server support the same transport protocols.

Although the RRAS Configuration Wizard automatically sets up installed protocols, you may need to use the RRAS snap-in to configure protocols installed after installing RRAS, and you may need to specify the routing behavior of the protocol.

TCP/IP remote access ports require a method to assign IP addresses to remote hosts. DHCP is the most easily managed method to do this. Remember to create a scope in the DHCP Manager specifically for remote access clients. You may also use a static address pool for client IP address assignment if you haven't installed DHCP on your remote access server. This feature operates like a mini-DHCP server using the DHCP protocol. If you use static assignment, be sure to allow a pool that is one address larger than the number of remote access ports, because RRAS always uses the first available address as the TCP/IP address of the RRAS adapter.

DHCP can provide all sorts of configuration information to remote access clients using DHCP options. Be sure you've set up DHCP to provide domain name and host name information to remote access clients.

Can PPTP Establish a Session with PPTP on a Remote Computer?

You may get one of the following error messages if your server is set to only accept 128-bit encrypted connections and the client supports only 40-bit security:

- RRAS could not negotiate a compatible set of protocols.
- The remote computer does not support the required encryption type.
- The PPP control protocol for this network protocol is not available on the server.

This error is also likely after the application of a service pack or the installation of the Routing and Remote Access Service update from Microsoft. Reapply the High Encryption Pack on the client and the server to correct this problem.

Is the User Account Information Correct?

The user account provided when dialing into RRAS is used only to check for dial-in permissions as set in the RRAS snap-in. The account provided must have specific dial-in permissions set in the RRAS snap-in to allow that account to dial in. Make sure that the correct user account exists on the remote access server or in the Active Directory and that it has dial-in permissions.

Domain security is a different matter. Once a connection has been established through RRAS, the local logged-on account information is used to check security permissions. This means that if you use different account information on the remote client, you may have network problems on the remote access server. There are two ways around this:

- Join the remote client to the domain and log in locally using a domain account.
- Create a local account with the same name and password as the domain account. This name and password will be passed through the remote access server for security on the remote domain.

These problems show up as typical user access or logon failures and should be fairly easy to troubleshoot.

User permissions through RRAS connections are slightly more complex because it's not always obvious which account is being used to grant permissions on the domain—it could be a domain account or a user account on the remote client, depending upon how you logged on.

Are RRAS Policies Applied Correctly?

For a user to complete a dial-up connection to an RRAS server, their user account must have dial-in permissions set in the Dial-In tab of their user Properties window in the Active Directory Users and Groups Console (see Figure 7.2). In addition, a Remote Access Policy must describe the conditions under which that user is allowed to connect, and those conditions must be met. In any other case, dial-in permission will be denied.

Figure 7.2   Set dial-in permissions in the user's Properties window.

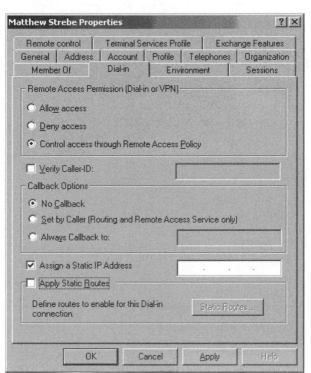

The following user account settings can be configured in the Active Directory Users and Groups snap-in on a per-user basis:

Remote Access Permission (Dial-In or VPN)   Allows this client to access the RRAS server remotely.

Verify Caller ID   Restricts a user to dial in only from a certain location. This prevents hackers from exploiting your dial-up server.

Callback Options   Allow the user to specify their number for callback or allow the network administrator to specify a fixed callback number. This prevents hacking and reverses the connection charge for long-distance dial-in.

Assign a Static IP Address   Allows users to receive the same IP address each time they dial in.

Apply Static Routes   Is an esoteric option mostly for the user accounts used by demand-dialing servers from branch offices.

> **NOTE** Many settings are grayed out in the Dial-In tab if the domain is running in Mixed Mode. Upgrade your domain to Native Mode in order to enable permission control through RRAS policies.

Remote Access Policies allow administrators to define the conditions under which dial-in users will be granted access to the network on a per-group basis. Policies can control numerous connection conditions, such as the days and times access will be granted, the types of connections (dial-up or VPN) that can be made, and the duration of connections.

When you install RRAS, a default policy allowing access to all users—if their user account allows access—is created. You should always test against this permissive policy to make sure you've got everything working before you begin creating more restrictive policies.

If you have users who can connect to the RRAS server but are not allowed to connect, review the conditions that apply to that user. If you can't tell exactly what's going on, consider removing RRAS policies and reapplying the default permissive policy. If the user still can't log in, it's not an RRAS policy problem.

Once the user can log in correctly with the default RRAS policy, you can create and apply more restrictive policies. Be sure to test your policies each time you add a new condition to make certain the policies behave the way you expect them to.

For complete information on creating and applying RRAS policies, refer to the online Windows help for Routing and Remote Access that is available from the RRAS snap-in.

Is Routing Operating Correctly?

If you can connect directly to the RRAS computer but cannot connect through it to other computers on the network, check the routing information for the protocol you're using in the RRAS console. Make sure RRAS is set to forward data through the RRAS server, and make sure that routing is enabled. If you've used the RRAS Remote Access Server configuration option, this should be set automatically.

Is Name Resolution Operating Correctly?

In Active Directory networks, make sure that DNS settings are correct and that DHCP is configured to send them to remote access clients. Once DNS is working correctly, locating domain resources through an RRAS connection should not be a problem.

For workgroups, if you can establish remote RRAS connections but cannot browse the Network Neighborhood of the remote network, set the workstation and domain properties of the remote client to match the network. If this doesn't work, use the Find

Computer option in the Start menu to search for the remote machine. Browsing often fails to function correctly over RRAS connections. Consider setting important host names in the LMHOSTS file if finding named resources is a consistent problem—although I've seen cases where this doesn't work either. Consult Microsoft's Knowledge Base online at support.microsoft.com for specific solutions to specific browsing problems.

The NetBIOS name of the connecting remote client must be unique on the network—conflicting names can cause all sorts of bizarre connectivity problems. Make sure remote clients have unique NetBIOS names.

If you're using RRAS to connect two distant offices on the same domain, make sure both remote access servers are also set up as WINS servers and are configured to replicate the WINS database correctly. This will make finding NetBIOS resources on the remote network quite a bit easier.

Summary

The Routing and Remote Access Service of Windows 2000 provides the following functions:

Network protocol routing for TCP/IP and IPX   Allows separate networks to transmit data amongst each other, and is required for dedicated connections to the Internet and other private networks.

On-demand establishment of dial-up networking connections   Allows small businesses and branch offices to utilize standard telephone lines or dial-up ISDN to "simulate" a constant connection. Demand dialing offers seamless and transparent connectivity to the Internet or private networks whenever it's needed.

Answering dial-up networking connections   Allows remote users to dial in to the network using modems from their home computers. Dial-up networking provides a least-common denominator for ubiquitous access from anywhere in the world utilizing the public switched telephone network.

Virtual Private Networking   Keeps network connections private by encrypting the contents of the stream. Windows 2000 provides two connection-oriented methods: PPTP, which works only with TCP/IP, and L2TP, which is capable of subsuming other protocols.

Network address translation   Shares a single IP address or small range of addresses amongst a much larger pool of private clients by using TCP port information to map internal client IP addresses to public services.

The functionality of RRAS is increasingly obsolete in the face of low-cost, dedicated devices that perform the same functions and the low cost of dial-up services provided by Internet service providers. However, in some uncommon circumstances, RRAS is the only good solution, and in those cases, it truly shines.

Case Study: RRAS to the Rescue

A "dot-com" client of mine had a very difficult problem: they needed to offer access to their Web site at trade shows using laptops. Marketing to an otherwise noncomputerized industry, they participated in numerous trade shows around the country that simply didn't have any sort of network wiring—no ISDN, no DSL, no cable modem, and certainly no T1 or Frame Relay links. At the time, wireless public access options did not exist that worked inside a building, so we were basically stuck: plain old-fashioned modems were the only solution. Of course, trying to demonstrate a Web site over a snail-slow modem connection would be unacceptable, but there seemed to be no options.

I knew we could use the multilink capabilities of RRAS to "bond" separate modem channels together into a single Internet connection, and I decided that this was really the only feasible solution. Figure 7.3 shows a network diagram of this solution.

The first step was to put together an RRAS server at their headquarters that would answer in-bound calls from the trade shows. We installed two PCI multitech 8-port multimodem adapters in the server, giving it 16 dial-in ports, and connected those to 16 standard phone lines. These lines were set up with a toll-free number on a "hunt-group" so they would all be reachable from the same number; the phone company simply "hunted" for the first non-busy line when a call came in. We configured the RRAS server to allow simple authentication and open routing since the server didn't contain any important data and was otherwise outside their firewall. We wanted to make the remote setup for the sales team as simple as possible because none of them had any real computer background. Hackers would only be able to steal free dial-up access if they came across the phone number, and with strong monitoring that wouldn't be a problem.

Figure 7.3 Using multilink and an RRAS server to create a single, high-speed network connection

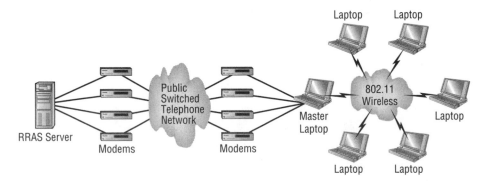

On the client end, we configured a "master" laptop with a quad-port serial PCMCIA adapter and four external modems (USB modems weren't quite as reliable in our testing as the tried-and-true serial modems). Four modems connecting back to the Web server in parallel using multilink provided connection speeds of 134.4Kbps—faster than the basic ISDN rate and nearly as fast as iDSL. To create a network of laptops, we also installed a PCMCIA wireless adapter that operated in the 2.4GHz band with a 1Mbps throughput rating and enabled Connection Sharing on that port.

The ultimate clients were simply laptops with wireless network cards. These computers connected to the Internet over the wireless network and through the master laptop. The wireless adapters allowed us to vary the number of client laptops depending upon the size of the show—often, we had eight laptops all running simultaneously in the trade show booths.

With 10 minutes of "prebrowsing" on the laptops to load bitmaps into cache, the Web speeds on the clients seemed as good as a T1 connection. Although we could have simply dedicated a modem to each laptop (as all the competitors did), we would not have gotten the high apparent speed. With the number of laptops we were using, most network traffic was very "bursty"—hitting the network hard for a moment and then idling for quite some time. Windows 2000 RRAS with multilink and connection sharing allowed my client to blow away the competition under the same environmental conditions—and setup was much easier for the sales team, since only one laptop needed any kind of configuration.

Part 2

Windows 2000 Network Planning

Topics Covered:

- Fundamentals of network planning
- Choosing network technologies
- Estimating the client load on servers and networks
- Designing physical cabling
- Choosing a server deployment methodology
- Active Directory Design
- Creating effective Group Policy
- Selecting useful security policies
- Large Scale Windows 2000 deployment
- Differences between client and server deployment
- Software Testing
- Migrating to Windows 2000
- Upgrading to Windows 2000

8

Network Design

Network design has become fundamentally easy because the market forces that represent choices made by network integrators in the past now dominate the industry to such a degree that other choices are no longer really even possible. For example, you will be using Ethernet on your network, you will be running that Ethernet over UTP and in larger networks, optical fiber as well, and you will be using either Windows 2000 or UNIX to provide all of your high-level networking services in new installations. Varying from these market-leading technologies will cost far more to provide the same level of network service, so it should only be done in rare cases where requirements are unique.

Not everything has become this simplified, however, and there are still numerous choices to make. This chapter presents a unified methodology for determining how to subdivide your internetwork into networks and subnetworks, how to lay out premises wiring and data-link equipment, and how to choose where you want to locate servers. Chapter 9 goes into depth on the software services you'll use on top of the physical infrastructure that this chapter will help you build.

This chapter details the following aspects of building or overhauling a network:

- Planning fundamentals
- Network design
- Selection of core technologies
- Estimation of network requirements

- Physical plant design
- Data-link and network protocol design
- Service design

Planning Fundamentals

Planning is a critical component of successful networking that is often ignored. Any effort to create a new system requires the following:

- A budget to constrain choices
- A goal to achieve
- A plan to achieve the goal within budget constraints

These fundamentals don't have the appeal (well, for us geeks anyway) of the more technical work to follow, but any attempt to start building a network without first laying this groundwork will only achieve its goals by accident.

Small networks will require proportionally less planning than large networks. In fact, if you've designed small networks in the past, you may not need to do any specific planning work at all.

Budgeting

The budget is the overwhelming constraint on your network. In the face of an unlimited budget, there's little need for design; you could simply buy the largest and fastest of everything, connect it all, and be done. Unfortunately, unlimited budgets are not common.

Budgeting changes considerably from organization, and no two organizations are in exactly the same financial position. Chances are, you already have an idea of which general category your budget position fits into: constricted, normal, or nearly unrestricted. These categories depend largely on your organization's overall financial strength and the importance of the network to your organization.

The best way to request a budget is to design what you would like to build under ideal financial circumstances. Create categories of equipment and software based on functional goals; for instance, one category might be the components that support dial-in remote access. Determine the overall price of the network and request that budget. After your finance people recover from the shock, you will at least have prepared them for what it will cost to get at least a working network. You'll be ready to scale down your requirements to meet your financial reality by eliminating specific categories of goals that are less important.

Total Cost of Ownership

Total cost of ownership (TCO) is financial jargon for the complete cost of a resource (like a network) throughout its entire useful life. Calculating the TCO for a resource is theoretically simple and is described by the following formula:

	Initial Cost
+	Maintenance Cost
−	Sale Value
=	Total Cost of Ownership

Installation cost is straightforward: determine the cost of the equipment and services necessary to install the network, and you're done. Sale value is also easy for computer and network equipment: assume you'll use everything until it breaks or is completely worthless, so just plug in a zero. Since you'll assume that every piece of networking hardware and software will be worthless in five years, assume that you'll bear the installation cost at least once every five years. Anything that lasts longer is a bonus.

Maintenance cost is the big unknown. It includes:

- Salaries of network staff (this usually includes you)
- Consultants
- Outsourcing services (ISP, communication charges, etc.)
- Replacement hardware (estimate 20 percent of the initial cost per year, 100 percent in five years)

The industry rule of thumb for estimating the maintenance costs for medium to large networks is six times the initial purchase price of the network per year. Smaller networks fare better; two to four times the purchase price is considered normal. Your estimates should be between three and six times the initial purchase price per year.

Because of the enormous recurring cost of maintaining a network, you should make maintenance cost your primary consideration when purchasing equipment. Time is money. Save both by choosing equipment and technologies that are easy to support and not likely to fail.

How do you estimate the maintenance cost of a network component? There's no standard method. Some components, like routers, seem to last forever and require no care. Others, like servers, often seem to require constant attention and intervention. The following sections will give you a sense of what to look for in hardware and software. They are all variations on the same theme: stick to the mass-market, low-priced equipment by avoiding small niche-market products and custom solutions.

WARNING   Be suspicious of any product that touts, as its primary advantage, a "lower total cost of ownership." Remember that the TCO for that product and the TCOs of its competitors in the ad you're reading were calculated by the manufacturer's marketing department. It's basically an admission that the initial purchase price is way higher than the competition and there's no other significant feature to talk about.

Choose Software That Is Easy to Install and Maintain   Ease of use is the mantra of low total cost of ownership. This is what makes Windows 2000 such a stellar performer compared to NetWare and UNIX, and why Macintoshes are still less expensive to own than similar Windows machines. Because most maintenance costs are tied directly to the payment of humans for their time, easy-to-use devices cost less.

Maintenance cost is what makes the TCO for Windows 2000 far lower than Linux, for example. Maintaining Linux requires consultants or specialized staff due to its cryptic UNIX command-line interface and its difficult installation and customization, whereas nontechnical clerical staff can be trained to maintain Windows 2000 servers in small networks.

Avoid Applications That Require Programming or Specialized Configuration   This includes GroupWare packages (such as Lotus Notes, GroupWise, and Exchange Server), highly customizable database applications (such as PeopleSoft), and any other sort of database application. The custom development required by these applications makes sense for only the very largest businesses—those with a billion dollars in sales or more—or for businesses where the passing of information forms the foundation of the business, so its handling is crucial. Even then, it's common in the development industry to present the best-case budget when competing for a job. The honest and meticulous consultant will always present a higher bid cost than less honest consultants, and therefore lose the consulting contract—so those willing to underestimate the costs always win in a typical lowest bidder selection. Cost overruns are typical for this reason, and most development efforts cost more than your entire network infrastructure combined.

Most standard business problems can be fulfilled by existing applications. I know it's heresy to make this suggestion, but if you have any control over operations, you should consider modifying your business practices to fit software rather than modifying software to fit your business practices. It's far easier to train people than to develop applications, and you'll probably find that the way you work now is less efficient than the way a mass-market application makes you work.

Try to plan for standard technologies like Internet e-mail, Web sites, and Usenet newsgroups rather than expensive GroupWare. These standard technologies are far easier to customize and have a much larger group of competing consultants, which drives down consulting prices. Of course, your business may actually require customized applications, but always scrutinize the need strongly; push for simpler technologies whenever possible. Remember: Everything will be obsolete in five years. Will you even be done customizing by then?

If you must use a customized GroupWare application, define your requirements closely and stick to those things you actually must have—don't waste effort adding frivolous features that only a few people will actually use. Once you have a detailed requirements document, create a list of test conditions that will satisfy the requirements (for example, "Edited document must be automatically forwarded to production department upon completion," and so forth). These test conditions explain quite clearly to everyone involved what the system must be able to do when it's finished and leave little room for "that's an extra feature at extra cost" haggling when the consultant wants to deliver incomplete software.

The requirements and test condition documents will form your request for quotes in your search for consultants. Make certain all candidates understand that the bid is a fixed price and that they must be able to complete the test conditions at the price they return. You don't have to be pushed into paying for cost overruns if the consultant has agreed in writing to a specific price.

Don't select the low-bid consulting group. Select the consulting group with the longest list of satisfied customers who has shown that they can develop a system according to a limited budget.

Reality Check: Notes from the Front

I was actually hired to arbitrate a disagreement between a customer of mine and their Lotus Notes developer. Both parties were to blame for the shoddy manner in which work proceeded.

The company gave a vague requirement to the consultant: "We want a work-flow system." The consultant, with no understanding of their business, returned a very encouraging price: $50,000. So they entered into a contract to develop the system. The developer returned an initial product that did little more than e-mail; users could pass information among themselves. They also installed a Domino e-mail server to integrate this system with the Internet.

The company demanded "more work" and gave the consultant many new requirements: the system should automatically forward certain messages to various groups of people and should be capable of storing a "knowledge base" of IT resources. The consultant performed the work and presented another bill: $200,000.

I was called in as a sort of expert witness to help the arbitrator determine how much, if any, additional money should be paid to the developer. Rather than stick the customer with an incomplete hodgepodge of functions and stick the consultant with six months of work without pay, I encouraged the arbitrator to recommend that the company perform a complete design specification for the system they wanted with the help of the consultant. The consultant would then complete that design at the lowest possible rate so long as the customer paid the current bill.

Upon completion, the customer had a very functional work-flow system that cost them $500,000 — 10 times the originally estimated price.

Never, Ever, Ever Develop Custom Software   Software development is an arcane art that is best left to large software publishers. Unless you are a software development house, you'll throw so much money at a custom software development effort that you'll probably lose your job before it's finished. It takes so long to develop applications that they're usually obsolete before they're finished. And even in the best case, the software quality is always lower than a mass-produced application. Think of software like a vehicle. Would you even consider building your own car? Of course you wouldn't. You shop for what's available and chose the model that comes closest to meeting your needs. Treat software the same way. Look at the software market and select the existing application that comes closest to meeting your needs. Then modify your existing practices to match the software.

There's nothing wrong with configuring or modifying existing software packages to tailor them to your environment—I wholeheartedly recommend that course of action. For example, creating templates for office documents, using macros to automate common tasks, and modifying menus to make them more useful are a normal part of software configuration.

The difference always comes down to development effort: if you can't complete your customizations in three man-months, you should take a serious look at whether or not it makes sense to outsource the problem.

Use Rapid Application Development Tools   If you absolutely have to develop your own software, use Rapid Application Development (RAD) tools. The idea is not to reinvent the wheel. If you feel you must develop software, use the tools that make it as quick and easy as possible. For example, there's no faster way to put together a database front end than with Microsoft Access or similar products, such as Alpha 5. Use these visual tools rather than developing a custom front end in C++. If you outsource programming, always negotiate a firm, fixed price up front and pay based on the achievement of easily identifiable milestones. Never get into a situation where you pay on a time basis for software, because the more time it takes, the more your developer gets from you, so your software will never be finished.

Avoid Specialized Hardware (and Software)   If you can't buy it off the shelf at a local computer store, think twice about purchasing it. Get your servers from a major national vendor (such as Dell, Compaq, or Gateway) that can provide replacements in a day or two. Avoid hardware that is so esoteric that it's hard to find, such as the machines mentioned below. Avoid the temptation to demand customized computers that will be difficult to replace. Of course, nobody sells routers and bridges in town, so you'll have to order that equipment specially. Don't feel like you have to order everything from a single vendor, though—I've never seen a case where one vendor competes well in the market for all the components of a network.

Forget using esoteric hardware such as Digital Alphas, Sun Ultras, and other high-end workstation and server hardware. Nowadays these machines are not much faster than standard Intel-based computers, they cost far more than their slight advantage justifies, and there's no easy way to repair them when they break. Because of their limited sales, consulting costs are high.

Avoid the Temptation to Build Your Own Computers and Servers   We all do it on occasion, and sure, you can get exactly what you want, but it takes more time than it's worth, the resulting computer has no system warranty, and it doesn't come bundled with any software. By the time you add up the costs of the individual hardware components, the operating system, and the installed applications, you'll find that a national direct marketer such as Dell is extremely competitive.

Existing Conditions

If you're lucky enough to be starting from scratch with your network, you're in the enviable minority. Most networks are born from at least an installed base of individual computers and office applications, which means that the network is handled less as an installation than a migration.

Existing conditions often will precipitate certain requirements (for example, to support specific applications, platforms, or work methodologies). Survey your organization to determine the following information:

How many computers are in use?   The answer will determine the size of your network, the number of servers you will need, and the quantity and type of data-link equipment you will require.

What types of computers are being used?   This answer will define the network operating system you should use, the transport protocols you can use, and some of the services you will need.

What special types of computing equipment, such as printers, are in use?   This step will identify additional special equipment, such as print servers, that might be required.

What contracted services, such as Internet or private wide area network connections, are in use?   This step will further isolate which network operating system you should use, as well as help you identify any third-party software that might be required.

What software is currently being used?   Some network-ready software will operate only under certain network operating systems. If your network is using this type of software, your choice of network operating systems may be limited.

Will existing local area subnetworks have to be integrated into the new network?   These existing networks will have to be compatible with the network you install, or they will have to be migrated to technologies that are compatible.

Performing an initial conditions survey isn't as hard as you'd think—it just takes leg work. The first step is a physical inventory. Identify each piece of IT hardware and determine how it's connected to the next piece. The result of this survey is a physical map that shows each piece of hardware and every physical connection. Using this map, determine the configuration of each piece of equipment.

Configuration is defined as the difference between the initial or default state of the machine and its current state. For bridges, routers, switches, print servers, and other dedicated devices, this usually consists merely of some IP setup information. For computers and servers, it consists of too much information to bother recording all of it, so record only the networking information and those services that the computer provides—services that can be accessed from the network.

By the time you're done with the device configuration survey, you'll know exactly what your network's current conditions are, and you can begin defining your goals for the upgrade.

Goals

When starting a network installation contract, I ask clients why they want a network. The answer to this question gives me the information I need to start planning for applications, services, and desktop requirements.

It always amazes me how many respond by saying that they don't know or that everyone else has one, so they must need one, too. Neither are good reasons to install a network, but answers like that really indicate that many people simply don't know what a network can do for their business.

If they don't know themselves, you must determine what the network needs to do by interviewing the people who will be using it and who will be responsible for it. Common goals include:

- E-mail
- Web access
- Sharing files and printers
- Group scheduling
- Work-flow management
- Customer support resources
- A Web site
- E-business

On Site: Interviewing Clients

Here are a few questions I ask clients about their networks in the planning phase:

- About how many computers will be attached to the network?
- What is more important: security or ease of use?
- Do you want to use the Internet? How (Web site, e-mail, e-commerce, etc.)?
- Will you be retaining a consultant, hiring employees, or maintaining the network with existing staff?
- What are your budget limitations?
- Will you be connecting to remote offices?
- Are there any specific applications you know you want to use?

Determining Your Requirements

Networks are the platform for providing shared computer-based services. So to determine your requirements, you simply need to determine which shared services you need, what platforms those services need to be compatible with, and how many users you need to support.

Forget about specific components such as Windows 2000, Cisco routers, Lotus Notes, and Compaq servers while you define your requirements—get down to basic services and general applications. You may find that your preconceived notions about what you thought you needed go by the wayside when you let your requirements guide you. Never let a salesperson define your requirements for you—the resulting system will only be ideal for their cash flow. Use the following questions as a guideline for developing your own requirements:

Compatibility   Is the network supposed to replace any existing systems? If so, you'll need to plan for migration from one platform to the other, which usually means that both platforms have to be available during some transition phase. Software to interface to or emulate existing systems is one of your network's requirements.

Applications   Is there a database to support? Are there specialized applications such as planning packages for materials requirements? Is GroupWare required? Will you need to host a Web site or e-mail?

Users   How many users will get networked computers? This number provides the magnitude of your network and will ultimately decide both your architecture and budget. Are there remote users, and if so, what is the ratio of local to remote users?

Connectivity   Will you need to connect to distant offices? How about the Internet for e-mail and Web service?

Platforms   What platforms need to be supported? Windows machines, DOS clients, Macintoshes, UNIX machines, and perhaps terminals attached to minicomputers are all clients you might expect to support. Esoteric clients may need special software or emulators to connect to the network—expect substantial additional cost in that case.

Services   What basic network services are required? File sharing is usually a must, as is print sharing. But what about shared faxing? Paging? Computer telephony?

Security   Does the business have proprietary secrets to protect? How about government contracts? Security will affect your choice of software and constrain your ability to provide or access some services.

Once you've got all your requirements down on paper, try to assess a vague cost for each one: expensive, valuable, inexpensive, easy, and so forth. Assign a numerical priority to all the goals from most important to least important. This will help you determine what to axe when your budget can't support it all.

Now that you've got your requirements down on paper, you'll have to do a bit of research to determine exactly what networked resources are required to fulfill your goals. I discuss specific methods for quantifying hardware resources in the following section.

Visualizing the Plan

Now that you've got your goals on paper, you'll need to create a network plan. Without getting into any specifics just yet, you should consider using a visual design tool such as Visio to help you plan.

By visually laying out servers and clients, you'll be forced to think deeply about the connectivity of each client, which will help you quantify all the necessary hardware and software to complete your network. Figure 8.1 shows a network laid out with Visio.

When finished, you'll have a diagram that can precisely explain your intentions to hired contractors and consultants, leaving little room for misunderstandings. You'll also have a handy check-off list to track progress and a source for documenting the system as it is installed. Once the network is finished, you'll have a map to your network that anyone can use to locate resources during troubleshooting.

Some of these software design tools are capable of connecting directly to inventory databases, which is a great way to make sure your maps are up-to-date and consistent with reality.

Finally, you can use your design schema as a data source for systems like HP OpenView and CA UniCenter, which are both great tools for keeping track of large networks.

Building a network from scratch can be a daunting task, even for experienced administrators. But there's no need to reinvent the wheel—network integrators have been building networks of all sizes for a decade. You can draw from their experience to design and build a network of any size.

Network Design

Network design can be approached methodically. Design a network in the following order:

1. Select core technologies.
2. Estimate network requirements.
3. Map the physical plant.
4. Plan the network connectivity.
5. Specify service and resource provisions.
6. Plan a network management scheme.

Figure 8.1 A network diagram created in Visio

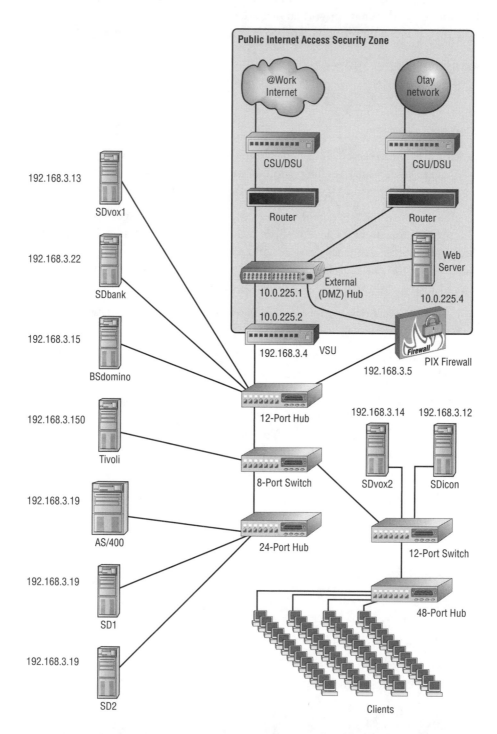

These design elements are approached on three scales, distinguished by the speed and distance at which the network must operate. By handling each scale of networking somewhat independently, the complete network design is broken down into manageable tasks. The three scales are as follows:

Subnetwork   A single LAN of usually 2 to 100 clients. Subnetworks are defined by the fact that all computers communicate on the same medium and can therefore address each other directly without going through a bridge or a switch. Subnetworks are also called *collision domains* in Ethernet and *rings* in Token Ring.

Network   Usually a network of 100 to 1,000 clients. Networks are defined by the requirement for data-link bridging between individual media, and that network broadcasts are forwarded to all participating computers. The key identifying aspect of a network is that all computers are within the same TCP/IP subnet. (Don't get confused here: an Ethernet network forms a single IP subnet because all computers in the network can communicate directly at the data-link layer.)

Internetwork   Usually networks of more than 1,000 clients that are defined by necessary routing between networks, which interrupts broadcast forwarding, so that some method of name resolution is required.

The following sections describe each of the scales in more detail. These scales are fluid—there's no reason, for example, that even a small network could not use routers for connectivity.

NOTE   Also bear in mind that the difference between subnetworks and networks is becoming completely arbitrary because of the use of Ethernet switches instead of hubs and broadcast media (such as coaxial cable). For the purposes of this discussion, subnetworks include the client computers and devices and the data-link devices (hubs or switches) that they're attached to. Networks then connect these workgroups together.

Subnetworks

Subnetworks operate as the data links between computers. A subnetwork consists of a single Ethernet, Token Ring, ARCnet, or FDDI Ring. The important characteristics of a subnetwork are that every device participating in the subnetwork can communicate directly with every other device and that the total bandwidth of the subnetwork is divided by the number of devices on the subnetwork, because only one device can transmit at a time. Subnetworks form the smallest accumulation of computers in your network, and they are physically limited by the distance that the link technology supports—100 meters for Ethernet over twisted-pair, for example. In order to create networks larger than the physical distance limitations of the network media, bridging or routing must be used to create networks or internetworks.

Networks

Networks are formed by bridging or switching more than one subnetwork together. *Bridges* are hardware devices that physically connect two subnetworks. When a computer on one subnetwork sends a packet to a computer on the foreign subnetwork, the bridge receives and retransmits that packet on to the foreign subnetwork. You can think of a bridge as a person standing in the doorway between two rooms, relaying bits of the conversations in each room to the other. *Broadcast packets* reach all recipients on the network. Broadcasts are used to locate computers on the network, to announce participation and network names, and for other protocol purposes such as transmitting error messages. In networks of more than about 2,000 computers, broadcasts consume far too much bandwidth, making it difficult for computers to transmit useful traffic. For this reason networks must be split and reconnected into internetworks.

Bridges rely upon the addressing mechanism of the data-link layer to distinguish between computers. Since the addressing mechanisms are different between different shared media types, bridges are only able to connect like subnetworks together. Because bridges can only connect like subnetworks (Ethernets to Ethernets, Token Rings to Token Rings), the entire network can consist of only one subnetwork type. For example, an Ethernet client cannot directly address a Token Ring client through any type of device, because their addressing schemes are not compatible. That function requires a higher-level protocol with a secondary addressing scheme such as IPX or TCP/IP. However, one protocol can be used to encapsulate packets of another protocol type and forward them between two similar networks. This sort of functionality is called *protocol encapsulation.*

Switches are multi-network bridges. A switch can simultaneously participate in many subnetworks and switch frames between them as necessary. Switches are easy to use and require little or no setup, but they are rarely ideal—in more complex networks they tend to retransmit more information than is actually required. However, switches have become so inexpensive that many companies now use them instead of hubs, which tends to improve network speed by eliminating collisions.

Internetworks

These are networks connected together by routers, which operate at the network layer and are therefore free from the constraint that only like networks can be connected. Routers can be used to connect any type of network together: Ethernets to Token Rings, leased lines to Asynchronous Transfer Mode (ATM) networks. For this reason, routing is generally more popular than bridging and is often used to connect subnetworks together directly. Routers are also less expensive than enterprise switches, and servers can perform double duty as routers if you are on a constricted budget.

Routers do require some manual configuration when they're installed and a very solid understanding of the protocols being routed (usually TCP/IP). For that reason, they may have a higher initial capital investment than switches, and they usually require more maintenance. Expanding a network may require revisiting all the routers in an enterprise if automatic routing update protocols such as RIP or OSPF are not in use throughout the network.

Selecting Core Technologies

Selecting the various technologies you'll use before you make specific design decisions is crucial, because each element of network design is too closely tied to the others to independently make these decisions. It's extremely difficult to design a physical plant without knowing which data-link technology you'll be using, for example.

The following sections present pragmatic solutions for each of the elements of design rather than exhausting the list of available options, because the market has made most of these decisions for you. Varying from these solutions is expensive, and you should only do so when requirements clearly call for an alternative solution.

Physical Plant

Physical plant decisions are easy right now: install the highest-grade unshielded twisted-pair (UTP) cable available for your subnetworks and connect the subnetworks together using optical fiber. Single-mode optical fiber is ideal, but multi-mode is acceptable for smaller networks and shorter distance runs (less than 2 kilometers).

These design choices are obvious because older physical plant technologies have all become obsolete due to the versatility and low cost of UTP. In the past, you had to select a data-link technology and then install the physical plant cabling mandated by that technology. This meant that premises wiring could not be installed when the building was originally constructed because the architect could not make network design decisions.

Because UTP is inexpensive and supports Ethernet, it has become the premises wiring of choice. Other data-link technologies have adapted to UTP, so that now all common shared-media data-link technologies can operate over UTP. UTP supports only two devices per link, so a cable must be run from a central location to each station location. Each of these cable runs is referred to as a *drop* in the industry, because the cable is typically run through ceilings and dropped down to the wall outlet for termination. The central locations are generally referred to as either *distribution frames* or *closets*.

Most UTP data-link technologies are designed to limit transmissions to 100 meters, so distances greater than that require a different cable type. You should consider using optical fiber links between subnetworks. Although it's possible to use coaxial cable to link closets, optical fiber is no more expensive than coaxial cable and allows much greater bandwidth and flexibility. Accordingly, all medium area network technologies run over optical fiber, including Ethernet, Fast Ethernet, FDDI, Gigabit Ethernet, and ATM.

Optical fiber to the desktop will eventually replace UTP as the cabling methodology of choice for two simple reasons: silica, the source material for optical fiber, is cheaper than copper, and optical fiber has vastly better data-transmission characteristics than copper wire. When economies of scale shift in favor of optical fiber, its significant bandwidth advantage will cause a sudden abandonment of copper wiring, and the recommendations I'm making now will sound as dated as a 19th-century textbook on electrical wiring. When this will happen is difficult to gauge, but we're probably still about 10 years away. At the moment, optical cabling is about twice the price of UTP cabling, and optical network devices are about 10 times the price of copper network devices.

Connectivity

Ethernet is the king of data-link technology. No other data-link technology is even remotely as inexpensive for the bandwidth, and there's no reason why any ever will be. Ethernet's simplicity makes it easy to work with, highly tolerant of faults (except when run over coaxial cable), and easy to design for. Ethernet is simple, cheap, and easy.

Ethernet comes in three speeds:

- Ethernet (10Mbps)
- Fast Ethernet (100Mbps)
- Gigabit Ethernet (1,000Mbps)

10Mbps Ethernet is considered obsolete for new installations but is still required for connecting to lower-speed devices, such as older computers, print servers, routers, and other network devices. Until 1996, 10Mbps Ethernet was the standard for connecting networks.

100Mbps Fast Ethernet is now the workhorse of networking. All your new designs should specify for connectivity to clients because it is vastly cheaper than its equivalent technologies and is highly reliable. 100Base-TX is the UTP variant; 100Base-FX is the optical fiber variant, which is useful for connecting closets less than 400 meters apart. Most 100Base-FX cards support a full-duplex mode that allows greater distance connections.

Beware the evil twin of Fast Ethernet: 100Base-VG AnyLAN. This technology is the mutant result of a number of silly compromises designed to make Ethernet incompatible with previous devices, harder to correctly install, and more expensive. Okay, granted that's not what the design specification called for, but that's what happened. 100Base-VG had some technically interesting ideas—guaranteed bandwidth (called *Demand Priority*), collision avoidance arbitration rather than collision-based arbitration, and other technical improvements—none of which were necessary and all of which added cost, complexity, and incompatibility. Fortunately, nobody bought 100Base-VG, so it's as expensive as all the other esoteric data-link technologies.

1,000Mbps (Gigabit) Ethernet is a point-to-point technology designed to link closets together over optical fiber while retaining protocol compatibility with standard Ethernet. 1,000Mbps Ethernet is not yet cost-effective for connecting directly to clients because the protocol is not shared, so clients cannot be connected together into shared media collision domains. I thought Gigabit Ethernet would remain expensive for some time, but adapters are already available at retail stores for less than $300 each. Because you can build routers and even switches out of standard PC hardware with just these devices, Gigabit Ethernet is already inexpensive enough to use as a standard data-link technology.

> **NOTE** A standards consortium has been announced for 10 Gigabit Ethernet, and some vendors have produced working prototypes. This technology should be available by 2002.

You will probably use other network technologies, such as Frame Relay or ATM, to connect to a wide area network. Your WAN service provider will mandate these decisions; you'll have to support whatever type of network they have. Usually, the service provider will suply a router to Ethernet that you simply connect to your network.

In rare cases, other data-link technologies such as FDDI might be more appropriate than Ethernet for network and backbone data links, but the extremely high cost of these options makes those cases rare. For example, FDDI would be a reasonable choice on a ship because of its automatic redundancy and its ability to route traffic on the counter-rotating ring in the event of damage. This functionality is worth paying for in extreme environments.

Network Protocols

Once you've selected your data link, decide which network protocols you will support on your network. There are four common network protocols:

- TCP/IP is by far the most common, and it is the protocol of the Internet and UNIX networking.
- IPX/SPX, developed by Novell, was the standard in local area networks until the Internet made TCP/IP more popular.

Windows 2000
Network Planning

PART 2

- NetBEUI is the original Microsoft/IBM LAN protocol for small workgroups.
- AppleTalk is required for file sharing among Macintosh computers.

Other less popular networking protocols exist, but they are so rare that they don't need to be discussed. The NetBEUI protocol in Windows 2000 cannot be routed, so it is not a true network protocol and not worthy of serious consideration in any but the smallest networks or as a troubleshooting protocol.

Nearly all routers support both TCP/IP and IPX/SPX, so choosing network protocols is mitigated by having only a few choices:

- TCP/IP is required for Internet access.
- IPX/SPX routes broadcasts, which can be problematic in large networks but makes name resolution much easier in small to medium networks. IPX/SPX is faster and easier to configure. However, Microsoft has deprecated support for IPX/SPX in Windows 2000 and recommends that all clients use TCP/IP.
- AppleTalk is required if you intend to support Macintoshes; otherwise it's not necessary.

That's all there is to it. Essentially, you should use TPC/IP. Windows 2000 still supports IPX/SPX, which is a much easier protocol to work with, but TCP/IP connectivity is so ubiquitous now that there's no compelling reason not to use it.

Service and Resource Provision

Service and resource provision describes the applications your network will provide and the servers required to provide them. Ask yourself why you are installing a network. Your answer will help you make appropriate service and resource decisions. For example, if you need a database, then you'll need a database server. That database server is a network resource. Common network resources include:

- File servers
- Network printers
- Web servers
- Firewalls
- Database servers
- E-mail/GroupWare servers

These service providers are a key element of your network and belong in your initial network designs. Why? Because they are the destinations for network traffic—the clients are all trying to communicate with these resources, so network traffic is shaped by their presence.

List each service provider in your network by the network operating system and applications it runs. If you have only vague ideas about which specific products you'll use to solve certain problems, stop and decide. Don't wait until after you have a network in place, because some service decisions can change the architecture of your network.

Network Management

Network management practices should also be finalized before starting on a network, because they often affect your decision to use specific equipment. The specific decision you need to make is whether you'll be using SNMP-managed devices.

SNMP-managed devices are connectivity hardware (hubs, routers, bridges, and switches) that have small computers built into them to respond to SNMP queries. Adding SNMP management typically adds about $500 per device.

I have never found SNMP to be worth the expense for troubleshooting or managing a network of 1,000 clients or less, but it becomes very useful for extremely large networks. Medium to small networks can certainly be easily managed without the automation provided by SNMP.

Enterprise management solutions such as CA UniCenter and HP OpenView can work with managed or nonmanaged devices, but they are most useful when used with managed devices.

Estimating Network Requirements

If you were going to build a warehouse to store engines, you could simply measure the size of each engine, determine how high you can stack them, quantify the maximum number of engines you'll ever need to store, add floor space for access, and build a warehouse of the exact size you need. Most architects would also add room for expansion. Another method would be to simply buy more space than you will ever need, but this approach obviously requires deep pockets.

Both techniques are used in networking, and, unfortunately, the second is more common. Many organizations waste a tremendous amount of money on hardware to guarantee that they will not have a capacity problem. In very small networks, buying more hardware than you need can actually make financial sense, because network architects may charge more to design a smaller network than the extra equipment costs. We will assume, however, that you intend to spend as little as you can to create a well-designed network.

The estimation method presented here is based upon the client load placed on two capacities: network and server. When you set out to design a network, the only information you bring with you is the scope of your problem as measured by a planned number of clients of each specific client type to support. A useful method to estimate network requirements must be able to take this information and answer these two important questions:

- How many servers will it take to serve these clients?
- How should the network be laid out to handle the load?

This method will help you answer both questions.

You will use this system both in the initial design stages to get an idea of how many servers will be required and later in the physical plant and service design stage to lay out network resources and locate servers physically.

Estimating Client Load

To estimate load capacities of networks, you need a system with which you can compare very different network technologies and relate them to client computer requirements, often without the benefit of knowing exactly how those client computers will be used.

Although no simple method will replace an experienced network integrator, a well-developed method can be useful for planning and estimating. A good working methodology will help you:

- Compare data-link technologies.
- Plan the network's physical layout.
- Predict the amount and type of hardware necessary to implement the network.

I've developed a simple method that will help you plan your network based upon the client load limit of various current data-link technologies. For example, a single 10Mbps Ethernet subnetwork can support a maximum of approximately 50 DOS clients. The same Ethernet subnetwork can serve 20 or so Windows NT workstations. These numbers provide the basis of a useful formula for estimating how many Ethernet collision domains you'll need, which in turn tells you how many hubs to buy, how many routers to connect them with, and so on.

Of course, these estimations are not absolute—the way the client is used will greatly affect its load on the network, and as technology changes, so will the load estimates for various clients. However, the law of averages comes to our aid by smoothing the usage characteristics of a single computer over the number of computers attached to the network. Unfortunately, averaging doesn't always work well. Consider the case of a diskless Windows computer that must boot its operating system from a network server. This client will usually demand far more from a network than a typical client because even its memory page file is being sent over the network.

You can use the method presented here if your operations conform to the common business uses of computers. If you are doing something you know will require more bandwidth, consider revising the client load values upward. I have presented worst-case capacities in this method, so resist the temptation to revise them downward.

Load Requirements of Typical Network Clients

The client load requirements shown in Table 8.1 were determined by dividing 100 by the maximum useful number of clients of that type that could operate on a single Ethernet segment.

Table 8.1   Load Requirements of Network Clients

Client	Metric	Explanation
Macintosh	1	Macintoshes usually require very little from a network, so I used a typical Macintosh client as the basis for the network formula.
DOS	2	MS-DOS machines tend to run simpler application software that does not demand much from a network.
Diskless DOS client	6	Diskless MS-DOS clients are much more demanding. These computers must use the network for every I/O command that would normally go to a local hard disk drive.
Windows 3.x	3	Windows is a more complex platform than MS-DOS, and applications built to run on Windows are more complex and network-aware.
Power Macintosh	3	Macintosh computers based on the PowerPC microprocessor are very fast. Although Macintoshes demand less from a network than most PC file-sharing schemes demand, these computers can hit the network pretty hard because of their speed.
Diskless Windows	9	Diskless Windows clients are extremely demanding of network bandwidth—more so than any other type of computer.
Windows 95, 98, or ME	4	Windows 9x is a powerful multitasking operating system that typically runs on fast client computers.
OS/2	4	OS/2 is very similar to Windows 95 in most respects. It runs on similar hardware and runs similar applications.

Windows 2000
Network Planning

PART 2

Table 8.1   Load Requirements of Network Clients *(continued)*

Client	Metric	Explanation
Windows NT Workstation or Windows 2000 Professional	5	Windows NT Workstation is the most powerful operating system available for PCs. Its ability to multitask multiple network applications smoothly requires much from a network.
UNIX or Linux workstation	5	UNIX workstations are usually used by bandwidth-intensive users such as programmers, graphic artists, and CAD operators.
UNIX X terminal	3	X terminals are diskless, but they operate as simple displays. Screen updates are sent from a compute server that actually performs the work requested by the user.
NetPC (Windows terminal)	2	Windows terminals are similar to X terminals in their use of bandwidth, but they are more efficient.
Web client	0.1	Web clients put very little load on a server if the Web application is designed properly.

Load Capacities and Requirements of Servers

A single server can only handle so many requests before it becomes bogged down. This typical load capacity can be used to determine how many servers of a specific type you'll need in a network.

To determine the load value your clients will place on servers, sum their client load numbers. Then, for each service you'll provide, multiply that sum by the service multiplier found in Table 8.2 to determine how much service capacity will be required. Finally, sum those service loads into a total service capacity requirement to get an idea of how many servers you'll need. Later in the planning process, you'll assign various services to specific servers based on the load that a specific service creates.

Once you've determined the total client service load for all combined functions, find the server hardware you're most likely to use in Table 8.3 and divide your total service load by the load capacity of that server. The result (rounded up of course) will tell you approximately how many servers you will need.

Table 8.2 Service Load Multipliers

Service	Multiplier	Explanation
File service	1	Loads are based on file service.
Print service	0.5	Printed documents are transmitted twice on the network: from client to server and from server to printer. But printing is fairly rare on most networks, so this traffic tends to be "bursty"—it's uncommon, but when it happens, it bogs down the network.
Terminal service	10	Acting as a compute server places a substantial load on a server. Use this value for Windows terminal servers or X clients (UNIX terminal servers).
Database service	0.5	Database service is typically more efficient than file service.
Web service	0.1	Web service is a fairly light load for a server.
E-mail	0.01	E-mail generates very little load on a server. Often a single e-mail server can serve an entire organization.
Router	0.2	Depending upon a server's place in the network, routing can be demanding.
Firewall	0.25	Firewalling is similar to routing but causes more CPU load.
Proxy	0.5	Proxy operations consume about twice the compute resources of stateful inspection firewalls.

Table 8.3 Load Capacities of Common Server Hardware

Server Class	Metric	Explanation
80386-33/16M/.5G	40	Serves approximately 20 DOS clients (running NetWare)
i486-66/32M/1G	80	Handles 40 DOS clients
Pentium-120/64M/2G	160	Handles 40 Windows machines

Windows 2000 Network Planning

PART 2

Table 8.3   Load Capacities of Common Server Hardware *(continued)*

Server Class	Metric	Explanation
Pentium Pro-200/128M/4G	320	Handles 80 Windows machines
Pentium II-400/256M/8G	640	Handles 128 Windows 2000 machines
Pentium III-800/512M/16G	1280	Sufficient for 60 NetPCs
Pentium 4-1G(2)/1G/32G	2560	Supports 25,000 e-commerce connections from Web clients

Table 8.3 shows the load capacities of various generations of server hardware. Each generation is twice as powerful as the previous generation. Use these figures as guidelines to interpolate the capacity of your hardware. For example, a Pentium-II 300 with 96MB of RAM and a 6GB disk would be directly between the Pentium Pro and the Pentium II listed, so it would have a load capacity of 480.

When calculating load versus capacity, remember that these numbers are maximum capacity estimates. Erring on the side of excess capacity is preferable to being tied to a slow network. You should try to avoid coming within 25 percent of the maximum values presented here if you want your servers to run smoothly at all times.

Load Capacities of Data-Link Technologies

Data-link technologies use various methods to arbitrate the sharing of media, which makes them difficult to compare. For example, although Token Ring has a faster bit rate than Ethernet, a client must wait for the token before transmitting, which can make Ethernet seem more responsive. Adding clients to a Token Ring will slow the network in a simple deterministic manner, whereas overloading an Ethernet can cause it to suddenly cease operating altogether. These differences make comparisons based on simple bit rate meaningless.

I chose to use the worst-case number of clients I felt could be usefully attached to a single shared-media network rather than use a comparison of raw throughput. I then applied this same value to the capacities of other types of networks that are not shared media, such as ATM, to show how these networks can be aggregated into large internetworks.

When creating internetworks, the capacity number used for a subnetwork becomes its load. For instance, a Fiber Distributed Data Interface (FDDI) ring with a capacity rating of 1,000 can be expected to handle up to 10 Ethernet networks, each with a capacity rating of 100. You would then use 1,000 to determine the load created by this network in the internetwork. Network data-link technology capacities are shown in Table 8.4.

Table 8.4   Load Capacities of Network Technologies

Network	Capacity	Explanation
Ethernet	100	Ethernet was used as the basis for comparison, because it is the most common network data-link technology. You can expect to attach 50 DOS clients to a single Ethernet subnetwork before it bogs down.
Token Ring (16Mb)	200	A single Token Ring can support roughly twice as many computers as a single Ethernet subnetwork. Because Token Ring degrades gracefully, you can continue to load a Token Ring past this point, but your network will slow considerably.
Fast Ethernet	500	Although the bit rate for Fast Ethernet is 10 times the rate of Ethernet, it cannot handle 10 times the traffic because of the delay involved in resolving collisions.
Fiber Distributed Data Interface	1,000	You can reasonably connect 10 Ethernet networks together on a single FDDI ring. This arrangement depends greatly upon where you've chosen to place your servers— centralized servers demand more from the backbone.
Gigabit Ethernet (1Gbps)	10,000	Gigabit Ethernet operates over FiberChannel at 1 gigabit per second. Although Gigabit Ethernet retains the Ethernet name, it is full duplex point-to-point and does not have collisions. It is perfect for a backbone technology in campus environments.
T1/E1	24/32	T1 (1.5Mb, U.S.) and E1 (2Mb, Europe, MX, South America) are telephony trunk standards commonly used for data transport. Frame Relay typically operates over these circuits but is sold in fractions of 56K (U.S.) or 64K (Europe). For Frame circuits, consider each fraction useful for one client.
T3/E3	672/512	T3 (45Mb) and E3 (32Mb) are aggregates of T1 and E1 circuits used in the same manner for higher capacity trunks.

Table 8.4   Load Capacities of Network Technologies *(continued)*

Network	Capacity	Explanation
ATM-155 OC-3	1,000	ATM is a switched-network technology; it is not shared. For this reason, you can count on being able to use about 80 percent of the bit rate for usable traffic so long as you maintain constant connections between servers.
ATM OC-12	4,000	ATM bandwidth increases linearly with speed. At 622Mbps, ATM OC-12 is sufficient for the most demanding backbone applications.
ATM OC-48 and (SONET)	16,000	ATM at OC-48 (2.2Gbps) is typically used for metropolitan area networks. This capacity is appropriate for metropolitan area high-speed links.
ATM OC-192	48,000	ATM at OC-192 (8.8Gbps) is used by the telephone companies for major trunks between metropolitan areas.
10 Gig Ethernet	100,000	At 10Gbps with no collisions and far less switching and framing overhead than ATM, 10 Gig Ethernet will be the capacity leader in campus area networks when it's available.

Reality Check: A Server Capacity Example

Determining service capacities using this method can be a little confusing, so let's break for two extended examples.

Standard Network

Let's say you have a client sum of 800, which represents 200 Windows machines. These machines create the following service loads:

- File service: 800

- Print service: 400

- Web service: 80

- E-mail service: 8

- Firewall service: 200

- Total server capacity: 1,488

After consulting Table 8.3, you find that you can break the problem down into a single Pentium III file, print, e-mail, and Web server and then install a Pentium Pro firewall. This may not be wise, however, because your network is probably going to be partitioned into multiple Fast Ethernets. You'll want at least two file servers, so two Pentium IIs will be more appropriate. Of course, some of the processors in this example are obsolete, so simply replace them with the most cost-effective processor you can purchase. You'll have extra capacity.

Windows Terminals

In this case, let's compute how many terminal servers it will take to operate a group of NetPCs. You have 32 NetPCs for a total client load of 64. Multiplying this by the server load factor for terminal service (10) gives you a total server load of 640 to support this function. Looking at your server hardware, you find that a Pentium II-400 class machine should be up to the task of serving this many NetPCs. Does this match reality? Based on my experience with Citrix Winframe (the product upon which the Terminal Service of Windows 2000 Server is based), it stretches a little thin (I'd call 25 a maximum for this hardware), but Microsoft claims in the guidelines set forth in "Windows Terminal Server Capacity Planning and Performance Analysis" that this should be well within the capacity of Windows 2000 Terminal Service. Windows terminals compute loads are extremely sensitive to the type of client software in use. For word processing, Microsoft's numbers might make sense, but browsing the Web would be a burden, even using our more conservative estimate.

Physical Plant Design

To properly design the physical plant, you must determine the physical location of network resources and determine which data-link technology you will use. With that information, you'll be able to design both the physical plant and the network connectivity. Use the following procedure to design the physical plant:

1. Map the locations of each network resource.

2. Group the resources into subnetworks as limited by the distance and connectivity limitations of the selected data-link technology.

3. Lay out the premises wiring that is necessary to link the resource on blueprints.

4. Link the subnetworks together using a high-capacity medium.

1. Map Resource Locations

It is easiest to map the physical location if you use a copy of the blueprints for your building. You should be able to acquire a set from your architect, landlord, or facilities group. In exceptionally rare cases, you may even be able to get them in an online format that can be imported into your design software. Figure 8.2 shows a blueprint in the first phase of design.

Figure 8.2   Start a network design with a blueprint of your building.

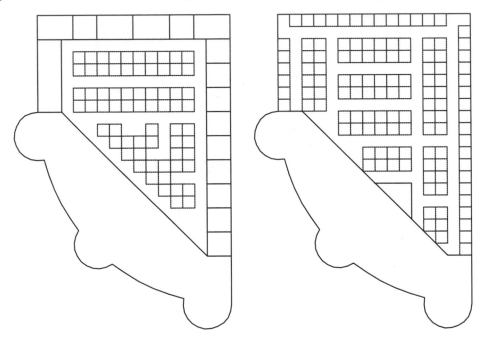

Often you may not know precisely where computers will be located in a new network. In this case, you should plan network drops as if they were power or telephone outlets—simply install at least two network drops per office (a similar frequency to telephone jacks) and more for larger rooms. The Electrical Industry Association and the Telephony Industry Association (EIA/TIA) guidelines set a maximum length of 80 meters for installed cabling; leave 10 meters on each end for jumpers from the wall or patch panel to the computer or hub.

Open bay cubicles can present a special challenge because there's no industry-accepted method for wiring through them to individual computers and because office furniture will probably not be installed when you design the network. Myriad options exist to solve this problem, from cubicle-mounted patch panels to prewired office furniture. None work well in my opinion, and they're all considerably more expensive than they are worth.

In my experience, the easiest way to design for open bay cubicles is to mount high-density, surface mount patch panels or wall boxes in the fixed locations closest to the cubicles. These locations could be in columns or in walls adjacent to a cubicle group. Sometimes no fixed wall is available, and you must use hollow power poles to bring the networking cables down from the ceiling. In this case, specify surface mount wall boxes on the power poles. When the furniture is installed, you can then use long (20-meter) jumpers that run through the wire ways of the cubicle furniture to connect individual computers to these high-density patch panels. When you install runs to open bay cubicles, your installed wiring should run no longer than 60 meters to allow for extra-long connection jumpers through the cubicles.

Map the location of network clients on your blueprints with symbols that specify the client load values, as shown in Figure 8.3.

Figure 8.3   Indicate client load values when mapping the location of network clients.

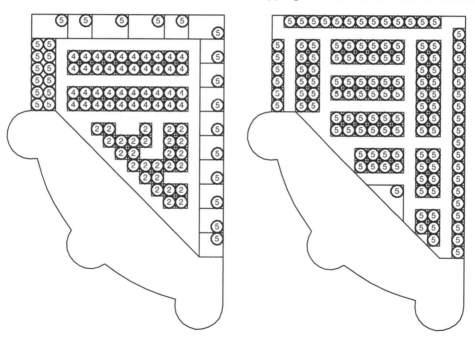

2. Group Your Resources

Grouping the individual units is an optimization problem for which there is no single solution. Different integrators will often select different routes and accumulations of computers based on their slightly different requirements and preferences. You should keep the following requirements in mind when grouping clients:

- Each client must be within the data-link distance limit of the closet (80 meters for Ethernet).

- Group clients by natural physical boundaries such as buildings, areas, and rooms. No grouping should cross large open areas such as atriums or halls.

- Try to group clients according to the number of ports on the hubs you'll be using.

Figure 8.4 shows clients grouped into both closets and Ethernet collision domains.

Figure 8.4   Grouping clients by closet and collision domains

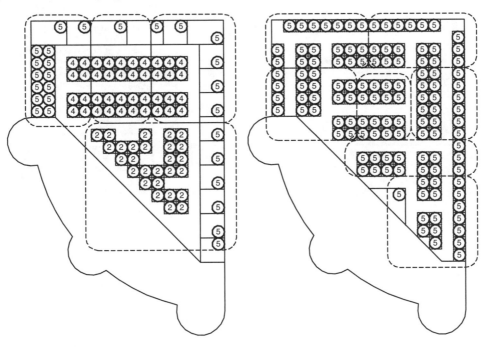

3. Lay Out Premises Wiring

Lay out the premises wiring as mandated by the location of units and the chosen link technology. This step is fairly obvious once you've grouped computers together, but selecting where to put the wiring centers isn't always obvious. In existing buildings, you may have to make trade-offs, such as sharing space with a mop or using cabinets installed in otherwise occupied rooms. Figure 8.5 shows an example of laying out premises wiring.

Figure 8.5   Laying out premises wiring

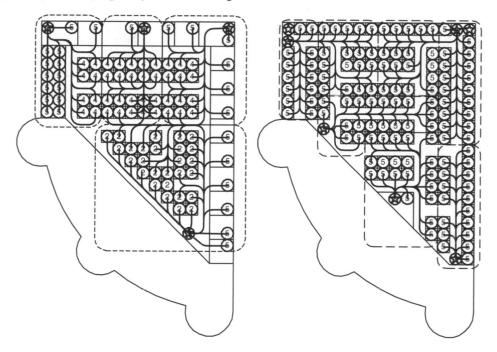

4. Link the Subnetworks

Link the subnetworks together using optical fiber—a medium capable of handling the combined traffic of the subnetworks. You can always select a backbone technology later, because all campus area backbone technologies operate over fiber. Two types of optical fiber are in use today: lower grade multi-mode fiber, which was originally used for local area networking, and higher grade single-mode fiber, which was designed for long distance telephony and costs about twice as much as multi-mode. Both types of fiber work well for the majority of campus area networking needs, but single-mode is more appropriate for backbone runs. Figure 8.6 shows an example of connecting closets.

Figure 8.6   Connecting closets

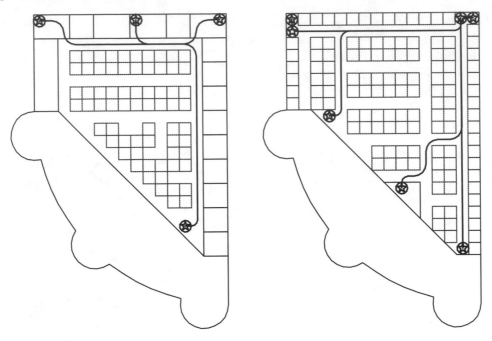

You will often have to connect buildings together in your network, which can present unusual challenges. If you happen to own the path between the two buildings, you can simply trench, install conduit, and pull the fiber through. Often it won't be that simple—you may be leasing the office space and have no ability to modify public areas. Or you may have a public street to cross. For these situations, you should consider wireless transports. A number of wireless options exist, but for backbone connections you won't want to use anything slower than 10Mbps Ethernet or perhaps 4-channel T1 microwave radios. In some circumstances, laser or infrared LED transceivers will work, but these options are easily obscured by smoke, fog, and rain and have serious line-of-sight constraints.

Data-Link and Protocol Design

Data-link and protocol design is easy if you do it in the proper order. Once you have the premises wiring laid out and your closets designed, you know exactly where you need to place hubs. To determine exactly how many hubs you'll need, simply count the number of clients you have in each closet and divide by the number of ports on the hubs that you'll be using.

You can use one of the following methods to connect closets together. Which method you choose depends somewhat on the level of efficiency you want to achieve, your budget, your ultimate design goals, and your level of expertise.

Using Switches to Connect Closets Together

This option is quite easily implemented and can be ideal for situations where clients will access a broad number of servers frequently. Figure 8.7 shows a network that uses a central switch to manage network access. This configuration is frequently called a *collapsed backbone* because the high traffic connection occurs on the back-plane circuit board of a single device. Remember that if you use this option, all data traffic in your network will go through this single bottleneck, which means you will have to have a very high-speed switch. Larger organizations cannot use collapsed backbones for this reason.

Figure 8.7   A switched network (collapsed backbone)

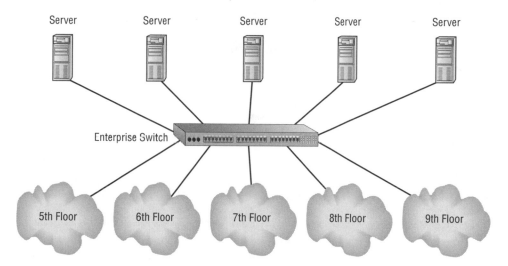

Using Routers to Connect All Closets Together

This option is harder to implement, but it is ideal when client access patterns are unknown or when link redundancy is a requirement. Routers work well in a variety of circumstances and scale reasonably well to large organizations. The fact that the Internet is based on this model shows that it functions on a large scale. Figure 8.8 shows a routed network.

Figure 8.8   A routed network

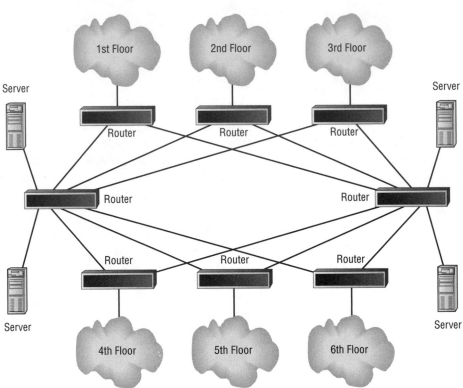

Using Servers As Routers

This option is very inexpensive and can be ideal for situations when most users will access only their primary server. For situations where users frequently access multiple servers, this configuration causes significant load on the server and is slower than dedicated switching or routing options. This solution can scale indefinitely, because if it is used properly, most traffic will stop at the server. Figure 8.9 shows a network where servers are used as routers.

If you can't tell which method is right for your situation, go with routers. They work reasonably well in all cases and can be reconfigured to work well in growth environments.

Figure 8.9   Distributed servers

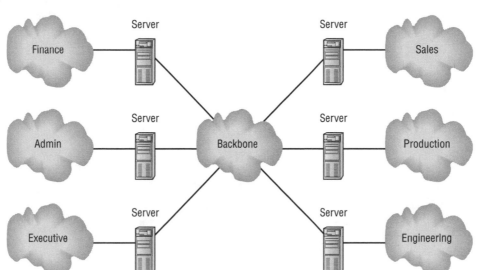

Service Design

Service design refers to the provision of network services such as file service, e-mail service, or database service. The location of these servers defines the routes that data traffic will have to take on your network, so plan carefully to prevent network bottlenecks.

You need to determine where you will locate your servers once you've grouped your clients into subnetworks but before you've determined how you will link those subnetworks together. You have two options:

- Centralizing all servers on the backbone
- Distributing servers to subnetworks

Centralized Servers

Many large organizations place all their servers in a central location and then build massive network infrastructures to route client data to and from these servers. This model has the advantage of centralizing the administration problems for servers to a single location. It makes it easy for functions such as archiving to take place and provides a single point of physical security. When these advantages are more important than cost, you should use this model. Keep in mind that it can become very difficult to keep the network operating at full speed using this model. Because all client traffic must be routed in and out of one location, your network can become bogged down. Figure 8.10 shows centralized servers in a switched network.

Figure 8.10   Centralized servers

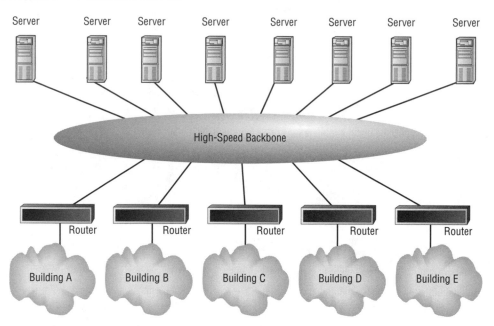

Distributed Servers

With this method, you place servers on the subnetworks or networks in which they are primarily used. This means that most clients will have a direct nonrouted connection to their primary server. Distributing servers creates administrative problems. Archiving is problematic if you have tape drives in every server, and it usually means you'll have to travel to different servers to perform routine administration. If you use distributed servers, plan on centralized archiving of the hardware and software and incurring additional costs for network management. You'll want to use SNMP management, and you'll probably want some sort of remote management software installed on servers so you can manage them from a central location.

With distributed servers, you can use your servers as routers by connecting them to both their local networks and the backbone with two network interface cards. This puts additional load on the server, but it eliminates the cost of a router.

This model is far more scalable than the centralized server model. Whenever you add new clients, you add a server with them. The only client traffic that gets routed to the backbone is connectivity to enterprise servers such as e-mail and database machines or Internet traffic. By eliminating typical file, print, and authentication traffic from the backbone, you'll find that you won't have nearly as much to worry about when you increase the size of your network. Therefore, you should prefer this method when cost outweighs administrative convenience and physical security. Figure 8.11 shows the distributed server model.

Figure 8.11   Distributed servers

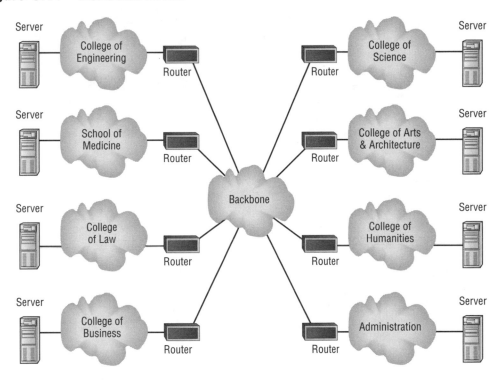

Windows 2000 Network Planning

PART 2

TIP   Choose centralized servers if you have a large budget and administrative convenience is more important than cost. Choose distributed servers if you are on a budget or if labor is more available than capital.

Summary

To design your network, state the goals you need to achieve and the constraints you are working within. Goals typically include providing an application to a set of users, connecting everyone via e-mail, or implementing a work-flow application. Constraints include budget, physical geography, and existing conditions.

Budget is your major planning constraint. The total cost of ownership shows what you'll pay to own a device, not just what you'll pay to acquire it.

Common mistakes in network planning are choosing technologies that are difficult to maintain, performing programming or considerable customization, developing software rather than changing work patterns to adapt to existing software, using specialized hardware and software, and building your own machines.

Existing conditions form the foundation of any new network plan. Clearly stating your goals, and checking them during every planning stage, is crucial to success. Requirements are the general constraints you'll use to narrow the list of candidate technologies, equipment, and software.

Network design is the process of determining the exact hardware and software required to accomplish the goal and specifying precisely how the hardware will be connected and how the software will be configured. Network design is best handled at three separate tiers: the subnetwork or workgroup, the network, and the internetwork of networks or backbone. The equipment you'll use at each tier will be increasingly fast and expensive.

Selecting core technologies used to involve a considerable amount of thought, but these days it's easy: use the highest category of unshielded twisted-pair available, currently Category 6, for your subnetwork wiring, and use single-mode optical fiber for the network tier and internetwork tier, except for those portions of the internetwork that are remote, where you should use either Frame Relay or Internet-encrypted tunnels. At the network layer, you have to use TCP/IP if you're going to use Windows 2000, but there may be some cases where you might want to use IPX or AppleTalk as well.

Estimating network requirements is most easily performed by using a methodology to guide you. Whether you create one based on your own experience or use the one presented in the chapter is irrelevant, as long as you have some standard to guide the process. A successful methodology will be able to predict the client load and will help you create the boundaries between subnetworks, networks, and internetworks.

Physical plant design is simple once you've mapped out the boundaries of your subnetworks. Stay within the designed distance rating for your data link (100m for Ethernet over UTP) and connect your subnetworks together using optical fiber. Your physical plant contractor can assist you with physical plant network design.

Data-link and protocol design is also easy: Use Fast Ethernet for everything that runs over copper and Gigabit Ethernet for everything that runs over fiber. Use routers to connect workgroups to the Gigabit Ethernet backbone. Use Frame Relay or IP tunneling to connect geographically separated networks.

There are two major schools of thought concerning service design: use expensive network links to centralize servers in a single location to reduce the administrative burden, or distribute servers out to workgroups in order to reduce the capital expenditure required to build the network. Which philosophy you choose depends on the size of your network and whether the long-term savings of centralization is more important than the reduced capital expenditure of distributed servers.

Windows 2000
Network Planning

PART 2

Case Study: Moving a Network

When one of my clients decided to move their operations to a new facility, I got together with their IT staff and recommended overhauling their network infrastructure.

Their existing platform consisted of numerous file servers distributed randomly throughout some departments on multiple platforms (UNIX and Windows NT). Their desktops had all been Windows 98, but most had recently been upgraded to Windows 2000. Server maintenance was a hassle because there was very little centralization of server hardware. Hubs were all centralized in one room, and the entire network consisted of a single 100MB collision domain.

They had been plagued for quite some time by bad network cabling and bandwidth problems caused by the "Frankenstein" growth of their network: the company had grown so quickly that computers were simply added to the network as necessary, and hubs were thrown in as needed to get users on the network. Consequently, there was no real logic to the network architecture, and with a single collision domain, access to server resources was slow. Many users stored vital company files on their own desktops for this reason. Many older PCs were still in use that couldn't really take the upgrade to Windows 2000 and had been creeping along, annoying the users.

Now that the company would be moving into a larger facility, it made sense to make a clean sweep of the network as well. We decided to keep only the client computers from the old network. We would replace all servers and network devices.

We sat down with the building's blueprints and took a look at the physical configuration of the network. Most of the building would be built out as open-space cubicles. The few offices that would be built would be placed together in one section. When I realized that most of the wiring would be run to cubicles, which nearly always involves long runs of network jumper cables through modular furniture trays, I suggested a departure from normal networking methodology.

Rather than installing individual UTP cables and terminating them in patch panels on the walls near the cubicles, where they would plug into jumpers for the final run to the computers, I suggested mounting 100Base-TX switches with a 1000Base-SX uplink on the walls in place of the patch panels. UTP jumpers would run directly from the hubs to the cubicle groups.

There would be no installed UTP—just a single pair of fiber to each cubicle group of about 24 clients. This meant we needed only about 1/20th the amount of installed cable, which made the all-fiber network considerably cheaper than the cost of a traditional, less-capable UTP plant. The fiber-optic network would run Gigabit Ethernet and be concentrated in a single Gigabit switch in the server room. We would need 16 ports on the switch to handle all the workgroups and servers.

Each new server would be built with a Gigabit fiber card and connected directly to the central switch. All the servers would be members of the same Windows 2000 domain, and a terminal server would be installed so that users on older clients could use Terminal Service rather than deal with the performance problems caused by their older hardware. Remote users could also access this server. The Terminal Service would nicely solve the recurring network access problems for the company's sales staff.

The installation went exceptionally smoothly. The simplified cable plant went in much faster than a UTP plant could have, and it tested out perfectly. We had no issues with distance, and we eliminated the possibility of electrical interference. We installed the new servers in place and brought them online in advance of the move-in, so we were easily able to cut server services over.

The only real problem was migrating file services from the legacy servers with a permissions structure intact in the space of a single weekend. We actually just copied all the files over, created a more sane directory structure, and applied an entirely new security structure. We then set up shares to mimic the familiar structure from the older platform.

Since the company shut their operations down for the move, we had a week in which to get all the clients physically installed and converted to the Active Directory. We put the entire sales staff on Terminal Service so that they would have consistency between home and the road. We reinstalled Windows 98 on computers that were older and problematic, loaded them with the Terminal Service client, and moved them into the sales department, thus freeing up some newer and more capable workstations for the production department.

In the end, we were able to increase the backbone bandwidth by tenfold, move to an all-switched architecture from a single collision domain, standardize on a single-service platform, and improve the usability of legacy clients—all in the space of about a week. Because of the savings in the cable plant, we were able to pay for the more expensive Gigabit Ethernet hardware. The entire project cost just about the same as an older all-UTP network but produced a far more efficient network.

9

Active Directory

Active Directory is a database service for Windows 2000 that can store and organize any information that client applications throughout an enterprise might need to access through their associated server application. Microsoft intends for all Windows-based server applications to eventually use the Active Directory as their data storage engine in much the same way that they currently use the Registry for configuration storage.

Active Directory is the central management structure for Windows 2000–based networks. Windows 2000 uses Active Directory to organize security principals such as users and computers, as well as to manage administrative objects such as shared folders and printers, into manageable collections called *Organizational Units* and *domains*. Domains are related to other domains in a parent/child hierarchical relationship within a DNS namespace called a *tree*. Trees can be linked together into a *forest*; the forest is the Active Directory. These structures together form the hierarchical structure of the Active Directory.

Active Directory is the major change to Windows 2000 Server from Windows NT Server, and the management paradigm is so dramatically different that you will need to make sweeping changes to your network in order to truly integrate it. The changes required, the learning curve, and the completely different management interface are why the rate of adoption of Windows 2000 by NT 4 users lags far behind the rate at which NT 3.51 users adopted Windows NT 4. These changes, however, make Windows 2000 far easier to manage.

Active Directory isn't nearly as complex from an administrative perspective as most people (including Microsoft) make it out to be. Once you understand the basic concepts and what Active Directory can do for you, you won't have much difficulty adopting and migrating to it. You'll find that administering a Windows 2000 network correctly takes about half as much effort as administering the same-sized Windows NT 4 network—perhaps even less once you're used to it.

In this chapter, I discuss Active Directory purely from the perspective of the Windows 2000 network administrator. I deliberately leave out information about the Active Directory Services Interface (ADSI, useful primarily to programmers) because that information, while informative, has little to do with the architecture, installation, migration, or maintenance of Windows 2000 for the vast majority of network administrators. You won't find discussions of LDAP, Distinguished Names, or modifying the Active Directory schema, because you can't use any of that information from the administrative interfaces included with Windows 2000. Once you understand *why* Active Directory works, understanding *how* it works is easy.

> **NOTE**   For detailed information about the structure of Active Directory and its programming interfaces, consult the "Windows 2000 Distributed Systems Guide" in the Windows 2000 Resource Kit or the "Active Directory Services for Windows 2000 Technical Reference," both from Microsoft Press.

Active Directory Defined

Active Directory is composed of a hierarchical database that stores information about the objects that make up your network: computers, users, security policies, and technically anything else someone writes an application to support. Because it is a database, it can be extended by Active Directory–enabled applications to store whatever other information the application needs to store.

Active Directory is unlike most databases in that it is hierarchical in nature rather than being a free-form relational database where relationships are described by keys stored along with the data. *Hierarchical relations* mean that records of information are related to other records of information through a parent/child structure; every record (except the root) has a single parent, and each record may have zero or more child records. Active Directory is particularly well suited to information that is frequently read but rarely written. Active Directory stores can be connected together into replication groups that will automatically update one another whenever information changes about a record so that each store has a complete copy of the entire database.

Reality Check: Just One Directory?

A serious maintainability problem looms in the future because of the extensible nature of Active Directory and the fact that Microsoft thinks that every application should store its data into it. In fact, Microsoft requires it for the Windows 2000 BackOffice logo program.

The root of the problem is that services (such as Exchange) can't be migrated easily among forests once their data is stored in an Active Directory. For example, the only Microsoft-supported method to change the name of your Active Directory root domain is to uninstall Active Directory from every domain controller in your domain and re-create a new Active Directory. Security hassles aside, it's impossible to do that with Exchange 2000 running on your network without destroying the Exchange data store. Problems like these will be exacerbated in the future when most third-party services are Active Directory–enabled—unless Microsoft releases real management tools that allow administrators to back up portions of the schema and restore them into other schemas.

For the time being, the choices you make now about the structure of your directory are far more inflexible than they should be at this early date in the deployment of Windows 2000. I predict that Microsoft will release a way to separate schemas and data by application about midlife in Windows 2000's life cycle, as this problem becomes more acute.

Windows 2000 uses Active Directory to

- Organize security domains into parent/child relationships.
- Automatically create trust relationships between related domains.
- Manage security accounts in the domain, a function formerly handled (in Windows NT) by the Security Accounts Manager (SAM) on the primary domain controller (PDC) and assisted by backup domain controllers (BDCs).
- Manage authentication between machines and users.
- Organize users, computers, and other objects into policy collections called Organizational Units.
- Enforce policies based on the organizational structure. Policies apply to the containers to which they are linked and to all the child containers and objects within it.
- Delegate network administration in a hierarchy.
- Distribute software automatically.

The Active Directory database can be used for any purpose. For example, Exchange 2000 extends the Active Directory schema (the definition of the structure of the database) to store its data, rather than implementing its own database as Exchange 5.5 and earlier did. Active Directory is based on the Exchange storage engine, which was implemented as a high-speed read-optimized replicating hierarchical database—just like Active Directory.

Architecture of Active Directory

Active Directory is a *hierarchical database*, which means that a hierarchy describes the relationships between objects in the database. The simplest definition of a *hierarchy* is a structure in which each object has one parent object, except for the root object at the base of the tree, which has no parent. Implied in this definition is the fact that one parent object may have many children. Hierarchies are often referred to as *trees* in computer science, but that term is given a specific meaning in Active Directory, so it should not be used to describe the directory itself.

Rather than describe the structure of the Active Directory from the root object down, I'm going to take the opposite tack and describe the Active Directory from the child objects up to the root. This way, I can discuss the firm concepts everyone understands before sailing into the abstract concepts of Active Directory.

It's important to note that the separate containers in the Active Directory are all physically implemented very differently. Some are security principals; others are not. Some can be linked hierarchically to containers of the same type; others cannot. Each type of container exists for a very specific reason—not simply to provide a different name to the next level of the hierarchy.

> **Object**   The data record that describes a managed resource, such as a computer or a user. Objects are created for every user account and computer in your organization. Each object may have many data attributes, each of which forms a "column" in the Active Directory. For example, a user has a first name, a last name, initials, a logon name, and a password, along with other stored information. If you laid out all the users in a list, each user would be one row, and the set of first names would form one column.
>
> In the Active Directory, security permissions can be set on a "per column" basis. This means that administrators could yield address-changing permission directly to the end-users themselves, but restrict access to changing phone numbers to members of the Facilities security group, and allow only administrators permission to change names.
>
> Security principals are managed in the Active Directory Users and Computers snap-in.

Organizational Unit   Containers used to group objects into managed units within a single domain. Organizational Units (OUs) are used to define group policy and administrative delegation for a collection of objects that should be managed together. Organizational Units are not security principals, but they are objects: they have no security identifier and cannot perform any actions in the system; they are merely containers in the Active Directory structure. Create Organizational Units when you want to apply different group policies to groups of computers or users, or when you want to delegate administration of groups of computers or users. Objects can be moved freely between OUs in the same domain.

Organizational Units can be organized into a hierarchy where a parent OU may have multiple child OUs. Objects cannot be members of multiple Organizational Units, so OUs should be used sparingly to match major management divisions in your company, such as departments, teams, and so forth. A domain always forms the root of a tree of OU structures.

Domain   The major security construct in Active Directory, just as they were in Windows NT 4. Computer and user accounts are actually stored by their local domain; other domains in the directory merely store enough data to enable logging in.

Domains are physically stored on *domain controllers*, computers that run the Active Directory service. Within a domain, all interior objects are replicated to every domain controller.

You should create new domains when you need to partition replication traffic for performance or security reasons. A single domain scales very well in Windows 2000. According to Microsoft, you should be able to comfortably serve at least 100,000 security principals in a single domain. Given that scalability, connection link speed is the only reason for most businesses to use multiple domains.

Tree   Describes the hierarchical parent/child relationship between multiple domains. Trees become meaningful whenever more than one domain exists in an Active Directory. If the two domains are within the same DNS namespace, then one domain is by definition the parent and the other is the child. Further domains are created as children to any existing domain in the domain tree.

There is no "tree" object; rather, the highest order parent domain in the tree (called a *root domain*) is the root object of a tree. Like OUs, trees are not security principals and have no actual logical object of their own.

The tree structure of an Active Directory defines the trust relationships between domains and defines the transit path that Kerberos authentication will take when a security principal from one domain accesses a security principal in another domain. In fact, trees are implemented simply as a collection of trust relationships that describe which domains are related to other domains. The structure of this relationship automatically defines the DNS name structure within the namespace.

Forest Simply a set of trees that share the same Active Directory schema and are related by trust relationships. There is no forest object or security principal; the Active Directory itself is the forest. The first domain created in the forest is the *forest root domain*, which is a domain that acts as the root object for all trees. Any tree having a bidirectional trust relationship with the forest root domain is a member of the forest.

Forests are not hierarchical. An Active Directory can have only one forest, so a parent/child relationship cannot exist between forests. Trust relationships between forests, when they exist, are not transitive.

Each forest has one Active Directory schema . You should only create a new forest when a business function requires a separate Active Directory schema. New forests are generally appropriate whenever a different corporation would be appropriate in a legal context.

In practice, you'll almost never plan to create more than one forest. The valid business reasons for doing this are extremely rare. The forest trust concept is designed primarily to allow two existing businesses with existing Active Directories structures to be connected together.

Two constructs are associated with the Active Directory that are not technically part of the Active Directory hierarchy because they can span the hierarchy in numerous ways—not just from parent to child:

Security group Security groups are not officially part of the Active Directory hierarchy because one security group can include security principals from any part of the directory.

Security groups are used to assign security permissions to NTFS file system files and directories, to the Registry, and to the Active Directory itself, as well as to define distribution groups for software and to filter the application of group policy.

Distribution groups exist simply for creating e-mail distribution lists. These groups are an optimization of security groups that don't require modification of the user's Access Token because they don't impact security, thus speeding the logon process. Why an e-mail group mechanism is built into an operating system that doesn't natively support e-mail is a mystery.

Sites *Sites* are collections of IP subnets that happen to be well connected, meaning that the domain controllers have at least a 500Kbps dedicated circuit always available between them. Note that the 500K circuit speed is merely Microsoft's recommended default setting; you can define the speed to be anything you want, and should consider link reliability as a possible reason to partition sites as well. Sites are designed to partition replication traffic along real geographic constraints, so that the Active Directory structure itself can remain relatively abstract.

Computers that host Active Directory databases are called *domain controllers*, and they are all basically peers—there is no single master like a primary domain controller, and all domain controllers are equal in their function, with slight exceptions. Each domain controller maintains information about its portion of the network (the portion below it in an Active Directory hierarchy), which is replicated to other domain controllers according to their participation in the directory.

Three *naming contexts* or *partitions* in the Active Directory exist that define precisely how replication occurs:

Schema Naming Context   Replicated to all domain controllers in the forest and can only be edited on the schema master—the forest root domain controller by default.

Configuration Naming Context   Replicated to all domain controllers in the forest and contains the complete hierarchy of domain controllers and trust relationships. Essentially, the Configuration Naming Context is what you're editing when you use the Active Directory Sites and Services or Active Directory Domains and Trusts management consoles.

Domain Naming Context   Replicated only to domain controllers within a domain and contains information about users, computers, shares, and Organizational Units—all the things you edit using the Active Directory Users and Computers management console.

Active Directory Design

Despite what you may have read about Active Directory design, developing a coherent directory strategy is neither confusing nor difficult. It doesn't require you to reorganize your business, and it doesn't have to take months of planning prior to getting started.

You should realize that most of the features of Active Directory are aimed squarely at larger businesses with tens of thousands of employees that span the globe. The vast majority of organizations (greater than 90 percent) that deploy Windows 2000 will never deploy more than one domain, because a single domain can contain many millions of objects and needn't be limited to a single site. Because most users will never require more than a single domain, I'm not going to belabor the architecture of Active Directory above the domain level. If you need to create a complex Active Directory architecture, consult Microsoft's Active Directory planning guides.

Nobody knows how well Active Directory services are really going to be accepted in the general business community or how many applications (outside of those engineered by Microsoft) will truly support Active Directory beyond its compatibility with LDAP services. Many people have likened Active Directory to Novell's NDS (NetWare Directory Services) architecture; Novell has only lost market share since introducing NDS because its inordinate complexity prompted migration to Windows NT.

Spend the minimum amount of effort required to get Active Directory working to help you to manage your IT problem. Create a single domain, and prepare yourself for the fact that you may need to reorganize your directory at least once in the future if your organization deploys Active Directory–based server applications. Don't waste your time trying to create a complex directory structure now when you don't know how you're going to use it in the future. Do the minimum required to get 2000 server deployed and controlling your network.

If you're excited about deploying an Active Directory–enabled network and you manage an exceptionally complex network, then by all means use Microsoft's guides to planning. If, on the other hand, your business already has collaboration software in place and you'll just be using Active Directory for its IT management features, then use this section as your guide to deploying it.

Simplified Active Directory Design

The simplest way to deploy a well-functioning directory is to match your existing business structure (both physical and logical) to analogous directory structures consisting of Organizational Units. Consider the following questions when planning your Active Directory design:

How many forests do you need?   Forget about using more than one forest. Unless your organization is actually a confederation of loosely associated businesses with legal separations between them, there's no good reason to create more than one forest. The vast majority of typical business should have only one forest.

Do you need more than one tree?   Most likely, you don't. Trees are designed to merge multiple DNS namespaces into a single Active Directory, which makes good sense in theory. But in the real world, nobody puts private network namespaces on the Internet. From your network, you'll never be able to log on directly to `client32.administration`
`.ny.ibm.com` because IBM firewalls every machine that they don't want the public to reach. Assuming that you do too, there's no point in having a noncontiguous DNS namespace on the private side of your network. Noncontiguous namespaces are for your public Web properties.

Simply put, your public Internet presence is an entirely different problem than your private namespace, even if you use the same second-level domain. In my network, www.connetic.net is a public machine. The forest root domain of my private network is inside.connetic.net, running Windows 2000 Server and acting as the DNS zone master for everything below it. The WWW, mail, and FTP services are all running on a pair of mirrored Linux boxes, and DNS for the public names are managed by my ISP.

You can use as many public namespaces as you need for marketing purposes. Many companies use different DNS namespaces on the public Internet, but the inside of a single corporation should always be a single DNS namespace. The only exception to this is the case of acquisitions or mergers, and even then, the namespaces should be merged as soon as it's convenient to do so.

So what about your public Web sites? Should you use multiple trees for them? In my opinion, you shouldn't even use Windows 2000 on your public Web sites. But platform preferences aside, there's very little reason to use Active Directory among a farm of Web servers and public database machines. Microsoft.com is the second largest Web site on the Internet, and it's comprised of just 30 machines. Unless you're Amazon.com, your public service problem is smaller than that (and if you are, you're running Solaris anyway). You won't need Active Directory to manage your public Internet presence.

No matter how many public domains your company manages, you should have one DNS namespace for your internal organization unless there's some overwhelming reason not to.

How many domains do you need?   The answer to this is at least one for each site that uses e mail for Active Directory replication because a permanent reliable circuit is not available. Beyond that, you shouldn't create administrative boundaries that will increase your workload unless you know you need to. Create one domain at your largest facility (the one containing the most security principals) and then attempt to connect each of your other branch offices to this domain. If you find you don't have the requisite connectivity, consider getting it before you consider splitting your domain. High-bandwidth circuits are expensive between sites, but you can use IPSec to secure communications over the public Internet to create virtual high-speed circuits without the connection or time charges. Consider modifying your network architecture before you saddle yourself with the increased administrative burden of unnecessary multiple domains. Remember that a single domain can span multiple sites even if they're not well connected. Use sites rather than domains to partition replication traffic.

Separate domains are required for sites that must use SMTP to replicate domain traffic because of distance or unreliable connections. If you have a site that can only connect via dial-up networking and a modem, you'll have to use SMTP replication and a separate domain. Separate domains should also be used for sites that have circuit connections slower than 128Kbps in order to reduce the scope of replication traffic and decrease replication frequency.

I recommend using just a single domain per site because you can use the OU structure to perform all of the Group Policy and administrative delegation you need. It's far simpler to move security principals around in a single domain. And, although Kerberos makes logging on to foreign domains easy, logons across domains can generate a considerable amount of traffic. Logging on to a single large domain requires just a single Kerberos request. Finally, it's easier to create a new domain than to remove one, so by starting with a single domain per site and then splitting domains when necessary, you'll know that you're always using the minimum possible number of domains.

The single domain model is appropriate in all of the following circumstances:

- Small- to medium-sized businesses
- Businesses that are not geographically spread out
- Small sites outside the headquarters, such as branch offices
- Users who frequently travel between sites

Valid arguments for a multiple domain model are as follows:

- Business is geographically dispersed where WAN links are too slow to handle single domain replication traffic.
- Remote networks can only be reached by SMTP e-mail.
- Significant political, legal, security, or business requirements force the partitioning of the network.

How do you form your Organizational Units?   Now that we've simplified the Active Directory structure to a single forest, a single tree, and a single domain for the vast majority of businesses, there is no need for significant worry about the remaining structure, since all objects can be moved freely between Organizational Units without hassle. This will allow you to manage OUs without being locked into your initial decisions. Voilà! You've just created your first Active Directory architecture.

Organizational Units should be formed by groups of users that share the same applications. In most companies, applications are common throughout departments, so departments make excellent Organizational Units. For example, engineers use CAD software, so Engineering would be a good OU. Sales people use sales-tracking applications, so Sales would make a good OU.

At this point, you've got all the containers most organizations will ever need for IT administration, and your Active Directory is designed. If you find you need additional

Organizational Units in the future, you can create them when the need arises. Figure 9.1 shows an Active Directory design for a medium-sized business.

Figure 9.1   The Active Directory structure is represented and stored as a hierarchy of domains and Organizational Units.

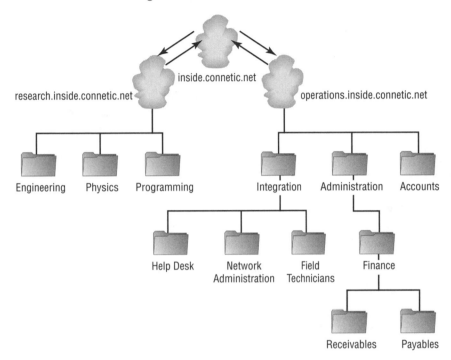

In general, you'll assign Group Policy based on the OU and delegate administration on a domain basis. You may want to create an extra OU in each domain that you use for administrative purposes, such as hiding IT resources that you don't want to show up in other places in the directory.

Domain Names

Your domain name structure should bear some resemblance to your Active Directory structure, but the two are not and should not be completely congruent.

The first differentiation should be between your publicly accessible (exterior) domain names and your private internal (interior) domain names. See the "DNS Configuration" section later in this chapter for more information about public and private DNS namespaces.

The root of your Active Directory should be a third-level domain name below your organization's primary registered second-level domain name. I recommend creating a specific third-level domain name to serve as the forest root domain, rather than using the second-level name. By creating a structural root domain, all other domains can be created as children to this domain, and that domain can serve as the root of a private DNS namespace. If you use your second-level domain name as the root of your Active Directory, you'll have a very difficult time separating public from private services and properly securing the private side.

You can also use the IETF `.local` domain to create your private namespace. Namespaces rooted in the `.local` domain will never be routable on the Internet, so for the interior of firewalled private networks, they can add a measure of security and reduce the length of your DNS names (`root.local` is much shorter than `root.corporate.connetic.net`).

Each public service, such as Web service or mail service, should have a third-level domain name associated with it. Privately, your fourth-level domain names should equate to domains and geographical locations—even if you have only one domain or geographical location. Using your site or internal domain name as a third-level domain name, even if you only have a single domain, will allow you to efficiently partition your exterior third-level domain names from your interior name(s).

Typical exterior third-level domain names include these:

- www
- mail
- ftp
- support

Typical interior third-level domain names include these:

- inside
- corp
- headquarters
- newyork
- rootdomain

You normally should not have exterior names below the third level. They're confusing to the public at large, and exterior names should represent services rather than specific machines or structures within your company.

Fourth and lower domain names within your company are entirely reasonable and will mimic your domain structure. I don't recommend using DNS domain names for anything below the domain level, except for the final level of domain names, which are, of course, the computer objects themselves.

Here are some examples of fully qualified domain names:

- `www.digitalwidgets.com` (exterior)
- `bjones.sales.saltlake.corporate.digitalwidgets.com` (interior)

Multiple Domain Considerations

Do everything you can to limit your network to a single domain; you'll have far less troubleshooting to deal with if you do. If you can't, consider the following suggestions for implementing a more complex Active Directory.

The most important domain architecture consideration for most users is the replication traffic across WAN links. Using a single site will reduce your administrative burden at the expense of creating extra replication traffic on your WAN links. How important this is to you depends on how fast, congested, and expensive your WAN links are.

Having a domain at each physical site will reduce the replication traffic across expensive inter-site WAN links because directory objects are not automatically replicated across domains. Usually, a site is the name of a campus, and for most companies, only one campus per city exists. If you must use the multiple domain model, try to create the fewest possible number of domains. Plan on mapping a fourth-level domain name for each site—for example, `sandiego.corporate.digitalwidgets.com`, `jersey.corporate.digitalwidgets.com`, and `newyork.corporate.digitalwidgets.com`. How you name them is up to you. By creating a domain for each site, you'll be able to take advantage of a cool feature of Active Directory—the ability to replicate information between domains via SMTP e-mail. This can relieve the replication load on congested WAN links by decreasing the frequency of replication traffic.

Also consider creating a special domain to host the forest root. The forest root is the first domain created within a forest, and it carries with it two special groups—Enterprise Administrators and Schema Administrators—which have special rights and privileges within the forest. If the domain that hosts the forest root is ever lost due to catastrophe or perhaps the sale of a portion of the company, these groups and their associated rights can never be recovered and a new forest must be created.

Creating a separate domain for the forest root also makes DNS configuration very easy, makes your DNS path coherent, and makes the Kerberos trust path easy to determine since only automatic trust relationships will be necessary.

You will need at least one domain controller for each domain, and you should have at least two. You should also place at least one domain controller at each site, and at least one domain controller at each site should be designated as the *global catalog server* (a domain controller that caches some information about every object in the forest). You should also have at least one DNS server at each site—which would ideally also be the domain controller—to reduce traffic on the network. For sites with more than 25 users, consider placing at least two domain controllers on site for fault-tolerance purposes.

DNS Configuration

Microsoft's default Active Directory setup in the Server Configuration Wizard is woefully inadequate in its default DNS configuration.

It presumes that:

- You have an existing DNS architecture that you're willing to scrap. Most large networks have a DNS architecture that they're happy with and don't want to migrate to or integrate with Windows 2000.
- If you don't have an internal DNS architecture, your network is not connected to the Internet. Most small networks use DNS to connect to the Internet and to host their public properties, but do not use DNS for internal name resolution on their network.

Neither of these two cases is correct for 90 percent of existing networks, and so the Active Directory Server Configuration Wizard actually screws up the majority of installations when it is used to create a DNS service.

Terminology: Domain Name Service (DNS)

The following definitions will clarify DNS:

Namespace A set of identifiers related to one another in an identifiable manner, usually a hierarchy. In a hierarchical namespace, child objects of the same parent have distinct names.

Domain A DNS namespace. The children of a domain may be another domain or a host. A DNS domain is not the same thing as an Active Directory domain, but Active Directory domains do have domain names.

Host A computer identified by a name. The host name along with the hierarchy of parent domain names forms an identifier which can uniquely identify any computer on the Internet or in a private network.

Root   The top of the DNS namespace hierarchy. In DNS, the root node has no name and is represented by a period (.).

Top-level domain (TLD)   The first level of children in the DNS namespace. On the public Internet, the TLD is either a country code (.us, .ca, .uk, and so on) or one of the major U.S. TLDs (.com, .net, .org, .mil, .edu, .gov). For private networks, any TLD can be used, but .local is reserved for private use and guaranteed to work. The release of new public TLDs is mangled by ICANN.

Second-level domain (2LD)   The next child domain after the TLD. This domain is normally the registered domain name of the company (ibm, apple, hp, sybex, and so on) and when combined with the TLD is the first level of domain name that could specify an actual host (sybex.com). Domains below this level are known as the third-level domain (3LD), fourth-level domain (4LD), and so forth.

Zone   A contiguous branch of the DNS hierarchy that is managed as a group by a DNS server. Examples of zones might be sybex.com, inside.connetic.net, or newyork.corporate.digitalwidgets.com. One DNS server can manage multiple, noncontiguous zones.

The Two Faces of DNS

In a perfect world, your organization would have only one DNS hierarchy, and the Internet root DNS servers would join it at the top-level domain to every other DNS namespace in the world. Anyone from anywhere would be able to query the IP address of any host on any network connected to the Internet.

In the early Internet, networks had (at least) two DNS servers reachable from anywhere on the network. On those DNS servers, the IP address of each machine available in the private network could be resolved. Public servers were merely those with conventional names like *ftp*, *gopher*, or *news*. The first Web consisted simply of internal machines named (by convention) *www*.

We don't live in that world anymore. Firewalls now form an absolute barrier to the internal portions of most networks; only universities tend to have widely exposed internal networks for historical reasons, and those are disappearing rapidly. The machines named *ftp*, *www*, and *news* now sit outside that barrier (or in a security zone of their own) and usually consist of a load-balancing server in front of an array of cloned servers.

Windows 2000
Network Planning

PART 2

When you register a DNS name, you're actually giving the registration authority the address of the DNS servers you've set up to resolve the registered name. So you must have publicly available DNS servers that can resolve the registered name for whomever asks for it.

On the inside of your network, you program each client, either manually or via DHCP, with the address of the DNS servers that it should both register its own name with and use to resolve DNS names.

You could use the same DNS server to serve both public and private clients. That's what was done for years until security problems made that methodology too dangerous. The problem is that a public DNS server publishes the names and addresses of the internal machines to any computer that requests it. Even if the firewall can't be breached, there's extremely valuable information about the interior of your network available for anyone to see.

Denial of service attacks could also be perpetrated from the Internet. If public DNS requests must be resolved against the same DNS servers upon which your company depends, a flood of DNS activity on your public services can drag down name resolution on your internal network as well.

The original solution to the security problem was *split DNS*—using the same server to serve both halves of the network separately. Split DNS isn't much better in reality. Because the machine is available on the public Internet, it is exposed to hacking attempts. If a split-DNS server is compromised, your internal network architecture is compromised as well.

Security is far more difficult to properly configure on a split-DNS server than on two separate servers. A security breach on a split-DNS server means that hackers get internal access to information about your internal network. A breach on a separate public server means only that you lose public name service.

I strongly recommend handling public and private DNS services on separate DNS servers. For most businesses, public DNS services should be handled by an ISP's DNS server, while private internal DNS names should be handled on the Active Directory domain controllers.

Configuring DNS When You Have an Existing UNIX-Based DNS Infrastructure

You can take one of four different approaches to DNS if you already use UNIX for DNS resolution:

- Upgrade BIND to be compatible with Windows 2000 and then configure Windows 2000 to use your existing UNIX infrastructure for DNS resolution.

- Manually enter DNS records for all your internal machines. This is burdensome.

- Separate Windows 2000 DNS from UNIX DNS by creating a new zone that will be automatically managed by Windows 2000 (for example, for the existing zone `law.utah.edu`, create a 4LD called `windows.law.utah.edu`) and configured to forward DNS requests onto the UNIX DNS architecture.

- Re-implement your UNIX DNS infrastructure using Windows 2000 and migrate to it.

None of these solutions are particularly easy to implement, and which one you choose depends upon the amount of UNIX expertise you have available to solve the problem.

Configuring UNIX or non-Windows DNS is beyond the scope of this book. Check out *DNS & BIND* by O'Reilly books for more information on configuring UNIX DNS servers.

Configuring DNS When You Have a Domain Name

If you have a registered domain name, you can simply create your Windows 2000 DNS namespace below it. Keep in mind that you can split the responsibility for a DNS hierarchy among DNS servers at any point in the hierarchy. Furthermore, the DNS servers don't necessarily have to be configured to perform zone transfers or replicate name information as long as they are both configured to forward to one another.

The default installation of DNS and Active Directory in Windows 2000 is rather broken. DNS, by default, is not configured, yet Active Directory relies upon it from the start. You're much better off manually configuring DNS before you install Active Directory on a server. The Active Directory Installation Wizard will automatically configure an existing DNS server to be an integrated DNS server during the upgrade to Active Directory. Use the following procedure to configure a new DNS infrastructure for most business networks:

1. Use a third-level domain name for your internal DNS domain.   Don't use your registered second-level domain name. For example, rather than using `connetic.net`, use `inside.connetic.net` or `corporate.connetic.net`. By using a third-level domain name, your internal network can be configured as the zone master for the 3LD and won't have to respond to every request for the 2LD that comes from the Internet; those requests can be left up to your ISP. If you used your 2LD, your internal DNS server would have to be configured to respond to every public request for `connetic.net`, which soaks up your bandwidth and compromises internal security. I recommend using a name to indicate the private side of a DNS namespace (as in `internal.connetic.net`, `root.connetic.net`, or `private.connetic.net`) with the intent that child domains be configured by site name (`sandiego.internal.connetic.net`) at the 4LD.

2. Set the DNS server to point to itself, before you install DNS.   This is crucial, because the DNS server will look to the DNS server entered as its "parent" for Active Directory replication and zone transfers. This is normally your ISP's DNS server, and they will begin to hate you if your server pesters their DNS server constantly. Your Event Log will fill up with mysterious DNS errors as well. The way to tell a DNS server that it's the top of an internal DNS tree is to point it to itself, as its own DNS server.

You also need to make sure that the computer's host name and DNS suffix are set correctly in My Computer or the System Control Panel. If the DNS suffix (domain name) is not set correctly when you start the Active Directory Wizard, the Wizard will not be able to find the DNS server, even if the DNS server is located on the same machine. The DNS suffix should be the same as the forward DNS zone that you'll create when you install DNS, and the same as the domain name you provide when you create the Active Directory.

3. Configure DNS.   Although you could simply use the Server Configuration Wizard to configure DNS at this point, it's best to configure it correctly before you install Active Directory so you know exactly how the configuration is going to proceed. Figure 9.2 shows the DNS Configuration Wizard. To configure DNS:

A. Install the DNS service using the Add/Remove Software Control Panel.

B. Start the DNS MMC console.

C. Right-click the root, and select Configure Server.

D. Select Yes, This Is the First Server if the question comes up.

E. Answer Yes to the forward lookup zones question.

F. Select Zone Type Standard Primary.

G. Enter the zone name. This is the DNS suffix you entered when you set the DNS server's DNS address (example: `internal.connetic.net`).

H. Use the default Create a New File with This File Name when asked about the zone file.

I. Answer Yes to create a reverse lookup zone.

J. Select Zone Type Standard Primary.

K. Enter the network portion of your internal IP address. This might be 192.168.10, or the private range of your assigned IP address space. It should match the length of your net mask, so if your internal network uses 192.168.10.0 and your net mask is 255.255.255.0, enter 192.1268.10.

L. Use the default filename for the zone file. Then click Finish.

M. Enable dynamic updates on the root DNS server by selecting the forward lookup zone, selecting Properties, and changing the Allow Dynamic Updates? answer to Yes. Do this for the reverse lookup zone as well.

Figure 9.2   The DNS Configuration Wizard makes installing DNS easy.

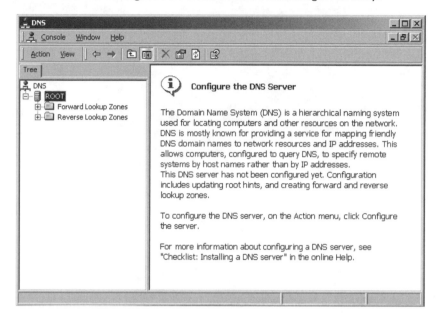

Windows 2000
Network Planning

PART 2

4. Configure forwarding.   Configure the root DNS server to query your ISP's DNS servers for all nonlocal domains. Figure 9.3 shows the Forwarders configuration panel. Here's how to configure forwarding:

A. In the DNS management console, right-click the root server, and select Properties.

B. Click the Forwarders tab, and check the Enable Forwarders check box. If the Enable Forwarders check box is grayed out, the DNS server is configured to host a root zone. Delete the "." root zone entry in the DNS Manager, restart the service, and try again. If that doesn't work, remove and reinstall DNS.

C. Enter your ISP's DNS server information in the IP Address field.

5. Integrate Active Directory.   Configure the internal root server using the Server Configuration Wizard, `dcpromo.exe`, or the DNS management console. Once this step is completed, the DNS server should be automatically reconfigured for Active Directory integration. You can check this in the Properties window for the DNS server in the DNS Manager snap-in.

Figure 9.3   Configuring DNS forwarding to look up unresolved domain names on the public Internet

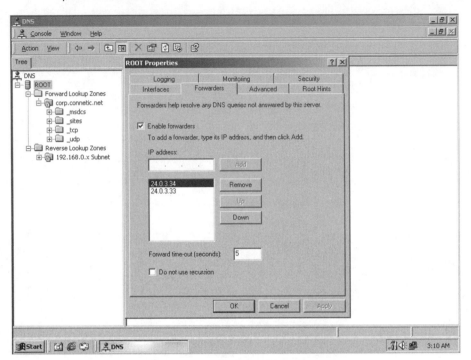

Configuring DNS When You Don't Have an Existing Registered Domain Name

The .local TLD is reserved by the Internet Engineering Task Force for use in private networks. The Server Configuration Wizard will suggest using this as your root domain if you don't have a registered domain name. For security purposes, this is fine; there's no way to resolve a .local domain name on the Internet, and there never will be. This means that machines in a private .local domain are not reachable from the Internet. Using the .local DNS TLD is similar to using the 10 or the 192.168 domain for IP addressing.

I have not used .local for a production network yet. As far as I've been able to test, I've found no problems with using .local in a Windows 2000 network as the TLD, even when the network is connected to the Internet. My research on the Internet hasn't turned up any solid examples of the use of .local domains, and the IETF's draft RFC is surprisingly short.

With proper DNS forwarding to actual DNS servers (those of your ISP, for example), internal clients have no problems resolving the standard TLDs (.com, .net, .org, and so on). And, considering the fact that your public services should handle name resolution differently than your internal network, it may very well be more secure to use the .local internal DNS TLD even if you have a domain name you've registered for public services.

Giving Up and Starting Over

If you've gone through the Active Directory Installation Wizard once and made the wrong choices, don't worry. You can uninstall and then reinstall Active Directory. In Windows NT, domain choices were hard to fix but not nearly as problematic as Windows 2000. In this section, I show you how to remove a current Active Directory installation in order to reengineer from ground zero.

> **WARNING** Destroying your current Active Directory information will delete all computer and user accounts. The computer accounts aren't a big deal; they'll be automatically re-created when the computers are reattached to the new domain, but losing user accounts could be problematic. Use the procedures for manual account migration discussed in Chapter 11 to assist with this problem.

1. Remove DNS if it is integrated with Active Directory.
2. Use dcpromo.exe to demote all Active Directory servers. On the last server, check the box to indicate that this is the last server in the domain so the domain structure will be destroyed.
3. Correct the DNS name service information on every domain controller to conform to your new planned DNS namespace.
4. Start over with the Server Configuration Wizard on the machine that you intend to be the Active Directory and DNS root machine.

On an Exchange 2000 server, this process is complicated by the fact that Exchange 2000 will only run on a network with Active Directory. You'll have to back up your data stores, remove Exchange 2000, and then reinstall it once you've set up the Active Directory infrastructure.

Managing Active Directory

Creating and configuring an Active Directory is surprisingly easy. Presuming you've got DNS set up correctly before you start, you can simply run the Active Directory Installation Wizard (dcpromo.exe) and answer a few questions to create a new forest, a new tree, and a new domain, or to add new trees and new domains to existing forests. Figure 9.4 shows the Active Directory Installation Wizard.

Figure 9.4 Use dcpromo.exe to create your Active Directory and add trees and domains to it.

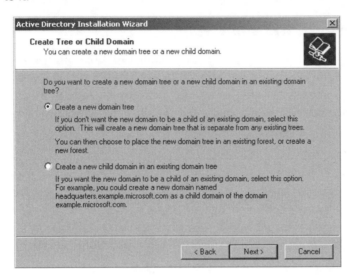

There's no real magic to creating an effective Active Directory interdomain structure or intradomain structure. The only slightly difficult part is correctly setting up sites for proper replication.

TIP Microsoft's online Active Directory administration help is surprisingly complete and well written. It gives complete introductory information about Active Directory management, and you should use it whenever you have a question about a specific function regarding the Active Directory snap-ins.

No central Active Directory tool exists to view the entire Active Directory hierarchy at once. This is because the two major upper-level components—forests and trees—aren't real objects (specific elements within the directory); they're simply special domains that host extra Active Directory information.

Three snap-ins are used for Active Directory configuration:

- Active Directory Domains and Trusts
- Active Directory Sites and Services
- Active Directory Users and Computers

You'll do most of your Active Directory configuration using the Active Directory Users and Computers snap-in. This snap-in controls the structure of a Directory within a single domain. It shows the OU hierarchy and the location of security principals within the domain and its OUs. This snap-in lists whichever domains you connect it to as peers irrespective of their actual parent/child relationship, which is unfortunate because if it did show the relationship between domains, you could build a single hierarchical view of your domain.

The Active Directory Domains and Trusts snap-in allows you to control the trust relationships between domains in a forest, but it doesn't show the hierarchy itself.

Sites and Replication

Windows NT 4 used *single-master replication* to propagate new user and computer accounts from the primary domain controller (the single master in a domain) to the backup domain controllers. New information flowed only one way, and because accounts could only be modified on the PDC (the User Manager for Domains, no matter where it ran from, was directly connected to the PDC and stored changes immediately to it), there was no problem with collisions. Windows 2000, however, uses *multimaster replication*, in which any domain controller can make updates to the Active Directory.

Collisions

Collisions occur when the same record is changed simultaneously on two different domain controllers in a Windows 2000 network. Because Windows 2000 uses multimaster replication for updates, and because those updates may take time to propagate to every domain controller in a complex network, it's quite probable that incompatible changes to the same record will eventually be made on two different domain controllers before they replicate to one another.

When collisions occur, Windows 2000 uses a rather simple formula to determine which update to use: On the first instance of a change, the controller with the latest time stamp wins. However, if the same change has been made multiple times on the same domain controller (because, for example, it was changed back by replication from another controller because it lost the time-stamp check), then the value from the domain controller that made the change the most times is kept. This rather simple mechanism ensures that in the vast majority of cases, the correct change will be used, and if it's not, that manual intervention will surely enforce the correct change. In the exceptionally rare case that the same change comes through from two domain controllers with the same time (in seconds) stamped and the same number of updates counted, then the Active Directory simply chooses one arbitrarily and relies on the fact that an administrator will correct the error through an additional update.

Windows 2000
Network Planning

PART 2

Replication

Windows 2000 automatically configures replication between domain controllers, and there's little reason to modify the defaults except in cases of extreme bandwidth constraints.

> **NOTE**   The mechanics of intrasite replication and intersite replication are covered in exhaustive detail in the "Windows 2000 Server Distributed Systems Guide," which is part of the Windows 2000 Resource Kit.

Normally, replication occurs whenever a batch of changes occurs in the domain. Windows 2000 actually queues up changes for a few minutes before it begins replication operations. Administrative updates to the directory usually occur at once, and there's no point in beginning separate replication sessions for each. Once a batch of changes has been made on a domain controller, it notifies its replication partners that it has changes, and the replication partners return contact to transmit the updates.

This system works fine in local area networks, but it's problematic over slower WAN connections because the updates can be quite large and can occur frequently. Updates can also occur many times over the same network if it has many domain controllers. The larger the network is, the more frequently replication traffic will occur. If the directory is being used for more than administration (for example, you have Exchange 2000 running on your network), then it's quite likely that replication traffic will be constant across slow WAN links. To cope with this problem, Microsoft uses the concept of sites to manage the scheduling of replication across slow links.

Sites

A *site* is defined as a set of domain controllers that are all connected to each other with links that have at least 500Kbps (Microsoft's recommended minimum) of available bandwidth. If connections between controllers are slower than this, then they should be partitioned into multiple sites. Sites must also consist of one or more IP subnets; if you're bridging across a slow WAN link so that all the computers can remain in the same subnet (a very bad practice that should be rare), you must partition each side into a separate subnet to create sites.

Replication within a site occurs automatically (and is uncompressed) whenever changes are made to the directory. Replication between sites is scheduled (and compressed for transmission) by administrators according to the demands placed on the WAN links. For each site, one domain controller is automatically designated as the *bridgehead server*. This server handles all intersite replication for the site. Since each site has only one bridgehead server, and since Active Directory uses "pull" replication (the receiver initiates the request for updates), replication over a WAN link is guaranteed to occur only once, no matter how many domain controllers exist in the remote network.

So, to create your site architecture, first create an accurate diagram of your network showing every local area network, WAN link, intersite dial-up connection, and so forth, including the speed of that link. Then draw boxes around the accumulated networks that are well connected such that the boxes are connected by slower WAN links only. Voilà, you have your site structure. Figure 9.5 shows this process.

Figure 9.5   Creating a site topology is simple using your existing network documentation.

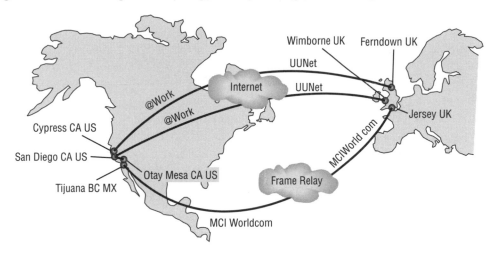

Once you've created your site structure, you can implement it using the Active Directory Sites and Services snap-in. When you start the snap-in, there will be an existing site named Default-First-Site-Name, which contains the root Active Directory controller. You should rename this site to match the site where you created the domain controller. You can then create sites that match the remaining sites in your network. I typically use the city name followed by the country code (as used in TLDcc domain names), except when more than one site per city exists, in which case I add a prefix such as the street name or some other site identifier. Examples include these:

- SanDiegoUS
- SaltLakeCityUS
- LondonUK
- TijuanaMX
- Lusk-SanDiegoUS

- Garnet-SanDiegoUS
- 700East-SaltLakeCityUS
- 5400South-SaltLakeCityUS

You must create site links along with the sites. *Site links* are used to create the schedule for replication between sites. When I create a site link, I specify the data-link type, the bit rate, and (if necessary for uniqueness) the sites that it links. This makes it easy to remember which sites participate in the link and what the bandwidth over the link is. For example:

- Microwave1500K-US2MX
- FrameCloud256K-US2EC
- DSL768K-SD
- Email-US-EC

Sites cannot be created without a link, and links cannot be created without at least two sites. This can lead to a chicken-and-egg problem where you may actually have to add dummy sites to a link in order to create it and then remove those sites and populate the link with the real sites. At the end of it all, you should have a site object created for each physical site and link objects that contain the sites connected to the link.

Once you've got your sites and site links created, you can modify the schedule allowed for each link. Figure 9.6 shows a relatively congested link that has been restricted to replicating during nonworking hours and lunch only.

After defining your sites and links, you can add server objects to each site in order to specify which servers belong in which sites. As an administrative convenience, you can create subnet specifiers that will automatically place domain controllers in the correct site based on their IP address when they are created. If you create your sites right after installing the first domain controller, the remaining domain controllers will automatically be placed in the proper site as soon as you install Active Directory on them. If you change the IP address of a server such that it would change the server's site, you must manually move the server in the Active Directory Sites and Services snap-in to match the change.

As a final note about sites, to reduce intersite queries from clients to servers, you should have at least one DNS server and one Global Catalog server at each site. *Global Catalog servers* maintain a copy of all the logon information in the forest so that logons don't have to proceed over WAN links. Both of these functions could be configured as ancillary duties of the bridgehead domain controller in order to simplify administration.

Figure 9.6   You can easily schedule when replication may occur over site links.

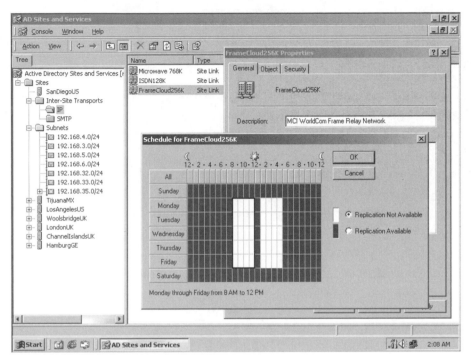

Summary

Active Directory is Windows 2000's central management structure. It is implemented as a hierarchical database of objects such as user accounts, computer accounts, shared folders, printers, services, and other domain information.

Windows 2000 uses Active Directory to perform domain logons, replicate data among domain controllers, create and manage trust relationships, and organize users and computers into manageable accumulations.

The Active Directory is organized into a forest of trees (each of which composes a DNS namespace) of domains related to one another in a parent/child relationship. Each domain contains a tree of Organizational Units culminating into computer and user objects. In a similar configuration, sites, site links, and server objects are used to manage replication between Active Directory domain controllers.

For the majority of users, a single domain architecture is appropriate. Multiple domains create administrative hassles, and since a single domain can handle millions of objects spread among numerous physical sites, there are very few good reasons why an organization would choose a multiple domain structure.

Proper DNS configuration is mandatory for the operation of Active Directory. Properly configuring DNS isn't particularly difficult, but a few snafus aren't particularly well spelled out in advance:

- Choose a unique third-level domain name below your company's registered domain name as the DNS root of your internal machines.

- Handle public and private DNS resolution separately on separate DNS servers.

- Make the root DNS server in your organization point to itself for DNS, and configure forwarders to query your ISP's DNS servers for public names.

- Configure the DNS server for automatic registration, and then install Active Directory to complete the process of creating an integrated DNS server.

The only tricky part to configuring Active Directory is properly defining and creating sites. The best starting point is to overview your existing network architecture. After reviewing your existing WAN links for upgrades and then implementing them, create a network map that shows each facility in your company and the links between them. Each facility is a site, and each WAN link shown on the network diagram will be implemented as a site link. Once you've created your sites and site links in the Active Directory Sites and Services snap-in, you can schedule how often you want replication to occur over each site link.

Case Study: Real World Active Directory Planning

In reality, Active Directory planning is quite simple: plan for a single domain, create sites based on WAN infrastructure, and map the business divisions or departments as Organizational Units in order to delegate authority and control Group Policy effectively. Sometimes, however, the existing conditions can make this simple plan difficult to implement, leaving you with tough choices to make about the structure of your directory. The following case study was my first ground-up Active Directory migration.

One of my clients was a smaller, multinational semiconductor manufacturer. Their existing network consisted of the following:

- A headquarters facility in San Diego with 35 users.

- A much larger manufacturing plant in Tijuana, Mexico, with 200 users connected by a T1 microwave radio to the San Diego headquarters site. The microwave bandwidth was split into 16 channels for voice and 8 channels for data, so we had 512K of bandwidth to Mexico.

- A small sales office in Los Angeles with 8 users was connected via ISDN.

- A few corporate officers and owners had 56K Frame Relay connections to their homes (strange, but true) because they worked out of their homes in Los Angeles and Orange County. These circuits were established before DSL existed.

- In the United Kingdom, another manufacturing plant with 30 users was located outside Woolsbridge and connected via 256K Frame Relay.

- A sales office in London with 12 users was connected via 128K Frame Relay.

- A finance office in the Channel Islands with 5 users was not constantly connected; their intermittent dial-up to the U.S. was used only to exchange e-mail and terminal sessions to the AS400-based financial application. This facility did not participate in the domain.

- Another sales office in Germany with 4 users was also connected via Frame Relay at 64Kbps.

Figure 9.5, earlier in the chapter, shows the architecture of the network.

The domain architecture was simple: a single Windows NT 4 domain existed with the PDC at the San Diego headquarters and a BDC at each location. The San Diego and Mexico facilities each had an additional BDC as well.

When we decided to migrate the network to Windows 2000, the bandwidth situation didn't look good according to Microsoft's planning recommendations. These links were already congested, and additional sporadic traffic would be problematic. Because of the low speed of the international connections, creating a separate domain for each site to minimize replication traffic seemed to make sense. Even scheduled connections using sites would probably generate too much traffic since we intended to administer everything from the headquarters site.

The connection to Mexico, while technically fast enough, was always jammed with data. Expansion was prohibitively expensive because of the complexities of licensing radio bandwidth in two countries. Cross-border physical circuits were inordinately expensive—in excess of $10,000 per month.

Rather than act in haste and deploy multiple domains at the outset, we decided to review the WAN infrastructure to see what could be done to improve bandwidth. The company's monthly telecommunications charges ran at around $30,000 per month even at these low data rates, because of the distances involved. Increasing bandwidth to the necessary 512K per site would have cost in excess of $100,000 per month. Frame Relay was already the least expensive WAN circuit that could be deployed across international borders, and their circuit charges were already competitive.

We decided to take a look at VPN technologies such as IPSec. If we could get a T1-rate Internet circuit at each site, and then run an IPSec VPN over the Internet, we could potentially reduce costs and increase bandwidth because we would not be paying distance charges for the circuits. But I'd been down the VPN route many times in the past, and I knew that when improperly implemented, VPNs were highly unreliable and chaotic in both their data rate and connection ability.

My experience told me that most problems with VPNs arose because of congestion on the Internet. To flow from one major ISP to another (for example, from UUNet to CerfNet), traffic must go through the very congested Commercial Internet Exchange (CIX) Network Access Points (NAPs).

The solution was to use a single ISP for all of the sites. UUNet, one of the oldest ISPs in the world (at the healthy age of 15), which was now a subsidiary of Worldcom, had connectivity to every site but Germany, the Channel Islands, and Mexico for about $2,000 per month. This meant that all of our traffic would flow only over their backbones, avoiding the congested CIX NAPs and the circuitous routes caused by routing among various ISPs.

UUNet was willing to put in a circuit to the Channel Islands, but the costs for that circuit would be about three times the price of any of the other circuits—$6,000.

As it turned out, the company was in the process of deprecating the Germany sales office, anyway, because it was simply too small and too remote to be well supported in any sense. The company felt it could better support its European customers from the London sales office.

As for Mexico, we decided to cut four voice channels over to the data circuit, which would give us 768Kbps between facilities and the occasional busy signal on the phone side, which was deemed less important now than when the connection was originally created. We added a low-cost, local, T1-rate Internet connection from a Mexican ISP to handle HTTP traffic and then filtered HTTP off of the microwave. Using two circuits, we were able to guarantee that business-critical data could get through over the private microwave link without blocking public Web access to users in Mexico.

We wanted rock-solid reliability from the VPN; it had to work at least as well as the Frame Relay circuits did. So we decided to use IPSec appliances from VPNet rather than Windows 2000's built-in IPSec. These devices could be placed at each site in parallel with a firewall to provide an emulated WAN link whether servers were up or not. Since they were solid-state devices and wouldn't be reconfigured once they were set up, they wouldn't be subject to the relatively frequent failure of a server.

The installation went well. Once the UUNet T1-rate DSL Internet circuits were in place, we put the VPNet boxes in place. After configuring them to work correctly with the firewalls, we ran both networks in parallel to prove out the reliability of the VPN. During the prove-out period, we eliminated the Frame Relay connections to the homes of corporate officers and replaced them with VPN boxes or client-side software running on inexpensive cable modems or DSL (whichever was available).

After three months without a hitch, we pulled the plug on the Frame Relay network. We were seeing nearly full T1 connectivity over the VPN, and the circuit charges were less than $10,000 per month. We now had the connectivity to establish just a single Windows 2000 domain using sites to schedule updates, so all of our architecture planning was complete.

Whenever possible, you should adapt your wide-area connectivity to the demands that Windows 2000 will place upon it, rather than adapting your domain architecture to the constraints of your WAN links. It's much easier to administer a simple domain and Active Directory structure, so you may be able to save the cost of an employee in the long run if you spend a little more on connectivity to make Windows 2000's technologies work for you.

24seven CASE STUDY

10

Deploying
Windows 2000

Deploying Windows 2000 in a large organization can actually be easier than in a small organization thanks to the wide array of automated remote installation tools available for and supported by Windows 2000.

You can perform a rollout installation of Windows 2000 in four ways:

- Direct installation from the original CD-ROMs
- Network installation using Remote Installation Service
- Network installation without using Remote Installation Service
- Disk imaging

I don't discuss direct installation from CD-ROM in this chapter because I covered it in Chapter 2. Direct installation is best for infrequent individual installations of Windows 2000 and is not well-suited for a mass rollout.

There's no reason to handle all your rollout requirements the same way, even if you're doing all the work at the same time. You may decide to use CD-based imaging for laptops, Remote Installation Service to roll out clients, and network-based disk imaging to roll out terminal servers. The point of any rollout effort is to get as much work done as quickly as possible, so make sure you're using the best method for each class of computers.

Choosing a Methodology

To decide on a deployment methodology, consider the following factors:

How many client computers are you rolling out to?   For less than 20 computers, it might not be worth your time to do the preparation work for a rollout. For more than 100 computers, Remote Installation Service is probably going to take longer than a weekend to complete.

Are laptop computers included in the rollout?   Laptops can be notoriously difficult to roll out because the vendors of rollout tools frequently fail to consider the special requirements of laptop hardware. Very few laptops can be supported by Remote Installation Service, and it's extraordinarily difficult to perform network-based rollouts to laptops because they often don't have standard network adapters. I've found it best to handle laptops as a separate rollout using CD-based imaging.

Are servers included in the rollout?   Remote Installation Service was not designed to image servers (there is an unsupported "hack" around this that I'll present later in the chapter), and domain controllers should never be imaged. Terminal servers and departmental file servers are good candidates for network-based imaging in larger environments.

Are your network adapters PXE compliant or supported by the PXE boot floppy? If they aren't, you can forget about using Remote Installation Service. Some type of disk imaging is your only resort in this case.

Remote Installation Services

Microsoft's *Remote Installation Service (RIS)* is a far more advanced version of Microsoft's earlier attempts at software rollout. Windows NT 4 included *sysdiff* for creating difference-based installation packages, but the software was difficult to use and provided very little benefit, since there was no good way to get a brand-new computer connected to the installation source. Most network administrators reverted to the age-old hard-disk cloning technique because it was faster and simpler.

Remote Installation Service solves many of these problems. RIS provides a method to start the installations using Intel and 3Com's Pre-boot eXecution Environment (PXE), which is built into new network adapters from 3Com, Intel, SMC, and a few other vendors. Computers with those network adapters can automatically download their operating system (and applications, if configured) from the network without having an existing operating system.

Microsoft also provides a PXE client creator program that will create a boot floppy that works with about 20 different PCI network adapters (from 3Com, Intel, SMC, and a few others—mostly vendors whose current product offerings are PXE compliant) to provide backward support for RIS where PXE-compliant network adapters are not present. Figure 10.1 shows the PXE boot floppy emulating a PXE network adapter.

Figure 10.1   The PXE boot floppy allows you to use RIS with certain non-PXE-enabled PCI network adapters.

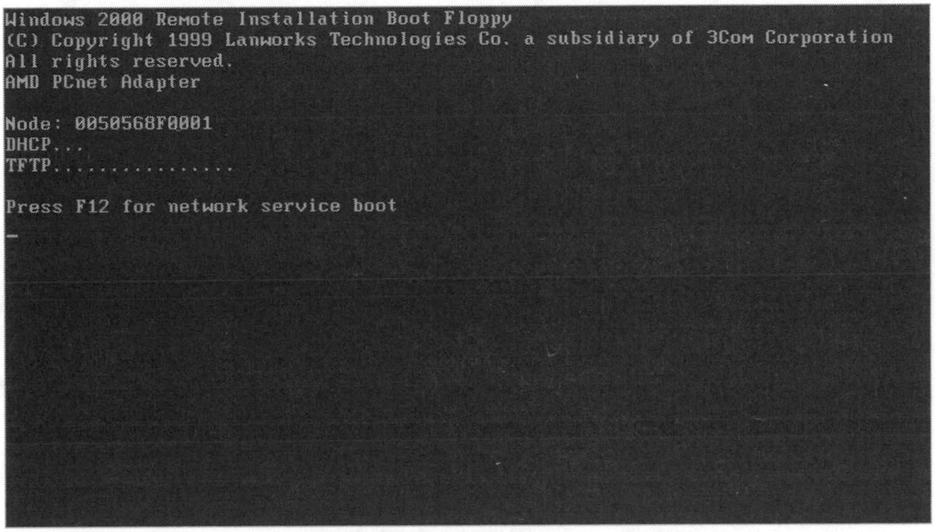

```
Windows 2000 Remote Installation Boot Floppy
(C) Copyright 1999 Lanworks Technologies Co. a subsidiary of 3Com Corporation
All rights reserved.
AMD PCnet Adapter

Node: 0050568F0001
DHCP...
TFTP...............

Press F12 for network service boot
_
```

RIS excels in installations of Windows 2000 Professional (it was not designed to install any other operating system) where computers are not homogenous and where the network adapters come with PXE BIOS ROMs. It is especially suited to environments with a frequent but not simultaneous need to install Windows 2000 clients.

How RIS Works

RIS is actually a package of technologies that Microsoft has integrated into a coherent whole. I'll explain the technologies as I explain the RIS process. Figure 10.2 illustrates the process described below.

1. When a PXE-compliant network adapter boots, it broadcasts a plea for a DHCP address on the local Ethernet broadcast domain along with its GUID or Ethernet MAC address (if it doesn't have a GUID).

2. The local DHCP server responds with an IP address, and the local RIS server responds with its address in the DHCP TFTP boot server field.

Figure 10.2 The client negotiates its boot information from a DHCP server, a RIS server, and an Active Directory server.

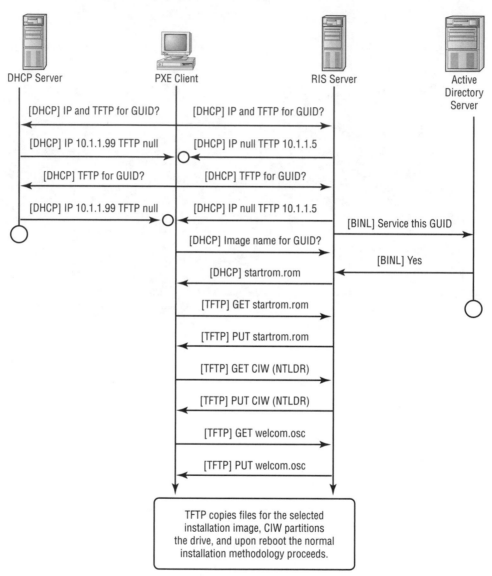

3. If the DHCP and RIS servers are running on the same machine, the response is combined into a single response. The client accepts both and proceeds with the boot process. Otherwise, the client ignores the first RIS response because it doesn't contain the client's IP address.

4. The client then repeats its request for a TFTP boot server, which both the DHCP server and RIS server respond to again.

5. The client ignores the DHCP server because its response doesn't (shouldn't) contain a boot server.

6. At this point, if the RIS server is configured to talk only to authorized clients, the RIS server will use the BINL protocol to contact an Active Directory server to request authorization to service the client by specifying the client's GUID. If the client does not have a GUID, a GUID is generated by using the client's Ethernet MAC address prefixed with zeros.

7. The Active Directory server checks its list of prestaged GUIDs (those that you entered when the client was shipped in) to determine if the client should be serviced by the RIS server that queried the Active Directory controller.

8. If the server declines to service the client because it is not authorized to by the Active Directory server, the client will repeat the DHCP plea for a TFTP boot server until it finds a TFTP server that is authorized to service it.

NOTE The TFTP server that ultimately winds up servicing a client may not actually be a RIS server; many disk-imaging software rollout tools also use PXE, DHCP, and TFTP to install their images. With careful planning and tuning, third-party boot servers can be made to operate correctly with RIS on the same network even if they don't support Active Directory.

---

9. The client uses DHCP-formatted queries to request the name of the boot image from the RIS server and establishes a TFTP session with the boot server to download the `startrom.rom` boot file.

10. `startrom.rom` establishes a TFTP session to download and run the *Oschooser* (also called the *Client Installation Wizard*, or *CIW*).

11. The Oschooser downloads the OSCML-formatted welcome, login, and subsequent screens to allow the user to identify themselves and select an operating system to download. The Oschooser welcome screen is shown in Figure 10.3.

Figure 10.3   The Oschooser welcome screen shows that everything is working normally in a RIS installation.

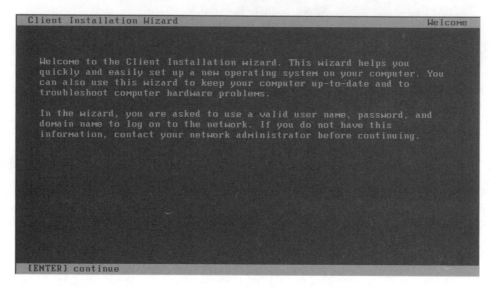

12. The Oschooser uses the information contained in the installation image template to determine whether and how to partition and format the computer's hard disk, and then it uses the normal Windows SMB protocol to copy the installation files from the RIS server to the local computer's hard disk drive.

13. The last important screen the user sees is the GUID information screen shown in Figure 10.4. At this point, the computer can actually be shut down and delivered. When restarted, the RIS installation completes automatically without asking the user any questions.

14. Upon reboot, the normal second-stage installation process for Windows 2000 begins, and the RIS server is no longer necessary.

As mentioned earlier, RIS servers can operate in one of two modes: *open response* to any client requesting service and *response only to clients with GUIDs* that have been entered into the Active Directory. Which mode you choose depends mostly on your security policy and the number of RIS servers you want to operate. If more than one RIS server is reachable from your client (either because you have multiple RIS servers in the Ethernet broadcast domain or because you're forwarding DHCP through routers), then you need to use GUID prestaging to determine which server will respond to the client. There's no other good way to make sure you know which server will respond. Also, if you have unusually high security requirements, you can use GUID prestaging to make sure no unauthorized clients are installed, although the installer will have to present a domain user account with the authority to perform remote installations when they run the Oschooser.

Figure 10.4   The GUID display screen indicates that the Oschooser has all the information it needs to complete the installation process.

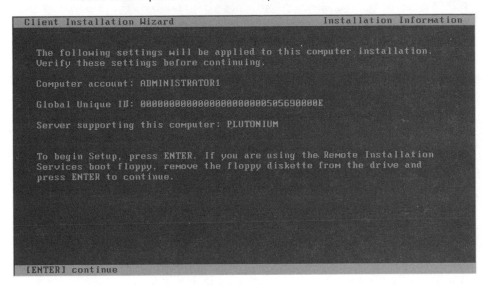

RIS installs the following services on the RIS server:

Boot Information Negotiation Layer (BINL)   Listens for DHCP requests and CIW requests. BINL actually implements the RIS-specific DHCP server and the RIS-specific CIW request protocol.

Trivial File Transfer Protocol (TFTP)   Is the TCP/IP protocol used by the RIS server to transfer files to the client. TFTP is the simplest file transfer protocol available over TCP/IP and is a standard part of most TCP/IP suites. TFTP is used for nearly all network boot protocols.

Single Instance Store (SIS)   Is a file system filter that allows a single instance of a stored file to appear as though it is stored in numerous places. SIS allows different RIS images to occupy only as much space as required by one copy of each unique file. SIS works by moving the single instance to its own storage area and creating links from the normal file system to the stored single instance of the file. The SIS store is contained in the \sis common store folder. SIS links are implemented as reparse points and are marked as sparse files so that the operating system reports the amount of space the file would take without actually taking it, which allows the quota service to properly account for size. Files do not need the same name to be identical; SIS will store only one copy if the contents of the files are the same. If a linked file is modified so that it is no longer identical, SIS automatically copies the file back to its original location and removes the SIS link reparse point.

NOTE   Be certain your backup software is compatible with the SIS store, or you'll be backing up every copy of a SIS-stored file rather than just the unique copy. The Windows 2000 backup utility is compatible with SIS.

WARNING   To restore a SIS volume (using file-based backup tools), the SIS service must be running on the volume prior to the restoration, or the restored data will not be compatible with SIS. Sector-based backup tools do not exhibit this problem.

SIS Groveler   Scans the SIS store to find duplicate files that are candidates to be merged into a single instance. Once candidates are identified, the Groveler compares the two files directly, and if they match, moves the files to the SIS store and creates links to the SIS store single instance.

Problems with RIS

Unfortunately, if you don't have PXE network adapters in your existing machines, and if the type of adapter you use (such as the very popular DEC adapters and the adapters built into Compaq and many other brands of computers) aren't compatible with the PXE boot floppy, you won't be able to use RIS. To guarantee compatibility with RIS, you should use Intel, 3Com, or SMC network adapters.

RIS supports the following non-PXE boot adapters:

- 3Com 3C900, 3Com 3C905 (all variants)
- AMD PCnet-based adapters
- Compaq NetFlex
- DEC DE450, DE500
- HP DeskDirect 10/100
- Intel Pro series (most variants)
- SMC 8432, 9332, 9432

RIS supports only a very few types of laptops. Laptops that require PCMCIA network adapters won't work. The PXE boot floppy supports only PCI network adapters, and PCMCIA network adapters cannot be PXE compliant because they're not built into the computer. Since about 80 percent of laptops on the market do not have built-in Ethernet ports, it's likely that this problem will affect your laptops. Among laptops with built-in network adapters that can use RIS are those that support their adapters as PCI devices that are supported by the PXE boot floppy (such as the Sony VAIO Z505 series) or that have PXE network boot support built in (such as the Fujitsu Lifebook S Series).

WARNING   Minor differences in the manufacture of a network adapter can cause the PXE boot floppy to fail. For example, I get a strange error that's not listed at support.microsoft.com on my Sony VAIO Z505 when I try to boot the PXE emulator floppy, even though the supported Intel Pro series network adapter is built in. I've received similar reports of problems with Compaq laptop built-in adapters as well. The only way to determine if a computer will work correctly with RIS is to test it.

RIS is not ideal for large rollouts. RIS reads the installation source files from a directory on the server's hard disk drive, and simultaneous connections to the service cause the server to slow down considerably. A server with copious amounts of RAM (more than 1GB) that isn't doing anything else can support about 25 concurrent installations. Less capable servers, servers that have other duties, or more widespread rollouts will cause further slowing. Unfortunately, most rollouts worth using rollout tools involve hundreds of machines.

One solution would be to have multiple RIS servers on your network, but that too has problems. RIS uses DHCP to connect PXE clients to RIS servers. Whichever RIS server responds first will "take" all the clients who request service. This is especially likely to happen on RIS servers that are also DHCP servers (because they respond in fewer steps) and on RIS servers that are configured to respond to unknown clients, because they respond to all clients, not just to those they're configured to respond to.

To get around these problems you can:

Disable all RIS servers from accepting unknown clients.   Assign client GUIDs to RIS servers in the Active Directory. In addition, ensure that none of your RIS servers are also DHCP servers. This option can cause more work than it saves, because you have to receive each new computer, unpack it to record its GUID, and then send the computer to whoever will ultimately receive it. You might as well install the operating system while you have it.

Place one RIS server on each Ethernet broadcast domain.   Configure routers not to forward DHCP requests. This is problematic if you wanted to use a single DCHP server on your internetwork and because the size of your broadcast domains may not be ideal for a single RIS server. It is probably the easiest way to build a RIS infrastructure throughout your network, however.

As with all network-based rollout tools, trying to perform a network installation over a WAN link is an expensive exercise in futility. For rollouts at remote sites, ether deploy a RIS server to the site or create CD-based rollouts that the end-users can install themselves (simply FedEx the CDs to the remote site).

> **NOTE** RIS requires a considerable number of services and computers to work correctly together in order to function, and this makes it extremely fragile. Hundreds of known issues exist with the service. Search TechNET for the Technical Guide to Remote Installation Service on microsoft.com for a complete explanation and list of known issues with RIS.

Methods

There are two ways to use RIS: deploy Windows 2000 in its default configuration, or create a completely configured client with applications and create a RIS-installable image to deploy the entire configuration.

OS-only installation   This only installs Windows 2000 Professional. When you install RIS, the RISetup program prompts for a Windows 2000 Professional CD-ROM to copy the default Windows 2000 installation files to the RIS remote installation share. You must provide a full version of Windows 2000 Professional; upgrade editions don't work.

Fully configured installation   You create installation sources, fully configured with the applications you installed on a prototypical client. You can create any number of installations on a RIS server, and thanks to the SIS service, the installations don't take up that much room because operating system and application files are stored only once, no matter how many installation images there are.

Of the two methods, fully configured installations make far more sense and save a considerable amount of time. The only time you should bother with operating-system-only installations are in environments where the users have full authority to install their own software and you have no idea what that software will be.

Disk Imaging

Disk imaging is the age-old method used by network administrators for rolling out computers of all types. Disk imaging is also called *disk cloning*, and it refers to making an exact copy of a hard disk drive in order to distribute operating systems and applications to computers throughout the enterprise.

In Windows NT, disk-cloning caused a troublesome problem; each cloned machine had the same *SID*—the unique identification number upon which computer-based security is based. Clients with the same SID could not differentiate users of one computer from users of another. Strange problems resulted, causing security failures and some application software to malfunction.

Manufacturers of imaging software studied the problem and released utilities that patched the Registry to change the SID. Microsoft did not support these patches, but they seemed to work.

About midway through Windows NT 4's life cycle, Microsoft finally caved to pressure from its largest customers and computer vendors and officially supported disk imaging. Microsoft released the first version of its system preparation utility, which essentially duplicated the final portion of the setup program upon first boot. This part of the setup recorded the CD key to create the installation's serial number and then randomly generated the computer's SID.

The Windows 2000 CD-ROM includes the System Preparation Tool, so it's now available for everyone to use.

Disk imaging really shines in mass client rollouts of 20 or more machines. For fewer than 20 installs, you're better off using RIS or manually installing clients. The preparation required to use disk imaging, the cost of third-party software or equipment, and the fact that you'll probably wind up opening the machines to remove their hard disk drives makes disk imaging more trouble than it's worth.

Disk imaging is great when you want to roll out servers. RIS does not support installing Windows 2000 Server, but there are occasions where rolling out servers is a good idea. For example, you may want to roll out terminal servers in mass numbers or be able to quickly deploy new terminal servers in case your load estimates were incorrect.

In circumstances where you are simultaneously deploying more than 20 servers of exactly the same type, disk imaging is also appropriate. I've never seen a circumstance where I thought it was appropriate to roll out domain controllers—a view supported by Microsoft, as the System Preparation Tool will not run on domain controllers. You can upgrade member servers to domain controllers after they've been rolled out, however.

How Disk Imaging Works

Disk imaging simply copies the contents of one hard disk drive to another. UNIX administrators have used it for years with the venerable DI command line tool that performs direct sector copies between SCSI devices. When Windows first came out, these administrators simply used the same tools and methods to roll out Windows that they'd always used to roll out UNIX machines.

Utilities specifically designed to perform hard disk sector copies from MS-DOS came on the scene just a few years later. Ghost, the first such tool, was simple to use: by putting the source and destination hard disks in a single computer, you could boot an MS-DOS boot floppy, run Ghost, and copy the two images.

Simple sector copies had problems, though. If the source disk was not exactly the same size as the destination disk, then the partition information would be wrong. So the sector copy tool vendors incorporated utilities to automatically or manually increase the size of the resulting partition. (Few can actually decrease the size, so create your images using partition sizes smaller than your smallest destination disk.)

Hardware vendors got into the act at this point, producing specialized computers designed for copying hard disk drives. Originally designed for computer vendors such as Dell, Sony, or Gateway who perform thousands of installations per day, these machines allow technicians in a computer production environment to perform one-to-many copies of a single hard disk—often to eight or more destination drives at the same time. It didn't take long for these tools to move into large enterprises.

The next innovation was imaging to and from files rather than using actual hard disk images. By creating a file that contained a hard disk image, one "master" hard disk could be used to install multiple different installations. The files could also be easily compressed to store more files on a single master hard disk.

Using image files also allowed sector imaging to be performed over a network. By connecting to a server (usually using TFTP or SMB), a client could be imaged without ever opening it up to remove the hardware. All that was required was an MS-DOS or proprietary network boot floppy compatible with the client's network adapter, or a server that could respond to network boot adapters.

The final innovation in disk imaging is *image multicasting*, where hundreds or thousands of clients can simultaneously receive their disk images without overburdening a single server. Using image multicasting, clients are network-booted (usually using PXE or another netboot protocol) and then wait for the server to transmit an image. Once all the clients are connected to the server, the server begins transmitting just a single image on the wire using either Ethernet or TCP/IP broadcast mechanisms. Every client connected to the server receives the same image and writes it down to its local hard disk. Because only one image is being transmitted, a single server can handle a practically unlimited number of simultaneous clients.

The most recent imaging packages have incorporated technology that allows administrators to create CD-ROMs of image files that boot the disk-imaging software. Many retail packages now have the ability to copy directly to an installed CD-R and to span large images across multiple CDs automatically. This allows administrators to perform disk imaging very conveniently and produce a set of installation CD-ROMs that will work on any computer. If the computer can't boot the CD-ROM, a boot floppy can be used to load the disk-imaging software.

Problems with Disk Imaging

The major problem with disk imaging in Windows NT—SID uniqueness—is not a problem in Windows 2000, thanks to the System Preparation Tool. That's not to say that disk imaging isn't without its problems, however.

Some computers, especially laptops, can be difficult to image without special hardware. It's difficult to make MS-DOS boot floppies that can mount PCMCIA network adapters and a TCP/IP stack in order to perform a network-based disk image without running out of memory. And, unless all your network adapters and laptops are the same, you'll have to make a new boot floppy for each class of computer. Putting together all the files necessary to perform this work under the long-obsolete MS-DOS operating system can be a challenge. You can overcome these problems by physically removing the hard disk drive—easy on some laptops but nearly impossible on others.

Depending upon the quality of your disk-imaging software, variations in drive sizes or types can cause serious problems. Early versions of disk-to-disk imaging software were not capable of resizing partitions to use the maximum size of the disk.

Problems with IDE disk BIOSes can make booting restored images larger than 2GB or 8GB (actually, the 1024 cylinder boundary) impossible (depending upon the machine and the operating system), and you won't know that until after you finish a test installation. These problems can be overcome by reducing the size of the boot partition to below the problem threshold for the computer in question, but it can take time to figure out what those thresholds are for each class of computer.

Hardware differences between the prototype installation machine and the destination machine can be problematic. Although Windows 2000—with its automatic Plug and Play detection of hardware—can solve many of these problems automatically, changes in the disk controller can cause the process to fail. End-users will also see numerous Plug and Play messages upon first boot and may be required to provide drivers to complete the hardware install. Use prototype installation machines that are the same as each class of installed computers to avoid these problems. If most of your machines are unique, RIS may be a better way to go because it performs the normal Windows 2000 installation.

Methods

There are a number of different ways to perform disk imaging, each of which is appropriate for different scales of rollout.

Traditional disk-to-disk cloning   Is best suited for small rollouts. Disk-to-disk cloning involves physically mounting the source and the destination drive in the same computer and using the computer to copy the sectors from one disk to the other. Disk-to-disk cloning requires the least preparation and is the most compatible method to use since it doesn't require special drivers in MS-DOS to complete. Disk-to-disk imaging tools typically cost about $30 per workstation.

CD-based imaging   Allows you to write images directly to supported brands of CD-ROM burners instead of to another hard disk drive. These solutions can span across as many CDs as are required to write the image, typically two to six depending upon how much software you install before you create the image. The software will even make the first CD-R bootable so the image can be restored simply without the hassle of putting together a boot floppy. To restore the image, simply insert the first CD-R in the set, boot it, and change the CDs when prompted.

CD-based disk imaging can be a hassle because you have to "baby-sit" the restoration to swap in subsequent CDs, which would waste valuable technician time for each installation. But restoring an image from a bootable CD is so simple that the end-user of the computer can perform the restoration rather than a trained technician. Using CD-based disk imaging, you can perform a rollout by simply distributing copies of the required image CDs directly to end-users. Even better, they can "repair" their computers later on if an errant software installation messes them up. End-users need only copy their documents up to the network and re-restore their computers. In my experience, CD-based disk imaging is the easiest way to perform rollouts to laptops because nearly every modern computer supports bootable CDs.

Network-based imaging   Involves downloading image files from the network and writing them to the local computer. Network-based imaging is much more suited to large rollouts because (like RIS) you don't have to open up every computer to remove its hard disk drive. Unfortunately, you will have to get the computers up on a TCP/IP network in MS-DOS, which is problematic these days. As MS-DOS slips into obsolescence, vendors have stopped creating MS-DOS drivers for modern network adapters.

Disk-imaging vendors haven't been sleeping, however. Many enterprise-imaging solutions support PXE and earlier TFTP-based network boot protocols, so clients don't have to have an operating system installed in order to connect to the network and download their source image.

Network broadcast or multicast imaging   Is the big brother of network-based imaging. Network multicast imaging relies upon the broadcast facility of the data-link (Ethernet) layer or the multicast facility of the network (IP) layer to simultaneously transmit an image to all the subscribed clients.

NOTE   The difference between *broadcast* and *multicast* imaging is simply which layer the connection occurs over: broadcast imaging occurs at the data-link layer and cannot be routed, whereas multicast imaging occurs at the network layer and can be routed. Which you use will depend on which third-party product you purchase to perform imaging. I refer to both methods as multicast imaging throughout this chapter.

With network multicast imaging, you can literally install thousands of computers simultaneously from a single source server, performing any size of rollout within just a few hours. It will actually take more time to run around and boot all the clients than to complete the body of network installations. There's no faster way to deploy a rollout. These tools are usually licensed on a per-seat basis for about $100 per client computer.

Hardware-based cloning   Refers to the use of a dedicated device to copy hard disks. These devices exist to fill niches (such as laptop upgrades through the PCMCIA port) or to speed rollouts. A $2,000 disk-imaging device can copy one source to eight destination drives simultaneously at speeds that are limited only by the hard disk drive; generally, the copy operation finishes in about 15 minutes. At that speed, you could deploy 200 clients in a typical workday—quite a few by any measure. Since hardware-based cloning doesn't require a license for each computer you clone to, it can be substantially less expensive than other cloning methods.

Vendor-supported imaging   Refers to buying computers with your client image pre-installed by the manufacturer of the computer. Large direct marketers such as Dell and Gateway provide this service for their account holders as a way to keep customers loyal. Essentially, you provide a hard disk with the image you want installed on all your new computers. Whenever you buy a computer, the vendor will copy your image to the computer's hard disk before it ships, so the computer will be ready for use as soon as it arrives. Best of all, this form of imaging is free. Unfortunately, you have to use the same vendor for all your purchases, and you have to make sure they actually perform the imaging; some vendors are much better than others about actually doing it.

Of all these methods, I use only three: network-based multicast imaging for large installations, CD-based imaging for small rollouts, and vendor-supported imaging whenever it's available. Of the above options, these three techniques are by far the simplest to perform.

Manual Network Deployment

It's possible to deploy Windows 2000 over a network without using any of these automation tools. In fact, it's pretty easy. All you have to do is copy the \i386 directory from a Windows 2000 Professional CD-ROM to a share on a server somewhere, and then browse to it from clients to run the winnt or winnt32.exe setup programs.

The browsing to it is the rub; without an operating system, how do you browse to a network share? The short answer is that you don't. Yes, it is technically possible to create an MS-DOS boot floppy to connect to the network and then run the winnt setup program, but that's usually considerably more effort than it's worth, and certainly harder than using disk imaging, RIS with compatible network adapters, or the bootable network CD-ROM.

However, if your computers can't boot CD-ROMs, don't have PXE-compatible network adapters, and wouldn't be convenient to disassemble for direct disk-to-disk imaging, this is probably your best bet. A number of models of laptops fit this profile, as well as most computers built prior to 1997. These platforms are probably too old to run Windows 2000 well, however, so consider deprecating them to Terminal Services clients or getting rid of them.

Upgrading from another version of Windows is another matter entirely. If you've already got a running installation of Windows (any version) connected to the network, manual network deployment is a great way to perform "upgrade rollouts." None of the methods discussed so far in this chapter are good for those who want to run the upgrade option in Windows 2000 because they overwrite your current computer configuration. If you want to use the upgrade installation option, manual deployment is the perfect way to do it.

Deployment

Should installations be performed by end-users or by IT technicians? The answer to this question will change everything about your rollout infrastructure.

If end-users can be trusted to complete their own installations, you can save a tremendous amount of time. In this scenario, computers are shipped directly to the end-user from the manufacturer. You "forward-deploy" installation servers throughout your enterprise so that they are reachable from anywhere. End-users simply turn on their machines, go through the netboot process to connect to an installation server, and download a preconfigured system image. This infrastructure allows clients or technicians to later rebuild a machine from scratch without removing it from its installed location. These are considerable conveniences, especially in very large environments. However, if even a small number (10 percent) of users fail at installation, the number of resulting service calls at the client station may be overwhelming during a rollout. You must have highly competent users in order to forward-deploy your installation servers.

If end-users (and I mean nearly all end-users) can't be trusted to complete their own installations, there's little point in forward-deploying installation servers because you'll be performing all your installations in your lab. In this scenario, new computers are shipped to the IT lab rather than to the end-user, configured and installed by technicians, and then moved out to their final location. Although it's more work up front for technicians, it always works correctly, is sustainable and maintainable, and is much easier to set up. Some people recommend starting the installation process in the lab and then deploying the client computers to the end-user for the completion. This is silly, because it requires both infrastructures to be in place, requires computers to be shipped through the lab anyway, and doesn't really save any time at all. The extra hour to complete the installation in the lab happens automatically, so there's no point in not letting it complete there.

Based on my experience as a consultant, it's rare to find end-users with the competence to configure Outlook correctly, much less select, install, and configure their own computers from scratch. I have found that configuring computers in the lab works a lot better than forward-deploying installation servers throughout an enterprise.

Deployment Infrastructure

Your deployment infrastructure consists of the machines used to store and transmit the installations, whether that transmission occurs directly to the destination hard disk or over a network. Once you've decided whether to forward-deploy installation servers or localize them in your IT lab/computer room and you've chosen either RIS or disk imaging, you're ready to install your service infrastructure.

Installing RIS

Installing RIS is easy, but there are a few steps:

1. Make sure your RIS server is a member of the Active Directory and can reach (or is) an authorized DHCP server.

2. Make sure a new empty volume of at least 2GB (and preferably much more) is available to create the RIS image store.

3. Install RIS using the Add/Remove Software Control Panel and reboot the computer.

4. Configure RIS using the Add/Remove Software Control Panel (click the Configure button next to the RIS service).

5. Supply a Windows 2000 Professional CD-ROM to provide a source for the base operating system installation.

6. Use the `rbfg.exe` tool to create PXE boot floppies as necessary.

That's pretty much it. At this point, you're ready to perform your test installations. Figure 10.5 shows the RIS Setup Wizard.

Figure 10.5   The RIS Setup Wizard shows the installation steps and its completion progress.

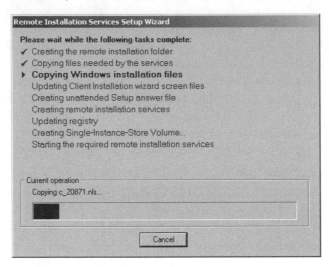

Establishing an Imaging Infrastructure

How you install a disk-imaging infrastructure depends on which infrastructure you use. For CD or direct disk-based imaging, your infrastructure will consist of a set of bench machines on which you install operating systems and applications in order to image them. You should use a system similar to each class of computer deployed throughout your organization to make sure drivers are correct for each machine.

If you're using Ethernet broadcast-based deployment, you need to have an image server on each Ethernet broadcast domain. If you're using TCP/IP multicast-based imaging, a single server in your enterprise might work as long as each client can reach it. Your routers must be compatible with the IGMP multicast protocol (and configured to support it) in order to use TCP/IP multicasting.

Performing Test Installations

Testing is requisite before any large-scale endeavor to make sure everything will work correctly and to make sure all the technicians know everything they need to know to succeed.

To test your deployment infrastructure, simply connect a new client to your installation servers and go through the installation procedure. This will prove out the installation process. If you're forward-deploying installation servers, be sure to connect from the most distant possible client to make sure your DHCP, Active Directory, and RIS services are available everywhere on the network.

Watch for problems such as clients connecting to the wrong RIS server if you have multiple servers installed. If any RIS server is configured to connect to unknown clients, it could interfere with GUID-based RIS installation.

Make sure each of your technicians has performed a test installation to ensure that they all know the ropes.

Creating Master Sources

Once you've got your installation server infrastructure online, it's time to create your *master sources*. The first step to creating master sources is determining what sources you need.

If you haven't already, survey your organization to create accumulations of users who all use the same software. These accumulations should be Organizational Units in your Active Directory; if they aren't, it might be wise to make them now. You can easily apply software distribution policy to Organizational Units.

Once you've identified functionally similar groups, list the applications used by each group. Then sort the groups from simplest to most complex, creating a new branch for each new application. The following list shows how images might be created for a medium-sized engineering and research firm.

Image Class Abstract for All Users:
Windows 2000 Professional
VNC
Office 2000 Professional
Lotus Notes Client
McAfee VirusScan
Adobe Photoshop
JetDirect
Image Class for Physicists:
Mathematica
Image Class for Engineers:
SolidWorks
AutoCAD
Visio Technical
Image Class for Finance and Administration:
Executive Staff software
MAS-90 client

Image Class for Executive Staff:
PowerPoint
Franklin Planner for Outlook
Palm Desktop
SolidWorks Viewer
Image Class for Payroll:
Finance and Administration
BofA Online Banking software
ADP Payroll software
Image Class for IT Staff:
TSAC
Windows 2000 admin tools
Visio Professional
WS Ping Pro
VNC Viewer
TeraTerm Pro
vmware

Start with a base installation of the software that everyone in your enterprise will use. At a minimum, this usually consists of the operating system, a Web browser, and an e-mail client. For most organizations, it includes office software such as Microsoft Office and perhaps some IT management tools such as VNC or Tivoli.

Once you've defined the various image classes, perform the installation that applies to all users and image it. Even though you may never deploy the class common to all users, you'll need to image it so you can quickly roll back to it to create the other classes.

Next, for each class, restore the image class common to all users, and then install the applications specific to the installation set. Once the applications have been installed, create a new image using either Sysprep for disk imaging or RIPrep for RIS installation. If there are derivative classes, such as the Finance and Administration and Payroll classes in the example list above, add those applications and image again to create their image classes.

Using Sysprep to Create a Disk Image

Sysprep is easy to use. Simply run the Sysprep program on a client installation to strip out its unique identifiers and prepare the installation for imaging. Once the computer has been shut down, it's ready to be imaged by your disk-imaging tools. Figure 10.6 shows the Sysprep utility being used to prepare a disk image.

Figure 10.6   Sysprep changes the computer's boot process to include the final portion of a normal Windows 2000 setup, including the Licensing Agreement shown here.

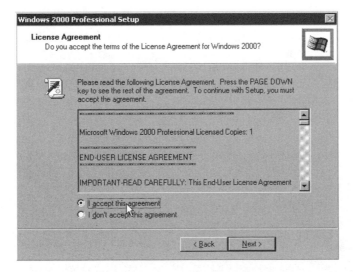

To install Sysprep, open the \support\tools\deploy.cab file and extract its contents to either the client being imaged (not recommended because it will appear in the final disk image) or a share on your image server. From the client that you will be imaging, run the Sysprep utility to prepare the computer for imaging. The utility can be copied to a floppy disk for clients that are not connected to a network. Figure 10.7 shows the only message Sysprep displays before preparing the installation to be imaged.

Figure 10.7   Simply click OK to prepare the installation for imaging.

WARNING   The Sysprep utility is easy to run and doesn't provide much warning about what it's going to do. If you install the utility on the computer being imaged, Sysprep will be rolled out to end-users along with all the other software in the image. An unsuspecting user might then run the utility and be surprised by the results. Although it's not harmful, it will probably require a call to technical support to get the GUID number required for reinstallation.

After the computer shuts down, do not boot the hard disk again until you've imaged it using your disk-imaging tools. Once it has imaged, you can boot it, run the setup process, and then install more applications to create derivative image classes by repeating the process. To return to a prior state to start with a new branch of image classes, simply restore an earlier image to the computer.

Using RIPrep to Create a RIS Image

Using RIPrep is easy. From the fully configured client, browse to the \\risserver\ reminst\admin\i386 directory on the RIS server and run the riprep.exe utility. In the RIPrep Wizard, enter the name of the RIS server you want to store the image to, a name for the image folder, and description text. Figure 10.8 shows the RIPrep Wizard in action.

Figure 10.8 RIPrep requires very little information to create an installation image.

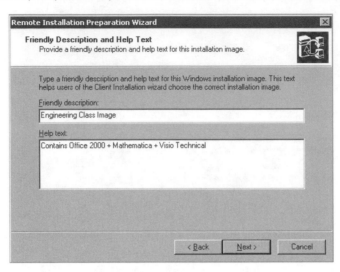

When you complete the Wizard, RIPrep will automatically create and upload the client configuration to the RIS server. Figure 10.9 shows RIPrep preparing a RIS client image.

Once you've completed creating the configuration image, you can install additional software for more complex installations.

Figure 10.9 RIPrep automatically copies partition information and files up to a RIS server for a custom installation.

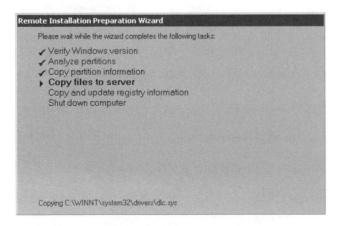

Deploying Servers

Server deployment is a totally different beast than workstation deployment. There is (or should be) about a 50:1 client-to-server ratio in your organization, so the client deployment problem is about 50 times larger than the server deployment problem. The largest network deployment I've ever worked on was 4,000 clients with 50 servers (an 80:1 ratio, appropriate in large environments), and that was just once. The overwhelming majority of server rollouts are considerably smaller than that.

So, for fewer than 50 machines, many of which are unique anyway, does any rollout methodology make sense? Should you bother trying to remotely install operating systems on servers using network-based disk imaging?

Network-based remote installation of any sort presumes that a server appears in your network, installed in place in a rack or server farm, without an operating system on it. Now, if some other agency other than your IT department actually received the server, unboxed it, validated it, inventoried it, rack-mounted it, attached it to your network, and powered it up, then remote installation might have some value. But to date, this has never happened on any network I've ever worked with.

Firstly, it's been a long time since I ordered a server that didn't ship from the factory with an operating system installed on it. Granted, I usually take exception to the way the operating system is preinstalled, but most vendors now allow you to send them an image of exactly what you want installed on your servers. In any case, installing an operating system on a modern server takes all of about 30 minutes. It takes more time to physically unbox, inspect, validate, inventory, and mount the server in its final location.

So given that you've got a bunch of administrative work that goes into a server just to attach it to your network, installing an operating system from a boot CD-ROM while it's sitting on your test bench being added to inventory and validated just isn't a hard enough problem to perform remotely, especially not with the cakewalk installation of Windows 2000 Server from a boot CD-ROM.

And, if anything goes wrong with a remote installation, you've just lost any time efficiency that would have been gained because you'll have to go retrieve the server to figure out what's wrong. And let's face it: if something is wrong with a server, you'll find out during the operating system installation. Simply installing a complex operating system is a pretty good system validation procedure. If that server has already been deployed before you find the problem, you'll have to un-deploy it to fix the problem. I've never deployed a production server before I'd installed and tested the services running on it in the shop, and I doubt I ever will.

Sometimes you may need to roll out a large number of servers in a short time—for example, in a new large installation, in the deployment of a new Web service, or during a network upgrade. In these cases, networked remote installation via imaging might be both faster and less troublesome than a CD-ROM-based installation—but I'm still skeptical. When we installed those 50 servers (this was in the days of Windows NT 4), we lined them all up in their racks in the computer room (they were centralized anyway), fired them up with the boot CDs in place, and just went round-robin from machine to machine answering the same question 50 times and then going back to the start. It took four hours to simultaneously install all 50 machines because they were all installing from separate concurrent sources. Windows 2000 would have taken less time because it asks fewer questions.

The Setup Manager, the third setup tool included with Windows 2000, can be very useful for setting up servers. I find RIS and Sysprep to be vastly superior for rolling out clients, but considering the unique requirements and lower rollout volume for servers, Setup Manager can be ideal.

Setup Manager allows you to easily create unattended answer files that work with the CD-ROM setup. You can copy the unattended answer file created by Setup Manager to a floppy disk, put the floppy and the Windows 2000 CD-ROM into a new server, and simply boot it. The CD-ROM setup will read the unattended answer file from the floppy and use it to answer the prompts during server installation. Complete instructions for using the tool are included with it, and you can find it in the \support\deploy.cab file on the CD-ROM along with Sysprep.

Finally, Microsoft's System Preparation Tool works on all versions of Windows 2000 Server as long as they are not (yet) domain controllers, so you can use it to perform image-based duplication of servers as well as clients, if I haven't convinced you that it's a waste of time.

Using Disk Imaging to Deploy Servers

Using disk imaging to deploy servers is just like using disk imaging to deploy clients, except that fewer of the machines will be exact duplicates. Also, you cannot duplicate domain controllers because the System Preparation Tool cannot run on them to make them unique (nor can any third-party SID changer I know of, but I'm sure someone will come out with one).

Certain types of servers can be handled in batches in large environments:

> **Terminal servers**   Make excellent candidates for imaged deployment because they shouldn't store unique information and will have much the same application set as clients.

Web servers   Are often deployed in large batches of clones, using the Load Balancing Service to switch between them. You may need to rapidly deploy more Web servers if your site suddenly becomes popular, so keeping an image master is a good idea.

Departmental file and print servers   Can be handled in batches in very large companies. These servers are usually forward-deployed right to the Ethernet broadcast domain being served so as to reduce load on the backbone, so they should be kept as standard as possible. If you do forward-deploy servers, be sure that they're backed up over the network rather than locally so you can replace them easily.

Deploying servers using disk-imaging techniques is exactly the same as deploying clients: create classes of servers based on major functional differences, deploy servers by class using disk imaging, and then customize each server once you're finished.

Manually Deploying Servers

Most servers should be manually deployed using the traditional CD-ROM installation method. Because servers are usually unique except in the largest environments, rollout techniques don't buy you much in the way of time savings.

Any computer that has to be backed up by a local tape device is a poor candidate for image-based deployment. These machines tend to be highly unique; they store unique data or they run unique services. Any type of machine that does not need local backup, and which there is more than one of, is a good candidate for image-based deployment. If the machine fails, a replacement can be created from the source image and immediately deployed. In the case of a forward-deployed file server, its shared files would have to be restored from tape, but that can be handled remotely once it is back in place on the network.

Manual CD-ROM-based installation is covered in complete detail in Chapter 2.

Summary

Deploying Windows 2000 throughout your organization doesn't have to be difficult. By selecting the right tools for your specific needs, you can create a deployment infrastructure that will make the job considerably easier than a batch of individual installations would be.

Windows 2000 supports four fundamental types of installations:

Installation from the original source CD-ROM   Installing or upgrading from the original CD-ROM is familiar to anyone who has worked with Windows 2000. It is the traditional method for installing an operating system on individual computers.

Installation from a network share   Installation from a network share is most useful when you intend to use the Windows 2000 upgrade feature to convert Windows 3.1, Windows 95, 98, Me, or NT workstations to Windows 2000. While it's technically possible to install from scratch using a network share, it's far less convenient than the other methods. To upgrade computers over a network share, simply copy the \i386 directory from an installation CD-ROM to a network share and run the winnt32.exe (or winnt.exe) located in the share on the computer you wish to upgrade.

Automated remote installation from a RIS server   RIS provides the ability to remotely install Windows 2000 on computers with PXE-compatible network adapters or on computers with network adapters supported by the PXE boot floppy that can be created using the rbfg.exe tool. By deploying a RIS server infrastructure along with DHCP and Active Directory servers, clients can connect automatically to a RIS server and download completely configured installations. Because computers must be PXE compliant or compatible with the PXE boot floppy, RIS won't be all that useful in many types of installations.

Disk imaging using the System Preparation Tool   Disk imaging is the traditional method used by network administrators to quickly deploy large batches of clients. Because of the variety of tools available, administrators can select from dedicated hardware imaging, CD-ROM-based imaging, disk-to-disk imaging, network-based imaging, and even network broadcast or multicast imaging that is capable of deploying thousands of clients simultaneously. The robust variety of tools make a good fit for just about any rollout requirements.

Case Study: Virtual Deployment

A client of mine was interested in adopting RIS for a rollout and subsequent user installations, but was somewhat leery of remote boot technology. If they decided to go with RIS, they would spend the extra money to specify PXE-compatible network adapters on all subsequent client purchases. They were also somewhat budget limited, and did not want to spend money on hardware for a test environment.

Knowing that vmware's network bridge emulated the AMD PCnet network adapter, and knowing that the adapter was on the PXE emulation boot floppy compatibility list, I felt that we might be able to simulate an entire deployment using virtual machines.

So we copied a preinstalled vmware image of a Windows 2000 Server domain controller that I'd already created, installed DHCP on it, created a secondary virtual disk for it, and installed RIS. The installation went smoothly, and we provided the Windows 2000 Professional CD-ROM for risetup.exe to copy into the virtual server. We then created a virtual floppy disk file and used the rbfg.exe utility to create the PXE boot floppy.

To create the client, I created a new empty virtual machine, configured it to boot the floppy, and copied the floppy file containing the PXE remote boot floppy image to the new client's directory. After configuring a few vmware settings, I fired up the floppy to see what would happen.

The PXE boot floppy ran, but it reported that it could not resolve IP address 255.255.255.255. I assumed it couldn't find the DHCP server, so I tested DHCP provisioning from a third Windows 98 virtual machine, but that didn't seem to be the problem. I checked the DHCP leases on the virtual server; it reported only the Windows 98 DHCP client.

Stumped, I fired up vmware's built-in packet sniffer (vnetsniffer.exe) to inspect the traffic from the virtual client. It showed numerous ARP attempts to a strange IP address: 51.210.101.58. After checking arin.net/whois to make sure the address wasn't something sinister, I decided it was probably caused by an uninitialized variable in the PXE boot floppy code that only expressed under the circumstance of being booted in a virtual machine. This was just a guess, but on a whim, I added that IP address to the virtual server's network adapter to see what would happen.

This caused the error message to change. Inspecting the sniffer, it was now clear that the client was receiving an IP address, but was not connecting to the BINL service to find the server. When I increased the priority of the server process and decreased the priority of the client process (to give the server more time relative to the client to respond to network requests) and rebooted the client, it came up to the F12 netboot prompt, and then worked normally.

We installed Windows 2000 onto the virtual client, configured it with applications, and then used RIPrep to transmit the client file back up to the server.

After seeing how easy RIS was to deploy and maintain, and considering that their rollout load would be minimal after the ini-tial burst, the client decided to allocate the budget for a dedicated RIS installation server. When we deployed the real-world RIS server, everything came up fine the first time, without the minor hiccups caused by different timings and initial conditions in the virtual environment.

11

Upgrading Networks to Windows 2000

Chapter 10 detailed rollout methods you can use when deploying a completely new Windows 2000 network. Those methods work fine for new installations of servers and clients, but what about the millions of existing Windows NT networks? What about migrating networks based on NetWare, or UNIX?

Microsoft's documentation on network rollouts is rather myopic. It usually assumes you're just deploying a brand new Windows 2000 network, or that you're upgrading from Windows NT 4 and that you are willing to trust Microsoft's upgrade utilities to perform the migration for you. For most people who need to upgrade a network, a mixture of upgrades and new installations is usually more appropriate.

In this chapter, I assume you're migrating from one of three server environments:

- A Windows NT domain
- A NetWare 3.x, 4.x, or 5.x network
- A UNIX network based on either PC-NFS or SMB file sharing

In all of these cases, I assume you have any or all of the following types of clients:

- Windows NT Workstations
- Windows 95, 98, or Me computers
- Windows 3.11 for Workgroups clients

- MS-DOS clients
- Macintosh clients
- UNIX NFS- or SMB-based clients

These network types cover everything I've seen in the last decade, so if this chapter doesn't apply to you, you should probably just buy new computers and go back to Chapter 10 to deploy a brand-new Network.

Migration Considerations

Can your network be migrated?

This seemingly simple question is the first thing you need to think about when you consider migration to a new technology. If your servers are based on Windows NT and your clients are all Win32 systems, the answer is probably yes. The further your existing conditions deviate from this standard, the less likely it is that migration will be feasible for you, and the more likely it is that you will have to deploy an all-new network if you intend to implement Windows 2000.

What would prevent you from upgrading other types of networks?

Incompatible application software   The primary reason that hinders network upgrades is incompatible application software that cannot be easily replaced. File-based databases can be very tricky to migrate to newer operating systems. Proprietary systems that rely upon unusual hardware or software, such as early computer integrated telephony solutions for call centers, scientific testing equipment, and applications that are no longer supported but upon which your business relies, can all keep you from upgrading to a new network infrastructure.

Legacy applications   If you're using legacy applications—for example, a Clipper file-based database running from a NetWare file server that will be accessed by MS-DOS–based clients—you will need to migrate more than just your operating systems and computers; you'll have to change the fundamental way you use applications. Your database, whatever it is, should be redeveloped for an SQL server, with a new client front end developed in C++, Java, Visual Basic, or dynamic HTML. If you use custom hardware for data acquisition that runs only under MS-DOS, you'll have a difficult time putting those machines on a network.

Of course, the ideal solution for these situations is to upgrade to newer technologies that are supported by Windows 2000, such as Lab View–based data acquisition, SQL databases, and TAPI-compatible computer telephony solutions. Unfortunately, these answers are only easy for IT people. They all require completely reengineering your business processes, retraining all the employees who use them, and spending thousands of dollars per seat to upgrade both hardware and software.

Migrating legacy applications is never easy and is often impossible. Your best approach when confronted with an obstinate legacy application is to put off migrating the network until the application can be completely redeveloped using modern methodologies. Redeveloping an application is risky and time consuming, so it should be done before you make changes to your network. That way, if you fail, a new and useless network that can't be used to run your legacy application won't magnify the cost of failure.

You may find some innovative ways to work around legacy applications. I've heard reports of file-based database applications that actually thrive on terminal servers, where users log on to the machine upon which the database is stored through terminals; files are kept local to the machine. Mainframe and UNIX applications can frequently be reached through terminal applications or Telnet from a Windows 2000 client. And MS-DOS–based test equipment can be set up in "partitioned networks," where the legacy applications run as they always have, and a Windows 2000 computer acts as a file-based proxy server to copy applications from NetWare or MS-DOS clients up to the Windows 2000 network. Proxies and gateway applications are routinely used to patch up migration problems in networks.

These solutions are always too specific to make general recommendations about, so you'll have to analyze your set of business applications in a test environment to determine whether or not you'll run into these legacy problems.

I've found the best way to test business-critical legacy applications for upgrading is to build a similar server machine (perhaps without fault-tolerant disk systems to keep the expense down) and then restore a recent backup tape onto it. This will give you a near-clone that you can use to test various migration strategies with impunity. You can use this test machine to create a complete "migration script" to work from when you modify the application or machine to connect to the new Windows 2000 network.

Choosing a Migration Method

You can perform a Windows 2000 network migration in two ways:

- Upgrade existing servers to run Windows 2000.
- Replace existing servers with new Windows 2000 servers.

Your choice of migration method depends largely on your existing infrastructure. If you're migrating from a Windows NT domain, then you have the option to upgrade your existing servers or to deploy new servers alongside your old servers. Otherwise, you'll need to deploy new Windows 2000 servers alongside your existing servers and then migrate services from the existing servers to the Windows 2000 servers.

Upgrading existing servers rarely makes much sense because by the time a new operating system is available, your server hardware is likely to be obsolete. It's also generally easier and less traumatic to deploy new servers alongside older servers so they both can be online during a transition period. In the specific case of Windows 2000, however, there is one mitigating reason to upgrade: preserving an existing Windows NT domain, share, permissions, profile, and policy infrastructure. But to do this, you only need to upgrade your primary domain controllers. You can replace all the backup domain controllers and member servers.

NOTE   There are two major components to any migration: servers and clients. There's no reason why you have to handle both components of a migration the same way. You can upgrade servers but roll out all new clients, or you can deploy new servers but upgrade existing clients. Keep this in mind as you read through this chapter to help determine which strategy is best for your situation.

Migrating your network to a new operating system gives you the opportunity to review the success of your existing network policies and make new choices about service deployment, security, and administration. If everything is running smoothly, then upgrading your existing network is probably a good idea.

If you're having any systemic problems with security, service deployment, server crashes, or unstable services, you should strongly consider simply deploying a new Windows 2000–based network and migrating services to it while your existing machines run alongside it. Deploying a totally new network infrastructure is easier then trying to fix systemic problems before or after upgrading.

The change to Active Directory is so sweeping that upgrading servers really doesn't buy you much except for automatic migration of domain accounts and user profiles. Even then, you'll wind up going back through all your accounts to add and modify information anyway. Considering that you've got a lot of work to do one way or another, you should consider simply starting from scratch and fixing all your problems in one fell swoop.

Choosing not to use the upgrade option on existing servers doesn't mean you aren't upgrading; it just means you're going about it a different way. If you deploy new Windows 2000 servers alongside your existing servers, you'll have to:

- Move domain accounts manually (or semi-automatically, as I'll explain later in this chapter).
- Recreate shares. (I'll present a hack for that as well.)

- Copy user profiles manually. (There's a good strategy for this as well.)
- Reapply permissions across files and shares (a good time to normalize your file directory structure and reestablish a correct permissions structure).
- Migrate services individually. (Make sure each service is working as it should, and that you're running the latest version of the service software.)

Each of these operations affords you the opportunity to analyze and fix problems you've had with your existing installation.

NT Domain Migration

It makes sense to migrate to a new domain whenever you know that your existing domain architecture isn't working the way it should, if you haven't used policies and roaming profiles anyway, or if you want to make a fresh start to solve systemic problems with existing servers.

Upgrading a Windows NT domain can save you time, especially in large domains. Upgrading your domain infrastructure will automatically import user accounts, shares, permissions, profiles, and policies, and it is usually a good idea. Upgrading is covered in the next section.

Creating a New Domain

Follow these steps to migrate to a new Windows 2000 domain:

1. Deploy new Windows 2000 servers.
2. Create the new Active Directory and share structure.
3. Migrate user accounts and profiles to Windows 2000 servers.
4. Connect clients to the Windows 2000 domain.
5. Migrate Print services to Windows 2000.
6. Migrate File services to Windows 2000.
7. Migrate applications to Windows 2000.

Deploy New Windows 2000 Servers   Creating a new domain is simple: build a new Windows 2000 server and install Active Directory before you connect it to your existing network. Windows 2000 won't let you use the "this is the first server in my network" option in the Server Configuration Wizard if it detects an existing Windows NT (or SAMBA) domain.

Once you have your new Windows 2000 server set up, connect the new Windows 2000 server to your domain and begin migrating services.

You don't have to deploy all your Windows 2000 servers at once. If your existing server hardware is capable of running Windows 2000 well, simply deploy one server first, migrate the services of the primary domain controller (PDC) to it, and then take your old PDC offline. Rebuild that old PDC into the next Windows 2000 server, replace an existing machine, and continue.

Some services (like File service) require a cutover, so you'll have to have your File service infrastructure in place before you can migrate that service. Whether or not you can use a "rolling rollout" to redeploy existing servers depends on how many of your machines have to be cut over simultaneously. With planning, you should be able to create a deployment schedule that will allow this. Keep in mind that you can also overburden a server for a short period of time if necessary and then use DFS to quietly offload file services to another machine once it's online.

At the end of a rolling rollout (and assuming a 1:1 machine replacement), you'll have one machine left. Dedicate it to a new Windows 2000 service you hadn't previously used, such as Terminal Services, or simply keep it as the test server you never had the budget to buy.

Create the New Active Directory and Share Structure   The migration to Windows 2000 is the perfect time to correct and normalize all your network structures: domain structure, permissions, shares, and so on. Spend some time on the Active Directory structure to be certain it will serve you well into the future rather than simply mimicking your existing domain structure. There will be no better time than now to get it right. Chapters 6 and 9 cover Active Directory in detail.

Migrate User Accounts and Profiles to Windows 2000 Servers   Migrating user accounts and profiles to Windows 2000 without using the upgrade option can be a bit of a hassle, but it's not impossible.

1. Move domain accounts by piping the `net user` command to a file at the command prompt, as in:

   ```
   net user >userlist.txt
   ```

2. Parse that text file with Word or any other text processor to create a single column list of user accounts, prefixed with `net user` and suffixed with a default password and the `/add` switch, as in:

   ```
   net user mstrebe changeme /add
   net user mwest changeme /add
   ```

3. Rename the text file to have a `.bat` extension and execute it on the new server to automatically recreate the base of user accounts on the new server.

4. Use the `net help user` command to see the other options you can append to the `net user` command to specify profile paths, home directories, password policies, and so on.

The new user accounts will all have the same password, so users should change their password upon first boot. Although I've never done it, it would be possible to use a password-auditing tool such as L0phtCrack on the legacy Windows NT domain to set users' passwords on the new Windows 2000 domain to match the users' existing passwords.

Migrating profiles from one server to another is easy: copy the profile directories on your old servers to your new servers when the profiles are not in use at the time of the cutover to the new domain. As long as the user account's profile path matches the location of the new profiles, that profile will be used the next time the user logs in.

Computer and user policy is so different from Windows NT to Windows 2000 that it doesn't make sense to try to migrate policies between the two operating systems. Survey your existing policy structure and recreate it using Windows 2000's Group Policy model. You will probably find it's easier to do what you originally intended using Windows 2000's hierarchical policies.

> **TIP** If you don't want to restructure your permissions architecture when you migrate to Windows 2000, you can use the Windows 2000 Server Resource Kit's ClonePrincipal utility to create exact copies of user accounts in your new domain.

Connect Clients to Windows 2000 Domains Connecting Win32 clients to Windows 2000 domains is easy: just change their domain association to the Windows 2000 domain in the Identification tab of the Network Control Panel (NT and 9*x*) or the Network Identification tab of the System Control Panel (Win2k pro). Figure 11.1 shows the Windows 2000 Network Identification tab.

You're far better off migrating all your 32-bit clients to Windows 2000 unless there's a good reason not to, however, and your job will be easiest if you perform the Windows 2000 Professional client rollout before you perform the server rollout. Upgrading clients to Windows 2000 is discussed in the "Client Migration" section of this chapter.

Migrate Print Services to Windows 2000 To migrate Print services to Windows 2000, simply delete the printer and its associated share on the legacy server, create a new printer and share on the Windows 2000 computer, and confirm the location of the printer share in the Active Directory.

The harder part is cutting existing clients over to the new server. I recommend a mass e-mailing to clients that includes the UNC path of the printer. By simply typing the UNC path to the printer into an e-mail message, any clients using Outlook or a similar e-mail program that automatically turns paths into links can simply click the link to install and connect to the printer. The message can contain instructions on how to delete the legacy printer connection as well.

Figure 11.1   Change a client's domain association using the Network Identification tab in Windows 2000 Professional.

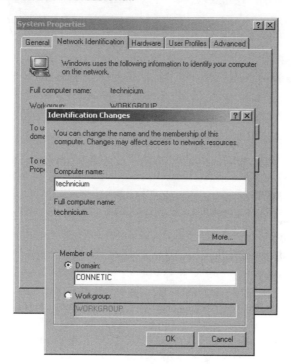

If clients are being rolled out as part of a network upgrade, include the printer's path in the default user profile of the installation image.

Migrate File Services to Windows 2000   Migrating File services to Windows 2000 requires a cutover—a point at which the legacy server goes offline and the replacement server goes online. This is necessary because you cannot allow users to access the same set of files on two different computers at the same time; it would be extremely difficult to determine where the last changed versions of files were stored.

Migrating files involves copying files from the legacy machine to the new machine, creating shares on the new machine, and publishing those shares in the Active Directory. It also involves changing any existing drive mappings on the client to reflect the new file share locations and informing users of the change.

To perform the file copy operation, simply put both computers on the same network and issue an XCOPY command (like the one specified in the "NetWare Migration" section later in this chapter) to copy files to the new server. You're not using existing domain accounts, so there's no point in copying permissions since they won't apply in the new domain anyway.

If you are going to upgrade your Windows NT domains to Windows 2000, be sure to perform your file copies using the /O option of XCOPY to copy over ACL and ownership information. The SIDs of migrated user accounts will be valid for the files moved over with ACL information thanks to the SIDHistory feature of Windows 2000.

Rather than change shares and drive mappings on all your clients, you can rename the new computer to have the same NetBIOS name as the legacy computer it replaces as well as the same share names. This will make your server migration invisible to end-users. To do this, the machines must have different names during the file copy operation or they cannot coexist on the same network. You can either rename the legacy machine before bringing the new machine online with the old machine's original name, or you can set up the new machine with a temporary name during the copy operation and then rename the new machine to match the legacy machine's name after it goes offline. Windows 2000 domain controllers cannot be renamed, so be sure to perform this operation prior to upgrading new servers to domain controllers.

If you decide to use new server names, you can send a mass e-mailing to clients containing a batch file that will run automatically when they click on it, or by including the commands in a logon script. By using the net use command, this batch file will automatically replace existing drive mappings. In the example below, the first line deletes the existing mapping for the Z: drive (assumed to be mapped to the legacy server) and the second line creates the new mapping.

```
net use z: /delete
net use z: \\server\share /persistent:yes
```

Using these methods, you can avoid manually visiting most of the workstations in your organization.

Migrate Applications to Windows 2000   The method you'll use to migrate applications to Windows 2000 depends entirely upon what the application is. Most Microsoft-provided BackOffice applications will run perfectly well on Windows 2000, but they're also all being replaced by Active Directory integrated updates (that usually include 2000 in the title).

Consider updating all your BackOffice applications to their "2000" versions when you perform your migration. There won't be a better time to do it, and you'll find it's easier to get all the confusion and training out of the way all at once. Once your users become accustomed to Active Directory, they'll be encumbered by applications that don't properly support it.

For third-party server applications, check with your vendor about Windows 2000 updates. Many popular accounting packages have problems running under Windows 2000 and have to be specifically patched or specially installed. Some don't work at all. Many vendors have different versions of their applications for Windows 2000 servers.

Essentially, you should plan on upgrading any piece of software that runs on your servers to a version made or at least tested on Windows 2000. Once the new version of the application is installed, you'll have to follow your vendor's recommendations for migrating your data from the legacy servers.

Upgrading the Current Domain

Most of Microsoft's recommendations for domain migration either assume that you don't have a network now or that you'll be using their migration method for moving your current domain structure to Windows 2000. This section summarizes Microsoft's various recommendations for upgrading an existing Windows NT domain or domains to a Windows 2000 domain.

I strongly recommend migrating to a single domain no matter how many domains you currently use. The justifications for using multiple domains in Windows 2000 are applicable to only the largest of businesses and organizations that are highly distributed (for example, military units) and which operate autonomously. These recommendations assume you want to migrate to a single domain architecture.

Here are the steps to migrating existing Windows NT domain or domains to Windows 2000:

1. Create a new Windows 2000 structural root domain.
2. Synchronize and back up existing domain controllers.
3. Upgrade the primary domain controller to Windows 2000.
4. Upgrade each backup domain controller to Windows 2000.
5. Switch from Mixed Mode to Native Mode.
6. Upgrade member servers to Windows 2000.
7. Reorganize the Active Directory.

Create a New Windows 2000 Structural Root Domain   A "structural domain" is simply a domain without any computer or user (resource) accounts; it exists to form the basis of the child domains below it and to act as the pinnacle of the Active Directory. Starting your domain migration by creating a new structural root domain rather than choosing an existing Windows NT domain to "bless" as the root domain will solve a lot of problems for you up front and allow you to concentrate more on the migration than on issues of structure.

Your new structural root domain will be the pinnacle of your Windows 2000 forest. All your existing domains will be upgraded as child domains of this domain. Once you've upgraded all your domains and made the switch from Mixed Mode to Native Mode, you'll be free of the size restrictions inherent in Windows NT 4 domains, and you can restructure your domains as you see fit.

Setting up a new structural root domain will of course require a new server. You can reuse an existing server, but you will have to wipe out its current operating system and reinstall from scratch; this is not an upgrade operation. I recommend purchasing a new server for this function. You can decide later whether to move file, print, and account resources onto this machine when you restructure the Active Directory at the end of your domain migration.

This machine should also run the Windows 2000 DNS service and act as the DNS root for your organization. Basically, this computer should be configured using the Active Directory Wizard as the first domain controller in your network with all the default settings.

Keep in mind that the Active Directory Promotion Wizard assumes that you want to completely overhaul your DNS infrastructure and use Windows 2000's Dynamic DNS server. It also assumes that it will be the root of the DNS domain tree. If you use the Wizard to update your first server to include an Active Directory–integrated Dynamic DNS server, be sure to add a delegation of authority for the DNS name of the domain to the authoritative parent DNS server. This server may belong to your ISP, so you may need their assistance to make this change.

If you are currently not using DNS, this is usually okay. If you already have a DNS architecture implemented in Windows NT 4 or are using BIND on UNIX servers, the default settings of the Active Directory Wizard will not work correctly for you. BIND version 8.2.2 or later is compatible with Active Directory. Earlier BIND versions and the DNS server from Windows NT 4 do not work correctly with Active Directory and should be replaced with Windows 2000's Active Directory–integrated DNS service.

There are too many ways DNS could be set up in your enterprise to cover all the possibilities in this book, so I can't make any specific recommendations about how to migrate your existing DNS infrastructure if you have one. Microsoft's white paper on DNS migration is available at www.microsoft.com/technet.

Synchronize and Back Up Existing Domain Controllers   Before you jump into upgrading, synchronize all your backup domain controllers with their respective primary domain controllers. This will ensure that they all have current account information if something goes wrong with the upgrade process. In addition, it's always wise to back up any machine before performing an operating system upgrade on it.

Upgrade the Primary Domain Controller to Windows 2000   Now that you have a new Windows 2000 structural root, you're ready to begin the process of upgrading your existing Windows NT domains into the new Windows 2000 domain.

When you upgrade a primary domain controller, the Active Directory installation process copies the user accounts, groups, and computer accounts contained in the Security

Accounts Manager (SAM) into the Active Directory. Once a Windows NT PDC is upgraded, it becomes the Windows 2000 PDC Operations Master (or PDC emulator) in a Mixed-Mode Windows 2000 network.

During the upgrade to Windows 2000, select the option to join the existing domain tree that was created when you installed the new structural root server. This will create a hierarchical transitive trust relationship with the structural root server and will ensure that you don't have any problems with trusts between your existing domains as they're upgraded to Windows 2000. Once you've updated all your domains, you will probably want to reorganize your legacy domain structure into a single domain (or at most one domain per site) and convert existing domains at a single site into Organizational Units. This will allow for considerable administrative convenience. Chapter 9 covers Active Directory recommendations and procedures in detail.

Upgrading the primary domain controller is easy. Here are the steps:

1. Synchronize all backup domain controllers (BDCs) to the PDC, and take one BDC offline.

2. Perform a full backup of the PDC.

3. Run WINNT32, and select the Upgrade option on the PDC.

It's wise to disconnect a BDC from the network prior to the PDC upgrade. If something goes wrong, you can put the BDC back online immediately to restore domain availability to the way it was before you attempted to upgrade the BDC.

Upgrade Each Backup Domain Controller to Windows 2000   You should upgrade backup domain controllers to Windows 2000 as soon as possible after your primary domain controllers are running in order to make the switch to Native Mode as quickly as possible. When you upgrade a Windows 2000 backup domain controller, you need to be certain that the machine can reach the upgraded domain controller for Windows 2000. If it cannot, it will assume that it is the first Windows 2000 domain controller and attempt to assume the Global Catalog server and Operations Master roles, which will conflict with the existing domain controller and cause you to have to start over on the second machine.

Keep in mind that there's little reason to use the upgrade option on a BDC except as a convenience, unless you need that BDC to service NetLogon authentication attempts. You may find it beneficial to install BDCs from scratch, especially if you're using third-party service applications on the machine.

Switch from Mixed Mode to Native Mode   Once all the domain controllers in your network have been upgraded to Windows 2000, you can switch from Mixed Mode (where Windows 2000 domain controllers will replicate with Windows NT 4 backup domain controllers) to Native Mode, which allows only Windows 2000 servers to participate in domain operations. The switch to Native Mode opens up the special features of Active Directory, such as support for huge domains, Kerberos authentication nested groups, and RRAS policies.

Native Mode applies only to domain controllers, not to member servers or workstations. These machines can continue to run Windows NT 4 after the switch to Native Mode and can be upgraded according to your rollout schedule.

Upgrade Member Servers to Windows 2000   Upgrading member servers to Windows 2000 is similar to upgrading clients: just run the upgrade option of the Windows 2000 setup, and you're off and running. Be sure to check with vendors of any applications you may be running on your member servers to make certain they'll operate correctly after the upgrade. If you don't have any other way to tell, run a full backup of the machine, perform the upgrade, and then revert from tape if you encounter any insurmountable problems.

Reorganize the Active Directory   Once you have upgraded all your domains to Windows 2000, you can set about the task of normalizing your Active Directory into a more coherent structure. The upgrade will leave you with resource and account domains added to your Active Directory as they were in your Windows NT 4 domain structure. You can use the Active Directory management tools to reorganize the domain into a more coherent structure for your users once all this information has been accumulated in one place— the Directory itself. Specific recommendations on Active Directory structure are contained in Chapter 9.

NetWare Migration

Migrating from NetWare is pretty easy thanks to Microsoft's Migration tools. Services for NetWare 5 includes two tools that can automate the migration of an NDS tree to an Active Directory and another tool that can automatically migrate files for you. Information on Microsoft's Services for NetWare and other NetWare tools is available at www.microsoft.com/windows2000/guide/server/solutions/netware.asp.

Gateway Services for NetWare (GSNW) allows Windows 2000 servers to "reshare" NetWare volumes so that they can be seen by clients of the Windows 2000 machine. Unfortunately, the overhead is substantial; you'll find that the considerable latency of the service makes it less than valuable for its intended purpose. Also, GSNW can only reshare a single NetWare server at a time. I prefer to obviate the NetWare gateway by migrating all user files over the course of a weekend, but there are cases where that's simply not possible and the Gateway Services for NetWare makes sense.

The other purpose of GSNW is to provide a NetWare redirector for Windows 2000 servers. This redirector is what will allow your Windows 2000 servers to attach directly to NetWare servers to siphon off the files they serve. Thanks to the redirector, moving file service is as simple as performing a (really long) XCOPY command.

Migration Steps

The basic steps to migrating a NetWare network are as follows:

1. Deploy new Windows 2000 servers.
2. Migrate the NDS structure to Active Directory.
3. Attach clients to the Windows 2000 network.
4. Migrate Print services to Windows 2000.
5. Migrate File services to Windows 2000.
6. Migrate applications to Windows 2000.
7. Shut down NetWare servers.
8. Remove NetWare redirector from clients.

Deploy New Windows 2000 Servers   Deploying new Windows 2000 servers alongside your existing NetWare servers is the first step in any migration from a foreign operating system to Windows 2000. How to do it is well covered in the rest of the book, so I won't belabor the point here.

Migrate NDS and User Accounts to Windows 2000   Microsoft provides two important tools to assist NetWare users with the move from NDS to Active Directory: Microsoft Directory Synchronization Services and Microsoft File Migration Utility. Both are part of Microsoft's Services for NetWare 5 package, which is specifically designed to assist NetWare supervisors with the migration to Windows 2000. If you have a complex NDS directory that you need to migrate, get these tools and use them. They are not expensive, and there's no easier way to perform an NDS migration.

On the other hand, if you're migrating a small NetWare network that doesn't have a complex NDS structure, you may find it's faster to use scripting tools to re-create your user accounts and to move files over using the time-honored techniques presented in this section. Moving user accounts is simple: capture a list of users using the NetWare command line tools, munge the text into a batch file for creating new user accounts as shown in the section on creating new Windows 2000 domains, and run that batch file on your new Windows 2000 machine.

Client Migration   During the client migration, client computers are connected to both the legacy NetWare network and the new Windows 2000 network. You can take as long as you want to perform this portion of the migration because users will not be relying upon the services of Windows 2000. Simply start at one end of the company and begin attaching client computers to the new Windows 2000 network while preserving their ability to log in to the NetWare network.

If you have legacy clients (for example, DOS) that won't support the upgrade to TCP/IP or the Microsoft Client for MS-DOS (which is much larger than the NetWare redirector), you can use the File and Print Services for NetWare package (FPNW) that comes with Services for NetWare to allow a Windows 2000 server to appear to be a Novell NetWare server to these legacy clients. This is a better option than keeping legacy operating systems and servers around to serve legacy clients.

Print Services Migration   Because Print services are a less-important network service, you can test the migration waters by migrating them first. If you run into serious problems trying to migrate printers, the migration is just going to get worse as you move into file and then application migration, so you need to take a step back and reevaluate your migration plan, your staff readiness and training, and the commitment of your user base to help make the migration work.

Migrating printers is a simple process. Because Windows 2000 can treat a NetWare print queue as a print device, you'll be able to hook your Windows 2000 servers to the NetWare print servers directly, and then migrate clients to the Windows 2000 print server at your leisure. Once you've got all the clients migrated to the Windows 2000 print server from the NetWare print server, you can disconnect the NetWare print queue and connect the Windows 2000 server directly to the print device. Using this methodology, you're not constrained to changing everything overnight, and you don't have to worry about multiple servers vying for a printer's attention.

File Migration   Unlike most other portions of a migration, File services must be "cut over" from one server to another. The same set of files must never be available on the network from two different servers, because invariably different users will connect to different servers, causing some file changes to occur on the old set of files and some to occur on the new set. Because there's no good way to determine what happened after the fact, you need to make sure this situation can't happen.

If for some reason you don't want to use Microsoft's File Migration Utility in the Services for NetWare package (for example, because you don't have the Services for NetWare package), you can use the old-fashioned way: bulk file copies on the command prompt. Hook up the new Windows 2000 servers with the Gateway Services for NetWare so they can directly attach to the NetWare network. Then copy files over using XCOPY from a command prompt when users are not accessing the network. Useful permissions information won't move over when you perform the bulk file move, so be prepared to re-create the permissions structure.

Why XCOPY? Because the graphical file copy method will fail whenever a file copy fails for any reason. XCOPY can be made to tolerate the failure of individual files without terminating the bulk copy operation. This way, you can copy most of the files and then figure out what went wrong with those copy operations that failed, rather than trying to fix problems one at a time and trying the entire copy operation again.

I use the following XCOPY command when migrating files between servers:

```
XCOPY source dest /e /v /h /k /y /c >copylog.txt
```

The switches have the following effects:

/e	Recurses into subdirectories to copy all files, including empty directories
/v	Verifies file copies
/h	Copies hidden and system files
/k	Copies MS-DOS attributes
/y	Suppresses overwrite confirmation
/c	Continues if errors occur

The >copylog.txt portion of the command redirects output that would normally go to the screen to a file called copylog.txt. This is important, because you'll want to search through this log to discover any errors that might have occurred during the copy operation so you can manually move those files over.

Once you've moved the files to the new server, unplug the NetWare servers from the network so users can't accidentally gain access to the files. If that's not an option, you'll have to use some other method to restrict access to the server, such as changing file permissions to allow only the supervisor to access anything or removing drive mappings on all the clients.

Application Migration   Migrating applications that run on a NetWare server to a Windows 2000 server isn't possible. (Okay, you could use vmware to host a NetWare server on a Windows 2000 server, but that's not realistic.) Applications can really only be replaced by an equivalent application that runs on Windows 2000.

Fortunately, the vast majority of NetWare servers don't run any specific applications; they just provide File and Print services, which are easy to migrate. Unless your business is based on a server-side NetWare application, you won't have to worry about application migration.

Don't get confused about file-based databases such as dBase, Clipper, FoxPro, MS-Access, and file-based accounting applications. These database products don't run on the server; they simply store files on the server. Technically, these applications can be migrated to a Windows 2000 server by copying the files and making sure drive mappings and paths on the clients remain the same. Application migration in this sense only applies to programs that actually execute on the server hardware.

That said, migrating file-based applications can be tricky because Windows 2000 and NetWare make different assumptions about File service, and sometimes those assumptions can make big performance differences or prevent an application from running at all. Check with your application vendor to see what problems they know about when migrating file-based database products to Windows 2000. Don't accept silly answers like, "We don't support Windows 2000." Threaten to move off their platform if they won't help you find out what could go wrong in migration, and then be prepared to do it if they are recalcitrant.

When migrating a legacy application, consider whether you really need to. Your formerly overburdened NetWare server may be breathing a lot easier with File and Print services migrated to a Windows 2000 server. If your applications are truly important to your business, consider simply leaving them on your NetWare servers and running a hybrid environment. You obviously already have the talent to operate NetWare servers, so there's no need to throw the baby out with the bath water just because you've decided to go to Windows 2000.

Choosing new applications to replace your NetWare server applications is beyond the scope of this book, but it's not really that difficult. Call the vendor of your current product. Unless they're on their way out of business, they've probably got a Windows version of their application software. If not, call their competition. Somebody does, and that vendor can help you migrate from your existing NetWare application to theirs.

Shut Down NetWare Servers   After you've obviated the services of your NetWare servers, you should shut them down. I recommend shutting down legacy servers right after you've cut their services over to a new machine—especially for services that store data, such as File service. This prevents some users from accidentally (or otherwise) reverting to the old server after the complete data set has been migrated. Those users will wind up losing their data when the old servers finally go offline.

Perform a final backup before you shut down your NetWare servers. Then, keep your servers in state after you shut them down. If there is a serious problem with the migration, you may need to revert to the NetWare servers to get back to work. Beware: if you do wind up going back to the NetWare servers, you'll have to perform most of the migration again.

Remove NetWare Redirector from Clients   Once you've determined that the migration is a success, you can remove the NetWare redirector from clients whenever it is convenient. Since it's not particularly important that you remove the redirector in most cases, you can simply leave it until a technician happens to visit the desktop for another purpose.

If you're using Services for NetWare to service NetWare clients because you need to keep MS-DOS client computers on your network, you should continue to do so. Microsoft's

Client for MS-DOS is considerably larger than the NetWare redirector (by about 100K), and since memory in MS-DOS is always at a premium, you should continue to use Services for NetWare to emulate a NetWare server rather than migrate clients to the Client for MS-DOS.

UNIX Migration

Migrating from UNIX can be very difficult, especially if you are using an NFS-based network. There are two important types of UNIX networks: (1) pure UNIX networks, where the servers and workstations all run UNIX, and (2) hybrid networks that have UNIX servers and Windows clients, Windows servers and UNIX clients, or both.

Microsoft provides a package called Services for UNIX that is essentially an NFS client, server, and gateway along with some administrative and convenience utilities. The Services for UNIX package does not include an LDAP migration tool for Active Directory or a file migration utility like the Services for NetWare package does. Microsoft must realize that in many cases, Windows will coexist with UNIX rather than replace it. Services for UNIX operates with many flavors of UNIX, including Solaris, HP-UX, and Linux.

If you have UNIX or any other type of non-Windows workstations, you'll be deploying an entirely new network. You'll only be migrating documents between the servers. To do that, you'll need a file-sharing protocol in common between the two server operating systems. Your options are FTP, NFS, and SMB. Of the three, I recommend using SMB, because the tools to add SMB to UNIX servers are free and easy to use. You can also easily use the NFS services that come with Services for UNIX, but those tools aren't free and are more difficult to acquire.

Microsoft's tools and Services for UNIX are available at www.microsoft.com/windows2000/sfu.

Migration Steps

The basic steps to migrating a UNIX network are as follows:

1. Deploy new Windows 2000 servers.

2. Migrate minor TCP/IP services to Windows 2000.

3. Attach UNIX clients to the Windows 2000 network.

4. Migrate Print services to Windows 2000.

5. Migrate File services to Windows 2000.

6. Migrate applications to Windows 2000.

7. Shut down or repurpose UNIX servers.

Deploy New Windows 2000 Servers   Deploying Windows 2000 servers in an existing UNIX environment can involve a considerable amount of planning because there are minor services that can be effectively served by either Windows 2000 or UNIX hosts. You need to decide before you deploy Windows 2000 whether you'll be moving crucial services such as DNS to Windows 2000 or leaving them on UNIX hosts. The big question, of course, is whether or not you intend to completely replace your UNIX hosts. This discussion assumes you will, so skip any of these recommendations if they don't make sense in your specific case.

The major service problem in migrating UNIX networks to Windows 2000 is DNS and the existing DNS name structure. Individual hosts inside your network already have DNS names that you may want or need to reuse on Windows 2000 hosts. You can usually only repurpose an existing DNS-named UNIX host with a Windows 2000 machine if you intend to completely replace all the network services of that UNIX host with services of Windows 2000.

To solve this problem, I recommend using a different DNS hierarchy for the Windows 2000 network than you used for the UNIX network. Then you can deploy all your Windows 2000 servers without any conflicts. You can use firewalls to redirect public services such as Web and mail service once you cut those applications over. For internal services, you can change DNS names once services have been moved over to Windows 2000 so that the old service name (for example, `files.production.mycorp.com`) will point to the new Windows 2000 file server.

Migrate TCP/IP Services   You will likely migrate myriad other TCP/IP services:

> **Web service**   Deciding to migrate your public Web services is a topic for an entire book. Simply put, you may decide to redeploy your entire internal network and keep your public Web services on UNIX because of the complexity of your existing Web application. Or your application may be so simple that it merely involves moving a set of HTML files. The only similarity between UNIX Web strategies and Windows Web strategies is HTML. All the database and active content strategies differ greatly, so it's best to treat a public Web transition as an entirely different effort from an internal network migration.

> **POP3 and SMTP service**   Windows 2000 doesn't come with an e-mail service, so migrating to Exchange from a sendmail UNIX host is technically a topic for a different book. That said, the cutover is pretty easy: deploy the new exchange server, make sure all your users have downloaded their e-mail from the UNIX host if they use IMAP, and then redirect the SMTP and POP3 ports on your firewall to point to the new e-mail server. Once you've got Exchange handling e-mail, you can deploy

Outlook on individual desktops and hook it up in "corporate mode" so it uses the Exchange server's MAPI handlers to trade contact and scheduling information.

DHCP   DHCP is also easy to migrate: Print out the conf files that show how you've got existing DHCP services running, and shut down the service on the UNIX hosts. Then bring it up on your Windows 2000 hosts and create analogous scopes. Simple, and you can even do it during the workday.

Attach UNIX Clients to the Windows 2000 Network   If you will be keeping UNIX hosts on your Windows network, install SAMBA (www.samba.org) to provide them with the ability to access Windows 2000 file shares. At the time this book went to press, the latest patch levels of SAMBA do not completely support Windows 2000 domains or direct SMB over TCP/IP, so although you don't need to run in Mixed Mode, your SMB servers will not be able to participate in domain security. They can connect to Windows 2000 computers as workgroup machines by providing a valid domain name and password.

Once you've got SAMBA deployed on UNIX hosts throughout your network, you'll be ready to move files from your UNIX file servers to Windows 2000.

Migrate Print Services to Windows 2000   Migrating TCP/IP Print services to Windows 2000 is rather simple. Most TCP/IP printers don't need to be handled through a central server, and in UNIX environments, they usually aren't. You can't really centralize TCP Print services for UNIX hosts if you intend to keep them in your network, so there's really no point in centralizing them for Windows 2000 hosts either. Simply set your Windows 2000 clients to print directly to the TCP/IP printers, and you'll be done.

Migrate File Services to Windows 2000   The best way to migrate File services from UNIX to Windows 2000 is to install SAMBA on your UNIX file servers and then open up your Windows 2000 file shares on the UNIX machine and move the files to Windows 2000 from the command prompt.

You could use FTP to do the same thing, but that takes quite a bit more up-front configuration on the Windows 2000 servers; you have to make FTP virtual roots that match the locations of each of your file shares. The simplicity of this operation once it is set up may appeal to you, and if for some reason you don't want to use SAMBA or PC-NFS, FTP is your only option.

When you've moved the files over, be certain to shut down the SAMBA, NFS, or FTP services you used on the UNIX server to share the files so clients don't accidentally log back in to the UNIX server and update files. You should probably copy the files over a weekend to make sure you don't have any problems with file versioning due to overlapping use of two different servers.

Migrate Applications to Windows 2000   Unlike NetWare hosts, UNIX servers frequently run special-purpose TCP/IP applications. And unlike NetWare hosts, the vendors of these applications may have no intention of ever providing a Windows 2000 environment because UNIX is not an obsolete operating system.

In these cases, you've got to decide whether to keep your existing UNIX application server or convert your operations to a competing product that runs on Windows 2000. Keeping the existing UNIX application server usually makes the most sense, especially since most UNIX apps have clients that either run on Windows directly, through an X-Windows server (in X, the terms *client* and *server* have meanings opposite from the normal usage), or through a Telnet client. You can use VNC as a free pseudo-X server for Windows computers that need to run applications on UNIX servers.

Shut Down or Repurpose UNIX Servers   The last step in a server migration is to shut down and remove the old servers. Old NetWare servers are pretty much worthless, but old UNIX servers can be recycled to create remote-access dial-in servers, firewalls, VPN endpoints, routers, Web servers, DHCP servers, DNS servers, and so forth. If you still run any UNIX servers, repurpose all your obsolete machines to support the services they support. Consider using UNIX machines for your public services, such as SMTP relays to protect internal Exchange servers. There are plenty of uses for old UNIX machines, even if they're slow by today's standards.

Client Migration

This section covers migrating client workstations to participate in a Windows 2000 domain. Chapter 2 covers upgrading Windows clients to Windows 2000.

Windows NT and 9*x* Clients

Moving or connecting Win32 clients (Windows 95, Windows 98, Windows Me, and Windows NT) to Windows 2000 domains is a trivial four-step process:

1. Convert user profiles in the old domain to local profiles.   This is only necessary if you are using roaming profiles in your Windows NT 4 domain and you've decided not to upgrade your servers from NT Server 4 to Windows 2000. If you upgrade your servers, roaming profiles will automatically be upgraded as well.

2. Connect the computer to the new domain.   Connecting Win32 computers to the domain is trivial. Simply change or create the domain affiliation in the Identity tab of the Network Control Panel, specify a domain account with the authority to add computers to the domain, and reboot the computer.

3. Copy local user profiles to the new domain and reconvert them to roaming profiles.   Log on to the computer as a domain administrator, open the System Control Panel, select the user profile you want to copy, click the Copy Profile button, and enter the UNC path you want to copy the profile to. This UNC path should match the "user profile" UNC path for the intended user's user profile in the Active Directory Users and Computers snap-in.

4. Install the Active Directory Client for Windows 2000.   This service allows the client to connect to the Active Directory and participate in much the same way as a Windows 2000 computer would.

NOTE   Windows NT 3.1 cannot be upgraded to Windows 2000. Considering the rarity of that operating system, this is unlikely to cause anyone any problems.

Windows 3.11 Clients

I recommend either replacing Windows 3.11 clients with modern computers and operating systems or deploying terminal servers and converting these computers into Windows terminals. Windows 3.11 is long obsolete; all the reasons for continuing to use it amount to inertia, and network upgrades provide an opportunity to get the ball rolling again to finally eliminate these legacy machines.

Windows 3.11 is a reasonable platform for the Terminal Services client. These computers are undoubtedly older 386 and 486 computers that would struggle to run a 32-bit operating system, and their users are not accustomed to particularly fast response anyway, so they are perfect for reuse as terminals. You can expect to deploy one terminal server for every 20 to 100 terminals depending upon the performance demands of the applications you run.

NOTE   Windows 3.11 cannot be upgraded to Windows 2000 Professional; however, it can be upgraded to Windows NT Workstation 3.51, which can subsequently be upgraded to Windows 2000 Professional—assuming the machine it's running on meets the minimum requirements for Windows 2000 Professional, which is highly unlikely.

MS-DOS Clients

Upgrading MS-DOS clients to work in Windows 2000 networks is cumbersome because the TCP/IP stack for MS-DOS is considerably larger than the NetWare redirector. In most cases, the Microsoft Client for MS-DOS will take more memory than your MS-DOS computers can spare and still run their applications. If you can't replace these computers with Win32 computers or convert them into Windows Terminals (Citrix sells a Windows Terminal client that runs directly on MS-DOS), then you should consider either running IPX as an alternate protocol along with Services for NetWare on your network or not upgrading your network at all.

Macintosh Clients

To support newer Macintosh clients in a Windows 2000 network, all you have to do is install the Services for Macintosh service. It is not necessary to install the AppleTalk protocol unless you will be supporting older Macs that cannot use AFP over TCP/IP.

Macintosh clients do not need to install any software to access Windows 2000 servers running Services for Macintosh, but they can install the UAM, which provides support for encrypted passwords on the network. AppleShare passwords are unencrypted by default.

Windows 2000 also includes Print Services for Macintosh, which allow Mac users to "see" any Windows 2000 shared printer as a Macintosh-compatible PostScript printer. Print Services for Macintosh automatically converts the Macintosh-submitted print job to the correct format for the print device.

UNIX Clients

You've got two options for UNIX clients that you want to support in a Windows 2000 domain: you can make the UNIX clients run SMB to access Windows 2000 file shares, or you can make the Windows 2000 servers run NFS to provide native NFS file sharing for UNIX.

Which is better? SMB, in my opinion. SMB is a faster file-sharing protocol than NFS because it supports numerous optimizations that NFS doesn't. Overall, it's about twice as fast in normal operations than NFS. SMB support for UNIX is also free from www.samba.org. As this book goes to press, the SAMBA client is not capable of authenticating with a Windows 2000 server in Native Mode because SAMBA is currently equivalent to a Windows NT 4 machine. The SAMBA-TNG code fork is working hard to make SAMBA completely Windows 2000 compatible, so by the time you read this, support may be available.

Installing Services for UNIX may be best in your situation until SAMBA is fully compatible with Windows 2000. Services for UNIX provides an NFS-compatible file server that UNIX hosts can connect to for file service. Most print services are already compatible with the UNIX LPD printer daemon, so they don't need to go through a Windows 2000 Print server.

Summary

There are two vastly different sides to a network migration: the server side and the client side. The server side involves updating servers to run a new operating system, migrating applications from one platform to another, and re-creating or migrating the security infrastructure of your network. The client side involves visiting each machine in the network to connect it to the new server infrastructure, which often means installing software on the clients.

Choosing to migrate a network to Windows 2000 is a serious undertaking that requires planning and foresight. Jumping into an upgrade without understanding the issues can cause considerable problems. Not properly weighing the various upgrade options can cause you a lot of wasted effort if tools exist that can automatically handle the problems you're dealing with.

Fortunately, Microsoft provides several tools and add-on software packages to assist in the migration to Windows 2000 from a number of other operating systems:

- Services for NetWare will help migrate NetWare Directory Services (NDS) structures, bulk-move files with permissions intact from NetWare servers to Windows 2000 servers, and even emulate NetWare servers for clients that can't be migrated.

- Services for UNIX provides a complete NFS client, server, and gateway package to allow UNIX clients and servers to participate in a Windows network. Services for UNIX also provides an Active Directory–integrated NIS server package for UNIX machines that use the NIS domain security service. Password synchronization and a number of UNIX utilities round out this package, which is designed more for cooperation than migration.

- Services for Macintosh provides a complete AppleShare server that can operate over AppleTalk or TCP/IP to support Macintosh clients. Print Services for Macintosh appears as a standard LaserWriter printer to Macintosh clients and converts PostScript print jobs for output to any Windows-based printer.

Windows 2000 even comes with upgrade tools for earlier Windows environments, including the PDC emulator that allows for Mixed-Mode domain operations during a Windows 2000 deployment and robust upgrade installation packages for both servers and clients. The 16-bit Terminal Services client can even be considered something of an upgrade tool that will allow the oldest Windows computers to participate usefully on a Windows 2000 network.

Migrating to Windows 2000 can be done seamlessly and with minimal impact on end-users, but that goal requires more attention to planning and preparation than actual upgrade work. Choosing server-side solutions to emulate older environments can go a long way toward smoothing out migration problems. Understanding your upgrade and migration options before you choose a methodology will solve most of your problems before they happen.

Case Study: Moving from UNIX

One of my small clients had a rather atypical network: a Linux file server running SAMBA providing service to Windows 98 clients. They called me in to assist with the transition to an all–Windows 2000 network. They had been quite happy with their Linux file server, reporting that it had never had a problem in the two years of its installed life, but they needed to move to an integrated contact management solution since they'd outgrown the Net Folders feature of Outlook. Exchange 2000 was their selected solution, and it only ran on Windows 2000. They decided to migrate their entire network rather than work in a mixed environment.

Client Migration

I decided to migrate the client workstations to Windows 2000 first. As it turns out, this was probably a bit of a mistake; if we had upgraded the Windows 98 clients to Windows 2000 with the Windows 2000 server already online, the Windows 2000 Professional upgrade process would have automatically created a roaming profile for us based on the user's Windows 98 settings. By upgrading desktops first, we had to create roaming profiles manually.

For the desktop computers, we used the Windows 2000 upgrade option. It worked seamlessly, with the exception of a conflict with some anti-virus software, which the compatibility checker reported and we removed prior to the upgrade. The upgrade option had very little impact on users.

We did run into a strange problem, however. As it turns out, the version of SAMBA running on the client's Linux server was not compatible with Windows 2000 in the domain mode. We solved the problem by setting the Windows 2000 computers to workgroup mode with the same domain name, but the problem did cause some minor password and account problems. We could have updated the version of SAMBA on the Linux server, but we elected not to since we'd be taking that machine down shortly anyway.

Laptop Installation

For laptops, we performed clean installations of Windows 2000 using sector-based disk imaging and platforms created using the System Preparation Tool. On one laptop, we installed the operating system and all the user applications, but we avoided installing drivers specific to the hardware of the laptop. We then imaged this to a spare hard disk using Apricorn's clever PCMCIA-to-IDE interface adapter and the EZ-GIG sector-imaging boot floppy that works with their PCMCIA card. This operation worked flawlessly and we didn't have to remove laptop hard disk drives, with the exception of two Compaq Presario laptops. Those machines had PCMCIA controllers that didn't work with the PCMCIA hard-disk-imaging software and didn't work with Windows 2000. Since there were only two machines, my client retired the computers and purchased new ones, but this issue would have been a showstopper if it happened on all the laptops.

Server Setup

Once we had the clients upgraded and working correctly, we installed Windows 2000 Server on a new machine. The installation went perfectly, thanks in part to the fact that the Compaq SmartArray RAID controller in the server was supported on the Windows 2000 CD-ROM. When the server was online, we installed Exchange 2000.

User Accounts

To migrate user accounts, we used /etc/passwd to retrieve a list of user accounts and created a batch file to re-create them on the Windows 2000 server. Since my client maintained a low security posture, we simply set all the passwords to the same known password and typed it in for users when they first logged in to the domain. After that, users could change to their own password.

Once the accounts were available on the new machine, we went around to each client computer and joined it to the Windows 2000 domain. During this "seat visit," we also turned their local profiles into roaming profiles and copied them up to the domain controller, and then connected their Outlook clients to the Exchange server. They would continue using the Linux-based SMPT/POP3 e-mail server during the transition, so we left their e-mail setups in place.

File Copy

At this point, both servers were online and clients could use either one of them. Drive mappings still pointed to the file shares on the Linux server, and we waited for a weekend to change this. Starting on Friday evening, we logged all the client machines out of both servers and started a file copy on the new Windows 2000 machine using XCOPY at the command prompt, piping the results to a text-based log. Once the operation was started, we went home and let the copy proceed through the night.

On Saturday morning, the copy was finished, and when I examined the log, I was surprised to find that we hadn't had a single problem file. At that point, we shut down the SAMBA daemon on the Linux server to make sure its shares would not be available to clients. We then re-created the share structure on the Windows 2000 server and created a batch file to delete and remap the shares on clients. At each client, we simply ran this batch file from a floppy, and the job was complete.

On Monday morning, everyone was back to work as usual, and we set about the problem of creating a permissions structure for their server since none had existed in their Linux environment.

At that point, we unplugged the Linux server's network adapter, but left it powered and in place in case there were any problems with migration. After two weeks without a snag, we shut down the machine and removed it.

Part 3

Windows 2000 Every Day

Topics covered:

- Client support best practices
- Support tools built into Windows 2000
- Third-party support tools
- Maintaining servers
- Monitoring servers
- Using remote administration
- Establishing an effective support organization
- Building a help desk

12

Supporting Clients

In a normal network, client support, also known as desktop support, consumes more time than all other network administrative duties combined. The reasons are simple: there are a lot more client computers than there are servers or dedicated network hardware, and the majority of people who use those computers are not computer experts, so they can accidentally cause malfunction.

Reducing the client support burden is the easiest way to reduce your overall administrative burden. Consider this: if you spend 40 percent of your resources supporting servers and 60 percent supporting clients, then cutting your client support burden by 50 percent would yield a 30 percent savings in overall administration resources—that's your time and your company's money. Reducing administrative burden by 50 percent is fairly easy to do in companies where few measures have been taken to do so.

This chapter is divided into three sections. "Support Best Practices" covers the theory behind many client support techniques. "Windows 2000 Client Support Tools" covers those resources already at your disposal to ease the client support burden. Finally, "Third-Party Tools" covers the invaluable tools you should acquire to make your support burden easier.

Support Best Practices

In the dawn of time, there were no networks. There were only large monolithic computers with hundreds of dumb terminals attached to them. The terminals performed no function of their own—they merely transmitted keystrokes and echoed responses on the screen over a simple, directly connected serial cable. The central computer did everything.

Desktop management was easy. If a terminal broke, you replaced it. If a user didn't know what the F4 key did, you sent him to training. The administrator's most arduous duty was mounting the nine-inch tape for backup each night. Applications were not added to existing computers—rather, new computers were brought online to support any required additional functionality. Customization didn't exist. Order reigned supreme.

Times have changed. Desktop computers have moved computational power out to every individual user. Spacious local hard disks host a seemingly endless array of cryptically named operating system files, application files, and user files. Networks transmit volumes of data so sporadically that useful measurement can only be taken over large time periods. Servers are arranged in tiers, with myriad purposes and overlapping duties.

In these new times, employees, forever free from the bounds of a flashing green cursor, soar with new productivity. But alas, the administrator's job has become so burdensome that the labor to fix this dizzying cosmos of equipment is far more costly than the equipment itself. They fear the day when failure might occur—simply determining what went wrong could take days. Chaos rules.

Fear not. A middle ground between centralized computing and distributed processing exists. Employees can be free to innovate as networks allow, and administrators can retain control of network resources and fix problems in a timely and controllable fashion. With planning and foresight—or money and hindsight—client administration can be controlled fairly easily.

The basic principle behind controlling the costs of client management is the concept of the replaceable desktop computer. If you can simply replace a broken computer, rather than fix it, without burdening your user or taking too much time, then you can move all of your troubleshooting and repair efforts into your shop. By maintaining just a few "spare" computers that can be swapped immediately in place of a malfunctioning computer, you'll get your users back to work faster than any other method—and that, remember, is the goal. You can then repair the broken computers when you have spare time or simply use them as spares.

Controlling client resources to reduce administrative burden doesn't mean stifling users. I've heard hundreds of users complain about "net nazis"—overzealous administrators who make policies where none are necessary and force their vision of control upon the unfortunate souls who use their network. This sort of administrative power struggle results in an adversarial relationship with users, who will then look for any reason at all to cast blame upon the IT group. Disgruntled users will circumvent security and feel justified in doing so and will passively resist all future control mechanisms.

Effective control doesn't imply policy implementation based only on your desire to simplify your administrative problem. The network doesn't exist to give the IT staff a job to do, it exists for the users. Keep this fundamental principle in mind when you negotiate policies with your users. You'll find that the majority of your users don't want or need a free hand to customize their computers—they just want to get their work done. Those workers who desire more freedom from constraint should probably get it, depending upon their job function. But you can negotiate a tradeoff of administrative burden: if they break their computers, they have to fix them or accept a more restricted desktop if they cannot. Most "knowledge workers" are experienced computer users who can make their own decisions about hardware platforms and software applications. Don't make policy decisions in a vacuum, because you must have the support of your users in order to implement sustainable control policies.

In this section, I will discuss the theoretical bases for reducing the administrative burden through centralization, reduction of the problem, replicated effort, and security.

Centralize Customization

Customization is the reason you can't easily replace computers in typical environments. Every desktop in your environment is somewhat customized. It has its own set of files, its own applications, its own operating system, its own configuration, even its own set of hardware.

If client computers weren't customized at all, you could simply replace them when they broke. One desktop would be as good as any other. Employees could use any computer to access their resources, because whatever customized file they needed would be on a server.

Given that customization is the root of client support problems and that the only customized component in a computer is the hard disk, then controlling access to (or even the presence of) the local hard disk in a client computer is the key to reducing client administration throughout your entire organization.

Customization-restricted clients store all created data and user configuration on central servers. This makes the desktop computer completely replaceable. Users can log in to any computer, not just the one they usually use. Broken machines can be replaced in minutes, and hard disk failure becomes just another replaceable component. New clients can be brought online quickly by cloning existing machines. The workstations do not need to be backed up, thus reducing the scope of your backup operations.

This line of reasoning explains the five major options that already exist for controlling clients:

- Windows terminals
- Diskless workstations
- Controlled-access clients
- Standard workstations
- Unsupported workstations

These five desktop options represent five different levels of administrative control: from strictest, least useful, and most easily managed to relaxed, unfettered, and difficult to manage. Which method is most appropriate for your network depends mostly on the needs of your users. In most organizations, a mix of at least two types of desktops is usually appropriate across the strata of your organization.

Windows terminals   Functionally the same as terminals of old, they don't process any of the user's work on their own. Windows terminals merely display data sent from a central computer (a terminal server) and transmit keystrokes and mouse movements. Windows terminals share the compute power of a single terminal server. Unlike the terminals and mainframes of old, however, desktop applications are not designed for terminal servers—they're designed for complete computers. Modern desktop applications are extremely wasteful of compute resources, and for that reason, a single powerful server can only reasonably support about 50 computers (and even then response will be sluggish). Windows terminals are only appropriate for desktop applications that are not compute or display intensive (Word processing or database entry). Graphical, mathematical, or I/O heavy applications are not suited to this environment.

Terminal Services for Windows 2000 allows you to disable the most wasteful features of the desktop operating system, such as Active Desktop. For many applications (Microsoft Word, for example), shutting off background features such as spelling and grammar checking can dramatically decrease the compute load of the application. Preventing things such as file search operations also helps considerably.

TIP Use your old 486 and Pentium class computers as Windows terminals to extend their useful lifetime.

Diskless workstations   Regular PC computers that lack a hard disk drive. They boot a special ROM embedded on the network adapter to connect to a remote-boot server, from which the operating system is loaded. This solves the problem of loading a single CPU with too many computing jobs, because each client has its own processor. Because diskless workstations do not have local storage, all file access must be transmitted over the network. Although a considerable amount of disk access is obviated using RAM-based caching, diskless workstations put about three times the load on the network that a normal PC does. However, with good network design, that's not really a problem. Diskless workstations also can take a bit of time to boot in the morning if all the computers are started at the same time. Diskless workstations are most suited to users who work with a well-defined set of lightweight desktop or office applications. Diskless workstations are not well suited to applications that involve heavy disk use, such as graphical rendering, CAD, scientific modeling, or software development.

NOTE   Windows 95 is the only 32-bit Windows environment capable of being booted over the network. Windows 98, Me, NT, and 2000 all require a local hard disk drive. This restriction eliminates the option of remote booting for many organizations.

Controlled-access clients   Normal PCs that use a combination of user profiles, strict policy, and security to prevent users from storing files on them or modifying their configuration. Think of controlled-access clients as diskless workstations with disks. The local hard disk is used for booting, loading applications, storing computer configuration information, and storing temporary files. User configuration and user-created files are stored without exception on centralized servers. Because the configuration is locked down, the computer can still be swapped out with a replacement in a very short time. Users may or may not be restricted in their desktop activities— their personal configuration choices are simply stored on the server instead of the local client using the profiles mechanism. Controlled-access clients are similar to diskless workstations in their application, but they can be used for more disk-intensive applications such as graphical rendering.

NOTE   Only Windows NT and Windows 2000 have the security control necessary to implement controlled-access clients correctly, although you can get close with Windows 98 and Me. When I implement controlled-access clients on 95, 98, and Me, I make sure that users understand that any files they store on their local computers will be lost if the IT staff has to fix their computer.

Standard workstations   Normal PCs connected to a network using the traditional redirector method. No specific control is implemented. These computers are the traditional workhorses of the network environment. These days, however, a standard PC is a lot more hardware than most office tasks actually require. Standard workstations are most appropriate for compute-intensive applications such as graphics, rendering, scientific modeling, and programming. Fortunately, the users who work with these applications usually are expert computer users.

Windows 2000
Every Day

PART 3

Unsupported workstations   If your business employs scientists, engineers, or programmers, these groups probably perform research using esoteric operating systems. Or you may have a department that needs to run a small application requiring an unusual operating system (often the case with scientific, engineering, or accounting software). These operating systems require an entirely different set of skills to support than the Windows and Macintosh clients normally found in businesses, and they consume an inordinate amount of support time because they're difficult to manage under even the best of circumstances. But rather than fighting the deployment of these systems, you should simply make it clear that the IT department is not responsible for supporting them in any way. Support should be the responsibility of either the users or the vendor providing the custom application, or it should be outsourced to a consulting group that specializes in the operating system.

Your environment probably requires a mix of the above client technologies. The two most popular and easily implemented are the controlled-access client and standard workstations. The more esoteric costs of thin clients and remote-boot workstations makes them about as expensive as a medium-power standard PC—a single hardware platform you could use to implement both controlled-access clients and standard workstations for those few users that really need them. If you give standard workstations to all users with minimal controls in place, you'll have constant desktop-support hassles.

Sage Advice: Force Centralized File Storage

Do not allow users to store their files and documents on their local computers. This is anathema in a network environment because it makes it impossible to quickly swap out client machines. It also leads to disarray and confusion about the location of files and makes it impossible to share files effectively in your group.

Move the My Documents Desktop folder by right-clicking it and browsing to a new location on the network. Most applications will then save documents to the network rather than the local hard disk.

Implement roaming profiles to store Desktop and application data (such as outlook.pst files) by specifying the UNC path to each user's centrally stored roaming profile in the user's account information in the Active Directory Users and Computers snap-in. If your users have local profiles, you can easily copy them to the server. Log on to the computer as an administrator, and then use the System Control Panel's User Profile pane to select the user's profile and copy it up to the server. The next time the user logs in, the same profile they use locally will be downloaded from the server.

If users complain that working on files over the network is too slow, upgrade the network. 100MB Fast Ethernet is fast enough for the most demanding engineering applications. Although programmers can make heavy demands of a network, they spend most of their time editing, not compiling. The occasional extra minute to compile a large application is worth the collaborative environment that working directly from the server fosters. In the worst case, use Gigabit Ethernet. In a well-designed network, it is just as fast as local disk access, and switched Gigabit Ethernet over copper is now down to $500 per station.

If your company is in the removable cartridge hard disk habit, get out of it. It never ceases to amaze me that people store their work files on a Zip disk rather than on the server, but I run into this insanity all the time. Files are lost to hot car seats, poorly labeled cartridges make files difficult to find, and two people can't work on the same group of files at the same time. If laptop users must use removable media, use CardFlash semiconductor memory, which is nearly impervious to data loss, and allow only one cartridge per person. This way, files must be moved to the server to make more room on the cartridge rather than be left to languish forgotten in desk drawers.

If your users must work from home, set up virtual private networking. It's more consistent, reliable, and sustainable than removable cartridge hard disks. A modem can download a 1MB file in about five minutes, which isn't a big deal when performed at the beginning and end of a work session. Removable cartridge hard disks only make sense when a work-at-home requirement exists for truly huge files.

Finally, for users who take files with them on a laptop, do what I do on my personal laptop: use solid state flash memory to store user-created files. Flash memory, usually in the form of a PCMCIA or (more commonly) CardFlash with a PCMCIA adapter, is the ideal removable medium for laptops. Since the memory is solid state, dropping the laptop won't damage the stored files. Neither will soaking the laptop in water, sitting on it, or even moderate fire damage. The available capacity (64MB is typical at the time of this writing) is plenty for even the largest work files, yet small enough to force users to occasionally move data to the network where it belongs, either by connecting the laptop to the network or by mounting the flash memory module in a desktop reader. By not storing files on the laptop's internal hard drive, laptop users can still benefit from the same ease of computer replacement that their desktop peers enjoy.

Windows 2000
Every Day

PART 3

Reduce the Problem

Reduce the scope of your management problem by standardizing software and hardware. Although this sounds very obvious, most of my clients allow users to choose their own applications: the CEO uses WordPerfect, while most everyone else uses Word. Document-format issues abound, and data is lost because of it. Yet everyone blames the software rather than the silly notion that minor differences between applications are more important than standardization.

Hardware standardization is even more important. If you want to replace computers quickly, the new computer must be able to boot the same operating system configuration as the old one. This doesn't mean that every computer must be of the same class or manufacture—it means that certain key components and platform choices should be standardized. For example, it's more important that your client computers use Windows 2000 Professional, boot IDE devices, and have the same network adapter than that they all be Dell Dimensions.

Larger companies typically purchase computers in larger batches, which makes standardizing on a few classes of computer easy. Smaller companies may have difficulty enacting specific hardware standards, because computers are typically purchased on an as-needed basis.

Hardware Specifics

Companies that cannot purchase large numbers of the same model should enact strict standards for the following client computer component:

- Disk controller

It's important, although not crucial, to standardize the following list of components for ease of repair. These components are not crucial because Windows 2000 Professional and Windows 95/98/Me can automatically detect them.

- Network adapters
- Video adapters

TIP You should phase out use of Windows NT 4 Workstation as soon as possible because of its inability to automatically detect hardware. Upgrading to Windows 2000 is quick and easy, and will cut your support burden dramatically.

These next computer components are not dependent upon specific drivers, so you have considerable flexibility in choosing them:

- Processor (assuming the same family)
- RAM
- Motherboard (assuming the same number of processors)

- Hard disk (assuming the same disk controller technology)
- Keyboards, mice, and control devices
- CD-ROM (assuming the same disk controller technology)

It's easy to maintain these standards if you select commonly available hardware for the standard components. You can either order computers to your exact specification, or you can order them without the two key driver devices—video adapters and network adapters—if you want to enforce a homogenous driver environment across all your platforms.

Restricting your hardware is considerably simpler with Windows 2000 than it was in a Windows NT environment. Plug and Play allows the operating system to more easily detect the video and network drivers. For this reason, it's not nearly as important to stick with the exact same video and network adapters as it was with Windows NT. Your requirements for Windows 2000 clients should be relaxed to those adapters that are included in the Windows 2000 default driver set located in the drivers.cab file. These drivers can be configured without intervention by the end-user, which is the ideal case.

Other more esoteric hardware (such as tape backup devices, removable media hard drives, sound cards, multimedia devices, and scanners) should not be part of your hardware specification. These peripherals are either not necessary in a network environment (for example, desktop tape backup) or can be added to a desktop like an application (for example, desktop scanners). Choose connectivity technologies such as USB or Firewire devices for external desktop peripherals (such as scanners) so they can be added to desktop computers without opening the computer up. Most end-users are capable of adding USB and Firewire devices to their computer without help.

Sage Advice: Client Hardware Standards

For the three important driver-controlled hardware devices, follow these practices:

- For Windows NT clients, network adapters should be selected based on a common manufacturer or a common chipset used by numerous manufacturers. For example, the DEC 21140 Tulip chipset is driver-compatible across more than 20 manufacturers. For Windows 98 and 2000 clients, simply choose adapters with drivers that are shipped on the operating system CD-ROM. They'll be automatically detected and configured upon first boot.

- Video controllers are more difficult to standardize, because video requirements vary widely among users. Video is not nearly as important for configuration, however, because all video adapters support the VGA lowest common denominator, which can be used until a new driver is installed.

- Disk controller technology is easy: use EIDE. Though SCSI is still slightly faster in its fastest configurations, it isn't worth the minor increase in speed for clients considering the driver differences among controllers. A few off-brand UltraDMA-33 and UltraDMA-66 chipsets are not compatible with Windows 2000's built-in IDE driver, but these chipsets are rare and easily avoided. Windows 2000 also does not support UDMA Mode 5, the mode implemented by ATA100 controllers. If you use these controllers with Windows 2000 service packs 0 or 1 (those current when this book went to press), corruption of system files can occur that will render the machine nonbootable. The Windows 2000 Repair Installation will fix the problem without data loss, but the machines will not be stable until Microsoft fixes the problem. Hum this mantra: "IDE for desktops, SCSI for servers." You should absolutely avoid RAID-0 solutions, either in hardware or software, for client workstations. While they can dramatically improve disk performance, these solutions dramatically reduce the reliability of the machine. Workstations using RAID-0 are far more likely to suffer from hard disk failure because there are more disks to break, and the failure of any one of them will cause the computer to fail. If disk performance is especially important, use a RAID-1 mirroring solution that can read from both sides of the mirror simultaneously.

Work More, Walk Less

In a standard help desk environment, users submit a trouble report by phone, via e-mail, or through a Notes or Exchange application, and a request for help is logged. The user waits around for a support technician to arrive and diagnose the problem. Upon determining the problem, the technician returns to the IT department to get the hardware or software tools needed to fix the problem, goes back to the client, and performs the repairs. Technician time spent: about two hours. User time spent waiting: about six hours. This means that a support technician can handle about four incidents per day, and that, on average, those four incidents result in 24 hours of lost user productivity.

Compare this to a just-in-time help desk that uses remote tools to solve these problems. The user calls the help desk via telephone or ICQ. The technician pulls up a real-time network map, selects the client, and opens a remote control session to that client. The technician can immediately see the specific error message the user is reporting and can initiate soft fixes remotely. The technician can perform software installation from server software sources, reconfiguration, virus checks, or diagnosis over the remote link. In the event of a hardware problem or a computer that cannot be reset by the user to a booted state, the technician logs out a spare client that's been pre-configured with the operating system and application package and replaces the defective computer, which is returned to the IT department for diagnosis and repair whenever time allows. Total average IT time spent: 15 minutes. Total user time spent waiting: 15 minutes. This means that the average support technician can perform 32 trouble calls per day, which results in eight hours of lost user productivity. The serious savings comes from the fact that a single support technician can perform the work of eight(!) support technicians from the previous model.

Remote control software can be used to perform routine maintenance (software installation or the application of service packs) and administration as well. Remote control interfaces such as the free open-source cross-platform VNC from AT&T's Olivetti Research Laboratory or the remote agents for packages such as NetWizard, Tivoli, CA UniCenter, or HP OpenView can increase the efficiency of an IT operation by an order of magnitude.

> **TIP** Stop reading, go to www.uk.research.att.com, and download VNC. It's free; it runs across UNIX, Macs, PC platforms, and even Windows CE and Palm computing devices. Remote control connections can be established either from the controller or the controlled computer. Of course, any remote control software introduces security problems, so be sure your security architecture won't allow this software to be used for evil (in other words, you've got a strong firewall in place).

Train Users

User training is the other side of increasing IT efficiency. By training users to run their computers effectively, you can eliminate a significant portion of the trouble calls to your help desk. Proper training also allows users to respond to verbal direction from support technicians to fix or diagnose problems over the phone.

This discussion of training addresses only the benefit to network administration, but the improvement in user efficiency at their job is phenomenal. A typical $100 training class for an application is repaid in just a few hours of user efficiency, so it's a fairly easy business case to make.

Sage Advice: Train First

Train new employees to use their computers and applications before they begin working and have periodic training refreshers or more advanced courses for existing applications.

You may encounter resistance in upper management to training employees. I've heard ridiculous justifications such as, "Trained employees have to be paid more," "I don't want to train people and have them leave the company," and "We can't afford (or don't have time to) train everyone." In extreme cases, management flat-out won't pay for professional training courses, and there's nothing a network administrator can do about it.

Or is there? You can personally develop training courses for the applications and systems you use in your network. Pass out network-specific user guides. Put up an intranet Web site with click-through training based on screen shots of applications and a frequently asked question guide. You can even put up a click-through troubleshooting guide that culminates in very specific e-mail trouble requests being posted to your support technicians.

Hold training seminars yourself. Keep them short and task-oriented, and, if necessary, hold them during lunch. Users will appreciate the training, and you'll see a significant reduction in trouble incidents.

Of course, these measures take time to put together up front, but proactive planning to avoid problems always does.

Windows 2000 Client Support Tools

Windows 2000 comes with a numerous tools you can use to reduce your administrative burden and create a uniform environment for users. These tools include:

- Intellimirror file-based replication
- Windows Installer application deployment system
- Group Policy
- User profiles
- Remote Installation Services

These tools are discussed in the following sections.

Intellimirror

Intellimirror is Microsoft's new name for their old replication service. The replication service that shipped with Windows NT 4 was highly disappointing—it could replicate only entire files, between only two locations, and only when the files were closed. In addition, the replication service replicated the entire file, not just the changed portion. And, if the file was changed in both locations, the replication service could not replicate it.

Intellimirror is essentially the same service, except that you can now use the Active Directory to store replicated directory information and replicate between multiple directories. It also works on the workstation version of the operating system. All of its other weaknesses remain, however.

Just as with Windows NT 4, Microsoft made broad claims of usefulness before the replication product shipped and has been backpedaling ever since as the problems inherent in its simplistic architecture emerged. They now recommend Intellimirror for just four situations:

Application deployment with Windows Installer As with all administrative tasks, the ideal is to find one method that works for everything. Windows Installer and Intellimirror can only install applications packaged with the new .msi installation format, which currently includes only Microsoft applications and a very few early adopters. The Windows Installer can also deploy simple .zap installation script files, which you will have to create to facilitate the deployment of third-party applications. Search the Microsoft Web site for more details on the .zap installation script format. If you continue to use any applications developed before Windows 2000, you'll have to use a third-party remote installation package such as Tivoli or NetWizard to deploy them or create your own .msi packages with the limited WinInstall LE package included with Windows 2000. And if you're doing that, there's no reason to bother using Intellimirror and Windows Installer. Perhaps in a few years this recommendation will change, but I doubt it.

Replicating roaming user profiles among domain controllers This portion of the Intellimirror service makes some sense at first glance, until you do the numbers. Roaming profiles have a downside: they are typically quite large, because applications such as Outlook store all Outlook data in them, and because they contain everything on the Desktop, which is where most users store their active documents. Because of the size of a typical roaming profile, using Intellimirror to replicate profiles from server to server becomes increasingly difficult as the number of users increases. Consider the following: Microsoft's own internal testing shows that the average office user needs about 25MB of space for their profile. If you replicated the profiles of 1,600 users, you would need 40GB of storage space on every server those profiles were replicated to. Obviously, roaming profiles cannot scale indefinitely; an organization of 10,000 users using roaming profiles across the enterprise would require "profile servers" in every location, each having 250GB of storage space. You need to be extremely careful about how you use Intellimirror to replicate profiles in your organization to prevent them from overrunning your storage space.

Backing up user files on workstations to a server automatically Here's a better idea: don't let users store files on their local workstations. If you're managing your connected desktops properly, you don't have this problem anyway. Theoretically, using the offline folders feature of Intellimirror—where a user's My Documents folder is redirected to a network share and then mirrored back to their local desktop—would help users work through a network outage. But in my decade of desktop administration, I've never let users suffer through more than about four hours of downtime per year. I can't imagine a situation where network outages are common enough to require this sort of workaround.

Backing up user files from laptops that are frequently disconnected from the network This recommendation makes some sense, but synchronization issues abound. In reality, this only makes sense for files that other people don't need to use. Here's the problem: Laptop users frequently work on files that other people need to use as well, such as field reports, business plans, spreadsheets, and so forth. People in the office have no idea that a replicated version of a spreadsheet is being carried around, so they modify that spreadsheet. When the replicated spreadsheet comes in from the field, a conflict exists. Both files have been modified, and there's no easy way to merge the two modified documents back together. In my experience, it's extremely difficult to get users to understand exactly what's really happening with automated replication, but they seem to understand handing files around on removable media pretty well. Give your laptop users PCMCIA or CardFlash media cards, have them store their files on that, and have them handle moving files to the network manually.

WARNING I installed Intellimirror on my laptop so that I could work with files offline. Since then, I've had infrequent problems with blue-screen crashes when I log out or shut down and the synchronization begins if there's no network connection to the server. To date, this hasn't caused any problems or data loss, but it's certainly frustrating. My computer has no other problems, and when I disable Intellimirror, the problem doesn't occur. As of this writing, no Knowledge Base articles cover the problem.

Early reports from Intellimirror adopters show that rather than reducing the total cost of ownership of the network, the replication system has merely increased the administrative burden. Because it does not perform any of its intended functions seamlessly and without intervention, it basically costs as much administrative work as it saves.

Until Microsoft improves Intellimirror functionality and enables it to deploy any application, you're better off sticking with disk imaging and the class-based application rollout methods described in Chapters 3 and 10.

Don't let the offline folders feature of Intellimirror (basically, the "briefcase" in reverse) lull you into thinking that it's now okay for users to work from their own hard drives.

While Intellimirror certainly makes it safer, it's still not completely seamless, and it doesn't work for files that need to be shared among users. You're far better off having people work directly on the network shares the way they always (should) have.

Group Policy

Policies are sets of rules that you create to control how users are allowed to work with their computers and how their computers operate. Policies are physically composed of groups of Registry settings that are applied to the Registry during startup and after a user logs in. Any aspect of computer behavior that can be controlled using the Registry can be managed using policies.

Using the Group Policy feature, you create the controlled-access clients that help you reduce your support burden. As such, group policies are among the most important long-term administrative tools available to Windows 2000 administrators. Spend some time learning and understanding group policies in your test environment or on virtual machines so you can apply them usefully in your environment.

Group policies can only be applied to Windows 2000 computers. Clients that run Windows NT and Windows 98 must be managed using the System Policy editors (`poledit.exe`) that come with those two operating systems. The NT/98 policies are not stored in the Active Directory and cannot be applied with the flexibility of Group Policy. If you intend to use Group Policy to manage your network, you should complete the upgrade to a homogenous Windows 2000 network as quickly as possible.

Group Policy is an extension of the Windows NT and Windows 95/98 concept of System Policy, a collection of Registry settings that are applied when a user logs in and which restrict the activities of that user. Group policies are stored in the Active Directory and can be applied as Active Directory containers to wide groups of users and computers.

Group Policy can also be used to control many group-based administrative functions in addition to computer- and user-based configuration. Group Policy is also used to control Windows Installer–based software installation and other administrative tasks that are based on aggregations of users.

There are two types of policies:

User policies Restrict the activities of the logged-on user. User policies are applied when the user logs on and before logon scripts are processed. The policies are applied in hierarchical order, starting with the site policy and ending with the last Organizational Unit (OU) policy that applies to the user. User policies are applied to the HKEY_CURRENT_USER (HKCU) Registry hive.

Computer policies   Modify the local computer's environment. Computer policies are applied immediately after network connections are established and before startup scripts are run, followed by the presentation of the logon prompt. Every Windows 2000 computer has one local policy by default, which is managed through the Group Policy snap-in. Computer policies are applied to the HKEY_LOCAL_MACHINE (HKLM) Registry hive.

Because of the flexibility of group policies, multiple policies will frequently apply to a single session. For example, separate, specific policies may need to be applied to the local computer, the logged-on user, and the department in which the user works. Multiple policies are applied in order of increasing specificity, starting with the local system policy or NT 4 policy, and then the site policy, domain policy, and OU policies in their hierarchical order. In general, the last-applied policy "wins" when a conflict in policy exists. This means that OU policy overrides domain policy, which overrides site policy, which overrides local system policy.

WARNING   The more group policies that apply to a user or computer, the longer it will take to start the machine or log in. Minimize the number of policies that apply to users as much as you can.

Creating a Group Policy

Creating a policy is easy, but the process is somewhat encumbered by the Windows 2000 user interface. Use the following steps to create a group policy.

1. To create a group policy that applies to a site, launch the Active Directory Sites and Services administrative tool. For domain and OU policies, launch the Active Directory Users and Computers administrative tool.

2. Right-click the appropriate Active Directory container (Site, Domain, or OU), and select Properties.

3. In the Properties window, select the Group Policy tab, and click New.

4. Type a name for the policy, and press Enter to create it. Notice at this point that the window can list any number of group policies.

5. Policies are applied in the order (and therefore, with the precedence) shown in this policy list. Click the Up and Down buttons to change the group policy application order for this Active Directory container.

6. To modify a policy, double-click it to launch the Group Policy Editor snap-in. The policy will be applied to all users and computers within this Active Directory container.

Figure 12.1 shows the Group Policy Properties window for an Organizational Unit.

Figure 12.1   The Group Policy portion of an Active Directory container Properties window allows you to create and manage group policies.

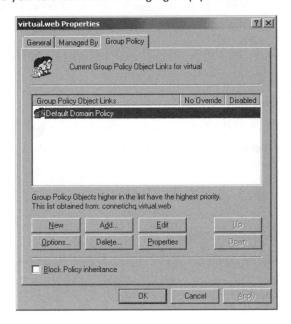

Redirecting Directories

Perhaps one of the most important management features of Group Policy is the ability to redirect the user profile directories that would normally be stored on the local computer to a network share. This eliminates many of the problems associated with user profiles and takes the bulk of profile data off the local machine, where they're neither backed up nor available to the user on other machines. These folders are:

- Application Data
- Desktop
- Start Menu
- My Documents
- My Pictures

Technically, you can redirect folders in two ways: redirect all users to a single location or redirect based on security group membership. I recommend that you use only single location redirection and that you create multiple Organizational Units with separate group policies if you need to separate users. This method is simpler to manage, easier to document, and more consistent with the Active Directory philosophy.

WARNING   A user's Start Menu folder in their profile only reflects the applications on the machine they normally use (the one on which the application was installed). Unless your machines are directory for directory the same on every computer, users will have problems running programs from the Start menu. This is one of the primary reasons I recommend class-based imaging rather than individual application installation for deploying applications.

To redirect profile folders to a network share, use the following procedure:

1. Open the appropriate group policy, and click User Configuration ➢ Windows Settings ➢ Folder Redirection.

2. Right-click the profile directory you want to redirect (you should redirect all of them in turn), and select Properties.

3. Choose Basic redirection, and then enter the UNC path to the share you want the folder redirected to (see Figure 12.2). You should always use the %username% variable to specify the logged-on user in your UNC path; otherwise, all users will be redirected to the same folders, mixing their settings and application data. An example of a proper redirection path would be:

    \\titanium\groupsales\%username%\desktop

   where titanium is the server name, groupsales is the share name (named after the group policy—a convention you should consider following for folder redirection), %username% is automatically substituted for the name of the logged-on user when the path is interpreted by the system, and desktop is a subfolder used to keep the various redirected folders separate. The correct folder name for each folder will not be created inside this path, so you must specify it in your group policy.

4. Once you've created the folder redirection, select the Settings tab, and check the option to copy the user's Desktop to the profile location. This way, they'll retain the settings they've already created rather than having to start over with a new profile.

NOTE   In a rather bizarre chain-o-failures, Group Policy will not be correctly applied to a machine that can't reach its listed DNS server, because the machine will not be able to retrieve its own name in order to pass it to the Group Policy server. This occurs because the client uses DNS to retrieve its own name—rather than access its local Registry—and will happen even if the Group Policy server can be reached through other name resolution methods.

Figure 12.2   Redirecting profiles to a network share

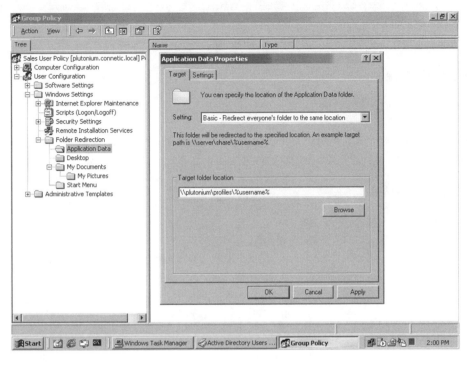

Troubleshooting Group Policy

Windows 2000 can create a log file that will allow you to trace down problems with Group Policy on the local machine. In order to enable logging to the file %SystemRoot%\Debug\UserMode\Userenv.log, use the Registry editor to create the following entry, and then restart the computer:

Key	HKEY_LOCAL_MACHINE\SOFTWARE\Microsoft\Windows NT\ CurrentVersion\Winlogon
Value	UserEnvDebugLevel
Value Data	0x10002 (Hex, DWORD)

You should only enable this logging feature while you are solving the problem, as it will reduce logon performance. Remove it by deleting the Registry key.

There are far too many known problems with Group Policy to attempt a comprehensive troubleshooting methodology in this book, so whenever you're having problems that you can't quickly resolve—such as a group policy not being applied or only being partially applied—go to support.microsoft.com, enter "Group Policy" as the search keywords, and read every article that seems even remotely related. Creating effective group policies and applying them in different scenarios is well covered in the Windows 2000 Server Resource Kit.

User Profiles

User profiles allow more than one user to customize a Windows 95, 98, NT, or 2000 client and retain their settings from one machine to the next (of the same type). Start menu, Desktop, and Control Panel configurations, and a number of other user-specific data, are stored in separate directories based on the logon name of the user. The Registry is customized upon logon with the configuration specific to that user, so the user's environment is unique for them.

There are three types of user profiles:

Local profiles   Stored on the client computer in the %systemroot%\profiles directory (upgraded computers) or the %systemdrive%\Documents and Settings directory. Changes to local profiles are stored locally.

Roaming profiles   Stored on a network share and downloaded when the user logs on. Changes to roaming profiles are transmitted back to the server when the user logs off.

Mandatory profiles   Cannot be changed permanently by the user and must be available for the user to log on to the client. Mandatory profiles can be used to make sure users cannot misconfigure their Desktop environment. Technically, the user can change a mandatory profile, but the changes are not saved to the server and will be erased the next time the user logs on.

Roaming profiles allow a customized user environment to be downloaded from a server at each logon, so the user's environment stays the same no matter what computer the user logs on to. For this reason, roaming profiles are an important part of the "replaceable client" philosophy of desktop management. Because even user configurations can be stored on a central server, desktop computers can be truly replaceable with minimal impact on users.

NOTE   The difference between a profile and a policy can be confusing. Keep this simple difference in mind: *policies* apply Registry keys to the Registry. *Profiles* download files to the computer. Both are key aspects of the replaceable client management technique.

With Windows NT and Windows 98 profiles, the "downloadable" part often creates problems because many large files (such as your outlook.pst file) are stored in profile directories. Because the profile is downloaded at each logon, the logon can take a significant amount of time—I've seen profiles that take 15 minutes to download. Windows 2000 solves this problem by allowing administrators to redirect the profile directories to a server share using Group Policy, thereby obviating the download time.

Roaming profiles do have a downside as discussed in the section on Intellimirror: they are typically quite large, there's one for every roaming user, and using Intellimirror to replicate them from server to server in your environment will take extraordinary amounts of storage space. Therefore, you should only replicate roaming profiles for users who actually roam frequently as part of their job.

Roaming and mandatory profiles are stored on a central server's network share. Upon logging on, the user's profile Registry file is downloaded and applied to the Registry, and the profile directories are copied to the local machine. The location of the profile on the server is defined by the profile path in the Active Directory Users and Computers administrative tool for every individual account.

Profiles are implemented through a combination of configuration Registry settings and directories. Profile settings for the currently logged-on user are applied to the HKEY_ CURRENT_USER Registry hive from the ntuser.dat (or ntuser.man for mandatory profiles) file stored in the user's profile root directory. The following settings are applied to the Registry:

- Windows Explorer settings
- Persistent network connections (drive mappings and network printer settings)
- Start menu settings
- Control Panel settings
- Application data
- Standard accessories configuration

A profile directory is maintained for each user of the machine, for a default user that serves as a source when new user profiles are created, and for all users. The "all users" profile directory contains items that should remain consistent for all users.

The profile directory for each user contains the following:

Application Data   Stores anything an application needs to keep for each user

Cookies   Stores data from Web sites that apply to that user

Desktop   Stores the files, folders, and shortcuts that appear on the Desktop

Favorites   Stores shortcuts to the user's most-often-used directories

Local Settings   Stores files that are a part of the user profile but which are not needed for roaming, such as the URL history, temp directory, and temporary Internet files

My Documents   Stores the user's office documents

NetHood   Stores persistent network connections

PrintHood   Stores networked printer shortcuts

Recent   Stores shortcuts to recently used documents

SendTo   Stores shortcuts, batch files, and scripts that can be applied to files to perform various common tasks

Start Menu   Stores shortcuts to applications in a hierarchy that appears as the Start menu browse tree on the Desktop

Templates   Stores template documents for office applications

ntuser.dat   Stores the Registry hive applied for this profile

---

WARNING   Users should avoid storing large files on the Desktop when roaming profiles are implemented unless you've redirected the Desktop to a network share, because the files on the Desktop are copied between the server and client at every logon. Logon time is a direct function of the size of the profile, so keep it as small as possible.

Roaming profiles for Windows 95/98 and Windows NT are partially compatible with roaming profiles for Windows 2000. The application directories are similar with some exceptions. Windows 95/98 supports creating shortcuts to Desktop files rather than downloading them as Windows NT and 2000 do. The Registry files are different, because the Registry structures of the two operating systems are not compatible. Information contained in the Registry will not be the same between the various platforms.

Remote Installation Service

The Windows 2000 Remote Installation Service (RIS) allows administrators to install Windows 2000 remotely to client computers that have network adapters compatible with Pre-eXecution Environment (PXE). PXE is a network adapter boot BIOS standard developed by Intel for supporting remote-boot computers. Microsoft uses this technology to deliver automated Windows 2000 setup and files to computers remotely over the network.

Remote Installation Service works by broadcasting a plea from a PXE client to a RIS server for a boot image. The server responds with a boot image that when booted attaches back to the RIS server and begins installing Windows 2000. The Windows 2000 installation proceeds according to the installation script created by the network administrator on the RIS server.

RIS is covered in complete detail in Chapter 10.

Third-Party Tools

A confusing array of software and hardware tools exists to assist in the administration of networks. Most of them are worthless. In this section, I discuss the tools that (in my experience) significantly improve your administrative efficiency.

I've found four categories of network tools to be very helpful in the administration of networks:

Common tools   Regular applications applied to network administration and appropriate for any size network environment

Remote control tools   Appropriate for smaller networks (fewer than 500 clients)

Desktop management software   Appropriate for medium-sized networks (200 to 2,000 clients)

Enterprise management software   Appropriate for large networks (more than 1,000 clients)

The numbers overlap because the functionality of the tools overlaps and there is no firm point at which you should switch from one technology to the next.

Use Common Tools

Tools for diverse functions, such as network documentation, help desk support, network monitoring, and remote management, all purport to improve administrative efficiency. The chosen tools and the available budget vary widely and depend on the size of the organization. Some of these more esoteric tools do have a place in larger organizations, but for most organizations, most proprietary network management tools are a waste of money. Fortunately, generic, low-cost tools are available for the common functions required in smaller networks.

For network documentation, use HTML-generating word processors and graphical tools such as Visio. These tools are cheap and commonly available. You can purchase Visio off the shelf at any software retailer. I use the full-blown Visio Enterprise, which is capable of scanning an SNMP network and creating detailed network maps automatically, but at

$1,500, that might be a bit much for your budget. Fortunately, Visio Professional, which includes everything you need to do it manually, is only about $400.

For client configuration and equipment control, you can create a simple Microsoft Access database if you can't get an application developed for an enterprise SQL server. No organization's configuration and control log is larger than a desktop database tool can handle.

Help desk software? Use e-mail. It's easy, it provides a tracking log, and it carries a complete history of the communication between the end-user and the support technician. Use the "reply with previous message" feature to keep the complete communiqué in a single e-mail message. This will serve as a cradle-to-grave log of the support session—including what actions the technician took to solve the problem. At the end of the troubleshooting session, have the technician forward the completed e-mail session to an e-mail account specifically created to store the sessions long term. You can use those e-mail messages as the basis of a troubleshooting database.

Want to deploy forms so that users have to provide a standard set of answers? Try generating an HTML form and setting the post method to a specified address (for example, mailto:support@connetic.net) with an encoding type of "text/plain." This will transmit through the client's e-mail software as an e-mail message, but it will contain a set of fields to be filled out. The Web form can be served from a server or even from a local file on their desktop. The following code shows an HTML example of how this works.

```html
<html>
<head>
<meta http-equiv="content-type" content="text/html;charset=iso-8859-1">
<meta name="generator" content="Adobe GoLive 4">
<title>Technical Support Form</title>
</head>
<body>Technical Support Request form<p>
<form name="FormName" action="mailto:support@connetic.net"
method="post" enctype="multipart/form-data">
<p>Your Name:<input type="text" name="name" size="24"></p>
<p>Department: <input type="text" name="department" size="24"></p>
<p>Extension: <input type="text" name="extension" size="24"></p>
<p>E-mail Address: <input type="text" name="e-mail" size="24"></p>
<p>Description of Problem:</p>
```

```
<p><textarea name="problem" cols="40" rows="4"></textarea></p>

<p>How does this problem impact your ability to work?:</p>

<p><input type="radio" value="annoying" name="triage">It's annoying.
</p>

<p><input type="radio" value="workstop" name="triage">I can't work
because of it.</p>

<p><input type="radio" value="multiworkstop" name="triage">I can't work
and that's holding up other people.</p>

<p><input type="radio" value="netfailure" name="triage">This problem
keeps many people from working.</p>

<p><input type="submit" name="submitButtonName">

</form>

</body>

</html>
```

The above HTML code will generate a local e-mail message in the user's outbox which does not require a server application or even an HTTP connection to a Web server. The code above generates an e-mail message with the following text attachment, which can be read by humans or parsed by machine:

```
----------------------------7d028514210d6

Content-Disposition: form-data; name="username"

Matthew Strebe

----------------------------7d028514210d6

Content-Disposition: form-data; name="department"

Engineering

----------------------------7d028514210d6

Content-Disposition: form-data; name="extension"

234

----------------------------7d028514210d6

Content-Disposition: form-data; name="e-mail"

mstrebe@home.com

----------------------------7d028514210d6

Content-Disposition: form-data; name="problem"
```

```
There's a hedgehog living inside my computer.
---------------------------7d028514210d6
Content-Disposition: form-data; name="triage"
workstop
---------------------------7d028514210d6
Content-Disposition: form-data; name="submitButtonName"
Submit Query
---------------------------7d028514210d6--
```

Do you want to centralize troubleshooting knowledge into a quick-access database? Use the Web. Each time a support technician solves a specific problem that hasn't been solved before, have them write up a quick document describing the problem, its symptoms, and its resolution. Link it into your troubleshooting "database" through a set of diagnostic click-through links based on the symptoms of the problem that get increasingly specific as the technician drills down. Use Internet Information Server's Index Server mechanism to provide a search interface, and you're done. You can even link it through to Microsoft's Knowledge Base on the Web if your network is constantly connected to the Internet.

Remote Control Software

In smaller networks, it doesn't make sense to pay $500 per client for a desktop management solution when you can use simpler, commonly available tools to perform the same function.

Windows 2000 Server provides remote management with a special administration mode for Terminal Services. By running the Terminal Services client, you can remotely administer any Windows 2000 Server. You can use NetMeeting's Desktop Sharing service to gain access to Windows 2000 Professional computers remotely.

VNC is the perfect tool for remote client support if you want a lighter, more flexible tool than NetMeeting. Written by programmers at the Olivetti Research Laboratory in the UK (and now owned by AT&T), this software is open-source, which means you can download the software for free, including the programming code if you feel like modifying it. VNC is also cross-platform—it runs on every major computing platform available today. Best of all, rather than installing a service that could be exploited by hackers, users can simply run the VNC service when they need to. Users can even initiate a reverse connection that is answered by the support technician. This feature allows the client to open connections from inside network-address-translated and firewalled portions of a network. I know of no other remote control package with this functionality.

NOTE VNC is freely available at www.uk.research.att.com.

Desktop Installation and Rollout Software

Desktop management, such as Attachmate NetWizard or Tivoli Director, is the next step up from remote control software. In addition to support for remote control of desktop computers, it adds provisions for package-based rollouts of applications. Administrators can create application packages stored on central servers that can be automatically downloaded to client computers and installed without the intervention of the local user. Typically, installation packages can be downloaded on demand by the user, on demand by the network administrator, or based on a calendar schedule to spread the load of the software distribution. Desktop management software is fairly expensive, costing about $500 per supported desktop.

Of course, Windows 2000 provides the Remote Installation Service and the Windows Installer, but those only work for the applications that support Microsoft's new .msi installer package format. Because they can't be used for everything, they're less useful than third-party solutions, in my opinion.

A lower-price solution is to maintain a few "image classes" of software using networked image installation software, such as Ghost or DriveImage. Then, whenever a new version of software or an additional application is necessary, you can load the existing source image onto a prototype desktop machine; perform the installation, upgrade, or configuration change; and then re-create the source image. You can then reinstall affected desktop clients with the newly updated source image.

WARNING When you install applications controlled by the Windows Installer, such as Office 2000, make sure you actually launch each application, create a document, and save it while logged in as the administrator before you deploy the image. If you don't, the installer will pop up in front of your users and demand access to the installation source files.

For example, you could have an office application's image consisting of the operating system and Microsoft office, e-mail, and other required basic applications. Another image could build on that but add programming environments for software developers. A third image might be based on the office application's image but include supported graphics design software. And a fourth image could include CAD/CAM applications for engineers.

After you've got the operating system and applications installed, but before you image the disk, run the Windows 2000 System Preparation Tool. This will remove system-specific information from the Registry—such as the computer's name and security identifier—and prepare the system to run a Wizard upon first boot so that the user can supply this information. This eliminates one of the hassles of Windows 2000 imaging: remembering to apply a new SID and computer name with a third-party tool.

WARNING   Some OEM editions of Windows 2000 don't work correctly with the System Preparation Tool because they don't require the entry of a CD key. This prevents the user from completing the System Preparation Tool. In this case, you'll need to buy a regular version of Windows 2000 Professional upon which to base your image classes.

Sage Advice: Restoration Made Easy

If you use image-serving software to perform operating system and application rollouts, tape an envelope to the side of each client computer containing a CD-R that boots to MS-DOS and then executes the image download software that will restore the image contained on the CD to the computer. This way, clients can update their own computers simply by inserting the CD. After the image is installed, they reboot their computer and go back to work. You can talk inexperienced users through the steps over the phone and eliminate a trip to the desktop. You can even use this tactic to restore accidental misconfiguration or problems caused by software corruption or viruses.

If your desktop image is larger than you can fit on a CD, have the MS-DOS boot image connect to the network to download the image from a server or use newer imaging software that can span images across multiple CDs.

Network Control Software

The final tier of network management software includes major management platforms such as CA UniCenter and HP OpenView. These products create an entire network-management software infrastructure that integrates SNMP device configuration management, visual network monitoring tools, remote control, archiving, and software rollouts all into one centrally controlled system. These systems are component-based, and an entire industry of software add-ons exists to perform every imaginable network administration and management task.

Well-configured installations of these products are an amazing technical feat and a joy to behold (if this sort of thing excites you). They're also hideously expensive, costing anywhere from $25,000 on up for basic platform options and about $500 for every client, depending on the options you install. Their cost is easy to justify for larger organizations, because they'll save you a tremendous amount of money in recurring support costs. However, they're exceedingly difficult to install correctly; have an experienced integrator perform the installation for you if you decide to go this route. It's also easy to go hog wild with feature options that cost extra and don't really reduce the administrative burden, so make sure you can justify all the expenses you'll incur with these products.

If these products are out of your range, you'll just have to make do with lower-level documentation tools—like Visio—that don't maintain a real-time connection to the network and rely upon your diligence in keeping the documentation up to date.

Summary

The methods and tools you use to perform client support will have by far the most dramatic impact on your time, budget, and nerves as a Windows 2000 administrator. Windows 2000 has made impressive gains in client administration, especially with Windows 2000 Professional, which is significantly easier to manage than any of its predecessors.

The client support methodologies you will use depend on the types of clients you use. Windows terminals, which perform all compute operations on terminal servers rather than on clients, can reduce administration dramatically for certain types of problems. Remote boot workstations were very popular in the past for reducing administrative burden, but because they are not supported by Windows 2000, the sun is setting on this very useful technology. Controlled-access clients are now the norm for desktop support, where network policies are centrally managed as components of the Active Directory.

Microsoft's built-in client management tools are a mixed bag: some are very effective, other simply trade one set of problems for another.

Group Policy is a significantly improved version of the System Policy that was available in earlier versions of Windows. Group Policy allows administrators to specify—at hierarchies in the Active Directory—computer and user policies that will be applied to every object in the container to which the policy is applied. This allows administrators to make broad and sweeping changes to the way computers are used and managed in the enterprise with just a few minutes of administrative effort.

Roaming user profiles are useful for users who need to use multiple computers in the enterprise. By providing a way for a user's documents, environment, and application data to follow them from computer to computer, users can be freed from using only a single desktop. Roaming user profiles help implement a completely replaceable desktop environment, which is the goal of proper client management.

Intellimirror is a set of replication technologies that manage the replication of user profiles, application installation sets, and user data throughout the enterprise to allow ubiquitous access to it. Unfortunately, the many restrictive properties of the service make it appropriate only for certain, rather uncommon, business practices. Better management practices exist for nearly all of its intended purposes.

Third-party client management software exists in three tiers: small networks, medium networks, and large networks. Essentially similar, small-network tools include network documentation tools, imaging tools, and remote client control. Medium-sized tools add automated policy-based application deployment. Enterprise large-network tools complete the network management function with network device control tools and real-time network monitoring and mapping tools.

No matter what type of network environment you operate in, researching the various options yourself, setting up a test lab, and rolling out class-based clients and central file storage will allow you to achieve replaceable client nirvana.

Case Study: Penny Wise, Pound Foolish

A client of mine decided they were spending too much money on IT—with a staff of only 100 people, they had 10 IT technicians. Ten percent of the company payroll was spent supporting computer systems, amounting to about $500,000 per year. They asked me to figure out how to reduce their IT costs (basically making me the IT hatchet man, but that's consulting).

I surveyed their current practices and determined the following:

- A Frankenstein network architecture existed. A few servers connected to a large switch, which was, in turn, connected to a sprawling Ethernet network of various grades and ages—some switched Category 5 Fast Ethernet, some 10Base-T over Category 3 wiring, and some 10Base-2 over coaxial wiring with media converters.

- Most clients were older 486-class computers, and, in some cases, workers made do with 386-class computers. Clients used a hodgepodge of operating systems: MS-DOS, Windows for Workgroups, Windows 95, Windows NT, and test installations of Windows 2000. The really funny part was that both the executive staff and IT staff had brand new Pentium II computers running Windows NT Workstation over Fast Ethernet, while all the task workers basically got along with whatever they had on their desks when they got their jobs. The IT staff was in the habit of responding to the executive staff's problems while ignoring the problems of those people who had no authority over them.

- The staff spent most of their time replacing outdated Ethernet cards, reformatting hard disks, reinstalling Windows 95 from floppy disks (because the computer didn't have a CD-ROM reader), and trying to track down faulty cable connections (because portions of the network ran over 10Base-2 Thinnet coaxial cable). Needless to say, spending eight hours of IT time troubleshooting a Thinnet Ethernet card is a complete waste.

I wrote up my findings and suggested the following:

- Replace every computer in the organization that hadn't been purchased in the last year with a machine conforming to at least a Pentium II 300MHz with 32MB RAM and a 2GB hard disk. These machines at the time cost about $1,500. Replacing 50 computers cost $75,000.

- Install a new Category 5 cable plant throughout the organization to support a migration to Fast Ethernet. $150 per drop for 75 drops totaled about $11,000.

- Replace the network architecture with 100MB workgroup hubs having Gigabit Ethernet links to a central router. Seven 16-user hubs at $3,000 each totaled $21,000.

- Install Gigabit Ethernet adapters in the centrally located servers. Three servers at $500 per NIC totaled $1,500.

- Install a Gigabit Ethernet central router. A 12-port bridge/router cost $24,000.

- Purchase Tivoli's Director IT management suite, including application rollout, inventory management, and remote control software. The cost for this installation was $30,000.

- Use profiles and policies to make certain users store their files on servers so their computers could be easily replaced.

- Cut the IT staff (one director, three network administrators, and six technicians) to one administrator and two technicians (after we got the new network implemented, of course). Total savings: $350,000 per year.

The bottom line is that the capital expenditures for my specification came to $165,000. The company saved that amount within six months of implementing my advice, and the remaining staff assured me that their jobs were far less hectic, affording them the time to set up a company intranet site. Lest the job-cutting aspect of this case study seem overly drastic, the staff that were laid off took their new enterprise management implementation skills with them and quickly found new, better-paying jobs.

13

Supporting Servers

Supporting servers is considerably different than supporting clients, even if the hardware and operating system are very similar. The support tasks are different because only one person is affected when a client goes down. When a server crashes, nobody can work, so heads roll—starting with yours.

Server support encompasses three broad aspects:

- Administration
- Maintenance
- Monitoring

Because this entire book is about administration, I'll take this opportunity to focus on remote administration. Maintenance is the judicious application of preventative measures to forestall or eliminate many common failures. Monitoring is the continual process of measuring server activity in order to detect and respond to failures or potential failures as soon as possible.

The simple requirement that production servers cannot go down during working hours makes their administration vastly different than clients. For this reason, you cannot

- Try "risky" administrative tasks—those that you've seen crash a computer or that you've never before performed.
- Perform any task you know will result in a reboot requirement during working hours.

- Install new software without testing it first.
- Install software that isn't absolutely necessary.

Servers that must be up 24/7 can be the ultimate administration nightmare; they theoretically can't be rebooted any time during their production lifetime.

This chapter is all about how to manage that problem and how to reduce your server administration costs.

Scheduling People

Keeping servers up and happy doesn't have to be difficult, but you should get used to the fact that in most environments, you'll probably need at least one network administrator working on the weekends to perform administrative tasks that can't be performed during the week. In the environments I manage, I give most network administrators Friday off and ask them to work on either Saturday or Sunday. Mondays always seem too hectic for time off, and if anything goes wrong on the weekend, you'll need to be in on Monday anyway.

I try not to ask people to work late whenever it can be avoided. Working late is very hard on people with families. Although most single people have no problem with it, those with families are put between a rock and a hard place—they either disappoint their families, or they ask to be excused when others are working. Weekends give you more time to get things done than nights anyway, and people can adapt their lives to a regular schedule. Be sensitive to the various religious needs of people that you manage; most consider the Sabbath to be Friday (Islamic), Saturday (Judaic and Seventh-Day Adventist), or Sunday (most Christian denominations). Your policy should allow network administrators to choose which of those days they need off.

I know of a few companies that schedule regular IT staff times from 10:00 A.M. to 7:00 P.M. This means that an early-morning problem might have to wait two hours for a network administrator to arrive, but that rare case is more than made up for with the two hours of nightly administration that occurs after hours. This also allows the IT staff to avoid rush hour.

In larger environments, consider scheduling everyone across a range of start times from 6:00 A.M. to noon. This gives you broad coverage for emergencies, puts everyone on site during core hours when meetings can be scheduled, and gives some flexibility to employees to choose what's best for them and their families. Each person's schedule should be as regular as possible. Don't get in the habit of asking those who should get off at 2:00 P.M. to work an extra hour or two to get something done while everyone else is around, while allowing those who are scheduled to get off at 9:00 P.M. to leave at 7:00 P.M. because everything is handled. Inequity in "real" work hours will cause discord faster than any other management problem I know of.

Finally, you can use the comp time concept to allow workers to accrue the extra hours they've worked and then take that time off later on. This allows workers the greatest personal freedom while ensuring (if properly managed) that time spent and compensation are fair.

Server Installation

Server installation isn't as much about installing an operating system (Windows 2000 Server or any other) as it is about deploying new capabilities on your network. Let's face it: you're not installing Windows 2000 because you enjoy installing software but because it performs some useful function for your network. In essence, you are not deploying servers—you're deploying services. Keeping this concept in mind will help you to keep your services architecture well in order and downtime to a minimum.

Deploying New Services

Deploying new services means installing software on your servers. Unfortunately, the installation of new software is by far the most likely reason why stable servers crash.

As businesses become more reliant upon their networks, simulation and testing of the production environment has become critical. When I first began working with networks, the network was more of an administrative convenience than a work necessity. Because business processes were all still paper-based, computers were used mostly for interoffice e-mail, printing, and office program file storage. Server downtime was routine, and workers expected a few hours of "unplanned" downtime per month.

Things have changed. These days, every operation of a business is online, and the network serves as the nervous system of the business. When a user's computer is down, it's likely that they will not be able to perform any useful work at all. When a server is down, hundreds of users can be affected.

As you know, servers can crash for all sorts of silly reasons when you install new services. I've installed video drivers that made a server unstable, I've tried to start services and had machines crash, and I've had numerous problems with applications that caused a server to crash on startup after they had been installed.

You simply cannot find out about these problems on a production server anymore. Installing an application only to find out that it causes some esoteric problem on your server that prevents it from booting can launch you into a days-long downtime nightmare.

Simulate and Test

You can avoid all these problems with proper testing and simulation. To operate a test lab, you'll need at least one typical client and a typical server. It's best to have one exact clone of every machine in your network. This of course is most easily achieved if you buy computers in large batches. If your budget doesn't support exact clones, near clones work well. The more hardware differences there are between your test equipment and your production equipment, the less likely it is that your testing will discover problems, so keep it as close as possible.

Your test network should never be attached to your production network, because you'll be using the same IP addresses, domain names, and network names on your test network as you use on your production network. You don't want the "Evil Kirk" version of your domain controller confusing everything on your network and bringing services to a standstill because of IP, name, or SID conflicts.

To create a simulation environment, simply take last night's tape backup of the server you intend to install software onto and restore it onto your closest matching test server. Once the "Evil Kirk" server is up and running, install the new service application and record any glitches you run into. Feel free to do things you'd never do in the production environment to see how the service reacts. Finally, attach your test client to the server and run the client side of the application, making sure everything works normally. If you have a scriptable client or the service has a load-testing application, use multiple clients to perform load testing in the simulation environment.

Once you've gone through the installation on the simulation server, you can install the service with confidence on the production server. The simulation server is then freed up for whatever other simulations are necessary.

vmware   You should be aware of an amazing piece of software called vmware, which allows you to run multiple simultaneous i386 virtual machines on a single computer, complete with a networking environment and hardware bridges to the hardware on your computer. A virtual machine is a simulated computer environment that can run software inside the virtual machine independently of software that runs on the real computer. The vmware virtual machine allows you to create complete client/server test environments on a single computer so you can test both sides of an application easily.

The vmware hardware environment is simulated and does not represent the actual hardware you'll be using on your servers or clients, so you should perform final testing on real computers, unless you can suffer the slight risk of accidental downtime. vmware is available for purchase and evaluation at www.vmware.com.

Consider Alternatives to Installing Software

Often, there are alternatives to adding services to existing computers that might be safer, easier, and more cost effective. These alternatives are

Add a new server.   Depending upon the service, it's often best to add an entirely new server rather than adding a service to an existing server. This is especially the case when the service will take up a considerable amount of compute power, memory, or disk space. Some services, such as terminal, Web, and database servers, are so power hungry that they should almost never be deployed on existing servers. But in these days of cheap hardware, even relatively minor services are candidates for their own hardware. DNS and WINS name services, DHCP, and domain controller services are strong candidates for their own servers simply because they're crucial to the proper operation of your network. If you deployed these services on their own set of "minor services" servers, you would have a lot more flexibility in bringing down other dedicated-purpose file and print servers momentarily during the day if necessary.

Add a dedicated network appliance.   Many dedicated network appliances exist for services such as file storage, network address translation (also called Connection Sharing in Windows 2000 Professional), DHCP, and even e-mail and Web services. While introducing these devices will cause different additional network administration tasks, they can be used to prop up areas where your existing servers are weak—and they are highly reliable. I believe that the future of networking is with dedicated-purpose network appliances rather than the monolithic multipurpose super-servers of today, because they spread out the fault-tolerance problem, they're scaled to the services they provide, and they are far less expensive than general-purpose servers.

Use an alternate operating system.   Some functions are simply easier to solve with other operating systems than they are with Windows 2000. E-mail is the perfect example. Although Exchange has become more stable in recent releases, it's a heck of a lot more software than organizations need if they're just using its Internet e-mail functionality. For e-mail, UNIX-based servers are both more reliable, less expensive, and less "maintainy" than Windows-based mail servers. You should probably consider AS/400 servers for financial applications because of their rock-solid reliability. It's rare that any one operating system does everything well, and Windows 2000 is no exception.

There are many important considerations beyond administrative convenience when selecting an alternative to deploying Windows 2000 services. You should at least consider the alternatives before you add services to existing machines.

Windows 2000
Every Day

PART 3

Remote Administration

If you have servers in more than one location, remote administration is a necessity. The time you save just walking around is considerable. Windows 2000's built-in support for remote administration is implemented using Windows 2000's Terminal Services functionality, which provides complete remote control of the server. Windows 2000 also provides Telnet services that can be used for remote administration, but these lack security and complete functionality and should be avoided in most installations.

Aside from the Terminal Services functionality of Windows 2000, you can use many of the service snap-ins to control computers other than the one the snap-in is running on. And you can use frame-buffer remote control software such as NetMeeting's Remote Desktop service, VNC, or pcAnywhere to perform remote administration as well.

Terminal Services Administration Mode

Windows 2000 plugs a glaring administrative hole in Windows NT by using the Terminal Services service in administrative mode. Administrative mode is essentially the same thing as regular Terminal Services mode, except that it does not require the Terminal Services Licensing Manager, and the server is not optimized (in the Registry) for Terminal Services.

To use Terminal Services in administrative mode, you simply install the terminal service on the server to be administered and run the Win32 Terminal client program on the controlling computer. You can create the Win32 (and Win16) Terminal server client disks using the Terminal Services Client Creator administrative tool (installed in the Administrative Tools Start menu when you install Terminal Services), or you can simply distribute the files located in `C:\winnt\system32\clients\tsclient\net\win32` and run the `setup.exe` program therein. The new version of the Terminal Services client, Terminal Services Advanced Client, can be downloaded from Microsoft's Web site.

Connecting to a server is simple, and you can use IP addresses in the Server Name input box to connect. Figure 13.1 shows a Windows 2000 server being remotely administered by a terminal client.

You will use Windows 2000 Terminal Services routinely to administer your servers; in fact, at many new client sites, I no longer install monitors, keyboards, and mice permanently on servers. Once a server is installed and running, I use Terminal Services exclusively for management. I do keep a USB keyboard and mouse along with a flat-panel monitor locked up for when network access is lost, but console access is rarely necessary these days. You should always install Terminal Services on new servers in Administrative Mode.

Figure 13.1   Remotely administering a Windows 2000 server using Terminal Services and a Windows 2000 terminal client

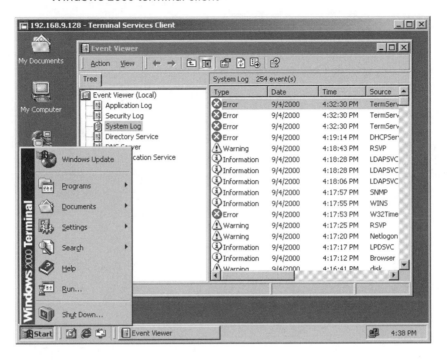

VNC

I personally use and recommend VNC for all remote management, even of Windows 2000 servers when Terminal Services are available. I mentioned VNC in Chapter 12 where Net-Meeting is the only built-in option for desktop support, but why use VNC instead of Terminal Services on a server? Here are five very good reasons:

- VNC is considerably smaller and puts less compute load on the server.
- VNC is ubiquitous; the same tool can be used to manage all the computers in your enterprise, not just Windows 2000 servers, and not just PCs running Windows.
- VNC is free, open-source software and is highly stable.
- VNC is always available via a quick download as long as you are connected to the Internet, and it can be used to control another machine without performing an installation. The "client" portion can be run from floppy disk if necessary. I've used VNC to solve a customer's problems with a Windows 2000 server in San Diego from my brother's Macintosh in Seattle while on vacation.

- VNC can be started in a secure "reverse connection" mode, where a local administrator or support technician can initiate the remote control session from the server that will be controlled, out through network-address-translating firewalls, to a host anywhere in the world—securely and without breaching firewall security or opening a nonsecure conduit through the firewall. Terminal Services cannot establish a reverse-initiated session, so firewalls have to be specifically configured to allow occasional exterior support, thereby opening a potentially very dangerous security door.

Enough said. You can download VNC at `www.uk.research.att.com`.

pcAnywhere

pcAnywhere is the granddaddy of remote control applications and the most popular. If you're going to use a simulated-console, remote control application other than VNC or NetMeeting, use this one. It's easy to use, has tons of features (such as screen resize and color interpolation when the resolution of the client doesn't match the server), and is inexpensive compared to most enterprise solutions.

Despite these strengths, pcAnywhere pales in comparison to VNC, except that it works well with modems. VNC operates only over TCP/IP, so you have to use PPP and RAS connections to establish a session, whereas pcAnywhere can perform remote administration irrespective of the network settings on either machine.

Make absolutely certain you have a strong firewall policy if you use applications such as pcAnywhere over the Internet. As with all remote administration tools, you should also use encrypted tunneling so hackers can't discern that you even have remote administration software running on your servers. Although pcAnywhere has password blocking, it's not strong enough to keep hackers out, so don't rely upon it.

Enterprise Solutions

Most medium-sized enterprise management tools, such as Attachmate's NetWizard or Tivoli Director, include remote control software similar to pcAnywhere. Generally, these tools are reincarnations of formerly independent software products that were put out of business by Symantec's offering and then purchased by these enterprise management companies to add remote control functionality to their products. As such, they're (in my experience) generally inferior to pcAnywhere, but if you're going to use the enterprise management tool anyway, you've already got their remote control software.

Enterprise solutions of this class typically include support for automated software installation to clients and hardware/software inventory keeping. You may or may not need these tools depending on the complexity of your problem. In my opinion, they aren't worth the cost when you consider the free alternatives, such as Windows 2000's own Group Policy–based software installation. I've never had to deal with an inventory problem so large that a reasonably simple database and a good update policy couldn't deal with it effectively—even when I was in the military and had to track very nearly every electrical device and piece of software we used.

Likewise, software distribution is easiest if you teach users how to install the software they need to use, and then, when you've put something new on the network, e-mail links to the executable `startup.exe` file with any necessary explicit instructions to the candidate users. The user simply clicks on the link to begin the installation and can read through the steps you promulgate in the e-mail as the installation progresses. I find this to be easier even than Group Policy–based installation, which is covered in Chapter 12.

You really don't have to worry much about "overinstallation" as long as you're using network license control applications that can tell you what your peak actual usage is. Casual users who install but then don't use applications will have very little effect on your license meters. When you use policies like these, even a massive software rollout is as easy as sending an e-mail message to a distribution list. Use Windows terminals for task-based workers who can't be trusted to figure out a setup program.

Maintenance

Server maintenance is a necessary evil. Servers that can be installed and forgotten about do not really exist because of the speed at which capacity is used up in our rapidly growing movement to an information society. Hard disks fill up, servers are outgrown and overloaded, and hardware fails.

The key to good administration is not to be surprised by these events when they happen. A methodical routine for maintenance ensures that you'll find problems before they get out of hand. This means that you can plan for downtime around *your* schedule, instead of putting your company on a work stoppage while you try to troubleshoot a crashed server in the middle of a workday. You'll spend more cumulative time on preventative maintenance than you would have spent on corrective maintenance, but you'll save everyone else's time, and that's what network administration is all about.

Planned Maintenance

You can avoid a lot of unexpected troubleshooting and server crashes by performing routine, planned, preventative maintenance on your servers. Scan the operations manual for each component that is included in your server (both hardware and software) to find planned maintenance items. Make complete lists of every periodic task listed, and add them to a more general list.

Use automated monitoring software to perform the following tasks:

- Ping servers frequently to make sure they're up.
- Use a service monitor to be certain mission-critical services are working.

Weekly maintenance should include the following:

- Check hard disk capacity for each volume. Record the weekly usage and keep a trend calendar of disk usage so you can plan for disk upgrades.
- Check the peak memory and page file usage statistics in performance logs for cases of large or unexpected increases in memory use.
- Check the System, Security, and Application Logs in the Event Viewer for unexpected entries.
- Review any Application Logs for services that do not make use of the Event Viewer.

Monthly maintenance should include the following:

- Clean tape backup mechanism if required.
- Review the permission structure of the disk using the CACLS command-line utility.
- Review share permissions.
- Review TCP/IP security settings.
- Review user accounts, deleting those that are obsolete.
- Install any service packs and service application updates or patches that have been tested and scheduled for installation.
- Manually delete any leftover temporary files.
- Reboot the server if possible.

Yearly maintenance should include tasks that require planned downtime:

- Evaluate the server for a complete upgrade. Is it keeping up with current demand, or has it become an increasing maintenance hassle?
- Open the machine and vacuum-dust the interior of the case, paying special attention to the power supply and exposed slots.
- Test the floppy disk drive by formatting a disk and copying files to it, and then reading those files on another machine.
- Run a complete hardware diagnostic program from a DOS boot floppy. Use the same software you use to validate new equipment.
- Perform a complete read and rewrite test for all disks after a complete system backup. Grown defects appear most often during write operations, so this test should get them all at once.

- Perform a hard test of your RAID system by pulling a hard disk out during operation (after a complete backup, of course) if your RAID system supports hot swapping. If not, shut the machine down and disconnect a drive, and then reboot it. Make sure your RAID system still performs as it did when it was originally installed.

- Upgrade the CPU to the highest performing model that will work in the same socket.

- Double the amount of installed RAM until the motherboard can hold no more. You may want to move lower-capacity memory modules to clients and replace them with fewer modules of the highest available capacity.

You should seriously consider simply replacing servers rather than performing yearly downtime maintenance. I know of some companies that are in their fourth year of operations on the same set of servers because they purchased exceptionally expensive computers up front and have maintained them well. But the usual case is to purchase typical servers, operate them for two years straight with no physical maintenance at all, and then simply replace them rather than upgrade them. Both methods work, and both have about the same total cost of ownership. The method that works for you depends mostly on your individual organizational requirements.

Scheduling Maintenance

When you plan to take a server down for maintenance, you should obviously do it when the server isn't needed for any service purposes. If you use Windows 2000 Server's clustering or third-party fault-tolerance or load-balancing software, this isn't an issue; you can simply choose a time during the day when the load is reasonably low and take down one of the servers, confident that the other server(s) will take up the slack.

But if you're like most network administrators, you'll have to wait for evening or weekend hours to take servers down. This can cause some strain—most network professionals are salaried, and working during the nights or weekends may mean working without compensation.

You can install new software and service applications during the day, but do not allow rebooting until the end of the day. After normal user traffic has dropped off, simply reboot the server, verify that everything is running correctly, and go home. You don't have to reboot a server immediately after installing new software; you just have to reboot it before the new software will work correctly. This doesn't work with upgrades to existing services, because these services usually must be stopped to allow the upgrade and then restarted, which will put the new files immediately into use without loading their attendant Registry settings. Although Windows 2000 requires considerably fewer reboots than Windows NT, you won't know if rebooting a new service is necessary unless you test it.

Attempt to start new services using the Service Control snap-in rather than rebooting. Nine times out of ten, a reboot isn't really required when a third-party application says it is; software setup programs call for it because it's easier than explaining how to start a service manually. Unless a server installs drivers, a reboot is usually not actually necessary.

Upgrading Servers

Server upgrades are never easy or convenient because you must take a server offline to upgrade it. Even rather simple software installations can require a reboot, because most of Windows 2000's operating system components only read Registry information when they're booted. Although Windows 2000 has reduced the reboots required for simple things like changing TCP/IP addresses and it no longer prompts for unnecessary reboots after installing services, you're still highly likely to have to reboot after new hardware is detected and after the installation of third-party software.

> **TIP** You often don't need to reboot a server after installing or modifying an existing service even if the setup program says you need to. You can usually just stop and restart the service. There's no way to tell whether this will work except to try it, but it's safe to try. If it doesn't work, just go ahead and reboot. For sensitive production environments, test the service on your test machines.

Server upgrades take two forms: hardware and software. Hardware upgrades, such as upgrading a microprocessor or adding RAM, can be quick and painless. Other hardware upgrades, such as changing out a motherboard that requires a different HAL, can require you to perform a repair reinstallation.

> **TIP** Some high-end servers now allow you to install PCI cards in special ACPI-compatible PCI slots without shutting down or rebooting the server. This only works if the server specifically supports the cards, so don't be tempted to try it unless you know your server provides support.

Software upgrades are usually fairly simple, even when they require an operating system reinstallation, because companies know that their reputation for quality generally rests on how easy it is to install their software.

Adding Storage

Adding hard disk space to a server is generally pretty easy. In fact, if your system partition is in a different partition than your shared directories, you can simply create a spanning volume set across drives using the Disk Administrator. This does make your volume less reliable because it will fail if any disk fails, so consider the likelihood of disk failure before you use volume spanning.

If you need to migrate to a different storage subsystem altogether (for example, if you're moving to a RAID pack), you can do it the hard way or the easy way.

The hard way is to install the new storage subsystem as the bootable disk, install a fresh version of Windows 2000, reinstall all your application software, copy user files back from the old drive, and reestablish shares. Or, you could run a full system backup to tape, remove the old drive system, install the new drive system, install a new copy of Windows 2000 and your restoration software, and then restore the tape.

The easy way is to leave the original storage bootable and then install the new storage. Next, install the disk driver for the new storage controller, if necessary, edit the boot.ini file to be able to load the operating system from the new storage, and then use Windows 2000's mirroring software to sector copy the entire disk from the old to the new. Once the mirror is finished, shut the server down and remove the old storage system.

If for some reason you can't use mirroring, use a disk-cloning utility, such as DriveImage.

Most RAID controllers have their own BIOS setup programs that allow you to define how the disks attached to the controller are used. The entire RAID pack then appears to the operating system as a single, normal hard disk. You'll be able to use the mirroring technique or a disk-cloning utility to migrate from your older storage system.

Migrating to a New Version of Windows 2000

Upgrading an existing server to Windows 2000 is easy—all versions of Windows 2000 can automatically handle any necessary migration through the setup program's upgrade option.

A simple upgrade isn't usually the best option, though. First, there's no reason to upgrade a server just because a new version of an operating system has been released. Unless you have a specific reason to upgrade a working server, don't waste the time or the money. Upgrades need to be part of a comprehensive network update, not a piecemeal update because new software was released.

Compelling reasons to upgrade include significant performance improvements, security fixes or enhancements, or new features that you need. Although it has a new interface and many new services, Windows 2000 is substantially the same operating system as Windows NT 4. Unless you need the service's Active Directory, it may be quite some time before an upgrade to Windows 2000 Server is necessary.

I'm not suggesting that you never upgrade a server, but by the time an operating system is actually obsolete, the hardware it's installed on usually is obsolete, too. Rather than upgrading an existing server to a new operating system, consider migrating your server to an entirely new hardware and software platform. And if you do this, you can continue to use your old server for some less-demanding task, such as print service, e-mail service, a router, or a RAS server. Windows NT 4 domain controllers cannot be a part of a "pure" Windows 2000 network, so you'll eventually wind up upgrading these servers to Windows 2000 after you've migrated away from using them as your primary enterprise servers.

Changing Basic Logic

Changing the motherboard of an existing server is usually not a problem because most motherboards work with the standard PC HAL. If you change your motherboard and find you can't reboot, you can perform a repair installation to install the correct HAL for the machine. You may have to replace the system key in the Registry to make sure the correct settings are maintained after the installation.

Upgrading a single processor is no issue at all as long as your motherboard supports both the old and the new processor. However, if you add a processor to a single-processor computer, you'll have to upgrade the HAL using the Device Manager. Simply right-click the HAL device (usually *Standard PC* under the Computer device tree), select Properties, select the Driver tab, and click Update. The driver files listed for this device are all various HALs required for different types of computers.

Adding RAM to a server is also no problem as long as your motherboard supports the extra RAM. Be wary of mismatched RAM, however. Using SIMMs from different manufacturers can cause random crashing on Windows 2000 machines. Even DIMMs, which only need to be installed one at a time, are very sensitive to differences between manufacturers. Also be aware of the differences between EDO, ECC, PC100, PC133, RDRAM, and other types of memory. Make absolutely certain that all the memory in your server is compatible with your motherboard, that the motherboard is configured correctly for the RAM, and that all the memory is from the same manufacturer. If after installing new memory your server begins crashing, even at long intervals, suspect the newly installed memory first.

Adding Servers

When you add servers, don't just add a server to shore up some needed capacity in file or application services without examining the service structure among your current servers. For example, if you're adding a new file server because your primary server has run out of disk space, don't just add another file server and leave your original server handling Exchange, IIS, the original file service, and print sharing. Use the System Monitor to determine the service load on your original server and split them between the two machines. You may find that the best way to correctly share the load is to use both machines for file and print service, and then have one machine run Exchange and the other run IIS for intranet service. Or you may find that one machine should share files, and all the other services should run on the other machine. Adding servers without examining your network load will create a Frankenstein network that is a patchwork of services with nonoptimal network loading.

Larger networks usually concentrate specific service applications on their own servers and then have numerous identically configured servers for groups of users. For example, a medium-sized enterprise might have a central Exchange server, a central intranet server, and then a file and print server for each workgroup.

Monitoring

Monitoring has two purposes: to measure load in order to predict impending problems and to monitor attempted misuse. Windows 2000 has a number of very strong utilities to support both of these monitoring goals. It amazes me how many Windows 2000 administrators never use them.

Third-party monitoring tools exist, but few do anything you can't get done with Windows 2000's built-in utilities. Most are hideously expensive and not worth the money. Beyond a good firewall (which you can't pay too much for), most security tools are a waste of time. It's easy to get caught up in security hysteria and spend a boatload of money on expensive monitoring tools that really don't improve your security posture more than a simple investment in a good security book does. I shamelessly recommend mine, *Windows NT 4 Network Security,* published by Sybex, 1998, and *Firewalls 24seven*, published by Sybex, 1999.

Security monitoring is not an optional component of server management—it's a necessity. At the very least, use Windows 2000's tools to monitor your machine. Don't let anyone have free rein on a network you depend on and are responsible for. Security and security monitoring are discussed in detail in Chapter 6. Network-monitoring tools are discussed here.

Windows 2000 Utilities

Windows 2000 comes with a number of utilities that can be used to monitor the network in addition to their usual purpose. A description of each of these tools follows.

The Network Monitor   The Network Monitor that comes built into Windows 2000 (and is installed as an optional component during setup) is indispensable for deep security monitoring and troubleshooting. You'll use the tool only rarely, but when you need to see exactly what's going on in a network communication, it's indispensable.

Ping   Ping is the granddaddy of network-monitoring tools. It is the simplest, the oldest, and by far the most useful monitoring tool available, in my humble opinion.

Ping is simple: by typing

```
ping 127.0.0.1 -t
```

(replace the local host IP address with the address you want to test), Ping will generate continuous ICMP echo packets destined for the intended host until you press the break key. If a route exists and the host is operating (and not ignoring echo commands), you'll get a reply message from the machine. Because Ping is ubiquitous and relies upon functionality built into all TCP/IP devices, it can be used to monitor the continued presence of any TCP/IP device on your network.

netstat   The `netstat` command is another indispensable network-monitoring command. It displays the current connection status of every TCP session on your computer. With the -a switch, `netstat` will display the ports your computer is listening for connections on.

What good is this? It's an immediate indicator of Trojan horse activity, for one thing. Any Trojan horse, virus, or worm that allows a computer to be exploited must either listen for connections or create a connection back to a hacker's listening computer. Both of these activities can be monitored using `netstat`. To get a feel for what `netstat` can do for you, issue the following command at the command prompt:

```
netstat /?
```

Resource Kit Tools

The Resource Kit contains a bunch of little tools that are extremely useful for server and network administration. Each of these tools is somewhat supported by Microsoft, though many were written by third-party vendors and purchased by Microsoft for inclusion in the Resource Kit. The tools are described in the accompanying Resource Kit documentation.

Third-Party Utilities

Although Windows 2000 has the strongest support for network and security monitoring of any network operating system I've seen, you'll need some third-party utilities on occasion. I've found the following tools to be very useful.

SysInternals   SysInternals is the public-service side of Winternals LLC, a company composed of two Doctors of Computer Science who have a highly developed sense of charity to go along with their brilliant programming minds. Although they charge for some of their more useful tools, they give a number away for free, including the source code, simply to advance the art of programming for Windows 2000. Their tools are written primarily for programmers, but some of them have very definite troubleshooting and monitoring purposes in normal networks. Check out SysInternals at `www.sysinternals.com`.

Filemon   Filemon shows all file activity on your server in real time. Filemon is useful for those times when you cannot figure out a cryptic "file not found" message from a program; Filemon will show you what file the application was looking for when it failed out. It can also be used to glean information about a new service or to get an idea of which applications are repeatedly using the disk.

> **WARNING**   Filemon puts a tremendous CPU load on your server. Don't use it during production uptime unless you have a problem you can't debug any other way.

Regmon   Regmon shows you all the Registry activity that occurs on your server in real time. When you start Regmon, it begins logging all Registry accesses to the screen. It's wonderful for fixing problems with Registry corruption and for decoding how a specific application uses its Registry settings.

> **WARNING**   Like Filemon, Regmon puts a tremendous CPU load on your server. Only use it during times when extreme CPU load is not going to interfere with the normal services the computer provides.

Because so much Registry activity occurs on a normal machine, you will quickly get lost in the quagmire of Registry activity unless you use filters. Filters allow you to specify exactly which processes you are interested in monitoring and which types of Registry access you are interested in.

> **TIP**   Launch Regmon before you install new software, and then keep a filtered log of all the new keys that the setup program created during the installation and that the application created the first time it was run. Save this info as a text file so you can manually remove the Registry keys created by the application in the event that it doesn't uninstall completely.

TCPView   TCPView is a "must-have" security-monitoring utility. It shows the real-time status of TCP connections. Every connection established to the server is shown by its port number and the IP address and port of the remotely connected host. It basically has the same functionality that is provided by the netstat program that ships with Windows 2000, but it has a prettier interface.

It would be great, for security purposes, if this program had a facility to log all new TCP connections to a file with their resolved names and ports.

Other Tools

A number of other small tools are very useful for security and network administration.

Servers Alive?   A shareware application that pings, at a specified interval, a list of TCP hosts. Should a server fail to report, you can specify how you want to be alerted. Servers Alive? can also probe specified TCP services so that you can be alerted when a certain service (for example, Exchange) freezes on a server, although Windows 2000's built-in service monitoring will handle this eventuality as well. Servers Alive? includes strong support for alerting and alert escalation; in combination with a paging gateway, you can be immediately alerted to any change in your network's status. Servers Alive? belongs in the toolbox of all serious network administrators. Get it at www.woodstone.nu/salive.

Ws-Ping Pro   WS-Ping Pro from www.ipswitch.com is a great utility for performing network surveys. By "pinging" every device in an IP network, WS-Ping Pro will give you a complete map of network addresses in use. By including a "port scan" of the ports those devices are listening on, and then telneting to devices and ports you don't recognize, you can determine what just about every device on any network is with a little bit of practice. I use WS-Ping Pro constantly when surveying new customer's networks.

Summary

Deploying servers in an enterprise environment is more difficult than deploying clients because most servers are unique in the services they provide and the data they store, whereas (in a well-managed environment) clients are not. For this reason, servers always require considerably more administrative effort on a per-machine basis than do clients.

Servers are merely platforms for services, so your approach to server deployment should be service-centric rather than platform- or hardware-centric. This means that rather than trying to pack as many services as possible on a single machine, you should consider where the service is required, how much compute time it will take, and whether your existing servers can handle the load. Deploying more servers is easier than fine-tuning existing servers to extend their capability.

Deploying new applications is highly likely to cause problems with your servers. Simulation and test environments can help you to find these problems before they cause problems for your users. By maintaining an effective simulation lab and testing software before you deploy it in a production environment, you can save yourself a tremendous amount of work down the road.

Remote administration is now built into all versions of Windows 2000 Server using Terminal Services. The Terminal Services client is both easy to use and highly effective for remote administration. However, the inability to manage Windows 2000 Professional clients from the same tool opens the door for other remote administration tools such as VNC, which can remotely administer nearly all the computers in your enterprise irrespective of the software manufacturer.

Maintenance is the continual process of preventing potential problems. Creating a maintenance schedule for a server is technically simple but can be some work to carry out. To create a maintenance schedule, examine the documentation for each device and application installed on a computer and note all the repetitive maintenance requirements for each. You have some flexibility in scheduling maintenance since even the best estimate is an estimate, so you should group your maintenance tasks into weekly, monthly, semiannual, annual, and biannual periods so they can be handled together.

Upgrading certain components of a computer, such as basic logic, processors, and RAM is easy as long as you aren't at the end of the life cycle for that product family. Other components, such as hard disks, are so difficult to upgrade completely that you're usually better off simply migrating to a new server. The expense of the disk subsystem in a server is usually about 50 percent of the price of the machine anyway, so hard disk migrations rarely make sense unless you have considerable excess capacity available in your disk subsystem. Windows 2000 now allows you to add external Firewire devices to easily increase your storage capacity. These solutions can be used as stop-gap measures to allow you more time between server upgrades.

Monitoring your servers allows you to predict certain problems, and it alerts you immediately to failure. The sooner you know about problems, the sooner you can act to prevent or repair them.

Case Study: Convenience Upgrade

A small business client of mine was on a very constrained budget but needed a server upgrade. Their Windows NT 4 server was bursting at the seams. After analyzing their existing server—a Pentium II-300 with twin 18GB SCSI hard disk drives—I determined that they could probably extend the life of their existing machine by replacing the motherboard and processor, increasing the amount of memory, adding new hard disks, and putting in a newer and more capacious backup mechanism. After updating all those components, however, they would be merely a case and a power supply away from a new server.

I presented my analysis to the customer, noting that purchasing a new server would give them a new warranty, and that they could use their old server for a database-driven intranet, which they had been considering. Given the benefits, they decided to purchase a new server rather than upgrade their existing server.

The talk then turned to software upgrades: a new server would provide an excellent opportunity to upgrade to Windows 2000 Server. Of course, here's where the additional cost came in: they'd have to purchase an additional server license and upgrade CALs for all the clients. However, they would eventually have to make this move anyway. By purchasing an additional CAL rather than an upgrade CAL, they'd be able to keep two servers online. The client approved this too.

The client was highly concerned about the migration of data and user accounts, however. They had a complex permissions structure and their data was highly sensitive to accidental disclosure within the company. They also had a fairly complex share structure and several user accounts.

I decided that using Windows 2000's upgrade option from Windows NT Server would be best, even though we would be moving to a new server. We purchased the server, a Pentium III-800 with 512MB RAM and twin 73GB hard disk drives.

To perform the upgrade, I waited until the weekend and then shut down the old server and removed the nonbooting mirror disk. This allowed me to leave the existing server in a bootable configuration for immediate restoration if necessary. I placed the mirrored disk in the new server and used PowerQuest Drive Image to copy its contents to the primary disk in the new server and expand the size of the data partition to the extent of the new drive.

I then booted the new server to Windows NT Server 4, inserted the Windows 2000 Server CD, and performed the upgrade installation. Once the installation was finished, I ran the Active Directory Upgrade Wizard to create a new forest root domain. I left the old server powered off but ready to boot in case of an emergency.

For backup, we decided to take an innovative approach I'd been testing on my own network: backing up to inexpensive, high-capacity Firewire hard disks rather than tape. For only $400 per 80GB drive (close to the cost of similar-capacity tape media alone), we created a rotating backup policy using two devices, where one device is attached to the server for backup while the other is safely offsite. Backups are performed incrementally during the week and fully on the weekend. The devices are switched on a weekly basis after the full backup, so at any time during the week, files can be restored from up to two weeks prior. File archiving is performed manually using permanent CD-R media from a workstation.

On Monday, the network users noticed no apparent difference, other than faster responses from the server.

The biggest difference has turned out to be manageability. Their server closet is adjacent to the conference room, and they previously had it open nearly all the time for routine administrative tasks such as tape changing and making bulk permissions changes. By using the Terminal Services client and the new Plug and Play mechanisms for backup, the doors on the server closet are now almost always closed.

24seven CASE STUDY

14

Information Technology Management

Contrary to popular opinion, Information Technology (IT) management is far from black magic or controlled chaos. In fact, it's one of the most deterministic business fields I've ever dealt with. This chapter will show you how to select technologies appropriate for the size of your business, how to organize an IT division, and how to implement new systems.

Often—especially in small- or medium-sized businesses—the roles of IT manager and network administrator are both performed by the same person. That person probably hasn't worked in a larger IT environment and may not have experience managing large systems. Growth environments can be intimidating, especially for isolated administrators who have little contact with the industry beyond catalogs and Web sites. This chapter will present the basic facets of large-scale IT management toned down for the small- or medium-scale business where management and administration are one and the same.

This chapter may not seem immediately appropriate for every reader of this book. Those who work for small businesses will find it more immediately beneficial than those in the trenches at a large business. But most IT directors and chief information officers of tomorrow will come from the ranks of network administrators today, so if you don't need the information presented here right now, chances are you will need it sooner than you think.

Management Scales

Approaches to IT vary widely depending upon the size of the implementing organization. Because sophisticated solutions are expensive, they're usually out of the range of small- and medium-sized businesses. Other solutions are targeted toward these smaller scales. IT management solutions are traditionally divided into three scales based on the size of the business:

Small business solutions   Defined by a small number of users (typically up to 25) using a single server at a single site.

Medium business solutions   Bounded by a somewhat fuzzier top end, although most network analysts would consider the boundary to be between 1,000 and 2,000 clients, with up to 25 or so servers. The business may exist at a single site or might have a headquarters and a number of satellite offices.

Large business solutions   Support thousands of users and multiple sites or large campuses that operate as autonomous interconnected networks.

Oddly enough, networks seem to cost about $3,000 per desktop initially—no matter how large your company is or what you try to do to contain costs. Because IT equipment and service costs have been coming down as inflation goes up, this number has remained remarkably unchanged for about a decade.

If you've ever toured the IT department at a company larger than yours and seen an HP OpenView–based network operation center with real-time updated network maps showing the immediate status of every client in the network, you may have come away thinking that if you don't use those tools, you're managing IT incorrectly. That is not the case: small businesses have different requirements and different measures of success. The goal of all IT management is to make the appropriate information tools available all the time to everyone who needs them in the company at the lowest possible cost. Techniques vary. The following sections delineate the scales that most software vendors create solutions for. Read the descriptions of the businesses carefully, because you may find that although your business does not fit directly into the seat count for a certain scale, its management practices will fit perfectly.

Small-Sized Businesses

Small businesses are traditionally construction contractors, medical offices, law and other professional consulting firms, contract manufacturers, and other firms that operate with a tight binding between specific customers and jobs. Small businesses do not advertise beyond their geographical region and are usually privately held.

In most small businesses, network administration is usually a corollary duty for someone in business administration or who has shown a propensity for figuring out computers. Many small businesses outsource IT support to consultants who stop in on a regular or as-needed basis.

Two types of products target small businesses:

- Limited versions of larger scale product suites are generally discounted in the hope that the customer will not switch to a competitor when the business grows.

- Specific-purpose utilities are written by smaller software houses or individuals to address a particular need. These small-scale tools are not integrated, so the small business IT manager typically has a "toolbox" of unrelated tools used for specific purposes rather than a monolithic, integrated management suite. This set of small tools is entirely normal and appropriate for this scale.

Because of the limited scope of the small-business IT management problem, most management tools generally are not necessary. That's convenient because many management tools are priced outside the budget of small businesses anyway.

Most small businesses do not have dedicated IT staff. IT management in small businesses tends to be very routine. A single server supports standard PCs in a single Ethernet collision domain. The network either has an Internet server/firewall and a dedicated Frame Relay or DSL connection (if the business is really hip) or relies on dial-up networking to connect to the Internet. Security is usually ignored beyond the logon password, and the server runs for years without assistance. It just sits under the Xerox machine, humming away. Most service calls are to fix user-caused misconfiguration, and the most demanding IT problem might be to get Mathematica to work with the latest service pack on Windows 2000 clients. Figure 14.1 shows a typical small business network.

Figure 14.1   A typical small business network contains a server, a multiplicity of clients, and a dedicated Internet connection.

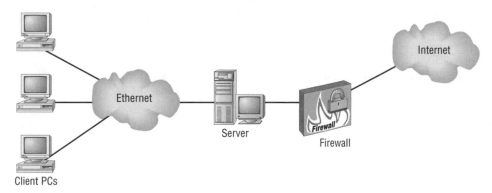

Windows 2000
Every Day

PART 3

Check out small business management tools at:

- www.uk.research.att.com
- www.ipswitch.com
- www.powerquest.com

Medium-Sized Businesses

Typically, medium-sized businesses still have a centralized IT management philosophy, because the companies, in general, retain a very centralized corporate management philosophy—one site is the headquarters, and if other sites exist, they are satellite or branch offices. Businesses that typify this structure include banks, military units, insurance companies, component manufacturers, and other operations that produce services or products independent of a specific customer. Medium-sized businesses advertise in very targeted channels, such as trade magazines to specific customers, if at all.

High-end management tools such as CA UniCenter and HP OpenView are still outside the range of what these businesses need or can afford. A large selection of medium-scale management tools exist for functions such as remote administration and software rollout. Tivoli Director, NetWizard by Attachmate, and Microsoft's Systems Management Server are good examples of these tools. Medium-sized businesses generally have an IT director, a number of technicians, and usually at least one network technician at each site.

A medium-sized network typically consists of a single "well-connected" (i.e., high-speed) network with multiple servers, a few wide-area connections connecting branch offices (which are themselves configured like small businesses), and possibly some esoteric components such as a wireless bridge between buildings in a business park (when rights to run a cable could not be acquired). Client computers in a medium-sized business are typically heterogeneous, having been purchased on a per-employee basis rather than in large batches (large business) or when the company was formed (small business). This factor often makes the medium-sized business the most challenging IT environment. Figure 14.2 shows a typical medium-sized network.

Check out medium-sized business management tools at the following Web sites:

- www.tivoli.com
- www.attachmate.com
- www.microsoft.com/smsmgmt

Figure 14.2   A medium-sized network usually contains multiple servers, a high-speed back-bone network, and remote sites.

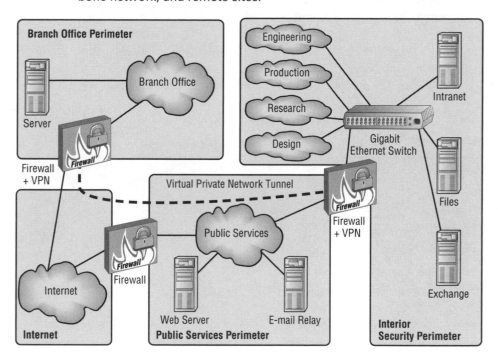

Large-Sized Businesses

Large-sized businesses typically distribute IT management to match the distributed nature of the business. These businesses never have the effort of the entire company dedicated to a single product, contract, or customer, and they are usually involved in the mass production of consumer goods. Most government agencies operate in the same manner as large businesses. Large businesses advertise in the mass media and are usually publicly traded.

For large businesses, sophisticated directory services are required to manage access to resources, and a large IT staff is nearly always required. Large businesses usually have a chief information officer (CIO) or chief technology officer (CTO)—which one depends on the market focus of the company—and an IT director and network staff at each site. Large businesses may be highly integrated, or because of acquisition or politics, they may have vastly different networked systems between sites. Often, integrating existing IT resources is the biggest challenge for large business managers.

Large business networks consist of wide-area connections between multiple sites, each of which operates as a small- or medium-sized network. It is extremely rare to encounter truly massive networks in a single high-speed facility—although this does happen in large complexes such as hospitals, certain military facilities, and in businesses that own their own large buildings. In these cases, the networks are designed like medium-sized networks gone massive—numerous centralized servers with a higher-speed backbone such as ATM or Gigabit Ethernet. Figures 14.3 and 14.4 show two different large business networks.

Figure 14.3   Large distributed networks are simply many medium-sized networks connected via a WAN.

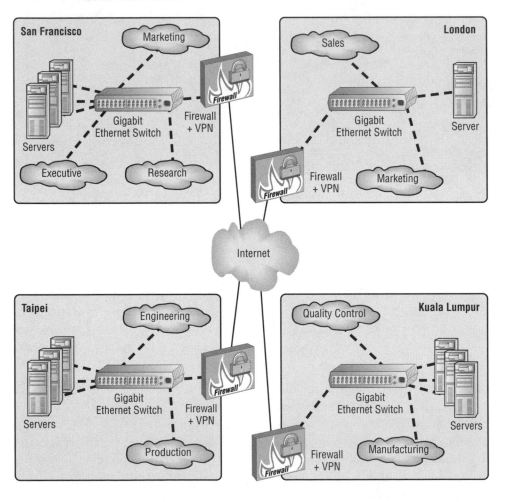

Figure 14.4   Large centralized networks use massive central switches to provide high-speed access for all users to all resources.

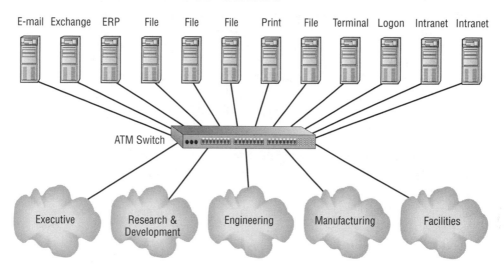

Check out large business management tools at the following Web sites:

- www.cai.com
- www.openview.hp.com
- www.tivoli.com

Selecting Core Technologies

The core technologies you build your network around will define the character of your network, the nature of your support operation, and the capacity of your business to perform its work. For these reasons, selecting core technology is the most important network decision you'll make.

You probably already have a network, but that doesn't mean you can't reengineer it, often using the same hardware you already own.

The most important core technology that you'll choose is your majority client, based largely on these basic types:

- Standard PCs are most appropriate for scientific, engineering, design, development, or CAD work.

- Remote-boot PCs are most appropriate for a wide array of standard business functions such as word processing, finance, communications, and presentation.

- Windows terminals are most appropriate for light, task-based work (database access or data entry).

Flexibility is the antithesis of ease of use; standard PCs are both the most flexible and the most difficult to support. Windows terminals are the least flexible and the easiest to support. Remote-boot PCs strike a middle ground between the two.

With standard PCs, you are free to run any client operating system you want. With remote-boot PCs, you are limited to MS-DOS or Windows 95 (Windows 3.11 for Workgroups, Windows 98, and Windows 2000 cannot be reliably remote booted). Windows terminals are even more limited; they run on the terminal server only, providing an execution environment most similar to Windows 2000 Professional.

TIP Some Windows terminals can remote boot either Windows 2000 Terminal Services for a Windows execution environment or X-Windows for a UNIX-execution environment.

Standard PCs place the lowest overall demand on network servers. Remote-boot workstations place a substantial load on servers and the network while booting but behave pretty much as normal computers once booted. Windows terminals do not place much of a load on the network, but they seriously burden the CPU and memory resources of the terminal server.

Organization

IT is a unique function within any business. Most business functions are compartmentalized into their discrete arenas with very little informal contact between divisions—the Accounting department accounts, Marketing markets, Manufacturing makes, Sales sells, and Human Resources does whatever the heck it is they get paid to do. IT is a different beast. IT staff works closely with all operations in the business.

Because IT doesn't perform work associated with direct revenue or even an easily quantifiable result, there's very little natural feedback for when the job is "well done." Given this vacuum of feedback, a very common problem often arises: IT departments make policies about the use of computers in order to make their own work more efficient, with very little concern for how it impacts the users of the system. For example, an IT department may

- Centralize all files on file servers—a worthy goal with many important benefits, but one that doesn't work for people who need to take laptops home to work.
- Use an HTTP proxy rather than a firewall for security purposes, which blocks the NNTP protocol used by Research and Development to keep up-to-date on scientific news.

- Decide to support only Windows computers, which leaves the programmers who develop for Linux out in the cold.

IT doesn't exist to make the job of IT easy, nor does it exist to give the IT director a fiefdom over which to reign; IT exists to keep business processes flowing as quickly and efficiently as possible. IT management exists to solve problems, not create them.

It's easy for IT directors to direct—it's quite difficult for them to accept feedback from users who know less about computers and networking. This generally results in an environment where IT management makes technology decisions independent of user requirements. In environments like this, everyone winds up with a Windows terminal on their desk that runs pathetically slow because the IT department got all their usage metrics out of some book (okay, some other book) rather than rolling out a proper load-testing network first.

An outsourced IT firm has to put customer service first, or they will lose work. In-house IT departments should also put customer service first, but because there's no good way to force them to, they usually gravitate toward working as efficiently as possible for them selves. This leaves users locked into systems that may run well but may not be the best fit for their needs.

Run your IT organization like an independent consulting firm. Treat every user on the network like they are your customers, because they are. Respect their opinions—they are the ones who will have to live with the decisions the IT staff makes. Act as if your entire organization could be fired if enough people were dissatisfied with the way the network ran. Above all, teach technicians to be friendly and courteous to users. Remember—it's their network. You just run it.

Effective IT organization is usually structured in four tiers:

Help desk   The first line of support. Via telephone, remote control software, or e-mail, these technicians receive and immediately respond to user problems in the network. Most organizations can centralize help desk support, even when offices are remote. If a help desk technician cannot solve a problem, the issue is escalated to desktop support.

Desktop support   Dispatched by the help desk whenever an issue cannot be resolved remotely. These technicians examine the client computer for hardware failures and software misconfiguration. There is usually one desktop support technician per site or per 100 or so client stations (depending on the support requirements of the desktop technology). In smaller sites, multiple support tiers may be collapsed into an individual who covers any or all roles. They can fix the problem, replace the malfunctioning machine, or escalate to the next level of support.

Network administrators   Dispatched either by desktop technicians or by the help desk during problem deluges. Network administrators examine the health of the whole network entity, including servers, data-link devices, and the physical layer to map the extent of the problem and then solve it. Short-term problems never escalate beyond the level of network administration. Pandemic network problems are escalated to management for permanent architectural solutions.

IT management   Makes strategic core-technology decisions, evaluates and selects applications, and creates the architecture of the network. IT management decides when and how to bring in outsourced consulting staff. IT problems don't normally escalate past IT management to business management except when a management deficiency exists.

From the user's perspective, trouble calls are handled like this: Upon being confronted by a technical problem that they cannot solve, they "access" the help system, either by submitting an e-mail to a standard address, calling a support phone number, or using some instant messaging network tool to report the problem. A help desk operator immediately answers the call and performs troubleshooting triage to determine if the problem is a user training issue, a malfunctioning application, a malfunctioning operating system, or malfunctioning hardware. Based on his assessment, he will either attempt to solve the problem by talking the user through a solution or by remote controlling the machine. If he fails to solve the problem, he will "escalate" the ticket to a desktop support technician, who will be dispatched to look at the problem directly. The vast majority of problems will be solved in these two tiers. Figure 14.5 shows the flow of events in a *worst-case* trouble ticket scenario.

Staffing

Hiring IT staff is something like picking good watermelons—except that you have less information to go by, because you aren't allowed to thump people to see how they sound. Resumes, especially among the brighter applicants of the IT world, only discern which applicants know how to write the best resumes.

There is only one qualification a junior (help desk or desktop support) IT applicant must have—a nimble mind. Computer technology moves too quickly to assume that you can learn a specific skill and be done with learning forever. Information technologists must be able to adapt to an environment that changes completely every two years.

I don't want to decry specific experience. It's important, especially in troubleshooting situations, and when you can get both experience and intelligence in an applicant, good for you. When choosing between the two, go with the more intelligent, less experienced applicant. Be sure you quiz an applicant well enough to discern how much of his resume is real experience and how much of it describes things the applicant has merely seen or heard of.

Figure 14.5   Trouble calls start out at the help desk and escalate through the support organization, potentially reaching the IT management tier if they cannot be solved
by subordinate personnel.

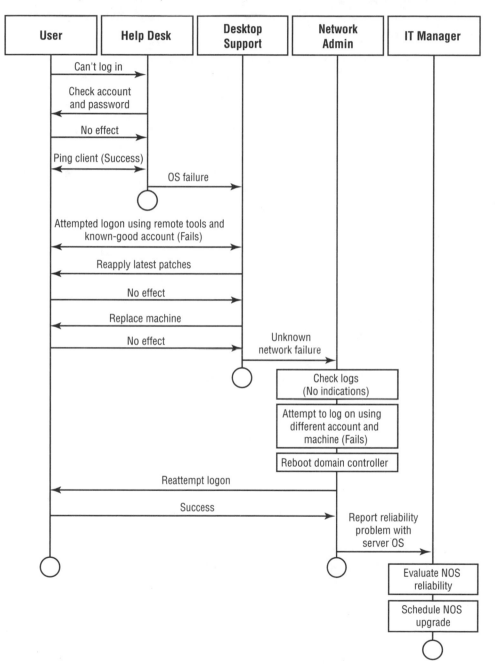

But when experience becomes too specific, such as hiring someone based entirely on their AS/400 experience, you should consider simply outsourcing those portions of your network's problem that require that specific experience to a firm that handles more than one customer. I've never seen a mainframe or a mini that needs the constant attention of a dedicated employee.

Beware of substituting certifications or degrees for either experience or aptitude. A certification or degree alone merely says that an applicant has the persistence to achieve a long-term goal. Certifications are a useful discriminator to narrow the field of applicants if you have some overwhelming response to an opening. But once an applicant is in the door, consider their certifications and diplomas meaningless and look strictly at aptitude and experience.

Higher-level staff (in other words, network administrators and IT management) should be stolen from your competition if they can't be raised within your organization. Good network administrators and IT managers are in constant demand, so the odds of finding a good one by placing ads in the paper are pretty slim.

Institute a policy of hiring candidates—even your IT upper management—only after a short-term contract with the company, say six months long, has been fulfilled. IT management has recently become the job of choice for former middle managers that were laid off in the early '90s following a particularly severe storm of management consultants. Some are excellent; others merely have excellent resumes. Let them show you their talents before you permanently hire them. Better yet, hire your employees from a technical staffing company. Quality is worth the extra cost.

Don't fall into the trap of letting your staff's qualifications choose your network technology. I have clients who are reluctant to upgrade their Novell NetWare networks solely because their staff (who already know Windows 95 inside and out) is reluctant to learn Windows 2000 or UNIX. That's ridiculous. Staff training follows technology, not the other way around.

I'm a fan of training IT staff through the ranks rather than hiring people into upper-level IT management. This works especially well if the business is growing, because IT staff can grow along with the business. Unfortunately, IT staff tend to have a rather myopic view of the world outside their network, so it's easy to get a feedback loop in your technology path, where familiar technology is preferred over more optimal solutions. For this reason, it's imperative that your IT staff participates in the IT community at large through magazines, Web sites, and trade shows.

TIP   I know trade shows have a bad reputation as a boondoggle, but IT trade shows, especially NetWorld+Interop, really do a lot to broaden the horizons of IT staffers. I go to them regularly and so should you. (And, hey, you can get this book signed!)

The four levels of IT support staff match the four tiers of IT organization:

Help desk staff/trainers   Should understand the use and function of the desktop operating system and all of the installed applications. They should be able to troubleshoot basic problems (such as saving files in various formats and printing) and should be able to discern the difference between a training deficiency and an actual computer problem.

Desktop support technicians   Should understand the operation of computers and operating systems. They should be able to build and troubleshoot computers using typical components, and they should be able to install operating system and application software without assistance. They should know how to troubleshoot the various levels of network connectivity and what to do when a client can ping a server but can't log in.

Network administrators   Should be subject matter experts in the server operating systems they support. They should be certified in the network operating systems they support, and they should be able to completely rebuild a server from scratch. Network administrators should understand how to measure a network's performance in the critical areas of network load and server responsiveness and should know the architecture of your network inside and out.

IT managers   Should be well versed in all aspects of information technology, including mainframes, client/server applications, database management, and client technologies. The idea that any MBA can read *IT Management for Dummies* and become a CIO is silly. The IT manager should be the most experienced technician in your company, not the executive who first purchased a Palm V Organizer. Good CIOs don't have much time for golf. Select IT managers with experience implementing specific systems and those who've worked firsthand with database management systems.

Outsourcing

Consulting in many business arenas has been reduced nearly to the point of a joke—nobody is actually ever unemployed anymore, they just consult. Carpetbaggers abound in the area of management consulting, and they've given a bad connotation to the word.

In computer and network services, however, consulting is a vibrant and important sector of the industry. It does not make sense to hire people for a number of installation- and configuration-related problems that your company will never again have once your systems are in place. Consultants are especially appropriate in the following areas:

GroupWare   GroupWare integration, which includes developing Lotus Notes and Exchange applications, establishing e-mail services, and setting up help desk and newsgroup software. If you can, avoid customizing software by purchasing off-the-shelf software that already performs the function. If you must customize GroupWare applications, have consultants do it for you rather than hiring staff.

Web and e-commerce   Development for both your Internet and intranet sites. Don't hire Web developers unless you sell Web services. And don't make the mistake of thinking that because you can write XML by hand in emacs that you're a qualified user interface expert and a graphic designer. Hire professionals.

Enterprise/Manufacturing Requirements Planning (ERP/MRP)   Software to run the production side of manufacturing businesses. These packages all require subject matter experts to install and configure them correctly.

Database   Development at all scales, from simple Access or Filemaker applications all the way up to Oracle Enterprise solutions. Larger businesses whose product is (in one form or another) data should hire their own database developers and produce their own solutions; organizations that use databases to encode their business logic and provide work-flow management should outsource. The difference is defined by constantly changing database requirements versus a relatively fixed database requirement.

Office software   Training can be important for businesses that deal with documents as a matter of course (such as law and professional firms) and for small businesses that are able to use Office applications to drive their business processes. Although these applications run perfectly well out of the box, getting a good trainer/consultant to teach everyone to use these tools to their potential is more than worth the investment.

Software development   Should be outsourced if it can't be avoided—unless your firm is a software development company. And you shouldn't consider developing software, even then, unless the software falls specifically in the realm of your company's expertise.

Security   All IT personnel should strive to be computer security experts in my opinion—but it can take quite a while to fully understand the theory and operation of network security. If you feel you don't have a complete handle on the security problem, then you should have consultants shore up your defenses until you do.

The idea behind all these consulting suggestions is to determine what you and your staff can do well and what isn't worth the time it takes to learn. If you're only going to do it once, outsource the effort. You'll get a better product in less time for less money and without the headaches.

Smaller businesses should strongly consider outsourcing all their IT requirements and hiring just one or two employees to manage the outsourced companies, control security directly, and act as a liaison between users and the outsourced companies.

Outsourcing all your IT has a number of advantages:

- You can concentrate on your business, not IT.
- IT resources and costs grow or contract linearly with the company. When you need more support, buy more. There's no hire/fire cycle to worry about.
- You get real experts without being stuck with anyone less than competent. If you don't like an outsourced company for any reason, don't use them again.
- You can save serious money if you have a smaller business that doesn't need full-time staff.
- You know you're getting the best value because you can always hire competing companies.
- You can hire more than one company to do network designs and then choose the one that best matches your needs.

However, outsourcing also has some problems:

- Responsiveness may suffer, since technicians will usually have to be dispatched from a distance.
- IT people are never around when anything breaks, so more troubleshooting is generally required.
- Some companies may have significant turnover and therefore may have no memory of your network.
- Costs can spiral out of control if you pay on a time-spent basis.

Most of these problems can be contained simply by finding the right support provider and negotiating a firm, fixed-price retainer based on the size of your network rather than the amount of time the company spends at your site. I run my consulting firm based only on fixed-price monthly retainers and contracts. My customers love the controlled and budgetable cost, and I get paid whether I show up or not, so the better their network runs, the more I can make. It's a win-win situation.

Budgeting

IT budgeting is something of a black art. Determining the costs of a network (or surveying the value of an existing network) is a fairly simple exercise, but determining how much money it's going to take to keep that network running is less clear.

Most large businesses plan for six times the price of the initial investment per year to support their network. However, I have small business customers who spend only 25 percent of their initial capital investment in support every year. That's quite a wide variance and testament to the difficulty in determining the recurring costs of network maintenance.

I've always found it easiest to compare networks based on how many clients are supported. (Supported clients are called "seats" in the industry, because presumably everyone has to sit down in front of whatever device they use. Bizarre, but that's how jargon in the computer industry works.) Planning for support costs then is most easily performed by thinking about the hard costs of supporting each individual client on a yearly basis—a unit I call the seat-year.

You can presume a few things about network maintenance:

- Every computer will be obsolete in three years. This means that you need to plug in one-third the cost of a new business-grade computer ($1,000) per seat-year.
- Every operating system will be upgraded at least once every three years. This totals, on average, $50 per seat-year.
- Software applications should be upgraded every two years or so. Figure that it should cost $200 per seat-year for application upgrades.
- Desktop/help desk/training support costs will run about $40 per computer per month. That's about $480 per seat-year.

This totals about $1,750 per seat-year to support one client.

There are two major components remaining: the network infrastructure and the service computers. Most physical layer, data-link layer, and network layer hardware (bridges, routers, hubs, and switches) have a useful lifetime of about 10 years. Divide the total cost of your network hardware by 10 and apply that as a yearly replacement/upgrade budget item. For a typical network, connectivity costs about $50, which translates (assuming a 10-year useful life) to just $5 per seat-year, which is really lost in the noise of these other calculations anyway.

Servers are another matter: they're expensive. Networks generally require a server for every 50 or so clients. The service life of a server can be stretched to three years, but that's pushing it harder than pushing clients out to a three-year replacement cycle. Assuming you pay an average of $10,000 per server (including hardware, software, and Client Access Licenses), and you replace them every three years, you'll need to spread $3,333 among 50 clients, which leaves a mere $66.66 per seat-year.

All these calculations make a number of presumptions, so we wind up with numbers that seem a lot more precise than they really are. But they are useful for getting us into the budgetary ballpark, which is right around $2,000 per seat-year, just to maintain the status quo, which is 66 percent of the initial installation cost. Figure 14.6 shows a typical IT budget and how it's divided by cost areas.

Figure 14.6   A typical IT budget allows for hardware, software, contracting and consulting, salaries, tools, and user training.

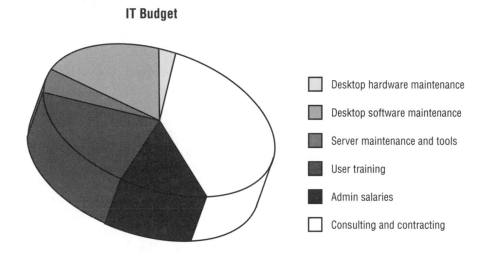

IT Budget

- ☐ Desktop hardware maintenance
- ☐ Desktop software maintenance
- ☐ Server maintenance and tools
- ☐ User training
- ☐ Admin salaries
- ☐ Consulting and contracting

This budgetary figure doesn't include the extra burden ERP/MRP or custom databases put on your budget. These support costs vary too wildly for me to attempt to put a real cost on them, but you should be able to get a very solid idea from the consultants that you use to put these systems in.

Evaluating Total Cost of Ownership

Total cost of ownership for the various client technologies is remarkably similar. If we break down each of the major client types by cost, we find something like Table 14.1.

Table 14.1   Comparative Costs of Client Technologies

Component	PC	Windows Terminal	Remote Boot
Monitor, keyboard, mouse	$500	$500	$500
Box	$1,500	$800	$1,300
Operating System license	$100	$150	$100
Client Access License	$40	$40	$40
Total (rounded to the nearest $100)	$2,200	$1,500	$2,000

By client cost alone, Windows terminals would seem to make the most sense. But that's not the whole story. Remote-boot PCs require a boot server that can serve about 35 clients, assuming it has no other duties. Windows terminals require a terminal server for every 20 machines. Since these machines are in addition to normal file servers, there is no associated cost of this nature for standard PCs. So to level the TCO playing field among the various client types, we must add 1/35th the price of a $7,000 server to remote-boot PCs, which equals $200. Similarly, 1/20th the price of a $7,000 server must be added to the price of a Windows terminal ($350). Adding these costs to the price of each client type levels the playing field considerably.

The total cost of ownership for all client types is roughly the same—about $3,000 per seat for typical business purposes with client licenses for office software and applications. The real difference between the client technologies lies in the recurring cost of administering the different technologies.

When choosing the types of clients, most people will choose general-purpose PCs because they are a safe, initially inexpensive, well-known solution that you can always get to work correctly. That's not always the right choice. Depending upon the size of your business, use the following guidelines to plan for client types:

- Small-sized businesses usually prefer standard PCs because of their flexibility and availability—they work when the network is down, and they can be purchased from any computer retailer.

- Medium-sized businesses can make good use of any of the technologies and should select their technology based primarily on the needs of the users—PCs for heavy-duty use, remote-boot computers for typical functions, and Windows terminals for task-based workers.

- Large-sized businesses should make their client decisions based mostly on the needs of users. Because of the size of the management problem, easily supported technologies such as remote-boot computers and Windows terminals will play a larger role, and because they can be purchased in bulk, their cost advantage can become significant.

Implementing Systems

Implementing any new system, or upgrading existing systems, doesn't have to be a chaotic morass. With a little planning and foresight, you can reengineer your entire network without so much as a hiccup in the daily operation of the company. The following are the phases of system installation:

- IT evaluation
- Test installation

- Training
- Back-end rollout
- Client rollout
- Cutover
- User support

Each of these distinct phases is important to the process in the order it's presented. Short-cutting these phases will make a system implementation more difficult.

IT Evaluation Phase

The entire IT organization becomes familiar with the new system during installations of the IT evaluation phase test, during test configurations, and with technical support from the manufacturer. The purpose of the IT evaluation phase is to make sure the entire IT organization is prepared to support the new product and is familiar enough with it to troubleshoot even unexpected problems.

Take as much time as you need during the IT evaluation phase to become comfortable with the product. Rushing new technologies into production environments is asking for trouble and serious delays. Your rollout will go smoothest when your IT staff is comfortable with the new products.

The IT evaluation phase should include at least one complete simulation. The simulation should mimic the function of your entire network, with multiple clients, routed connectivity between machines, and anything else your network includes.

> **TIP** I use VMWare to perform full-scale IT evaluations on a single high-performance machine. VMWare creates virtual computer environments so complete that the virtual machines actually go through a complete boot process in a window on your computer, and you actually have to install the operating systems you want to use inside the virtual machine. You can literally install any *x*86 computer operating system "in a window" on either Windows NT or Linux installations of VMWare. I've had simulations consisting of a Windows 2000 Server, four Windows 2000 Professional clients, a Windows 98 client, and a RedHat 6.1 mail server all running on a single machine and communicating with each other in order to find compatibility problems between Linux and Windows. Check out the evaluation version at www.vmware.com.

Test Installations

Never, ever, ever install new technologies directly in your network without first performing a test installation. Test installations are limited-scope rollouts to more sophisticated users in order to determine how the product functions in a production environment. Your test installation may, in many cases, be entirely within the IT department, but it can also include small groups in other divisions if these groups are technically oriented and can work through configuration problems. Candidate groups would be software developers, scientists, and engineers.

A test installation is simply a small-scale rollout of new IT systems in a limited environment to make certain that the software will perform as expected in the real world and that the IT staff knows for sure how to install and troubleshoot the system, so that the actual installation isn't waylaid by unforeseen problems. In addition to the commonsense reason of working out all the kinks in advance, performing test installations keeps your learning curve to yourself, not exposed to everyone else in the company.

Besides building a database of technical support problems, you'll be able to use this phase to monitor the performance of the product in an environment that more closely matches the environment of your whole network, yielding far more accurate usage statistics than any synthetic loads or virtual machine installations could provide. The usage characteristics you determine during this phase will determine the exact server-to-client ratios that you'll use in your full-scale rollout.

Don't finish your test installation phase until you have determined the precise performance characteristics of the new technology in your environment, compiled a support database that is extensive enough to handle most user problems during and after the rollout, and completed a training course and materials for standard users. Once these functions are complete, you're ready to move on to the training phase.

Wide-Scale User Training

Wide-scale user training is the next step in an organized implementation. By training users before the technology arrives at their desks, you've made them comfortable with the coming change, and you seduce them into anticipating the new system. Thus, when the new product arrives, users are prepared to use it, excited to have it, and ready to begin working immediately. You'll preempt passive resistance to the new methods, and you'll avoid users who try to blame the IT division for whatever problems they have with the new system. By simply preparing users in advance, you can avoid the appearance that the IT division simply makes policy without user feedback—even if you do.

Developing a training session is pretty easy if you base it upon an outline of the product's functionality. I usually start with a PowerPoint presentation (training is the only thing I use PowerPoint for) designed to be displayed with a projector system, because I find dark rooms tend to lull people into hypnotic acceptance.

1. Describe the purpose of the new software, including why the company feels it's necessary. Users need to know why changes occur if they're going to accept them.

2. Provide an overview of the system, using a logical map of how the various departments and external users (such as business partners and customers) will use the system. Usually, a work-flow diagram that describes how the major roles will use the major portions of the system is best.

3. Describe how the new system will assist users in their jobs, using screen shots of the product to familiarize them with its look and feel. Point out whiz-bang features that will save users time and effort. This section should be the meat of the presentation.

4. Describe how the system will be installed, being sure to point out any work interruptions or significant changes the users should expect. These are the things people will (justly) complain about. By making sure people know about them in advance, you won't upset them.

5. Explain the project timeline, when users can expect to see the new system, and when they can expect to begin using it.

6. Make sure everyone knows who to talk to about problems they might have with the system.

During the training session, be prepared for millions of silly questions aimed squarely at debunking the new system from people who'd rather not change, or amazingly detailed questions from those who fear that they won't be able to adapt to the new system. ("Yes, but after I've created my monthly usage reports, what will the hotkey for sorting them by SKU number be?") Don't be sidelined by these questions during mass training sessions; tell everyone they can schedule one-on-one training with an IT staff person, if they need to, when the product is installed for them. Most people will be able to figure out how to integrate the new product into their work without help. Remember that the purpose of the wide-scale user training is not so much training as it is eliciting support for the new system among users by eliminating their fear, uncertainty, and doubt.

Back-End Rollout

If your system is client/server, the rollout will have two phases: first the servers and then the clients. Rolling out servers is easy because there's no demand on the new systems. You can move the back-end servers into production using only the test rollout group or the IT division for system validation. Once the back-end servers are in place, tested, and online, you can begin the client rollout.

Client Rollout

Now you're ready for the full-scale rollout. Depending on the type of system you're implementing, you may either replace an existing system, upgrade a system, or add a system alongside a legacy system that will be removed when the rollout is completed. In any case, the rollout is the period where client stations are individually updated to the new system.

Whenever possible, use automation tools to perform the rollout. IT management software such as Attachmate NetWizard, Tivoli, HP OpenView, and CA UniCenter are all capable of creating installation packages that can be automatically deployed to users *en masse*. Generally, these systems take so much effort to prepare that they're only useful when deploying 250 or more seats, but for large installations, they can save a tremendous amount of time.

Even in situations where you won't be using full-scale IT management software to perform rollouts, you can still use automation to get the job done more quickly. Use e-mail to send each user a link URL to the setup package on the server. The end-user can then open the mail, click the link, and wait while the automated installation takes place. This method is by far the most effective I've ever seen for reducing IT burden during a client rollout. You will have to create installation scripts and use software that can be scripted, but since the new Windows Installer service is completely scriptable, you'll be able to use this method with most new software in the near future.

Windows 2000 supports a whole slew of new installation features, including the Remote Installation Service (RIS), which uses PXE-compatible remote-boot network adapters (or the remote-boot floppy disks from Microsoft) to automatically attach to a server and begin installing Windows 2000 Professional. I always recommend using disk cloning with the System Preparation Tool, but RIS may be easier in circumstances where a PXE remote-boot architecture already exists.

In situations where e-mail and automated installation is not possible, you may be able to use remote-control software such as VNC or the NetMeeting Remote Control service to control the user's machine directly and attach to a central shared directory that contains the application to be installed. You'll find you can work about 10 times faster using remote tools than by having desktop technicians visit each client in person.

Client rollouts proceed in this order:

1. Create the typical client installation. Usually, you would create a prototypical client installation on one machine and then create an installation image or package containing the complete new system. In instances where imaging is not possible or recommended, this step may merely yield a step-by-step installation sequence for desktop support technicians to follow when they install the system. The installation sequence instructions should include test procedures to make sure the system works correctly and should culminate with a sign-off for each system that the desktop installer uses to certify that he has completed the entire installation correctly.

2. Using the prototype installation, install the system software on the client hardware if possible. This is not possible with upgrades or with terminal or remote-boot computer deployment, but it should always be performed in advance for general PC client rollouts.

3. Place any new client hardware at each user location. There is no way to avoid physically visiting each desktop, but for light items (less than 20 pounds) you might be able to get each user to pick up their own hardware. This is a good reason to consider deploying laptops instead of desktop computers if everything else is equal.

4. For software-only deployments, deploy the software to each client computer *en masse*, either via an e-mailed link or by using remote installation tools. In the worst case, have desktop support technicians visit each desktop to install the software.

NOTE Hardware rollouts will always take far more time than software rollouts, because every client station must be visited. Software-only rollouts can often be completed in a day if you have the right infrastructure for it. If you don't, they're much like hardware rollouts, because you'll be visiting every desktop.

Rollouts do not have to be a frenzied IT activity where nerves are worn thin by late workdays and a rushed pace. The rollout doesn't have to occur any faster than the IT evaluation phase—take it easy and save your energy for the support phase after the cutover.

Cutover

Cutover is the moment when all users simultaneously stop using the old system and begin using the new system. Cutover is necessary whenever the new system is not compatible with the old system—it creates a demarcation that prevents some information from going to the old system while other information is processed by the new system.

If the new system was used with testing information prior to the cutover, that test information must be deleted immediately prior to the cutover. Cutover is usually performed over a weekend to give the IT staff time to test the production system before work starts on Monday. The apparent difference to typical users is that they used the old system on Friday and the new system on Monday.

The old system should be taken offline during the cutover to prevent users from reverting to it in the mistaken belief that they should do that if they have problems with the new system. After the old system is offline, there may be a data migration to the new system or an archival process, depending on how the information processed by the old system should be managed in the future.

Cutovers usually involve the following sequence of events:

1. Test the back-end to be certain it performs correctly.

2. Test the deployed client hardware and software, either remotely or by visiting each desktop. The test should prove that the clients will be able to attach normally to the

back-end when the cutover occurs. For large installations (more than 250 installations), a representative test of 5 to 10 percent of desktops is appropriate unless you run into problems among the sample group, in which case you should begin testing all of them.

3. Perform the cutover by activating the back-end and shutting down the legacy system. Be prepared to reactivate the legacy system in the event of an unforeseen failure in the new system.

4. Validate the new system by having everyone perform a few days to a few weeks of work with it.

5. Visit each desktop on a time-available basis to remove any legacy hardware.

Once the old system is offline, any legacy client hardware or software can be removed from users at the leisure of the IT department.

Help Desk/Desktop Support

The period directly following the cutover is always the most frenetic period of a system implementation. It is during this period that the IT staff finds out that it really was necessary to sort monthly usage reports by SKU number and has to have the consultant add that functionality to the system. User-training problems will abound.

If you're consulting a system integrator for the installation, consider paying for supplemental support from their staff, because you'll find your staff is probably less prepared for the onslaught than you thought.

The key to handling the support phase after cutover is good preparation. Have your help desk in place with procedures that don't rely on the newly installed system to get help. For example, don't implement an e-mail system and then stipulate that users should send e-mail to the help desk to get support.

Don't immediately dispatch desktop support staff for every call. Assign priorities to each support incident and have your staff handle them in priority order. The key here is not to waste your time helping the facilities manager, whose job doesn't impact anyone else, while the production line sits idle awaiting support. Base your support priorities on the criteria of minimizing work stoppage. Is it a work stoppage issue, or can the user work around it? If it's not a work stoppage, prioritize it below problems that are.

Priorities should always be assigned by the number of users affected and in the following order:

- Work stoppages or issues that cannot be worked around
- Serious usability issues that can be worked around

- Productivity improvements
- Convenience features

How many other people depend on this specific user's work to continue theirs? Obviously those who cause a bottleneck in the workflow for others are the highest priority. Note that this isn't the same question as how many people work for the affected user—management above a working group typically doesn't interfere with daily operations, so don't waste your time getting executives online until you've knocked down all the bottleneck users in your organization.

Summary

Good IT management is not particularly difficult—in fact, it's very routine. IT management can be very different between small, medium, and large businesses, so it's most appropriate to talk about those three scales somewhat differently. Everything from the types of servers, types of clients, management software, and even management style can be completely different among these scales:

- Small businesses typically have a single server and a single site.
- Medium-sized businesses typically have multiple servers and up to a few thousand clients. They may be concentrated at a single site or distributed among multiple satellite offices of a single headquarters building.
- Large businesses typically have multiple large sites, each of which is the size of a medium-sized business. Large companies with tens of thousands of users at a single location are very rare.

IT organizations are most effective when they're apportioned into support layers, where lesser skilled technicians handle easier problems and forward (or "escalate" in support jargon) the tougher issues to more experienced technicians. This allows an IT department to leverage employees of nearly all skill levels while still providing correct and appropriate support to all users. This method also keeps junior technicians from being forced to handle problems that are over their heads, thus minimizing the potential for personal failure. In smaller businesses, these tiers are often collapsed so that one or just a few people handle them all, but the tiers should still be kept in mind for when the company grows and so that new hires aren't immediately expected to know everything.

The support tiers are as follows:

- Help desk support to answer phone, e-mail, and perhaps chat inquiries immediately to solve application and training problems.

Windows 2000 Every Day

PART 3

- Desktop support to handle problems with individual client computers and the installation of client software.

- Network administrators to handle servers; data-link and network layer devices such as hubs, routers, and bridges; and more complex software systems such as database, MRP, and IT management software.

- IT management to make strategic decisions about the network architecture and selecting systems, and to act as a last resort before consulting help is called in to solve persistent problems.

Outsourcing is a necessary part of nearly every well-run IT organization. Outsourcing specific problems such as esoteric systems, application or software development, and training is almost always more effective and less costly than trying to train in-house personnel to manage these same functions. Outsourced experts retain far more specific knowledge of the systems they support than any jack-of-all-IT-trades could ever hope to have, and they can work far more quickly for that reason.

Budgeting and cost analysis are a major portion of an IT manager's job. Correctly taking all cost factors into account when analyzing systems can make seemingly expensive systems seem inexpensive and can reveal the true costs of inexpensive systems. Case in point: Linux, while free, is so difficult to maintain as a desktop operating system that it only makes sense for those rare cases where the users are computer experts.

Finally, implementing systems is what IT is really all about. System implementation can be easy and systematic no matter how large or small an implementation is. By following a strict regimen of evaluation, testing, and user training before the rollout, and by providing additional support after the rollout, you can make even sweeping changes to your IT infrastructure seem relatively painless and easy.

Case Studies: IT Management Techniques

These miniature case studies highlight various approaches to IT management and their effects on staff, systems, and budget. These case studies are examples of how *not* to manage an IT department, because the rest of this chapter provides the positive example.

Each of these case studies points out IT departments with serious systemic problems: it's not the people who are bad; it's the way the department is structured that is bad. They highlight common problems, such as management by the latest fad, decentralization, and IT insulation from user problems caused by over-centralization.

To avoid these problems, you need to strike an appropriate balance between centralized IT management and decentralized management. The best way to do this is to operate the way an outside IT support firm would—keeping the customer's needs as the top priority. When you follow this paradigm, centralization and a host of other problems take care of themselves.

"Healthy Competition"

I once had a customer who had two separate IT directors—both with equal power and the same set of responsibilities. The idea was that they were supposed to compete against one another so the company would always have the best implementation at the lowest cost. A management consultant came up with this glimmer of brilliance.

The net effect was that the two IT directors hated each other. They had to hire consultants (like me) to make even the most mundane decisions because they could not agree on how the department should operate. The network became schismatic, with each director taking control of the portions they installed or supported. They'd deny documentation to each other, foment dissent within the ranks, and work to make the other look bad. It was by far the most dysfunctional IT organization I've ever seen. Don't be tempted to do this.

"Not without My Budget"

A major public university (which shall remain nameless) does not have a dedicated IT staff. Rather, each college funds its own networking operation and staff. A good friend of mine was the director of one of these college network operations. Being distributed as they were, his staff was small and so was the problem: he supported about 500 clients and perhaps 10 servers. His staff regularly attended meetings, and he had his own desk and coffee mug. He was paid a miserable wage ("not much money for the network this year"), but he had just finished college, so he didn't need much money.

The net effect of this lack of structure is that no college has a truly professional staff. No central point of operations exists—even for controlled access to the Internet; effectively, every server in the university is a public host on the Internet, and they routinely suffer major hacking breaches. There isn't even a common e-mail standard or basic platform—some colleges use UNIX, some NetWare, and some Windows. Many have PC clients, others have Macintoshes, and still others use Windows or X terminals.

24seven **CASE STUDY**

The university as a whole pays for more IT staff than any organization I've seen, but some colleges languish with too little support while others pay people to drink coffee and write e-mail systems from scratch. Worst of all, nobody involved thinks there's anything wrong with this.

"The Occupation Army"

A major pharmaceutical company has a lovely IT department. This department supposedly operates as an independent organization, but each division must pay directly for the staff they support. The divisions have no power to compel the IT staff to do anything, but they are compelled to pay them. The support procedure works like this: requisitions for equipment are made by the local divisions who will have to pay for it, but all equipment purchases are actually made by the central IT department. IT has veto authority over all in a vain attempt to control the proliferation of platforms in the company. Support requests also go through the central IT office for dispatch. Even though an on-site technician is always dispatched to look at the problem, local employees cannot request assistance directly.

I entered the picture because it became easier for a group of programmers at one site to outsource their department's IT problems than it was to get support from the on-site staff. Because the programmers had control of their own budget, the IT staff couldn't stop them from doing outsourcing, but the programmers still had to pay the on-site staff. They decided to retain me and pay them, because at least that way the problems that they had been living with for months on end while the local staff sat

around awaiting the proper authorization from the East Coast would be solved.

"Testing Is a Waste of Time"

Not performing test installations can lead to a tremendous amount of wasted time and animosity with the end-users. I recently worked with another consultant who was assisting his client with deploying a hardware-based VPN. As their general-purpose IT outsourcing firm, I agreed to drive to another city about two hours away to install the remote end of the VPN hardware. The consultant was certain that there would be no problems, so I traveled out, installed the hardware, configured it for Internet access, and waited for him to get the VPN established from the headquarters site. And I waited. And I waited. Late that night, he gave up, declared the box bad, and asked me to bring it back down.

So I traveled back, and he asked me to drive back up with another box. I refused and told him to make sure he could get the VPN established between the two boxes in a test environment in one room, so that we could simply plug in a completely functional VPN at the remote site rather than experience the same problems repeatedly. He resisted the idea, claiming it would just waste time, but I made it a condition of my continued assistance, so he acquiesced. After two days of failing to get the VPN to work reliably in the test environment, he gave up and called in the manufacturer's support engineers, who determined that the problem was old firmware, and, after updating it, got the VPN running in short order.

Had we tested in the first place, I would not have wasted a trip, and he would not have looked incompetent in front of his client.

Part 4

Troubleshooting and Optimization

Topics Covered:

- Windows 2000 performance-monitoring mechanisms
- Architecture optimization
- Optimizing your network
- Optimizing Windows 2000 servers
- Methodical troubleshooting
- Determining where fault lies in a complex system
- Troubleshooting axioms
- Troubleshooting tips for networks, servers, and clients
- Troubleshooting the Windows 2000 Registry
- Finding help online
- Analyzing client load on servers and networks
- Physical plant design
- Network architecture choices

15

Performance Optimization

Performance optimization is the process of finding the resource that slows your network the most, speeding it up, and then starting over by finding the new slowest resource. This cycle of finding the speed-limiting factor or bottleneck, eliminating it, and starting over with the next bottleneck will allow you to reach the natural performance limit of your network in a simple, methodical way.

Windows 2000 provides a comprehensive set of tools for finding and eliminating bottlenecks in both servers and networks. Windows 2000 provides low-level support for performance monitoring by including counters in every object that can be meaningfully measured. This performance information is used to tune Windows 2000 automatically by changing various thread priorities, caching characteristics, network timings, and many other factors.

You use the Performance Console to measure system performance through object counters. You can use the Performance Console to find bottlenecks (performance-limited resources) in your server. The Performance Console enables you to inspect the value of the object counters in real time so you can see how various activities affect the resources of your server.

NOTE   The Performance Console is actually an MMC console configured with two snap-ins: the System Monitor and Performance Logs and Alerts.

To effectively find bottlenecks, you must look at the overall performance of your computer under a typical load. Using more general counters and averages will give a good indication of where to look for specific bottlenecks. Processor performance, memory performance, and disk performance are the three major capacities that you should check. For servers, you should also pay particular attention to the network subsystem, especially if the other three subsystems are not showing bottlenecks.

Windows 2000 also includes the Network Monitor, which captures packets, broadcasts, or multicast frames that are being sent to or from the server it is installed on. The Network Monitor included with Windows 2000 is a limited version of the same tool that ships with Systems Management Server (SMS, a Microsoft BackOffice application that can be purchased separately). The SMS version can capture network packets from the entire network, not just those involving the server. You can filter captured data based on the protocol used, the computer address, and the protocol properties. Filtering allows you to take a large amount of information and display only the frames that match your criteria.

By using the Performance Console to tune the performance of individual servers and the Network Monitor to tune the performance of your network, you can increase the speed of your network and stave off major hardware upgrades until the system reaches its natural limit.

This chapter first covers performance theory, then discusses the practical aspects of architecture, network, and server optimization, and ends with a section on optimization shortcuts and best practices.

Performance Theory

You can improve the performance of a single component in any system in two ways:

- Reduce the load placed upon the component.
- Increase the capacity of the component.

Reducing the load placed upon the component could require changing how the component is used, adding other components to share the burden, or removing functionality. Increasing capacity generally requires upgrading to hardware that can perform more work, but it might also require tuning the component to work more efficiently with available resources.

In a system, the complex interactions between components can make it difficult to ferret out which components are the cause of undesirable effects. However, systematic measurement of the load across all the components of a system will make it obvious which components are responsible for limiting performance.

These components that limit performance in a computer are called *bottlenecks*. For example, slow memory limits the speed at which a processor can manipulate data—thus limiting the computer's processing performance to the speed that the processor can access memory. If the memory can respond faster than the processor, the processor is the bottleneck.

A slow hardware resource, such as a hard disk drive, causes the microprocessor and system RAM (both fast) to wait for the resource to complete I/O requests. Thus, during disk I/O, the speed of the hard disk is the bottleneck.

Although you cannot make your hard disk faster (except by replacing it with a faster one), you may be able to reduce the number of times the computer needs to access it, or you can limit the amount of information that is transferred. You may also be able to spread the load across many hard disk drives, thus dividing the time you spend waiting for drive access by the number of drives available.

In your network, the users of client computers should be the bottleneck. To achieve performance nirvana, their computers must be more responsive than the users need, the network data link must be more responsive than the clients attached to it, and the servers must be more responsive than the networks to which they are attached.

Eventually, you will find a limitation that you cannot overcome. This point is the natural limit of your system, and finding it is the ultimate goal of performance tuning. If you need speed beyond the natural limit of your system, you will need to upgrade the hardware resource causing the limitation.

Ferreting out bottlenecks involves a little understanding of how computers and networks work, and it requires some software. Even the best system engineers can only guess at what causes a complex system to run slowly unless they have proper monitoring tools.

Measuring System Resources

To find a bottleneck, you must be able to measure the speed of the different resources in your system. Measurements enable you to find the one resource that is performing at its peak and, therefore, causing the bottleneck.

> **NOTE** Hardware resources operating at their maximum performance level are the bottlenecks.

Troubleshooting and Optimization

PART 4

Different resources require different measurements. For example:

- Network traffic is measured as a percentage of utilization.
- Disk throughput is measured in megabytes per second.
- Interrupt activity is measured in interrupts per second.

To compare resources, you must use measurements that are equal. In most cases, Windows 2000 provides a basic "percentage of processor time spent doing this" measurement that you can use to compare dissimilar resources.

To find a bottleneck in a network, you use the System Monitor's network counters and the Network Monitor to determine whether your data-link layer is sufficient for the number of computers on it. With an Ethernet or Fast Ethernet network, a sustained network utilization of 30 percent or more is an indication that you need to consider either splitting that network into two or more subnetworks or moving to a faster data-link technology. If your network is not experiencing excessive utilization, servers that are too loaded to respond quickly to client requests may be causing slow performance. Perhaps the servers are not optimized for their tasks, or perhaps they simply aren't powerful enough to handle their duties for the number of clients attached.

To find a bottleneck in a server, you first run the System Monitor (I discuss this later in this chapter in the section "Performance Monitoring"). You then need to put your server under a typical load, for example, by attaching multiple clients to your network file server and copying files. Then you should run your server application and put it under a load by doing whatever normally makes your server slow.

The System and Network Monitors will suggest a few broad measures that will show you where to search more deeply to find the exact bottleneck. For example, if after measuring processor time and disk time, you see that the disk is running at its peak, you know to concentrate on disk-related measurements. Or if the Network Monitor shows that the network is under excessive load, try to find the clients that are transmitting excessively and determine if their traffic is appropriate. If it is, you should either split your subnetworks further or upgrade to a faster data-link technology.

> **NOTE** Make certain you've found the bottleneck before concentrating on detailed performance monitoring. Since performance-limited resources hide behind other, slower resources, you won't be able to see the difference if you make changes to objects that are not the true bottleneck.

Eliminating Bottlenecks

Finding a bottleneck is only half the battle. Eliminating it (making the component fast enough so that something else becomes the primary bottleneck) may involve changing a Control Panel setting, or it may involve replacing every cable in your network and the devices that connect to them. You will have to determine how to relieve the load placed on the resource.

Usually, you will be able to look at more detailed measurements to determine the specific activity that is bogging down your network. For example, if your network utilization is high, you should then use the Network Monitor to determine which computers are generating that load and why. You may find that you have a malfunctioning device on your network that is generating spurious traffic or that your replication or backup scheme is generating far more network traffic than you suspected. These problems can be easily corrected. Sometimes, however, you'll find that your network simply isn't fast enough, and major architectural changes are in order.

TIP   When troubleshooting, make only one change at a time. Otherwise, you will not be able to tell which change fixed the problem.

Achieving maximum performance from your network is a continuing process. Once you have eliminated the major bottleneck in your system, you start over and eliminate the next new bottleneck. Your system will always have a bottleneck, because one resource will always cause other resources to wait for it.

You continue to eliminate bottlenecks until:

- You make your computer so fast that you never need to wait for it.
- You upgrade or replace components.
- You realize that you can't afford to buy any more new components and settle for what you have, knowing that it is as fast as it will get.

Architecture Optimization

The process of optimizing system performance consists of three categories of optimization: architecture, network, and server. *Architecture optimization* affects every aspect of your network system—not just physical data-link speed, server performance, or application speed. Architecture optimization is the process of making the entire system as efficient as possible.

Troubleshooting and Optimization

PART 4

To differentiate the processes of architecture and network optimization, think of freeways: a network optimization approach would build more freeways, whereas an architecture approach would change the environment to effect working at home or living closer to work.

Architecture optimization produces the greatest overall benefit. Network optimization produces the next best benefit to performance, and server optimization is the least beneficial. Oddly, these three components of system optimization become increasingly complex and difficult even as their returns decrease.

Redesigning an existing network is considerably more difficult than putting an effective architecture in place to begin with, but even that is not particularly difficult in most cases, because the optimization usually involves only the connections between workgroup collision domains. Therefore, only networking equipment and servers are involved.

Architecture optimization involves these key components:

- Creating the least amount of network traffic possible by selecting the client hardware and application software that generate the lowest amount of network traffic while performing the necessary work. For task-based work, this may require using terminal servers or highly controlled workstations, or it may require loading applications on the local hard disk rather than over the network.

- Making network traffic travel the shortest possible distance by placing file or terminal servers in workgroups on the same collision domain as their supported clients.

- Using content-efficient protocols for data that must, by its nature, travel long distances to centralized network resources. Do this by selecting data-dense protocols, such as e-mail and client/server databases, rather than less efficient word processors and file-based databases.

- Making effective use of caching and data replication to push frequently accessed non-changing data as close to the data subscribers as possible. For example, use HTTP proxy servers on workgroup file servers to cache the corporate intranet site, and make them domain controllers so they can perform logons locally. Put user profiles on the server closest to the users. Use Intellimirror technology to synchronize files between poorly connected sites rather than allowing file access to travel over slower WAN links.

Architecture optimization provides the greatest return on your investment, so be sure to start with architecture before proceeding to network optimization.

Network Optimization

Because the speed at which network clients can work is usually tied to the speed at which they can access the network, the speed of the network limits the speed of every computer attached to it. Many factors affect the responsiveness of a network from the point of view of client computers, but the two factors that have the most impact are

- The availability of network bandwidth
- The responsiveness of network servers

Measure your network performance before you measure the performance of individual servers. The network performance measurement will first tell you whether your network is a bottleneck, and if not, it will tell you which network resources are the bottlenecks.

If too many computers are competing for a single, shared media subnetwork, if the computers are able to process data faster than the data rate (or bandwidth) supported by the network data link, or if the network servers are too loaded down to respond quickly, then the speed of network clients will be limited by the network. This problem is most apparent when you run network-limited clients, such as Windows Terminals or diskless workstations. Standard workstations are less limited, because they do not rely on the network for their system and application files.

Conversely, if the network is immediately available in most cases, if the data-link bandwidth is greater than the amount of data that the client can process, and if the servers are able to respond quickly to client requests, then the clients will not be limited by the speed of the network. Therefore, a fast network requires that the data rate of the data-link technology exceeds the ability of the clients to process data, that competition to access shared media networks is not excessive, and that servers be fast enough to respond to all simultaneous client requests.

Improving network performance is rarely easy. When networks begin to run slowly, speeding them up can be very difficult. You can improve network performance in two ways:

Reduce traffic   This option is best when circumstances permit it, because it works regardless of your current network architecture and may not require any physical changes. Reducing traffic may involve localizing servers inside departmental subnetworks or migrating network applications to lower-bandwidth Internet client/server protocols. You can also reduce traffic by splitting subnetworks—you may find that replacing hubs with switches can solve Ethernet bottleneck problems without expending much effort, although this does constitute a physical change in your network architecture.

Increase speed   This option works very well, but it is also very expensive; it requires the replacement of every data-link device on the network. This option should be regarded as a major network infrastructure change and should be implemented gradually.

These two reciprocal methods are described in detail in the following sections. Reducing traffic is actually an architecture optimization, although its performance-improving aspects give it the character of a network optimization, while increasing speed is purely network optimization.

Reducing Traffic

There is no systematic way to reduce network traffic. You must monitor your network using the tools discussed later in this chapter and decide whether you can relieve the traffic load on your network. However, you can look for the following problem areas:

Users that generate excessive traffic (in excess of their peers)   Find out why. If they don't have a valid work-related reason, encourage them to stop. The recent proliferation of custom multimedia Internet services such as RealAudio, Napster, and streaming video can have dramatically adverse effects on your Internet bandwidth. Eliminate them unless they are necessary for work.

Diskless workstations running Windows   These stations generate an enormous load on networks. Hard disks are very inexpensive compared to the cost of a network upgrade, so consider adding hard disks to these machines and booting the operating system locally. Or consider using Terminal Services for diskless machines, which are comparatively frugal with network bandwidth.

Network loading of applications that could be stored locally   Although I recommend the central installation of applications for ease of administration, decreasing the load on your network may be a higher priority for you. This trade-off is typical of the many cost, performance, and ease-of-use compromises you will make.

Inefficient client applications that rely on data stored on the network   Replace them with true client/server applications. An example would be to migrate an Access database that is stored on a server to a client/server database using an Access front end and an SQL server back end.

The wasteful practice of using Office applications (for example, Word and Excel) to store or transmit data in your environment   The documents created by these applications are huge compared to their information content. E-mailing them as attachments around your network causes an unnecessary burden on every resource involved. Encourage people to use bandwidth-conserving technologies, such as e-mailing links or text, using databases, and storing content in HTML (Web pages) rather than in Word, Excel, and PowerPoint for internal communications.

Identifying Top Talkers

Reducing your network load usually involves identifying which computers generate the most load, determining why, and reducing that load, if possible. Repeating this process until you cannot relieve the load any further will reduce traffic to the extent possible.

Routers, bridges, and servers normally generate the most apparent load on the network. Servers usually respond to each client request, so they normally generate about 50 percent of the load on a network. Bridges and routers are actually forwarding data from other networks, but their Media Access Control (MAC) addresses will appear in the Network Monitor as the source of the traffic.

If you see multiple IP addresses coming from single MAC address when you are using a packet sniffer (such as the Network Monitor) to monitor network traffic, you are probably looking at traffic coming through a bridge or router. (It is possible for multiple IP addresses to be bound to a single adapter in Windows NT, 2000, and UNIX, but this usage is rare.) Inspect source IP addresses to determine which devices are truly using the most bandwidth.

Splitting Networks

Unless your network is far behind your traffic requirements, you will get a lot of mileage out of simply splitting your shared media networks into multiple subnetworks joined by switches, routers, or servers that perform the routing service.

Splitting networks is analogous to building more freeways. In theory, doubling the number of collision domains cuts the traffic on each network in half. However, that method works only when you can guarantee that both sides of the conversation are on the same subnetwork. For example, if you split your network but place two computers that spend most of their time communicating on the network on different subnetworks, you haven't solved the problem. Their traffic will simply be retransmitted on both subnetworks.

You have to make sure you've isolated the same subnetworks computers that spend time talking to each other, which is why basing subnetworks on some real grouping of individuals, such as by department, usually works well. These users—and by extension, their computers—will spend most of their time communicating internally.

While you can easily split up your collision domains using Ethernet switching at the data-link layer, you'll be better off in the long run to design a routed network architecture where smaller collision domains are connected together via routed links to a high-speed backbone. These networks are far more deterministic in their traffic patterns, and unlike switches, IP routers don't "forget" rarely used addresses in their address tables.

Besides that, routed networks support multiple simultaneous paths to the same destination for network redundancy. Switches must be implemented in a true hierarchy that is by its nature not redundant. Network redundancy allows you great flexibility in performing work on live networks (you can take down sections that have redundant alternate routes) in addition to fault tolerance.

Splitting Subnetworks with a Centralized Server   The vast majority of all network traffic in client/server local area networks is between clients and servers. Peer-to-peer networks may be communicating with other computers on the network, making splitting subnetworks difficult. However, because most clients spend the majority of their time communicating with a single server, you can usually make the server a part of each subnetwork. Figure 15.1 shows a network that puts a single server on each subnetwork, thus efficiently multiplying the total bandwidth to the server without upgrading to a higher-speed network.

Figure 15.1   A central server on multiple subnetworks can eliminate network bottlenecks in small networks.

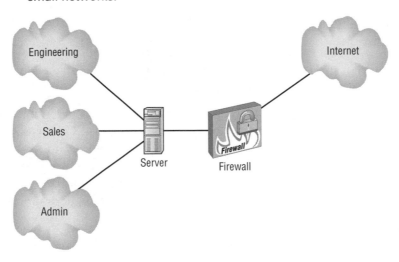

Servers Local to Subnetworks   This solution isn't quite as easy when you have more than one server, but you can still identify the server that each client usually talks to and put that client on the same subnetwork as that server. Then, by attaching all your servers to a single high-speed subnetwork, you can route any traffic for other servers over a higher-speed link rather than upgrading the link technology of your entire network. The configuration in Figure 15.2 shows a high-speed backbone between servers localized to subnetworks.

Figure 15.2   Many connected departmental servers can communicate directly with their subnets.

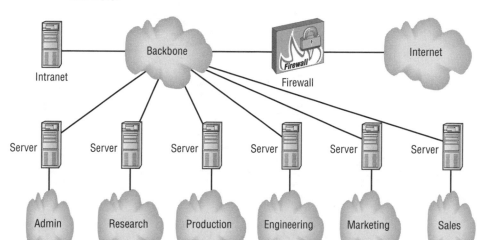

Servers on a High-Speed Backbone   When clients must access many different servers without preference (this is rare), you may need to implement servers on a high-speed backbone, using dedicated routers to attach client subnetworks. This architecture has the disadvantage of requiring expensive routers to attach to the backbone. It also requires every packet transmitted to a server to traverse the backbone, which forces the backbone to deal with the vast majority of all the traffic on the network. Figure 15.3 shows servers on a high-speed backbone.

In some situations, clients must access not only their departmental server but also many other servers (for example, an intranet server, a messaging server, and an Internet gateway). An obvious solution would be to simply put all the servers on a backbone and route to them, but that configuration might not be the best solution. Even if the clients spend only 25 percent of their network time communicating with their departmental server, you are better off directly attaching them to it and using it to route to a backbone that contains the other servers. Remember that every packet you keep off the backbone makes the backbone faster. For example, a network with four departmental servers that can deal with 25 percent of their clients' requests without forwarding them to the backbone will cut backbone traffic in half. That load reduction can stave off migrating to a higher-speed network technology for years.

However, routing can be a significant performance hit for servers. Whenever you configure servers to perform a routing function, you should monitor them periodically to ensure that they are not causing a significant network bottleneck. If they are, you should move the server inside the department and use a dedicated bridge or router to perform the routing function.

Troubleshooting and Optimization

PART 4

Figure 15.3 Many servers on a high-speed backbone

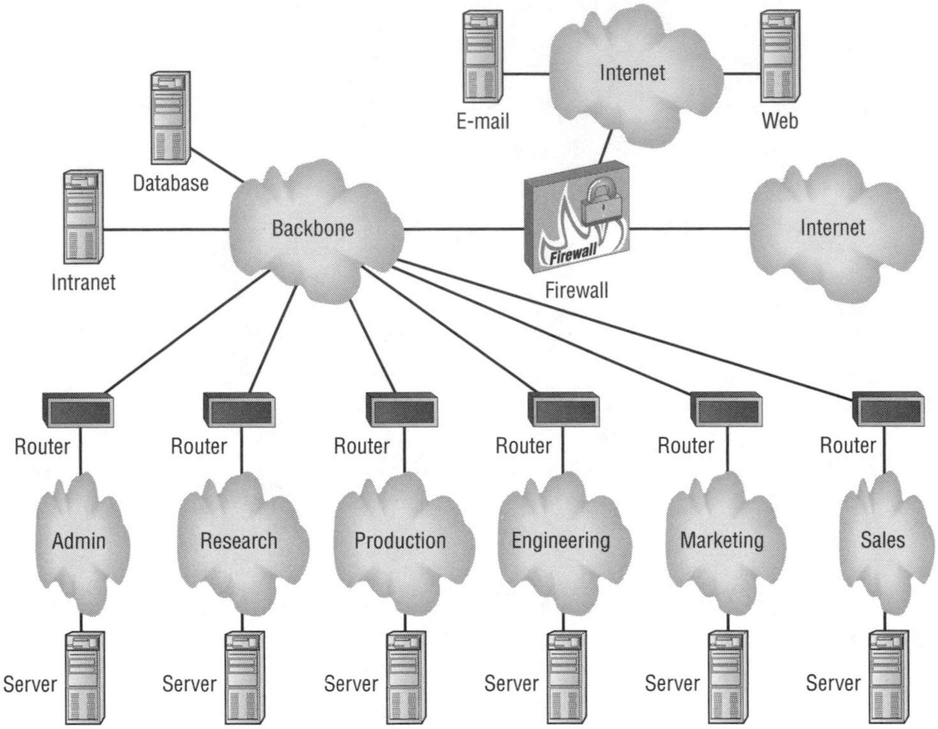

Increasing Speed

If you can no longer reduce traffic or efficiently divide subnetworks, you will have to upgrade the physical data-link network protocol. Usually, this upgrade involves moving from Ethernet or Token Ring to Fast Ethernet or Fiber Distributed Data Interface (FDDI).

Remember that you may not have to upgrade your entire network. You may be able to simply upgrade your backbone technology, the links between servers, or certain subnetworks or users to higher-speed networks. Use the Network Monitor to identify top talkers on your network and migrate those users to faster protocols first.

Fast Ethernet

Fast Ethernet is simply regular Ethernet at 10 times the raw throughput. Fast Ethernet runs at 100Mb rather than 10Mb. The two major varieties of Fast Ethernet are 100Base-X, which is a regular Ethernet at a higher speed, and 100Base-VG (AnyLAN), which uses a similar but incompatible access method that can guarantee throughput even in heavily loaded networks, making such applications as real-time voice or video over the network reliable.

Three varieties of 100Base-X Fast Ethernet exist:

- 100Base-TX runs over standard Category 5 twisted-pair wiring on two pairs.
- 100Base-T4 runs over Category 3, 4, or 5 twisted-pair wiring on all four pairs.
- 100Base-FX runs over one pair of multi-mode optical fiber.

You must use special media converters to adapt from any one type of cable to another. Some hubs include media converters or transceivers that do the job for you. Most 100Base-FX adapters and some 100Base-TX adapters can operate in a special mode called Full Duplex, which allows them to transmit and receive data simultaneously and eliminates collisions on the wire (however, collisions still occur inside hubs). This technology not only doubles the capacity of Fast Ethernet to 200Mbps, it extends the distance limitation of 100Base-FX from 400 meters to 2,000 meters.

Gigabit Ethernet

Gigabit Ethernet is the next order-of-magnitude improvement for Ethernet—it runs at 10 times the speed of Fast Ethernet over a single pair of optical fibers or four pairs of Category 6 UTP. Gigabit Ethernet does not support collision detection or multiple access—it is point-to-point only. That said, Gigabit Ethernet can be effectively switched, and since switches are now nearly as inexpensive as hubs, Gigabit Ethernet can be effectively "hubbed" by using high-density switches.

> **NOTE** As this book goes to press, an industry consortium is finalizing the standard for 10Gig Ethernet.

Fiber Distributed Data Interface (FDDI)

FDDI is essentially 100Mb Token Ring over fiber-optic cable with a second counter-rotating ring (the data flows in the opposite direction) that provides a measure of fault tolerance in case of cable faults. A copper variant called CDDI runs over the same Category 5 twisted-pair wiring that Fast Ethernet runs over.

FDDI is the oldest high-speed network technology in common use. Early problems with fault tolerance features were solved long ago, and although it remains expensive, FDDI is very stable and can support operations at metropolitan area distances.

Asynchronous Transfer Mode (ATM)

ATM is the new telephony standard for wide area telecommunications links. Because it supports different guaranteed levels of service for voice, video, and data networking at very high

Troubleshooting and Optimization

PART 4

data rates, ATM has become a compelling new option for campus area transports. ATM standards using the same frame technology have been defined for the following data rates:

- ATM-25 runs at 25Mbps and is intended as a competitor to Fast Ethernet in local area networks.

- STS-3 runs at 155Mbps over fiber or Category 5 twisted-pair wiring as an alternative to Fast Ethernet or FDDI in high-speed workstations or network backbones.

- STS-12 runs at 622Mbps over fiber as a campus area transport.

- STS-48 runs at 2.2Gbps over fiber as a metropolitan area transport. Few computer networks will implement this speed, but they may be attached to telephone networks operating at this speed.

- STS-192 runs at 8.8Gbps over fiber as a long-distance intercity transport. Only telephone companies will install this grade of ATM.

NOTE   OC (Optical Carrier) grades are equivalent to STS (Synchronous Transmission Signal) speeds. STS refers to the digital bit rate, whereas OC refers to a specific STS rate over optical fiber carriers. STS-N rates are multiplied by 51.84Mbps to determine the aggregate bit rate.

The compelling factor in ATM is that the same frame technology can be switched among any of the data rates listed above by relatively simple switches. Unfortunately, the ATM standards are still not completely defined, and you may have trouble getting devices from different manufacturers to operate properly. Be certain to choose equipment that the manufacturers guarantee to be compatible before purchasing any ATM equipment. Current ATM switches for the enterprise are extremely finicky and require considerable administrative effort compared to their Ethernet counterparts, which are maintenance free.

FiberChannel

FiberChannel was developed as a high-speed peripheral interconnection bus for disk arrays and mainframe computers, but its very high data rate (256Mbps or 1Gbps) makes it compelling as a point-to-point, full-duplex, server-to-server connection. FiberChannel is essentially the SCSI protocol serialized over a pair of fibers.

The Network Monitor

The Network Monitor monitors data sent over the network. Data is sent through the network in frames or packets, each containing header information that identifies the protocols being used to send the frame, a destination address, a source address, and the data. Each package must contain a source and destination address to be delivered correctly.

Most people don't make a habit of opening packages not addressed to them. The network is the same way. By default, a network card will ignore any packet that is not addressed to its computer. On the other hand, network monitors really don't care to whom a packet is sent. They are able to capture all packets on the network.

Network monitors use a special mode, called *promiscuous mode*, that is supported by most modern network cards. Promiscuous mode allows the network adapter to capture all the data packets on the network. Special promiscuous mode drivers work by capturing the data of every packet, as opposed to capturing only packets that are addressed to the computer network card.

The Network Monitor that ships with Windows 2000 Server is not a fully functional network monitor. It is a limited version of the Network Monitor that ships with SMS. Instead of being able to capture all the network packets, this version of Network Monitor can capture only frames involving the server that it runs on, including

- Frames sent from the server
- Frames sent to the server
- Broadcast frames
- Multicast frames

Because the Network Monitor that ships with Windows 2000 Server is not fully functional and does not capture every network packet, the server's network card driver does not have to run in promiscuous mode. Network Monitor is able to use the network driver interface specification that your network card uses. The frames that are detected are then copied to the server's memory in a capture buffer. Using the NDIS standard instead of promiscuous mode reduces the CPU load by up to 30 percent.

In contrast, the Network Monitor that ships with the SMS product is able to capture all packets on the network, regardless of the source or destination computer address. The SMS server must use a promiscuous mode network driver.

Server Optimization

You may never have to deal with manual performance tuning, because Windows 2000 tunes itself very well for most users and most situations. Unlike many operating systems, you will not have to manually adjust arcane environment variables to improve Windows 2000 performance. Windows 2000 takes care of that for you. The tuning you will need to do to optimize Windows 2000 performance involves determining which hardware resources are under the greatest load and then relieving that load. Windows 2000 comes with some very powerful tools to assist you, but because of the self-tuning nature of Windows 2000, you may never have to use them.

Windows 2000 automatically provides the following optimizations:

- Multiprocessing to divide the load evenly amongst multiple processors
- Memory optimizations to expand the size of available RAM
- Caching disk requests to obviate disk access and increase I/O speed

These optimizations are discussed in the following sections.

Multiprocessing

Multiprocessing divides the processing load across several microprocessors. Windows 2000 uses *symmetric multiprocessing*, a technique in which the total processor load is divided evenly among processors. Simpler operating systems use *asymmetric multiprocessing*, which splits the processing load according to some criterion other than load. Usually, those operating systems put all system tasks on one processor and all user tasks on the remaining processors. Support for multiprocessing varies by product:

- Windows 2000 Professional ships with support for two processors.
- Windows 2000 Server ships with support for four processors.
- Windows 2000 Advanced Server ships with support for eight processors.
- Windows 2000 Datacenter Server ships with support for 32 processors.

Scheduling and resource assignment among processors takes computing time. Because of this load, two processors are not twice as fast as one. A Windows 2000 system with two processors generally runs at about 150 percent of the speed of a one-processor system, depending on the type of programs run. An application that has only one thread cannot be run on more than one processor.

In many computing problems, threads depend on results provided by other threads. This circumstance is like a relay race in which a runner (thread) must wait for the baton (results) before starting. Obviously, splitting these threads among processors doesn't make the application run any faster. Multiprocessing works best with large computing data sets that can be broken into chunks and solved independently of one another.

You can use multiprocessing to improve the performance of CPU-limited applications, such as Windows 2000 Terminal Services, which puts a heavy demand on terminal servers. Other applications (for example, databases) or Internet application servers can also soak up a lot of compute time. It is probable that you will have to upgrade your motherboard in order to add more processors. That's usually not a problem, because motherboards generally cost less than the processors you put in them.

One modern processor is more than enough for more mundane server operations (such as file and print services); these functions demand more from disk and network resources.

If you determine that your processor is the bottleneck, you will need to upgrade to a newer microprocessor or computer or upgrade to multiple processors. If you can't get a microprocessor that is twice as fast to work in your computer, don't bother upgrading the microprocessor. Upgrade the entire computer.

Memory Optimizations

Page swapping, while useful to at least keep a server running, is a good indicator that you should add memory. In fact, with RAM as cheap as it is these days, you should add enough memory to your servers so that they do not swap to disk under normal operating conditions. This will provide optimal memory performance.

The more memory you have, the less time the system spends on page swapping. Windows 2000 systems with less than 64MB of memory will spend a significant amount of time swapping pages to the virtual memory page file, especially if they are running more than one application at a time. This swapping activity slows the computer dramatically, because hard disks are very slow (but also very cheap) compared to physical RAM. Microsoft recommends at least 128MB for anything but the lightest loaded Windows 2000 Servers, and I recommend at least 256MB for any server handling more than 20 simultaneous connections of any sort. A server with 50 or more simultaneous users should have at least 512MB.

The faster page swapping happens, the lower its impact on system responsiveness. To speed this process, Windows 2000 supports simultaneous writing to more than one hard disk for its virtual memory paging file. Since physical drives can operate simultaneously, splitting the virtual memory swap file among different disks allows Windows 2000 to divide the time spent processing virtual memory swaps by the number of physical disks. You can use the System Control Panel applet to assign a portion of the page file to each disk in your server.

Windows 2000 allows you to split your swap file among volumes on the same physical disk, but there is no performance-related reason to do so. In fact, this configuration increases swap time by forcing the drive head to move much more than normal during swapping. You should set only one swap file per physical disk and avoid putting the page file in fault tolerance volumes, such as mirrored partitions or stripe sets with parity. You should also consider setting the initial and final sizes for the swap file to the same number (physical RAM plus 12MB unless you have a reason to do otherwise) to prevent your page file from becoming fragmented if Windows 2000 increases its size automatically.

Caching Disk Requests

Windows 2000 uses disk caching to reduce the amount of input/output traffic to the hard disk drive. Caching works by reserving a portion of memory as a staging area for hard disk reads and writes. When data is read from the disk, it is stored in the cache. If the same data needs to be read again, it is retrieved from the very fast memory cache, rather than from the slower disk.

Actually, disk read operations don't just bring in the data requested. Entire clusters are transferred from the hard disk to the memory cache, because read and write operations are most efficient at the cluster size. Consequently, a good portion of the data located on the hard disk immediately after the data that is requested also comes into the memory cache. Because read accesses tend to be sequential, the next read request is likely to be in the cache.

The disk cache is also used for write operations. The Windows 2000 file system (NTFS) doesn't write data to the hard disk immediately. It waits for system idle time so that it will not affect the responsiveness of the system. Data writes are stored in the memory cache until they are written to disk. Often, especially in transaction-oriented systems such as databases, new changes supersede data written in the cache even before it is written from the cache to the hard disk. Consequently, the write cache completely eliminates the need to write that data to the disk.

Data writes waiting in the cache can also be read back if they are subsequently requested, which allows yet another cache-related optimization. The type of caching used in Windows 2000 is called *write-back caching,* as opposed to *write-through caching,* which immediately writes data to the disk while preserving it in the cache for subsequent rereads. Write-through caching is used in operating systems that cannot otherwise guarantee the integrity of data on the disk if power is lost while data is in the cache waiting to be written to disk.

NOTE   The caching schemes used in hardware to make your microprocessor run faster operate on exactly the same cache theory as presented here.

Windows 2000 uses all the memory that remains free after the running processes have the memory they need as a disk cache. Windows 2000 dynamically changes the amount of memory assigned to the disk cache as new processes are started to ensure the optimal performance boost from caching. Windows 2000 balances the amount of disk cache and the amount of virtual memory page swapping to optimize the use of physical memory.

Performance Monitoring

The Windows 2000 Performance Console is an amazing tool that provides the ability to inspect the performance of just about every process and resource that occurs in your computer. The Performance Console allows you to determine the exact cause of every performance-related problem your computer experiences.

Performance and the Performance Console are broad topics. An entire book could be dedicated to the various features and the workflow theory used to discern where and why bottlenecks occur. Windows 2000 automatically makes most adjustments for you though, so for most tasks, that level of detail is not required to make your computer run well. So this section explains how the Performance Console works and tells you which indicators to watch in order to quickly narrow down performance problems. You cannot harm your system by experimenting with the Performance Console, so feel free to see the effect of the different low-level indicators.

Heisenberg's uncertainty principle states that to measure quantum phenomena is to change it. This principle is also true of performance monitoring. Running the System Monitor and Performance Logs and Alerts tools in the Performance Console takes a small amount of CPU time, and enabling disk monitoring also slows input/output requests slightly. Therefore, you cannot measure system performance without causing the performance to change slightly. In almost every case, this change in performance is slight and will have no undesirable effect on your measurements or the validity of your conclusions, but you should be aware that it is happening.

Object Counters

Each Windows 2000 software object is monitored by counters that increase incrementally each time that object performs a function. For example, each time a network device driver reads a packet, the device driver increases the packet's read counter by 1 and the byte's read counter by the size of the packet. Also, each time the processor switches threads, it updates the time spent in that thread in a counter used for that purpose.

Counters permeate all Windows 2000 objects, and they allow meaningful measurement to occur by accounting for everything that happens. Windows 2000 uses many of these counters to measure performance for its own automatic optimizations. Table 15.1 shows the low-level system objects that you can monitor with the Performance Console.

Table 15.1 Windows 2000 Object Counters

Object	Purpose
Cache	Microprocessor level 2 cache performance
Logical disk	Mass storage performance, including network storage

Troubleshooting and Optimization

PART 4

Table 15.1   Windows 2000 Object Counters *(continued)*

Object	Purpose
Memory	Memory performance and usage
Objects	Process and thread counts
Paging file	Virtual memory usage
Physical disk	Hard disk drive performance
Process	Executing process performance
Processor	Microprocessor performance
System	Windows 2000 performance
Thread	Individual thread performance

You will also see objects for each network service you have installed. Actually, any software can be written to register performance monitoring counters with the system, so you may see even more counters than are shown here.

Processor Performance

The microprocessor is generally the fastest component in a computer. In Pentium II class and higher computers, the microprocessor is rarely the cause of a bottleneck unless you are running scientific, mathematical, or graphical software that puts a heavy load on the floating-point unit of the microprocessor.

The following performance objects can be monitored to profile processor performance:

Processor ➤ % Processor Time   Shows the current utilization of the microprocessor(s). The microprocessor does not become a bottleneck until you see a sustained 80 percent or better level of utilization when watching the Processor ➤ % Processor Time counter in the System Monitor. If after tuning your computer to eliminate processor bottlenecks, it still runs in this zone, you need to upgrade to a faster (or just another) microprocessor. This counter shows how busy the microprocessor is. The processor will spike to 100 percent at times—this spike is normal and does not indicate a bottleneck. As long as the processor normally runs somewhere between 0 to 80 percent, your processor is sufficient for the workload. After adding this counter, let the computer idle for a moment. Then move your mouse around on the screen and notice the effect on the Processor ➤ % Processor Time measure. Dramatic, isn't it?

Processor ➤ Interrupts/Sec   Measures the rate of service requests from peripheral devices. An unusual amount of activity on this counter without a corresponding increase in activity in the computer indicates that a hardware component is malfunctioning and is sending spurious interrupts. This counter should operate continuously between 100 and 1,000, but spikes up to 2,000 are acceptable.

System ➤ Processor Queue Length   Counts the number of threads waiting for attention from the processor. Each thread requires a portion of microprocessor time. Many threads running simultaneously may exceed the supply of processor time, causing the microprocessor to become a bottleneck. A sustained thread queue that is greater than 2 indicates a processor bottleneck; too many threads are standing in line awaiting execution, which bogs down the processes that rely upon those threads.

Disk Performance

Disks affect computer speed more than any other component. Booting, application loading, storing and retrieving data, and virtual memory swapping performance are all tied to the speed of your disk, because disks are so much slower than the processor or memory. For these reasons, the speed of your disk(s) affects the overall speed of your computer.

Because disks affect so many aspects of your server's overall performance, increasing disk speed is by far the best optimization you can make to improve overall system performance. But to increase disk performance, you should add copious amounts of RAM. Unallocated memory in Windows 2000 systems is automatically used as a disk-cache by the operating system, so adding RAM to disk-bound systems can dramatically increase performance. Windows 2000 can make good use of all the RAM you give it, so if you hit a disk bottleneck, your easiest solution will be to add as much RAM as possible to see if that eliminates the problem before you migrate to a new disk subsystem.

As with all performance monitoring in Windows 2000 Server, you can use the disk monitor to profile your disk activity. However, your computer also comes with a performance indicator that works in any operating system: the hard disk drive light. If your disk light is on most of the time under normal working conditions, you need to add RAM to decrease paging. If paging is already not a problem, you need to move to RAID. If you've already got fast RAID in place, you need to split the function of this computer across two or more machines. You can't avoid these solutions, and all the performance monitoring on the planet isn't going to uncover a different answer.

Redundant Array of Independent Disks (RAID)

RAID works on the same theory as stripe sets. The difference is that a RAID controller replaces your regular SCSI controller and makes the striped volume look like one physical disk to Windows 2000. (See Chapter 3. "Storage and Fault Tolerance," for a discussion of *stripe volumes* and related technologies.)

RAID controllers include a microprocessor that handles breaking up and recombining the disk data so that the computer's microprocessor doesn't have to. Most RAID controllers also use some RAM as a cache to increase the speed of transfers to and from the controller. This cache works the same way as the Windows 2000 cache described in the earlier section, "Caching Disk Requests."

RAID controllers essentially perform the same service as stripe sets, but because they relieve the computing burden of stripe sets from the processor and add a memory cache dedicated to disk transfers, they can help relieve processor bottlenecks. Unfortunately, RAID controllers can be very expensive, so they are generally used only in servers.

A new breed of less expensive, processorless RAID-0 and RAID-1 controllers exists. These controllers are actually just hard disk controllers with BIOSes that implement a disk striping or mirroring function and come with drivers that support that striping or mirroring for Windows 2000. Because no computation is required for either of these functions, they are both fast and effective. RAID-0 controllers reduce fault tolerance because the failure of any single disk will cause the pack to fail, so make sure you have a strong backup policy in place or an online standby server to tolerate the higher likelihood of failure.

Physical versus Logical Disk Performance

Windows 2000 monitors two different disk objects: logical disk and physical disk. *Logical disk* measures the performance of volume which may span several physical disks. *Physical disk* measures individual disk performance. Both are important to the performance monitoring process.

The logical disk object can measure the performance of network connections that are mapped as drives and the performance of volume sets and stripe sets that cross physical disks. You will use the logical disk object to uncover bottlenecks initially and then move to the physical disk object to uncover the reasons why that bottleneck is occurring.

Physical disk measures only real transfers to and from actual hard disk drives or RAID sets. These measures isolate performance differences between disks in your system and provide detailed information about the specific performance of a certain disk.

Disk counters cause measurable performance degradation by distracting the processor at critical input/output periods. Logical disk counters are disabled by default; physical disk counters are enabled. If you attempt to monitor physical or logical disk performance without enabling the appropriate counters, you will not see any disk data. When you have finished monitoring disk performance, remember to disable the disk performance monitors. Leaving them enabled serves no purpose and slows your machine down.

To enable or disable disk performance counters, use the `diskperf.exe` command prompt tool with the following options:

-y	Start both physical and logical performance counters.
-yd	Enable physical disk performance counters.
-yv	Enable logical disk performance counters.
-n	Disable all disk performance counters.
-nd	Disable physical disk performance counters.
-nv	Disable logical disk performance counters.

Monitoring Disk Performance

In Windows NT 4, you had to enable physical disk performance counters using the `diskperf.exe` command-line utility. In Windows 2000, disk performance is enabled by default. The following are important counters you'll want to watch:

Memory ➤ Pages/Sec   Indicates how many page swaps are written to the disk. Leave this counter showing in the Performance Monitor while watching the % Disk Time to see how dramatically page file performance affects your overall performance.

Logical Disk (or Physical Disk) % Disk Time   Shows how much processor time is spent servicing disk requests. It is a good broad indicator for determining whether your hard disk drive is a bottleneck during activities when you would not normally expect to wait for your hard disk drive. Note that this counter is a processor metric, not a physical disk metric. Measure this counter against Processor ➤ % Processor Time to see if disk requests are eating up all your processor time.

Logical Disk (or Physical Disk) Disk Bytes per Second   Shows how fast your hard disks are transferring data. Turn this counter on and then copy a large directory of files between disks to get a good baseline of the speed at which your disk or disks run.

Logical Disk (or Physical Disk) Average Disk Bytes per Transfer   Shows the size of the average transfer. Average transfers that are larger make more efficient use of disk hardware and execute faster; smaller transfers cause the computer to work too hard to write them to disk.

Current Disk Queue Length   Shows how much data is waiting to be transferred to the disk. Many processes must wait for disk requests to be serviced before they can continue. A long disk queue indicates that many processes are being delayed by disk speed.

When you interpret performance data, keep the following information in mind. Pages/Sec should be consistently less than 20, or excessive paging is taking place, and you need to add RAM. All counters that have the word *Queue* in them have an acceptable threshold value of 2 or less.

You need to upgrade your processor (or add another one) under the following circumstances:

- Processor ➤ % Processor Time exceeds 75 percent.
- System ➤ Processor Queue Length exceeds 2.

You need to add RAM under the following circumstances:

- Memory ➤ Pages/Sec exceeds 20.
- Memory ➤ Available Bytes is less than 4MB.
- Memory ➤ Committed Bytes exceeds physical RAM.

You need to upgrade your disk subsystem under the following circumstances:

- Physical Disk ➤ % Disk Time exceeds 50 percent.
- Physical Disk ➤ Disk Queue Length exceeds 2 continuously.

Summary

In my networking practice, I've found the following optimizations to be the most useful. They're specific in nature, but they solve a wide variety of problems and are fairly easy to implement.

Buy and use dual processor servers.   Although a second processor only improves CPU performance by about 50 percent, it guarantees that no single thread can utilize 100 percent of your available computing power. This will make any heavily loaded server more responsive.

Use RAID-1 mirroring for the system disks of every server, unless you're already using RAID-5.   Mirroring not only provides fault tolerance for your system volume, it doubles the read rate, cutting boot and access time nearly in half.

Upgrade your servers to the latest processor technology.   Because you can upgrade processors, motherboards, and RAM without many hassles, you should stay in the habit of upgrading your servers about once every two years.

Add RAM to your servers.   256MB of RAM is common for servers these days. The more memory your servers have, the faster they'll respond on your network.

Use 10K-RPM hard disk drives, the vast majority of which are SCSI.   These disks transfer data at a real rate of 25 to 50 percent faster than 7200RPM and 5400RPM drives. Most servers are disk limited, so use the fastest possible hard disk drives.

Use SCSI hard disk drives.   SCSI hard disks are capable of optimizing disk requests to handle those near the drive head before those that are far away, thus eliminating many seeks across the surface of the disk. IDE disks—even UltraDMA100 disks—are designed for single-user desktop computers. They handle all requests in order, thus slowing over-all access speed on the same speed of disk by half on heavily loaded servers.

Add servers.   You should probably have one multipurpose server for each group of approximately 25 to 50 clients depending on how much traffic your users generate. That server should be the location of the user's home and profile directories, the domain controller from which they log in on, the router between them and the rest of the network, and a proxy for Web and intranet sites. If this means you would have a large number of servers, just treat them as a higher-level client—make them all the same and use workstation rollout techniques to manage them.

Use Gigabit Ethernet on your backbone.   A single 100MB network connection for a modern server is okay for file servers, but is usually a bottleneck for application servers. Use Gigabit Ethernet for the central database, the Web, and the domain con-trollers on your backbone. Connect your backbone to multihomed workgroup serv-ers with a gigabit adapter up to the backbone and Fast Ethernet out to a maximum of four workgroups per server.

Upgrade your network to Fast Ethernet.   If you don't have Category 5 cabling installed, either install Category 5 wiring or use 100Base-T4 to operate over Category 3 or 4 wiring.

Migrate from a switched Ethernet architecture to a routed TCP/IP architecture.

Routing gives you a lot more flexibility once you take the time to implement it. You can create multiple data paths to support redundancy in the face of failure, too.

Switch from diskless workstations to policy-controlled normal workstations.

This will allow you to remove the operating system and application load from your network and put it where it belongs—in the computer. Don't use centrally stored applications either—it's a waste of bandwidth. Remember the ideal: push data out as close as you can to its ultimate point of use.

Spend money on servers rather than clients.   Clients don't need voluminous hard disks; they only need enough to load the operating system and applications—approximately 2 GB these days, which is what Windows 2000 Professional requires. Clients rarely need top-of-the-line processors or a lot of RAM. Any Pentium MMX with 64MB of RAM is sufficient for running office applications. Put your budget money into server RAM and hardware RAID for servers instead. You'll be ahead with both money and performance.

Troubleshooting and Optimization

PART 4

Case Study: Compute Bound Problems

A customer of mine used a Windows 2000 Professional workstation to run heat-stress analysis on modeled components using a technique called *finite state analysis*. The process involved designing three-dimensional software models of their product and then running an application designed to perform the analysis on the models. Using a Pentium-II 450MHz computer with 128MB RAM and a 12GB UltraDMA IDE hard disk, a single analysis took about 10 hours. This, unfortunately, meant they could run only a single analysis per day without investing a significant amount of money in additional software.

They asked me to determine how they could use their existing resources to perform more analyses. The scientist performing the analysis was considering installing a RAID array in the machine to improve its performance.

Using the Task Manager for a quick look at processor load and RAM usage, I determined that their software put a 100-percent CPU load on the microprocessor and allocated the entire amount of remaining physical RAM in the computer (but not virtual memory, which it seemed to avoid using). About five hours into the process, the hard disk would begin heavy activity for quite some time.

These numbers basically meant that the problem was bound by the speed of the processor. The heavy disk activity was likely the result of the process writing out its first batch of results to free up memory for the next batch.

They were already using the fastest processor available at reasonable cost (they didn't have a Pentium III machine yet, but at that time they were expensive and weren't significantly faster anyway), so they had nowhere to go for raw speed improvement, but they could add more processors to the computer. Using the System Monitor, I determined that their software ran in just a single thread. The heat-stress analysis software was not multithreaded, so it would not be able to make effective use of another processor.

Because of these problems, it seemed that there was nothing they could do to improve computing performance: the software was limited to using a single processor, and they already had the fastest processor available.

So I looked next at disk-swapping. Obviously, the analysis my customer wanted to solve didn't fit entirely into memory, because the software would begin writing results out to disk before it had finished. This meant that if I could eliminate disk writing, I might be able to speed the analysis.

I borrowed a 128MB DIMM from a sister machine, installed it in the analysis machine, and ran the analysis again. This time, the analysis completed in half the time! The program was designed to use as much physical memory as was available before it began swapping to disk, so by doubling the amount of RAM in the machine, I was able to forestall the slower disk process. Further increasing the amount of RAM in the computer lowered the analysis time even more, so they are now able to perform many times more analyses per day, even though they couldn't increase the processor speed.

16

Troubleshooting Theory

Networks are incredibly complex. Network software is even more complex than network hardware and computers, and network operating systems are the most sophisticated pieces of software that programmers can create. Making such complex and sophisticated things foolproof is virtually impossible, so although Windows 2000 is as robust as any operating system you will encounter, you will occasionally need to fix problems with your servers. Often, network problems can seem like server problems, so you need to develop the skills to quickly determine what components are likely to be at fault whenever a fault condition occurs.

Troubleshooting is a skill like any other. You can apply certain general principles to any troubleshooting situation, but you must know how the specific system you are troubleshooting works if you want to be able to diagnose faults. As with any other skill, you get better at troubleshooting with practice.

This chapter introduces you to some general computer troubleshooting principles and then shows you how to troubleshoot computer hardware, Windows 2000 operating system software, and network connections. The next chapter, "Practical Troubleshooting," applies the principles you learn in this chapter by teaching you the most common problems. Through practice, you'll be able find and fix the myriad of glitches that will arise day to day.

The Troubleshooting Process

Troubleshooting is the methodical process of eliminating faults from a system. Although troubleshooting a computer is difficult, you can quickly isolate the culprit by following a few basic rules that focus your troubleshooting efforts on the components most likely at fault.

Troubleshooting a network involves the following fundamental steps:

1. Determine the component that is most likely at fault.

2. Change the hardware or software configuration of the suspect component.

3. Test to see whether the configuration change has eliminated the problem.

If a hardware failure caused the fault, you will have to replace (or repair, but that's rare these days) the failed component. If a software configuration caused the fault, you will have to reconfigure your system to eliminate the fault. In some cases, you may not be able to reconfigure your system, because the configuration problem involves the denial of some service that is required to reconfigure the faulty component. If you run into this catch-22, you may have to reinstall the operating system on the server or client that is faulty.

> **NOTE** Working on electronic devices, including computers, can be dangerous. You should only attempt to troubleshoot a computer if you are very familiar with electrical safety, electronic equipment, and computer hardware.

Focus is important in troubleshooting. Making random changes in a system, just hoping something will work, is a good way to waste a lot of time and to create more problems, especially with untracked changes. Focus on a specific component, and test it thoroughly. If you are not able to correct the fault, restore the original configuration before moving on to another component.

Troubleshooting is relatively easy when you are dealing with only one fault, as is generally the case with a hardware failure. Software failures, however, are usually a lot more complicated. You may be faced with a situation in which two or more simultaneous problems are causing a fault. Correcting only one fault at a time will change the symptoms but will not correct the problem. For example, suppose your modem doesn't work. You have a hardware conflict because your modem is set to the same IRQ as your LAN adapter, which caused your modem software to automatically detect the wrong modem. You will have two problems (a hardware setting and a software configuration) to fix before you can operate your modem. Correcting one or the other problem will not allow you to use your modem.

> **TIP** Rotating between symptoms indicates that there is more than one problem.

Troubleshooting is either quick and easy—as in the case of a simple failure when you are pretty certain what is wrong—or long and complex—for example, when you return to work to find a computer that went down during the night and refuses to reboot. Often you will come upon more than one fault; each fault has to be resolved to progress to the next fault. This sequence is the natural cycle of troubleshooting.

TIP   Partial success usually indicates a complex failure involving two or more faults.

The rest of this section covers the general principles of troubleshooting that apply to any system. Following these guidelines will help you quickly determine what is at fault in your system. However, no book or set of rules will really help you find a problem unless you understand the system you are troubleshooting.

Windows 2000 software has been thoroughly debugged by Microsoft. However, bugs exist in all nontrivial software, especially in the less frequently used areas. Nonetheless, Windows 2000 runs, and it runs well. All of its services operate properly. If you have a persistent problem with a Windows 2000 machine, it is likely caused by less-than-compatible hardware or improperly configured software.

TIP   Bugs are most likely to exist in rarely executed code.

Windows 2000 is very specific about which hardware it will work with. Early in Windows 2000's design cycle, Microsoft chose not to support all hardware devices that can be added to a PC because of the security holes DOS-mode drivers allow—and because Microsoft could not possibly write drivers for all the PC-compatible hardware that exists. If you are having a problem with a new Windows 2000 installation, chances are good that you are using hardware that does not appear on the Windows 2000 Hardware Compatibility List (HCL).

TIP   Bugs are more likely the fault of a third-party driver than of Windows 2000 standard components. Consider these drivers as primary suspects when troubleshooting.

A Needle in the OSI Stack

Complex systems, such as computers, operating systems, and networks, are designed and constructed in layers. In a layered system, simpler constructions provide a foundation upon which more complex constructions can rely. Layers of these interdependent

Troubleshooting and Optimization

PART 4

constructions provide, at their top, the amazingly complex functionality that you experience when you use the system.

Layers arise in system design partly because it's too difficult to create the ultimate functionality of the system from scratch and partly because systems evolve over time. As a system is used, new functionality becomes available, which is layered atop the existing functionality, to provide new utility.

Imagine trying to conceive of and implement Windows 2000 as a single unified program. Such a task would be far too difficult for even a software giant like Microsoft to accomplish, and the resulting program would be practically unmodifiable. It would take far longer to implement and would be impossible to add new functionality to it without rewriting it.

Monolithic (nonlayered) system design is part of the reason NetWare's functionality lags so far behind Windows 2000 and UNIX, why far less third-party software is available for the operating system, and why Windows NT/2000 has nearly completely supplanted Novell in the network operating system market.

Novell takes far longer to release significant operating system upgrades than their competition. Novell designed the original version of NetWare as a single program and has basically rewritten every significant upgrade from scratch rather than building upon an existing platform. NetWare 2.*x* was scrapped and rewritten for 3.*x*, which was basically rewritten for 4.*x*, which represented Novell's first attempt at layered design.

Windows 2000, on the other hand, has merely evolved from the original Windows NT 3.1 source code. Windows NT 3.5 was an evolution of Windows NT 3.1. It fixed a number of bugs, changed the functionality of some basic components, and added TCP/IP support. Windows NT 3.51 fixed more bugs, added more comprehensive TCP/IP support, and extended file system features. Windows NT 4.0 added the user interface from Windows 95, and Windows 2000 merged usability components like Plug and Play (for example, USB), better PC-card support, as well as enterprise network features such as Active Directory. The layered design philosophy on which Windows 2000 is based is why Microsoft's operating system is far more nimble.

Figure 16.1 shows the architectural differences between Windows 2000 and NetWare. While NetWare can be divided into layers, the layering is abstract, and the functionality is truly contained within a single large application. In Windows, each layer represents independent drivers that can be replaced or changed at any time with software developed by third parties.

Figure 16.1   Windows 2000 is a kernel-based layered operating system, whereas NetWare is a monolithic operating system with a few modular components.

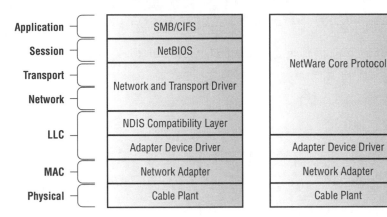

The price for layered design is speed and efficiency. NetWare remains faster than Windows 2000 for basic services (such as file and print), because service requests don't have to "drill down" through layers of APIs and through security checks. On the other hand, NetWare is far less secure and lacks support for many less common services (USB, for example) because they're more difficult to develop since the operating system doesn't provide a standard interface for layered drivers and services.

Design layers make troubleshooting far easier because you can start the troubleshooting process at the bottom layer of the system and work up to the top. By validating the proper operation of each layer, you eliminate numerous components that could be at fault.

When you troubleshoot, start at the bottom layer and verify that the symptoms of correct operation occur. Because of the complexity of these systems and the fact that many elements of a layer may be tolerant of faults, a faulty component in a layer may not be obvious if the layer seems to operate correctly. These sorts of problems require more rigorous testing but can still be approached on a layer-by-layer basis.

> **NOTE** Advanced troubleshooters can use a "binary search" troubleshooting method where you start at the middle layer and then go down or up the layers depending upon where your testing takes you. This cuts the search time down dramatically, but you have to be completely familiar with all the layers before you can use this methodology.

Troubleshooting and Optimization

PART 4

Computer Hardware Layers

Computer hardware can be divided into layers for troubleshooting purposes. Figure 16.2 shows a dependency diagram for modern PC computers.

Figure 16.2 For a computer component to function, all the components below it in the diagram must be functioning correctly.

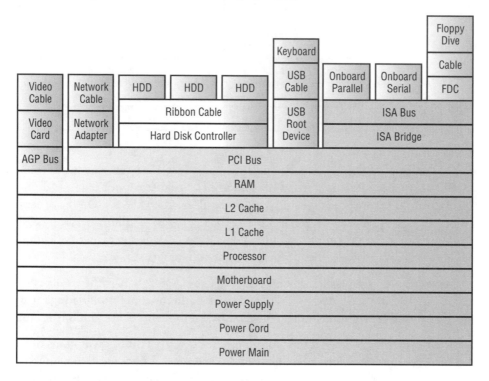

Processor, motherboard, video Must operate correctly for the computer to turn on. Note that many server BIOSes no longer require video adapters to start for systems such as UNIX that can be completely managed from a serial terminal.

RAM, caches Must operate correctly for the computer to execute software.

Hard disk controller Must operate correctly to load software.

Hard disk drive(s) Must operate correctly to reliably store and retrieve software and data.

Peripheral hardware Must be in place to provide the peripheral service, such as attachment to the network, printing, or access to CD-ROMs. This is the first layer that is not necessary for the computer to boot correctly, and the last troubleshooting layer. If the computer boots correctly, your hardware failure is most likely in this layer.

Computer Boot Phases

Understanding the computer boot process can dramatically simplify troubleshooting. Computers boot in the following phases:

POST   The power on self-test must correctly complete before the computer will relinquish control to the BIOS. The POST tests for the presence of memory, a video adapter, a keyboard, and other components the BIOS will need in order to start.

Computer BIOS   The Basic Input/Output System must be in place to identify and load the operating system from a mass storage device. The BIOS is also responsible for enumerating Plug and Play and PCI devices, assigning resources to Plug and Play–compliant hardware for the initial boot, and for providing an interface for selecting the boot device. The final act of the computer BIOS is to identify the booting hard disk controller (which is by default the hard disk controller with the lowest IRQ level or the controller specified in the BIOS). Modern BIOSes allow you to specify other devices, such as CD-ROM, from which to boot.

Hard disk controller BIOS   The hard disk controller BIOS enables the hard disk controller to load the master boot record and to provide an interface to allow the loading of sectors until a more appropriate driver can be loaded by the operating system. The hard disk controller BIOS is physically located on the hard disk controller and is specific to each model. Motherboards which have embedded hard disk controllers combine the hard disk BIOS with the computer BIOS. Technically, any device may have a boot BIOS. For example, network adapters may be equipped with a "Boot PROM" containing a BIOS that can provide a network identity (an IP or other network layer address) and load a boot image from a remote-boot server.

Master boot record   In the Microsoft/IBM partitioning schema, the master boot record is the first stage boot loader. It loads a table of partitions and then reads the boot sector for the partition marked active and executes it. Many operating systems don't comply with this specification and simply boot the operating system directly from the master boot record sector. Windows 2000 with Basic partitioning complies with this specification; Windows 2000 with Dynamic partitioning does not and does not allow booting multiple operating systems from the same disk.

Boot sector   The bootstrap routing must load and execute properly to bring the operating system in from disk. Boot sectors are specific to the particular operating system being loaded. Bootstrap routines load either the operating system kernel and (at least) the hard disk controller device drivers into memory or a third-stage boot loader.

Boot loader   In Windows 2000, the boot sector loads the NTLDR boot loader, which examines the computer's hardware environment, sets some environmental variables for the NT kernel, and then loads the kernel and the kernel mode device drivers. The final act of the boot loader is to start the kernel, and the screen turns from black to blue. In Linux, LILO is the boot loader. In Windows 98, MS-DOS 7 is the boot loader.

Kernel load   The operating system must operate to provide its services. If there are problems with the kernel load phase in Windows 2000, the computer will *blue-screen* (crash and display debugging information).

Drivers load   Most peripheral components require drivers, whether those drivers are built into the system or provided separately. During the drivers load phase, problems with drivers will be noted in the Event Log if the problem is not critical to the boot process. If the computer depends upon the driver to boot, the computer will blue-screen.

Services load   Executable files that provide wide-ranging operating system services and act as part of the system load next. Problems with services are noted in the Event Log. Services are never critical to the boot process, but certain exceptions will cause blue-screen crashes during the boot process because the computer's state becomes too corrupted to continue loading normally.

User interface start   Once system files are loaded, connections from the local console and/or the network can be made to establish user sessions. At this point in Windows 2000, the WinLogon process is called to allow the local user to log on to the computer, and the NetLogon service begins providing networked users the ability to log in.

Failure usually occurs in the startup phase of the failed component. For example, if your system crashes during the services load phase, a service has failed. The service may fail because it or the data upon which it relies is damaged, or because a previously loaded component has failed, but the failure was not critical until a dependent service started.

Network Layers

Network connectivity can be divided into the following layers (in this order) for troubleshooting (see Figure 16.3):

Physical layer   The cable infrastructure must be able to transport data reliably for communication to exist. Test the physical layer with cable test devices. Wireless devices can be fiendishly difficult to test at the physical layer; usually, testing them at extremely close range is all you can do to validate the physical layer. The test equipment required to validate the physical layer of a wireless device is generally too expensive.

Data link   The network interfaces, hubs, repeaters, and bridges must be functioning correctly for data to be transmitted between machines. Test data-link layer equipment by passing information between known-good machines or by using data-link layer echo test software provided by the network interface manufacturer. Manufacturers such as 3Com and Intel provide data-link layer test software with their network interface adapters.

Network protocol   The transport protocol software on the end-systems and routing, gating, and firewalling functions of intermediate systems must be functional and correctly configured for reliable communication to occur. Test the network and data-link layers using the IP Ping utility and other IP network utilities such as ARP and ipconfig.

Session management   The operating system's session establishment, logon, and higher-level transportation software must be operational and configured correctly for network services to operate. If the network layer is functioning correctly, session layer (and above) problems occur for one of only six reasons.

- The session layer service or a host service upon which the service depends is not installed. (Install the service to correct this problem.)

- The service is not bound to the network adapter to which the attaching host is connected. (Correct the binding.)

- The service files are corrupted or are the wrong version. (Reapplying the service pack will fix this problem.)

- The Registry settings for the service are corrupted. (Un-install and reinstall the service to fix this problem. Some services may require an operating system reinstall.)

- The service is performing correctly but is denying service to the account because of a permissions problem. (Log on as an administrator to test this, and correct permissions for the requisite account to correct the problem.)

- The service cannot be reached from a client because another network service (such as name resolution, routing, or proxy services) is misconfigured.

Figure 16.3   The troubleshooting process begins at the bottom layer of the network and proceeds up to the top.

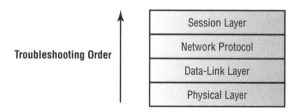

In the remaining portions of this section, I discuss these troubleshooting layers in detail.

New Networks

New networks can create a number of troubleshooting problems: bad routing tables abound, cabling may not be completely tested or working, bad connectors can prevent links from working, and even power sources can be problematic.

Troubleshoot network problems from the physical layer up. Always insist on a full cable test report for newly installed cable, including a Category 5 network scan. Don't let a cabling contractor tell you that cable scans aren't necessary, or they already did a continuity test. Full 100MHz cable scans with a wire map showing that all pairs are properly wired for UTP will keep you from wasting days of your time troubleshooting intermittent network failures. For optical fiber, insist on OTDR traces showing 3dB or less of insertion loss. Be suspicious of any spikes or drop-outs in the trace that can't be explained. Insist on cable scans.

Test workgroup and enterprise hubs and switches as you bring them online one at a time. Don't wait until you've got an entire network set up before you start testing end-to-end connectivity, because any malfunctioning component can make the entire system seem bad. Use laptops to test as you install.

Routing can be a real bear, especially in new networks. Make sure you understand TCP/IP routing before you start installing equipment, and make a complete network map on paper showing how everything connects together along with assigned network numbers, subnet masks, and gateways. Build your routing tables for each device on paper before bringing them online. Use a routing protocol such as RIP or OSPF (at least) to allow routers to determine optimal routes automatically.

Once you have your network equipment online, perform end-to-end throughput testing using laptops before you put servers in. Be sure you know your network is operating before you complicate your troubleshooting problem with additional hardware.

New Computers

Brand-new computers from any major manufacturer will work correctly with Windows 2000—right out of the box. If you have serious problems installing Windows 2000 on a new computer, you should suspect a hardware failure, because all new computers are designed to work smoothly with Windows 2000.

There is one exception to this rule: computers that you specify the components of or build yourself. You may find you have considerably more trouble installing Windows 2000 on these machines. At fault is usually the disk controller technology—some RAID and SCSI controllers can be very difficult to work with under Windows 2000 even when they come with drivers.

If you are building a computer from scratch, save yourself a lot of time by getting it working correctly under MS-DOS or Windows 95 before trying to install Windows 2000. Better yet, save yourself even more time by buying a complete computer with Windows 2000 factory-installed. If you can't buy Windows 2000 preinstalled, check the Microsoft Web site (`www.microsoft.com/windows2000/upgrade/compat`) for computers listed on the Windows 2000 Hardware Compatibility List. Microsoft has certified that these computers will run Windows 2000 properly.

If you are determined to build your own computer, study the Windows 2000 Knowledge Base on the Microsoft Web site so you can avoid buying hardware that is known to cause problems under Windows 2000. Pay special attention to the specific types of SCSI adapter and motherboard you purchase. The HCL is also included on the Windows 2000 installation CD-ROM.

WARNING Avoid SCSI controllers that are embedded on the motherboard, because they frequently require drivers that only the motherboard manufacturer can provide, which are not as well tested than the generic drivers provided by the OEM for its controller boards.

New Windows 2000 Installations

Windows 2000 is exceptionally easy to install. Most new computers, even those you build, will be able to install Windows 2000 without any issues at all. If you have problems with a device on a fresh install, you should seriously consider replacing the device, because you'll continue to have problems with it any time you decide to upgrade or reinstall the operating system.

Be certain that you don't have any interrupt, DMA channel, or memory port conflicts before attempting a Windows 2000 installation. This is easily accomplished by specifying only PCI components for new computers (because Windows 2000 permits resource sharing for PCI devices), unless you absolutely must have an ISA board installed. PCI devices are automatically Plug and Play–compliant, and (except in rare cases where two devices demand overlapping resources) Windows 2000 will be able to automatically assign resources that do not conflict.

If you have a hardware conflict, turn on PCI Plug and Play compatibility if it is allowed in your BIOS and force an ESCD update in the BIOS to reassign interrupts. This can be performed manually by moving a PCI device from one slot to another. Remove all hardware that is not necessary for the operation of the computer, such as modems, sound cards, and (if possible) your network adapter. This step reduces possible sources of conflict when you install Windows 2000. Once the operating system is running, you can add these components one at a time to be certain they are configured correctly.

If you are using SCSI devices, be aware that many common SCSI adapters have compatibility issues running under Windows 2000. Check the Windows 2000 Knowledge Base using the search key "SCSI Adapters" for a rundown of the compatibility issues of certain controllers. Also, with some SCSI controllers, the Windows 2000 loader can have a hard time finding your boot drive if you have an active IDE bus and SCSI devices set on ID 0.

Axioms of Troubleshooting

Finding the component at fault is the primary purpose of troubleshooting. Once you know exactly what is wrong, fixing the problem is usually trivial. Following is a list of axioms for general troubleshooting that will help you quickly isolate and repair hardware and software faults in Windows 2000 (or any other system):

- Be patient.
- Know the system.
- Isolate the fault.
- Check the most recent change.
- Check the most common failure point.
- Check things that have failed before.
- Perform easy tests first.
- Make assumptions to guide your troubleshooting.
- Use what you know.
- Change only one setting at a time.
- Track the changes you make.
- Try to make transient failures repeatable.
- Try to isolate individual faults in multiple fault malfunctions.
- Resort to permanent changes last.

Be Patient

Patience is not just a virtue when troubleshooting, it's an absolute necessity. When you are under time pressure to get a system working, you are better off using another computer to fix the problem, if possible. If you can't, you will just have to forget about your deadline because rushing through the troubleshooting process usually doesn't work. You will save yourself more time in the long run by taking your time to troubleshoot than by frustrating yourself with rushed efforts that don't work and may introduce additional faults. Most troubleshooting efforts will take hours.

Know the System

You can't troubleshoot unless you know your system. Troubleshooting is the process of diagnosing symptoms, postulating causes of the failure, and testing your hunch by making configuration changes. If you don't understand the symptoms you see, the rest of the troubleshooting process breaks down, and you will be unable to make a reasonable diagnosis.

If you are reading this chapter first because you have a Windows 2000 computer that isn't working, you should turn back to page one and start reading there. The knowledge you gain about the inner workings of Windows 2000 from the rest of this book will help you diagnose your problem.

Isolate the Fault

The fastest way to determine fault in a malfunctioning computer is to remove what you know is working from the list of suspect components. Narrowing your search will help you focus on components that could be at fault and keep you from making changes in other working portions of the system. For example, if you can reliably see information on the screen, most of the hardware in your computer is working properly. You can eliminate the processor, motherboard, RAM, video card, and monitor from your list of suspect components.

In many cases, you will be able to isolate a component quickly by validating many components at a time. For example, a computer that boots completely probably does not have any failed hardware components.

Check the Most Recent Change

If you've just changed something and your computer no longer works properly, it doesn't take a rocket scientist to figure out that the most recent change caused the problem (or exacerbated an existing, unexpressed problem). This logic would normally go without saying, but when a malfunctioning computer frustrates you, it's easy to forget.

In addition, a fault might not show up immediately, and you may have to think about what you changed last. Or someone else might have changed something on the computer that you are not aware of.

Often users accidentally break something when they try to make a change to their system and then pretend not to know what is wrong to avoid embarrassment or liability. You should try to foster an environment where users will not be afraid to come clean with this information, because ultimately it will cost you a lot more time to try to get to the bottom of a fault if you don't know about recent changes.

Here are some suggestions to facilitate troubleshooting in a corporate environment:

- Implement security on workstations to prevent users from being able to configure a system incorrectly.

- Try to change policies that hold your co-workers liable in some way for accidental damage to a computer, or they will never help you troubleshoot anything.

- Make sure your clients understand that your ability to work quickly will save them money.

I frequently run into cases where rebooting a server causes some function to fail. Administrators who have manually started an executable rather than configuring the computer to start the executable during the boot process cause this problem. This is most common with software such as MAS-90 or Lotus Notes that operates as a service but isn't written to the services specification, so it has to be started manually. Windows 2000 allows administrators to specify executables they want to run as services. Use this feature to make sure that every service your servers provide starts automatically without human intervention when the computer boots.

Check the Most Common Failure Point

This is another rather obvious point, but it is an important axiom of troubleshooting. Hard disks have become very reliable lately, but they are still the third-most-likely-to-fail component in a computer, after the monitor and the floppy disk drive. Unlike monitors and floppy disk drives, a crashed hard disk will quite probably make your computer useless. Hard disks are also complicated enough that the failure might not be obvious. Hard disk faults can also be a software problem that looks like a hardware problem.

Connectors and cables are also common failure points. Cables inside computers can become loose if a computer is moved or subject to vibration. PCI bus card edge connectors are very sensitive to movement compared to ISA bus cards, and single inline memory modules can also come loose easily. Check all these components when you have a mysterious hardware failure that keeps your computer from booting.

Peripherals that rely on jumpers for option settings are susceptible to loose jumpers. Check to make sure no jumpers are missing and that they are firmly seated in their correct positions if you suspect a component is faulty.

Check Things That Have Failed Before

If you have a component that has failed or disconnected in the past, chances are that it will do so again. If you are experiencing the same sort of failure symptoms as you have in the past, the first thing to check is the component that failed before.

If you find that a recently replaced component has failed again, some other component may be causing that component to fail.

Perform Easy Tests First

If you don't have any idea what might be wrong, you should start by checking components that are easy to test. This process is most easily accomplished if you have a computer that you know is working and is configured similarly. You can swap easily removable components between the two computers to see if the fault moves with the component.

> ***TIP*** Check BIOS settings if you have a problem with any hardware embedded on the motherboard.

Quick software reconfigurations should be performed before more lengthy or sweeping changes (for example, reinstalling the operating system or swapping out a hard disk).

Make Assumptions to Lead Your Troubleshooting

When troubleshooting, you will refine or redefine your initial diagnosis as you work. This diagnosis will lead in the direction of failed components. For instance, if your computer boots but does not come up on the network, you can assume one of the following:

- The network software is configured incorrectly.
- Another piece of hardware conflicts with that network adapter.
- Another computer has a conflicting IP address or computer name.
- The network adapter has failed.
- The network adapter cannot reach the network because of a cable fault.
- A network service like routing or name resolution is improperly configured.
- The server is down and not responding.

You can test each of these hypotheses to determine the true cause of the problem.

Use What You Know

You might know the events that precipitated a failure without realizing it. For example, in the network scenario previously described, you can use your knowledge of the computer's environment to guide your troubleshooting.

For example, if the computer used to work fine on the LAN but stopped networking after a new sound card was installed, the LAN adapter and the sound card are conflicting. If the computer stopped networking after a recent remodel, there's a good chance that a cable was broken or unplugged during the construction. Or if a network administrator has been reading this book and playing with the Registry, there's a chance the networking software is no longer configured correctly for your network.

Change Only One Setting at a Time

This axiom is very important. Often, especially with software configuration troubleshooting, you are tempted to try something, see if it works, try something else, and see if that works. Unfortunately, this haphazard process causes you to unwittingly change configuration information that may, in turn, produce another fault. You can easily fix the original fault but introduce another without even realizing it.

Each time you make a change, restore the original settings if the change didn't correct your problem—*before* continuing on to your next test.

When you make changes to the Registry directly, export the keys you're changing before you change them. If your changes fail to correct the problem, import the original settings to restore the original configuration. If you make changes to a configuration file, copy the file with a new name before you make any changes. To restore your changes, delete the file you modified and rename the copy of the original back to its original name.

> **WARNING**   Be aware that a file may not have the same permissions as its parent directory. When you make a copy, the copy will inherit the permissions of the parent directory, which could possibly be different than the original file. If you then delete the original and rename the copy, you will have changed the permissions settings for the file. Use the CACLS program to make sure the original and the copy have the same permissions before you modify anything.

Track the Changes You Make

Write down each change you make. You need a way to keep track of the multiple changes you implement simultaneously in an effort to solve a complex problem. A change log also allows you to update the computer configuration report you keep on all your computers. Table 16.1 shows a sample change log for a troubleshooting session.

Table 16.1   A Sample Change Log

Time	Setting	Initial State	Change to	Effect
9/1/00 11:21	USB flash reader driver	None	Installed	Computer crashes on boot.
9/1/00 11:30	USB flash reader driver startup type	Automatic	Disabled	Computer stable.

Table 16.1   A Sample Change Log *(continued)*

Time	Setting	Initial State	Change to	Effect
9/1/00 11:40	USB flash reader driver	Installed	Removed	Computer stable, flash reader nonfunctional.
9/7/00 15:30	Updated flash reader driver	None	Installed	Computer stable.

Try to Make Transient Failures Repeatable

Transient failures indicate either an environmental variable failure (such as a loose connection) or conflicting software that causes the faulty condition when in certain states.

If you suspect an environmental fault, try to exacerbate the condition to make the fault stable. If you suspect a software fault, try stopping services and unloading running applications until the fault disappears. Then begin restarting services until you can get the fault to reappear.

Try to Isolate Individual Faults in Multiple Fault Malfunctions

Unusual symptoms (those you don't see in this chapter) usually occur because more than one fault is present. To get a computer up in a multiple-fault malfunction, you may have to correct each fault simultaneously if the faulty components are dependent upon one another. This makes troubleshooting exponentially more difficult. If you can isolate a fault by removing a hardware component or stopping a software service that allows you to determine one of the factors in the malfunction, you will be able to concentrate on that factor until it works correctly.

If you cannot isolate an individual fault in a multiple fault situation, you should start with the basic troubleshooting procedures of validating the proper performance of your hardware and then reducing the complexity of your software by stopping unnecessary services and unloading running software. This reduces the complexity of the environment and narrows down the list of suspect components. When you have reduced the running software environment to the minimum level required to operate, reintroduce components until the fault appears again.

Resort to Permanent Changes Last

Permanent changes, such as replacing hard disk drives, reinstalling the operating system, or deleting files, should be your last resort. All of these repairs will take a long time to implement and will reset your security permissions, shares, and network names. Be certain you are replacing the component at fault before making these drastic repairs.

Troubleshooting and Optimization

PART 4

Summary

As with most aspects of computing, troubleshooting is a deterministic field that is learnable. You don't have to be a guru in order to fix even tough problems with Windows 2000.

The natural layering of computer systems provides a convenient way to partition your troubleshooting efforts. By validating whole layers, you can bypass those portions of a system that are contained within the functioning layers and concentrate your efforts on components that operate within the layers that are malfunctioning.

If you follow the general principles I listed earlier in the chapter, under "Axioms of Troubleshooting," you will almost always find the problem in a timely manner and without further messing up your system.

Troubleshooting Windows 2000 is actually easier than troubleshooting its predecessor, Windows NT, because the Plug and Play functionality in Windows 2000 automatically obviates many of the most common types of errors.

Case Study: When Debugging Goes Awry

This case study is going to take a somewhat different tack than the other case studies in this book. In this example, I ignored my own advice and let an incorrect presumption lead me into a three-month struggle with a crashing server. This specific case study deals with Windows NT 4 Server, but the exact same thing would have occurred in Windows 2000, and it's an especially good example of how ignoring the axioms of troubleshooting can lead you astray.

In this case the server was mine (thankfully), built to my specifications to replace my current office server, an aging dual Pentium 200 with a 10GB IDE RAID-0 disk pack based on a Promise Technology FastTRAK controller. I bought the new machine without disks, because I intended to migrate the RAID pack from the old machine—that was the point behind buying a custom configuration rather than an off-the-shelf computer.

To perform the migration, I backed up the computer to tape, shut down the old server, extracted the disks, RAID controller, tape, CD-R, network adapters, and all the other high-value equipment; and installed them in the new machine. I was prepared to reinstall Windows NT Server, because the new machine had a single processor and the old machine had two, so the HALs would be different.

I booted the machine and, sure enough, got an error message about the HALs. So I set it to boot the CD-ROM and went through an upgrade. Everything seemed fine.

When I rebooted, the machine crashed (blue screen: "IRQL not less than or equal"), indicating a problem in `ntfs.sys` or `ntoskrnl.exe` each time I tried to get it up. I tried to reinstall again, but could not get all the way through the CD-ROM installation without crashing.

The fact that the machine crashed in `ntfs.sys` led me to believe the problem was caused by the RAID controller—perhaps it was not tested to function in a PC100 (100MHz RAM bus) machine. The controller was not listed on the Hardware Compatibility List, but it had worked well in the other machine.

The volume on the RAID pack had become increasingly corrupt through these failed installs—leading to actual volume structure damage that, in my mind, further vilified the RAID controller or its driver.

So I called the RAID controller manufacturer and was told a number of things to check on the pack. I deleted the pack, low-level formatted each of the drives, re-created the pack, and performed a fresh installation. The installation crashed part way through—just as it had earlier.

By this point, I decided it had to be the RAID controller, so I purchased and installed a single large disk big enough to hold the contents of the RAID pack. I set the BIOS to boot from that disk and installed the operating system. It worked fine. So I restored the backup tape, and that worked, too. I left the RAID controller installed with disks running, just to test it, and put the server back online.

It seemed to work fine when being used as a server, but it would blue-screen crash randomly whenever I launched applications on it—same thing in `ntfs.sys` or `ntoskrnl.exe`. I presumed the problem was the RAID controller still extant in the system, so I removed it and unloaded the driver.

The problem continued unabated, if not more frequently. I was stumped. The controller was out of the picture completely, yet the problem didn't go away. So I pulled out the Performance Monitor and began profiling the use of the server when I launched applications on it. I found that the server crashed whenever an application caused the allocation of more memory than physically existed on the machine—whenever the swap file came into heavy use. So I disabled large caches in the Registry, and voilà! The problem went away.

Except that the applications still crashed—it just didn't show a bluescreen. Access violations abounded. I remained perplexed.

So I stepped back, took a deep breath, and thought about the system. The errors I now saw clearly indicted the memory subsystem, so I replaced the RAM with higher-quality memory, at a cost of about $200. The machine hasn't had a problem since, even after putting the RAID controller back in and moving the operating system to it. It had been the RAM the entire time.

What did I do wrong?

- I assumed that the machine from the manufacturer was built correctly, even though I know that incomplete computers can't really be tested.

- I jumped to a conclusion about a portion of the system that was very difficult to troubleshoot and test without first checking the easy things. I had memory in another computer I could have swapped in at the beginning in five minutes—just to see what would happen—or I could have moved the RAID pack and disk set into anther computer to test it, especially since I ignored the fact that it had been working correctly in an older machine.

- I knew that new unproven components are far more likely to be failure components than older proven components, but I failed to test the new components in another machine. Had I moved the RAM into another computer, the crashing problem would have moved with it.

- I didn't resort to permanent changes last—I tackled them first. This caused a serious delay.

- Finally, I knew from earlier experience that Windows NT is highly sensitive to proper RAM timings and compatibility between the motherboard and the memory. I ignored this in my untested certainty that the RAID controller might have a problem operating in a newer computer.

Had I followed these basic tenets of troubleshooting, I would have solved this problem in a single day rather than several weeks.

17

Practical Troubleshooting

Practical troubleshooting is a skill born of practice—and lots of it. Although you can learn and adopt a troubleshooting methodology by reading a book, you won't find the answer to every problem specifically delineated in any single work. It's simply not possible for me to explain enough explicit errors to cover everything you might run into. What I can do is explain those things you are most likely to see and teach you how to search for answers to the problems I can't cover.

This chapter is divided into three general categories: network troubleshooting, computer hardware troubleshooting, and software troubleshooting specific to Windows 2000.

In this chapter, I expand on the principles of troubleshooting explained in Chapter 16, "Troubleshooting Theory." I offer specific troubleshooting advice that assumes you understand general troubleshooting concepts. If you've opened the book to this chapter to fix a specific problem, you may find you'll need to read Chapter 16 first, if not the rest of the book.

Troubleshooting Networks

Entire networks never completely fail unless acted upon by an external factor, such as power loss or flooding. When an external factor does cause multiple faults, it's usually quite obvious what happened (by the damp carpet or the crater-shaped hole where your building used to be). In most situations, however, only a single component of a network fails in any fault situation. Because networks tend to fail one piece at a time, and because the voltages transmitted on normal network cables are so low that even a malfunctioning device won't damage other devices attached to the cable, you can usually be certain that once you've found the problem, you'll be able to fix it. Lightning strikes can cause power surges on network cables, thus causing all the equipment attached to the affected cable to fail—but, again, that's usually fairly obvious. And with modern UTP wiring, only two devices are attached to any one cable.

That said, it is possible (though rare) for networks to suffer from a cascading failure, where a failed or misconfigured device subsequently causes other devices to fail or become misconfigured. A bad routing table entry could be automatically propagated by a routing protocol such as RIP or OSPF. A device with a bad power supply could cause a circuit breaker to fail, thus shutting down other devices on the same circuit. A virus could spread to many computers throughout your enterprise. These failures, though sweeping, are always simply the same failure multiplied by a number of devices. Once you figure out what's wrong on one device, you'll be able to quickly recover the others.

So the trick to troubleshooting networks is to quickly isolate the failed component and then troubleshoot that component.

Network failures can be broken down into the following four categories:

Client problems   Affect only a single client. Other computers will work normally on the network.

Server problems   May deny access to the server to everyone on the network and for that reason can be confused with data-link problems. Ping from one peer to another without involving the server to validate the cable plant and data-link equipment.

Data-link or network routing faults   Occur with hubs, bridges, routers, switches, and network interface adapters. These faults fall into common categories such as addressing problems, misconfiguration, incompatible frame types, and outright component failures.

Cable faults   Include breaks, shorts, grounds, or loose connections that cause spurious faults. Most difficult network faults that involve random numbers of computers, partial or temporary loss of a server, or other nondeterministic faults are cable faults.

I explain each of these types of faults in detail in the following sections, and then I discuss specific troubleshooting recommendations and sequences.

Client Problems

Client problems are easy. If the problem affects only a single station on your network, it's a client problem. Use the following steps to find the fault in a client-based problem:

1. Validate the cable running to that client by attaching another known-good client to the same outlet and jumper cable—or better yet, use a cable scanner to validate the entire run and the jumpers.

TIP Keep a wiremap cable scanner handy to make sure you've got proper connectivity on your UTP cables. These devices cost less than $50 and can save you hours of troubleshooting by finding cable faults quickly. Even better are true cable scanners, but at $2,000 and up, they're only appropriate for larger installations. They can be rented, however.

---

2. Make sure the network interface adapter is installed correctly and is not conflicting with another device in the computer. MAC address conflicts are exceptionally rare in Ethernet networks, but IP conflicts abound in statically assigned IP networks. Look for conflicting NetBIOS names as well—random failures can occur if two computers have the same NetBIOS name in a NetBIOS namespace.

TIP Windows 98 and 2000 will not use an IP address if they've detected it elsewhere on your network. If you can't get an assigned IP address to "stick," that might be why.

---

3. Make sure the correct driver is installed and configured to work with the hardware resource settings of the network interface adapter. Network adapter failures can be very strange, so try using a different network adapter if you suspect there's a problem with the one you have.

TIP Keep a USB Ethernet adapter handy to quickly troubleshoot adapter problems in Windows 2000 machines without having to open them up.

---

4. Check to make sure the proper transport protocols are installed and that any addresses, frame types, or network numbers are set correctly.

TIP Always use DHCP in TCP/IP networks. It will save you months of network layer troubleshooting by simply avoiding the whole issue of addressing conflicts.

---

5. Use the Ping tool in TCP/IP networks, or the IPXPING tool in NWLink networks, to see if the server is reachable from the client.

TIP   Use the –L option in Ping to make sure that big packets are making it through. Distance, cable faults, or certain routers or firewalls can chop up large packets, so pings will work but useful-size packets won't. Also use the –T option to send packets repetitively over a long period to get a feel for the overall percentage of success or to find sporadic problems.

---

6. Make sure the client software is properly installed and configured and that the client computer has been properly named and identified as a member of the correct domain or workgroup.

TIP   If more than one workgroup shows up in your domain browser, at least one of your computers is on the other workgroup. If you only have a single workgroup in your organization, that computer won't be accessible.

---

7. Try adding the NetBEUI protocol to two computers on the same subnetwork to see if you can share resources over that protocol if you are having problems with NWLink or TCP/IP, since NetBEUI is automatically configured correctly.

TIP   The simplicity of NetBEUI makes it ideal for troubleshooting network layer problems.

Server Problems

Server problems are just like client problems, but since they affect the one computer everyone is trying to talk to, nothing happens on your network. For this reason, a server problem may look like a data-link problem. When running through server problems, first check all the steps shown in the previous section, "Client Problems." Then try these steps:

1. Change two client computers to the same workgroup and share a resource from one to the other. If it doesn't work, move to data-link troubleshooting.

2. If you have another server available, verify that clients can attach to it. If they can't, move to data-link troubleshooting.

3. Troubleshoot the computer hardware to validate that the server is operating correctly.

4. Replace the network adapter with an adapter from a different manufacturer using a different driver.

5. Use Backup to create an emergency repair disk, and reinstall Windows 2000 Server using the Repair option. Remove any third-party drivers and services except those absolutely necessary to operate the server.

6. Check for name resolution problems: conflicting NetBIOS names, problems finding a WINS or DNS server, names being overridden in the LMHOSTS or HOSTS file, and propagation of name broadcasts through routers if you aren't using WINS or DNS. If you can't ping a machine using its DNS or NetBIOS name but you can ping its IP address, you've got a name-resolution problem.

NOTE   Duplicate Windows names on your network can cause some serious and bizarre problems. For example, if a newly installed client has the same name as your server, other clients on that network will lose their ability to communicate with the server's higher-level services (server services) but will still be able to ping the server and access lower-level network services. Check for name conflicts whenever you have problems with file or print sharing. A similar set of problems can be caused by duplicate TCP/IP addresses.

Data-Link Problems

Data-link problems occur when a device that connects the network together physically or logically fails. These faults are relatively common, especially in larger networks having many data-link devices. Data-link faults usually affect entire subnetworks, generally denying access to the network or other subnetworks, depending upon the function of the specific device. Use the following steps to validate your data-link equipment:

1. Put a client right next to your server, attach it via a single cable to the server (it must be a crossover cable for UTP or fiber networks), and try to log in from there.

2. Take each hub in the affected areas of your system and verify with your collocated client and server that you can attach to the server through each port of each hub. This will quickly validate the proper operation of your hubs.

3. If you have two subnetworks that cannot connect to each other, replace the bridge between them.

4. If you suspect a router may be at fault, reboot it. Some routers will allow you to use the Telnet tool to check the configuration of the router.

5. Routing problems can be difficult to track down. Use Ping and Tracert to figure out where packets are stopping. Routing problems usually only happen when someone has been messing with routers, so you'll usually know what's happened.

Troubleshooting
and Optimization

PART 4

Cable Faults

Cable faults are rather common in network environments. Jumper cables that attach computers to wall outlets are always underfoot, so they often get run over by office chairs or pulled out of their sockets. Contractors working in ceiling areas may accidentally cut or kink network cables. Cables that are under stress may eventually break under the strain. Unfortunately, you have no way to fix damaged cable in most installations, so all you can do is determine that the problem is in fact a bad cable and call in a cabling contractor to fix it. That's why this section is last—you should correct all other possibilities before assuming that you have a cable fault. Use the following steps to identify cable faults:

1. Determine how many computers are affected and in what areas. Since cable faults generally affect only a single cable, check the one cable that the affected computers rely upon.

2. Try using another computer at the failed station location to determine if it's really a cable fault. If a known-good computer doesn't work at that location, it's probably a cable fault.

3. Validate the data-link devices between the failed station and the server using the troubleshooting steps for client problems and data-link problems.

4. Disconnect the cable on both ends of the link. Use a cable tester to check for continuity, shorts, or grounds.

5. Run a temporary long jumper between the computer and the closest hub or other data-link device. If the computer starts working with the long jumper, you have a cable fault.

6. Have a cabling contractor come in to repair the damaged cable.

Troubleshooting Computer Hardware

In order for your software to run correctly, the hardware in your computer must be operating correctly. Whenever a hardware component is possibly at fault in a malfunctioning computer, you should validate it is operating correctly before you attempt to correct software faults.

The few simple troubleshooting techniques presented here will help you quickly isolate common hardware problems. These techniques are not all-inclusive, nor do they in any way replace the general techniques presented in the previous section. These techniques are simply the culmination of a great deal of troubleshooting experience.

DOS As a Troubleshooting Tool

Windows 2000 requires a completely functional hardware and software environment from a computer just to boot. Windows 2000 probes hardware and exercises the entire system as it comes online. Consequently, any number of faults will prevent Windows 2000 from starting at all. Simpler operating systems, such as MS-DOS, can operate on a computer that is significantly degraded. A floppy disk that boots a simple operating system can be an invaluable troubleshooting tool. (The Windows 98 Emergency Boot Disk is the perfect tool for troubleshooting Windows 2000, as it loads generic CD-ROM drivers and provides access to FAT32 volumes. With third-party NTFS drivers for DOS, it can be used like a recovery console to rename, delete, and restore files.)

In addition, quite a few DOS-based hardware validation tools are available. You can use these tools to inspect hardware, check for hardware conflicts, and validate the proper operation of a number of computer components. These tools can be run from a floppy disk on a system that doesn't boot Windows 2000 at all.

Remember, however, that MS-DOS will not have access to NTFS file system partitions. The DOS partition and format tools will not be able to modify an NTFS partition. Use the Windows 2000 repair console to perform disk check operations and to gain file system access to NTFS drives.

The following is a short list of components to consider suspect under a range of troubleshooting issues. Check these in order to progressively narrow your search. Remember that complex faults (those involving more than one specific failure) may not fit into any one category. Also, many software problems can look like hardware faults until you test the component under a different operating system, such as MS-DOS.

Power

If nothing happens when you turn the computer on, check the power cords and switches. Even in the worst failure situation, you should at least hear the fan spinning in the power supply. If you hear the fan in the power supply, check if the microprocessor fan is spinning. If it is, you probably don't have a power supply problem. See if you can hear hard disks spinning—if they're running, you definitely don't have a power supply problem.

WARNING   Never install or remove anything while the power to your computer is on. Dropping a screw onto a powered motherboard will probably destroy it and some of your peripheral cards. Some ATX power supplies do not have "hard" power switches in back that can be turned off to ensure that no power reaches the motherboard. Unplug these power supplies whenever you have the computer's case open to be certain the computer is off.

Motherboard, Processor, RAM, and Video

The computer's motherboard, processor, RAM, and video adapter must all operate correctly for the computer to complete the power-on self test (POST) performed by the BIOS each time you turn the computer on. If you see the normal boot screen after turning on your computer, these components are probably all working correctly. If they are not, you may hear a few beeps (POST codes), or there may be no activity at all. Some computers can operate with a bit of failed RAM. These computers will either give an error message while testing RAM or will not count up to the entire compliment of memory.

If you suspect a problem with any of these components, remove and reseat the video card and memory modules. Processor failures are very rare—I've never seen one occur. The only way to test for a processor failure is to swap in a known-good processor of the same brand, model, and speed rating. Motherboard failures are also rare and very difficult to validate. Verifying the processor, RAM, and video adapter in another computer of exactly the same make is usually easier than swapping out the motherboard.

TIP   Problems with mismatched RAM show up in Windows 2000 as blue screens ("IRQL not greater than or equal is the most common error"), or they show up as access violations in applications that you know work correctly. Replace your RAM with matched high-quality memory and you'll see your problems go away.

BIOS Configuration Problems

With many computers, it is possible to set BIOS information incorrectly. The BIOS determines such critical parameters as how fast RAM memory is accessed, what type of hard disk drive is attached, and how interrupts are assigned to PCI slots. Incorrectly configuring your BIOS can very likely degrade its performance or keep it from working at all.

WARNING   If you don't understand a BIOS setting's purpose, don't change it without recording its present value so you can change it back.

When you suspect a hardware conflict or a problem with the video, memory, processor, or the motherboard, check your BIOS parameter settings before you replace anything. The manual that came with your computer or motherboard should show the proper settings for your computer. If it does not, check with the manufacturer's technical support.

Failing all else, you can usually use a BIOS Default Settings option to get your computer working, although generally at a lower-than-optimal speed. Use this setting to verify whether you are having a BIOS configuration problem and then tune parameters to increase the speed.

> **TIP**   Most motherboards have a jumper that will allow you to clear the CMOS BIOS memory area. Use this jumper to return a motherboard to factory defaults. Consult your motherboard manual to find this jumper and operate it correctly.

Hardware Conflicts

Hardware conflicts are by far the most common problem in PCs running any operating system. Hardware conflicts occur when two peripherals are configured to use the same interrupt, DMA channel, port address, or buffer memory.

> **NOTE**   Windows 2000 is not immune to hardware conflicts. Although PCI devices rarely have problems, Windows 2000 cannot reliably reconfigure ISA Plug and Play resources. To troubleshoot these problems, shut off all motherboard-integrated peripherals such as serial, parallel, and sound cards to free up resources, and then use the Device Manager to manually move the errant device to known-free resources before reenabling the integrated peripherals.

You troubleshoot these problems by removing all peripheral cards that are not absolutely essential to boot the computer. These peripheral cards include modems, LAN adapters, sound cards, I/O controllers, secondary hard disk controllers, CD-ROM controllers, and any other peripheral cards except video and your primary (boot) hard disk controller.

If your computer goes through a normal start-up process, reintroduce each peripheral card, starting with the secondary hard disk controller and adding each additional card in order of its importance to you. Turn off the power to the computer, install the card, and then check for a normal boot. Use the Device Manager to make sure a hardware conflict has not occurred. Repeat this process with each card until the problem reappears. When the problem reappears, the most recent card installed is either conflicting with an installed device, incorrectly configured, or has failed. I discuss the Device Manager later in this chapter.

Hard Disk Controllers and Drives

Hard disk failures are the most damaging of all computer component failures. All hardware components can simply be replaced. But because hard disks contain the most recent set of all the data you store on your computer, their loss means the loss of irreplaceable data. Every component in your computer can fail without causing significant data loss—except the hard disk. Hard disk problems fall into just a few categories:

- Power or bus connection problems
- Hardware configuration problems
- Incorrect BIOS information
- Failed mechanisms
- Failed hard disk controllers
- Bad sectors
- Data corruption caused by software

Following are symptoms and solutions for each of these problems.

TIP   Backing up your data to other media, usually tape, is the only way to recover completely from a total hard disk failure. If your data is important, back it up daily.

Power or Connection Problems

Power or connection problems are easy to find. Check to make sure each hard disk drive is receiving power. If the hard disk is spinning, it is powered up correctly. On IDE drives, make sure the cables are securely and correctly installed. If you can't tell which way the cable should fit, and the connector isn't keyed to prevent incorrect insertion, remember that the side of the connector with two notches mates to the side of the hard disk port that has a notch in the center. Make sure the cable is correctly attached to the motherboard/hard disk controller by matching the red striped side of the cable to the pin labeled *1* on the circuit board.

SCSI is slightly more difficult. A SCSI bus must be properly terminated, and the total cable length should be as short as possible. Proper SCSI termination is set when the devices at each end of the SCSI bus have termination enabled or a physical terminator is installed at the end of the bus. No device, including the controller card, should have termination enabled if it is not at the end of the SCSI bus. Often, one SCSI bus will have some internal components and some external components. In this case, the last drive attached to the internal bus should be terminated, the SCSI controller should not be terminated, and the last device on the external bus should be terminated. Refer to your SCSI adapter manual for more information on SCSI termination.

Modern SCSI is quite a bit easier if you follow a few simple rules: Use different SCSI busses for internal and external devices. Put terminators on the end of internal cables rather than on the last device. This will allow you to remove devices without wondering which one provided termination. Finally, use physical active terminators at the end of your external SCSI chain rather than using a SCSI device to provide termination for the same reason.

Hardware Configuration Problems

Drives can be incorrectly configured in ways that will prevent them from operating. Make sure that you don't have two devices on a SCSI bus with the same SCSI identification number. Also make sure that you don't have two IDE devices both set to master or slave. If you have only one IDE device, it should usually be set to master. If you have an IDE CD-ROM and an IDE hard disk on the same bus, the CD-ROM should be set to slave.

Some SCSI drives must be set to have the SCSI controller issue a start-up command before the disk will spin up. Make sure the controller is set to issue a start-up command to these disks. If your controller can't issue start-up commands, jumper the drive to start up at power-on.

Incorrect BIOS Information

In the past, you had to set the specific drive parameters for each hard disk in the BIOS so that operating systems knew how to partition and format the disk. Most modern controllers and motherboards are capable of automatically detecting hard disk geometry. But some computers have BIOS programs that are too old to recognize new large disks. In these cases, you should upgrade to a hard disk controller that can recognize the full capacity of your disk.

> **NOTE**   Automatic hard disk geometry detection is available on all modern controllers and motherboards. I've never seen a case where other settings were better.

Sector translation is provided in many IDE and SCSI disks to allow operating systems that have a 1,024-cylinder limit to access an entire large disk. You may need to turn on this feature to complete the MS-DOS portion of the Windows 2000 installation if your primary disk has more than 1,024 cylinders. Once you have turned on sector translation, it must remain enabled for that drive.

> **TIP**   Always set LBA mode for modern hard disks before you format the disk. You may later use sector copying software that will require LBA mode to access the entire disk.

Troubleshooting and Optimization

PART 4

Failed Mechanisms

Failed mechanisms are the worst hard disk problem you can have. This problem is caused when the hard disk spindle or head assembly physically breaks. Unfortunately, you cannot recover from this situation, and you will lose the data on that hard disk.

TIP   Because you cannot prevent hard disk failures, back up regularly to another mass storage device to prevent losing your data.

This fault is signaled by strange noises coming from your hard disk. If your disk is "knocking" when you try to access it, or you hear strange grinding or scraping noises, it is usually too late. Sometimes the disk will bind and fail to spin at all. This symptom can make a physical disk failure seem like a power problem.

NOTE   Hard disk failure is accelerated by local temperatures exceeding 150°F. Temperatures in this range cause the sealed bearing oil in the drive spindle to break down and eventually lose its viscosity, which in turn leads to rapid heating and expansion of the spindle until it physically seizes. You can avoid high disk temperature by specifying individually cooled hard disk enclosures for your hard drives. These 5.25-inch drive bays have fans and filters in front that constantly cool each drive. They cost less than $20 and can significantly lengthen disk life.

Failed Hard Disk Controllers

Hard disk controllers rarely fail, but they can conflict with other devices in your computer. Check these cards the same way you would check any other hardware conflict. If you seem to have no access whatsoever to your hard disk, or if during the BIOS phase of the boot process your computer tells you that you have a hard disk controller failure, check the seating and settings of your hard disk controller. Swap it with another hard disk of the same type, if necessary. If your hard disk controller is embedded on your motherboard, disable it and install a peripheral card hard disk controller set to the same interrupt, port, and DMA channel.

Bad Sectors

Bad sectors are a fact of life in hard disks. As hard disks age, they gradually lose their ability to store information. This gradual loss shows up as bad sectors, also known as "grown defects" in the hard disk industry. Hard disks typically ship from the factory with bad sectors, so all operating systems are capable of marking sectors bad. Sectors will usually fail on a write operation rather than a read operation, so the NTFS hot-fixing feature will usually keep you from having to worry about them.

When many sectors fail suddenly, you are about to experience a failed hard disk mechanism. This failure is signaled by unexplained loss of hard disk space during the normal operation of Windows 2000 as NTFS marks more and more sectors out of use. You may also experience unrecoverable read errors. You should see reports of sector failures in the Event Log. Transfer data off the disk as soon as possible and replace it with another hard disk.

Corruption

Data corruption is simply data stored on a hard disk that is incorrect due to a software or human failure rather than a hardware failure.

Corrupted Boot Sectors   This can occur when a file system installation is taking place, and the computer is interrupted by a power fluctuation. Sometimes boot sector corruption is caused by installing another operating system over Windows 2000. You can correct this problem by using the MS-DOS fdisk utility and issuing the `fdisk /mbr` command at the `C:\>` prompt.

The `/mbr` switch tells fdisk to write a new master boot record to the hard disk. You may also see this problem if you turn off sector translation in the BIOS of your hard disk controller. Try changing the sector translation setting before issuing the `fdisk` command. If you are unable to correct the problem by changing sector translation, change the translation setting back to its original setting and issue the `fdisk /mbr` command.

Unless you have the sector translation in a different state than when the disk was originally formatted, the `fdisk /mbr` command will have no adverse effect on your system—even if it doesn't correct the problem.

Corrupt Partition Tables   Partition corruption on Basic partitions usually occurs when you're replacing an operating system with another, resizing existing partitions using third-party tools, or writing down a partition image. These problems usually result in BIOS missing operating system errors or inaccessible boot device blue screens. The bad news is that the only reliable way to recover from a partition table problem is to remove existing partitions and repartition the disk, which inevitably involves reinstalling the operating system.

Windows 2000's new dynamic partitioning solves some long-standing problems with the original Microsoft/IBM partitioning scheme used by most other operating systems, but it introduces a few new problems as well. For example, dynamic partitions store information about all the partitions on every disk and information such as the computer's name. When you move disks to different computers and repartition them, Windows 2000 will attempt to "recover" this information and will display obsolete partition information on them. Even worse, if you install a system on a disk, the obsolete information can cause the install program to ratchet up the drive letter, so that your entire system will be installed on the D: drive or higher. Since you can't change the drive letter of the system drive, you'll have to wipe the disk and reinstall to fix it.

The only way to get rid of this obsolete information is to low-level format the drive using your SCSI controller's BIOS or use a utility such as IBM's Wipe or Zap disk tool to zero-out the hard disk. Download these free utilities at www.ibm.com.

Corrupted File Systems   NTFS has a number of built-in mechanisms to keep it from becoming corrupt. However, some problems, especially hardware configuration, can cause NTFS to become corrupted. NTFS will check for hard disk corruption each time you reboot your computer. NTFS corruption is very rare under normal usage.

FAT file system volumes are very likely to become corrupt over time with normal usage. You should use the Microsoft chkdsk utility frequently, at lease once a month, to detect and correct file system corruption on FAT and FAT32 formatted volumes.

Troubleshooting Windows 2000

Windows 2000 is a complex environment with myriad software components. But it does work correctly out of the box on systems with hardware that is completely supported and correctly configured. If you have one of those systems, a fresh Windows 2000 installation will always work.

This provides a good baseline for the operation of all further services. As a machine is customized with applications, user configurations, upgrades, and so forth, opportunities for misconfiguration multiply exponentially. It is usually the complex interactions between these software components that cause problems in servers.

You may run into situations where two pieces of software are mutually exclusive—because of their differing requirements, they cannot run on the same machine. This problem occurred frequently with Windows NT and is likely to occur with Windows 2000 as service packs are released. For example, the numerous security changes and API differences introduced in Windows NT Server 4 Service Pack 3 could prevent a firewall from working correctly. But Microsoft required Service Pack 3 to install the Option Pack that included Internet Information Server 4, so these two functions could not exist simultaneously. This unfortunate situation is fairly common in server applications, because many of them are written to the very specific network APIs that tend to change frequently between service packs.

Windows 2000 does include built-in mechanisms to prevent the common problem of DLL conflicts that afflict all other versions of Windows. Service pack differences, however, are likely to cause application incompatibility because applications rely upon the operating system APIs published at the time the application was published. Future updates that change these APIs cause incompatibilities.

The following sections detail troubleshooting information for the Windows 2000 boot process, general environment, and networking services.

Boot Process

After you have determined that the computer hardware is operating properly, you must be sure that Windows 2000 is being loaded correctly. This section first shows you some of the boot sequence errors and what they mean, then teaches you how to diagnose boot.ini problems, and finally explains how to use Windows 2000 boot disks and emergency repair disks to repair the Windows 2000 boot process.

Boot Sequence Errors

The boot sequence is a complicated process. If one of the boot components is damaged or removed, or your boot.ini file is incorrectly configured, you may see one of the following messages (in which case you need to use a boot disk or an emergency repair disk to fix the boot sequence).

- The following message indicates that the NTLDR file is missing or corrupt (or that you've left a nonbootable floppy disk in the disk drive bay, and your BIOS is set to prefer floppy boots):

  ```
  BOOT: Couldn't find NTLDR

  Please insert another disk
  ```

- If this message repeats after you have selected the Windows 2000 operating system on the boot menu, then ntdetect.com is damaged or missing:

  ```
  NTDETECT V1.0 Checking Hardware

  NTDETECT V1.0 Checking Hardware
  ```

- This message indicates several possible problems: (1) the Windows 2000 operating system is damaged or missing, (2) the boot.ini file is missing and Windows 2000 was installed in a directory other than \winnt, or (3) boot.ini is directing the operating system loader to a location that does not contain a valid ntoskrnl.exe:

  ```
  Windows 2000 could not start because the following file is missing
  or corrupt:

  \<winnt root>\system32\ntoskrnl.exe

  Please reinstall a copy of the above file.
  ```

- This problem can occur when you partition free space on your hard disk if the partition number that contains Windows 2000 changes. Edit the boot.ini file to reflect the new partition number that contains Windows 2000.

- The following message indicates that the boot sector is missing or corrupt for a dual-boot operating system:

  ```
  I/O Error accessing boot sector file

  multi(0)disk(0)rdisk(0)partition(1):\bootsect.dos
  ```

- This message indicates that the Windows 2000 entry in boot.ini points to a missing or malfunctioning device or to a disk partition that does not contain a file system recognized by the Windows 2000 boot loader:

  ```
  OS Loader V5.00

  Windows 2000 could not start because of a computer disk hardware
  configuration problem.

  Could not read from the selected boot disk. Check boot path and
  disk hardware.

  Please check the Windows 2000 documentation about hardware disk
  configuration and your hardware reference manuals for additional
  information.
  ```

- This next error occurs for several reasons: (1) the Windows 2000 loader cannot access the hard disk upon which your Windows 2000 partition is stored, (2) the Windows 2000 loader is confused about which hard disk controller to consider the primary device, (3) the disk driver cannot correctly control the hard disk, or (4) the sector alignment is different than it was when the operating system was installed, which can occur with image copies or other esoteric circumstances:

  ```
  STOP: 0x000007E: Inaccessible Boot Device
  ```

Because a number of SCSI adapters do not conform to the complete SCSI standard, they may cause this problem, but if your adapter is on the Windows 2000 Hardware Compatibility List, then this isn't the problem.

STOP messages are also heralded by the infamous "blue screen" of Windows NT crash fame. Due to circumstances Microsoft does not report until the problem has been corrected in a downloadable service pack, these screens very rarely indicate a serious failure from which Windows 2000 is not able to recover. These problems are usually related to I/O, and the bug that crashed the computer probably resides in a driver. If you have a problem with a STOP message blue screen, log on to the Windows 2000 Knowledge Base and use the search key "STOP:" to find the bugs Microsoft knows how to correct.

If you have just added a SCSI controller to a Windows 2000 computer that boots from an IDE hard disk, make sure that no SCSI device is set to ID 0 (or otherwise disable bootable SCSI hard disks). This setting will prevent the SCSI controller from attempting to boot the disk and will prevent the Windows 2000 DETECT portion of the boot loader from assigning the SCSI adapter a bus number of 0, thereby causing boot.ini to refer to the wrong partition.

The Windows 2000 Boot Floppy

Your Windows 2000 server will normally boot from its hard disk drive. You may have installed Windows 2000 into the boot partition of your hard drive, in which case the boot files and the operating system all reside in the same volume, or you may have installed Windows 2000 on another partition, in which case the boot files will reside in the boot partition, separate from the operating system.

A third boot configuration is possible for Windows 2000. You can create a floppy boot disk that contains the boot files needed to start the Windows 2000 operating system. Booting from a floppy is slower than booting from a hard disk, but a floppy boot disk can be very useful when your computer is not booting properly.

To create a boot floppy, format the floppy disk in Windows 2000. This will write a Windows 2000–specific boot sector to the floppy. Then copy the following files to the disk:

- boot.ini
- ntldr
- ntdetect.com
- ntbootdd.sys (if it exists)

If the problem you are experiencing booting Windows 2000 is because one of the boot files listed above is missing or corrupt, you can boot Windows 2000 with the boot floppy disk you have previously created. Then you need to copy the files from the floppy disk to your boot drive (the C: drive). This process will restore the missing or corrupted files and allow the boot process to proceed normally.

The ntbootdd.sys file is the driver used by your hard disk controller if your hard disk controller's BIOS is not INT13-compliant and therefore uses the SCSI() boot.ini syntax rather than the multi() syntax. If you need to replace this file, copy the driver file (such as aic78xx.sys) from the driver floppy provided by the manufacturer to your boot floppy and rename it ntbootdd.sys.

Using the Windows 2000 CD to Fix Problems

Problems with a Windows 2000 server are often caused by a corrupt installation or Registry setting. What exactly does *corrupt* mean in this case? Quite simply, it means that one or more things—either a component of the operating system or a Registry setting—is either missing or not behaving as expected.

What causes corruption? Well, mucking around deleting files or Registry keys is one obvious cause, but sometimes corruption is caused by more typical and necessary practices:

Patches   Software vendors often feel free to patch an operating system when they need an extra bit of functionality. This patch might work fine with a very specific version of a DLL, but it can begin to cause problems after installing a service pack or updating the operating system. This sort of corruption is especially common with firewall software. Service packs themselves have been known to cause corruption problems.

Installing or removing software   Occasionally, an uninstall program can be a little too aggressive in removing Registry keys and files that might be used by other programs.

Incompatible applications   Applications and drivers often change operating system Registry settings when they're installed, and, on occasion, applications may need to set the same Registry setting to different values or install a DLL with the same name but different functionality in the same location. Windows 2000 can automatically fix this problem by identifying applications that use DLLs with the same name and forcing those DLLs to be installed in the application directory rather than in the operating system directories. Why Microsoft ever specified that application-specific DLLs should be placed in the system directories in the first place is a mystery that has caused untold thousands of hours of troubleshooting.

Poorly written programs   Vendors frequently fail to thoroughly test software before shipping it. While the software probably worked fine on their hardware, it may encounter compatibility problems with your hardware or more commonly with software you already have loaded. Removing the software doesn't necessarily remove the entries it made in the Registry or the files it installed in system directories.

This is one major reason why you must always simulate application deployments to production servers on test machines that are as similar as you can afford them to be. Finding these problems on a test machine makes you a guru. Finding them on a production server makes you the cause of unplanned downtime.

Hardware failure   Disk controllers and hard disks that are going bad can cause an amazing amount of corruption in a very short time. Writing incorrect data to the disk can cause pernicious problems with an install. You'll usually know about these problems soon after they start happening, but probably not in time to do anything about it.

Old configuration information   Changing the hardware on a server requires installing new drivers, but administrators often fail to remove old drivers, services, and software. These obsolete bits of code still try to start and usually fail, and they soak up time and memory in the effort. In some cases, they can also cause compatibility problems or kernel crashes (blue screens), too.

Microsoft now provides three separate methods to troubleshoot nonbooting Windows 2000 computers:

- Safe Mode
- The Recovery Console
- Repair Installation

At least 90 percent of all nonbooting Windows 2000 problems occur because you installed either a service pack that causes incompatibility problems with existing services or because you've installed a new service that has compatibility problems with your existing software or hardware. In either case, you installed something, you rebooted, and the server never came back.

When you're confronted with a server that cannot boot all the way, or crashes shortly after you log in, you should use these three troubleshooting tools in the order presented here to attempt to resolve the problem. These solutions are all increasingly complex and increasingly dangerous to your existing installation, so always attempt them in this order.

Using Safe Mode

Safe Mode is another excellent troubleshooting mechanism borrowed from Windows 95. Safe Mode is conceptually very simple: by selecting Safe Mode early in the boot process, you tell Windows 2000 to load only Microsoft drivers and not to start the extra devices or services specified in the Registry, Startup batch files, or the Startup program group. This prevents any of these programs from crashing the server and provides a complete running Windows 2000 environment for you to troubleshoot within. You can disable services, delete files, and even uninstall errant applications (usually the one you just installed) while in Safe Mode.

Getting to Safe Mode is easy: just press F8 during the boot process when the NT boot loader tells you to. Figure 17.1 shows the Safe Mode selection screen, with the Windows 2000 Advanced Options menu.

Figure 17.1   Windows 2000 Safe Mode is reminiscent of Windows 95.

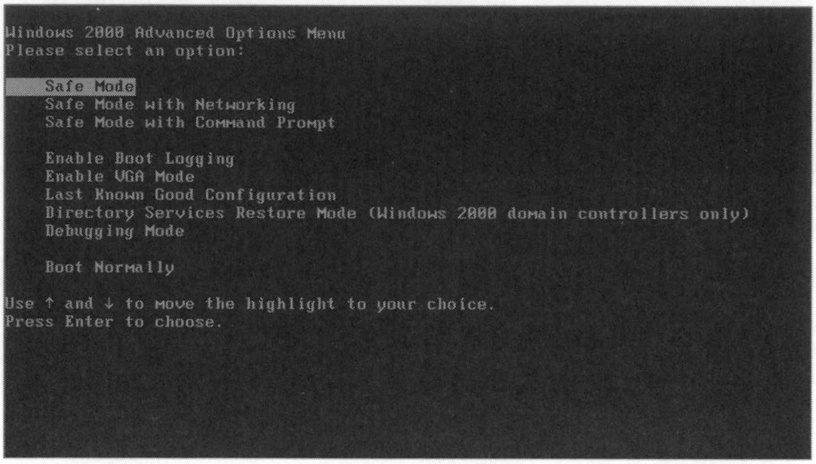

```
Windows 2000 Advanced Options Menu
Please select an option:

    Safe Mode
    Safe Mode with Networking
    Safe Mode with Command Prompt

    Enable Boot Logging
    Enable VGA Mode
    Last Known Good Configuration
    Directory Services Restore Mode (Windows 2000 domain controllers only)
    Debugging Mode

    Boot Normally

Use ↑ and ↓ to move the highlight to your choice.
Press Enter to choose.
```

The various options are:

Safe Mode   Starts Windows 2000 without any unnecessary device drivers and using the safest possible drivers for necessary devices such as vga.sys for video.

Safe Mode with Networking   Starts Windows 2000 as above but includes the network drivers to provide access to your network. If this mode doesn't work but Safe Mode does, your problem is with a network driver.

Safe Mode with Command Prompt   Starts Windows 2000 but loads cmd.exe as the shell rather than explorer.exe. This can help you troubleshoot problems with Explorer or Internet Explorer, programs loaded in the System Tray, or programs in the startup directory.

Enable Boot Logging   Causes Windows 2000 to write a log file to %systemroot%\ntbtlog.txt.

Enable VGA Mode   Starts Windows 2000 using your current video driver in 640×480×16 mode. This mode is compatible with all monitors and can be used to fix the screen resolution if you've set a resolution that the monitor can't handle. You can also troubleshoot problems with your display driver.

Last Known-Good Configuration   Starts Windows 2000 with the Registry control set that is known to have completed an entire boot process normally. Keep in mind that Windows 2000 doesn't establish the "last known-good" control set until the system has completely settled, about 5 minutes after a normal boot. I discuss control sets in Chapter 18.

Directory Services Restore Mode   Is required to perform a directory services restoration on a domain controller.

Debugging Mode   Transmits debugging code information over COM2. A terminal program on COM2 will display information that the designers of Windows 2000 and third-party developers use to debug their applications.

Boot Normally   Is self-evident.

You'll save yourself a lot of time if you always start with Safe Mode to troubleshoot a nonbooting machine. The only time you should step down to the Recovery Console is when the computer still crashes when you try to start using Safe Mode with Command Prompt.

Using the Recovery Console

Microsoft has finally caved to the fact that low-level, pre-GUI access to an operating system is frequently necessary to fix problems. Originally, Microsoft's contention was that any NT operating system corruption problem could be solved by reinstalling using the Repair option and providing an emergency repair disk. This worked reasonably well until they patched the NTFS file system driver in Service Pack 4 to be upward compatible with the forthcoming Windows 2000. At that point, the original Windows NT installation CD could no longer recognize post–Service Pack 3 NTFS partitions, so they could no longer be repaired. This left NT pros high and dry, with no recover options other than tape restoration, and third-party tools that provide an NT-compatible command line, such as ERD Commander, became a virtual necessity.

Microsoft has built this functionality into Windows 2000, and it's pretty cool. Using the Recovery Console, you can remove errant drivers (the number one cause of unbootable systems), fix Registry problems, and change service startup settings. Figure 17.2 shows the Recovery Console right after booting to it.

To start the Recovery Console, boot the Windows 2000 installation CD, and select the Repair option. Then select the Console option, and select the Windows 2000 installation that you would like to log on to. After you provide the administrator's password, the install process will stop, and you will be left at a command prompt for Windows 2000. This command prompt is entirely different than the Safe Mode with Command Prompt option that you can select from the Windows 2000 Advanced Options menu. That command prompt is actually the cmd.exe program running under the full Windows 2000 operating system, with access to all running programs and no restrictions on its operation—but it requires a substantially functional installation to reach. The Recovery Console, on the other hand, doesn't require much of anything from the existing installation other than that it actually exists.

Figure 17.2   The Recovery Console allows low-level access to a Windows 2000 installation.

```
Microsoft Windows 2000(TM) Recovery Console.

The Recovery Console provides system repair and recovery functionality.

Type EXIT to quit the Recovery Console and restart the computer.

1: C:\WINNT

Which Windows 2000 installation would you like to log onto
<To cancel, press ENTER>? 1
Type the Administrator password: *******
C:\WINNT>_
```

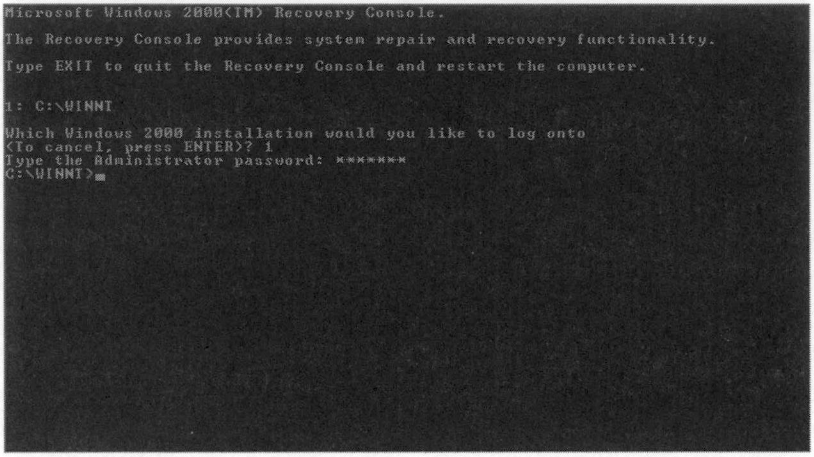

TIP The Recovery Console is still missing a bunch of handy commands that the Windows 2000 version of ERD Commander (from www.sysinternals.com) handles, such as file and Registry editing, unlimited copying (the Recovery Console has restrictions to hinder hackers), and most important of all, resetting forgotten administrative passwords. You'll save its cost in a single recovered password incident.

The Recovery Console has its own unique set of commands, listed below. No other commands work in the Recovery Console.

ATTRIB   Is essentially the same command as the MS-DOS attrib command. ATTRIB changes the read-only, system, hidden, and compressed attributes of a file.

BATCH   Executes commands specified in a batch file. Because the Recovery Console is not a complete command prompt environment, it cannot automatically execute *.bat files, and it can execute only batch files that contain only Recovery Console commands.

CD/CHDIR   Is the same as the CD command prompt command.

CHKDSK   Runs the CHKDSK command on the drive specified. Use the /R switch to attempt repairs on the disk.

CLS   Clears the screen like its command prompt counterpart.

COPY   Copies files between disks, but not to removable media. This restriction is designed to prevent hackers from copying data files off a server. COPY also does not support wildcards and will automatically expand compressed files copied from the Windows 2000 installation CD. A Registry setting will enable copying to floppies and copying between any locations in the volume, as discussed in Chapter 18.

DEL/DELETE   Deletes files but is restricted to operating within the system directory and the root directories of hard disks, removable media, and the local installation source.

DIR   Displays the current directory listing but is restricted to operating within the system directory and the root directories of hard disks, removable media, and the local installation source.

DISABLE   Disables the service or driver listed as the command parameter.

DISKPART   Runs the Windows installation FDISK utility for partitioning hard disk drives. You can use the command with parameters to specify the partition you want to create (use HELP DISKPART for syntax) or type DISKPART to get a user interface. The user interface is the same as the Installation program disk partitioning utility.

ENABLE   Enables the service specified as a parameter using the start type specified as the second parameter. Valid start types are:

    SERVICE_BOOT_START

    SERVICE_SYSTEM_START

    SERVICE_AUTO_START

    SERVICE_DEMAND_START

EXIT   Exits the Recovery Console and restarts the computer.

EXPAND   Expands the compressed file specified as the first parameter. This will unpack installation files from the source CD. The COPY command will also perform this function.

FIXBOOT   Writes a new boot sector on the partition specified by a drive letter. The master boot record loads the boot sector for the active partition. That boot sector then loads the OS loader (NTLDR). Use FIXMBR to rewrite the master boot record.

FIXMBR   Writes a new master boot record to the device specified or to the boot device if no device was specified. Unlike the MS-DOS FDISK /MBR command, FIXMBR is capable of writing a master boot record to any drive attached to the system.

FORMAT   Formats partitions for use with Windows 2000. Use the /FS: switch with NTFS, FAT, or FAT32 to specify a file system. Use /Q for a quick format.

HELP   Shows the syntax for the specified Recovery Console command.

Troubleshooting and Optimization

PART 4

LISTSVC   Lists the services and drivers installed on the computer, including the service names you'll need for the ENABLE/DISABLE commands, the startup type, and a human-readable description of the service or driver.

LOGON   Allows you to log on to various installations of Windows 2000 on the local machine as the administrator. The LOGON command ran when you first started the Recovery Console to get the administrative password. LOGON does not allow you to log on as various different users.

MAP   Displays drive-letter-to-device name mappings for all hard disks installed in the computer for which active device drivers are present. You can use MAP ARC to display the correct ARC (boot.ini) syntax for each device as well, which is invaluable in correcting problems with the boot.ini file.

MD/MKDIR   Creates a directory but is restricted to operating within the system directory and the root directories of hard disks, removable media, and the local installation source.

MORE/TYPE   Displays the contents of the specified text file.

RD/RMDIR   Deletes a directory but is restricted to operating within the system directory and the root directories of hard disks, removable media, and the local installation source.

REN/RENAME   Renames a file but is restricted to operating within the system directory and the root directories of hard disks, removable media, and the local installation source.

SYSTEMROOT   Performs a CD to the current system root directory, usually C:\winnt.

If you've ever troubleshot a failed Windows NT server, you can see that these commands provide the necessary tools to recover from the vast majority of problems that prevent a Windows NT system from booting—especially the DISABLE command for shutting down errant services or device drivers that cause the computer to crash before the boot process is completed. You can also use the COPY command to replace driver files and DLLs from the installation CD-ROM, and the DELETE or RENAME command to remove corrupted files or third-party drivers that cause problems.

You should attempt to use the Recovery Console to fix a nonbooting server before you attempt to use the Repair Installation option. It's potentially much faster if you know what you're going after. If you really have no idea what's wrong, you should probably use the Repair Installation option, as it will usually not cause any additional harm.

Using the Repair Installation

The Repair Installation of Windows 2000 can solve all sorts of problems. I don't want to sound cavalier here—reinstallation can also introduce problems and is, at the very best, a time-consuming process. But many problems simply can't be solved any other way, because files and Registry settings must be restored to their original states or at least known-working states for the computer to function. Unless you happen to possess a complete and correct diagnosis of the exact problem, you won't know exactly which files or Registry settings are needed or where they should go.

Reinstalling Windows 2000 in a domain isn't as damaging as it used to be. Keep in mind, however, that reinstalling Windows 2000 on the computer you created the forest root domain on will cause you to irrevocably lose the Enterprise Admins and Schema Admins groups. Keep good backups of this machine for that reason.

Reinstalling Windows 2000 is similar to an original installation except that you choose the Repair option rather than the New option during the initial setup. When you select the Repair option, you'll see a screen that asks which areas of the Registry should be replaced. You replace a hive by selecting that option, which will cause the setup program to replace that section of the Registry with default information. Figure 17.3 shows the Repair Installation options of Windows 2000.

Figure 17.3   The Windows 2000 Repair Installation option allows you to repair common problems that can prevent Windows 2000 from booting.

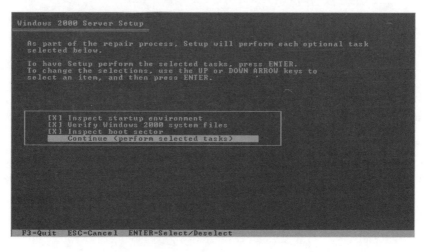

The options and their consequences are as follows:

Inspect Startup Environment   Checks the boot files to make sure they're the same ones created originally and ensures that the ARC paths listed in the boot.ini file are correct.

Verify Windows 2000 System Files   Compares the files on your hard drive to the files on the Windows 2000 installation CD-ROM and optionally replaces them.

Inspect Boot Sector   Automatically fixes problems with the partition boot sector (not the Master boot record, however).

When a Windows 2000 installation goes completely south, you may not have a Registry remaining to work with. In this case, the setup program will inform you that it cannot find an existing Windows 2000 installation. If this happens, you have three options: either restore from tape; reinstall Windows 2000 completely, create all new user accounts, and reinstall all applications; or perform a repair installation and hope the \repair directory is accessible to the Windows 2000 CD-ROM.

General Windows Environment

If you are sure that you have no hardware problems, and your Windows 2000 server boots properly but you still experience difficulties, you will need to troubleshoot the running operating system. Windows 2000 provides an excellent environment for troubleshooting—you can view almost any aspect of the operating system with tools provided by Microsoft. The tools you will most often use are the Device Manager, which gives you control over all the hardware in your system, and the Event Viewer, which records problems detected by Windows 2000. You can also use the System Monitor to find programs that are using more resources than you might expect and degrading the performance of your machine. Use of the Performance Monitor is covered in Chapter 15, "Performance Optimization."

Troubleshooting with the Device Manager

The Device Manager is a powerful troubleshooting tool that migrated to Windows 2000 from Windows 95 along with Plug and Play. The Device Manager gives you nearly complete control over the way device drivers are installed and over the resources used by hardware in your computers.

The Device Manager is actually an MMC snap-in launched from the Hardware tab of the System Control Panel, which is most easily reached by right-clicking the My Computer icon. The Device Manager snap-in is also part of the default Computer Management console. You can create your own MMC console with the Device Manager installed in it by launching mmc.exe and adding the Device Manager snap-in manually. When you do this, you'll see an option to manage any other computer reachable on your network. This option lets you view devices and resources on other computers but not change settings on remote computers, so its value as a remote administration tool is dubious. You can add as many different computers as you want to a single console. Figure 17.4 shows the Device Manager.

Figure 17.4   The Device Manager is actually an MMC snap-in that can be added to any administrative console.

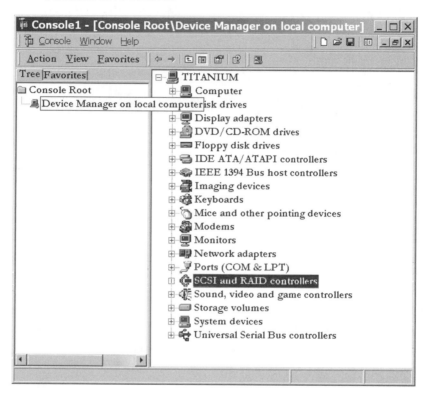

The Device Manager presents a tree view of device types at the top level. You can use the View menu to show devices by the following options:

Devices by Type   Devices are grouped by the type of device. This is the default view.

Devices by Connection   The tree structure represents the ports and busses through which each device is actually connected.

Resources by Type   DMA, IRQ, Memory, and I/O settings are easily viewed and compared.

Resources by Connection   Dependent device resources are grouped under their parent devices.

The View menu also contains the Show Hidden Devices setting, which you should always have checked. This setting shows all loaded device drivers, which allows you to remove errant software device drivers such as those installed by virus scanners or other low-level application software. The ability to remove these drivers is crucial to proper troubleshooting.

All visible device types indicate actual devices present in your system. You can right-click devices to enable, disable, uninstall (remove the driver), or select properties. The Properties window allows you to change advanced settings, which vary by device, to reinstall the device driver, and to change device resources for ISA Plug and Play devices.

Many devices have custom property tabs available in their Properties windows. For example:

- The Advanced tab in the Properties window for USB devices will show you the USB bandwidth allocation for devices on that bus. The tab for USB hubs will show you how much power various devices draw and how many ports are available.

- The IRQ Steering tab of the Standard PC device (under Computer) allows you to disable IRQ Steering if necessary. IRQ Steering allows Windows 2000 to reassign PCI IRQ resources. If IRQ Steering is disabled, then only the computer BIOS may assign IRQ resources. IRQ Steering is especially important for USB and Card-Bus devices added to the system after it has been booted. If IRQ Steering is disabled, Windows 2000 may not be able to use these devices.

- Modems have a number of extra tabs in their Properties windows for diagnostics, sound volume settings, initialization strings, and so forth. You can also enable log recording connection attempts and view the log to troubleshoot failed connection attempts.

- The Advanced tab for Network Adapters contains parameters to fine-tune server performance. Max out the Extra Receive Buffers settings to improve many aspects of server performance by up to 20 percent. Changing these settings will cause a network disconnection and immediate reconnection.

- The Printer Port Settings tab lets you determine whether or not the port uses an interrupt in Windows 2000. Not using an interrupt preserves IRQ resources. Using an interrupt can improve performance with some devices.

Be sure to explore the Properties windows of devices on your machines to familiarize yourself with their advanced features.

Troubleshooting with the Device Manger is pretty simple. If a device doesn't work, use the Device Manager to uninstall the driver and try to install it again. If that doesn't work, and the device is an ISA Plug and Play device, try moving the resources manually to settings that show no conflicts in the Device Conflicts window at the bottom of the Resources panel of the device's Properties window.

If none of these tactics succeed, physically remove all hardware that is not necessary to boot the computer, and then reinstall components one at a time in the order that they are important to you. This will allow you to install the maximum number of important peripherals that Windows 2000 can successfully support on that particular computer.

Troubleshooting with the Event Viewer

Rather than reporting nonfatal error messages on screen during operation, Windows 2000 adds a record to the Event Log. This technique keeps users from being bothered by annoying messages that they may not have the permissions to fix and, more importantly, keeps a written log of all error messages for you to review. If you've ever had a user call you to fix an error and then not remember what the error was, you'll appreciate the Event Log. You review the Event Log with the Event Viewer, shown in Figure 17.5.

Figure 17.5   The Event Viewer lets you track event messages in several specialized logs.

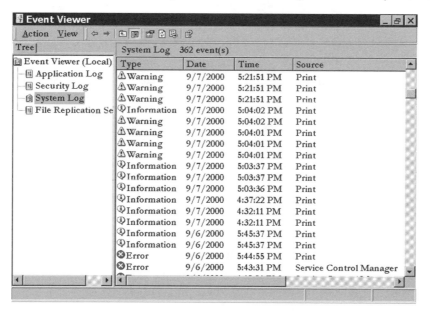

You should begin all troubleshooting sessions by reviewing the Event Log with the Event Viewer. Quite often, the Event Log will tell you exactly what is wrong. Three separate system logs are maintained by the Event Viewer by default:

System Log   System events are recorded by the Windows 2000 services.

Security Log   Security events are recorded when they occur. Security events are designated by your audit and user policies.

Application Log   Application events are recorded by applications other than the operating system.

Additional logs can be added to the Event Viewer by other services. An example of this is the File Replication Service Log that is normally present in the Event Viewer along with the three standard logs.

The log that an application uses is entirely up to the application, so you'll find lots of annoying thematic overlap. Just get in the habit of checking both the System and Application Logs, because it's not always clear where error messages will show up.

Events in the Event Log are recorded with three priorities:

- Informative messages are marked with a blue icon containing the letter *i*. These events are supposed to be for your information only and should not affect the operation of your server.

- Alerts are recorded with a yellow icon containing an exclamation mark (!). These events indicate that your computer is operating in a degraded condition or that some noncritical resource is not operating correctly.

- A red stop sign indicates a critical warning. Something serious is wrong with your computer or configuration, and it will cause denial of a service.

The Security Log has two event icons:

- A key shows passed audit policy events.
- A padlock shows blocked audit policy events.

You should check your Event Log any time you suspect something isn't working correctly in your system. You should check it periodically (at least once a month), even when things are working fine.

Because many services fail due to underlying problems, a single problem might have four or five associated error messages from various portions of the system. Network adapter failures would typically show a Service Control Manager error and various other service errors, because services that rely upon that adapter will also fail.

Note that drivers and the kernel cannot log messages to the Event Log because the Event Log service runs outside the kernel. All kernel and driver problems that don't cause a blue-screen crash will show up as Service Control Manager errors because higher-level services that use the functionality of failed devices also will not start.

Troubleshooting Security Problems

If a user cannot access a program or existing data on a computer, chances are that the user does not have sufficient permissions to do so. To troubleshoot security problems, log on as the administrator and attempt the same operation. If you can perform the operation, the problem is a security problem. You can either assign the user permissions to use the resource, or you can move the resource to an area where the user has sufficient permissions.

Sometimes even the administrator can't use or delete a visible resource. In this case, either there is no ACE granting the Administrator access or the resource was created and assigned permissions under a previous installation of Windows 2000 that has since been overwritten. The old administrator account that no longer exists is now the owner of the resource. Because Windows 2000 assigns a new security ID to the new administrator during the new installation, no current user has permission to use or delete this resource. Fortunately, Windows 2000 provides a way around this problem. The administrator can take ownership of any resource and then reassign permissions as necessary. Chapter 6 provides complete information on troubleshooting security problems in Windows 2000.

Network Services

Troubleshooting network services can be rather difficult, because the complex interactions between all the modules often cause problems themselves. In fact, it's usually the bindings between services and drivers that are the cause of networking problems.

These interactions are controlled by the Registry, and it is Registry "corruption"—misconfigured or missing Registry keys—that causes the vast majority of Windows 2000 service problems. This is such a large topic that Registry troubleshooting is covered separately in the next chapter. This section contains a common, quick methodology for restoring network services between computers.

Generally, most networking problems can be solved by removing the networking service components and transport protocols, rebooting, reinstalling them, reapplying the latest service pack, and rebooting again. This restores Registry settings to their default values.

Make sure the computer is communicating on the network by pinging another computer. If you can't ping another machine on your network, you've got a problem with either your adapter, driver, cabling, or TCP/IP stack. Validate the cable by connecting a working computer to it and logging it. Validate the adapter and driver by removing and reinstalling the driver. Validate the TCP/IP stack by removing and reinstalling it. Remember to reapply the latest service pack after you do so. If you still can't ping another computer at this point, try replacing the adapter with one of another model.

Once you can ping another machine, try to connect from the client or server in question to a resource on the other end-system that uses a low-level service, such as FTP or HTTP. For example, try pointing a Web browser on the client to a Web site on the server, or a Telnet client to the Echo Simple TCP/IP service on the machine. Proving out a connected TCP/IP path is a very good reason to use simple TCP/IP services on a server.

Also make sure you can reach the computer by pinging both its IP address and its DNS or NetBIOS name. If you can't ping the name, you've got a name resolution problem to fix before you troubleshoot further.

Once you've validated a complete round-trip path between the end-systems, try again to use the higher-level network services. If you cannot log in, try an administrative account. Make sure all the normal networking services are running on both machines and that the Event Logs show no errors. Determine which of the end-systems is actually having the problem by using a known-good third system to connect to each.

Once you've identified the problem machine, try removing and reinstalling all network services. This quite frequently solves bizarre service problems because it re-creates the dependency settings in the Registry.

If you cannot manually remove a network adapter, protocol stack, or service, then the computer's Registry is definitely corrupted. You'll have to manually remove the service or driver from the Registry, as explained in Chapter 18. In extreme cases where you've definitely ruled out hardware failure, you may need to reinstall Windows 2000 in its repair mode.

Troubleshooting Resources

Once you have exhausted your own knowledge and skills, and the diagnostic utilities provided by Microsoft give you no more useful information, you will need to turn to other resources for help.

The TechNET CD and the Microsoft Knowledge Base Library are invaluable for Windows 2000 troubleshooting. Beg, borrow, or steal access to these resources if you must, because you won't get far without them. You can also ask others for help on the Internet or through online services.

Windows 2000 help files   A good first-line troubleshooting resource. These help files are based on Microsoft's experience with customer support, so they include specific troubleshooting help for the problems that are most often reported to Microsoft. You stand a good chance of finding a help file that can walk you through the steps for fixing software configuration problems.

TechNET   Microsoft distributes this CD-ROM to technical support professionals who subscribe. It contains much of the same information found on the Microsoft Web site, but it is far faster because your searches are not limited by the speed of your modem. You can subscribe to the TechNET CD-ROM service by calling (800) 344-2121. MCSEs get a free subscription to TechNET for one year after obtaining their certification. TechNET can be searched online at search.microsoft.com.

The Internet   By far the best troubleshooting resource for any computer problem. The cumulative experience of thousands of Windows 2000 experts is available through both Microsoft-sanctioned and third-party resources. Unless you are working with an experimental release of Windows 2000, you can presume that someone else has had the same problem you are having. There's a good chance they posted a question on a news group that was answered by someone who knew what to do about it.

Direct from the manufacturer   Most hardware manufacturers also maintain Web sites that contain current versions of their Windows 2000 drivers. If you are having a problem with a third-party driver, check the vendor's Web site for an updated driver. If you can't find the site, use Google to search for it.

Microsoft Knowledge Base   The Microsoft Knowledge Base is the official repository for support information about all Microsoft products, including Windows 2000. The Knowledge Base is an accumulation of answers to technical support questions received by Microsoft since Windows 2000 was first released. You can access this database at support.microsoft.com.

Search engines   Web search engines provide a very fast method to find information about Windows 2000 and troubleshooting. Frequently, you can find answers from people who have had the same problems you are having. These search engines are provided free of charge by corporations who are interested in furthering the development of the Internet and the World Wide Web. The largest index and search engine providers are presented here. Many others exist, and you will find links to them through these providers:

- www.yahoo.com
- www.google.com
- www.excite.com

Summary

Troubleshooting is a methodical process, albeit a frustrating and slow one at times. When you troubleshoot in the correct order, you can quickly determine the problem domain, isolate the faulty component, and take restorative action.

Troubleshooting and Optimization

PART 4

Troubleshooting networks is pretty simple. By determining which devices in a network are affected, you can isolate the single point of failure that is affecting those devices. For example, if all the clients on a single subnet cannot attach to the network, then either the hub that creates the subnet is at fault or the router that connects it to the rest of the network is. Start troubleshooting in the middle, at the network layer with the Ping command. If you can ping, troubleshoot up the OSI stack into the session, application, and user layers. If you can't, troubleshoot down through the network, data-link, and physical layers.

Troubleshooting clients is a bit trickier; you have to determine whether you're encountering a hardware problem or a software problem. With the exception of disk failure, hardware problems are easy to troubleshoot and fix. Disk problems almost always take days to resolve.

Troubleshooting software usually means troubleshooting Windows 2000, which has a wide array of new and highly useful troubleshooting tools. Windows NT Server 4 had essentially run out of troubleshooting options by Service Pack 4, thus incurring the wrath of NT network administrators. Microsoft apparently got the message and included both a Safe Mode for quick and painless problem solving and the Recovery Console, which allows very low-level access to Windows 2000 installations. The repair option has also been streamlined to reduce the problems it can cause.

Finally, Plug and Play support gives Windows 2000 complete control over installed devices, unlike Windows NT. With NT, you had to configure devices manually or in their BIOS and then tell Windows NT drivers what their parameters were. Windows 2000 finds the devices and controls their configuration. If you need to manually change anything, you specify the change using Windows 2000. This level of control over hardware prevents numerous problems from occurring in the first place and makes solving the problems that do occur much easier.

Case Study: Use the Right Tool for the Job

Recently, a customer asked me to upgrade a few of their laptops. To cut costs, they had purchased inexpensive laptops designed for the home market, Compaq Presarios. These laptops were based on the Cyrix MediaGX integrated processor, which contains most of the logic of a PC motherboard on a single chip.

I installed Windows 2000 without a hitch, but when it came time to add the PCMCIA network adapter, a strange thing happened: the dongle light briefly illuminated, but the laptop did not recognize the hardware. Nothing happened at all, in fact. I was somewhat taken aback—even if the hardware wasn't recognized properly, I had expected the Plug and Play subsystem to at least report the additional hardware.

When I opened up the Device Manager, no devices showed installation problems, but the device I'd just installed didn't show up. To be honest, I was a little lost. I tried manually installing the device driver, but that didn't seem to help—it just showed up as a device with an error.

Going back to my old school MS-DOS troubleshooting tactics, I decided to look for a device conflict. I knew we were using a 16-bit PCMCIA adapter, so it would go through the ISA bridge and be handled as an ISA device. This created the potential for IRQ, port, and memory conflicts.

I booted to the laptop's BIOS and disabled all the built-in peripherals: the on-board audio adapter, serial ports, printer port, and USB adapter. After saving this configuration, I booted the laptop normally. This time, the laptop correctly recognized the adapter, and I was able to install the device driver.

The Device Manager now showed that the adapter was occupying IRQ 5—the same one used by the on-board audio device. I used the Device Manger to manually move the IRQ to the unused IRQ 3 (this computer had only one serial port) and to ensure that the port address would be unused as well. After this, I rebooted the laptop and reenabled the on-board devices. They all came up correctly under Windows 2000 after that.

The MediaGX processor handles all of its internal devices—including sound, video, and all the ports—as ISA devices, so Windows 2000 cannot steer conflicting IRQs off to enable new devices. I did exactly what PCI Steering does automatically for PCI devices. PCI Steering doesn't work for ISA devices, however, so I had to reassign IRQs manually. I recommended to my client that from then on, they purchase business-grade machines that are more compatible with modern operating systems.

24seven **CASE STUDY**

18

The Registry

Don't fear the Registry. It's big, it's Byzantine, and it's fragile—it's understandable that many Windows 2000 administrators avoid it, but sooner or later you'll have to get comfortable with its structure and use if you're going to maintain a Windows 2000 system. This chapter will cover why and how the Registry is organized, how you should work with it, and some general troubleshooting procedures that are fairly common. The appendix is a detailed encyclopedia of Registry settings you can use as a reference when you have a specific problem or when you're rooting around looking for some specific configuration.

WARNING Standard Registry warning and disclaimer: Changes in the Registry settings can cause your computer to become misconfigured, and the computer will no longer behave as expected. You may have to reinstall Windows 2000. Proceed with caution and at your own risk. And don't run with scissors.

The Registry is a unified database of program configuration settings. All programs installed on a Windows 2000 machine and written to the Win32 programming specification (including the operating system) store their configuration information in the Registry. Using Registry editors, you can customize, correct, and even misconfigure Windows 2000 or any installed applications.

The Registry is also the biggest design flaw of Windows 2000, in my opinion. (The other contestant in the major design flaw race is the dynamic link library architecture.) The centralized nature of the Registry and the fact that it does not work with standard file-handling tools cause the following problems:

- Applications cannot be reliably copied between machines, because there's no uniform way to tell which Registry keys are associated with which applications.

- Applications usually cannot be moved because Registry keys store their fixed location for internal reference. Moving an application will usually cause it to work incorrectly.

- Applications must be specifically installed and uninstalled, which would not be necessary if Registry data and DLLs were located in the same directory as the application. If applications did not require installation, network clients could simply begin using network-stored applications, rather than require a network technician to install them. Application rollout tools and many enterprise management tools would not be necessary.

- Backup and restore operations are not simple file-copy operations—special API calls must be used to back up and restore the Registry.

- You cannot completely delete an application by simply deleting its file system directory. If the application's Registry data is corrupt, you may not be able to use its uninstallation tool either, which means you may never be able to completely remove a malfunctioning application.

- Damage to Registry files can cause widespread application failure—the Registry is a single point of failure.

Microsoft originally used the Registry architecture because they wanted applications to be able to modify the configuration of other applications. and so that read/write access to the Registry could be speed-optimized easily. While this sounds like a good idea, it makes it possible for poorly written software to mess up perfectly good software, a problem that happens all the time. And the speed optimization could easily be handled by simply reading the configuration settings of running software into memory and then letting the Virtual Memory Manager page the settings back out to disk. In fact, Registry access isn't fast enough to support many applications—IIS4 was reengineered to use its own high-speed Registry, called a *metabase*, because Windows NT's Registry slowed down its ability to respond to numerous client requests. Windows 2000 and IIS5 inherited this design. My point that applications should have their own Registries is basically proven by Microsoft's own example of spinning off application-specific Registries when the centralized Registry failed to meet their requirements. Unfortunately, we're stuck with the Registry and all its flaws for quite some time. Sadly, it's better than the maze of text settings files used in earlier versions of Windows and in UNIX.

WARNING   Don't mess with the Registry on a production server. Do all of your testing of Registry effects on a test computer before making any changes in the field.

To learn about the Registry safely, download the 30-day evaluation edition of vmware at www.vmware.com, and then install a copy of Windows 2000 in a virtual machine using the option for undoable disk storage. Inside the virtual machine, you can mess around with the Registry with complete impunity, because you won't be crashing the system upon which you rely. With the undoable disk option, you can simply "undo" any change that causes the installation to become unusable so you won't even have to reinstall. You'll find that once you've got a virtual machine to play with, the hesitation to experiment will go away, and you'll be a Registry hacker in no time.

The Registry Structure

The Registry is a simple hierarchical database, which means that elements of the database can themselves contain elements, thus creating a tree-structure hierarchy. The elements in this case are called Registry keys. *Keys* are named entities that may contain named data elements (called *values*), much the way that folders contain files in a hierarchical file system such as NTFS or FAT. The values contained in the Registry keys have a reference name, a data type, and a value associated with them. Figure 18.1 shows the structure of the Registry.

Windows 2000 and the applications that run on it use the Registry to store configuration information. This is data that must persist from one running session to another, because the data is used to provide operating parameters for the software that depends upon it.

Any Win32 application can create, store, change, and retrieve values from the Registry. Registry keys are secured objects, so they have an access control list and can be locked to prevent modification. However, most are not locked, and administrators have wide access to the Registry to make changes.

Specific Registry keys and values only have context for the applications that use them. They mean nothing to other applications, and although most keys have reasonably obvious human-readable names, their purpose is inscrutable if you don't understand which applications use them and what the values they contain do. For this reason, you will usually need a guide to the Registry settings to explain them or at least specific directions on how to add, change, or delete keys to perform a specific change. Changing or deleting keys without understanding their purpose is a recipe for disaster. Windows 2000 cannot

Figure 18.1 The Registry is a hierarchical database of name/value pairs.

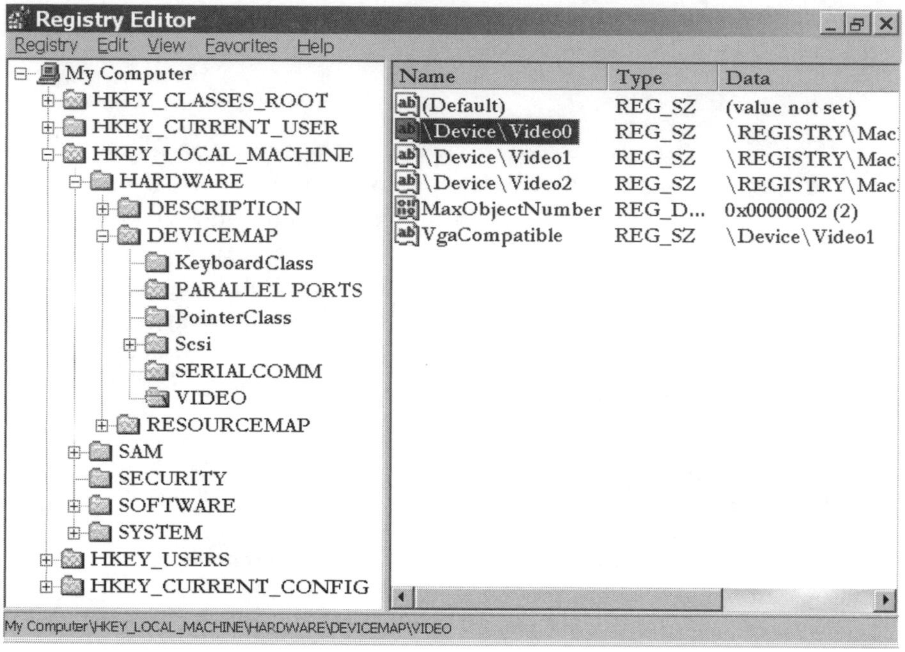

completely boot if a combination of specific keys are missing or changed, and applications will not behave normally if keys they rely on are missing or changed. Never delete or modify a Registry key unless you understand its purpose and you know what the effects of the change will be (or you're willing to live with the unknown consequences).

The structure you see in the Registry when you load a Registry editor is actually created at boot time when the system loads files called *hives*, which actually permanently store the Registry keys. The hives store various types of Registry keys, as described below:

HKEY_LOCAL_MACHINE Stores the Registry keys that are created by applications (including Windows 2000's services and Explorer). Nearly all the hive files (SAM, SECURITY, SOFTWARE, SYSTEM) are contained in the HKLM key. This key stores very nearly every useful troubleshooting key that you'll work with.

HKEY_CLASSES_ROOT Stores application dependency data (for example, Explorer extension associations and OLE class registrations).

HKEY_CURRENT_CONFIG Stores dynamic changes that will not be permanently stored to the HKEY_LOCAL_MACHINE\SOFTWARE and HKEY_LOCAL_MACHINE\ SYSTEM keys.

HKEY_CURRENT_USER   Points to the logged-on user's user profile in the HKEY_ USERS key. This key contains Desktop settings, Control Panel configurations, and other settings that are specific to the current user.

HKEY_USERS   Stores user profiles and all the information they contain as above.

Hives are either automatically created at boot time or when a user logs in, or they are stored in one of the hive files located in the %systemroot%\system32\config directory.

Some Registry keys are merely pointers to other locations in the Registry. For example, the HKEY_CURRENT_USER key isn't a copy of the current user's profile from HKEY_USERS, it's a pointer to it. When you change a value in HKEY_CURRENT_USER, that value actually changes in HKEY_USERS. You can think of HKEY_CURRENT_USER as shorthand notation for the specific key of the logged-on user. Other keys, such as HKEY_CURRENT_CONFIG and HKEY_LOCAL_MACHINE\SYSTEM\CurrentControlSet work this way as well.

Control Sets

Windows 2000 stores the system configuration (Registry settings that control how drivers and services run) in keys called *control sets*. There are usually at least two control set keys that have a numerical enumeration suffix, as in the following:

ControlSet001

ControlSet002

Two "meta" keys also exist:

- CurrentControlSet is a pointer to the control set used to boot.
- Clone is a copy of the CurrentControlSet that the system actually operates from.

The SYSTEM\Select key contains values that show which control sets are used for what purpose:

Value	Description
Current	The current control set
Default	The default control set used at start-up
Failed	Any control set that cannot be booted
LastKnownGood	The control set used if the Last Known Good option is used at start-up

You should usually manipulate the CurrentControlSet Registry key to ensure that you are manipulating the correct control set.

Troubleshooting and Optimization

PART 4

Registry Tools

Every program that modifies a configuration setting for any piece of software, system or otherwise, is a Registry tool. Registry tools make use of the Registry as a named value store by using special function calls built into Windows 2000 to create, change, and delete Registry values.

The Control Panel is the primary Registry configuration tool that you should use to configure your Windows 2000 machine. Aside from being easier to use than the manual Registry-editing tools, different versions of Windows 2000 may store Registry values in different places. Using the Control Panel ensures that you always change the values you intended to change.

Unfortunately, a number of configuration settings have no associated Control Panel, and some Registry corruption problems cannot be solved by higher-level Registry editors (for example, the Control Panel or a piece of applications software).

RegEdt32 and Regedit

To handle cases where no alternative to changing a Registry setting exists or when a Registry corruption problem prevents the standard tools from working with the Registry, Windows 2000 comes with two general-purpose Registry editors. Each of the following Registry editors has features that the other does not have, so you'll probably use both on occasion, although most people favor one or the other for routine editing:

RegEdt32   The original Windows NT Registry editor. It opens five different windows for the various top-level keys rather than presenting them all in a hierarchy. For security reasons, `regedt32.exe` can be used to modify access control lists for Registry keys or to load and unload hives from other installed copies of Windows 2000. The text export function of RegEdt32 creates files that can be read by system administrators but cannot be reimported.

Regedit   The Windows 95 Registry editor that is included with Windows 2000. It opens the entire Registry as a single hierarchy, so it's easier to browse, and it includes automatic search features that are missing in RegEdt32. It allows you to import and export text files of Registry settings for program installation or for changing Registry settings in batches. Regedit cannot modify Registry security, nor can it load or unload hives. This tool works the same way in all 32-bit versions of Windows.

Some claim that Regedit should not be used for editing the Windows 2000 Registry, citing the fact that you cannot modify Registry security with it. That argument is silly. Regedit would not be included with Windows 2000 if it didn't have a purpose, and you'll rarely if ever change the security setting of Registry keys. I personally prefer Regedit, because I can easily browse the entire Registry hierarchy, and I can use the same interface on all versions of Windows. In Regedit, I can also save the keys that I'm about to edit to a text file—if I realize that I made a mistake, I can simply reimport the text file to revert to the original settings. RegEdt32, on the other hand, has a read-only mode that will prevent you from accidentally changing anything while you browse.

Figure 18.2 shows Regedit. Figure 18.3 shows RegEdt32. Notice the difference in the menu structures.

Neither Registry editor has a Start menu item associated with them. You can either create a shortcut to the editor or use the Start ➤ Run facility to run them by name.

Loading and Unloading Hives

It is possible to directly load Registry hive files—not textual representations of Registry files. For example, you may need to do this if you have to repair a nonbooting Windows 2000 machine using another installed copy of Windows 2000. In the newly installed copy of Windows 2000, you can directly import the Registry hives from the directory containing the misconfigured Windows 2000 system. Then you can correct the Registry settings in the old Registry hive and resave the hive to reboot the crashed machine.

Figure 18.2   Regedit displays the entire Registry as a single hierarchy.

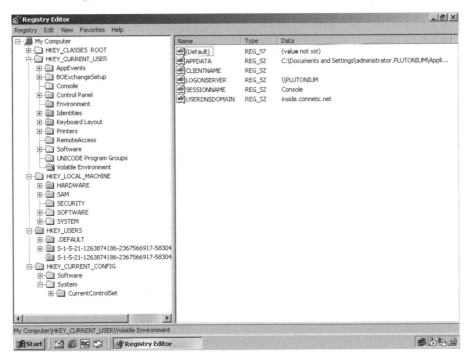

Troubleshooting and Optimization

PART 4

Figure 18.3   RegEdt32 displays the Registry as five different hierarchies.

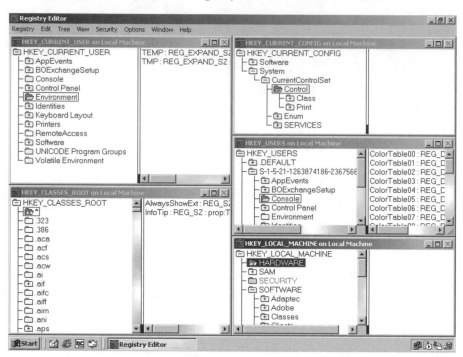

You can't load a Registry hive with the same key name as an existing hive in your Registry, because the configuration settings for the other installation will not be the same as the settings that are required for the running operating system.

Follow these steps to load a Registry hive:

1. Activate `regedt32.exe`. (Registry hives can only be loaded using this editor.)

2. Select the key under which you wish to load the hive. This should usually be the key where the hive would be loaded anyway.

3. Select File ➢ Load Hive.

4. Select the path to the hive file. Windows 2000 system hives are stored in `%WINNTROOT%\System32\config`.

5. Enter a new name for the hive, such as "othersystem." The hive will be added to the Registry editor.

6. Make any changes you need to the Registry settings in this hive.

7. When you are finished, select the hive, and then select File ➢ Unload Hive. This will remove the hive from the Registry and save it back to the disk.

Saving and Restoring Registry Keys

For individual keys and settings, the Registry editor supports reading and writing textual representations of Registry keys. You can use this functionality to automatically create and maintain groups of Registry settings. This functionality would be required when distributing new applications. The text files created by the Registry editor have the extension .reg and are automatically associated with the Registry editor in Windows Explorer. When you click on a REG file, its keys are automatically loaded into the Registry. The structure of a REG file is something like the INI files used in earlier versions of Windows. The following text is an example of a Registry key exported to a REG file:

```
Windows Registry Editor Version 5.00


[HKEY_LOCAL_MACHINE\SYSTEM\CurrentControlSet\Services\Tcpip]
"Type"=dword:00000001
"Start"=dword:00000001
"ErrorControl"=dword:00000001
"Tag"=dword:00000004
"DisplayName"="TCP/IP Protocol Driver"
"Group"="PNP_TDI"
"Description"="TCP/IP Protocol Driver"


[HKEY_LOCAL_MACHINE\SYSTEM\CurrentControlSet\Services\Tcpip\Parameters]
"NV Hostname"="VAIO"
"NameServer"=""
"ForwardBroadcasts"=dword:00000000
"IPEnableRouter"=dword:00000000
"Domain"=""
"Hostname"="VAIO"
"SearchList"=""
"UseDomainNameDevolution"=dword:00000001
"EnableICMPRedirect"=dword:00000001
"DeadGWDetectDefault"=dword:00000001
"DontAddDefaultGatewayDefault"=dword:00000000
"EnableSecurityFilters"=dword:00000000
```

```
"AllowUnqualifiedQuery"=dword:00000000
"PrioritizeRecordData"=dword:00000001
```

As you can see, the file starts with a text tag identifying the version of the Registry editor and then contains one or more Registry key entries. Each key is enclosed in square brackets. Values are enclosed in parentheses, and value data is defined with an equal sign followed by the data.

WARNING   If you double-click on a *.reg file in Windows Explorer, Windows 2000 will ask you if you want to add the contents of the file to the Registry. Do not click Yes unless you intend to add its contents to the Registry. Do not import *.reg files from anyone you do not know.

Group Policy

When you make configuration changes through Group Policy in Windows 2000, the changes are made to the Registry when the computer boots (computer policy) and when a user logs on (user policy). The process works like this: Every Active Directory container that the user is a member of may contain a group policy. A *policy* consists of a set of Registry keys and values that implement the specified changes. When a user logs in, the policies are applied in hierarchical order (the hierarchy being the Active Directory hierarchy of the containers), overwriting one another as they are applied.

Unlike System Policy in Windows NT, which permanently applied system policy settings that often caused permanent damage to Windows NT installations, group policy settings are not stored in the hives that make the Registry persistent. They're stored temporarily only for the duration of that user's session (user policy) or until the computer is rebooted (computer policy).

Computer policies are usually applied to the Registry in the following locations:

- HKLM\SOFTWARE\Policies
- HKLM\SOFTWARE\Microsoft\Windows\CurrentVersion\Policies

User policies are usually applied to the Registry in the following locations:

- HKCU\SOFTWARE\Policies
- HKCU\SOFTWARE\Microsoft\Windows\CurrentVersion\Policies

Technically, policies can make changes to any part of the Registry. The keys above are simply those that Microsoft has set aside for the specific purpose of storing policy information. The \SOFTWARE\Policies keys are the preferred locations and store the bulk of policy change information. The \SOFTWARE\Microsoft\Windows\CurrentVersion\Policies keys are used primarily by Internet Explorer. The appendix details the use of these keys.

Management Snap-Ins

Many of the MMC snap-ins used for configuration are really just Registry editors that present human-readable explanations for keys and that limit the scope of the presented keys to a specific function. In Windows NT 4, most management interfaces abstracted the Registry setting through specific dialog boxes. In Windows 2000, Microsoft has done away with that abstraction for the sake of efficiency and coherency; it actually makes more sense to simply set the Registry values directly.

The Management snap-ins are very similar to the Registry editors. In fact, they are a more sophisticated Registry editor that provides a purpose-oriented (system control, in the case of the group policy editor) hierarchy for browsing Registry keys.

The keys displayed and configurable in the various Management snap-in's editor are loaded from .adm files contained in the %systemroot%\inf\ directory. These files contain a script that defines the settings available in the policy editor and which Registry keys they modify. You can modify these ADM files with a text editor if you want to use the Management snap-ins to edit other Registry keys. The following text is an example of a Registry setting described in a Management snap-in:

```
CATEGORY !!NetworkConnections  ;Machine
    KEYNAME"Software\Policies\Microsoft\Windows\Network Connections"
    POLICY !!ShowSharedAccessUi
        EXPLAIN !!ShowSharedAccessUi_Help
        VALUENAME "NC_ShowSharedAccessUi"
            VALUEON NUMERIC 1
            VALUEOFF NUMERIC 0
    END POLICY
    END CATEGORY ;NetworkConnections [more]
```

The identifiers that begin with !! are macros which are expanded based on values that appear at the bottom of the ADM file.

Scripting with reg.exe

Windows 2000 includes a command prompt tool call reg.exe that allows administrators to modify the Registry using plain batch files. By calling REG with a command parameter and the name of the key involved, you can perform nearly any possible Registry operation in a script. You can set up REG as a logon, logoff, startup, or shutdown script to make widespread changes to client computers in the domain. REG supports the following operations, whose functions are obvious:

REG QUERY

REG ADD

REG DELETE

REG COPY

REG SAVE

REG RESTORE

REG LOAD

REG UNLOAD

REG COMPARE

REG EXPORT

REG IMPORT

Issue REG <COMMAND> /? at the command prompt for help on each operation.

Third-Party Tools

The Windows 2000 Resource Kit provides two tools—regback.exe and regrest.exe—to back up and restore the Windows 2000 Registry from within a running Windows 2000 environment. These tools offer a functionality similar to the system state backup function of the backup program.

A number of high-speed Registry search tools exist. The only time I've ever needed to use a tool of this nature was when I installed Windows NT on the D: drive and later decided to change it to the C: drive using the Disk Administrator. Suddenly no settings files could be found, so I used a high-speed search-and-replace Registry editor to change every instance of D: in the Registry to C:, which fixed the problem. Windows 2000 doesn't allow you to change the drive letter of the system volume, so this isn't a real option any more.

I can't really recommend doing widespread search-and-replace operations in the Registry. You might inadvertently change some setting that is not related to your intent but that matches the search criteria. Check out www.download.com if you're interested in third-party Registry search utilities.

Hacking the Registry

I've discussed Registry editors, but I haven't really mentioned why you would need them. In a perfect world, you wouldn't need them, because every Registry setting you'd want to change would be available in an MMC snap-in. In reality, you frequently have to fix things that Microsoft didn't know would break, so you'll be in the Registry often.

There are innumerable reasons why the Registry becomes corrupted. Common reasons include failed software installations, a crash in the midst of a batch of Registry setting changes, and the failure of software uninstallers to remove all the necessary Registry keys.

TIP   Instead of deleting Registry keys, export them to a text file first, and then delete them. That way you can reimport them if you've made a mistake.

In any case, there are a number of reasons why you might have to directly modify Registry settings. Although the Registry is huge and in many cases oddly structured, you can quickly develop a feel for which portions of the Registry are relevant to the troubleshooting and configuration processes. Once you're comfortable with the Registry, the chances that you will cause Registry corruption by incorrectly deleting keys is significantly reduced.

Fixing Windows 2000 Machines That Can't Boot

Installing new services (or forgetting to apply the latest service pack) on Windows 2000 machines occasionally can cause the machine to crash before it is entirely booted. Since the computer crashes during the boot problem, you cannot fix the problem from that version of Windows 2000. There are five solutions to this problem:

1. Reinstall Windows 2000. This is the longest and most intrusive method.

2. Install another copy of Windows 2000 onto the same disk and use that copy to repair the originally installed version.

3. Move the computer's hard disk into a working Windows 2000 machine and make the necessary changes to fix the problem.

4. Boot the Windows 2000 CD-ROM to the Recovery Console and attempt to solve the problem.

5. Run a repair installation to reset the operating system to Service Pack 0.

Assuming you're going to use the second or third method, you can then use the procedure for editing the failed computer's Registry that is described in the earlier section, "Loading and Unloading Hives." The system hive file contains all driver and adapter information that might need to be changed.

To change the startup value for a service or driver in a nonoperational system, use the Registry editor to browse to the `ControlSet001\services` (or the current control set as defined by the value *Current* in the system hive). Browse to the service or driver you suspect is causing the problem, and change the `Start` value to `0x4` (Disabled).

> **TIP** From the Repair Console, you can use the enable and disable commands to change the startup type of a device or service to prevent the service from crashing during the boot process.

An easier method to deal with newly installed drivers or adapters is simply to rename the driver or service executable or DLL. This will prevent the service from attempting to start (and subsequently crashing) Windows 2000. You'll then be able to use the system's own Registry-editing tools to remove the corrupted driver information.

Repairing Higher-Level Applications

Applications installed in Windows 2000 seem to suffer Registry corruption far more often than they should. The usual method for dealing with this problem is removing and reinstalling the application, which works fine most of the time.

However, this doesn't work all the time. If the uninstallation program doesn't remove all the corrupted Registry keys, the second installation will be just as corrupt as the first. The solution here is to manually find and remove those keys after uninstalling.

Then there are those times when uninstalling an application would cause a lot of work or when an application simply can't be removed. In those cases, you will probably need to get technical information from the publisher of the application about its Registry settings so you can add or change them manually.

Adding Functionality

Windows 2000 has a number of features that don't have an associated Management snap-in but which can be really useful. Some of these features are associated with Windows 2000 Resource Kit programs, but most of them are just hanging out in the Registry waiting to be enabled by an intrepid Registry guru. You'll come across these little nuggets of functionality in Tips and Tricks books and Web sites, in Microsoft's technical databases, and on occasion by simply playing with the Registry.

Cool Trick: Explorer BMP icons

You can force Explorer to display the contents of a BMP file as the icon rather than using the default MS Paint icon by changing the following Registry key:

    HKEY_CLASSES_ROOT\Paint.Picture\DefaultIcon

Change the (default value) entry to %1 in place of the mspaint.exe,1 entry. The change will take effect immediately. Now all your BMP icons will be tiny representations of the pictures they contain.

Manually Removing Software

You will often find that software developers don't spend much time getting their uninstallation software working correctly, so you'll frequently have to remove software manually.

Application

For the vast majority of applications, you can remove all their Registry settings by deleting the HKEY_LOCAL_MACHINE\SOFTWARE*<Vendor Name>**<Product Name>* key.

You usually shouldn't delete the vendor name key because vendors use that single key for all their software. Delete the key associated with the product name instead.

If the program has created an association to a file type, you should have to delete that association in the HKEY_CLASSES_ROOT key. If the software has installed any drivers or services, treat them as shown in the next section.

Services and Drivers

Services and drivers are located in the same place in the Registry and handled the same way. To disable a service or driver (less permanent and more stable than removing the key), browse to the following Registry key and change the Start value to 4 (disabled):

```
HKEY_LOCAL_MACHINE\SYSTEM\CurrentControlSet\Services\<Service Name,
Driver Name, or Adapter GUID>
```

This is equivalent to using the Drivers or Services Control Panel to set the start-up type to disabled. Network adapters are shown by their GUID, which you can determine by copying the value into the Clipboard and then searching on it. Or, you can compare the IP address listed in the tcpip subkey with the IP addresses of adapters in your system.

Printers

Sometimes you must manually remove and reinstall printers.

To delete a local (My Computer) printer, stop the spooler service using the Services Control Panel, delete the following Registry keys, and then restart the spooler:

```
HKEY_LOCAL_MACHINE\SYSTEM\CurrentControlSet\Control
\Print\Environments\Windows NT x86\Drivers
```

Troubleshooting
and Optimization

PART 4

```
\Version-3\<Printer Name>
```

```
HKEY_LOCAL_MACHINE\SYSTEM\CurrentControlSet\Control
\Print\Printers\<Printer Name>
```

To delete a network printer, stop the spooler service using the Services Control Panel, delete the following Registry keys, and then restart the spooler:

```
HKEY_CURRENT_USER\Printers\Connections\<Server Name>
HKEY_LOCAL_MACHINE\SYSTEM\CurrentControlSet\Control\Print
\Providers\LanMan Print Services\Servers
\<Server Name>\Printers\<Printer Name>
```

Important Registry Keys

Only a few portions of the Registry are extremely useful for troubleshooting. Following is a list of important Registry keys and their uses. You should study the function of these keys in the appendix.

HKEY_CURRENT_USER   This key stores environment settings that apply to the current user. You can edit these keys more conveniently using the Control Panel or the Group Policy editor than using the traditional Registry editors, but some keys don't appear in either of those tools.

HKEY_LOCAL_MACHINE\SOFTWARE   This key contains keys for installed software applications. Subkeys identify the software publisher, and each publisher's subkeys identify individual products. Deleting the keys for products will usually eliminate most of the Registry settings for the product unless there are document extensions located in HKEY_CLASSES_ROOT.

HKEY_LOCAL_MACHINE\SOFTWARE\Microsoft   This key contains keys for software published by Microsoft—including Windows 2000 itself. I think it's silly to establish important system keys inside a key used for more pedestrian purposes, but that's the way Microsoft decided to do it.

HKEY_LOCAL_MACHINE\SOFTWARE\Microsoft\Windows\CurrentVersion   This key contains keys that apply to all 32-bit versions of Windows, including Windows 95 and Windows 98. Most of these keys address user-interface options and options related to Windows Explorer.

HKEY_LOCAL_MACHINE\SOFTWARE\Microsoft\Windows\CurrentVersion\Run
This key contains a list of programs that should be executed by Windows Explorer after it launches. This is the place to look for those annoying auto-start programs that you can't find in the start-up folder.

HKEY_LOCAL_MACHINE\SOFTWARE\Microsoft\Windows NT\CurrentVersion   This key contains keys that apply only to Windows 2000. Most of these keys apply to executive services, subsystems, and network settings.

HKEY_LOCAL_MACHINE\SOFTWARE\Microsoft\Windows NT\CurrentVersion\ Winlogon   This key contains values that control the logon process. Check it out in the appendix.

HKEY_LOCAL_MACHINE\SYSTEM\CurrentControlSet\Control   This key contains control values for the kernel and executive services of Windows 2000.

HKEY_LOCAL_MACHINE\SYSTEM\CurrentControlSet\Services   This key contains keys for every installed service and driver. You'll edit this key to control errant services and drivers, so make sure you're familiar with it.

Summary

The difference between a typical Windows 2000 user and a Windows 2000 guru is knowledge of and familiarity with the Registry. If you want to be a guru, you need to know the Registry inside and out.

The Registry is a unified, hierarchical database of name/value pairs that stores configuration information for the Windows 2000 operating system and for installed drivers, services, and applications. Registry keys denote specific branches in the hierarchy. Registry keys only have meaning to applications that use the keys.

The top branches of the Registry are called hives, which are actually physically stored in different files in the system root directory. Branches of the Registry may actually be pointers to other portions of the Registry that provide a common means to redirect applications to contextual keys. For example, HKEY_CURRENT_USER actually is a pointer to whichever key inside HKEY_USERS specifies the logged-in user.

The two primary Registry editors included with Windows 2000 are RegEdt32, which allows the modification of Registry security settings, and Regedit, which has search and import/export features. Many of the Microsoft Management Consoles are actually implemented as scripted Registry editors as well, providing plain text descriptions of Registry features.

Troubleshooting
and Optimization

PART 4

There are numerous reasons why you might be required to manually edit the Registry as a Windows 2000 administrator. You may need to

- Manually remove errant software.
- Disable a service or driver.
- Enable a feature that has no management interface.
- Repair an application that has been corrupted.

Despite the size and complexity of the Registry, there are only a few well-known areas with keys that you can usefully modify. These areas are where Windows 2000 stores many of its feature-driven Registry keys. Less configurable areas of the Registry store linkage information and undocumented keys for low-level services and drivers.

The appendix is an all-but-complete listing of Registry keys included in Windows 2000. Most of the keys you'll ever need for troubleshooting purposes are listed there.

Case Study: Fixing an Unsuccessful Uninstallation

A customer called me when their Windows 2000 server began crashing after they uninstalled Adaptec EZ-CD Creator. Apparently, an employee thought that making backups to a CD-R directly on the server would be clever, so he installed a CD-R burner and Adaptec EZ-CD Creator. The busy servers couldn't dedicate enough time to keep the CD burner's buffer from underrunning and wasting the CD-R, so the employee uninstalled EZ-CD Creator and deleted all the Adaptec files.

Upon reboot, the server blue-screened repeatedly. They could boot it in Safe Mode, but that didn't solve the problem and allowed no access to crucial services.

When I arrived, the server was off. I booted it and noted that the crash occurred in a driver called cdr4_w2k.sys. I knew this wasn't a default system driver, so I assumed it was the CD-R driver for EZ-CD Creator 4. I rebooted the server in Safe Mode, opened the Registry Editor, and browsed:

HKEY_LOCAL_MACHINE\SYSTEM\ CurrentControlSet\Services\Cdr4_2K

and set the Startup Type to 4, which disabled the service. Upon rebooting, the server started normally, except that it had no CD-ROM drives available. This problem was fixed with a search of Adaptec's technical support Web site.

It took about 10 minutes to solve the problem, and most of that time involved waiting for the server to reboot.

Appendix

Useful Registry Keys

The Registry is a massive collection of individual values for nearly every program installed on your computer. The impetus for writing this appendix was simple—searching Microsoft's archives and the Web for the purpose of a Registry key is tedious and often difficult to do unless your machine is working correctly. And if that were the case, you likely wouldn't be hunting down the value of a Registry key.

While I have tried to document the entire basic structure of the Registry in Windows 2000, I did not describe every single Registry key. I've intentionally left out Registry keys that can't usefully be modified by hand and that are not helpful for troubleshooting. I've concentrated on those keys that are highly relevant to troubleshooting or which represent some interesting functionality. Many keys are inscrutable, created automatically by the system and unmodifiable, or simply should never be edited manually. On the other hand, Windows 2000 provides lots of little functions that don't have a management interface, so you have to edit the Registry manually to enable or disable these functions.

Where specific important values are present, a table of values and their associated description (or in some cases, the data they contain) is included. Values in parentheses are the default value for the key. Keys often have a default or unnamed value that is associated with the key. This value is expressed using the @ symbol in Registry export files and, by default, in this text.

Much of the information in this chapter is of little value to most people—but some of it is highly valuable to nearly everyone. If you want to see the inner workings of Windows 2000 for yourself, you can read through the entire appendix. If you just want to jump ahead to the good parts, skip to those entries denoted by the star symbol (★).

HKEY_CLASSES_ROOT   Maintains Explorer file associations for document extensions and file types. HKEY_CLASSES_ROOT is actually a pointer to HKEY_LOCAL_MACHINE\SOFTWARE\ classes.

Each document extension type is represented by a key of the same name; this key contains a value that associates the extension with an abstract file type. Each file type contains keys and values that associate activities with icons, such as Open or New. (The remaining glossary entries for this key are representative rather than exhaustive, as most keys for this hive do not vary.)

Some document extensions contain ShellEx or ShellNew keys. These keys describe the functionality of the right-click context menu. For example, the presence of a ShellNew key with a NullFile value and an empty string data will cause Explorer to list the document type in the New context menu and to create a new blank file in the current Explorer location.

HKEY_CLASSES_ROOT\<.ext>   Identifies the abstract file type that handles the extension. May also include a MIME type identifier called Content Type.

HKEY_CLASSES_ROOT\<.ext>\ShellEx\<CLSID>   The CLSID (OLE Class Identifier) of the application that handles this extension.

HKEY_CLASSES_ROOT\<.ext>\Shell\<Selection>\Command   Command line text that executes when this context menu item is selected.

HKEY_CLASSES_ROOT\<Abstract File Type>   Descriptive name of this file type.

HKEY_CLASSES_ROOT\<Abstract File Type>\CLSID   The CLSID (OLE Class Identifier) for this file type.

HKEY_CLASSES_ROOT\<Abstract File Type>DefaultIcon   Path to the default icon for this file type.

HKEY_CLASSES_ROOT\<Abstract File Type>\Shell   Default context menu selection from the subkey types.

HKEY_CLASSES_ROOT\<Abstract File Type>\Shell\<Selection>   String containing the context menu text.

HKEY_CLASSES_ROOT\<Abstract File Type>\Shell\<Selection>\Command   Command line text that performs the menu action.

HKEY_CLASSES_ROOT\<Abstract File Type>\Shell\<Selection>\ddeexec   DDE (Dynamic Data Exchange) parameter text that performs the action specified.

HKEY_CLASSES_ROOT\<Abstract File Type>\Shell\<Selection>\ddeexec\ Application   The OLE registered application that handles the DDE action.

HKEY_CLASSES_ROOT\CLSID   Contains the class identifiers (CLSIDs) of registered Component Object Model (COM) (formerly OLE) types. CLSIDs refer to a number of COM components of the Explorer interface, such as the Control Panel, permanent Explorer Desktop components, and any other display object that is not handled in the same manner as a standard folder or file.

HKEY_CLASSES_ROOT\hlp   File type association for the .hlp extension. The values for help files are shown in these keys as an example of how extensions are handled, not because these keys are especially important.

Value	Data
(default)	Abstract file type key. (hlpfile)

HKEY_CLASSES_ROOT\hlpfile   Executable file activity association for the hlpfile abstract file type.

Value	Data
(default)	Plain-text description of the abstract file type. (Help File)

HKEY_CLASSES_ROOT\hlpfile\DefaultIcon   Defines the displayed icon for the hlpfile extension.

Value	Data
(default)	Resource file containing the icon image and the image index. (%SystemRoot%\System32\shell32.dll,23)

HKEY_CLASSES_ROOT\hlpfile\s\Shell\Open\Command   Defines the shell action to perform when the Open command is applied to a help file (.hlp). The %1 environmental variable contained in the string refers to the first parameter, which Explorer sets to the path and filename of the activated help file.

Value	Data
(default)	Shell command that launches the executable file that performs the Open command for the hlpfile file type. (%SystemRoot%\System32\winhlp32.exe %1)

HKEY_CLASSES_ROOT\Interface Contains interface descriptions for Registry COM components.

HKEY_CURRENT_CONFIG This key contains information about the loaded hardware profile. The information contained in this key is used by currently executing software and should not be manually edited. Nothing in this hive is useful for troubleshooting, in my experience.

HKEY_CURRENT_USER This key contains policy settings that apply to the current user. It is a pointer to the profile key located in HKEY_USERS of the person logged in.

The key HKEY_USERS\.DEFAULT specifies settings that will apply to the computer when no user is logged in and will be copied to form a template when new users are added.

HKEY_CURRENT_USER\AppEvents This key enumerates system events (user- or system-initiated application interface messages) and their associated labels and sounds. You can disable the sounds associated with various application and system events by removing the associated value under the \SCHEMES key.

HKEY_CURRENT_USER\Console Contains values defining the visual layout of the command prompt. These values can be changed by modifying a shortcut to the command prompt.

HKEY_CURRENT_USER\Control Panel\Accessibility Contains values defining the settings of the Accessibility Options Control Panel. The values correspond directly to their counterparts in the Control Panel.

HKEY_CURRENT_USER\Control Panel\Appearance\Schemes Defines the color schemes available in the Display Control Panel. Each value is the name of the scheme, and its corresponding data is a record containing the color and size settings for that scheme.

HKEY_CURRENT_USER\Control Panel\Colors Defines the colors used by the various elements of the Windows Desktop as set by the current scheme and modified by the user in the Appearance panel of the Display Control Panel.

You can change the color of the default logon screen by changing the background value of HKEY_USERS\.DEFAULT\Control Panel\Colors.

HKEY_CURRENT_USER\Control Panel\Current Defines the currently selected color scheme.

HKEY_CURRENT_USER\Control Panel\Cursors Defines the paths to the cursor bitmap paths for each cursor context as set in the Mouse Control Panel.

HKEY_CURRENT_USER\Control Panel\Desktop

This key contains values that control how Windows Explorer operates. The list below highlights some of the more interesting values in this key.

Value	Data
AutoEndTasks	1 = Kills apps at shutdown without asking. (0)
CoolSwitch	(1) = Enables Alt+Tab switching.
CoolSwitchColumns	Number of icon columns in the switch panel. (7)
CoolSwitchRows	Number of icon rows in the switch panel. (3)
CursorBlinkRate	Cursor blink rate in milliseconds.
DragFullWindows	(1) = Drags windows with contents. (0) = Drags outline.
FontSmoothing	Amount of anti-aliasing to perform on fonts. (2)
GridGranularity	Defines the size, in units of 8 pixels, of an imaginary grid in which to position windows on the screen. (0) = No grid.
HungAppTimeout	Milliseconds to wait for response from hung application. (5000)
IconSpacing	Horizontal pixels between icons. (75)
IconTitleFaceName	Font to use for icon titles. (MS Sans Serif)
IconTitleSize	Font size for icon titles. (9)
IconTitleWrap	(1) = Wrap long icon names.
IconVerticalSpacing	Vertical pixels between icons. (75)
MenuShowDelay	Milliseconds to delay automatic menu drop-down. (308)
Pattern	Selected background pattern.
ScreenSaveActive	1 = Screen saver enabled.
ScreenSaverIsSecure	1 = Requires password to clear screen saver.
ScreenSaveTimeOut	Seconds until screen saver activation.
TileWallpaper	1 = Tiles wallpaper. 0 = Centers wallpaper.
WaitToKillAppTimeout	Milliseconds to wait before option to end hung application. (20000)
Wallpaper	Path to selected wallpaper.
WheelScrollLines	Intellimouse wheel lines to scroll. (3)

HKEY_CURRENT_USER\Control Panel\don't load   Lists the Control Panel (*.cpl) files that should not be included in the Control Panel.

HKEY_CURRENT_USER\Control Panel\Infrared   Contains values used to control the Infrared port as managed in the Infrared Devices Control Panel.

HKEY_CURRENT_USER\Control Panel\International   Constants associated with internationalization variables as set in the Regional Settings Control Panel.

HKEY_CURRENT_USER\Control Panel\Keyboard   Keyboard settings defined in the Keyboard Control Panel.

HKEY_CURRENT_USER\Control Panel\Microsoft Input Devices   Contains values specific to mice that use the Microsoft driver.

HKEY_CURRENT_USER\Control Panel\Mouse   Mouse settings defined in the Mouse Control Panel.

HKEY_CURRENT_USER\Control Panel\Patterns   Color masks to create the various patterns that are available in the Display Control Panel.

HKEY_CURRENT_USER\Control Panel\PowerCfg   Defines the various power configurations available in the system and the currently selected power profile.

HKEY_CURRENT_USER\Control Panel\Screen Saver.<screen saver>   Settings specific to various Control Panels.

HKEY_CURRENT_USER\Control Panel\Sound   Enables the system speaker and extended sounds.

HKEY_CURRENT_USER\Control Panel\Sounds   Contains values used to control the Sounds and Multimedia Control Panel.

HKEY_CURRENT_USER\Environment   Contents of the user's environment variables such as TEMP and PATH.

HKEY_CURRENT_USER\Printers   Contains user settings for installed printers. These values should be changed using the Printers Control Panel.

HKEY_CURRENT_USER\RemoteAccess   Contains a list of defined dial-up networking connections established for this user along with the settings required to establish the connection.

HKEY_CURRENT_USER\Software This key contains all user-mode application software settings that are specific to users. Most of these keys are maintained by third-party applications. Each vendor creates a key named after their company the first time a product of theirs is installed. Each installed product creates a key named after the product to maintain its Registry keys and values.

HKEY_CURRENT_USER\Software\Microsoft\Windows\CurrentVersion\Explorer
This key contains values affecting the operation of Windows Explorer.

Value	Data
DirectoryCols	Contains a list of column widths for the default directory view in Explorer. Delete this key to reestablish standard column widths.
IconUnderline	Controls the underlining of icons based on the cursor position.
ShellState	Affects how Internet Explorer interacts with Windows Explorer.

**HKEY_CURRENT_USER\Software\Microsoft\Windows\CurrentVersion\Explorer\
AutoComplete** Controls the functionality of the IntelliSense AutoComplete feature.

Value	Data
Use AutoComplete	AutoComplete enabled. (yes)

**HKEY_CURRENT_USER\Software\Microsoft\Windows\CurrentVersion\Explorer\
BrowseNewProcess** Controls whether the explore functionality of Explorer is run in a new process or the same process.

Value	Data
BrowseNewProcess	Explores in new process. (yes)

**HKEY_CURRENT_USER\Software\Microsoft\Windows\CurrentVersion\Explorer\
RecentDocs** Contains keys that define the menu of recent documents in the Start menu.

**HKEY_CURRENT_USER\Software\Microsoft\Windows\CurrentVersion\Explorer\
Shell Folders** Defines the physical paths to the various shell folders for the current user. Standard values when logged in as the administrator are the following:

Value	Data
Administrative Tools	(C:\Documents and Settings\Administrator\Start Menu\Programs\Administrative)
AppData	(C:\Documents and Settings\Administrator\ Application Data)

Value	Data
Cache	(C:\Documents and Settings\Administrator\Local Settings\Temporary Internet)
Cookies	(C:\Documents and Settings\Administrator\ Cookies)
Desktop	(C:\Documents and Settings\Administrator\ Desktop)
Favorites	(C:\Documents and Settings\Administrator\ Favorites)
Fonts	(C:\WINNT\Fonts)
History	(C:\Documents and Settings\Administrator\Local Settings\History)
Local AppData	(C:\Documents and Settings\Administrator\Local Settings\Application Data)
Local Settings	(C:\Documents and Settings\Administrator\Local Settings)
My Pictures	(C:\Documents and Settings\Administrator\My Documents\My Pictures)
NetHood	(C:\Documents and Settings\Administrator\NetHood)
Personal	(C:\Documents and Settings\Administrator\My Documents)
PrintHood	(C:\Documents and Settings\Administrator\ PrintHood)
Programs	(C:\Documents and Settings\Administrator\Start Menu\Programs)
Recent	(C:\Documents and Settings\Administrator\ Recent)
SendTo	(C:\Documents and Settings\Administrator\ SendTo)
Start Menu	(C:\Documents and Settings\Administrator\ Start Menu)
Startup	(C:\Documents and Settings\Administrator\Start Menu\Programs\Startup)
Templates	(C:\Documents and Settings\Administrator\ Templates)

HKEY_CURRENT_USER\Software\Microsoft\Windows\CurrentVersion\Explorer
SmallIcons   Controls whether to use small or large icons.

Value	Data
SmallIcons	Uses small icons. (yes)

HKEY_CURRENT_USER\Software\Microsoft\Windows\CurrentVersion\Explorer
tips   Controls the start-up tips program (tips.exe). Change these values for the default
user to eliminate tip window start-up for new users.

Value	Data
Show	Doesn't show tips. (0)

HKEY_CURRENT_USER\Software\Microsoft\Windows\CurrentVersion\Explorer\User
Shell Folders   Controls the path to various directories associated with the user shell.
You can set these values to a shared UNC path to use a common folder for all users.

Value	Data
AppData	%USERPROFILE%\Application Data
Cache	%USERPROFILE%\Local Settings\Temporary Internet Files
Cookies	%USERPROFILE%\Cookies
Desktop	%USERPROFILE%\Desktop
Favorites	%USERPROFILE%\Favorites
History	%USERPROFILE%\Local Settings\History
Local AppData	%USERPROFILE%\Local Settings\Application Data
Local Settings	%USERPROFILE%\Local Settings
My Pictures	%USERPROFILE%\My Documents\My Pictures
NetHood	%USERPROFILE%\NetHood
Personal	%USERPROFILE%\My Documents
PrintHood	%USERPROFILE%\PrintHood
Programs	%USERPROFILE%\Start Menu\Programs
Recent	%USERPROFILE%\Recent
SendTo	%USERPROFILE%\SendTo
Start Menu	%USERPROFILE%\Start Menu
Startup	%USERPROFILE%\Start Menu\Programs\Startup
Templates	%USERPROFILE%\Templates

Appendix

HKEY_CURRENT_USER\Software\Microsoft\Windows\CurrentVersion\Internet Settings   Controls various Internet Control Panel settings.

Value	Data
AllowCookies	(1) = Allows Web browsers to post informational cookies to the local machine.
AutoConfigProxy	Name of the proxy auto configuration DLL. (wininet.dll)
DisableCachingOfSSLPages	1 = Does not cache secure socket layer pages. (0)
DisconnectIdleTime	Time before Auto Disconnect.
EmailName	(IEUser@)
EnableAutodial	1 = Automatically dials a dial-up networking entry when establishing a TCP/IP connection.
EnableAutodisconnect	1 = Enables Auto Disconnect.
EnableHttp1_1	(1) = Enables HTTP 1.1 extensions.
EnableSecurityCheck	1 = Enables security warnings.
FtpDefaultExpiryTimeSecs	Undocumented. Probably: default time to expire FTP cache.
GlobalUserOffline	Controls whether IE5 starts in online (0) or offline (1) mode. Set this value to 0 (online) if you cannot change IE5 to online mode manually.
HttpDefaultExpiry TimeSecs	Undocumented. Probably: default time to expire HTTP cached pages.
MimeExclusionListForCache	List of MIME types that should not be cached. (multipart/mixed multipart/x-mixed-replace multipart/x-byteranges)
NoNetAutodial	1 = Prevents IE from invoking the Dial-Up Connection Manager automatically.
ProxyEnable	1 = Use Proxy to connect to Internet.
ProxyHttp1.1	(1) = Proxy HTTP 1.1 requests.
SecureProtocols	Defines the security protocols in use.
SyncMode	Determines how often Internet Explorer checks for new versions of Web pages. (3) = Every time you visit a page. 2 = Once per day. 0 = Never.

Value	Data
Trust Warning Level	Controls the trust warning level. (High)
User Agent	Controls the text that IE5 uses to negotiate compatibility with remote Web servers. You can change this text to individually identify Web browsers in your organization. (Mozilla/4.0 (compatible; MSIE 5.0; Win32))
WarnonBadCert-Recving	(1) = Warns when invalid or expired certificates are received.
WarnOnPost	(1) = Warns when posting.
WarnOnZoneCrossing	(1) = Warns when moving between Internet zones.

HKEY_CURRENT_USER\Software\Microsoft\Windows\CurrentVersion\Internet Settings\Cache   Controls the type and amount of content Internet Explorer will cache.

HKEY_CURRENT_USER\Software\Microsoft\Windows\CurrentVersion\Internet Settings\Cache\Content   Controls the number of HTML pages Internet Explorer will cache.

Value	Data
CacheLimit	(0xffa0) = Maximum number of Web pages to cache.
CachePrefix	("") = Text prefixed to stored Web pages.

HKEY_CURRENT_USER\Software\Microsoft\Windows\CurrentVersion\Internet Settings\Cache\Cookies   Controls the number of cookies IE5 will cache and how they will be identified.

Value	Data
CacheLimit	(0×2000) = Maximum number of cookies to store.
CachePrefix	(Cookie:) = Text prefixed to stored cookies.

HKEY_CURRENT_USER\Software\Microsoft\Windows\CurrentVersion\Internet Settings\Cache\History   Controls the number of visited sites IE5 will cache.

Value	Data
CacheLimit	(0×2000) = Maximum number of history files to cache.
CachePrefix	(Visited:) = Text prefixed to history files.

HKEY_CURRENT_USER\Software\Microsoft\Windows\CurrentVersion\Internet Settings\Url History   Controls the number of URLs IE5 will cache for the purpose of displaying visited links in an alternate color.

Value	Data
DaysToKeep	(0x14) = Days to maintain clicked links.

HKEY_CURRENT_USER\Software\Microsoft\Windows\CurrentVersion\Policies
Contains user settings set in Group Policy. For each value, the setting is enabled by setting a DWORD value of 1 or disabled by setting a value of 0. For a complete discussion of Group Policy, see the entry at HKEY_CURRENT_USER\Software\Policies.

HKEY_CURRENT_USER\Software\Microsoft\Windows\CurrentVersion\Policies\ ActiveDesktop   Controls policy settings for the Active Desktop. These settings are configurable using Group Policy.

Value	Data
NoAddingComponents	Disables the addition of Desktop components.
NoChangingWallPaper	Disallows the changing of wallpaper by the user.
NoCloseDragDropBands	Disables toolbar drag-and-drop and closure.
NoClosingComponents	Disables the closing of Desktop components.
NoComponents	Disables all Desktop components.
NoDeletingComponents	Disables the deletion of Desktop components.
NoEditingComponents	Disables the editing of Desktop components.
NoHTMLWallPaper	Disables HTML wallpaper.
NoMovingBands	Disables the resizing or moving of toolbars.

HKEY_CURRENT_USER\Software\Microsoft\Windows\CurrentVersion\Policies\ Explorer   Controls policy settings for Windows Explorer. These settings are configurable using Group Policy.

Value	Data
ClassicShell	Enables the shell from NT 3.5.
ClearRecentDocsOnExit	Clears history of recent docs on exit.
DisableTaskMgr	Prevents user from running the Task Manager.
EnforceShellExtensionSecurity	Allows only approved shell extensions.
LinkResolveIgnoreLinkInfo	Does not track shell shortcuts during roaming.

Value	Data
NoActiveDesktop	Does not use Active Desktop.
NoActiveDesktopChanges	Does not allow changes to the Active Desktop.
NoAddPrinter	Disables the user's ability to add printers.
NoChangeStartMenu	Disables drag-and-drop changes to the Start menu.
NoClose	Disables Shutdown option.
NoDeletePrinter	Disables the user's ability to delete printers.
NoDesktop	Hides all Desktop items.
NoDrives	Hides removable media drives in My Computer.
NoDriveTypeAutoRun	Controls the CD-ROM AutoRun feature. (0xe19dfae8)
NoFavoritesMenu	Hides Favorites menu in Start menu.
NoFileMenu	Disables File menu in shell folders.
NoFind	Hides Find option in Start menu.
NoFolderOptions	Hides Folder Options settings.
NoInternetIcon	Hides Internet Explorer Icon.
NoLogoff	Disables Logoff option.
NoNetConnectDisconnect	Removes Map Network Drive and Disconnect Network Drive.
NoNetHood	Hides Network Neighborhood.
NoPrinterTabs	Disables the General Details printer tabs.
NoRecentDocsHistory	Does not record history of recent docs.
NoRecentDocsMenu	Hides Recent Documents in Start menu.
NoRun	Hides Run option in Start menu.
NoSaveSettings	Does not save changes to Explorer settings.
NoSetActiveDesktop	Removes Active Desktop settings.
NoSetFolders	Disables changes to printers and Control Panels.
NoSetTaskBar	Disables changes to Taskbar and Start menu.
NoStartBanner	Disables start banner.

Appendix

Value	Data
NoStartMenuSubfolders	Hides program folders.
NoTrayContextMenu	Disables right-click contact context menu in the System Tray, Start button, and Application buttons.
NoTrayContextMenu	Disables Taskbar context menu.
NoViewContextMenu	Disables all context menus in Explorer.
NoViewContextMenu	Disables the context menu in shell folders.
RestrictRun	Runs only specified Windows applications.

HKEY_CURRENT_USER\Software\Microsoft\Windows\CurrentVersion\Policies\ Network Controls policy settings for the Network Control Panel and the My Network Places Desktop icon. These settings are configurable using Group Policy.

Value	Data
NoNetSetup	Disables the Network Control Panel.
NoNetSetupIDPage	Hides the Identification page in My Computer.
NetNetSetupSecurityPage	Hides the Access page.
NoEntireNetwork	Disables the Entire Network option in My Network Places.
NoWorkgroupContents	Disables workgroup contents in My Network Places.

HKEY_CURRENT_USER\ Software\Microsoft\Windows\CurrentVersion\Policies\ System

Value	Data
NoDispAppearancePage	Appearance page of the Display Control Panel is not available.
NoDispBackgroundPage	Background page of the Display Control Panel is not available.
NoDispCPL	Display Control Panel is not available.
NoDispScrSavPage	Screen Saver page of the Display Control Panel is not available.
NoDispSettingsPage	Settings page of the Display Control Panel is not available.
DisableRegistryTools	Disables Registry editors.

Value	Data
NoSecCPL	Disables the Passwords Control Panel.
NoPwdPage	Disables the Change Passwords page.
NoAdminPage	Hides the Remote Administration page.
NoProfilePage	Hides the User Profiles page of the System Control Panel.
NoDevMgrPage	Hides the Device Manager page of the System Control Panel.
NoConfigPage	Hides the Hardware Profiles page of the System Control Panel.
NoFileSysPage	Hides the File Systems button of the System Control Panel.
NoVirtMemPage	Hides the Virtual Memory button of the System Control Panel.

HKEY_CURRENT_USER\Software\Microsoft\Windows NT\CurrentVersion   Controls software settings specific to Windows 2000 and the logged-on user.

HKEY_CURRENT_USER\Software\Microsoft\Windows NT\CurrentVersion\ Extensions   Contains a list of filename extensions and the commands used to launch the programs associated with those extensions. The extension is the key name, and the command is the data.

HKEY_CURRENT_USER\Software\Policies   The preferred location for the application of user-based group policy. Group Policy is a mechanism that allows administrators to specify numerous overlapping Registry settings files to be applied to the Registry of a computer during the boot (for computer policies) or logon (for user-based policies) process. This key is reserved for user-based policies.

This key contains only some certificate manager keys by default unless group policy is applied to the computer. Group policy Registry settings and their meanings are contained in .adm files. The following files can be opened and read to determine the various keys, associated values, and intended purposes that will be applied inside this key when group policy is applied:

```
C:\WINNT\inf\system.adm
C:\WINNT\inf\inetres.adm
C:\WINNT\conf.adm
```

Other .adm files may exist on your server; perform a file search operation to find and read them.

Appendix

HKEY_LOCAL_MACHINE   Contains keys pertaining to the configuration of the computer. Most useful troubleshooting and configuration keys are found under this key.

HKEY_LOCAL_MACHINE\HARDWARE   This key contains the hardware resources detected by the BIOS, the `ntdetect.com` boot loader, and the Plug and Play subsystem. The values in this key are dynamically created each time the computer boots.

HKEY_LOCAL_MACHINE\SAM\SAM   This key contains a pointer to the `HKEY_LOCAL_MACHINE\SECURITY` key that contains the Security Accounts Manager database. Each user and group entry is listed by the account's security identifier. This key is normally secured and not visible unless you are running the security context of the system.

HKEY_LOCAL_MACHINE\SECURITY   The security key contains the Security Accounts Manager database of users and groups for the local machine accounts, as well as data required for domain security and policies. The structure of the security key is undocumented, and the internal structure of the key is protected by an access control list. You can change permissions using RegEdt32 to view the internal structure of this key, but you should only make changes to this key using the Local Users and Groups snap-in.

HKEY_LOCAL_MACHINE\SECURITY\Policy\Secrets   This key stores public and private keys for various services in Windows 2000, such as DHCP, Terminal Services, and back-end services such as SQL Server or Exchange Server.

HKEY_LOCAL_MACHINE\SOFTWARE   Contains a key for the manufacturer of every installed application. Under that key, each manufacturer's installed products are enumerated. These keys store configuration data specific to each application.

This key also contains the `Microsoft\Windows` and `Microsoft\Windows NT` keys, which contain numerous keys and settings critical to the operation of the system. Since these elements are not applications and cannot be uninstalled, it is interesting that Microsoft chose to enumerate them under the `SOFTWARE` key rather than in a special key of their own.

HKEY_LOCAL_MACHINE\SOFTWARE\Classes   This key is the actual storage location for `HKEY_CLASSES_ROOT`, which is a pointer to this location.

HKEY_LOCAL_MACHINE\SOFTWARE\Microsoft\ADs\Providers   This key lists the Active Directory namespace providers, such as LDAP and IIS, which are installed as part of the directory. All installed namespaces for the Active Directory are listed here.

HKEY_LOCAL_MACHINE\SOFTWARE\Microsoft\ADs\Providers\<PROVIDER>\ Extensions\<extension>\<CSLID>   This key lists the CSLID for each extension of an Active Directory provider. Information on how to use and modify these keys will come from the vendor that provides the extension.

HKEY_LOCAL_MACHINE\SOFTWARE\Microsoft\Windows\Help   Contains an entry for every installed help file, which associates the file with a physical file path.

HKEY_LOCAL_MACHINE\SOFTWARE\Microsoft\Cryptography   Contains keys used by the CryptoAPI to control the registration of cryptographic service providers. A subkey is present for each registered cryptographic service provider.

Value	Data
MachineGuid	The Guaranteed Unique Identifier used by the CryptoAPI to generate machine-specific keys.

HKEY_LOCAL_MACHINE\SOFTWARE\Microsoft\MMC   Contains keys used to configure the Microsoft Management Console, including the list of registered snap-ins.

HKEY_LOCAL_MACHINE\SOFTWARE\Microsoft\SystemCertificates   Contains security and encryption certificates stored by the system for the Public Key Infrastructure. Adding or removing certificates should only be managed through the Certificates Manager or a service designed to work with the PKI.

HKEY_LOCAL_MACHINE\SOFTWARE\Microsoft\Windows\CurrentVersion   This key stores data used by the Win32 environment.

Value	Data
CommonFilesDir	Location of the Common Files directory.
DevicePath	Location of the .inf files used for device driver installation.
MediaPath	Location of the Media directory.
MediaPathUnexpanded	Location of the Media directory using the %SystemRoot% environment variable.
PF_AccessoriesName	Name of the Program Files Accessories directory.
ProductID	Product ID number.
ProgramFilesDir	Location of the Program Files directory.
ProgramFilesPath	%ProgramFiles%
SM_AccessoriesName	Name of the Accessories Start menu item.
WallPaperDir	Location of the Wallpaper directory using the %SystemRoot% environment variable.

HKEY_LOCAL_MACHINE\SOFTWARE\Microsoft\Windows\CurrentVersion\Explorer\Desktop\NameSpace   Contains a list of CLSIDs that define the icons permanently installed on the Desktop (Recycle Bin, The Internet, InBox, and so on). Deleting these keys will remove the Desktop icons.

Appendix

**HKEY_LOCAL_MACHINE\SOFTWARE\Microsoft\Windows\CurrentVersion\Explorer\
FindExtensions**   Defines the entries that appear in the Start ➢ Find menu.

**HKEY_LOCAL_MACHINE\SOFTWARE\Microsoft\Windows\CurrentVersion\Explorer\
RemoteComputer\NameSpace**   Contains a list of CLSIDs that define the icons available to remote users of this machine (Printers and Scheduled Tasks are enabled by default).

**HKEY_LOCAL_MACHINE\SOFTWARE\Microsoft\Windows\CurrentVersion\Explorer\
Shell Folders**   This key contains values that identify the file paths of the Desktop, Start Menu, Programs, and Startup directories for all users.

Value	Data
Common Administrative Tools	C:\Documents and Settings\All Users\ Start Menu\Programs\Administrative Tools
Common AppData	C:\Documents and Settings\All Users\ Application Data
Common Desktop	C:\Documents and Settings\All Users\ Desktop
Common Documents	C:\Documents and Settings\All Users\ Documents
Common Programs	C:\Documents and Settings\All Users\ Start Menu\Programs
Common Start Menu	C:\Documents and Settings\All Users\ Start Menu
Common Startup	C:\Documents and Settings\All Users\ Start Menu\Programs\Startup. If this value is missing, Explorer will open all folders in the root directory by default. Correct this problem by re-creating the value with this data: %ALLUSERSPROFILE%\Start Menu\Programs\ Startup.
Common Templates	C:\Documents and Settings\All Users\ Templates

**HKEY_LOCAL_MACHINE\SOFTWARE\Microsoft\Windows\CurrentVersion\Explorer\
StartMenu**   This key contains values that control how the Start menu functions. Most of these values can be set by right-clicking the Taskbar, selecting Properties, clicking the Advanced tab, and then checking the features you would like to use.

HKEY_LOCAL_MACHINE\SOFTWARE\Microsoft\Windows\CurrentVersion\Explorer
Tips Contains a series of values that define the Windows tip text that appears in the Tip of the Day dialog box at start-up.

HKEY_LOCAL_MACHINE\SOFTWARE\Microsoft\Windows\CurrentVersion\Explorer
User Shell Folders Specifies the path for Start ➢ Programs entries in the common groups division. This value can be configured using Group Policy.

Value	Data
Common AppData	%ALLUSERSPROFILE%\Application Data
Common Desktop	%ALLUSERSPROFILE%\Desktop
Common Documents	%ALLUSERSPROFILE%\Documents
Common Favorites	%ALLUSERSPROFILE%\Favorites
Common Programs	%ALLUSERSPROFILE%\Start Menu\Programs
Common Start Menu	%ALLUSERSPROFILE%\Start Menu
Common Startup	%ALLUSERSPROFILE%\Start Menu\Programs\Startup
Common Templates	%ALLUSERSPROFILE%\Templates

HKEY_LOCAL_MACHINE\SOFTWARE\Microsoft\Windows\CurrentVersion
Installer Contains keys that identify the Windows Installer (.msi) packages installed on the local computer.

HKEY_LOCAL_MACHINE\SOFTWARE\Microsoft\Windows\CurrentVersion\Policies
Stores keys and values created by the applied group policies that restrict access to the local machine. The policies in this key are interpreted by Windows Explorer. For more details, see the entry under HKLM\SOFTWARE\Policies.

HKEY_LOCAL_MACHINE\SOFTWARE\Microsoft\Windows\CurrentVersion
Reliability The operating system writes a time stamp to this key every five minutes (or as otherwise defined by the TimeStampInterval value) that is used to log the time the server crashed in the event of an abnormal shutdown.

Value	Data
LastAliveStamp	0 = Disables time-stamp logging, otherwise date and time of last valid time stamp.
TimeStampInterval	(0x0) = Time-stamp interval.
ShutdownReason	A code indicating why the previous shutdown occurred.

Appendix

★ **HKEY_LOCAL_MACHINE\SOFTWARE\Microsoft\Windows\CurrentVersion\Run**
Contains the paths to Explorer extensions, such as Tray items, that run each time Explorer is started. This value is configurable using Group Policy.

HKEY_LOCAL_MACHINE\SOFTWARE\Microsoft\Windows\CurrentVersion\ RunOnce   Contains the paths to programs that should run the next time that Explorer starts. Generally used to complete installations after a reboot, this key should normally be empty.

HKEY_LOCAL_MACHINE\SOFTWARE\Microsoft\Windows\CurrentVersion\Setup
Contains information about the current setup of Windows. Used by the Add\Remove Programs Control Panel to determine which Windows components are currently installed. This key is largely deprecated in Windows 2000.

HKEY_LOCAL_MACHINE\SOFTWARE\Microsoft\Windows\CurrentVersion\ SharedDlls   Contains a list of shared DLLs, each with a counter datum enumerating the number of installed applications that use the DLL. Upon uninstallation, an application decrements the counters of each DLL it uses. When a DLL counter reaches zero, the user is prompted to delete shared DLLs no longer in use.

★ **HKEY_LOCAL_MACHINE\SOFTWARE\Microsoft\Windows\CurrentVersion\Uninstall**
Contains an entry for each application that can be uninstalled using the Add\Remove Programs Control Panel. If you have manually deleted an application, remove its entry under this key to eliminate its presence in the Add\Remove Control Panel list.

★ **HKEY_LOCAL_MACHINE\SOFTWARE\Microsoft\Windows NT\CurrentVersion**
This key contains values entered or identified during the original operating system installation.

Value	Data
CSDVersion	Identifies the current service pack level as a string.
CurrentBuild	Identifies internal build versions. (obsolete)
CurrentBuildNumber	The operating system build number. (2195 for Windows 2000)
CurrentType	Identifies the kernel in use, either Uniprocessor or Multiprocessor.
CurrentVersion	Operating system version number. (5.0 for Windows 2000)
DigitalProductID	A munged version of the CD-KEY typed in when the product was installed.

Value	Data
InstallDate	Installation date. (dword)
PathName	Operating system installation path. (=%windir%)
ProductID	Product unique number.
ProductName	Microsoft Windows 2000.
RegisteredOrganization	Organization name entered by the user during setup.
RegisteredOwner	Owner's name entered during setup.
SoftwareType	Identifies type of software.
SourcePath	Path to the installation i386 source directory. Change this value if you copy the i386 to your hard disk.
SystemRoot	Path to the Windows 2000 System directory.

**HKEY_LOCAL_MACHINE\SOFTWARE\Microsoft\Windows NT\CurrentVersion\
Fonts**   Contains an entry for every installed font that associates the font name with a physical file path.

**HKEY_LOCAL_MACHINE\SOFTWARE\Microsoft\Windows NT\CurrentVersion\
FontSubstitutes**   Contains entries describing acceptable replacement installed fonts for fonts that are not installed (usually Macintosh fonts).

**HKEY_LOCAL_MACHINE\SOFTWARE\Microsoft\Windows NT\CurrentVersion\
Hotfix**   Contains keys identifying installed hot-fixes by their Knowledge Base unique ID.

★   **HKEY_LOCAL_MACHINE\SOFTWARE\Microsoft\Windows NT\CurrentVersion\
NetworkCards\<Adapter #>**   Contains keys enumerating the installed network adapters. Each key is named for the bind order of the network adapter (1...*n*). Values for each adapter are as follows.

Value	Data
Description	Text description of the adapter.
Hidden	1 = Adapter does not appear in the Network Control Panel.
InstallDate	Date of installation. (dword)
Manufacturer	Text identifying the manufacturer.
ProductName	Text identifying the product.
ServiceName	The GUID that refers to the network card.
Title	As Description value above but prefixed with the bind number in brackets.

Appendix

HKEY_LOCAL_MACHINE\SOFTWARE\Microsoft\Windows NT\CurrentVersion\ Perflib\009 The ACL for this key controls which users have permission to remotely monitor this computer's performance using the System Monitor. 009 is the language identifier for English—internationalized versions will be different.

HKEY_LOCAL_MACHINE\SOFTWARE\Microsoft\Windows NT\CurrentVersion\ Ports Port setting information as defined in the Ports Control Panel.

HKEY_LOCAL_MACHINE\SOFTWARE\Microsoft\Windows NT\CurrentVersion\ ProfileList\<User SID> Contains an entry for each profile stored on the local machine. Keys are identified by the SID of the user. Profiles only exist for users who have logged on locally or whose profiles have been moved to this machine. Use these keys to identify the SID of a user by account name. Values for each profile are as follows.

Value	Data
ProfileImagePath	Path to the location where this profile is stored. Change this entry to move the profile to another location.
ProfileLoadTimeHigh	(0x1c0509e)
ProfileLoadTimeLow	(0x578daa20)
RefCount	(0x1)
Sid	Munge of the user account SID. Key name provides a human-readable SID.
State	(0x100)

HKEY_LOCAL_MACHINE\SOFTWARE\Microsoft\Windows NT\CurrentVersion\ Terminal Server Used to control the settings for Terminal Services, including default values for terminal sessions.

HKEY_LOCAL_MACHINE\SOFTWARE\Microsoft\Windows NT\CurrentVersion\ Terminal Server\Install\Software Mimics the structure of the HKEY_LOCAL_MACHINE\ SOFTWARE key for programs that need to maintain different settings for terminal software than for software that is run locally. The settings in these keys override settings in the local machine software key for software run by terminal users.

★ **HKEY_LOCAL_MACHINE\SOFTWARE\Microsoft\Windows NT\Current Version\ Winlogon** Used to set configuration data related to interactive logons.

Value	Data
AllocateCDRoms	1 = Restricts CD-ROM access to interactively logged-on user.
Allocatedasd	1 = Restricts removable hard disk cartridge access to interactively logged-on user.
AllocateFloppies	1 = Restricts floppy access to interactively logged-on user.
AltDefaultDomainName	Domain name shown when no network connection is available.
AltDefaultUserName	User name shown when no network connection is available.
AutoAdminLogon	1 = Performs auto logon using DefaultUser and DefaultPassword entries.
AutoRestartShell	1 = Restarts shell process (explorer.exe) if it is closed or crashes.
CachedLogonsCount	0 = Disables caching of domain logon credentials on local machine. (10)
DCacheUpate	This value is undocumented.
DebugServerCommand	Yes or No.
DefaultDomainName	Domain in which DefaultUserName is defined.
DefaultPassword	Text password for auto-logon user.
DefaultUserName	Name of user to automatically log on, if any.
DeleteRoamingCache	1 = Deletes cached copies of roaming profiles.
DisableCAD	1= Ctrl+Alt+Del is not required for logon. Setting this value can compromise security.
DisableLockWorkstation	Disables the Lock Workstation button.
DontDisplayLastUserName	1 = User Name field cleared in logon dialog.
LegalNoticeCaption	Title for the legal notice dialog box, if any.
LegalNoticeText	Text of the legal notice dialog box, if any.
Passwordexpirywarning	Days prior to warn users that their password is going to expire. (14)
PowerdownAfterShutdown	Sends API command to power off machine after shutdown.

Value	Data
ReportBootOk	0 = Disables the automatic (default) start-up acceptance, which happens after the first successful logon. Do not change values in the BootVerificationProgram key unless you need a custom verification program to satisfy specific start-up criteria at your site.
RunLogonScryptSync	1 = Runs logon scripts synchronously (logon scripts must complete before the shell will be loaded).
SFCDisable	1 = Disables the System File Checker (sfc.exe), which protects against overwritten system files.
Shell	Filename of shell executable.
ShowLogonOptions	Enables logon options button. (1)
Show	0 = Off, or time in seconds to wait for user profile information before the default is accepted.
ShutdownWithoutLogon	1 = Enables shutdown button in logon screen.
SlowLinkDetectEnabled	1 = Automatically detects slow network connections.
SlowNetworkTimeout	0 = Off, or time in milliseconds to wait before slow network is determined.
System	Undocumented.
Userinit	(C:\WINNT\system32\userinit.exe) = Specifies executables to be run by WinLogon when a user logs on. These executables are run in the user context.

HKEY_LOCAL_MACHINE\SOFTWARE\Microsoft\Windows Scripting Host Contains a list of installed scripting hosts and their associated extensions.

HKEY_LOCAL_MACHINE\SOFTWARE\Policies The preferred location for the application of user-based group policy. Group Policy is a mechanism that allows administrators to specify numerous overlapping Registry settings files to be applied to the Registry of a computer during the boot (for computer policies) or logon (for user-based policies) process. This key is reserved for computer-based policies.

This key contains very few keys by default unless group policy is applied to the computer. Group policy Registry settings and their meanings are contained in .adm files. The following files can be opened and read to determine the various keys, associated values, and intended purposes that will be applied inside this key when group policy is applied:

C:\WINNT\inf\system.adm

C:\WINNT\inf\inetres.adm

C:\WINNT\conf.adm

Other .adm files may exist on your server; perform a file search operation to find and read them.

HKEY_LOCAL_MACHINE\SYSTEM   Contains values that pertain to the operation of the kernel, the executive, services, and drivers. These keys are usually critical to Windows 2000's ability to boot, so you should be especially cautious when changing them.

HKEY_LOCAL_MACHINE\SYSTEM\Clone   Contains the working copy created at boot time of the current control set. This copy of the control set is the copy actually used by the operating system while it runs. It is locked and unchangeable while it is in use by the operating system. When you make changes to the current control set, they are not effective until reboot because the version actually in use is the Clone key.

HKEY_LOCAL_MACHINE\SYSTEM\ControlSet00x   Each of the control sets is a different system configuration. 001 is usually the originally installed control set. 002 is usually the LastKnownGood control set. You may have additional control sets, especially if you've had boot problems with your machine in the past.

★   **HKEY_LOCAL_MACHINE\SYSTEM\CurrentControlSet**   CurrentControlSet is a pointer to the ControlSet00x that is current. Make changes in this key to guarantee that they'll be used the next time you boot your system.

HKEY_LOCAL_MACHINE\SYSTEM\CurrentControlSet\Control   Contains settings for the kernel, executive services, and drivers that are required for the proper operation of Windows 2000.

Value	Data
CurrentUser	Contains the name of the variable used to represent the user. (USERNAME)
RegistrySizeLimit	Maximum size the Registry can grow to. (25 percent of the PagedPoolSize)
SystemStartOptions	Options specified on the boot.ini command line.
WaitToKillService-Timeout	Allows you to specify a length of time that the Service Control Manager must wait for services to complete the shut-down request. (20000)

HKEY_LOCAL_MACHINE\SYSTEM\CurrentControlSet\Control\BackupRestore Contains keys used by the Windows 2000's built-in backup program to determine which files and Registry keys should not be backed up or restored. These values can be changed through the backup program's user interface.

HKEY_LOCAL_MACHINE\SYSTEM\CurrentControlSet\Control\BootVerification-Program Contains the filename for programs that establish a last known good configuration upon successful boot. The default of no entry should not be changed except by software specifically designed to perform this function.

HKEY_LOCAL_MACHINE\SYSTEM\CurrentControlSet\Control\Class Contains keys that provide information to the Device Manager to identify Plug and Play hardware. A key is present for every class of hardware that the system knows about. Each device appearing in the Device Manager is represented in these keys.

HKEY_LOCAL_MACHINE\SYSTEM\CurrentControlSet\Control\Class\<CLSID> Describes a class of hardware, and contains values that determine how to display the class in the Device Manager and how setup should be handled. Every class of devices is represented in these keys whether they are installed in the system or not.

HKEY_LOCAL_MACHINE\SYSTEM\CurrentControlSet\Control\Class\<CLSID>\ <instance> One instance key in the form "0000" through the number of installed devices is present to describe each device appearing in your system. In each instance, values representing the properties of the device's driver are present. Instances are only present in the Registry if a driver has been loaded for this device because it once appeared in the system. Removing the instance for a device is equivalent to uninstalling it in the Device Manager.

Value	Data
DriverDate	Driver release date.
DriverDateData	Driver data metadata.
DriverDesc	Description of the device.
DriverVersion	Driver version.
InfPath	Name of the INF file that describes this device.
InfSection	Label of the section in the INF file that describes this device.
MatchingDeviceId	Generic class of the device.
ProviderName	Vendor of the device driver.

HKEY_LOCAL_MACHINE\SYSTEM\CurrentControlSet\Control\ComputerName\ ActiveComputerName The contained value ComputerName is the active name of the computer. Do not set this key directly; use the System Control Panel to change the computer's name.

HKEY_LOCAL_MACHINE\SYSTEM\CurrentControlSet\Control\ComputerName\ ComputerName The contained value ComputerName is the name that the ActiveComputerName key will receive upon next boot.

HKEY_LOCAL_MACHINE\SYSTEM\CurrentControlSet\Control\ContentIndex Registry settings pertaining to the Content Index service. Microsoft does not specifically document these values, but their use is generally obvious from the value name if you understand the function of the Content Index.

HKEY_LOCAL_MACHINE\SYSTEM\CurrentControlSet\Control\CrashControl Settings that determine how to handle kernel dumps (blue screens). These values are set in the System Control Panel.

Value	Data
AutoReboot	1 = Reboots automatically.
CrashDumpEnabled	1 = Writes memory dump file.
DumpFile	Path to the memory dump file. (%SystemRoot%\MEMORY.DMP)
LogEvent	1 = Sends event to System Log.
MinidumpDir	%Systemroot%\Minidump = Path to the mini dump file.
Overwrite	1 = Overwrites the memory dump file automatically.
SendAlert	1 = Sends alert on network.

HKEY_LOCAL_MACHINE\SYSTEM\CurrentControlSet\Control\CriticalDeviceDatabase Contains keys that identify those devices necessary for the system to boot. These devices are used instead of the keys identified in the Device Database whenever you select the Safe Mode boot option.

HKEY_LOCAL_MACHINE\SYSTEM\CurrentControlSet\Control\DeviceClasses Contains keys that relate device hardware identification strings provided by the Plug and Play system to the software CLSIDs used by the system to identify drivers.

HKEY_LOCAL_MACHINE\SYSTEM\CurrentControlSet\Control\FileSystem Implements system policy concerning file systems.

Value	Data
NtfsAllowExtended CharacterIn8dot3Name	1 = Allows extended characters in 8.3 filenames. This can cause problems on computers that do not use the same code page.

Appendix

Value	Data
NtfsDisable8dot3Name-Creation	1 = Does not create 8.3 filename hashes for long filenames. Disabling short name generation on an NTFS partition will improve the performance of directory enumeration, but may cause problems for 16-bit applications.
NtfsDisableLastAccessUpdate	1 = Disables updating last access time. This can speed file system performance on disk-bound systems.
NtfsEncryptionService	Efs = Name of the service used to perform file encryption.
Win31FileSystem	1 = Disables long filename support on FAT volumes. (0)
Win95TruncatedExtensions	(1) = Truncates extensions longer than three characters in the NT command prompt. File operations specifying a three-character extension will be applied to files containing longer extensions (for example, dir *.htm will list both *.htm and *.html files). This may cause unexpected application of commands to files.

HKEY_LOCAL_MACHINE\SYSTEM\CurrentControlSet\Control\GroupOrderList
Defines the load groups that drivers and services may be members of and sets the order in which those groups are loaded. The Group value of a driver or service defines which of the groups listed in this key that driver or service belongs to.

HKEY_LOCAL_MACHINE\SYSTEM\CurrentControlSet\Control\hivelist   Defines the disk location of the various Registry hives. One value per hive is listed. Default entries for a logged-on administrator are listed here.

Value	Data
\REGISTRY\MACHINE\HARDWARE	("") = Contains a null entry (the default) because the hardware list is built dynamically rather than read from a file.
\REGISTRY\MACHINE\SAM	\Device\HarddiskDmVolumes\ PhysicalDmVolumes\BlockVolume1\ WINNT\system32\config\SAM

Value	Data
\REGISTRY\MACHINE\SECURITY	\Device\HarddiskDmVolumes\ PhysicalDmVolumes\BlockVolume1\ WINNT\system32\config\SECURITY
\REGISTRY\MACHINE\SOFTWARE	\Device\HarddiskDmVolumes\ PhysicalDmVolumes\BlockVolume1\ WINNT\system32\config\software
\REGISTRY\MACHINE\SYSTEM	\Device\HarddiskDmVolumes\ PhysicalDmVolumes\BlockVolume1\ WINNT\system32\config\system
\REGISTRY\USER\.DEFAULT	\Device\HarddiskDmVolumes\ PhysicalDmVolumes\BlockVolume1\ WINNT\system32\config\default
\REGISTRY\USER\<Logged on SID>	\Device\HarddiskVolume1\Documents and Settings\Administrator\ NTUSER.DAT
\REGISTRY\USER\<Logged on SID>_Classes	\Device\HarddiskVolume1\Documents and Settings\Administrator\Local Settings\Application Data\Microsoft\ Windows\UsrClass.dat

HKEY_LOCAL_MACHINE\SYSTEM\CurrentControlSet\Control\Keyboard Layout
Contains selections for DOS international keyboard layouts. Use the Keyboard Control Panel to modify the information in this key.

HKEY_LOCAL_MACHINE\SYSTEM\CurrentControlSet\Control\Keyboard Layouts
Contains paths to various keyboard control libraries for various languages. Use the Keyboard Control Panel to modify the information in this key.

★ **HKEY_LOCAL_MACHINE\SYSTEM\CurrentControlSet\Control\Lsa**   The Local Security Authority manages authentication and auditing functions for the local computer. Most of these values have serious implications and should not be implemented without a solid understanding of their use. Search the TechNet CD-ROM for more information regarding their proper use.

Value	Data
AuditBaseObjects	1 = Enables auditing of base objects. Also enables auditing of system objects in the Local Security Policy or Group Policy to begin tracking base object use.

Appendix

Value	Data
Authentication Packages	Name of the authentication package library. (msv1_0)
Bounds	This value is undocumented.
CrashOnAuditFail	1 = Forces NT machine to shut down when the audit log is full. Only administrators can log on, and they must clear the log or reset this value to allow other users to log on.
FullPrivilegeAuditing	Enables auditing of all user privileges, especially use of backup and restore.
Incompatibilitylevel	0 = Sends both NT and LM password hashes. 1 = Sends LM only if server requests. 2 = Does not send LM hash. LAN Manager hashes are far less secure than NTLM or NTLMv2 hashes.
LsaPid	Processor ID of the running lsa.exe process.
Notification Packages	Contains a null-separated string of password filter DLLs. Default value is FPNWCLNT KDCSVC (null) (null); you can add PASSFILT (null) (null) to enable stronger password filtering. FPNWCLNT is the File and Print for NetWare client; KDCSVC is the Kerberos Authentication Service.
RestrictAnonymous	1 = Prevents anonymous users from enumerating shares or viewing account information.
Secureboot	Provides additional security for password hashes stored in the Registry to defeat password crackers such as L0phtCrack. 0 = SysKey additional hashes disabled. 1 = Loads SysKey hash from Registry. 2 = Enters passphrase. 3 = SysKey on floppy. Do not change this flag unless you're working from complete SysKey instructions.
Security Packages	Service name of installed logon providers. This is a reg_multi_sz value. Default data is (kerberos msv1_0 schannel).
Submit Control	1 = Allows system operators to schedule AT service commands.

HKEY_LOCAL_MACHINE\SYSTEM\CurrentControlSet\Control\Network   Contains keys that create the bindings between network adapters, clients, services, and transport protocols. A key identified by fixed CLSIDs exists for each of those four classes of network services.

HKEY_LOCAL_MACHINE\SYSTEM\CurrentControlSet\Control\Network\ {4D36E972-E325-11CE-BFC1-08002BE10318}   Contains keys that enumerate each network adapter installed in the system by CLSID.

HKEY_LOCAL_MACHINE\SYSTEM\CurrentControlSet\Control\Network\ {4D36E973-E325-11CE-BFC1-08002BE10318}   Contains keys that enumerate each network client's bindings.

HKEY_LOCAL_MACHINE\SYSTEM\CurrentControlSet\Control\Network\ {4D36E974-E325-11CE-BFC1-08002BE10318}   Contains keys that enumerate the bindings for each network service.

HKEY_LOCAL_MACHINE\SYSTEM\CurrentControlSet\Control\Network\ {4D36E975-E325-11CE-BFC1-08002BE10318}   Contains keys that enumerate the bindings for each transport protocol.

HKEY_LOCAL_MACHINE\SYSTEM\CurrentControlSet\Control\NetworkProvider\ Order   Provides the order in which networks should be accessed.

Value	Data
ProviderOrder	A string containing the order in which network providers should be accessed. (LanmanWorkstation)

HKEY_LOCAL_MACHINE\SYSTEM\CurrentControlSet\Control\Nls   Contains values for code pages and internationalization language files for the system.

HKEY_LOCAL_MACHINE\SYSTEM\CurrentControlSet\Control\NTMS\OMID\Tape   Contains keys that identify the locations of various tape media service DLLs.

HKEY_LOCAL_MACHINE\SYSTEM\CurrentControlSet\Control\PnP   Contains a key listing PCI chipsets with which Windows 2000 is compatible, along with PCI routing configuration information for each chipset.

HKEY_LOCAL_MACHINE\SYSTEM\CurrentControlSet\Control\Print   Contains print spooler control values and subkeys identifying installed printers, drivers, and print monitors. Some settings under this key can be made by opening the Printers Control

Appendix

Panel, selecting the Add New Printer icon, and selecting Server Properties in the File menu.

Value	Data
BeepEnabled	1 = Beeps every 10 seconds when a remote job error occurs on a print server.
DisableServerThread	1 = Print spooler does not transmit shared printer information to other print servers.
MajorVersion	Print provider version. (0x2)
MinorVersion	Print provider minor version. (0x0)
PortThreadPriority	Priority for the port thread in the spooler service. (0x0)
PriorityClass	Priority class for the port thread in the spooler service. (0x0)
SchedulerThreadPriority	1 = Higher than normal. 0 = Normal. FFFFFFFF = Lower than normal.

HKEY_LOCAL_MACHINE\SYSTEM\CurrentControlSet\Control\Print\Environments
Defines file locations and names for driver DLLs and help files for various NT/2000 platforms.

HKEY_LOCAL_MACHINE\SYSTEM\CurrentControlSet\Control\Print\Environments\ <Platform>\Drivers\<Print System Version>\<Printer Name>   A key is listed here for each printer on the system. Version-2 printers are Windows NT 4 compatible. Version-3 printers are Windows 2000 compatible.

Value	Data
Configuration File	Filename of the print driver configuration DLL.
Data File	Filename of the print driver data file DLL.
Datatype	Undocumented.
Dependent Files	Null-separated list of files upon which this printer driver depends.
Driver	Filename of the print driver.
DriverDate	Driver date machine-readable binary.
DriverVersion	Driver version machine-readable binary.
HardwareID	Manufacturer-specific hardware value.
Help File	Filename of the printer HLP file.

Value	Data
Manufacturer	Manufacturer name.
Monitor	Name of the print monitor (if not default).
OEM URL	URL for Internet support.
Previous Names	Undocumented.
Provider	Microsoft Windows 2000.
TempDir	(0x0)
Version	Print system version.

HKEY_LOCAL_MACHINE\SYSTEM\CurrentControlSet\Control\Print\Forms   Contains a list of values defining various paper sizes.

HKEY_LOCAL_MACHINE\SYSTEM\CurrentControlSet\Control\Print\Monitors\ <Monitor Name>   Associates a monitor name with a monitor driver DLL.

Value	Data
Driver	A string containing the filename of the print monitor driver.

HKEY_LOCAL_MACHINE\SYSTEM\CurrentControlSet\Control\Print\Printers\ <Printer>   Contains a key for each installed printer. Key names differ based on the printer, but values below each key are relatively static. These values are the same for all printers.

Value	Data
Attributes	Printer attributes. Values for the bitmask are undocumented. (8)
ChangeID	(0x2208)
Datatype	Spooler data type. (RAW)
DefaultDevMode	A character string sent to the printer to identify its operating mode.
DefaultPriority	Default priority. (0)
Description	Contents of the Printer Description field.
dnstimeout	(0x3a98)
DsKeyUpdate	(0x40000007)
Location	Contents of the Printer Location field.
Name	Name of the printer in the Printer Control Panel.
Parameters	Printer-specific parameters.

Appendix

Value	Data
ObjectGUID	Not documented.
Port	Port to which print requests are directed.
Print Processor	Print processor for this printer.
Printer Driver	Identifies the printer driver for this printer.
Priority	Printer priority.
Security	Printer security data as set in the Printer Control Panel.
Separator File	Path to the file containing a page to be printed to separate print jobs.
Share Name	Printer's shared NetBIOS name.
SpoolDirectory	Spool directory if other than the default.
StartTime	Printer accepts jobs starting at this time. (0) = Always available.
Status	Printer status.
TotalBytes	Bytes transmitted to printer since installation.
TotalJobs	Print jobs handled since printer installation.
TotalPages	Pages printed since installation.
TxTimeout	Seconds to wait before sending timeout error message.
UntilTime	Printer rejects jobs after this time of day. (0) = Always available.

**HKEY_LOCAL_MACHINE\SYSTEM\CurrentControlSet\Control\Print\Printers\
<Printer>\DsDriver**   Printer values that define the capabilities of the print device.

Value	Data
driverVersion	Driver version.
printBinNames	String defining the friendly names of the printer bins.
printCollate	Flag indicating whether the printer is capable of collating documents.
printColor	Flag indicating whether the printer is color (1) or black and white (0).
printDuplexSupported	Flag indicating whether the printer can print on both sides of the page.
printLanguage	Printer language (PCL, PostScript, etc.).

Value	Data
PrintMaxResolutionSupported	Maximum printer resolution in DPI.
printMaxXExtent	
printMaxYExtent	
printMediaReady	Friendly name of the loaded paper size.
printMediaSupported	Friendly names of supported paper sizes.
printMemory	Value indicating the amount of RAM installed in the printer.
printMinXExtent	
printMinYExtent	
printNumberUp	Value indicating how many pages the printer can put on a single page using the N-up print feature.
printOrientationsSupported	Friendly names of supported page orientations. (PORTRAIT, LANDSCAPE)
printPagesPerMinute	Speed of the printer. Equal to printRate if printRateUnit is PagesPerMinute.
printRate	Printer speed as defined by the printRateUnit.
printRateUnit	Unit of measure for the printer speed. (PagesPerMinute)
printStaplingSupported	Flag indicating whether the printer can staple collated documents together.

HKEY_LOCAL_MACHINE\SYSTEM\CurrentControlSet\Control\Print\Printers\ <Printer>\DsSpooler   Values that control spooling for the printer.

Value	Data
description	Printer description.
driverName	Printer driver name.
flags	Device-specific flags.
location	Printer location.
portName	Printer port name.
printEndTime	Printer end of availability.
printerName	Printer name.
printKeepPrintedJobs	Flag indicating whether finished jobs should be kept in the spool directory (1) or deleted (0).

Appendix

Value	Data
printSeparatorFile	Print separator file.
printShareName	Printer share name.
printSpooling	Printer spool preference. (PrintAfterSpooled)
printStartTime	Printer beginning of availability.
priority	Printer priority.
serverName	Print server name.
shortServerName	Print server NetBIOS name.
uNCName	Printer's UNC name. Slashes are doubled.
url	Printer share's URL.
versionNumber	Spooler version.

**HKEY_LOCAL_MACHINE\SYSTEM\CurrentControlSet\Control\Print\Printers\
<Printer>\PnPData**   Values that allow Windows 2000 to recognize the printer when it's attached to a local port.

Value	Data
HardwareID	Printer hardware ID.
Manufacturer	Printer manufacturer name.
OEM URL	URL to printer manufacturer.

**HKEY_LOCAL_MACHINE\SYSTEM\CurrentControlSet\Control\Print\Printers\
<Printer>\PrinterDriverData**   Contains information used by the print subsystem to control the specific printer referred to by the printer driver. These values may vary depending upon the capabilities of the print device.

Value	Data
DependentFiles	Other drivers upon which this printer driver depends.
FeatureKeyword	Driver-specific feature string.
FeatureKeywordSize	Length of FeatureKeyword.
Forms?	Handled forms.
FreeMem	Printer available memory.
InitDriverVersion	Driver version.
JobTimeOut	Job timeout.
Model	Manufacturer's model.
PrinterData	Printer-specific initialization data.

Value	Data
PrinterDataSize	Length of PrinterData.
Protocol	Driver-specific protocol number.
TrayFormSize	Length of TrayFormTable.
TrayFormTable	Listing of trays available to the printer.

★ **HKEY_LOCAL_MACHINE\SYSTEM\CurrentControlSet\Control\Print\Providers**
Contains control values for the LAN Manager print provider and a key defining that provider. Other network providers install their own print providers here.

Value	Data
EventLog	A bit flag indicating what classes of error messages should be logged in the Event Log. Sum values to combine. 0 = No event logging. 1 = Errors only. 2 = Warnings only. 4 = Information only.
LogonTime	Time at which the printer becomes available.
NetPopup	1 = Enables that annoying pop-up dialog box whenever anyone prints through the local print server.
NetPopupToComputer	1 = Enables transmission of pop-up dialog box to the computer where the user is logged in.
Order	A string containing the order in which print providers are checked for service fulfillment.
RestartJobOnPoolEnabled	1 = Allows jobs to a local printer to be restarted if an error occurs.
RestartJobOnPoolError	600 = Seconds to wait before restarting jobs if an error occurs.
RetryPopup	1 = Retry pop-up on fail.

HKEY_LOCAL_MACHINE\SYSTEM\CurrentControlSet\Control\PriorityControl
Contains the value that controls the priority boost given to the foreground application. This value is normally set in the Performance tab of the System Control Panel.

Value	Data
Win32PrioritySeparation	Quanta separation value.

Appendix

HKEY_LOCAL_MACHINE\SYSTEM\CurrentControlSet\Control\ProductOptions

Identifies which version of the operating system is running on the machine, and the information is used by a number of services to determine optimizations and limitations. Changing this value is a violation of your End User License Agreement with Microsoft.

Value	Data
ProductSuite	Indicates whether Terminal Services are installed on the local machine. (Terminal Server)
ProductType	LanmanNT = Windows NT Server 4. WinNT = Windows NT Workstation 4 or Windows 2000 Professional. ServerNT = Windows 2000.

HKEY_LOCAL_MACHINE\SYSTEM\CurrentControlSet\Control\Redbook   Contains values specific to various CD-ROM readers which are used to optimize their read performance.

HKEY_LOCAL_MACHINE\SYSTEM\CurrentControlSet\Control\SafeBoot   Contains keys that control which drivers and services will be loaded for different Safe Mode levels.

Value	Data
AlternateShell	The shell program to load when Safe Mode with Command Prompt is selected. (cmd.exe)

HKEY_LOCAL_MACHINE\SYSTEM\CurrentControlSet\Control\SafeBoot\Minimal
Contains keys that specify the devices to load for Safe Mode.

HKEY_LOCAL_MACHINE\SYSTEM\CurrentControlSet\Control\SafeBoot\Network
Contains keys that specify the devices to load for Safe Mode with Networking.

**HKEY_LOCAL_MACHINE\SYSTEM\CurrentControlSet\Control\ScsiPort\
SpecialTargetList**   Contains keys that identify certain SCSI hard disks that must be handled specially.

**HKEY_LOCAL_MACHINE\SYSTEM\CurrentControlSet\Control\SecurePipeServers\
winreg**   The permissions set on this key in RegEdt32 define the remote access permissions to the Registry. To restrict Registry access from the network, set permissions on this key. This key contains only one value, which must be present for the Registry server to handle permissions properly.

Value	Data
Description	(Registry Server)

HKEY_LOCAL_MACHINE\SYSTEM\CurrentControlSet\Control\SecurePipeServers\ winreg\AllowedPaths Contains a value defining the Registry paths available to remote users or services irrespective of the security settings on the winreg key. This allows you to define specific Registry paths available to remote users who would normally be restricted by the permission settings on the winreg key.

Value	Data
Machine	Allowed Registry paths, null-separated.

HKEY_LOCAL_MACHINE\SYSTEM\CurrentControlSet\Control\SecurityProviders Contains a value that defines the security provider DLLs installed in the system. Security providers may have unique data that is defined below this key and identified by the name of the security provider service.

Value	Data
Security Providers	List of security provider DLLs, comma-separated string.

HKEY_LOCAL_MACHINE\SYSTEM\CurrentControlSet\Control\ServiceGroupOrder Contains a null-separated byte array that defines the order in which drivers are loaded into memory.

Value	Data
List	Null-separated byte array that lists the names of services and drivers in their load order.

HKEY_LOCAL_MACHINE\SYSTEM\CurrentControlSet\Control\ServiceProvider\ Order Defines the way the Win32 API will use name service providers when resolving a network name.

Value	Data
Excluded Providers	(0) = List of identifiers of name services that should not be used when resolving names.
ProviderOrder	Order in which major protocols will be used for name resolution.

HKEY_LOCAL_MACHINE\SYSTEM\CurrentControlSet\Control\Session Manager Defines values used by the kernel during its operation and during the boot process.

Value	Data
AllowProtectedRenames	(0x1) = This value is undocumented.

Value	Data
AutoChkTimeOut	Seconds to delay running BootExecute program, thus allowing user to bypass by pressing any key. Default (10) if nonexistent.
BootExecute	Specifies programs to run after the kernel load phase of the boot process. (autocheck autochk *)
CriticalSectionTimeout	A debugging parameter for timing out deadlocked thread conditions in the kernel. Deadlock timeout is not normally used.
EnableMCA	(0x1) = This value is undocumented.
EnableMCE	(0x0) = This value is undocumented.
ExcludeFromKnownDlls	This value is undocumented.
GlobalFlag	Global flags are used by the executive for purposes such as debugging and disabling subsystems.
LicensedProcessors	Number of processors the Windows 2000 product is licensed to use. Changing this value can cause a kernel mode exception at boot time. (4)
ObjectDirectories	Specifies object directories to create during start up. (\Windows\RPC Control)
PendingFileRename Operations	2000 will copy files specified in this key before booting the operating system, so files constantly in use can be replaced. See Knowledge Base article Q181345.
ProcessorControl	(0x2) = This value is undocumented.
ProtectionMode	1 = Base operating system objects should be secured at C2 level. See Windows 2000 Server Resource Kit.
RegisteredProcessors	Number of processors this NT product will use at most. (4) Defaults are 2 for NT Workstation, 4 for NT Server, and 8 for Enterprise Server. (4 is default for this product.)
ResourceTimeoutCount	Specifies four-second ticks until resources time out. Retail versions of NT never time out.

HKEY_LOCAL_MACHINE\SYSTEM\CurrentControlSet\Control\Session Manager
AppCompatibility   Defines code segments used to patch NT-compatible applications for proper operation under Windows 2000.

HKEY_LOCAL_MACHINE\SYSTEM\CurrentControlSet\Control\Session Manager
AppPatches\<Application Name>   Defines code segments used to patch commercial applications for proper operation under Windows 2000.

HKEY_LOCAL_MACHINE\SYSTEM\CurrentControlSet\Control\Session Manager
DOS Devices   Contains symbolic links created during start-up as an interface for MS-DOS devices.

Value	Data
AUX	(\DosDevices\COM1)
MAILSLOT	(\Device\MailSlot)
NUL	(\Device\Null)
PIPE	(\Device\NamedPipe)
PRN	(\DosDevices\LPT1)
UNC	(\Device\Mup)

HKEY_LOCAL_MACHINE\SYSTEM\CurrentControlSet\Control\Session Manager
Environment   Contains a list of environment system variables available to all users. These values can be modified in the System Control Panel's Environment tab.

Value	Data
<Environment Variable>	<Environment Variable Data>

HKEY_LOCAL_MACHINE\SYSTEM\CurrentControlSet\Control\Session Manager
Executive   This key is undocumented. It appears to contain values relating to the way the executive allocates its own threads and their priorities.

HKEY_LOCAL_MACHINE\SYSTEM\CurrentControlSet\Control\Session Manager
FileRenameOperations   Used by the system to perform file-rename and delete operations during the boot process before the files are locked for use. Little additional documentation exists, and Microsoft recommends that the system maintain these entries.

HKEY_LOCAL_MACHINE\SYSTEM\CurrentControlSet\Control\Session Manager
KnownDLLs   Associates library short names with the actual filenames of the DLL.

Value	Data
<Driver Name>	<Corresponding DLL file name>

Appendix

**HKEY_LOCAL_MACHINE\SYSTEM\CurrentControlSet\Control\Session Manager\
Memory Management**   Contains values that control how Windows 2000 allocates and
uses random access memory.

Value	Data
ClearPageFileAtShutdown	1 = Zero-fill page file at shutdown.
DisablePagingExecutive	1 = Kernel and drivers cannot be paged to disk.
IoPageLockLimit	Specifies the maximum number of bytes that can be locked for I/O. 0 = Uses default of 512K. I/O-intensive machines may benefit by increasing this value in increments of 512K.
LargeSystemCache	1 = Prefers file caching and page applications to disk. On nonfile servers, this causes excessive paging activity. Set to 0 for higher application performance and reduced paging activity.
NonPagedPoolQuota	Size of the nonpaged memory pool in bytes. 0 = Automatic. Changing this value can cause wide-ranging failure due to inability to automatically allocate memory.
NonPagedPoolSize	Size of the nonpaged memory pool in bytes. 0 = Automatic. Changing this value can cause wide-ranging failure due to inability to automatically allocate memory.
PagedPoolQuota	Size of the paged pool. 0 = Automatic. Changing this value can cause wide-ranging failure due to inability to automatically allocate memory.
PagedPoolSize	Size of the paged pool. 0 = Automatic. Changing this value can cause wide-ranging failure due to inability to automatically allocate memory.
PagingFiles	String containing the path to the page file, the current size, and the maximum size. For example, C:\pagefile.sys 27 140.
PhysicalAddressExtension	(0x0) = This value indicates whether the new, expanded memory scheme that allows paged access to memory beyond the 4GB barrier is in use.

Value	Data
SecondLevelDataCache	Amount of processor's second-level cache to use. 0 = 256K. Change this value to the actual size of your second-level data cache to increase performance. (Pentium II = 512)
SystemPages	Number of page table entries for PCI cards. 0 = Automatic.

HKEY_LOCAL_MACHINE\SYSTEM\CurrentControlSet\Control\Session Manager
Power   Defines the AC and DC power policies for the power management subsystem.

HKEY_LOCAL_MACHINE\SYSTEM\CurrentControlSet\Control\Session Manager
SFC   Defines the names of the Program Files directory and the Common Files directory.

Value	Data
CommonFilesDir	C:\Program Files\Common Files
ProgramFilesDir	C:\Program Files

HKEY_LOCAL_MACHINE\SYSTEM\CurrentControlSet\Control\Session Manager
SubSystems   Maintains a list of application subsystems and their locations.

Value	Data
Debug	Location of the Debug driver if installed. ("")
Kmode	Location of the Win32 subsystem driver. (%SystemRoot%\system32\win32k.sys)
Optional	Null-separated list of optional subsystems. (Os2 Posix)
Os2	Location of the OS2 subsystem executable. (%SystemRoot%\system32\os2ss.exe)
Posix	Location of the POSIX subsystem executable. (%SystemRoot%\system32\psxss.exe)
Required	Null-separated list of mandatory subsystems. (debug windows)
Windows	Location of the Win32 subsystem. Includes some named parameters. (%SystemRoot%\system32\csrss.exe ObjectDirectory = \Windows SharedSection = 1024,3072,512 Windows = On SubSystemType = Windows ServerDll = basesrv,1 ServerDll = winsrv:UserServerDllInitialization,3 ServerDll = winsrv:ConServerDllInitialization,2 ProfileControl = Off MaxRequestThreads = 16)

Appendix

HKEY_LOCAL_MACHINE\SYSTEM\CurrentControlSet\Control\Setup Contains values established by the Windows NT setup program relating to the console video type, keyboard type, and pointer type.

HKEY_LOCAL_MACHINE\SYSTEM\CurrentControlSet\Control\SystemResources Contains keys that enumerate the system bus types and reserve resources for busses that are not Plug and Play compatible.

HKEY_LOCAL_MACHINE\SYSTEM\CurrentControlSet\Control\Terminal Server Contains information used to configure the terminal server for Windows 2000. Information on tuning these values is available at support.Microsoft.com. The various keys below the Terminal Server key are used to define connection timings, user overrides, Terminal Services add-ins, and keyboard layouts.

Value	Data
DeleteTempDirsOnExit	1 = Delete temporary directories upon logoff.
FirstCountMsgQPeeksSleepBadApp	Value used by the terminal server to determine if an ill-behaved Win16 or Win32 app is using too much idle CPU time. The value represents the number of times the app queries the message queue while idle.
IdleWinStationPoolCount	Number of idle RDP sessions to maintain.
Modems With Bad DSR	List of modems that don't properly set the Data Set Ready line.
MsgQBadAppSleepTimeInMillisec	Amount of time bad apps are suspended.
NthCountMsgQPeeksSleepBadApp	Once an application has been determined to be ill-behaved, this is the number of message queue queries the terminal server will allow before it sleeps the application again.
PerSessionTempDir	1 = Different temp directory for each session.
ProductVersion	Terminal Services version. (5.0)
TSAppCompat	1 = Enables application compatibility mode.
TSEnabled	1 = Terminal Services are enabled.
TSUserEnabled	1 = TS users are made a member of the TERMINAL SERVER USER group (permissions compatible with TS4).

HKEY_LOCAL_MACHINE\SYSTEM\CurrentControlSet\Control\Terminal Server\ AddIns   Contains a list of Terminal Server add-ins that extend the functionality of the Terminal Server service, such as the drive mapping service or the file copy service. Check Knowledge Base articles Q244732 and Q244725 for more information about this key.

HKEY_LOCAL_MACHINE\SYSTEM\CurrentControlSet\Control\TimeZoneInformation Contains values that define the computer's relation to Greenwich mean time (GMT).

Value	Data
ActiveTimeBias	Current offset from GMT in minutes.
Bias	Standard offset from GMT in minutes.
DaylightBias	Offset from GMT during daylight savings time.
DaylightName	Text name of the daylight savings time zone.
DaylightStart	Daylight savings start date.
StandardBias	Offset from GMT during standard time.
StandardName	Text name of the standard time zone.
StandardStart	Start date of the daylight savings time zone.

★ **HKEY_LOCAL_MACHINE\SYSTEM\CurrentControlSet\Control\Update**
Changes the policy file update mode.

Value	Data
UpdateMode	0 = Policies will not be applied.
	1 = Policies are applied automatically from the validating domain controller.
	2 = Policies are applied manually from a specific UNC share.

HKEY_LOCAL_MACHINE\SYSTEM\CurrentControlSet\Control\VirtualDeviceDrivers
Contains all Virtual DOS Machine (VDM) virtual device drivers from vendors who wish to provide virtual drivers for their Windows-native drivers. Very few vendors actually do this, and the key contains no useful data by default.

HKEY_LOCAL_MACHINE\SYSTEM\CurrentControlSet\Control\Windows   Contains values that control the operation of the 32-bit Windows subsystem.

Value	Data
CSDVersion	Undocumented. May display the current service pack version in the second byte.

Appendix

Value	Data
Directory	Defines the system variable that points to the system directory. (%SystemRoot%)
ErrorMode	Controls how Windows 2000 handles a class of internal errors called hard system errors. 0 = Errors are displayed in series, and dialog boxes wait for a response from the interactive user. 1 = Nonsystem errors are handled as usual. System errors are written to the Event Log. No user intervention is required, and no dialog box is displayed. 2 = Errors are written to the System Log, and no dialogs are displayed.
NoInteractiveServices	Nonzero value will prevent services from interacting with the logged-on user irrespective of service's interactive flag. (0)
ShutdownTime	Contains the date and time of the last shutdown.
SystemDirectory	Defines the location of the Win32 system directory. (%SystemRoot%\System32)

HKEY_LOCAL_MACHINE\SYSTEM\CurrentControlSet\Control\WOW Contains values that control the operation of the 16-bit windows subsystem (Windows on Windows or WoW) that runs in the Virtual DOS Machine (VDM).

Value	Data
Cmdline	Path to the executable used to create VDMs. (%SystemRoot%\system32\ntvdm.exe)
DefaultSeparateVDM	Specifies whether to run each 16-bit executable in a persistent shared-memory environment (no) or in a separate VDM for each 16-bit application. Speed your machine when not running VDMs and protect them from one another by setting this value to yes.
KnownDLLs	List of known 16-bit DLLs installed in 2000, which replace DLLs of the same name that have been provided by vendors.
LPT_timeout	Printer timeout in seconds. If no printing activity from the VDM occurs within this period, the print handle is closed and spooling can begin.

Value	Data
SharedWowTimeout	(0xe10) = Timeout before a shared Windows on Windows (16-bit subsystem) is closed.
Size	Size of VDMs in MB. 0 = Automatic.
Wowcmdline	Path to the executable used to create WoW VDMs. (%SystemRoot%\system32\ntvdm.exe -a %SystemRoot%\system32\krnl386)
Wowsize	Size in MB of the WoW VDM.

HKEY_LOCAL_MACHINE\SYSTEM\CurrentControlSet\Enum   Contains hardware configuration tree for data for devices and drivers. During the Plug and Play enumeration of hardware at boot and whenever hardware is added or removed, a key for each device is added to this key. The data appearing here is visible through the Device Manager, where it can be modified.

HKEY_LOCAL_MACHINE\SYSTEM\CurrentControlSet\Hardware Profiles   Contains hardware configuration data specific to a certain profile. Also appears in HKEY_CURRENT_ CONFIG.

HKEY_LOCAL_MACHINE\SYSTEM\CurrentControlSet\Services   Contains keys representing every driver and service installed in the system. Modifications to the keys contained herein will change how the system boots on its next power cycle.

HKEY_LOCAL_MACHINE\SYSTEM\CurrentControlSet\Services\<Adapter GUID>\ Parameters\Tcpip   Contains TCP/IP protocol entries specific to a network adapter. Although adapters are simply drivers, these keys can only be added to adapter drivers and so are categorized separately.

Value	Data
DontAddDefaultGateway	1 = Disables the creation of a default route for LAN adapters when PPTP is installed.
PPTPFiltering	1 = Enables PPTP filtering for this adapter.
PPTPTcpMaxDataRetransmissions	The number of times a PPTP packet will be retransmitted without acknowledgment. Value should be set higher than the default TCPMaxDataRetransmissions value to prevent dead gateway detection on congested links.

Appendix

★ **HKEY_LOCAL_MACHINE\SYSTEM\CurrentControlSet\Services\<Driver>**
Contains keys specific to loaded services and drivers in Windows 2000. Contains start-up and control information for the drivers and services loaded by Windows 2000.

Value	Data
Autorun	(1) = Automatically runs the autorun CD-ROM file (CD-ROM only).
DependOnGroup	Driver groups that must be started before this driver or service can run.
DependOnService	Name of any services that must be loaded before this service.
Description	Description of the driver or service.
DisplayName	Display name of the driver or service.
DriverVersion	Revision number of the driver.
ErrorControl	Determines what will happen if a driver fails to load during startup. Options are: 0 = Ignore and continue booting. 1 = Normal. Continue booting, but display a message indicating the failure. 2 = Severe. Switch to LastKnownGood, or if already in the LastKnownGood, continue. 3 = Critical. Fail the attempt to start up.
Group	Identifies the driver group to which this driver or service belongs.
ImagePath	Path to the driver.
ObjectName	Logon name of the account that runs the service when Type = 0×10 or the driver object that is used to load the driver if Type = 0×01 or 0×02.
RequestedSystem-Resources	Contains memory, IRQ, and DMA resources requested by the device.
Start	Controls if and when the service or driver will be loaded during the boot process. 0 = Boot. 1 = System. 2 = Automatic. 3 = Manual. 4 = Disabled.

Value	Data
Tag	Load order within the service or driver group. This tag is equal to the driver's position in the GroupOrderList.
Type	Service or driver type. 0x1 = Kernel device driver. 0x2 = File system kernel device driver. 0x4 = Adapter arguments. 0x10 = Win32 service. 0x20 = Process sharing Win32 service.

HKEY_LOCAL_MACHINE\SYSTEM\CurrentControlSet\Services\<Driver>\Enum   The purpose of this key is not documented. It probably has to do with the Plug and Play assignment of the hardware adapter that is bound to the driver.

HKEY_LOCAL_MACHINE\SYSTEM\CurrentControlSet\Services\<Driver>\Linkage   Determines how services and drivers interact. They are detailed more fully in the Windows 2000 Resource Kit. Generally, you should not modify these values.

Value	Data
Bind	Names of system objects created by the driver.
Export	Exported object interfaces.
Route	Path through the binding protocol.

HKEY_LOCAL_MACHINE\SYSTEM\CurrentControlSet\Services\<Driver>\Linkage\ Disabled   Contains information about disabled service interactions, just like the previous key.

HKEY_LOCAL_MACHINE\SYSTEM\CurrentControlSet\Services\<Driver>\ Parameters   Contains keys and values specific to the service or driver.

HKEY_LOCAL_MACHINE\SYSTEM\CurrentControlSet\Services\Alerter\Parameters   Contains values specific to the Alerter service.

Value	Data
AlertNames	Specifies the user names of those to whom administrative alerts should be sent.

Appendix

**HKEY_LOCAL_MACHINE\SYSTEM\CurrentControlSet\Services\AppleTalk\Adapters\
<Adapter>** Contains values specific to AppleTalk-compatible network interfaces on the computer.

Value	Data
ArpRetries	Number of address resolution tries.
DdpCheckSums	1 = Use DDP checksums.
DefaultZone	Default zone if this adapter seeds the network zone information.
NetworkRangeLowerEnd	Low end of the network number range if this adapter seeds the network.
NetworkRangeUpperEnd	High end of the network number range if this adapter seeds the network.
PortName	AppleTalk protocol name specific to this adapter.
SeedingNetwork	1 = This adapter seeds the network.
ZoneList	Zone list to seed the network with.

**HKEY_LOCAL_MACHINE\SYSTEM\CurrentControlSet\Services\AppleTalk\
Parameters** Contains values specific to the AppleTalk service.

Value	Data
DefaultPort	The network on which Services for Macintosh names are registered. This is, by default, the first network adapter found. Change this to the network adapter attached to the Macintosh network if SFM stops working after a network adapter installation.
DesiredZone	Specifies the AppleTalk zone of the server. Default zone for the network is used if this value is not present.
EnableRouter	1 = Route AppleTalk to all interfaces. Microsoft recommends not using this feature unless absolutely necessary.

★ **HKEY_LOCAL_MACHINE\SYSTEM\CurrentControlSet\Services\Browser\Parameters**
Contains values specific to the Browser service.

Value	Data
IsDomainMaster	Set this value to True to make the computer a preferred master browser.
MaintainServerList	Yes = This computer is a browse server. No = This computer is not a browse server. Auto = This computer may negotiate to become a browse master.

HKEY_LOCAL_MACHINE\SYSTEM\CurrentControlSet\Services\DHCP\Parameters\ Options   Contains keys identifying the Registry locations of DHCP service parameters.

HKEY_LOCAL_MACHINE\SYSTEM\CurrentControlSet\Services\EventLog\<Event Log>   Contains values identifying and controlling the Event Logs. Each Event Log may have subordinate keys identifying the services and applications that send events to that log, along with parameter data.

Value	Data
File	Path to the application Event Log. (%SystemRoot%\ system32\config\AppEvent.Evt)
MaxSize	Maximum file size of the Event Log. (0x80000)
Retention	Specifies that records that are newer than this value will not be overwritten. This is what causes a log full event. This value can be set using the Event Viewer. (604800) (7 days)
Sources	List of applications that send messages to the application Event Log.

HKEY_LOCAL_MACHINE\SYSTEM\CurrentControlSet\Services\EventLog\<Event Log>\<Source>   Contains keys identifying and controlling the sources of Event Log messages.

★ **HKEY_LOCAL_MACHINE\System\CurrentControlSet\Services\LanManServer\ Parameters**   Contains values that control the functions of the server service.

Value	Data
CacheOpenLimit	(0x0) = This value is undocumented.
EnableFCOpens	1 = Combines MS-DOS file control blocks into a single open operation. May be necessary for older MS-DOS network applications.
enableforcedlogoff	(0x1) = Forces logoff when logon hours expire.
enablesecuritysignature	1 = Enables SMB message signing. SMB message signing can be used to prevent SMB packet forgery. (0x0)
EnableSoftCompat	1 = Map compatibility open request to normal open request. Some MS-DOS network applications may require this.
GUID	This is a binary value.

Appendix

Value	Data
IRPstackSize	Allocated stack size for the SRV service to share to 2000 clients. Not present = default (4). Gradually increase this value if you get Not Enough Server Storage Is Available to Process This Command errors.
Lmannounce	1 = Enable browser announcements to LAN Manager 2.*x* clients.
NullSessionPipes	List of null session pipes that are exempt from anonymous use restrictions.
NullSessionShares	List of shares that can be attached to by anonymous (null session) clients.
OplockBreakWait	Seconds to wait for client to respond to an oplock break request. Lower values detect dead clients faster but risk losing cached data. (35)
requiresecuritysignature	(0x0) = Ignores sessions that do not use SMB message signing.
ScavTimeout	Time that the scavenger remains idle before waking up to service requests.
Size	(0x3)
ThreadPriority	Server thread priority in relation to base priority.

★ **HKEY_LOCAL_MACHINE\SYSTEM\CurrentControlSet\Services\LanManServer\Shares**
Contains a value for each file and print share on the computer.

Value	Data
<Share Name>	String parameter list of maximum users, path to share, share permissions, and share type.

**HKEY_LOCAL_MACHINE\System\CurrentControlSet\Services\LanManWorkstation\
Parameters**   Contains values relating to the network redirector. Most of these values pertain to file locking and caching operations and should only be changed by application developers to tune their applications.

Value	Data
BufFilesDenyWrite	(1) = Buffer shared files opened only for read access.
BufNamedPipes	(1) = Buffer character named pipe operations.
BufReadOnlyFiles	(1) = Buffer shared read-only files.

Value	Data
CacheFileTimeout	Maximum time a close file will be left in the cache. (10)
CharWait	Time to wait for a named pipe to become available. (3600)
CollectionTime	Maximum time that write-cached data will remain in a character mode pipe. (250)
DormantFileLimit	Maximum files to leave open on a share after an application has closed them.
enableplaintextpassword	1 = This machine will transmit passwords without encryption. This is required to log on to third-party SMB servers such as SAMBA.
enablesecuritysignature	1 = Sign SMB packets.
IllegalDatagramResetTime	Window for merging illegal datagrams into one log entry. (60)
KeepConn	Maximum time a connection can be dormant. (600)
LockIncrement	Rate at which the redirector ramps back failed lock operations from OS/2 applications. (10)
LockMaximum	Maximum number of nonblocking requests a server will receive from an application.
LockQuota	Maximum read bytes for applications using lock-and-read operations (4,096)
LogElectionPackets	1 = Generate events when browser receives election packets.
MailSlotsBuffers	Maximum MailSlots buffers. (5)
MaxCmds	Maximum work buffers. Increase for applications that use more simultaneous network operations. (15)
MaxCollectionCount	Writes smaller than this number of bytes are buffered to improve performance. (16)
NumIllegalDatagramEvents	Maximum number of illegal datagram events to log within IllegalDatagramResetTime. (5)
OtherDomains	Other LAN Manager domains to be listed for browsing.

Appendix

Value	Data
PipeIncrement	Rate at which Workstation service backs off failing nonblocking pipe reads. (10)
PipeMaximum	Maximum time to back off failed nonblocking pipe reads.
ReadAheadThroughput	Throughput required before Cache Manager enables read-ahead buffering.
requiresecuritysignature	1 = Only speaks to servers that are signing SMB packets.
ServerAnnounceBuffers	Maximum buffers used to process server announcements. (20)
SessTimeout	Maximum short-term outstanding operation time. (45)
SizCharBuf	Bytes written into character mode buffers. (512)
Use512ByteMaxTransfer	(0) = Uses server-negotiated buffer size rather than a maximum of 512 bytes per request.
UseLockReadUnlock	(1) = Carries out automatic locks and unlocks after read and write operations.
UseOpportunisticLocking	(1) = Uses opportunistic locking.
UseRawRead	(1) = Uses raw reads.
UseRawWrite	(1) = Uses raw writes.
UseUnlockBehind	(1) = Uses opportunistic unlocking on the client.
UtilizeNTCaching	(1) = Uses Cache Manager to cache the contents of files.

**HKEY_LOCAL_MACHINE\SYSTEM\CurrentControlSet\Services\MSFTPSVC\
Parameters** Contains parameters pertaining to the FTP service.

Value	Data
AllowGuestAccess	1 = Allows guest access.
AnnotateDirectories	1 = Enables directory annotation. This displays the contents of the file named .ckm located in the annotated directory.
EnablePortAttack	Undocumented.
InstallPath	Installation path of the IIS services.

Value	Data
MajorVersion	IIS version.
MinorVersion	IIS Minor version.

HKEY_LOCAL_MACHINE\SYSTEM\CurrentControlSet\Services\MSFTPSVC\ Parameters\Virtual Roots Contains the list of FTP service virtual root directories.

Value	Data
<Directory Root>	Path to directory root.

HKEY_LOCAL_MACHINE\SYSTEM\CurrentControlSet\Services\NDIS\Parameters
The solitary value in this key determines how deferred procedure calls (DPCs) generated by interrupts are handled in multiprocessor systems. Because DPCs are cascading events from interrupts, the local processor cache will already contain the local processor information required to handle the DPC in many cases. For this reason DPCs should usually be handled on the processor that handled the interrupt for maximum efficiency.

Value	Data
ProcessorAffinityMask	Bitmask for processors that will handle shared interrupts in a multiprocessor system. (0xFFFFFFFF) = Distribute DPCs across all processors. 0 = Handles DPCs on the processor that handled the source interrupt.

HKEY_LOCAL_MACHINE\SYSTEM\CurrentControlSet\Services\NetBT\Parameters
Contains values that are specific to the NetBIOS over TCP/IP driver.

Value	Data
BcastNameQueryCount	Times to retry broadcast name queries. (3)
BcastQueryTimeout	Time between BcastNameQueryCount in milliseconds. (750)
BroadcastAddress	Global parameter to set the broadcast address for all subnets.
CacheTimeout	Time to cache names in the remote name table in milliseconds. (600000)
DhcpNodeType	DHCP-provided NodeType. Not user configurable.
DhcpScopeId	DHCP-provided ScopeID. Not user configurable.
EnableDns	1 = Queries DNS for names after other lookups fail. (0)
EnableLMHOSTS	1 = Searches LMHOSTS for name resolution. (0)

Appendix

Value	Data
EnableProxy	1 = Acts as proxy name server for bound NetBT networks. A proxy name server allows broadcast client. (0)
EnableProxyRegCheck	1 = Denies name broadcast name registrations that are different than the existing name to address mapping.
InitialRefreshTimeout	Initial name registration refresh timeout.
LmhostsTimeout	Timeout value for DNS and LMHOSTS name queries in milliseconds. (6)
MaxDgramBuffering	Maximum memory to use for outstanding datagram transmits. (0x20000) (128K)
NameServerPort	TCP/IP port to listen for name service packets. (137)
NameSrvQueryCount	Times to retry name queries to a WINS server. (3)
NameSrvQueryTimeout	Time between NameSrvQueryCount. (1500)
NbProvider	RPC parameter indicating the transport used by NetBT. (_tcp). Do not change this value.
NodeType	Node type for name resolution: 1 = b-node. 2 = p-node. 4 = m-node. 8 = h-node.
RandomAdapter	1 = Randomizes IP address in responses to name queries to load balance between two adapters on the same net.
RefreshOpCode	Forces NetBT to use a specific name refresh packet opcode. This key is not well documented and should be left in its default state.
ScopeID	NetBIOS DNS name scope for the node. * = Null scope. Overrides DHCP.
SessionKeepAlive	Interval between keep-alive packets in milliseconds. 0xFFFFFFFF = Disable keep-alives. (3600000) (1h)
SingleResponse	1 = Only supplies IP address from a single interface in name query responses.

Value	Data
Size/Small/Medium/Large	Size of the name table (NetBIOS name cache) used to store local and remote names. 1 = 16 (small). 2 = 128 (medium). 3 = 256 (large).
TransportBindName	Partial path to the transport object. Do not change this value. (\Device\)
WinsDownTimeout	Time to wait before retrying to contact a WINS server in milliseconds. (15000)

HKEY_LOCAL_MACHINE\SYSTEM\CurrentControlSet\Services\NetBT\Parameters\ Interfaces\Tcpip_{GUID}   Contains the list of adapters bound to NetBT.

HKEY_LOCAL_MACHINE\SYSTEM\CurrentControlSet\Services\NetLogon\ Parameters   Contains values specific to the NetLogon service.

Value	Data
DBFlag	Enables logging of NetLogon service to netlogon.log in the NetLogon share directory. Used only for debugging builds of Netlogon.dll.
DisablePassword Change	1 = Disables weekly machine account password change initiation from workstations or member servers. Machine accounts normally change passwords automatically every seven days. See Knowledge Base article Q154501 for information. (0)
ExpectedDialupDelay	Seconds before interactive logons time out, declaring domain controller cannot be found.
PulseInterval	Frequency at which domain controllers transmit changes to the SAM in seconds. Decrease this value for cost/per/transmit WANs. (3600) (1h)
Randomize	Wait seconds before BDCs should respond to PDC update messages. This is a form of collision avoidance. (30)
RefusePassword Change	1 = Refuses requests for weekly machine account password change from workstations or member servers. (0)

Value	Data
RequireSignOrSeal	(0) = Requires Signed or Sealed channel. This should only be set if all domain controllers in all trusted domains support signing and sealing (i.e., are updated to SP4).
Scripts	Location of logon scripts. (%SystemRoot%\system32\repl\import\scripts)
SealSecureChannel	(1) = Encrypts all outgoing secure channel traffic if domain controller supports it.
SignSecureChannel	(1) = Signs all outgoing secure channel traffic if domain controller supports it.
SysVol	Path to the system volume. (C:\WINNT\sysvol\sysvol)
SysVolReady	Flag to indicate the status of the system volume. (1)
TrustedDomainList	List of domains that this domain controller trusts.
Update	Yes = Fully synchronizes the SAM among domain controllers upon start-up. (No)

HKEY_LOCAL_MACHINE\SYSTEM\CurrentControlSet\Services\NWCWorkstation\NetworkProvider   Contains network provider values for the gateway or client services for NetWare (CSNW).

Value	Data
Class	Bitflag determining the network services provided by this redirector. (11)
DeviceName	Object name of the device driver. (\Device\nwrdr)
Name	Provider description. (NetWare or Compatible Network)
NWCompatible-Authentication	(1) = Uses NetWare-compatible authentication.
ProviderPath	Path to the network provider DLL. (%SystemRoot%\System32\nwprovau.dll)

HKEY_LOCAL_MACHINE\SYSTEM\CurrentControlSet\Services\NWCWorkstation
Parameters Contains values for the gateway or client services for NetWare redirector.

Value	Data
CurrentUser	SID of the logged-on user.
DisablePopup	1 = Disables NetWare broadcast messages equal to CASTOFF ALL in the NetWare redirector.
MaxBurstSize	Maximum packets to burst before requiring acknowledgement. 0 = Burst mode off.

HKEY_LOCAL_MACHINE\SYSTEM\CurrentControlSet\Services\Nwlnklpx\NetConfig
<Adapter> Contains values specific to the NWLink IPX-compatible, TDI-compliant transport protocol for each installed network adapter.

Value	Data
AdapterName	Name of the NWLink adapter.
BindSap	Ethertype for Ethernet II frame types. (33079)
EnableFuncaddr	(1) = Uses IPX Functional Address for Token Ring adapters.
MaxPktSize	0 = Automatic.
NetworkNumber	IPX network number for this adapter.
PktType	MAC frame type. 0 = Ethernet II. 1 = Ethernet_802.3. 2 = 802.3. 3 = Ethernet SNAP. 4 = Arcnet.
SourceRouteBcast	Source route to transmit packets to the broadcast MAC address. (0) = Single route. 1 = All-routes broadcast.
SourceRouteDef	Source route to transmit packet to a unique MAC address that does not appear in the source routing table. (0) = Single route. 1 = All-routes broadcast.

Appendix

Value	Data
SourceRouteMcast	Source route to transmit packets to the multicast MAC address. (0) = Single route. 1 = All-routes broadcast.
SourceRouting	(1) = Enables source routing for Token Ring adapters.

HKEY_LOCAL_MACHINE\System\CurrentControlSet\Services\NWLinkIPX\Parameters Contains values specific to the NWLink IPX-compatible, TDI-compliant transport protocol.

Value	Data
ConnectionCount	Number of times an SPX probe will be sent when connecting to a remote node before an error occurs.
ConnectionTimeout	Time in half seconds between connection probe transmissions.
DedicatedRouter	1 = Computer is dedicated to router and has no services running on it.
DisableDialinNetbios	1 = IPX does not forward NetBIOS type 20 packets over RAS connections. Some NetBIOS applications may require enabling to operate properly.
DisableDialoutSap	1 = IPX does not transmit SAP announcements and responses on RAS connections.
EnableWANRouter	1 = Routes IPX broadcasts over RAS links.
EthernetPadToEven	1 = Pads Ethernet frames to even length for older ODI cards. (1)
InitDatagrams	Number of datagrams initially allocated by IPX.
KeepAliveCount	Retries keep-alive probe before timing out. (8)
KeepAliveTimeout	Time between keep-alive transmits in half-seconds. (12)
MaxDatagrams	Number of datagram buffers allocated by NWLink. (50)
RipAgeTime	Delay before requesting RIP update in minutes. (5)
RipCount	Retries RIP request before giving up. RIP is the IPX automatic routing table update protocol for IPX similar to RIP for IP. (5)

Value	Data
RipRoute	(1) = Enables IPX RIP updates.
RipTableSize	Number of entries in the RIP table. (7)
RipTimeout	Time between RIP requests in half-seconds. (1)
RipUsageTime	Delay before deleting old routing table entry in minutes. (15)
SingleNetworkActive	1 = Both RAS and network adapter cannot be active at the same time. Allows CSNW to locate NetWare servers through RAS link. (0)
SocketEnd	End range for auto-assigned sockets. (24575)
SocketStart	Start range for auto-assigned sockets. (16384)
SocketUniqueness	Number of sockets to reserve when auto-assigning a socket. (8)
SourceRouteUsageTime	Delay before deleting Token Ring source routes. (15)
VirtualNetworkNumber	Computer's virtual network number.
WindowSize	Seed value for SPX allocation field. (4)

HKEY_LOCAL_MACHINE\SYSTEM\CurrentControlSet\Services\NwlnkNb\ Parameters   Contains NWLink NetBIOS values. This key was named NWNBLink in versions before NT 4.0.

Value	Data
AckDelayTime	Start value of the delayed acknowledgment time. (Default or no entry is 250.)
AckWindow	Frames to receive before acknowledgment. Can be set to zero for fast links. (Default or no entry is 2.)
AckWindowThreshold	Specifies how many milliseconds an ACK roundtrip should take. If the time exceeds the threshold, automatic acknowledgments are necessary. If set to zero, AckWindow is relied upon. (500)
BroadcastCount	Number of times to transmit a broadcast. (3) Broadcast count is doubled if Internet is enabled.
BroadcastTimeout	Time between transmission of find-name requests in half-seconds. (1)
ConnectionCount	Number of times to send a connection probe. (5) Doubled if Internet is enabled.

Appendix

Value	Data
ConnectionTimeout	Half-seconds between connection probes during session initiation. (2)
EnablePiggyBackAck	1 = Receiver automatically acknowledges upon detecting the end of an inbound NetBIOS message. (1)
Extensions	1 = Uses NWNBLink extensions.
InitialRetransmissionTime	Milliseconds between initial transmission retries. (500)
Internet	1 = Packet type is 0x14 (WAN broadcast) rather than 0x04. Also doubles the timings of numerous connection flow control settings.
KeepAliveCount	Number of attempted session-alive packets before timing out. (8)
KeepAliveTimeout	Half-seconds between session-alive packets. (60)
NbProvider	Object name of the NetBIOS network provider (_ipx). Do not change this value.
RcvWindowMax	Number of packets that can be received before acknowledgment. (4)
RetransmitMax	Retries before timing out due to bad link. (8)

HKEY_LOCAL_MACHINE\SYSTEM\CurrentControlSet\Services\NwlnkSpx\ Parameters Contains values for the SPX services of the NWLink transport driver.

Value	Data
ConnectionCount	Times to probe when connecting to a remote node before erroring out. (5)
ConnectionTimeout	Time between probe attempts in half-seconds. (2)
InitialRetransmissionTime	Wait for acknowledgment delay before sending probe in milliseconds. (500)
InitPackets	Initial packet buffer allocations. (5)
KeepAliveCount	Keep-alive probes before timing out. (8)
KeepAliveTimeout	Time between keep-alives in half seconds. (12)
MaxPackets	Maximum packet buffers that SPX will allocate.
MaxPacketSize	Maximum packet size that SPX will negotiate with a remote node. (4096)
RetransmissionCount	Probes to send waiting for data ACK. (8)

Value	Data
SpxSocketEnd	Auto-assigned socket end boundary. (32767)
SpxSocketStart	Auto-assigned socket start boundary. (24576)
WindowSize	Seed value for SPX socket allocation field. (4)

**HKEY_LOCAL_MACHINE\SYSTEM\CurrentControlSet\Services\NwlnkRip\
Parameters**   Contains values for the NWLink RIP routing information protocol.

Value	Data
NetbiosRouting	Controls IPX NetBIOS broadcast forwarding. 0 = None. (2) = Forwards from RAS client to the network. 4 = Forwards from network to the RAS client. 6 = Both 2 and 4.

**HKEY_LOCAL_MACHINE\SYSTEM\CurrentControlSet\Services\RasMan\
Parameters**   Contains values for the RAS Manager.

Value	Data
Logging	1 = Logs all RAS communications to %systemroot%\ system32\device.log.

★ **HKEY_LOCAL_MACHINE\SYSTEM\CurrentControlSet\Services\RasMan\PPP**
Contains values for the Point-to-Point Protocol.

Value	Data
DisableSoftware Compression	1 = Disables software compression. (0)
ForceEncrypted Password	(1) = Uses CHAP for authentication. 0 = Uses PAP.
Logging	1 = Logs all PPP events to %systemroot\ system32\ras\ppp.log.
MaxConfigure	Times to retry configure_request packets before giving up. (10)
MaxFailure	Times to retry configure_nak packets without sending a configure_ack packet before assuming that a PPP session cannot be established. (10)
MaxReject	Times to retry config_rejects before assuming that a PPP session cannot be established. (5)

Appendix

Value	Data
MaxTerminate	Times to retry `terminate_requests` before giving up. (2)
Multilink	(0x0)
NegotiateTime	Window for PPP session establishment before giving up and disconnecting the line. 0 = Never hang up. (150)
RestartTimer	Window in seconds for transmission of `configure_request` and `terminate_request` packets before timing out and starting over. (3)

HKEY_LOCAL_MACHINE\SYSTEM\CurrentControlSet\Services\RemoteAccess
Controls the configuration of the remote access service of RRAS. The keys in this key define accounting service providers, authentication providers, and protocol bindings to interfaces.

HKEY_LOCAL_MACHINE\SYSTEM\CurrentControlSet\Services\SimpTcp
Parameters Contains values that control the simple TCP/IP services. These values are undocumented but fairly obvious.

Value	Data
EnableMultipleThreads	1 = Spawns new thread per connection.
EnableTcpChargen	1 = Enables chargen service over TCP.
EnableTcpDaytime	1 = Enables daytime service over TCP.
EnableTcpDiscard	1 = Enables discard service over TCP.
EnableTcpEcho	1 = Enables echo service TCP.
EnableTcpQotd	1 = Enables quote service over TCP.
EnableUdpChargen	1 = Enables chargen service over UDP.
EnableUdpDaytime	1 = Enables daytime service over UDP.
EnableUdpDiscard	1 = Enables discard service over UDP.
EnableUdpEcho	1 = Enables echo service over UDP.
EnableUdpQotd	1 = Enables quote service over UDP.
IoBufferSize	Buffer size (per connection?) (8192)
MaxIdleTicks	Maximum idle time (milliseconds?) before a nonresponsive socket is killed. (600000) (10m?)
MaxTcpClients	Maximum clients for all simple TCP/IP services. This prevents simple services from being exploited by certain denial of service attacks. (16)

Value	Data
QotdFileName	Filename containing quotes to serve. (%SystemRoot%\ system32\drivers\etc\quotes)
SelectTimeout	0000012c

HKEY_LOCAL_MACHINE\SYSTEM\CurrentControlSet\Services\SNMP\Parameters\ PermittedManagers   Contains incremental values starting at 1. Data is the text of a permitted manager.

HKEY_LOCAL_MACHINE\SYSTEM\CurrentControlSet\Services\SNMP\Parameters\ TrapConfiguration\Public   Contains incremental values starting at 1. Data is the text of a trap configuration.

HKEY_LOCAL_MACHINE\SYSTEM\CurrentControlSet\Services\SNMP\Parameters\ ValidCommunities   Contains incremental values starting at 1. Data associated with each value is the text of the valid community.

HKEY_LOCAL_MACHINE\SYSTEM\CurrentControlSet\Services\Tcpip\Parameters
Contains values used by the TCP/IP TDI-compliant transport protocol.

Value	Data
AllowUnqualifiedQuery	(0x0)
DatabasePath	Path to Internet configuration files HOSTS, LMHOSTS, networks, protocols, services (%SystemRoot%\ System32\drivers\etc)
DeadGWDetectDefault	(1) = Changes to backup gateway if transmits through current gateway seem unresponsive.
DefaultTOS	Default type of service parameter for outgoing IP packets. See RFC 791. (0)
DefaultTTL	Default time-to-live value for outgoing IP packets. (128)
Domain	DNS domain of local host.
EnableICMPRedirect	1 = Redirects in response to ICMP redirect messages. Set to 0 for increased security against TCP/IP session hijacking. (0x1)
EnableSecurityFilters	1 = Security filtering enabled. (0)
ForwardBroadcasts	Ignored parameter.
Hostname	DNS name of local host.

Appendix

Value	Data
IPEnableRouter	1 = This host acts as a router. (0)
NameServer	List of space-separated IP addresses of name servers.
NV Domain	Defaulted to DNS domain name.
NV Hostname	Defaulted to host name.
PrioritizeRecordData	(0x1) = Enable subnet prioritization instead of round-robin address return for DNS name responses.
SearchList	List of DNS domains to append to failed simple name resolutions. Use com net org for Internet hosts if you don't use DNS for WINS resolution. ("")
UseDomainNameDevolution	(0x1) = Use DNS Devolution to find hosts. Devolution appends the local computer's DNS suffix to the names of host names being searched for and then removes domains until the host is found.

HKEY_LOCAL_MACHINE\SYSTEM\CurrentControlSet\Services\Tcpip\Parameters\ PersistentRoutes   Contains a list of persistent routes programmed using the route command. The value contains all information, and the data field is null. Value follows this syntax:

```
<destination address>,<mask>,<gateway>
```

HKEY_LOCAL_MACHINE\SYSTEM\CurrentControlSet\Services\Tcpip\ ServiceProvider

Value	Data
Class	(8) = TCP/IP provides name service.
DnsPriority	DNS name resolution priority versus other name resolvers. (2000)
HostsPriority	Hosts file name resolution priority versus other name resolvers. (500)
LocalPriority	NetBIOS name cache name resolution priority versus other resolvers. (499)
Name	Transport name. (TCP/IP)

Value	Data
NetbtPriority	NetBT (WINS) name resolution priority versus other resolvers. (2001)
ProviderPath	DLL for name resolution. (%SystemRoot%\System32\ wsock32.dll)

★ **HKEY_LOCAL_MACHINE\SYSTEM\MountedDevices**
Stores information about disks, partitions, and volumes as maintained by the Disk Administrator. Values under this key should never be directly edited.

HKEY_LOCAL_MACHINE\SYSTEM\Select   Identifies which control set is current and which is LastKnownGood.

Value	Data
Current	ControlSet that is current. (1)
Default	ControlSet that is the default start-up control set. (1)
Failed	ControlSet that failed and caused fall-over to LastKnownGood. (0)
LastKnownGood	ControlSet last known to boot completely besides the current control set. (2)

HKEY_USERS   Contains all active loaded user profiles. HKEY_CURRENT_USER is a pointer to one of these profiles. See values under HKEY_CURRENT_USER.

Appendix

Index

Note to the reader: Throughout this index **boldfaced** page numbers indicate primary discussions of a topic. *Italicized* page numbers indicate illustrations.

Shortcut	Method
Map network drive	Right-click My Network Places, and select Map Network Drive. *or* Right-click share in Explorer after browsing to another computer, and select Map Network Drive.
Move shortcut within Start and Programs menus	Click and hold shortcut, drag to new location, and release. Folders will expand after a delay.
Move Quick Launch toolbar to side of screen	Drag vertical slider bar on Quick Launch toolbar in Taskbar to left or right side of screen. Drag and drop again to snap toolbar to vertical edge of screen.
Move, size, or close program window that exceeds size of screen after changing resolution	Right-click program's button in Taskbar. Select Maximize to place program window correctly on screen.
Network and dial-up connections	Right-click My Network Places, and select Properties.
Open All Users shortcuts	Right-click Start button, and select Open All Users, or select Explore All Users.
Open logged-on user Start menu shortcuts	Right-click Start button, and select Open.
Organize Start menu	Right-click Programs menu, and select Sort by Name.
Pause printer	Right-click Printer icon, and select Pause.